D1570084

The Yale Edition of the Complete Works of St. Thomas More

VOLUME 7

LETTER TO BUGENHAGEN

SUPPLICATION OF SOULS

LETTER AGAINST FRITH

Published by the St. Thomas More Project, Yale University,
under the auspices of Gerard L. Carroll and Joseph B. Murray,
Trustees of the Michael P. Grace, II, Trust,
and with the support of the Editing Program of the
National Endowment for the Humanities
and the Knights of Columbus

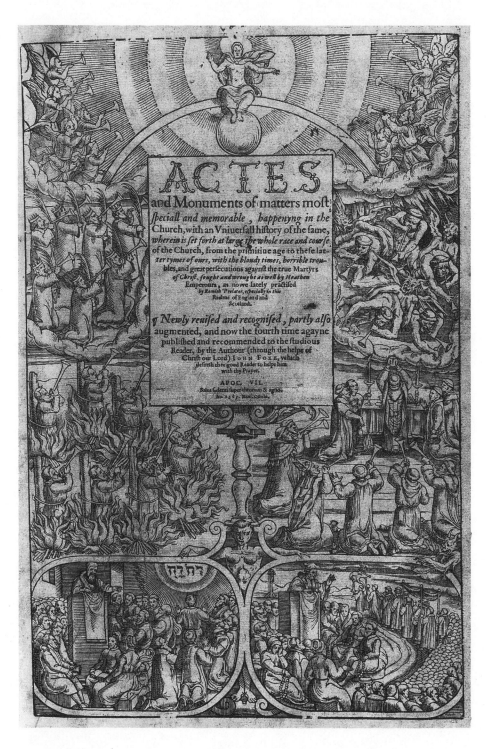

Title page, John Foxe, *Acts and Monuments,* London, 1583 (reduced)

The Complete Works of
ST. THOMAS MORE

VOLUME 7

Edited by

FRANK MANLEY

GERMAIN MARC'HADOUR

RICHARD MARIUS

and

CLARENCE H. MILLER

Yale University Press, New Haven and London

Set in Baskerville type by The Composing Room of Michigan.
Printed in the United States of America by
Vail-Ballou Press, Binghamton, N.Y.

Library of Congress catalogue number: 63-7949
International standard book number: 0-300-03809-7

The paper in this book meets
the guidelines for permanence and durability
of the Committee on Production Guidelines
for Book Longevity of the Council on
Library Resources.

10 9 8 7 6 5 4 3 2 1

For Louis L. Martz
A laborer in the vineyard
of the Yale Edition of St. Thomas More
From the earliest hour
With admiration and gratitude
For his learning, guidance, and support

ACKNOWLEDGMENTS

Like all the other volumes of the Yale edition of More, this one owes most to the labors and the heritage of Richard Sylvester, who fathered the whole enterprise and fostered it for so many years. The dedication of this volume is a token of gratitude for the long-standing and continuing contribution of Louis Martz. Of this "bright asterism," "these twi-lights, the Dioscuri" of the More edition, we may say, with Ben Jonson, that

> *fate doth so alternate the design,*
> *Whilst that in heaven, this light on earth must shine.*

Frank Manley wishes to acknowledge the assistance of Clarence Miller and Germain Marc'hadour in helping him polish and correct the translation of More's *Letter to Bugenhagen*. Clarence Miller also edited the commentary, cutting the excess and generously supplying additional references from his rich store of information about the period. Louis Martz read the introduction with his usual good sense, grace, and feeling for style and was able to suggest some transpositions that improved it immensely. Ralph Keen and other members of the staff of the More Project were cheerful and indefatigable in insuring the accuracy of the texts. And there are other debts as well—debts that go back thirty years or more to an afternoon at Louis Martz's house, in the garden, under the blooming apple trees, when I first met Dick Sylvester. We were both young assistant professors at Yale, our wives were both pregnant for the second time, our lives were still mostly before us, and Dick asked me to join the More Project, which was just getting under way at the time, and in so doing changed my life in ways that I cannot even measure. Since then Dick has died, cut off just as the promise was being fulfilled; I have moved away from New Haven; and the More Project is now drawing to a close. These are the last few sentences I expect to write about St. Thomas More, and it is fitting perhaps that I use them to acknowledge in some public fashion outside the limits of my own heart and memory some of the people I have met and learned to love while working on the project all these years. The first and most important of these is Louis Martz, to whom this volume and so much else about the More edition is dedicated. He gave me my first job and then went on to give me his friendship and the opportunity to work with him on one of More's greatest books. To Edwine Martz, for her gentleness, courtesy, and unfailing good humor and hospitality. To Richard Marius, for his high spirits and irrepressible gaiety. To Germain Marc'hadour, for his charity and devotion. To Clarence Miller, who led us all out of darkness after Dick died. To Joy Sylvester and Patrice and Paul and Peter and, last but not least, my god-child, Sara, who shared their home and affection with me. And to Tom Lawler, Dick Schoeck, Helen Whall-Seligman, Elizabeth Coffin, Jim Lusardi, Garry Haupt, Bill and Margaret Wimsatt, Floyd Watkins, Bill Dillingham, and Trudy Kretchman—for good times and good fellowship. And finally to my family—Carolyn, Evelyn and Mary, Thrower and Ralph, Mary Catherine, Peter, Michael and David and Matthew—who in their various ways put up with all this. To all these, my sincere love and affection.

Germain Marc'hadour renews his thanks to the many generous people whose support he acknowledged in the opening pages of the Yale edition of *A Dialogue Concerning Heresies*. His debts for the *Supplication of Souls* began earlier, when in 1959 he tried out on his mother a French translation of it; and they ended much later with the gentle goading of Ralph Keen and Clarence Miller and their substantial contributions to his commentary. He is also very grateful to Louis Martz, Raymond Lurie, Michele Margetts, and Katherine Gardiner Rodgers for their generous and invaluable help in shaping his introduction and polishing its documentation.

Richard Marius offers his thanks to the staff of the Harvard Libraries. He also is very grateful to Ralph Keen for his patient and indefatigable help in getting things right and to Clarence Miller for providing the commentary for *A Letter against Frith*. He also acknowledges a large debt to Stephen Foley, whose labors on the Yale edition of *The Answer to a Poisoned Book* made his own labors much lighter.

Clarence Miller wishes to thank Ralph Keen, his hardy helper and good right arm, whose unfailing assistance everywhere in the volume, from illustrations through appendices, has been invaluable and indispensable. He is especially grateful to his co-editors in this volume, all "old hands" of the Yale edition who did not rest on their Morean laurels but returned to the fray in yet another campaign. He also takes this opportunity, his last in the preface of a More volume, to acknowledge, with deep gratitude, his long and large debts to Richard Sylvester, Louis Martz, and all the other Yale editors, helpers, and supporters, who have brought the great work so close to its final fruition. He is also grateful for grants from the Mellon Foundation at St. Louis University, which enabled him to work for extended periods at the More Project.

We offer our thanks to Jay Williams and Mary Alice Galligan of the Yale University Press, to our manuscript editor, Ann Hawthorne, and to our indexer, Mary Ellen Curtin, all of whom helped us over difficult terrain toward the goal of an accurate and usable volume. As usual, we owe a large debt of gratitude to the assistants at the More Project: Raymond Lurie, Katherine Gardiner Rodgers, and Michele Margetts.

Finally, we are grateful to the Knights of Columbus for their generous support of our edition.

F. M., G. M., R. M., and C. H. M.

Atlanta, Ga.; Angers, France;
Cambridge, Mass.; St. Louis, Mo.

CONTENTS

Acknowledgments   viii

List of Illustrations   xiii

Introduction   xv

Letter to Bugenhagen   xvii
By Frank Manley

  Circumstances of Composition
    Bugenhagen's *Letter to the English*   xvii
    More's *Letter to Bugenhagen*   xxx
  Rhetorical Strategies
    Bugenhagen's *Letter to the English*   xxxvi
    More's *Letter to Bugenhagen*   xlii

Supplication of Souls   lxv
By Germain Marc'hadour

  The Two Supplications
    The Date of Fish's *Supplication* and More's Reply   lxv
    The Political Setting   lxvii
    The Twin Issues: Theological and Economic   lxix
    Scripture in More's *Supplication*   lxxiv
  The Dogma of Purgatory
    Place or State?   lxxxvii
    Conciliar Definitions   xci
    Jean Gerson on Purgatory   xcvi
    John Fisher on Purgatory   ciii

Letter against Frith   cxviii
By Richard Marius

  The Early Career of John Frith   cxix
  Henry VIII's Approach to John Frith   cxxviii
  Frith's *Christian Sentence*   cxxxiii
  More's Defense of the Real Presence against Frith   cxxxix
  Frith's Counterattack and Death   clii

The Texts   clx
By Clarence H. Miller

    Letter to Bugenhagen   clx
    Supplication of Souls   clxi
    Letter against Frith   clxviii

Texts

    Letter to Bugenhagen, with a translation by Frank Manley   1
    Supplication of Souls   107
    Letter Against Frith   229

Commentary   259

Appendix A, John Bugenhagen's *Epistola ad Anglos*   393

Appendix B, Simon Fish's *A Supplicacyon for the Beggers* with John
    Foxe's Sidenotes   407

Appendix C, John Frith's *A Christen Sentence*   423

Appendix D, *The Story of Simon Fish* from John Foxe's *Acts and
    Monuments*   435

Appendix E, Popular Devotions Concerning Purgatory,
    By Germain Marc'hadour   445

Appendix F, The Printer's Copy for the *Supplication of Souls* in the
    1557 *English Works,* By Ralph Keen   455

Appendix G, Table of Corresponding Pages   483

Glossary   491

Index   517

ILLUSTRATIONS

Title page, John Foxe, *Acts and Monuments*, London, 1583 (*STC²* 11225). Courtesy of the Beinecke Library, Yale University.

frontispiece

between pages

Supplication of Souls (1529¹; *STC²* 18091), sigs. c_1v-c_2. Courtesy of the McAlpin Collection, Union Theological Seminary, New York

clxiii–clxiv

facing page

Title page, *Letter to Bugenhagen* (Louvain: Fowler, 1568). Courtesy of the Huntington Library, San Marino, California

2

Title page, *Supplication of Souls* (1529²; *STC²* 18092), Courtesy of the Beinecke Library, Yale University.

109

Richard Hunne hanged in his cell, from John Foxe, *Acts and Monuments* (London, 1563; *STC²* 11222), sig. Nn_4v. Courtesy of the Beinecke Library, Yale University.

132

Title page, Otto Brunfels, *Precationes Biblicae* (Strasbourg: Johann Schott, 1528). Courtesy of E. P. Goldschmidt & Co., Ltd.

176

between pages

Supplication of Souls (1529¹; *STC²* 18091), sigs. h_2v-h_3. Courtesy of the McAlpin Collection, Union Theological Seminary, New York.

185–86

facing page

Christ in Limbo, by Albrecht Dürer (*Passio Domini Nostri*, Nürnberg: Hieronymus Holzel, 1511), plate xi. Courtesy of the John M. Wing Foundation, the Newberry Library, Chicago.

186

Title page, *A Letter against Frith* (1533; *STC²* 18078). Courtesy of the Folger Shakespeare Library, Washington, D. C.

231

facing page

The Last Supper, by Albrecht Dürer (*Passio Domini Nostri*, Nürnberg, Hieronymus Holzel, 1511), plate ii. Courtesy of the John M. Wing Foundation, the Newberry Library, Chicago.   236

Johann Bugenhagen, by Lucas Cranach the elder. Courtesy of the Staatliche Lutherhalle, Wittenberg.   395

between pages

Supplication of Souls (1529²; *STC*² 18092), sigs. F₁v and F₄v. Courtesy of the Beinecke Library, Yale University.   467–68

INTRODUCTION

LETTER TO BUGENHAGEN

Circumstances of Composition

BUGENHAGEN'S *LETTER TO THE ENGLISH*

JOHN BUGENHAGEN'S *Epistola ad Anglos* was first published by Simpertus Ruff at Augsburg in 1525. It was translated into German almost immediately and went through three German editions and two additional Latin editions before the end of the year—a total of six separate editions in two languages within a few months.[1] Its success was extraordinary. In February 1526 it was reprinted at Cologne by one of Luther's foremost opponents, John Cochlaeus, who, like More, incorporated the text in his own argument and responded to it point by point.[2] Shortly before that More had written his own reply and decided to put it aside, never to be printed in his lifetime.[3] In 1536, the year after More's death, Bugenhagen's *Letter* was finally translated into English, perhaps by William Tyndale,[4] and was thus made available to the ordinary Englishman. But by that time it no longer mattered. The occasion had passed. There was no need to urge the English to join the Reformation because it had already happened. The cause for which More had fought and died was already lost.

In 1525, the year in which he wrote the *Letter to the English*, Bugenhagen was best known as a friend and close associate of Luther's, a man very near to the center of power in Wittenberg. In fact, More thought

---

[1]Georg Geisenhof, *Bibliotheca Bugenhagiana: Bibliographie der Druckschriften des D. Joh. Bugenhagen*, Quellen und Darstellungen aus der Geschichte des Reformationsjahrhunderts 6 (Leipzig, 1908), pp. 215–21 (nos. 181–89); cited hereafter as "Geisenhof." Bugenhagen's *Letter* is reprinted as Appendix A of this volume.

[2]*Epistola Iohannis Bugenhagii Pomerani ad Anglos. Responsio Iohannis Cochlaei* (n.p., 1526; Geisenhof, no. 189); cited hereafter as "*Responsio Cochlaei*." The dedication to Hermann Rinck, Wolsey's agent in Germany, is dated February 10, 1526, at Cologne.

[3]The reply was first published by Fowler in 1568, thirty-three years after More's death.

[4]No. 4021 in *A Short-Title Catalogue of Books Printed in England, Scotland, & Ireland and of English Books Printed Abroad 1475–1640*, compiled by A. W. Pollard and G. R. Redgrave (London, 1926; cited hereafter as *STC*); second edition, revised and enlarged by W. A. Jackson, F. S. Ferguson, and Katharine F. Pantzer, 2 vols. (London, 1976–1986; cited hereafter as *STC²*). See William A. Clebsch, *England's Earliest Protestants, 1520–1535* (New Haven and London, 1964), p. 25, n. 1; cited hereafter as "Clebsch."

of him as its bishop (74/27, 102/31–32). Born on June 24, 1485, at Wollin in Pomerania, Bugenhagen attended the University of Greifswald and graduated in 1502. In 1504 he became headmaster of the municipal school at Treptow. In 1509 he was ordained to the priesthood and from 1517 to 1521 served as lector in scripture and patristics at Belbuck. Deeply influenced by Luther's *De captivitate Babylonica* and *De libertate Christiana* and desiring to know the author better, Bugenhagen gave up his position at Belbuck and moved to Wittenberg in 1521. Shortly afterward, in October 1522, he renounced his vow of celibacy and married Eva Rörer, sister of George Rörer, thus becoming one of the first reformers to marry. The following year, on the personal recommendation of Luther, he was elected pastor of the city church of Wittenberg by unanimous vote of the senate of the university and members of the city council. He remained official pastor of the city for the next thirty-four years.

Next to Melanchthon, whom he is said to have resembled in his moderation, Bugenhagen was probably the most important member of Luther's inner circle. He officiated at Luther's wedding to Katherine von Bora in 1525, stayed in Luther's home, and for many years was his confessor, friend, personal adviser, chief lieutenant, and counselor. His writings were relatively unimportant and consisted primarily of scriptural commentaries and translations of the Bible into Low German. He assisted Luther with his German Bible and wrote a number of polemical works against Catholics, Zwinglians, and anti-Trinitarians. None of these broke new ground, and his main talents seem to have been his gift for friendship and his ability as an administrator. In his later years he functioned primarily as a church organizer and was instrumental in establishing Lutheranism in northern Germany and Denmark. Between 1528 and 1544 he wrote church orders for Brunswick, Hamburg, Lübeck, Pomerania, Denmark, and Schleswig-Holstein. In Denmark in 1537 he officiated at the coronation of Christian III, consecrated seven "bishops" as overseers of the Danish church, and reorganized the University of Copenhagen. He died at Wittenberg on April 20, 1558, twelve years after Luther, twenty-three years after More.[1]

---

[1]On Bugenhagen see Hermann Hering, *Doktor Pomeranus, J. Bugenhagen* (Halle, 1888); Karl Vogt, *Johannes Bugenhagen Pomeranus* (Elberfeld, 1867); the article by Gustav Kawerau in *The New Schaff-Herzog Encyclopedia of Religious Knowledge*, 13 vols. (New York and London, 1908–14); and *Theologische Realenzyklopädie*, 11 vols. (Berlin and New York, 1977–82), 7, 354–63.

Bugenhagen, then, was, as Fowler describes him, "a man of no small reputation among Protestants" (2/6–8, 12/3–5).[1] More himself links him with Lambert, Karlstadt, and Oecolampadius as one of the leaders of the Reformation (see, for example, 14/36–37), but he was hardly that. Neither an original thinker nor a theologian, he was best known for his friendship with Luther and his official, almost symbolic position as chief patriarch of Wittenberg. Why then did he presume to write his *Letter to the English* as though it were an official pronouncement or one of Paul's epistles? What could he possibly have hoped to accomplish? He had no previous connection with England and was so little known outside Germany that Cochlaeus—a suspicious man when it came to Lutherans—thought it must be some sort of trick. There were no Lutherans in England, Cochlaeus noted: there would be no one there to listen to him. Besides, Lutheran books were forbidden. Who then in England could read it? The real audience, Cochlaeus concluded, were not the English, but the Germans. Bugenhagen was trying to strengthen the Lutheran position in Germany by attempting to convince the people that the king of England and the entire English nation were prepared to join the Lutheran cause: "Per mathematicam uero hanc epistolam tuam decepti credant nunc. Regem illum simul cum tota gente sua in partes concessisse uestras."[2]

The author, then, was relatively unknown in England, and the *Letter* itself was simply a pamphlet, no more than a few pages in length. It broke no new ground, addressed no new issues, raised no new questions. It merely asserted basic Lutheran doctrine, particularly the concept of justification by faith alone. How are we to explain the popularity demonstrated by six editions in two languages in a few months and almost immediate attacks by two of Luther's foremost Catholic opponents? What was it in the *Letter* itself or in the circumstances of its composition that gave it a significance beyond its apparent importance? And what is that significance? More and Cochlaeus, it turns out, were both confused as to Bugenhagen's ultimate purpose. Bugenhagen himself was confused, acting most probably on certain false rumors transmitted to Luther by Christian II of Denmark. But once released, whatever the author's original intention, Bugenhagen's *Letter*

---

[1] The description seems defensive, for if Fowler thought Bugenhagen a worthy opponent, he would not have thought it necessary to explain who he was. On the other hand, he may have been speaking ironically, Protestants being for recusant Catholics a rather specialized group to be famous among.

[2] *Responsio Cochlaei*, sig. C5v.

to the English became caught up in certain events in England in the mid-1520s that altered the way it was perceived. It became touched, however mistakenly, by the intensity of the moment.

Before 1525 England appeared to be squarely in the Catholic camp. The bull *Exsurge Domine,* which excommunicated Luther, was published on June 15, 1520. It accused Luther of reviving the ancient heresies, listed forty-one heretical articles among his published works, and ordered his books sought out and destroyed—"eradicated from the memory of man" as the Edict of Worms was later to put it. Public burnings of Luther's works were held almost everywhere in Europe— at Rome in the Piazza Navona, at Naples, Louvain, Cologne, Mainz, Leipzig. Accordingly, in England on the morning of Sunday, May 12, 1521, a procession of notables led by Thomas Cardinal Wolsey, archbishop of York, assembled at St. Paul's Cathedral in London. The archbishop of Canterbury made a short speech and Wolsey gave the blessing. The assemblage then repaired to St. Paul's Cross, where in the presence of thirty thousand onlookers Wolsey ascended a platform covered with a canopy of cloth of gold and in company with the papal nuncio and ambassadors of the Holy Roman Empire and the Venetian Republic watched while Luther's books were burned. John Fisher, bishop of Rochester, delivered a two-hour sermon publicly repudiating Luther on behalf of the English crown and branding him a heretic. His works were no longer permitted to be imported, and teaching his doctrines was forbidden. Fisher's sermon, which was published shortly afterward,[1] constituted the first English attack on Luther. The nation had publicly and politically taken a stand on the side of Pope Leo X and Charles V against the forces of Lutheranism.[2]

A few months later, in July 1521, Henry VIII published his *Assertio septem sacramentorum adversus M. Lutherum* (*STC* 13078), a defense of the church's sacramental system against Luther's attack in his *De captivitate Babylonica* (October 1520). The volume was an extraordinarily violent attack not only on the *De captivitate Babylonica* but also on Luther's own person, and Luther very soon replied in kind. In Sep-

---

[1]*STC* 10893. The text is most readily available in *The English Works of John Fisher, Bishop of Rochester,* Part 1, ed. J. E. B. Major, Early English Text Society, Extra Series no. 27 (London, 1876; reprint, 1935), pp. 311–48; cited hereafter as "Fisher, *English Works.*" Fisher's sermon was in English, but it was immediately translated into Latin by Richard Pace, royal secretary to Henry VIII, for wider dissemination.

[2]The best account of the bookburning of 1521 is in Carl S. Meyer's "Henry VIII Burns Luther's Books 12 May 1521," *The Journal for Ecclesiastical History,* 9 (1958), 173–87. See also Clebsch, pp. 9–19.

tember 1522 he published his astonishing *Contra Henricum regem Angliae.* Never before had a reigning monarch been subjected to such abuse by a commoner. Luther himself admitted that the book seemed to have the devil behind it.[1] The king's dignity had been debased, and, although some sort of response was obviously called for, it was just as obvious that Henry was not in any position to make one himself. Hence the real work of responding to Luther was entrusted to the most capable man at court, the author of the renowned *Utopia.*

More proceeded, Harpsfield says, according to the scriptural adage that one should reply to a fool according to his own folly.[2] He took up Luther's attack on the king point by point, confronting him with citations from his own works and the Bible, and then, after the fashion of the time, veering off into the most violent personal abuse. The book could hardly have been more offensive. It is a brilliant piece of Renaissance polemic, matching Luther in vulgarity and fulfilling in its rambling way all the expectations of the period. Luther was stung, but he did not know who had attacked him, since More concealed his own identity in an elaborate literary hoax reminiscent of *Utopia,* claiming that the whole thing was written by one William Ross.[3]

Henry VIII's *Assertio* and More's *Responsio ad Lutherum,* though written in Latin, were both essentially popular works addressed to a continental audience. They were not specialized theological treatises. That aspect of England's response was left to John Fisher, bishop of Rochester. Fisher's two vernacular sermons at the bookburnings of 1521 and 1526 were designed as the official doctrinal replies to Luther

---

[1]*Responsio ad Lutherum,* p. 725, vol. 5 of The Yale Edition of the Complete Works of St. Thomas More. For volumes of the Yale Edition, which are cited hereafter as *CW* followed by the volume number, see the bibliography.

[2]Nicholas Harpsfield, *The Life and Death of Sir Thomas More,* ed. Elsie Vaughan Hitchcock and R. W. Chambers, Early English Text Society, Original Series no. 186 (London, 1932), p. 106.

[3]More's name did not appear until the collected edition of his Latin works, the *Opera omnia* of 1565; no. 75a in R. W. Gibson and J. Max Patrick, *St. Thomas More: A Preliminary Bibliography of His Works and of Moreana to the Year 1750* (New Haven and London, 1961; cited hereafter as "Gibson"). The *Responsio* was first begun under the pseudonym Ferdinandus Baravellus on February 11, 1523, and was finished in time for Erasmus to receive a presentation copy at Basel in July of the same year. Almost immediately after its publication, however, More withdrew this first version of the book in order to add to the prefatory material and shift the scene from Spain to England. The name of the pseudonymous author was changed accordingly from Baravellus to the English-sounding William Ross, and a new section was added on the nature of the church and the question of papal primacy. The revised version was once again printed by Pynson. The preface was dated October 15, 1523. See *CW*5, 823–31.

on the part of the English church and state. These public pronouncements were followed by a series of theological works that examined the
central issues of Lutheranism—*Assertionis Lutheranae confutatio* (1523),
Sacri sacerdotii defensio contra Lutherum (1525), and particularly *Defensio
regiæ assertionis contra Babylonicam captivitatem* (1525). Fisher "established the terminology, chose the ground, and set the tone for the
doctrinal and ecclesiological debates which were the substance of the
English Reformation before the 'King's matter' became prominent."[1]

Ceremonial bookburnings, the direct involvement of the king, a
major theological response, and a scathing personal attack by the most
noted man of letters in the country—these were the steps taken in
England to combat Luther in the early 1520s. They have all the ear-
marks of a well-conceived government program—including the fact
that it did not succeed. For who can throw a net on the people? All
those directly involved were men of considerable power, prestige, and
influence. Their careers were well established. They were all associated
with the highest levels of government. But despite their passionate
conviction, they were not representative of the nation as a whole. In
1525 and the early months of 1526—at the very time when More was
writing his *Letter to Bugenhagen*—there was a sudden shift, a dramatic
outburst of Lutheran activity in England that far surpassed anything
that had gone before. Wolsey was quick to take retaliatory action, but
he did not have the ability or the imagination to do anything other than
repeat with variations what he had already done before. The Reformation had arrived at last in England.

At Cambridge a group of thirty or more Lutheran sympathizers—
clergymen and fellows of the university—met regularly to discuss the
new gospel.[2] Their meetings were so open and so well known that the
place where they met, the White Horse Tavern, was popularly known
as "Germany." On December 25, 1525, a member of this group, Robert
Barnes, prior of the Augustinian friars at Cambridge, was bold enough
to carry the process a step further by preaching a sermon on Luther's
postil or commentary on the gospel for the day.[3] The evidence is less

[1]Clebsch, p. 31.
[2]John Foxe, *Acts and Monuments*, 8 vols (London, 1843–49; reprint, New York, 1965) 5,
416 (cited hereafter as "Foxe"); cited by Philip Hughes, *The Reformation in England*, 3 vols.
(London, 1954–56), *1*, 133 (cited hereafter as "Hughes"). Hughes gives a list of names of
the thirty sympathizers, among them William Tyndale, George Joye, Robert Barnes,
Miles Coverdale, Thomas Bilney, Hugh Latimer, Cranmer, and Frith. See also
Confutation, CW 8, 1370.
[3]The best account of the strange career of Robert Barnes is by James Lusardi in
Confutation, CW 8, 1367–1415.

conclusive, but Hugh Latimer seems to have preached a second Lutheran sermon at Cambridge on the same day.[1] At Oxford the archbishop of Canterbury asked Wolsey to appoint a special commission consisting of Fisher and Tunstal to stamp out Lutheranism there.[2] The intellectuals were, as usual, the first to be tainted. There were outbreaks at both universities. Soon the disease would be epidemic.

Around the same time, late 1525 and early 1526, the first sheets of William Tyndale's translation of the New Testament were smuggled into England.[3] Cochlaeus, always concerned with English affairs, was the first to sound the alarm.[4] On the face of it there would seem to have been some connection between the appearance of an English New Testament and a heightening of Lutheran activity in England. One senses the beginning of a new phase: the Reformation was now moving out to the people. But even if there were no real connection in the sense of a plan or conspiracy, there was still the deeper relatedness of events themselves, tilted and moving in the same direction like strata of underlying rock, beyond the comprehension of any one man or any one group of men. On October 12, 1524, for example, Cuthbert Tunstal, bishop of London, called the booksellers in the city together and solemnly warned them against importing and selling unlicensed foreign books.[5] The warning had nothing to do with Tyndale's New Testament, but it seems to indicate that books such as Tyndale's—heretical material of all sorts—were currently being imported in sufficient numbers to concern the authorities. By early 1526 the flow of heretical books had increased to such an extent that there was serious discussion of issuing a royal proclamation to stop it. Instead of being directed against booksellers and other members of the trade, it was to have been directed against the population as a whole. Anyone possessing hereti-

---

[1]Clebsch, p. 26.

[2]Hughes, *1*, 133.

[3]Completed between May 1524 and July 1525, during Tyndale's stay in Wittenberg, the translation was printed by Peter Quentel at Cologne and, when interrupted by the authorities there, finished at Worms in 1525. Based on Erasmus' Greek New Testament, Tyndale's translation is an independent piece of work, but it shows traces of phrasing taken from Luther's German Bible. Sheets of the interrupted quarto edition, completed at Worms, arrived in England before the octavo, printed entirely at Worms. The octavo contains the bare text only. The quarto edition includes translations of Luther's prologues to various books as well as references to parallel passages and notes taken from Luther's translation. The quarto is thus much more controversial, much more identifiably Lutheran (Hughes, *1*, 144–45).

[4]Clebsch, p. 26.

[5]*CW 9*, xxvi–xxx and Commentary at 11/20.

cal books was to be ordered to turn them in to the authorities on pain of
excommunication. Anyone convicted of holding heretical beliefs was
to renounce them. If they refused, they would be burned at the stake.
It is not known if the proclamation was ever issued, but the proposal is a
good indication of the magnitude of the problem.[1]

By January 1526 things came to a head. Alarmed by the increased
Lutheran activity in the country, Wolsey requested permission from
the king to stage another ceremonial bookburning. Henry immediately
gave his assent, suggesting that John Fisher would be "moste meete to
make the sermond," as in 1521, "bothe propter auctoritatem, grauita-
tem, et doctrinam personae."[2] Accordingly, on Quinquagesima Sunday, February 11, 1526, at St. Paul's Cathedral, Wolsey staged his
demonstration. Outwardly the ceremony of 1526 might seem to have
been a conditioned response, an unimaginative repetition of the same
ritual that was supposed to have exorcised Luther in 1521, full of the
same English love of pomp and splendor, making the same point for
the same ostensible purpose; but inwardly it was anything but the
same. The ceremony of 1521 was England's official response to the
pope's excommunication of Luther, denouncing him as a heretic and
outlawing his publications. The bookburning was thus by and large a
symbolic action confirming England's unity with the universal church.
Among those participating were ambassadors representing the nations
of Europe. It was not entirely an English affair.

In 1526, however, there were no ambassadors. Their places were
taken by representatives of the English clergy—thirty-six abbots, pri-
ors, and bishops. It was specifically and dramatically English. The
baskets of books that were collected and burned were no longer taken
from open shelves in booksellers' shops. They were illegal imports,
contraband, gathered by forced entry and secret search, as in More's
raid on the Steelyard a few weeks before, on January 26, 1526, or the
search made at Cambridge among thirty prime suspects a few days
later.[3] Instead of the abstract idea of heresy occurring somewhere in
Germany, related to England only by politics and the universal nature

[1]CW 9, xxv.

[2]Clebsch, p. 27. See also Letters and Papers, Foreign and Domestic, of the Reign of Henry VIII, ed. J. S. Brewer, James Gairdner, and R. H. Brodie, 21 vols. (London, 1862–1932; reprint, Vaduz, 1965), 4/1, 433, no. 995; cited hereafter as LP. See also CW 8, 1377–78. Wolsey's original request to the king, made through John Langland, bishop of Lincoln, is now lost, but Langland's reply for the king, from which this quotation is taken, is still extant.

[3]Foxe, 5/2, 416.

of the church, there were now actual heretics present in England, some of whom were displayed for the occasion.

Robert Barnes was one of these. Shortly after preaching his ill-advised sermon on Luther's postil, Barnes had been taken up by the authorities at the university, examined, and then passed on to Wolsey, who forced him to renounce his beliefs, to kneel (together with five men from the raid on the Steelyard) on a separate stage at the book-burning, and to beg forgiveness while Fisher preached a pointed sermon on the gospel of the day—the words of Christ to the blind man: "Receive your sight; your faith has saved you."[1] While the books were burned, Barnes and the others were made to march around the fire three times carrying faggots, which they then cast into the flames. Afterward, in the culmination of the ceremony, they were given final absolution by Fisher and received back into the church.[2]

The difference between the bookburning of 1521 and that of 1526 is a measure of the distance England had come in those five years. The ritual of 1521 was largely ceremonial and symbolic, directed toward heresy abroad. Its message was addressed to Wittenberg. The ceremony of 1526, on the other hand, was much more functional and specific. It spoke to events currently occurring in England and was essentially a show of force on the part of the government. Forbidden books, such as Tyndale's New Testament, were not to be imported. Forbidden ideas were not to be harbored in the heart. It seems less like a bookburning than an *auto-da-fé*, directed not toward the abstract ideas printed in books but toward the men who possessed them. For those Englishmen who longed for spiritual reform and looked to Luther as a sign of new hope, the ritual of 1526 was an overt threat. Heresy, the government said, is now here at home among us. The warning was issued: it was not to be tolerated.

It was just at this moment, against this heightened sense of fear and alarm, that Bugenhagen's *Letter to the English* happened to bumble onto the scene. After 1525, when it became clear that heresy had made some inroads in the country despite the vigilance of the church and state, the atmosphere was so tense and tainted with hysteria that it was hardly the time to listen to what Bugenhagen undoubtedly intended as a Pauline, apostolic approach to the problem—mild, reasonable, irenic, low-key, and unctuously sanctimonious. To Henry VIII, Wolsey, and men like

---

[1]*CW 8*, 1382.

[2]The best accounts of the bookburning of 1526 are by Lusardi, *CW 8*, 1382–83, and Clebsch, pp. 26–30.

More—harriers of heretics—the fact that the *Letter* was written at all undoubtedly was taken as further evidence of the insane pride and arrogance of Luther and his followers.[1] Heretics were no longer content with meeting among themselves in secret cells, circulating forbidden books and forbidden ideas. They had now come out in the open like noonday devils—clear, plain, ugly as sin. Things had come together too neatly. To a loyal Englishman the events of 1525–1526 would have seemed like parts of a concerted effort: the presence of heresy at both universities, the appearance of an English New Testament circulating surreptitiously, stealing the minds and hearts of the people, and now this, an apostolic letter from one of the Germans, "a man of no small reputation among Protestants" (2/6–8, 12/4–5), urging instant conversion. When he was translating the New Testament, Tyndale had been with Luther at Wittenberg. Contacts were undoubtedly made, and now that the work was finished and was being smuggled into the country, the titular head of the Lutheran church—the Wittenbergian pope or bishop—writes like John the Baptist crying out to the people to make straight the way.

So it must have seemed to More. And there may have been some truth to it. The appearance of Bugenhagen's *Letter to the English* in conjunction with Tyndale's New Testament may have been too fortunate to be entirely fortuitous. And yet there is good evidence to suggest that it was not part of a Protestant plot. It was simply a mistake, a miscalculation, a bizarre, ironic accident based on a false rumor circulating in Wittenberg that suggested that England was ripe for the plucking. Henry VIII, Luther was told, had gone soft on Protestantism.

On June 21, 1525, just as the Peasants' Revolt was ending and the last bands were being exterminated, Luther wrote his friend George Spalatin, chaplain at the court of Frederick, duke of Saxony, inviting him to his wedding reception the following Tuesday. The wedding itself had already taken place on June 13. Half joking, Luther said that he wanted to see if Spalatin really approved of what he had done. In the last paragraph, almost as an afterthought, he mentioned that he was returning a letter Spalatin had sent to him. "I am sending you back the King of Denmark's letter," he wrote. "I actually know nothing about the books of the King of England. I will pray for him, though, as much as I can and will write him in due course. I haven't been able to

---

[1]More assumes Bugenhagen is absolutely crazy. See, for example, 22/16–24/4, 70/3–72/30, 84/15–29, 86/28–31. Some of this is rhetorical, but much of it is not.

get to it. You will let me know when you have the time and a messenger to carry the letter."[1] The Danish king referred to was Christian II, who had been dethroned in 1523 and shortly afterward spent some time with Luther in Wittenberg. He had written either to the Elector Frederick or to Spalatin himself to pass on the startling information that Henry VIII, the king of England, Luther's old opponent, was now inclined toward Protestantism. Hence Luther's promise to pray for him. Christian II also suggested that if Luther were to write a submissive letter and apologize to the king for abusing him, it would no doubt be taken in good faith. Luther promised to get around to it as soon as possible. Meanwhile, he had a marriage on his hands.[2]

The proper occasion did not present itself until September 1, 1525, when Luther wrote Henry VIII a letter as astonishing in its own way as the false report of Henry's own change of heart. In order to secure what he thought was an advantage, Luther utterly debased himself. He began by excusing the scurrilous book he had written against Henry by blaming it on others who had caused it to be rushed into print. They were the ones at fault, not he. As for himself, Luther offered to publish a recantation. Not only that, he would be honored to write another book entirely praising the king this time and explaining the details of the new gospel. Meanwhile he prayed that Henry's desire to foster the gospel would continue to grow and increase.[3]

Written in 1525 at roughly the same time, Bugenhagen's *Letter to the English* was probably inspired by the same rumor. How else are we to account for it? Bugenhagen was relatively unknown, and the English were hardly prepared for wholesale conversion. But if Bugenhagen had heard the rumor (as he undoubtedly had, since he was one of Luther's close advisers) that the Holy Spirit had descended on Henry VIII and so inflamed his heart that he now looked with favor on the new gospel, and if at the same time he knew of the readiness of Tyn-

---

[1] "Remitto literas regis Danorum. Ego vero de libris Regis Anglie nihil scio. Orabo quoque, quantum possum. Suoque tempore scribam; modo non licuit; monebis tu, cum ocium & oportunitas nuncii fuerit"; *D. Martin Luthers Werke: Briefwechsel*, 16 vols. to date (Weimar, 1930–), *3*, 540; cited hereafter as *WABR*.

[2] Erwin Doernberg, *Henry VIII and Luther: An Account of Their Personal Relations* (Stanford, 1961), pp. 49–50.

[3] *WABR 3*, 563. An English translation is available in Doernberg, pp. 50–53. The first edition of Henry's reply to Luther (*Literarum, quibus Henricus octavus respondit ad quandam epistolam M. Lutheri . . . exemplum, STC* 13084) was first published by Pynson on December 2, 1526. The English translation (*A copy of the letters, wherin kyng Henry the eyght made answere vnto a certayn letter of Martyn Luther, STC* 13086) was also published by Pynson but without date. It probably followed the Latin edition by a month or two.

dale's New Testament (as he may have), then it becomes a little more understandable and a little less preposterous that he would have composed such a document. Luther wrote a personal letter of apology to the king in his own hand, and the titular head of the church in Wittenberg followed it up with something like a general proclamation or Pauline epistle addressed to the people as a whole. The two may very well have been conceived of as a unit or at least as two aspects of the same thing.

The tone of Bugenhagen's *Letter* also suggests that he may have been suffering under some sort of delusion. Unlike most polemical works of the period, it is not a vicious attack on his opponents. It is an overview of Lutheran doctrine, or of what is essential in it. The tone may strike the reader as hypocritical, pious perhaps, and sanctimonious, but it is not personally abusive, not violent, not furious and insulting like a barking dog. And the reason may very well have been its connection with the rumor of England's imminent conversion. If he wrote in the shadow of such a possibility, Bugenhagen would probably have hoped to accomplish something more than mere insult. To convert a whole nation called for sobriety, high seriousness, spirituality, a reining in of the passions, not anger and aggression.

There are, moreover, curious resemblances between Luther's letter to the king and Bugenhagen's *Letter* to the king's loyal subjects. Luther has a special need to apologize and apologize profusely, and that takes up most of his letter. But in those sections where he speaks more broadly, he sounds surprisingly like Bugenhagen. They both say essentially the same thing. The only difference is that Bugenhagen has the opportunity to expand on it and explain it more fully. At one point, for example, Luther defends himself against the charge of heresy. How can it be heresy, he asks, to teach the doctrine of Christ crucified? That is the one, absolute, essential teaching of his on which all the others are based: "quidnam mali possim dicere, qui aliud nihil doceam, quam fide Iesu Christi, filii Dei, pro nobis passi et suscitati, salvos fieri oportere, sicut testantur euangelia et epistolae apostolorum. Hoc enim est caput et fundamentum doctrinae meae, super quod postea aedifico et doceo charitatem erga proximum, obedientiam erga politicos magistratus, tum crucifixionem corporis peccati, ut itidem praescribit christiana doctrina."[1] Bugenhagen says essentially the same thing. It is the main point, the constant refrain of his entire letter. Like Luther he begins by defending the reformers against various sorts of false rumors and lies

---

[1] *WABR 3*, 564.

that remain unspecified. He then focuses almost exclusively on what he calls the one main article of Lutheran belief underlying all others: "Est autem Articulus ille: Christus est Iusticia nostra. Nam is factus est nobis a Deo sapientia, iusticia, satisfactio, redemptio" (42/34–44/2).[1] For those who are led by the spirit of Christ, Bugenhagen says, are the sons of God. Echoing Luther's reference to charity, obedience, and continence, he refers to such men as good trees producing as it were without effort good fruit in their season. They worship God properly, keep all the sacraments Christ instituted, and perform all sorts of charitable acts toward their neighbors, loving even their enemies (80/7–28).[2]

These are both excellent summaries of the Lutheran concept of justification, and one would naturally expect them to be somewhat similar. It would be surprising, in fact, if they were not. And yet, sketchy as Luther's statement is, the similarities are too great to be entirely coincidental. If they were both written at the same time for the same general purpose, called forth by the same occasion, the connection between them would seem even more plausible.

Luther could go only so far in his letter to the king without awaiting the king's reply. Bugenhagen, however, could proceed at once and help consolidate their position by writing a little book of his own addressed not to the king, but to the people, explaining more fully what Luther could only touch on in his letter. By discussing essential Lutheran doctrine, focusing on the idea of justification, and showing how innocent it really was, how spiritual, how fundamentally Christian, Bugenhagen could go far in allaying English fear and suspicion. The full explanation would come later, when Luther wrote the book he promised to address to Henry, in which he would explain all his teachings in all their rich profundity.

If that was the plan, then something went haywire. Luther's letter never got to England—at least not on time. Although it was written on September 1, 1525, it was delayed for some reason and did not reach the English court until March 20, 1526, when we first hear of it in More's possession.[3] Since More was functioning at the time as the

---

[1]See Appendix A, 400/6–10.

[2]Appendix A, 402/7–35. Both also assume that they or any true followers of Christ will be persecuted for his sake. Luther quotes the second Psalm: "Quid mirum vero, si Caesar et aliquot Principes in me saeviunt? Nonne, ut Psalm. II. dicit: 'Adversus Dominum et Christum suum fremunt gentes, meditantur populi, conspirant reges terrae et conveniunt principes'?" (WABR 3, 564). Bugenhagen (16/9–10) refers to the beatitude in Matthew 5:11 ("Beati eritis, quum maledixerint vobis homines").

[3]William Knight wrote to Wolsey from Winchester that the king said that Sir Thomas More had the copy of Luther's letter (LP 4/2, 1084, no. 2420).

king's sole secretary, it is natural that the letter would have passed through his hands.¹ Bugenhagen, meanwhile, had already rushed into print. His *Letter to the English* went through a number of editions in quick succession and seemed an instant success. It flashed across the sky of Europe as suddenly and inexplicably as a meteor. Who could say what it meant? Without Luther's letter to the king, which would not surface until the following year, Bugenhagen's *Letter* seemed on the face of it so preposterous that one had to cast about to invent explanations. Since there was apparently no context, men were free to interpret it any way they wanted. To Cochlaeus it was a trick to delude the Germans. To Englishmen like More it was simply another example of the megalomaniacal lunacy of the heretics, who stirred once in the belly of the state and thought they already ruled the country. It was only later, when Luther's letter arrived at court, that it was possible to understand what had happened, but by that time it was too late. The connection was already broken. The whole court was agog with the news of Luther's latest insanity. His letter to the king was galvanizing. It required an instant reply. Meanwhile Bugenhagen was forgotten.

MORE'S *LETTER TO BUGENHAGEN*

MORE's reply to Bugenhagen was written sometime in the three-month period from December 1525 to February 1526.² At the time he was serving primarily as humanist-in-residence at court and as private secretary to Henry VIII. As such, he was required to be in constant attendance on the king as he moved in progress throughout the country from Greenwich to Ampthill to London to Windsor to Brideswell.³ More was forty-eight years old. His family was settled on his estate at Chelsea, which he had purchased just the year before—his gallery, his gardens, his orchards, all the pleasant, comfortable things his wife enumerated for him in the Tower just before he was executed. In September 1525 his two youngest daughters, Elizabeth and Cecily, were married at Willesden in the private chapel of Giles Alington,

---

¹More served as the only royal secretary to Henry VIII from shortly after September 1522 until the middle of 1526. Before that time, beginning in 1518, he shared the duties with the official secretary, Richard Pace. See John A. Guy, *The Public Career of Sir Thomas More* (New Haven and London, 1980), pp. 15–17; cited hereafter as "Guy."

²More refers to Luther's *De servo arbitrio*, which was published in December 1525, but he had not yet heard of the first volume of Erasmus' *Hyperaspistes*, dated February 1526. See note on 84/23–29.

³For More's itinerary for the year 1525, see Guy, p. 19.

husband of Alice Alington, More's stepdaughter. In the same month, More gave up the office of undertreasurer of the Exchequer, which he had held since May 1521, and assumed the more burdensome, less remunerative duties of chancellor of the duchy of Lancaster and high steward to the University of Cambridge.[1] The following year Holbein was to visit[2] and paint the celebrated portraits of More and his family by which we now know them.

Somewhat deeper, closer to what we now perceive as the underlying drift or current of his life—"the fountain," as Othello calls it, "from the which my current runs"—are More's dealings with the heretics during this same period, particularly in the first two months of 1526, when the *Letter to Bugenhagen* was most probably written. In August 1525 More met with John Eck, one of the leading German polemicists. Eck was in London to assure continued English support against Luther. More gave him a copy of his *Responsio ad Lutherum,* which Eck duly noted as being a gift from the author,[3] and it may have been during this meeting that More first heard of Bugenhagen's *Letter.*[4] A few months later, as part of the government's crackdown on heresy, More led a raid on the merchants of the Hanseatic League residing in the Steelyard in London, and it is this event more than any other that forms the symbolic, figurative background to the *Letter to Bugenhagen.* The two events not only parallel each other in time, but they also complement each other on an emotional level. The anger from one flowed over into the other and helped intensify them both. Both were essentially acts of violence. The only difference is that one was more immediate and direct than the other.

On the evening of January 26, 1526, Thomas More and several other members of the royal council along with their retainers invaded the precincts of the Steelyard and posted guards at all the exits. More then called the merchants together and tried to calm their fears by reminding them that one of their fellows had just been imprisoned for

---

[1]Guy, pp. 24–27. The dates are slightly different in R. W. Chambers, *Thomas More* (London, 1935; reprint, Ann Arbor, 1958), pp. 214–15; cited hereafter as "Chambers."

[2]Holbein arrived in London with a letter of introduction from Erasmus to More sometime before Christmas 1526. See Stanley Morison, *The Likeness of Thomas More* (London, 1963), pp. 4–6.

[3]*CW* 5, 825.

[4]This suggestion runs counter to More's own account of how Bugenhagen's letter was delivered by hand to his door by some anonymous caller while he was away from home on a trip (12/6–29), but More's account may be an elaborate hoax. It is difficult to say how much truth there is in it.

clipping English coins.[1] Since November 1520 More had held a half-share in the keepership of the foreign exchanges,[2] and he used his position as a pretext to warn the merchants about the debasement of English coinage and particularly about the possession of vernacular Bibles and other Lutheran books. The king, he said, was more concerned about that than he was about the case at hand. Then he left.

The next day More appeared again, this time with two clerks. The merchants were divided into two groups, one for each clerk, and made to swear that they would destroy any forbidden books in their possession. Then their quarters were searched. As a result of the search, four of the merchants were taken into custody and interrogated by Wolsey. All confessed to having seen or having had in their possession at one time or another various German books of Luther's. None could read Latin. Most were ignorant of theology, but some confessed to holding views that were innocently tainted by heresy. One, Hans Reusell, thought the pope was the same as any other bishop. He had never heard of papal infallibility. Another, Helbert Bellendorpe, confessed to eating meat on three separate occasions because, as he said, sounding like Luther, the kingdom of God does not consist of meat and drink. Days of fast and abstinence were not instituted by Christ, but by the church.[3] After being interrogated, the merchants confessed and were ordered as penance to recant publicly at the bookburning scheduled at St. Paul's Cathedral on February 11, 1526, after which they would receive final absolution.

If the *Letter to Bugenhagen* is a corollary to the raid on the Steelyard, there is nothing in the work itself to indicate More's involvement. In fact he goes out of his way to disguise any possible connection. In the first few pages he describes how it came to be written. A manuscript of Bugenhagen's original letter was dropped off at his house while he was away from home on a trip. He had no idea who had sent it to him or why it was sent. He was no theologian, and he certainly had no interest in Luther. The account seems like a typical example of More's love of elaborate literary disguise. But how are we to take it? In the version of

---

[1] The best accounts of More's raid on the Steelyard are M. E. Kronenberg, "A Printed Letter of the London House Merchants (3 March 1526)," *Oxford Bibliographical Society, Publications,* New Series, *1/1* (1947), 25–32, and Carl S. Meyer, "Thomas More and the Wittenberg Lutherans," *Concordia Theological Monthly, 39* (1968), 246–56. This was not the first time More raided the Steelyard. He had invaded the precincts on Friday, December 22, 1525, under the pretext of checking on coinage. See *CW 6,* 456, n. 2.

[2] Guy, pp. 24–25.

[3] *LP 4/1,* 885, no. 1962.

the text we now have, in Fowler's printing, More is clearly identified as the author. His name is prominently displayed on the title page. But is that what More intended, or is it simply Fowler's attempt to cash in on More's fame? If More had published it in his lifetime, would he have issued it under his own name, or would he have printed it anonymously? Our answers to these questions significantly affect how we read the text. On the one hand, More would have used his real name and his real position in the world as something like a mask to conceal the fact that he was not an innocent bystander, a disinterested citizen, as he pretends, but the infamous William Ross, who had already written extensively against Luther. It is a brilliant idea: to use the truth as a form of disguise. The possibilities for irony are endless. Writing in Latin and addressing the same international audience who had read his famous *Utopia* ten years before, More would have been able to bring to bear against the Lutherans the full weight of his reputation without letting on that he had ever attacked Luther before or dirtied his hands in the controversy. If, on the other hand, More did not intend to identify himself on the title page, then the letter would simply have been taken as the work of an unknown Englishman, a representative member of the educated middle class, who had been finally driven to break his silence and speak out against the Lutherans.

With the evidence we now have, it is impossible to tell which of these alternatives is correct. It is tempting to believe that More would have used his own name simply because of the added sense of complexity and irony it brings to the text, but there is a strong likelihood that the title page as we now have it (as opposed to the one on More's manuscript) was drawn up by Fowler. But in either case, whether he speaks anonymously as a representative Englishman or whether he speaks in his own person, he still functions as something like the European spokesman for the entire English community.

But if that is the case—if More was serving as the mouthpiece or representative of the English nation—why did he not publish his reply to Bugenhagen? It seems likely that the manuscript was carefully prepared for publication. The Latin is polished and extremely effective, catching the emotions precisely. There are none of the logical gaps, hesitations, false starts, and digressions typical of a first draft. In fact it seems more finished, more unified, more focused than most of More's polemical works simply because of its brevity and the normal precision of More's Latin style. Fowler says that the manuscript he printed from was the author's own autograph copy carefully corrected in More's own hand as though to prepare it for the printer (2/10–12). Why then did More lay it aside?

There are a number of possibilities. Elizabeth Rogers suggests that
More simply became involved in other things, specifically the later
English controversies.[1] But that was two years down the line.[2] Louis
Schuster suggests that More did not publish it because he was waiting
for Bugenhagen to repent.[3] Germain Marc'hadour thinks that publication was probably rendered superfluous by Cochlaeus, who finished his
reply to Bugenhagen on February 11, 1526, about the same time More
completed his, so that when he received a copy of Cochlaeus he saw no
point in proceeding further. There is no evidence, however, that More
ever saw Cochlaeus' tract, and even if he did, he would undoubtedly
have realized that except for the form—the use of extensive quotation
followed by extensive reply—there was very little overlap. The intents
and purposes of each were entirely different. Surely there was room
for both.[4]

---

[1]Elizabeth F. Rogers, "Sir Thomas More's Letter to Bugenhagen," *The Modern Church-
man*, 35 (1945–46), 351, reprinted in *Essential Articles for the Study of Thomas More*, ed. R. S.
Sylvester and G. P. Marc'hadour (Hamden, Conn., 1977), p. 448; cited hereafter as
"*Essential Articles.*"

[2]More did not begin writing about Tyndale, Fish, and other English heretics until after
March 7, 1527/8, when he received a packet of books from Cuthbert Tunstal, bishop of
London, with instructions to still the raving babble ("insanae neniae") of their tongues
(*The Correspondence of Sir Thomas More*, ed. Elizabeth F. Rogers, Princeton, 1947, pp. 386–
88; cited hereafter as "Rogers").

[3]*CW 8*, 1154–55. This suggestion may have been modeled on the report that Fisher
delayed publication of his *Defensio regiae assertionis* two years while awaiting Luther's
repentance. One need only read the last paragraph of More's *Letter to Bugenhagen* to
realize how ambivalent the call for repentance there really is. The gesture is made, but in
such an insulting, unloving fashion that no one in his right mind would take it seriously:
"Abandon that ungodly sect, the most shameful that ever existed on earth. . . . Give up
your illegitimate bishopric. Send away that unfortunate girl you whore with in the name
of marriage. And spend the rest of your life in repentance for what you have done" (103–
04). The last paragraph of Bugenhagen's *Letter*, which More judiciously omits, makes it
abundantly clear how unlikely the possibility of repentance actually was.

[4]*CW 6*, 459, n. 2. More's reply is very different from Cochlaeus'. Cochlaeus writes as a
German veteran of the wars against Luther. For him Bugenhagen's *Letter* was a very
minor work, almost an outline—"libellus paruulus," he calls it, "immo uerius scheda
quaedam." Cochlaeus was a busy man. He was involved in other things and had no more
than a few hours to spend on it: "agere licuerit mihi, aliquot horas per biduum huic
negociolo suffurari" (*Responsio Cochlaei*, sig. A₁v). The result is a dull, plodding, unimaginative little book made up solely of counterpunches. It has none of the pressure of
English nationalism behind it, as More's does. Writing as spokesman for the entire
nation, More takes Bugenhagen's *Letter* very seriously and attempts to come to grips with
most of the central features of Luther's thought, particularly the doctrine of justification
by faith alone. More's reply is illuminated from within by an intensity of passion and a
sense of injustice and outrage entirely lacking in Cochlaeus.

The most likely explanation, however, the simplest and most
straightforward, is that More's *Letter to Bugenhagen* was undercut and
rendered obsolete almost as soon as it was written by the arrival in
England of Luther's astounding letter to Henry VIII. The *Letter to
Bugenhagen* was probably written in the first few months of 1526, when
More's activities against the heretics were at a white heat. Then, on
March 20, 1526, or a few days before, just as More would presumably
have been finished with Bugenhagen, Luther's letter arrived at court
like a bombshell (or an unexpected gift from God, depending on one's
point of view), and suddenly everything was changed. Up to that point
the king's hands were tied. He could not reply in his own person to
Luther's vicious attack in the *Contra Henricum* because he could not
allow himself to descend to Luther's own level of abuse. But this was
different. He was free to reply to a letter, especially one as superficially
humble, obsequious, and self-serving as this. The opportunity was too
good to miss, and a reply was drawn up almost immediately. More no
doubt had a hand in it. Like the *Assertio,* it was probably a collaborative
effort by More, Lee, Powell, and others.[1] By September 1526, copies

There is no convincing evidence that More knew or used Cochleaus' *Responsio.* The
arguments of each are entirely different. There are no echoes, no verbal similarities, no
carryover of ideas. Nevertheless, my friend and colleague Richard Marius has pointed
out to me that the way in which More divides Bugenhagen's text into bite-sized pieces
corresponds very closely to the way in which Cochlaeus divides the text. (They both
follow the same method of quotation and response.) Does this correspondence suggest
that More consulted Cochlaeus' pamphlet in drawing up his own reply? These corre-
spondences are simply what one would expect. They are based on logic and reflect the
way in which Bugenhagen divided his argument into organizational units. Anyone
would divide the text in much the same way. More interesting are the departures from
the progression of Bugenhagen's *Letter.* Cochlaeus proceeds from beginning to end
without any departures whatsoever. He quotes the entire text in the same order in which
it appears, whereas More allows himself more freedom. He varies the citations, skipping
a page or a paragraph, and then incorporating it later in another context, or even
ignoring it entirely if doing so suits his own purposes. More had a much bolder mind and
did not need Cochlaeus to show him how to divide a text into its logical components. He
was quite capable of dividing it to suit himself so as to advance the purposes of his own
argument.

[1]*CW 6,* 458. Germain Marc'hadour suggests that More acted as literary editor while
someone else, Edward Powell or Edward Lee, worked out the theological arguments.
The style, therefore, was More's, the content someone else's. This explains, Marc'hadour
says, both the similarities and the differences between More's *Letter to Bugenhagen* and the
king's letter to Luther. The divisions seem somewhat artificial, however, and many of the
stylistic resemblances Marc'hadour cites are not particularly convincing. There is no
doubt that More had a hand in the king's letter, but it is impossible to say what parts were
his and what parts someone else's. See also Doernberg, *Henry VIII and Luther,* p. 53, who
cites *LP 4/2,* 1060 (no. 2371) and 1479 (no. 3261).

were ready to be sent in the king's name to the princes of Germany,[1] and by the end of the year it was published in both Latin and English editions.[2] At Wolsey's insistence Luther's letter was printed first, then Henry's stern reply showing the world what a fool Luther was.[3]

By his letter to Henry, Luther had put himself in a disastrous position. Since he seemed to be suffering from the same lunatic delusion as Bugenhagen that England was ready to turn Protestant, what better person to disabuse him than the king himself? More and Bugenhagen might do for the preliminaries, but this was the main event. One crushing letter from the king would do more to destroy Lutheran hopes in England in 1526 than anything More could possibly devise. Judged solely as a piece of propaganda, as part of the battle for men's minds, the king's letter was immeasurably more important than More's simply because of the king's reputation and his symbolic role as head of state. Not only that, but if More published the *Letter to Bugenhagen,* it might detract from the king's own letter by going over some of the same ground. It would not do to enter into competition with the king, either in actuality or in the king's own eyes. Better to throw all one's energies into helping him frame an appropriate reply. For the time being—for a few years yet—one's hope lay with the king.

Rhetorical Strategies

Bugenhagen's *Letter to the English*

Bugenhagen's *Epistola ad Anglos* is divided into four main parts: (1) an introduction that defends the Lutheran sect against various unspecified rumors and lies; (2) a statement of the utter simplicity of Protestant doctrine, which, underneath its apparent diversity, teaches only one central article of faith: the belief that Christ is man's righteousness; (3) the effects of that teaching on moral life, the worship of God, and the sacraments of the church; and (4) a brief conclusion that reverts to the beginning and knits it all together.

---

[1] Rogers, p. 368.

[2] The Latin edition was published December 2, 1526; the English translation, in January or February 1526/7.

[3] Henry wanted to send his letter to the princes immediately, without waiting for a copy of Luther's letter to be made, but Wolsey did not agree: "aswel for that Luther, who is ful of sutelte and craft, herafter might percase denye that any such lettre hath been sent by hym unto the Kingis Highness, as that the said answer, not having the said copy adioyned therunto, shuld be, for want therof, to the reders and herers therof, sumwhat diminute and obscure and not perfitely perceyved by them that shal rede the same" (Rogers, p. 368).

The work is very brief, and the basic argument, by which I mean the rational, paraphrasable outline through which Bugenhagen moves, is so apparent that there is very little need to go over it here. What may not be so apparent, however, is the rhetorical strategy Bugenhagen uses. By rhetorical strategy I mean the inner argument, the attitudes Bugenhagen desires to instill in his readers, the message or messages he intends them to absorb—the ways in which he manipulates them, in other words, and the purposes of that manipulation. It is this, more than the argument itself, that More concentrates on in his response, opposing Bugenhagen's rhetorical strategy with a counterstrategy of his own.

The form is that of a Pauline epistle. In fact Bugenhagen begins by obliquely referring to Paul's letter to the saints at Ephesus (Eph. 1:1–2) in order to drive home the resemblance. It is soon apparent, however, that the "saints" in England whom Bugenhagen addresses, the members, that is, of the Lutheran community, who already accept the gospel of the glory of God, are not the real audience Bugenhagen has in mind. He is actually addressing those who reject the new gospel either because of the various rumors and lies told about the Protestant sects or because of their own ignorance and misbelief. It is as though St. Paul wrote not to the Ephesians, but to the devotees of the cult of Diana of Ephesus in order to convert them to Christianity. Except for a brief nod to the saints at the beginning and another reference at the end to round it off, Bugenhagen addresses this second audience almost entirely.

The purpose of the *Letter* is to convince this audience of the merits of the new gospel, and the first order of business is to disarm their objections by meeting head on the rumors and lies that distort their perceptions and keep them from accepting the new teaching. But note how Bugenhagen goes about it. He admits nothing. There are "vague rumors" and "lies,"[1] but what they are he never says. The closest he comes to dealing with it in fact is in the reference to "unchristian acts" (whatever they might be) performed "under the pretext of Christian liberty."[2] This is an oblique reference to the Peasants' Revolt, which had been raging in Germany for almost a year when Bugenhagen wrote that line. The country was in complete turmoil. One hundred thousand people were killed, and Luther was accused of causing their deaths by preaching the doctrine of Christian liberty and thereby stirring them up and offering them hopes of a new order. But Bugenha-

---

[1] Appendix A, 398/7–12.
[2] Appendix A, 398/13–14.

gen never identifies the reference. He leaves it intentionally vague and argues, or rather implies, that whatever it was, it had nothing to do with *real* Christian liberty. Those who performed such "unchristian acts" were not true Christians. "Not everyone who claims for himself the name of Christ," he says, "has put on Christ."[1] But the reverse is also true. The saints who glory in the gospel of God—the implication is clear—would not do such things, because they are the true followers of Christ.

By not specifying the false rumors and lies leveled against the Lutherans, Bugenhagen not only avoids having to repeat them and thus run the danger of reinforcing them in the mind of his audience; he also avoids having to deal with them at all. Not only that, but by not stating what they are, he creates the illusion that there are in fact no serious charges. And the same is true of his accusers. They are evil-hearted enough to invent such falsehoods in the first place, but they are also as vague as the accusations themselves, so vague as to create the impression that there are no opponents at all, not even the Catholic church, but merely unnamed enemies, as in the Psalms and the rest of the Old Testament, where the foes of Israel are identical with the unspecified enemies of God. Besides these shadowy figures, the agents of lies and slander, there are two other categories or groups of men who oppose the new gospel. The first are the weaklings, the "infirmiores," who have no strength of character and backbone: they are thus taken in by rumors and lies told about the Lutherans and reject them. The second group are the ignorant or less well educated, who are confused by the various theological arguments offered pro and con: they simply do not have the intellectual equipment to deal with them. There has to be a trick to it somewhere, they think. Surely there is poison hidden under all this disagreement.

Since there are in effect no real enemies and no real charges of any substance brought against the Lutherans, it follows that they must be suffering from a form of persecution, for the true church has always been persecuted. "This is our glory," Bugenhagen says, quoting St. Paul: "Nam gloria nostra haec est, testimonium conscientiae nostrae" (2 Cor. 1:12). Persecution is necessary to strengthen the soul. How else are we to experience in our own lives the force of Christ's beatitude: "Beati estis cum maledixerint vobis, et persecuti vos fuerint, et dixerint omne malum adversum vos mentientes, propter me" (Matt. 5:11)? Persecution is an essential part of Christian experience, for the son of

---

[1]Appendix A, 398/14–15.

man was reproved by the world and the teaching of the cross was esteemed foolishness.

The hypocrisy is overwhelming—at least it seemed so to More—but the rhetoric is brilliant. Bugenhagen knows very well the sort of things the Lutherans are accused of, the heretical beliefs and the civil disorders, but instead of confronting them directly and answering them as straightforwardly and honestly as possible, he turns the tables on his accusers so completely that to refuse to answer their objections or deal with them in any way whatsoever is to be taken as a virtue. To try to defend oneself, in fact, or even to offer an explanation would be downright unchristian. Better to suffer as Christ suffered.

The image Bugenhagen thus creates for himself (and by extension for all Lutherans) is that of a patient, pious man who suffers slander meekly for Jesus' sake and does not reply to his enemies with words of anger. He accepts the enmity of the world as part of the world's hatred of God. This is not a polemical work, he seems to insist. His enemies will not be attacked nor will his doctrines be defended. He simply wishes to be like Paul and to spread the word of God among those who thus far have failed to accept it because of their own weakness and ignorance. What Bugenhagen has to offer is a free gift of God's salvation given in love to his fellow man. The tone therefore is low-key, the purpose explanatory. "What poison then are you afraid of," he asks, "since we do nothing in secret and set all our works before the whole world to be judged?."[1] Unlike their opponents, who rely on human statutes and traditions, the Lutherans trust only in the palpable evidence of God's own word in scripture. Instead of a variety of doctrines, they teach only one basic article of faith that underlies everything they say or do, and that one article is this: that Christ is our righteousness.

Bugenhagen thus presents himself as a model Christian, whose reliance is on Christ alone. "For God made him our wisdom, justice, satisfaction, redemption."[2] He is our teacher, Bugenhagen says, and we accept as truth only what he has revealed to us with his own mouth.[3] This, then, is what Lutheran doctrine really amounts to: the simple teaching of Christ in the gospels—no more and no less. To reject Luther, therefore, is to reject Christ. The implications are clear enough. But in case anyone missed them, Bugenhagen spells them out. "Whoever does not grant us this," he says, speaking of the fact that

---

[1]Appendix A, 400/1–2.
[2]Appendix A, 400/9–10.
[3]Appendix A, 402/3–5.

Christ is our righteousness, "is no Christian."[1] By this time he has the
reader in a full nelson. If one agrees with Bugenhagen that Christ is
our righteousness, then he believes what Bugenhagen teaches, and he
is a Lutheran. If he does not, he is no Christian.

From that one article of belief, that Christ is our righteousness, all
other doctrines, all dogmas, all other professions of faith inevitably
follow: "But perhaps you will ask what we think and teach about morals, the worship of God, the sacraments, and things of this sort. I
answer that Christ who became our righteousness also became our
teacher."[2] The remainder of the *Letter* seems fairly straightforward. It
soon becomes apparent, however, that in referring to Christ as our
righteousness Bugenhagen is not speaking of the simple belief that
Christ is at the center of Christian experience. It is something more
complicated than that, something he never defines, never fully explains. It is as though he is speaking from within a closed system of
belief and uses ordinary terms in such a way that they become charged
with additional meaning. As Bugenhagen proceeds, it soon becomes
clear that what he is actually referring to is the Lutheran doctrine of
justification, by which faith and faith alone in one's righteousness
through Christ so transforms an individual that he becomes utterly
changed. "For those who are led by the spirit of Christ," Bugenhagen
says, "are the sons of God."[3] The verb he uses to describe this process is
"aguntur," which means not only "led," as we have translated it, but
also "moved," "touched," "stirred up," "agitated," "activated," or "driven," as by a compulsion. The spirit of Christ, which enters an individual through faith, interpenetrates his very being and possesses him,
as it were, so that he becomes the son of God. He has been justified or
made righteous by his faith alone, and from that point on, unless he
should happen to lose his faith, he is like a good tree that cannot fail to
bear fruit in its season. The process is fixed and unalterable: "Such a
one will live soberly, piously, and justly, adoring God in spirit and
truth. . . . About the sacraments he will believe what Christ taught and
established. He will serve his neighbor with instruction, advice, prayer,
material possessions, even at the cost of his life. And this not only for
friends, but also for enemies. Such are the things Christ taught us; the
nature of the spirit draws the hearts of believers to these things; and
these are the things we teach must be performed."[4] The key words

[1]Appendix A, 400/10–11.
[2]Appendix A, 402/2–4.
[3]Appendix A, 402/10–11.
[4]Appendix A, 402/11–19.

here are "corda credentium," "the hearts of believers"—those full of faith—who are drawn inevitably "by the nature of the spirit" to accept what Christ taught. It is as though belief calls forth belief, and not only that, but once the process has begun, almost compels it.

Bugenhagen explains this fundamental Lutheran doctrine so subtly, so delicately that the effect is almost subliminal. The reader is not even aware of it until it has already happened. Except for the word *iustitia*, which reverberates throughout and carries its own burden of meaning, there is no technical language, no jargon, no complex theological distinctions, nothing to perplex the reader or make him think he is hearing anything other than orthodox Christian truths articulated by a deeply spiritual man.

At the same time, subordinate to the primary argument, running concurrently with it, is an oblique attack on Catholicism and certain specific Catholic doctrines which seems to contradict the smooth rhetorical surface. Bugenhagen edges toward polemics, but the attacks are rarely given space of their own or developed fully. They occur primarily as negations in the midst of something else—as asides or innuendos in which Bugenhagen downgrades his opponents while going about the main business of explaining his own position. It is as though he cannot define one without simultaneously referring to the other with which it is inevitably joined in his mind. And so they both rise up together. Bugenhagen deals primarily with the concept of justification. The attack, therefore, centers on its opposite: the Catholic doctrine of good works. The Catholics, however, are never identified as such. Bugenhagen refers to them in various ways, but the reader himself makes the connection. Bugenhagen names no names. They are the opponents and no more than that, the enemies of God and the gospel, a conglomeration of heretical sects (by which he means the various religious orders), Pelagian heretics who seek grace in nature, not in God, self-justifiers, hypocrites, Pharisees, who make a show of piety, backbiters, members of the kingdom of Satan.[1] For them good works are simply an attempt to fulfill certain external forms without first experiencing a living faith in God, which gives the forms their only true meaning.[2] If left to itself, faith alone produces good works as naturally and spontaneously as a tree produces fruit in its season. Anything else is an empty show.

If one yields to Bugenhagen's rhetorical flow, one is utterly convinced by the time he comes to the last paragraph that the Lutherans

---

[1]Appendix A, 400/13–21.
[2]Appendix A, 400/28–31.

are the true followers of Christ, the bearers of the ancient gospel message, and their opponents are the enemies of God who have deformed and distorted it. In the conclusion Bugenhagen once again addresses the congregation of "saints," as in the beginning, and thus not only rounds off his letter but also creates the impression that he has been speaking to them all the while. This in turn justifies and to some degree validates the submerged allusion to Paul's epistles with which he began. It is not simply an allusion, one feels at this point. It is more like a real analogy. As in the early days of the church, the true gospel is being preached, and the spirit of God is moving among us.[1]

There is no need to doubt Bugenhagen's sincerity. The rhetoric is extremely convincing, and beyond that, or perhaps within it or through it, we glimpse the conviction of a man's entire life. At the same time, we are also aware of the fact that Bugenhagen is out to create certain effects and impressions and instill if possible certain attitudes in the mind of the reader. Unless a person agrees with him in the first place, he is bound to sense that he is being manipulated. Whether or not he had heard the rumor of Henry VIII's sudden interest in Protestantism, Bugenhagen was clearly seeking the main chance and using any means at his disposal to advance the Protestant cause and help bring about the conversion of England. It is possible, of course, to feel more than one way about something not only sequentially but also simultaneously, and Bugenhagen's motives for writing the *Letter to the English* were undoubtedly mixed. But if one looks at it too long from the perspective of what Bugenhagen hoped to gain, the impression begins to shift. The spirituality changes to hypocrisy, the piety to smug self-satisfaction, and the references to Paul begin to turn into something like mock heroic. This was undoubtedly how More saw it. The temper of the times allowed no other response. And in order to counter it, he fashioned a rhetoric of his own.

More's *Letter to Bugenhagen*

M ore's *Letter to Bugenhagen* does not seem to have a form of its own. In choosing to respond to Bugenhagen point by point, using the device of quotation and response, More committed himself to following the same pattern, the same general arrangement of material in more or less the same chronological order, and the form—whatever form it has— seems to be merely parasitic or symbiotic. There are times, of course, when More varies the order. The most significant of these is at 66/16–23

---

[1]Appendix A, 402/26–404/8.

where he quotes part of a passage out of sequence and then at 80/15–23 quotes it again, this time in sequence as part of a longer passage. The quotation is given in full and cited in this climactic position in order to strengthen a point More had been making and to show how the Protestants condemn themselves out of their own mouths. But generally More acts as Bugenhagen's shadow.

Nevertheless, within that rational, orderly sequence of quotation and response is another pattern or series of patterns that is not part of the rational argument and not entirely free from it either. These are the underlying motives, the particular concepts or attitudes that led More to embark on a reply in the first place and caused it to assume the shape or form it did. They are not always entirely rational, at least not in the same way the argument itself is rational. If the argument is linear, moving steadily toward its own completion, like a plot, the underlying forms and motives I am speaking of are essentially circular and repetitive. They cluster together and break the surface, appear for a moment, and then disappear only to circle back on themselves and reappear once again, intensified by each new repetition until finally the impression is created, the attitude upheld, and the work proceeds that much closer toward its goal.[1] We are reminded of what Louis L. Martz spoke of in another context as More's "art of improvisation": "It is an art that seems informal, extemporaneous, spontaneous. It allows for long digressions, excursions, and familiar asides, but in the end it reveals, lying under and within all its apparent wandering, a firm and central line, a teleological structure, based on a goal never forgotten."[2] It is this movement and the goal toward which it is directed that I would like to trace here, realizing all the while that it does not proceed in a neat, orderly fashion, but in fits and starts, now moving forward, now circling back on itself to gain momentum to move forward again. There are logical gaps, redundancies and repetitions, ideas brought up and then dropped, but all the while, despite the apparent lack of structure, we sense the presence of More himself, not bound in lockstep to

---

[1] I am not speaking here of those instances in which More adds to the argument, as when he broadens the section on rumors and lies by bringing up the whole question of authority in the church, which Bugenhagen never mentions; or later, when Bugenhagen discusses what he considers to be the one central article of faith (that Christ is our righteousness) and More goes on to expose it as a restatement of Luther's doctrine of justification by faith alone. I would regard both of these and any other additions of this kind as part of the paraphrasable content and not as part of the rhetoric with which it is treated.

[2] *CW 12*, lxi.

Bugenhagen (as Cochlaeus apparently felt himself bound), but free to
follow the patterns of his own mind. The dependence on Bugenhagen's argument runs like a backbone through the work, but within that
or through it or beyond it, we come in contact with other underlying
forms or shaping principles, which describe their own looser, less rational patterns of organization. Most have to do with rhetoric or what I
have called in speaking of Bugenhagen's *Letter* the inner argument.

The first of these is the use of the *persona,* which frames the work at
the very beginning and defines its form as a familiar letter written to
one Pomeranus (his real name is not even given), a figure of some
importance among the heretics at Wittenberg. On returning home
from a trip, More says, a servant of mine gave me a letter from you,
Pomeranus.[1] So it begins, and from that point on the whole thing
proceeds like a practical joke.[2] We know almost nothing about the
persona except what we can gather from the account of how he received
the letter and what prompted him to reply to it. He was minding his
own business, he says, when the letter was forced on him, addressed to
him neither personally nor generically ("neque nominatim, neque in
genere"). For it was addressed "To the saints in England," and he knew
he did not qualify for that. He was not even a Lutheran. As he turns the
letter over in his mind, wondering who might have sent it to him, he
comes to suspect that someone was trying to convert him to Protestantism. He had never taken a public stand on the issue of heresy, partly
because he was no theologian and partly because he figured it was not

---

[1]More treats the letter as a piece of hand-delivered mail, not a printed text available to
the public, and it may very well have been that the copy he received from Barlow or some
other source was a manuscript. We have collated copies of all the editions of Bugenhagen's *Letter* More might have used. None of them corresponds exactly to More's
quotations, and although some of the variants are to be explained by More's paraphras-
ing the text or arranging it to fit his own syntax, he was not in the habit of misquoting his
opponents or altering their texts at will. (Some of these minor differences are given in the
notes on 16/5–10, 26/1–4, 28/14–17, 32/10–14). The evidence for a manuscript therefore is strong. At the same time the idea of a manuscript letter delivered to More's house
fits in very well with the illusion More wishes to create, that he is responding to a familiar
letter with one of his own. Hence the address to Pomeranus that runs throughout the
text.

[2]More used the same device to considerably greater effect in *Utopia,* the *Responsio ad
Lutherum,* and the *Dialogue of Comfort.* See Thomas Stapleton, *The Life and Illustrious
Martyrdom of Sir Thomas More* (part 3 of *Tres Thomae* [Douay, 1588]), trans. Philip E.
Hallett (London, 1928) pp. 65–66 (cited hereafter as "Stapleton, *Life*"), and my discus-
sion of audience in the *Dialogue of Comfort, CW 12,* cxx–clxiv.

his business. He had other things to do (12/23–26). Some Lutheran must have taken that for interest or at least impartiality and thought he could be easily swayed, especially by something like Bugenhagen's letter, which seems on the surface so devout (12/27–29). He resolves, therefore, to answer Bugenhagen with a personal letter in order to make it clear once and for all that he is "too loyal a Christian ever to be a Lutheran" (14/3–4). Although he had not spoken out before, he can no longer restrain himself. More seems to insist that the *persona* is a representative, educated Englishman of a certain class. Bugenhagen wrote to the entire English nation, and this typical, ordinary Englishman, carefully devoid of all personal attributes and individual characteristics, speaks for all England.

And then the voice disappears. More no sooner sets up the *persona* than he drops it or forgets about it and steps forth in his own person and assumes control, absorbing the *persona* or abolishing it as soon as he begins to slog on through the tedious process of quotation and response that make up the body of the work. The high spirits and real sense of gusto that marked the beginning give way to the dark anger and hostility and barely suppressed violence moving through strict chains of reason that characterize the work as a whole. It is as though More had forgotten himself for a moment and then quickly remembered and returned to the same scurrility with which he had treated Luther in the *Responsio ad Lutherum.* But even that is not consistent, for if the *persona* disappears, it also returns periodically in somewhat altered form, perceived in a sudden rift of humor that runs for a few pages or in the homeliness of a metaphor. At times More warms to his subject, as at 52/26–54/22, where he is discussing the value of good works and becomes so involved in what he is saying that he forgets Bugenhagen, forgets his rage and anger, and focuses on the subject at hand. The voice we hear then is not that of the polemicist, but of an ordinary man. At other times the work is highlighted by a metaphor struck out like a match in the darkness, and we are suddenly reminded of another Thomas More. "I do not see anything except by light," More says at one point, trying to explain free will and the nature of grace, "and yet I assist the light to some extent when I open my eyes and focus them." More's mind seems to warm to the subject, and he immediately follows that image with another more graphic: "If someone lowers a rope in a well and pulls out a man who could not get out by himself, would it not be true that the man in the well did not get out through his own power? And yet he contributed something of his own by hanging onto the rope and not letting it get away. The freedom of

the will is similar to that" (50/16–20). If Lutherans believe good works
flow inevitably from faith, More says, why do they bother to teach
works at all? It is like a man casting a shadow. He's going to do it whether he wants to or not as long as he stands in the sunlight (90/5–7). As
for the miracle Luther speaks of, that so many men have rushed so
quickly into the life of freedom and sensual gratification he offers
them, that's about "as much like a miracle as rocks falling downhill"
(30/22–29). Metaphors like these illuminate the text and bring to it a
sense of ease and good humor, a down-to-earth homeliness that we
have learned to associate with More in other works. We are reminded
of the humor reported in so many of his conversations, the anecdotes
and merry tales scattered through all his written works and particularly
the *Dialogue of Comfort,* the elaborate literary hoaxes in *Utopia* and
elsewhere. It is one of his most appealing features and seems to proceed from the same deep source, the same irrepressible sense of high
spirits and gusto that appeared for a moment at the beginning of the
Letter to Bugenhagen in the use of the *persona* and then disappeared.

But not entirely. There are other times when the *persona* itself or
something very like it returns, and we glimpse what the work might
have been like if More had been able to restrain his anger and maintain
an ironic distance throughout. At 70/3, for example, More pretends
not to understand Bugenhagen. His ideas are so bizarre and so beastly,
More says, that he tried to interpret them in such a way that they
seemed—not good or honest, that was impossible—but less vile, less
harmful to God, less sacrilegious. For he was by nature a kindly man,
More says of himself, who pitied Bugenhagen and always tried to put
the best light on things. But try as he might he still could not make any
sense out of it (70/12–28). The passage goes on for three or four pages
with More offering one bizarre interpretation after another, asking
Bugenhagen if that is what he could possibly mean and then showing
how that could not be it because not even Bugenhagen is that absurd.
The section is one of the finest in the book. Bugenhagen is made to look
crazier and crazier as More's explications of what he could possibly
mean grow stranger and stranger. The whole thing is characterized by
rigorous logic used for the most implausible purposes, cut through
with irony and wild laughter. Bugenhagen is made to look so peculiar
that for a moment one can truly believe that he and the Protestant
movement he stands for do not pose a serious threat.

Then reality returns. It is as though More wakes up, and the humor
is put aside. He seems to realize suddenly that Bugenhagen is not a
figure of fun. The issue has gone beyond humor, which requires some
degree of detachment and disengagement for its effect. There are

serious issues at stake, and they cannot be laughed away.[1] It seems significant that this particular passage, where the humor runs highest and the laughter is loudest, is immediately followed by one of the most violent, hostile sections in the entire book. It is as though More recoiled from his own levity: "Who would not confound heaven and earth, sea and sky when he sees a Lutheran bishop—a man who has broken his vow, shattered his faith, violated the chastity of his priesthood, who wallows in continual incest, which he prefers to call marriage, who shakes his ass as he preaches about virtue—suddenly pontificate about the grave and weighty rules and regulations concerning the worship of God as if he were sent down to us from heaven?" (74/26–32). More's latent sense of anger and outrage catch up with him here and smother any further attempts at humor.

In one sense, of course, the violence and crudity are typical of Renaissance polemic and speak less of More than of the period itself. Luther's polemical works were no better in this respect than More's. In fact, they may have even been worse (or better, as the case may be). For Luther seems to have had a real talent for vulgarity and obscene invective. John Fisher, on the other hand, is singularly free from that sort of abuse, and so is John Cochlaeus in his reply to Bugenhagen's *Letter*, written at almost exactly the same time as More's. What is it in More that makes his invective so fierce in his reply to Bugenhagen?

The first thought that occurs is the hair shirt and the scourge More sent to his daughter Margaret wrapped in a cloth along with his last letter from the Tower just before his execution.[2] More was a complex man, and even if we do not attempt to get into the darker aspects of his personality it seems clear that the "discipline" More inflicted on himself with these instruments is not entirely unrelated to the anger and violence of his polemical works. It is the flip side of his faith, the rigidity and inflexibility of his absolute belief in God and the nature of his church that led More to stand up for what he conceived to be the rectitude of his own conscience and the salvation of his soul despite the opposition not only of his family, but of the entire English nation and

---

[1] By the time More wrote the *Dialogue of Comfort,* he had achieved that detachment, but only because he was in prison and had stepped out of his own life and was preparing himself for the life to come. His primary concern was to learn how to die without betraying his faith. He had put the world behind him. See *CW 12,* 37/8–40/10 and Commentary, 92/25–94/17 and Commentary, cxxxi–cxxxv. In his polemical works, except for *A Dialogue Concerning Heresies,* More's detachment and the humor that rose from it appear only sporadically in an occasional anecdote or humorous turn of phrase.

[2] Stapleton, *Life,* p. 206.

the massive power of its government and laws. Bolt would not have admired More as a modern existential hero certain of his own identity in the face of a meaningless existence[1] if it were not for this peculiarly medieval foundation of his faith that underlies the affable, easygoing surface of his personality. If More was not a "fanatic," in both the best and the worst senses of the word, he would not have been a saint and martyr. It is a matter of faith—a measure of his love of God.

It is also a matter of heresy. Sometime around 1526, the year in which More wrote his reply to Bugenhagen, he was speaking to his son-in-law, William Roper. An enthusiastic man, easily carried away, Roper was expressing his delight with the settled estate of England, "all in one faithe agreing together," compared to the religious dissent and turmoil on the Continent. (The Peasants' Revolt had just been put down in Germany the year before at the cost of 100,000 lives.) More agreed. "And yeat, sonne Roper," he replied, "I pray god . . . that some of vs, as highe as we seeme to sitt vppon the mountaynes, treading heretikes vnder our feete like antes, live not the day that we gladly wold wishe to be at a league and composition with them, to let them haue their churches quietly to themselfes, so that they wold be contente to let vs have ours quietly to our selves."[2] This is the More we all know and love—the gentle irony and balance of mind, the humorous image of treading heretics like ants. And yet the violence is not far away. The tone becomes serious. One cannot allow heretics to live quietly to themselves. The implications are clear. They must be eliminated. Beneath the banter and humorous exaggeration we glimpse the mailed fist. For if one believes, as More did, that the Catholic church was instituted by Christ on earth and is not only divinely inspired but guided by the Holy Spirit through time, then any deviation from its essential teaching is not only heretical, but probably, in an ultimate sense, demonic.

Thus the church, like More, has never been easy on heretics. According to Tertullian, heretics are like cheese. They clabber the sweet

---

[1]Robert Bolt, Preface...

[1]Robert Bolt, Preface to *A Man for All Seasons: A Play in Two Acts* (New York, n.d.), pp. x–xiv.

[2]William Roper, *The Lyfe of Sir Thomas Moore, knighte*, ed. Elsie Vaughan Hitchcock, Early English Text Society, Original Series no. 197 (London and Oxford, 1935), p. 35; cited hereafter as "Roper." A few years later More told Roper of his famous three wishes: "Nowe wold to our Lord, sonne Rooper, vppon condicion that three things were well established in Christendome, I were put in a Sack, and here presently caste into the Thames." Roper was all agog and asked what they were. Universal peace, More replied, a settlement of the king's "great matter" of his divorce, and "that wheare the Church of Christe is [at this presente] sore afflicted with many errors and heresees, it were setled in a perfect vniformity [of] religion" (Roper, pp. 24–25).

milk of doctrine in imitation of the psalm, "Coagulavit sicut lac cor
eorum." They are pigs with cloven hoofs (like the devil) who fail to
ruminate on the knowledge of God. The pearls of scripture cast down
before them are totally wasted. For they are possessed like Legion. All
the demons expelled from the gentiles entered into them in a rush and
drove them as if by instinct over the cliff into the sea of desire for the
things of this world. They are men of blood and sorrow whom God
detests. They gnaw at scripture like internal parasites and torture the
word of God. They are the enemies of truth who are so full of contention they cannot even agree with themselves.[1] Augustine is even more
severe. Persecution of heretics and schismatics, he says, should not
even be considered persecution, because it affects only the body, not
the soul. Hatred of heretics is a sign of great glory, for they are all
soldiers and sons of the devil. They are serpents hardened with dis-
dain, dogs, bulls, wolves, foxes dragging wildfire on their tails, pseudo-
prophets, thieves and robbers, wild reeds, chaff and straw, children of
concubines, and the dung of the church. The sin they commit is worse
than murder. It blasphemes God himself and is therefore the greatest
of all sacrileges. It exceeds all other sins, for it proceeds against the
Holy Spirit and is therefore hated by God. The lives they lead are
detestable. Christians either laugh at their vanity or view them with
sorrow, realizing that they also are men. If it were not for pride and the
desire to seem holy, they would not have become heretics in the first
place and worshiped only the shadows of things. Heresy springs full
grown from pride, but heretics themselves are stupid. They are always
uneasy and disquieted inside because the Holy Spirit allows them no
rest.[2] Even as gentle a man as John Fisher continues the litany. "Heresy," he says in an official condemnation of Luther, "is the sede of the
deuyll . . . the corruption of our hartes, the blyndyng of our sight . . .
the mourder of our soules."[3]

More is part of this same tradition. He agrees with Augustine that
heresy originates in pride, "the very mother of all heresyes." The
desire to seem holy drives heretics on until they sink deeper and deep-

---

[1]*Patrologiae Cursus Completus: Series Latina*, ed. J.-P. Migne, 221 vols. (Paris, 1844–
1903), *1*, 453, 814–15, 951, 959; 2, 19–20, 31–32, 35, 61–62, 64–65, 246–47, 434, 934;
cited hereafter as *PL*.

[2]*PL 33*, 38, 172, 219, 554, 891; *34*, 142, 176, 217, 823, 1721; *35*, 101, 684, 836, 1482,
1925; *36*, 55, 286, 1641; *37*, 682; *38*, 513; *40*, 715–16; *41*, 1545–46; *43*, 115, 333; *44*, 330.

[3]This condemnation was in Fisher's public pronouncement against the heretics at the
second bookburning staged by the government in 1526. Cited by Thomas Lawler in *CW*
6, 440.

er into hypocrisy.[1] "There is no faute," More says, echoing the traditional view, "that more offendeth god."[2] Heretics are the gates of hell,[3]
weeds that spring up in the fair field of the faith,[4] "the deuyls mar-
tyrs/takynge moche payne for his plasure/and his very apes."[5] Their
head is the Antichrist, "of whom these folk," speaking of the Lutherans, "be the fore walkers."[6] Luther's new gospel is in effect "the hole
hepe" of all past heresies gathered together[7]—the "most beestly" heresy "that ever sprange in Chrystes chyrche."[8] That is why it must be
exterminated. Agreeing with Augustine that "it is lawful / necessary /
and well done" to persecute heretics and burn them at the stake,[9] as
was the custom in England and other good Catholic realms,[10] More
argued that the church was not at fault in this. The heretics brought it
on themselves by their own "vyolent cruelte."[11] Ecclesiastical authorities do not desire the deaths of heretics. As long as they abjure and
forswear their false doctrines, they will be taken back into the church.
But if they do not, they are excommunicated, and the church simply
abandons them. The rulers of the temporal realm then take action on
their own because such men are perceived to be dangerous to the good
order of society. Their conversation is perilous to others, endangering
their immortal souls. Burning them at the stake, therefore, is no different from executing any other violent men of blood, psychopaths who
pose a danger to themselves and to other members of society.[12]

More's anger, then, and the violence and cruelty of the *Letter to
Bugenhagen*, are directed not so much against Bugenhagen as an individual—More had never seen the man and knew nothing about him—
as against heresy and heretics in general, defined according to the
traditional teaching of the church. Bugenhagen fulfills in his own person all the character traits—the spiritual, psychological, physiological
profile—of the typical heretic described by Augustine and the early

---

[1] *CW 6*, 423/4–18. Cf. Augustine, *PL 34*, 142, 176; *38*, 280.
[2] *CW 6*, 407/16–17.
[3] *CW 5*, 150/3–5.
[4] *CW 5*, 150/1–2.
[5] *CW 6*, 423/11–13.
[6] *CW 6*, 434/33–34. Cf. Augustine, *PL 40*, 686; *42*, 664.
[7] *CW 6*, 417/28–29.
[8] *CW 6*, 427/18–21.
[9] *CW 6*, 405/34–406/1. The entire chapter is relevant (406/32–418/9). Cf. also Augustine, *PL 35*, 1482.
[10] *CW 6*, 409/21–24.
[11] *CW 6*, 406/22–27.
[12] *CW 6*, 410/7–28.

fathers of the church. More's response, in other words, is inseparable
from the traditional violence of the institutional church directed
against those who imperiled its integrity and that of the society of
which it was a part. More claims this viewpoint as his own and assimi-
lates it so thoroughly that it is difficult if not impossible to distinguish it
in the end from all other elements of his personality—his passion, his
repressed anger and rage, his previous encounters with Luther, his
social class, his fundamental conservatism, and the hierarchical nature
of the society of which he was a part.

It is as though the danger is too serious for rhetoric or anything
other than the truth. Not knowing that Bugenhagen probably thought
he was addressing an audience of Englishmen already half-convinced
of what he was saying before he even began, More seems to have been
struck by the overwhelming sense of hypocrisy—"tam in speciem pia"
(12/28), as he describes it—and most of his efforts in replying to Bugenhagen are directed toward attempting to strip away the mask and
expose the true face of the demon hidden behind it. Bugenhagen is a
rhetorician manipulating the minds of the people with subtleties of
language, lies and half-truths, omissions, distortions, falsifications of
all kinds, in order to make himself appear holy and convince them
of the sanctity of Lutheran doctrine. More, therefore, will not answer
him with a rhetoric of his own, which in the circumstances would be
self-defeating, but with what he regards as the unvarnished truth. "I
will not use rhetoric to attack the wickedness of your words," More
says. "For there is no need for rhetoric to make a good man hate
someone who is so full of the breath, so full of the hissing of the ancient
serpent, so full of the raging fury of hell that he would not hesitate to
blaspheme openly, shamelessly, and maliciously against all other virtues except faith alone by designating and calling them hypocrisy and
wickedness, no matter how much they shine like piety" (68/21–28). In
saying that he will not use rhetoric, More, of course, is extremely
rhetorical. The denial of rhetoric is followed by an impassioned, rhetorical sequence of images linking by means of the repetition of "tanto"
Bugenhagen's breath with the hissing of Satan, the ancient serpent:
"tanto spiritu, tanto Serpentis antiqui sibilo, tanto cum tartareo fremitu." This is not a form of plain style, where the rhetoric is used to
conceal rhetoric. It is more open than that, more inflamed and passionate, as though More believed the rhetoric not to be rhetoric but a
heightened form of truth infused with emotion. In his efforts to unmask the heretics and reveal them for what they truly are, More uses
their own words against them, points to the inconsistencies and contradictions in their beliefs, and confronts them with their own deeds in

order to strip them bare and show their true nature. He does so with great emphasis on reason, logic, and common sense as aspects of the truth and the means to attain it. At the same time, the emphasis on reason is driven and at times undercut by great tides of anger and outrage as More responds passionately, with deep emotional conviction, to the arrogance, hypocrisy, and fundamental insanity of people who could believe such things in the first place and then tell such lies to cover them up. It is this attempt at unmasking, seen everywhere in the book, that constitutes More's principal response to Bugenhagen and his primary rhetorical strategy. Within the order of the argument—the use of quotation and response—it is this process of unmasking that constitutes the inner form of the work, uniting both passion and reason.

Toward the beginning, for example, Bugenhagen defends the Lutherans against the rumors and lies leveled against them. Although he admits that these vague accusations scare off many of "the weaklings"—the "infirmiores"—who might otherwise be converted, he is careful never to mention the precise nature of the accusations themselves, leaving them purposely vague. More is not so careful. The first step in stripping away the mask of hypocrisy is to show the reader exactly what the heretics are accused of, for their deeds reveal what they truly are more clearly than their words:

> Would you call it a lie if someone says your sect has destroyed a good part of Germany in riots, murder, looting, and arson? Do you dare call people liars who testify that your unholy doctrine is the cause of so many crimes, so many injuries, so much desolation? Inciting riots, setting laymen against clergy, arming the people against magistrates, inflaming the people against princes, plotting battles, disasters, wars, massacres—do you call that preaching the gospel? [16/16–25]

"You hurled a burning torch on all of Germany," More says later on. "You lit the wildfire that is now consuming the world, and you keep on fanning the wicked flames with your poisonous breath. All this is too well known to be concealed, too widely circulated to be denied, and too destructive to be tolerated. So how can you write so sanctimoniously, Pomeranus, and say . . ." (24/32–36). The accusations continue on almost every page of the book. More constantly reminds the reader of the discrepancy between words and deeds. Most of the accusations have to do with the Peasants' Revolt, as at 22/18–28, 98/15–26, 100/19–102/9. The last remaining bands of peasants had been massacred just a few months before, Luther was regarded as responsible for the uprising, and the events were still fresh in every-one's mind.[1] Where More is not reminding the reader of that, he is discussing the sex lives of the reformers. Most of them were priests who broke their vows of celibacy to marry incestuously with nuns. Luther himself had just succumbed a few months before, and this too is still fresh in More's mind. He keeps reverting to it: "Is it a lie," he asks Bugenhagen,

> to say that although you were a priest and had vowed to God never to marry, you have nevertheless taken a wife? Or to say that, although you want to be regarded as a bishop, you are a common fornicator every day of your life? Or is it a lie to say the same thing about your friend Lambert, who was a Franciscan, and many other Lutherans as well? Or is it a lie to say that Luther himself, when he was an Augustinian monk, engaged in whoredom, not marriage, with a nun dedicated to God for many years and then stolen from him? [28/18–26]

Even at the end when he offers forgiveness, More is unrelenting: "Send away that unfortunate girl you whore with in the name of mar-riage. And spend the rest of your life in repentance for what you have done" (102/32–104/2).[2]

The deeds of the heretics, then, reveal them for what they truly are, but they are also condemned by their own dogmas and beliefs. The truths of their heart speak out against them. There are five separate catalogues of Lutheran doctrine that punctuate More's reply at regular intervals like a chorus or the repeated words of a refrain. Germain Marc'hadour observes that because of the breadth of Bugenhagen's *Letter* More had a chance to deal with Lutheran doctrine in its "globality." "Hence the enumeration, at five different points, of the absurd, insane, or impious articles that make up the new gospel."[3] But the catalogues are also attempts on More's part to reveal Bugenhagen's

---

[1]See note on 22/18–24/32.

[2]In his *Thomas More, History and Providence* (New Haven and London, 1983), pp. 137–39 (cited hereafter as "Fox, *Thomas More*"), Alistair Fox argues that the real motives behind More's *Letter to Bugenhagen* were the Peasants' Revolt and Luther's marriage, both of which occurred in 1525. There is no doubt that these events and others like them loom large in the text and help explain its anger and rage, but in writing against the heretics More was moved by something more than mere threats of civil disorder and Luther's licentiousness. But even more dominant is More's outrage with Lutheranism in general, in all its aspects, and in particular the doctrine of justification by faith alone, which he saw as lying at its heart.

[3]*CW 6*, 457.

hypocrisy by reminding the readers of what the Lutherans really believe. He takes their own words and crams them down their throats. The second catalogue, at 44/8–24 is typical. Bugenhagen has just argued that Lutherans hold one primary article of belief that underlies all the apparent variety of their teaching. More reminds the reader that it is a little more complicated than that:

> If one were to grant you this, that Christ is our righteousness, does he also have to admit that the bread in the eucharist remains bread? That the mass is of no use to anyone? That the whole church has performed the sacrifice incorrectly up to now? That up to now it has used an impious and sacrilegious canon, and that the sacrament of orders is an empty lie? And . . . therefore a woman is fit to hear sins in the sacrament of confession? And a woman can consecrate the body of Christ? And this: . . . there is no purgatory? And no free will? And no human law a Christian has to obey? [48/8–18]

At 56/25–58/3 More uses a similar catalogue to show that Lutherans believe a good bit more than simply what Christ taught with his own mouth, as Bugenhagen argues. In every instance the catalogues are used to remind the reader that Bugenhagen cannot be taken at face value and that what he says must be placed in the total context of Lutheran belief. They serve the same function, in other words, as the reiterated references to the Peasants' Revolt and the sexual license of Luther and his friends: to remind the reader that Bugenhagen is not only a hypocrite. He is also a liar.

There seems to be little difference in fact between the beliefs of the Lutherans and the deeds they perform. More treats them both as though they were essentially the same thing. In the first catalogue, for example, at 16/25–37, the emphasis is on the verbs. Lutheran dogma and belief are not treated like passive articles of faith stored up in the minds of the faithful like jars on a shelf. They are dynamic principles of action by which the heretics *destroy* the sacraments, *reject* the saints, *blaspheme* the Mother of God, *scorn* the cross, *make light of* vows taken, *renounce* celibacy, *defile* virginity, *urge* marriage on monks and nuns.[1]

---

[1] In the original Latin the verbs stand out even more than they do in English. They are linked together rhetorically as a chain of infinitives: "An seditiones *mouere,* laicos in clerum *concitare,* plebem in Magistratus *armare,* populos aduersus Principes *incendere,* pugnas, ruinas, bella, strages *procurare* . . . *destruere* Sacramenta Christi, Sanctos Christi *spernere,* Matrem Christi *blasphemare,* Crucem Christi *contemnere,* vota Christo facta *vilipendere,* dicatum Christo caelibatum *soluere.*"

And, bringing word and deed together, they urge "these things not just with words, foul as they may be, . . . [they provoke] them as well with their filthy example." More is speaking not so much of the "globality" of Lutheran doctrine as he is of the globality of evil. Heresy, it was commonly held, was totally evil. The opposite of truth, it was similar to it in that it infected the whole man to such a degree that everything he said or did was essentially corrupt. If, therefore, a heretic tried to conceal his true beliefs behind a veneer of seemingly saintly actions, the hypocrisy would soon be exposed by the evil in his heart. And the same was true of his words. No matter how glorious they seemed, no matter how sanctimonious, they would soon be stripped away by the horror of his deeds. "Heresy did not admit of any compromise, any relative or tentative concessions," John Headley observes. "Without being dualistic, the age took a substantialist view of heresy. Heresy did not limit itself to a single doctrine but infected all doctrines held by the heretic, be they orthodox or not, and corrupted his moral life as well. Heresy was always essentially, substantially, one."[1]

Besides using the words and deeds of the Lutherans to discredit Bugenhagen, More also points out the inconsistencies and contradictions that riddle Bugenhagen's own argument. In doing this More places great stress on logic and reason. Since heretics were enemies of the truth, they were by nature irrational, possessed by forces beyond their control, incoherent, inconsistent, contradictory. And Bugenhagen was no exception. More therefore proceeds slowly, carefully, with great shows of patience through long, syllogistic explanations of the falsity of Lutheran doctrine and then, breaking the mood, lashes out in anger or exasperation. At 42/17–28, for example, More points out that if the fathers of the church were mistaken in matters of faith, then Bugenhagen has to admit that the gates of hell have prevailed against scripture. But if, as Bugenhagen admits, the gates of hell have never prevailed against scripture, then he has to agree that the fathers were right in matters of faith, and in admitting that, he condemns himself, for the fathers are opposed to everything he says. The compartments are airtight, the method rigorously applied.[2] More is not dealing with an ordinary opponent who like most men is full of good will but makes occasional mistakes in logic. He is dealing with a heretic who has no

---

[1]*CW* 5, 811.

[2]Sometimes too rigorously. The stress on reason is often so great that, like Macbeth, More "falls on the other" and ends up being not very convincing. At 58/33–60/8, for example, reason is held so tightly that it does not admit the validity of a greater psychological truth. At other times it is pushed so hard it comes out seeming sophistical.

good intentions, no innocent motives. Bugenhagen's errors in logic and instances of false reasoning are calculated attempts to deceive, arising from the evil in his heart. Word and deed are seen to come together once again, and Bugenhagen's shows of false logic are as unmistakable an expression of his moral corruption as any of the overt actions that led to the Peasants' Revolt.

For Lutherans, reason is not man's essential attribute, an instrument designed by God to enable him to seek the truth. It is simply another form of rhetoric used to manipulate the reader and lure him into accepting false doctrines. Hence More's emphasis on hypocrisy and the rhetoric of hypocrisy. He has no hope but to counter it with truth and no instrument but reason. At 90/8–12, for example, More points to a problem in the Lutheran doctrine of justification: "this teaching of yours is in many ways so horribly at odds with itself that one part contradicts the other." Bugenhagen, however, pretends that it all fits together. The difficulty, More says, is that "you are teaching one thing from the heart while wanting to seem as though you are really saying something else." Justification by faith alone frees a man from all further concern about sin. It is a passport to all sorts of licentious living.

> Still, in order to deflect a little of the hatred inspired by such insane teaching, you insert in passing now and then something contrary to what you wrote before, thus raising the question of whether your true beliefs are as crazy as what you write. But you have not handled it all that cleverly, Pomeranus. The cosmetic coating of virtue you carefully applied is easily wiped off. To let you see that this is no sooner said than done, we will consider right now what kind of fruit the people of your faction cannot but bring forth. [90/17–25]

Even scripture, the source of all truth, is not immune from this sort of manipulation. The Lutherans have nothing to set against the consensus of the church through all the ages, More says at one point, except Luther's crazy babbling. To make these ravings seem more acceptable and take on the semblance of truth, the Lutherans pretend to have arrived at their conclusions logically, proving them "by the indisputable evidence of sacred scripture" (36/25–38/3). But that is all a lie. Luther is possessed by an evil spirit, and his beliefs are the product of his irrational mind (86/18–27). Scripture is used simply to dress it up and make it seem like rational thought. More than that, the actual words of God in scripture, by which truths are revealed that lie beyond the limits of man's reason—even they are tortured and distorted by Bugenhagen and his brethren until finally there is no basis on which to stand. It is all hypocrisy and false seeming, rhetorical manipulation designed to lure men to their destruction. Lutherans collect passages of scripture that seem to support their beliefs, More says, and ignore others that argue against them. They quote passages out of context, and if that doesn't work, they simply change the quotations to make them fit. Or they misunderstand them. And finally, if confronted with a flat-out contradiction, they simply say that God was being ironic (84/15– 86/14).

More uses the actual deeds of the Lutherans and the profound irrationality of their doctrine to show the true hypocrisy of Bugenhagen's *Letter to the English,* but ultimately it is Luther himself or rather More's image of Luther, that provides the real revelation. As the work proceeds, it becomes increasingly clear that More is not concerned merely with Bugenhagen. He strikes through Bugenhagen at Luther. He is the one responsible for whatever the Lutherans have done in the past. The deaths of more than 80,000 persons rest on his soul. And it was his evil spirit, possessed by demons, that created a doctrine so profoundly wicked that it incorporates every heresy imagined by man (40/25–30). He is the fountainhead and source of all the challenges to vested authority and all the dissensions of the time. Bugenhagen simply creates an illusion; Luther is the reality behind it. To expose Bugenhagen, therefore, is to reveal Luther. And the opposite is also true. More uses Luther's own words and deeds throughout the book to unmask Bugenhagen, strip away his hypocrisy, and reveal the true nature of the new gospel.

At the heart of the book is the central issue of justification—the belief that Christ is our righteousness—which Bugenhagen describes as the ultimate foundation of all Protestant teaching. More correctly identifies this as the Lutheran doctrine of justification by faith alone, but note how he does it. The assumption throughout is that Bugenhagen is lying. He withholds the truth in order to deceive the unwary, making it seem as though he is not even speaking of justification. He simply implies that one who has faith in Christ will naturally shun vice and embrace virtue. But that conceals the greater part of the "mystic teaching" (58/16–19). "As I said," More continues, "you touch on this more timidly than Luther and shrewdly try to avoid the odium of such an assertion. You hide the fact that you preach the doctrine of faith so as to lure people to vice and unteach virtue. When you say that faith alone is sufficient, you want it to seem as though you mean that if one has faith he will naturally shun vice and embrace virtue" (58/27–32). It is only by reverting to Luther that we know for certain what Bugenhagen is getting at. For Luther is bolder and less hypocritical: "You conceal it in vain," More explains, "since it has been spread abroad through the whole world in the books of your master. Luther treats this opinion of your school more openly and explains it somewhat more boldly. He writes plainly that no sin can damn a Christian except the sin of unbelief" (58/18–23). More interprets this to mean that as long as a person has faith, he can go ahead and commit any sins he wants to, and his sins will be swallowed up or absolved by his faith (62/2–14). "If he had thought about it ten years," More continues, Luther "could not have explained it more clearly" (62/7–8). Bugenhagen tried to "trick out" this "ungodly belief" and moderate it for public consumption, but he cannot twist Luther's words to mean anything other than what they actually mean (62/15–25).

The best example of the way in which More uses Luther to expose Bugenhagen's hypocrisy, one that illustrates the entire process of unmasking, is the portrait of Luther we are left with just as the book ends, in the last few pages. This is the final summing up, the ultimate revelation, the teleological goal toward which the volume has been steadily moving, and it seems altogether fitting that the features we see on the face of the heretic that rises up before us unmasked are not those of Bugenhagen, but those of Luther. For he is the ultimate reality we have come to sense throughout the volume. The rest of it, More demonstrates, is a play of shadows, an illusion created by hypocrisy.

The section begins with a catalogue of the absurdities of Lutheran doctrines and quickly switches to a description of Luther. His beliefs always change for the worse, as was the case with indulgences, the power of the pope, and finally the eucharist. He was just about to do away with the real presence of Christ in the host when Karlstadt, Zwingli, and Oecolampadius beat him to it, arguing there was nothing there but bread. Luther, therefore, feared for his power. He wanted no one to surpass him in evil, and it was only his pride and envy that kept him from rushing to the same conclusion: "just as he was about to start, one sin kept him from committing another. It was only envy that restrained him from going ahead and preaching that ungodly heresy in public. . . . He preferred to dismantle what he had formerly built up (as anyone could see he was doing) rather than allow anyone else to become the heresiarch of any godless sect" (96/19–29). Then follows another catalogue of Lutheran absurdities. What does it actually matter, More asks, what Luther believes about the eucharist when he can believe all this other stuff? The next few pages (98/15–102/2) speak in general of Lutheranism and the Peasants' Revolt. Then at 102/3 More returns to Luther and the part he played in it. He was the instigator. He was the one behind it all: "He was the one who inflamed the peasants to every crime they committed; he armed them and egged them on. Then, when he saw that fortune had deserted them, he grimly cut them down by writing his

vicious pamphlets against them. He outlawed them and turned them
over to the nobles to be hacked to pieces. And that unspeakable politician
did all this in order to extinguish with the blood of those pitiful wretches
the fires of hatred directed against himself. He first stirred them up, and
then he sacrificed them" (102/3–9).

To unmask Bugenhagen, then, is to reveal the hideous face of
Luther. But what is it to unmask Luther? Is there still another mask
behind the mask he wears, or is he the thing itself? He stirred up the
peasants, as we have just seen, to take the heat off himself, and then
when it seemed the fight was going against them, he switched sides and
abandoned them to the princes. His only interest was in saving his own
skin. Like heretics from time immemorial, he is ridden by pride and
self-interest in imitation of Satan (20/10–16). As More depicts him,
Luther is so far gone in evil that it has overwhelmed any human feeling
or compunction he might have possessed, and it is difficult to conceive
of him as a mere man. He seems more like a vital power, a force not of
life, but in opposition to life, full of a sort of evil gusto, a power or
principle of destruction loosed on the world: "In council with you and
his other lieutenants he makes plans hour by hour, devising nothing
but how to incite rebellions, subvert the faith, uproot religion, profane
holy things, corrupt morals, prostitute virgins, and destroy virtue"
(24/24–29). The evil is so extreme and so total, so utterly incomprehensible, that it seems almost comic, and he ends up resembling a
figure in a farce. What do you do? Barabbas asks Ithamore in *The Jew of
Malta,* and Ithamore replies that he spends his time

> In setting Christian villages on fire,
> Chaining of eunuchs, binding of galley slaves.
> One time I was an hostler at an inn,
> And in the night time secretly would I steal
> To travelers' chambers and there cut their throats.
> Once at Jerusalem where the pilgrims kneeled,
> I strewed powder on the marble stones,
> And therewithal their knees would rankle so
> That I have laughed a-good to see the cripples
> Go limping home to Christendom on stilts. [II, iii, 200–9]

Ithamore is a Turk, born in Thrace, brought up in Arabia. That
explains what he does. But Luther is simply crazy,[1] besides being evil,
and part of the humor is related to that. One laughs at him as in

---

[1] The theme of insanity runs through the book. See, for example, 18/30–32, 20/12–
16, 30/22–29, 32/24–28, 36/24–38/3, 40/25–30, 70/3–11, 84/23–86/27, 90/17–20.

simpler, more primitive times people laughed at madmen and mental defectives. In the debate with Erasmus over free will, for example, Luther "runs around with a Sardonian laugh trumpeting victory, trophies, triumphs, claiming his reply is so perfect that neither devil nor angel could talk him down. It is easy for a wretch who babbles insane nonsense to shout in his madness that he has argued so brilliantly that no one could possibly refute him. What he replies to the *Treatise* seems absurd even to Luther himself. He knows ahead of time that he will be condemned. He knows it is capable of provoking only laughter or anger in anyone other than the partisans of his own heresy" (86/9–18).

And yet there is something more disturbing in Luther's madness. As in true insanity, there are rational motives involved. There is never any doubt as to Luther's intentions. He would have the people believe that Christ "came to grant them permission and complete freedom to give themselves up to all kinds of debauchery. And then, after they had led that sort of life on earth, he would give them eternal happiness in heaven" (68/32–36). And yet, crazy as he is, Luther knows better than that. His intent is to seduce the people, using their own weakness against them so as to destroy their souls and condemn them to hell. The madness lies not so much in what Luther says—though that seems crazy enough—as in his insane persistence in saying it. Like Bugenhagen he is willing to do anything to further his evil intentions. He lies, cheats, contradicts himself, plays the fool and the hypocrite, distorts sacred scripture, blasphemes God—even allows himself to seem crazy. But all the while the intent is not irrational, nor is it comic. Underneath it all is a steady direction, a set plan and purpose—something more awesome than mere craziness.

As is often the case with the truly insane, Luther seems in touch with mysterious forces beyond the reach of ordinary human experience. He is no longer in control of himself, but has been possessed, and what speaks through him is not his own spirit, but that of another. As the book proceeds, we finally come to realize that Luther is not the ultimate cause. There is something beyond him. Like Bugenhagen, Luther is finally a mask, except that his mask is the total human personality. The reality is otherwise. In the Introduction to *A Dialogue Concerning Heresies,* Thomas Lawler speaks of the "idea of heretical possession that More, Fisher, and Tunstal acquired during the heresy trials." Through their interrogations of heretics, they became convinced of "the devilish hold of heresy, which could reach so deeply into a man's soul that even after hours of patient pleading and discussion he would recant his recantation and begin to preach heresy again." In its last stages, Lawler suggests, it is a sickness of the spirit so virulent that it "was perhaps demonic."[1] In Luther's case—the extreme case of the arch-heretic—it was clearly so. More is quite explicit about it in the *Letter to Bugenhagen*. He comments in passing, for example, that Luther's treatise *The Slavery of the Will* just goes to show "how his own will was enslaved to a raving demon when he wrote that book" (84/26–29). A page or so later More returns to it again. Luther admits that he could never persuade anyone or win anyone over to his beliefs unless he was already predisposed to agree with him in the first place. It would seem to be a valid psychological observation. The metaphor Luther uses is that of "drinking in his spirit" by reading his books. More agrees: "By reading Luther's books they become possessed by the same spirit that makes him tremble with raving madness and, once they have rejected the faith of Christ, drives them mad too" (86/24–26). This is apparently the same thing Lawler terms "heretical possession." It passes from one man to another like a disease. But how literally are we to take it? Does More really mean that in reading Luther's books one drinks in the demonic and literally absorbs it into himself, becoming possessed by it as Luther was possessed when he wrote it? Or is that simply an elaborate way of saying that in reading Luther one is influenced by evil? Or is there any real difference between them? The literal and the metaphoric ultimately come together, just as they do in More's treatment of Luther. He remains a man even while we realize that he is possessed by forces beyond his own comprehension. There is no doubt that More believed in a literal devil who roams the world, as in the old prayer, "seeking the ruin of souls." There is also no doubt that he believed in the existence of the demonic as it manifested itself through men like Luther, who by their own volition become the agents of its will. The enemy within the individual's own heart and soul is identical with the enemy without, and both are to be seen as masks—agents or representations—of a more ancient power of evil. "Our wrestling is not against flesh and blood," as Paul said, "but against the principalities, against the powers, against the world rulers of this present darkness, against the spiritual hosts of wickedness in the heavenly places" (Eph. 6:12).

In the *Letter to Bugenhagen* More's term for this, for men like Luther, who become conduits through which the demonic enters into human existence, is "Daemonum satellites," agents of demons or their attendants, escorts, accomplices. "The divine goodness uses at times such agents of demons," More says, "to test the patience of good men in the church or punish the sins of the faithful. But God will be true to his

---

[1]*CW* 6, 444.

word and along with the temptation provide a way out, and eventually
he will wipe away every tear from the eyes of those who have mended
their ways" (100/19–24). Ironically, beyond his knowing, this particular passage would become one of the touchstones More kept returning
to for strength and consolation during his months of imprisonment in
the Tower just before he was executed, when he was called upon to test
his long-standing convictions and prove them true with his own life.
Henry VIII, Cromwell, Norfolk, and others who threatened him in
prison were no more than shadows, illusions, simulacra—outriders of
a more awesome power. "It is the mydday devill hym selfe," More says
in *A Dialogue of Comfort,*

> that maketh such incursion vppon vs, by the men that are his
> ministers to make vs fall for feare /. . . for his fasshion ys to set his
> seruauntes agaynst vs, & by them to make vs for feare or for
> Impacyence to fall / And hym selfe in the meane while com-
> passeth vs, runnyng & roryng like a rampyng lion ⌐about vs,⌐
> lokyng who will fall, that he than may devoure hym / . . . The
> devill it is therfor, that yf we for fere of men will fall, is rcdy to
> rone vppon vs & devoure vs."[1]

The suffering that More endured in the Tower was the product of
the same power that unleashed Luther and Bugenhagen in the first
place, and in each case the remedy is the same: the belief that God is
faithful and along with the temptation will provide a way out. "No
temptation has seized hold of you except what others have suffered
before you. For God is faithful and will not allow you to be tempted
beyond what you can endure, but along with the temptation will provide a way of escape so that you will be able to stand it" (1 Cor. 10:13).
In the Tower More's anger toward his enemies burned itself out or
became transformed by the grace of God into the theological virtue of
hope.[2] In 1526, however, in the *Letter to Bugenhagen,* More had not yet
reached that point of detachment or serenity or clarity of mind, and
the quotation from Paul cited above is immediately followed by a cry
for vengeance. Thinking of the 80,000 men and women massacred in

---

[1]*CW 12,* 317/25–318/9.

[2]Suffering from religious persecution himself, More has not banished anger and
concern for polemics. They surface at times, as at *CW 12,* 37/4–40/10 and 92/21–96/29,
but they are suffused with something else, something that checks the impulse—a desire
now to pray for others, to pray for forgiveness, combined with an occasional outburst in
the form of a submerged allusion to scripture or an oblique aside or a depraved negative,
denying interest even while pursuing it. See *CW 12,* cxxxi–cxxxv and clix–clxii.

the Peasants' Revolt, More becomes so overwhelmed that he is carried
for a moment beyond syntax: "But his wrath and indignation, you—
you, I say, you ungodly, cruel slayers of the faithful—with the breath
of his anger he will blow you to ashes and drive you like dust from the
face of the earth" (100/24–28).

The flaws in More's *Letter to Bugenhagen* are obvious and need no
special emphasis here. Like most of More's polemical works, it fails to
speak beyond the immediate concerns of its own age, primarily because More does not conceive of his opponents as men like himself
reaching out in their blindness and stupidity toward God. They are not
ordinary people driven by their own complex need for grace and a
sense of wholeness in their lives. They are idiots and madmen possessed by forces beyond their control and thus both more and less than
human. As heretics, they gave themselves over to evil and became
transfigured by it. The failure on More's part was a failure of human
understanding and compassion, but the fault was not his alone. The
church itself in the same period made the same mistake. It failed to
offer a proper channel for the desire for true spiritual renewal that
rose up within itself and was thus unable to deal with it except by fiat
and repression.

In his old age, when he had become a lesser man and the rage and
self-doubts that tormented him earlier had quieted, Luther remembered his old opponent Thomas More. Someone asked him if More
was executed "for the Gospel's sake or no?" It was a question only a
Protestant would ask. A Catholic would say "God," not "the Gospel."
And Luther answered,

> No, in no wise; he was a cruel tyrant; he was the king's chief
> counsellor; a very learned and wise man, doubtless, but he shed
> the blood of many innocent Christians that confessed the Gospel;
> he tormented them with strange instruments, like a hangman;
> first, he personally examined them under a green tree, and then
> cruelly tortured them in prison. At last, he opposed the edict of
> the king and kingdom. He was disobedient, and was punished.[1]

Luther is wrong, of course. More was not a torturer and hangman.[2]
But that is beside the point. What is important here is the perception.

---

[1] *The Table-Talk of Martin Luther,* trans. William Hazlitt (Philadelphia, n.d.), p. 376 (item DCXXV).

[2] Cf. More's own defense against such charges in *The Apology, CW 9,* and J. B. Trapp's comments in the Introduction to that volume, pp. xxx–xxxii.

Luther focused on rumors and the secondary meanings of More's polemical works, such as the *Letter to Bugenhagen,* and judged him to be a cruel and bloody man as violent as his words. And More mistook the ultimate purpose of Luther's rebellion as a blow against God. He did not understand the complex psychology of Luther's spirituality and the touching attempt always to strike through dead forms to the living faith beneath. Seen from this distance More and Luther are both larger than life, heroic figures. They stand out from all other men of their age in their purity of heart, the fervor of their faith, their love of God, and their willingness to follow the dictates of conscience despite the opposition of the entire world. What they did then exemplifies what the human spirit is capable of and thus consoles us all and gives us hope. But neither understood the other's deeper purpose. And so one was beheaded, and the other died a bitter, savage old man, almost a parody of himself. The real tragedy lies there.

SUPPLICATION OF SOULS

The Two Supplications

A. THE DATE OF FISH'S *SUPPLICATION* AND MORE'S REPLY

ACCORDING to John Foxe, Simon Fish's *Supplication for the Beggars* reached court circles around Candlemas, that is, February 2, 1529.[1] We may safely infer that More would quickly have known of this publication: he was officially sworn, and personally eager, to prevent the circulation of illegal literature. Fish's pamphlet was exactly the kind of book that Tunstal had commissioned him to read and refute. Whatever More's immediate reaction was to the pamphlet, he was still engaged with his *Dialogue Concerning Heresies*.[2] Not until its publication in June 1529 was More really free to concentrate on the issues raised by the "beggars' proctor."

More's *Supplication of Souls* provides no internal evidence for a precise dating of its composition. The invention and the penning of this work may well have spread over a considerable period of time. More was apt to draft sections of a work before he had determined its overall plan.[3] At any rate, the two books of More's *Supplication* appear to have been completed by October 24, 1529, for the heading tells us that it was "made" when More was still chancellor of the duchy of Lancaster. In the second edition of the *Dialogue Concerning Heresies*, the title page clearly distinguishes between More's successive identities: the book is ascribed to the chancellor of the duchy of Lancaster, its overseeing to the lord chancellor of England. There are signs of haste in the composition of More's *Supplication*, slips in accuracy that could easily have been caught; and even a small amount of leisure might have brought to More's attention the scene of St. Monica's death, which he was to ex-

---

[1]"Foxe," *4*, ii, 659. See *CW 8*, 1187–91, for Louis Schuster's detailed account of Fish's *Supplication* in the context of "More's Polemical Career."

[2]He was not free to enter a new arena by that time, *pace* Fox, *Thomas More*, p. 180.

[3]The composition of *The History of Richard III* continues to baffle its readers and editors (see *CW 2*, xxviii–xxix, l–lviii; *CW 15*, cxxxiii–cliii), as does *Utopia's* patchwork composition. The *Responsio ad Lutherum* changed its "economy" at a late stage; hence the many pages added to Book 1, chap. 10. More also began *The Debellation of Salem and Bizance* with the second part.

ploit at great length in the *Confutation*.[1] The book may have gone to press in early summer, immediately after the *Dialogue* was out of the printer's way, and the second edition may have preceded More's return from his overseas mission to Cambrai. This situation would explain why, unlike the *Dialogue*, the *Supplication* underwent no authorial revisions in the second edition. On the other hand, it is likely that the treatise was conceived and partly written during More's diplomatic mission with Tunstal to negotiate the Treaty of Cambrai (July 1— August 11, 1529). More and Tunstal were in perfect accord in their double task: to restore peace and to defend orthodoxy. They ordered Stephen Vaughan to search for heretics at Antwerp, where Tyndale would soon receive More's *Dialogue* and write his *Answer* to it. On the very day he signed the historic treaty, More wrote to Henry: "finally your Grace hath the p(eace) with thentrecours . . . sealed and sworne th(is day), the fyveth day of August . . . in the Cathedrall church of this t(owne of) Cambray, of whiche oure Lorde send good and long contin(uance)."[2] His presence at Cambrai is attested until August 11. On his return, he "rode immediately to the King at Woodstock,"[3] probably on August 22. We do not know whether he was free to enjoy a few days at home. Because Tunstal fell ill, More was constrained to report on the treaty alone.

The legal year began, as usual, on St. Denys's Day, October 8, with Wolsey in the seat of the supreme judge; but on that very day the cardinal was indicted of praemunire, and ten days later he surrendered the Great Seal. Another week elapsed before More, having received his appointment as lord chancellor, renewed his oath of office, which included a promise to suppress heresy.[4] By now the *Supplication* was evidently finished. If More had brought a manuscript home from the Continent, there would have been time for two printings before the end of September, the second resulting presumably from a large demand and from the desire to make the book available to members of the new Parliament. More's suppliants appear to have the legislators in mind when they dwell on the wisdom of former Parliaments and on the king's ability to overrule his subjects' desires (139/30–140/5).

---

[1] Some other obvious mistakes would have been corrected if More had had time for careful revision. In "the fyrste chapiter of Genesys" (146/10–11), the fault may not be perceptible, but an attentive reader will detect the omission of Paul in the recapitulation of proofs (194/4–8), a significant flaw given the importance of 1 Cor. 3. Even an error such as "whychy" (226/29) was slavishly reproduced in the second edition.

[2] Tunstal, More, Hacket to Henry VIII, Rogers, p. 419, lines 11–17.

[3] Rogers, p. 422, lines 6–7.

[4] Guy, p. 104.

THE POLITICAL SETTING

I N the autumn of 1529, when Wolsey fell from power, strong anticlerical tendencies among the English people and the nobility found an
opportunity to surge forward. Wolsey himself had long been a target
of these tendencies because of his unscrupulous accumulation of vast
wealth and power. To the adversaries of clerical privileges, he seemed
to embody all the abuses they most resented. With Wolsey gone, the
forces represented by the dukes of Norfolk and Suffolk (Norfolk being
the uncle of Anne Boleyn) found a threefold opening: lack of a powerful clerical opponent in the seat of civil power; Henry's infatuation with
Anne Boleyn; and his hope, through Anne, to provide the kingdom
with a male heir to the throne.

Wolsey's fall, though not formally accomplished until October, was
imminent throughout the summer; it had been foreshadowed by the
Darcy memorandum of July 1529. That document, deriving from the
Norfolk-Suffolk alliance, urged the sharp curtailment of clerical power
and in addition suggested the need "to view what of all temporal lands
the spiritual men hath, and by what titles, and for what purposes and
whether it be followed or no"; it also suggested "that it be tried whether
the putting down of all the abbeys be lawful and good or no, for great
things hang thereupon."[1] It was presumably such views as these, gaining headway in the summer of 1529, that led Thomas More to publish
his *Supplication of Souls* in answer to Fish's anticlerical pamphlet, which
had, if one may believe Foxe, reached the hands of Henry VIII himself
through the agency of Anne Boleyn.[2] Since Henry was already aware
of the plea for royal supremacy over the church contained in Tyndale's
Obedience of a Christian Man, Fish's tirade against the clergy, accusing
them of every abomination from extortion to adultery, and his plea for
confiscation of all their properties and income, made a potentially
dangerous appeal to a king already impatient of clerical delays in the
great matter of his divorce.

The correspondence of the papal legate, Cardinal Campeggio,
throws dramatic light upon the danger. His letter of April 3, 1529, to
Salviati relates discussions that may have been inspired by Fish's pamphlet.[3] Copies of a Lutheran pamphlet in English, says the cardinal,
have been "sown" about court these days. This *libretto* urges the kings
of England and France to bring the clergy back to the condition of the

---

[1] The Darcy memorandum is readily available in Guy, Appendix 2, p. 206.

[2] See p. lxv, n. 1, above, and Appendix D, p. 439, below.

[3] *Römische Dokumente zur Geschichte der Ehescheidung Heinrichs VIII von England*, ed.
Stephen Ehses (Paderborn: Ferdinand Schöningh, 1893), p. 73–78.

early church by taking away all their temporal goods. After Henry VIII broached the subject with him, in Wolsey's presence but apparently of his own accord, Campeggio said that the devil under the angelic garb was exposed by the reformer's intention to appropriate the goods of the church. He gave the king two reasons for not yielding to the pressure. First, he offered a juridical reason, namely, the antique determination that the church may justly own temporal goods, and that to believe otherwise is heretical. But, Henry remarked, are not these simply churchmen's decrees in favor of the church? It is time for the laity to step in and have their say. Your Majesty knows, Campeggio answered, that conciliar decrees are inspired by the Holy Spirit. Second, Campeggio offered an argument from the king's own interest: in pressing need he often avails himself of church money; this recourse will cease if his fattened lay subjects prove recalcitrant. When Henry referred to the evil life of the Roman court, the legate pointed out that, for all its failings, the apostolic see, unlike the churches of Greece and Asia, has always held firm the true Catholic faith. Campeggio also said he had not seen a copy of the *libretto*. This diminutive more fittingly describes the "Beggars' Book" than it does Tyndale's *Obedience*.

We can see, then, why Thomas More's answer to Fish's *Supplication* turned out to be more than ten times as long as Fish's incendiary pamphlet of barely sixteen pages. More is not answering one pamphlet; he is aiming, as in his *Dialogue Concerning Heresies,* published a few months earlier, to stem a widespread movement headed by a now powerful faction with direct and intimate access to the king. One notices, too, that Fish's attack on the doctrine of purgatory occupies hardly two pages in his pamphlet, whereas More devotes the entire second half of his treatise to a defense of this doctrine, and further emphasizes the point by presenting his pleas and arguments through the assembled voices of the souls now suffering in the fire of purgatory. It is true that this device wears thin in places and takes on real power only in the final pages, where the souls plead with the living not to be persuaded by such pamphlets to abandon their prayers for the dead and thus delay the release of the souls from their suffering. Indeed, More uses the device hardly at all when he is disputing such matters as Fish's allegedly precise statistical account of the income derived from begging friars, amounting, Fish declares, to 43,333 pounds, 6 shillings, and 8 pence.[1]

---

[1]*Supplication for the Beggars,* Appendix B, below, 413/21–23. See also 122/21–23, 124/21–24, 124/29–33, 125/20–21, 126/1–3.

Nevertheless, the device is important because it serves as a reminder, from beginning to end, that the attack on clerical property and income is basically, for More, an attack on established Christian doctrine, and thus involves far more than financial matters. This attack threatens the very life of the soul. Here, as in his other treatises of controversy, More sees clearly that these "new men" are attacking the foundations of the ecclesiastical establishment. If, for example, the doctrine of transubstantiation is false, then no priests are needed to enact the eucharistic miracle. If there is no real presence of Christ in the sacrament of the altar, then there is no need for ceremonies to celebrate and worship that presence. If the doctrine of purgatory is false, then the whole fabric of chantries and prayers for the dead becomes unnecessary. The result, More explains again and again, will be the sundering of the Christian community, which for More consists of both the living and the dead. Hence the vivid sense, at the close of More's treatise, of the nearness of the souls in purgatory to the living: the cry of the souls to the living stands as an emblem of More's sense of the Christian community. The dead need the help of the living; the living need the help of the dead.

Thus the refutation of Fish's charges against the clergy requires not only the social, political, and financial rebuttal given in the first part of the *Supplication of Souls;* ultimately, the refutation requires a defense implicit in the voices of the very souls in purgatory crying out for their release from the purifying fire. The king, as More points out (162/29–163/1), has long since taken his stand against the Lutherans; he is Defender of the Faith. Though the possession of church lands and the increase of royal power may be attractive to a grasping monarch, the thought that such proposals are prompted by heretics may give the king some pause.

THE TWIN ISSUES: THEOLOGICAL AND ECONOMIC

MORE, on reading the first two pages of Fish's pamphlet, could have recognized echoes of Tyndale's "wykkyd boke of obydyence" (162/1–2), for obedience itself is a refrain of the "beggars": "where was their obedience become?" and "Where is theire obedience become?"[1] they ask, speaking of the clergy; and, once the clergy are tamed, they tell Henry, "Then shall you haue full obedience of your people."[2]

---

[1]Appendix B, 415/34, 416/32–33.
[2]Appendix B, 422/24–25.

Another trait, characteristic of the reformers, is the copious use of holy scripture. Luther's teaching certainly permeates the book, perhaps via Tyndale's "wicked books" (161/34–162/2). Luther's solafideism inspires Fish's main objection to the very principle of indulgences: "remission of sinnes are not giuen by the popes pardon, but by Christ, for the sure feith and trust that we haue in him,"[1] and More will single out for attack this reliance on "onely fayth" (159/24, 174/27). Another major doctrine of Luther inspires Fish's rejection of purgatory: "there is not one word spoken of hit in al holy scripture."[2] A special point that underpins Fish's anticlericalism is Lutheran rejection of "holy orders," says More (154/14), who also hears the German's voice in "Then shall the gospell be preached" (155/19–20). It was indeed a concern of the early Reformation to preach the gospel and not the decalogue.

At the same time, economic factors were working to reinforce the Lutheran tendencies. The economic crisis that hit all of Europe in the third decade of the century, reaching its climax in the "laste .ii. dere yeres" (122/1) before 1529, coincided with the mounting assault against purgatory, from Luther's inconclusive "conclusions" of 1520 to his *Repeal of Purgatory* (*Der Widerruf vom Fegefeür*, Nürnberg, 1530). Anticlericalism provides the link between the two issues, the economic and the theological, that account for the bipartite division of More's answer. The acute, spasmodic phase of controversy to which we owe the books of Fish and More can be better understood if we survey the symptoms of the progress of the dual crisis in the preceding years. The intertwining of the two issues demonstrates that More, by devoting as much space to the doctrine of purgatory as to criticism of Fish's drastic economic schemes, is not taking his flight into some new Utopia, or burying his head in a vague underworld, to avoid facing the radical changes called for by the crisis.

Until the Reformation, purgatory was a devotional, not a polemical, subject. Opinions differed about details, as they still do among loyal Catholics. The application of pardons to the souls was much questioned by theologians but was almost taken for granted by the faithful and was readily asserted by pardoners. Despite Wyclif's calling it a folly to trust indulgences, the first datable piece of printing done in England was Sixtus IV's bull of 1476, the first papal document to extend the benefit of the pardon explicitly to the departed. Apart from doubts

---

[1]Appendix B, 420/11–13.
[2]Appendix B, 419/17–18.

concerning the pope's power beyond the grave, there was no heresy about purgatory except among the Waldensians and the Cathars.

By 1520, however, Luther had taken a few steps toward the revocation of purgatory that he would complete in 1530, and the demand for indulgences had begun to dwindle on the Continent. In October 1520, in his Brigittine monastery, Oecolampadius finished translating St. John of Damascus on "How Much the Good Works of the Living Profit the Dead."[1] The Greek father, of course, did not share the Latin vision of purgatory. But the West, too, had been divided: thus Ambrosius Catharinus, in his *Apologia* (Florence, December 1520), chided Luther for confused statements, and especially for relying on Tauler alone to make purgatory a temporary hell, full of anguish and despair. Henry VIII, in the *Assertio* (July 1521), held that Luther had all but rejected purgatory.[2] Luther's open rejection of this Catholic concept followed in 1522. In the summer of 1522, preaching on Dives and Lazarus, he claimed "we have no command from God to pray for the dead" and described the departed souls as asleep until Judgment Day.[3] More's 1523 *Responsio ad Lutherum* declared: "the king has proved both by the gospel and by reason that the successor of Peter can remit the punishment of purgatory."[4] More also pretended to quote Luther: "My heresy stands unconquered: that there is no purgatory."[5] Elsewhere, he commented on Luther: "I am not at all surprised if he has no fear of purgatory; there is indeed no reason for a person to be afraid of it who has had this sort of faith and lives in this manner."[6]

John Eck, who had faced Luther at the Leipzig dispute, finished *De purgatorio contra Ludderum*, which appeared in Rome.[7] On the other hand, in the *Epichiresis*, written in August 1523, Zwingli refused to see purgatory as implicitly asserted in the practice of praying for the

---

[1]John of Damascus, "quantum bona opera viventium defunctis prosint," in *Opera* (Basel: Henricus Petri, 1539), sigs. y4–z4v.

[2]*Assertio septem sacramentorum* (London, 1521), sig. b2: "Praeterea quid profuerit cum illo loqui, quibus subsidiis liberemur a purgatorio, qui totum ferme tollit purgatorium?"

[3]"Sermon von dem reichen Mann und dem armen Lazarus," in *D. Martin Luthers Werke*, 94 vols. to date (Weimar, 1883–), *10/3*, 176–200 (cited hereafter as *WA*), in particular p. 194: "Wyr haben keyn gepot von Got fur die todten zů bitten," and p. 191: "und (die todten) schlaffen auch noch drinnen biss an den iungsten tag."

[4]*CW* 5, 331.

[5]*CW* 5, 479.

[6]*CW* 5, 259.

[7]*De Purgatorio Iohan. Eckii contra Ludderum libri III* (Rome: Marcellus Franck, 1523).

dead.[1] The destiny of the souls, he says, is unknown to us.[2] From 1524 on, the production of pamphlets on the subject grew into a deluge. Nonetheless, on December 23, 1524, Clement proclaimed 1525 a holy year, the golden occasion for gaining the plenary indulgence in Rome; for 1526, he extended the privilege to all Christians who were unable to visit the Eternal City.

Now John Frith prepared to enter the field by translating portions of Luther's 1521 retort to Catharinus; Frith's version of *The Revelation of Antichrist* may have reached London while More's *Supplication* was still on the loom:

> Who is able to numbre the monstruous mervels / only of them that are departed. Good lord, what a see of lyes hath envaded vs / of aperinges, coniuringes and answers of sprites by the which it is brought to passe / that the Pope is also made the Kinge of them that are dead and raigneth in purgatorye / to the great disprofite of his prestes (if he continew) which haue all their liuinge / riches / and pomp out of purgatory.[3]

As Frith and Luther here imply, the cutting edge of the issue of purgatory was the money which belief in it brought to the priests. And this mercenary aspect became increasingly apparent during the 1520s because of the calamities afflicting Western Europe: droughts, epidemics (especially the as yet "anonymous" syphilis and sweating sickness), civil and foreign wars. This situation has been described in the Introductions to More's *Dialogue Concerning Heresies* and the *Confutation*.[4] We shall complete the picture by drawing on a rather neglected source: the diplomatic correspondence of Jean du Bellay, who represented Francis I at Henry VIII's court during the harsh years (1527–1529) which More repeatedly made the context of his first English works of controversy.

A few gleanings from du Bellay's dispatches reveal the mood of England during that "unseasonable" period. The country's economic plight is a recurring topic; and du Bellay spends a large portion of his letters to Montmorency trying to arrange for shipments of grain, both

---

[1] Ulrich Zwingli, *De canone missae epichiresis*, in *Huldreich Zwinglis sämtliche Werke*, ed. Emil Egli et al., 14 vols., Corpus Reformatorum 88–101 (Leipzig, 1905–59), 2, 556–608; cited hereafter as *CRZ*.

[2] *CRZ* 2, 593–94.

[3] John Frith, *The Revelation of Antichrist* (London, 1529), sigs. F₈–F₈v.

[4] *CW 6*, 455–72; *CW 8*, 1168–84.

for his household and for sale in England.[1] The English merchants
have conspired to buy nothing from the farmers, so that these, returning home with their wool and cloth unsold, might mutiny against the
war. But threatened with the Tower by an angry Wolsey, the merchants bought everything at the next market. "Wolsey is playing a
terrible game, for I believe he is the only person in England who wishes
a war with Flanders."[2] The sweating sickness has struck London in the
summer of 1528. The cardinal is taking refuge at Hampton Court
from the contagion and from his enemies. The king has dispatched
Anne Boleyn to her father's home in Kent and moves restlessly from
place to place.[3] There are not enough priests to bury the dead: "should
this last, corn will soon be quite cheap."[4] England is so utterly depleted
that, whatever may happen, no recovery can be expected for at least
two years. Du Bellay has run up debts[5] and is himself laid low by this
disease.[6]

Since Wolsey's fall was predictable even before Parliament was sum-
moned (August 9), the drastic measures advocated by Fish's beggars
recommended themselves to many future members of both houses.
The years of dearth, reaching their peak precisely in 1529, were forc-
ing civic and political action against the plague of beggary, and England was not alone in being tempted to rid itself of "poor beggars" by
seizing the alms of the "rich beggars."

Under these urgent circumstances, singling out Fish's brief attack on

---

[1]Jean du Bellay, *Ambassades en Angleterre de Jean du Bellay. La Première Ambassade (sep-
tembre 1527–février 1529). Correspondance Diplomatique*, ed. V.-L. Bourrilly and P. de
Vaissière (Paris 1905), pp. 32–33: "je croy que mondict seigneur le légat se trouveroyt
ennuyé si la chose ne venoyt à tel effect qu'il demande, car vous sçavez l'asseurance qu'il a
baillée au peuple, ouquel se trouve de jour à aultre augmentation de trouble et nécessité
pour la grant faulte de bled qui est en ce pays icy." See also p. 44.

[2]Du Bellay, *Ambassades*, p. 158: "Les marchans avoyent conspiré de ne venir plus à
l'estrade à fin que les paisans, retournans sans vendre leurs laines et draps, mutinassent le
pays. Il a mandé incontinent à aulcuns des principaulx que c'estoyt assez, qu'il les cog-
noissoyt et qu'il sçavoit bien où estoyt la Tour; ilz sont venuz crier miséricorde et ont
promis que au prochain marché, qui sera mercredi, il ne demourera pour ung escu de
marchandise qu'ilz n'acheptent à quelque pris que ce soyt; mais soyez certain, Monseig-
neur, qu'il fault qu'il joue de terribles mistères, car je pense qu'il est seul en Angleterre
qui veult la guerre en Flandres." See also Charles W. Ferguson, *Naked to Mine Enemies:
The Life of Cardinal Wolsey* (Boston, 1958), p. 391.

[3]Du Bellay, *Ambassades*, p. 304. See also J. J. Scarisbrick, *Henry VIII* (Berkeley, 1968),
pp. 210–12.

[4]Du Bellay, *Ambassades*, p. 305.

[5]Du Bellay, *Ambassades*, pp. 310, 324, 345.

[6]Du Bellay, *Ambassades*, p. 333.

purgatory in order to create an extended defense of the doctrine is in some ways a brilliant strategy, for More's *Supplication* shifts the ground of the argument to the economy of the afterlife—with an intimate appeal to the human concern for the souls of the departed fathers, mothers, sons, daughters, husbands, and wives. Moreover, it is a doctrine that does not require obscure theological arguments for its justification; its truth, More argues, is based upon the book that for the reformers is all in all, the Bible. Of all the doctrines of the church, it is one of the most thoroughly established, by every precedent and tradition known to Christianity.

Scripture in More's *Supplication*

More is readier than most Catholic controversialists of his day to confront the reformers on their chosen ground, the Bible. His *Responsio ad Lutherum,* for all its being a defense of Henry VIII's *Assertio,* is more scriptural than the king's book. If it already claims for the church the power to distinguish the Word of God from the words of men by establishing a catalogue of inspired writings and the authority to interpret the Bible, the 1523 book firmly bases these prerogatives on the New Testament itself: Christ himself tells his disciples to have recourse to the church for the fullness of truth. In 1526, when More urges Erasmus to redeem his pledge of a second volume defending free will, he reminds him that Luther must be encountered in the only arena he accepts: the written Word of God.[1] Scripture is also the largest single issue treated in *A Dialogue Concerning Heresies,* even though it is not one of the "diuers maters" listed on the title page.[2] The main novelty More faces in the *Supplication,* from the standpoint of biblical evidence, is the importance of an Old Testament witness, namely Maccabees: characteristically, he bases the authenticity of that pre-Christian source on the authority of Christ in the New Testament.

More proceeds by organizing ten biblical passages into a crescendo of proofs: four from the Old Testament and six from the New, climaxing with two sayings ascribed to Christ himself. Obviously, the pattern is by no means homogeneous in its formal details. As if verisimilitude made it indecorous for an agonized crowd of souls to achieve the neat regularity which would become a scholar at his desk, the ten proofs are

---

[1] *Opus epistolarum Des. Erasmi Roterodami,* ed. P. S. Allen et al., 13 vols. (Oxford, 1906–58), *6,* 442; cited hereafter as "Allen."
[2] In the Index of *CW 6,* the entries for "Scripture," "New Testament," "Vulgate," and "Written . . . word of God" fill more than two columns.

presented with considerable irregularity: the reference is or is not given, the Vulgate Latin is or is not quoted; the sentence is sometimes translated, sometimes paraphrased. Unlike the other eight, the two main texts, one drawn from Maccabees, the other from 1 Corinthians, are amplified through developments that remain firmly geared toward the "pryncypall purpose" (193/2). The seasickness parable (188/36–189/28), which at first seems to be a kind of psychological digression, is a very apt illustration of the nausea of sin. The exegesis of the sin against the Holy Spirit (191/14–192/21) is clearly functional: it is a reassuring sermon against despair, akin to the pages that deprecate pusillanimity and preach Christian hope in More's prison writings.[1]

One third of Book 2 is devoted to the scriptural demonstration of purgatory (176/9–194/30), and the theme reemerges with a discussion of apparitions (196/13–198/2), a short section on the second book of Maccabees (203/7–23), and a recapitulation of the proofs (210/23–28). The rationale for allotting the Bible such pride of place is that for Luther and his followers "no thynge is to be byleued for a sure trouth/ but yf it appere proued and euydent in holy wryt."[2]

More's first argument, from the life of Hezekiah (4 Kings 20:1–7, Isa. 38), is no proof proper, but "probable reason taken of the scrypture" (178/16–17). Its unusual length (176/21–177/28) reflects its role as a kind of methodological specimen: More demonstrates how to handle the documents of revelation, how to open the Old Testament with the key of prepossessed faith. Hezekiah's devotion is emphasized in Kings (4 Kings 18–20), Paralipomenon (2 Par. 29–32), and Isaiah (Isa. 36–39). He prays with Isaiah and they are heard; he does what is pleasing to God; he is a mighty smasher of idols and an enlightened reformer of the Temple liturgy; he involves the whole nation in the resumption of the Passover. He truly combines "holynes and connyng" (177/26). Like the godly princes More mentions in Book 1, he provided for the clergy of the Old Law, ordering the people "to give the portion due to the priests and the Levites, that they might give themselves to the law of the Lord" (2 Par. 31:4), and the laity's response was most generous.

The royal estate of Hezekiah may have had something to do with the souls' summoning him to bear witness against a "bill" submitted to England's king. A pious ruler, he had recourse to prayer as a weapon against Sennacherib. He was cured of a malignant boil by Isaiah's

---

[1]*Dialogue of Comfort* (CW *12*, 111–20) and *De Tristitia Christi* (CW *14*, 97–109).
[2]CW *6*, 149/12–13.

prayer and the application of a fig poultice. Hezekiah's prayer (Isa. 38:9–20) was treated as a psalm; its inclusion in the books of hours contributed to making his name famous or at least familiar.[1] The office connects the prayer especially with the liturgy of Easter Eve, since some of its phrases—such as "vadam ad portas inferi . . . non infernus confitebitur tibi"—can readily be accommodated to the entombed Christ awaiting resurrection. The link with purgatory is not obvious: More reasons it out of "the cyrcumstaunce" (177/24), meaning Hezekiah's righteousness, which made him likely to avoid hell, and his desire to do penance in this life. For this interpretation, More cannot claim backing from the unanimous opinion of the church fathers; he refers instead to "auncyent doctors" (176/26–27), with no definite article: these need not be as ancient as the church fathers proper.

From "probable reason" (178/16), the souls move to "playne and euydent textys" (178/18) with a brief sentence from what they rather vaguely call "the boke of the kyngys" (178/19–20), actually 1 Kings (that is, 1 Sam.) 2:6. This bringing back, *deductio (deducere) ad infernum (inferos),* is a common Old Testament phrase. More infers purgatory from it, but most interpreters construe it as "bringing man to death's gate and back to life again"; *ad infernum* appears to be interchangeable with *ad nihilum,* or *in lacum,* to designate the total impotence of the grave.

More's third proof (178/26–179/25) hinges on a long Latin sentence from Zech. 9:11, which he translates quite literally, including the rather awkward preterit "erat." The present "est" of other versions is more natural, and More himself uses it in a freer rendering further in his discussion: "where in ys no water" (179/14). In his translation he wisely leaves out the "quoque," which the absence of context makes redundant. His viewing "the dampned spyrytys" as "the very gaolers of god" (178/34–179/1) is consistent with other pages of the *Supplication* (for example, 221/8–16). This jail does not lack parallels in the Bible, including the New Testament (in 1 Pet. 3:19 a jail is the receptacle of "spirits" visited by the spirit of Christ). The prison metaphor will dominate several chapters in the *Dialogue of Comfort,* where Antony devotes thirty pages to it (*CW 12,* 250–80). The image of a "drye pyt of fyre" (179/3) will be contrasted by Frith against John Fisher's preference for Job 24:19, which combines extremes of freezing and burning. More

---

[1]The prayer is on sig. o7 of *Hore beate Marie* (Paris, 1530; *STC* 15963), a copy of which bears More's autograph prayer.

justifies the lack of water in Zechariah through the parable of Lazarus and the rich glutton (Luke 16:19–31; 179/4–12), a familiar scene regularly exploited by preachers because it was the gospel for the second Sunday of Lent. Catholic tradition, though, seems less sure than More that purgatory is "clerly proued by the playn wordys" of Zechariah here (179/24–25).[1]

Half of the space More devotes to the Old Testament proofs is claimed by the books of Maccabees (179/26–183/28). His souls stay faithful to their vague method of reference; although they quote from both 2 Macc. 12:39–46 and 1 Macc. 4:52–61, they usually speak of "the boke of the Machabees" in the singular,[2] and yet these books are by different authors and are strikingly different in tone.

The Maccabean writings in some ways form a bridge from the Old to the New Testament. They abound in intimations of Christian doctrine; they stress resurrection from the dead, the intercessory power of the saints, and the ability of the living to assist the dead by their prayers, alms, and sacrifices. In Augustine's view, the main ground for their full reception by the church was the example of "those who, like true martyrs . . . suffered their passion for the law of God."[3] He was alluding to the old Jewish lawyer Eleazar (2 Macc. 6:18–31) and the seven Maccabean brethren encouraged by their mother (2 Macc. 7:1–41). That some suicidal feats are not merely recounted but admired detracts nothing from the perfection of the eponymous hero, Judas Maccabaeus, "which was Goddes knyght," according to Chaucer,[4] a title that More amplifies into "the greate good and godly valyaunt capytayne of goddys people" (181/13–14). Both a fearless warrior and a shrewd negotiator, worthy as Roland and wise as Oliver, "good and holy" (179/30), he was one of the three biblical characters in chivalry's hall of fame, the Nine Worthies.[5]

---

[1]For example, the note to Zech. 9:11 in the Douay Old Testament (1609–10; STC 2207): "S. Ierom, S. Cyril & other fathers vnderstand this lake to be *Limbus patrum* from whence Christ deliuered the Sainctes of the old testament" (vol. 2, sig. 5O₃).

[2]Only in two instances is the plural used (181/10, 22), and even then the pronoun is in the singular (181/12).

[3]*De civitate Dei* 18.36; *Corpus Christianorum: Series Latina*, 176 vols. to date (Turnholt, 1953–), *48*, 632; cited hereafter as *CSSL*.

[4]"Tale of Melibee," *Canterbury Tales*, in *The Works of Geoffrey Chaucer*, ed. F. N. Robinson, 2nd ed. (Boston, 1957), B² 2847.

[5]J. Huizinga, *The Waning of the Middle Ages*, trans. F. Hopman (London, 1924), p. 61. In *Love's Labour's Lost*, he still holds his own with Hercules and Hector, Alexander and Pompey: "Judas I am, ycleped Maccabaeus" (V, ii. 591).

As they did with King Hezekiah, the souls simplify a "noble hystory" (181/22) by concentrating on the central personage. Where the Bible shows all the survivors of the battle concerned with the fate of their slain comrades and engaged in collective prayer even before Judas decides to take a collection and to have a sacrifice offered in Jerusalem (2 Macc. 12:39, 41–42), More makes Judas the seat of the fear, the prompter and organizer of the prayer. This synecdoche is a stylistic convention—"Caesar pontem fecit" is its paradigm in books of rhetoric—yet More may also, at this perilous juncture, have chosen it to conjure up, from the troubled days of the past, the exemplary figure of a reforming sovereign. Judas' main initiative was to make the suffrages for the dead truly public by entrusting them to the priests functioning in the Temple of Jerusalem. As head of the chosen people, he possessed a "sacre magesty" that in medieval Christianity was held to "approche priesthode . . . in dignitie."[1] In Christendom, as in Jewry, a legitimate ruler is endowed with the kind of aura which in the gospel enables Caiaphas to act as an inspired prophet (John 11:51), and which prompts Paul to apologize when he learns that the man he has rebuked is, though wicked, a bishop (Acts 23:5). More had used these two precedents for Henry VIII against Luther.[2]

To Judas, then, More naturally ascribes the fear lest the fallen, already punished by death for breaking the First Commandment (cf. Deut. 7:25), should take a worse fall after death. The hero's wisdom and holiness guarantee that this concern for the welfare of departed souls is not mere superstition, that the solidarity between the living and the dead receives manifest expression under the aegis of a pious prince who was the author of a new liturgical feast which was destined to continue and to be endorsed by Christ's own participation (181/13–21). Although purgatory is not mentioned, the doctrine it embodies is quite explicit here. It may surprise us that More does not quote the comment by which the author of the story draws a theological corollary from Judas' conduct:

> he took full account of the resurrection. For if he had not expected the fallen to rise again it would have been superfluous and foolish to pray for the dead, whereas if he had in view the splendid recompense reserved for those who make a pious end, the thought was holy and devout. This was why he had this atonement

[1] CW 2, 62/27–28.
[2] CW 5, 134/28–30.

sacrifice offered for the dead, so that they might be released from their sin. [2 Macc. 12:43–45][1]

These imperfect believers were the proper denizens of purgatory: stained by having carried and trusted amulets—"an abomination to the Lord your God" (Deut. 7:25)—they were nevertheless sufficiently attached to God to risk their lives in the defense of his law. Their posthumous relief takes the triple form for which the souls keep pleading: "prayoure/ almoyse/ & sacryfyce" (179/29). The impressive sum levied by Judas strikingly anticipates the mass stipends of Catholic Europe, the principal source of England's *valor ecclesiasticus,* and an eyesore for Fish and many avid readers of his pamphlet.

Opponents of praying for the dead, annoyed by these "playn and open wordys" (183/21), use them as proof that the books of Maccabees are "none holy scrypture" (180/14). Being but a Jew, they say, Judas ignores the redemptive sufficiency of Christ's blood, while his chroniclers' commendations and deductions rather disprove than prove the divine inspiration of the entire book—so "they deny yt for scrypture" (180/18–19). It is against this second "shyfte" (180/4) that More mobilizes his suffering souls.

The question of the scriptural canon looms large in the overall controversy and has received systematic treatment elsewhere in this edition of More's works.[2] All that needs to be stressed here is the difference between Protestant objections to these books of Maccabees and Luther's underrating of James's epistle. Luther's doubts about the "epistle of straw"[3] did not obtain confirmation among all of his fol-

---

[1]This quotation, from the Jerusalem Bible, imperfectly represents the last verse of chapter 12, which in the Vulgate reads: "Sancta ergo et salubris est cogitatio pro defunctis exorare, ut a peccatis solvantur." The Douay version, made from the Vulgate, has: "It is therfore a holie, and healthful cogitation to pray for the dead, that they may be loosed from sinnes." The Douay note Englishes the Greek original of verses 45–46 and cites the comments of Augustine and Bernard and formulas of Jewish prayer for the dead. It adds in the margin: "Iudas was high priest when he caused prayers and sacrifice to be offered for the dead. It was the general practise of the Church. And is yet obserued by the Iewes" (vol. 2, sigs. 6C$_1$v–6C$_2$).

[2]*CW* 5, 735–36, 741–42; *CW* 13, 113/1–8 and 150/2–10; also Germain Marc'hadour, *The Bible in the Works of Thomas More,* 5 vols. (Nieuwkoop, 1969–72), 4, 201–6; cited hereafter as "Marc'hadour, *The Bible.*" The sentence from Augustine, quoted countless times over the centuries and echoed by More dozens of times, reads: "Ego vero Evangelio non crederem, nisi me catholicae Ecclesiae commoveret auctoritas" (*PL 42,* 176). More's full rendering of it occurs in *CW 8,* 737/8–10: "Now as for me, I wold not byleue the gospell but yf the authoryte of the catholyke chyrche moued me therto."

[3]"Vorrhede" to the New Testament (1522), in *Die Deutsche Bibel, WA 6,* 10.

lowers: Tyndale's New Testament and Protestant Bibles through the centuries retained James. On the other hand, most post-Reformation editors of the Bible leave out or relegate to an appendix the books that the Jewish Synod of Jamnia (first century after Christ) excised from the Hebrew canon of inspired writings, among them Maccabees. The Sadducees, who denied the resurrection, could not accept 2 Macc. 7:9 or the apparitions related in 2 Macc. 15:11–16. The more influential Pharisees, although they had prepared Israel to believe in the resurrection, resented the new accents this doctrine assumed for the worshipers of the risen Christ and, moreover, hated pagan Rome, an ally of the Maccabees. Using the Septuagint version of the Old Testament, the Greek-speaking Christians accepted its full catalogue, which included Maccabees. Yet their apologists knew and wrote that it would be futile to draw arguments from books to which the Jews accorded no divine authority. Most of these books were recent accretions to the Bible, and some of them were composed in Greek, notably Wisdom— "Sapyence," as More calls it (181/31)—and 2 Maccabees. These were listed as authentic scripture in the catalogues drawn by the church at a succession of synods: Rome (382), Hippo (393), Carthage (397, 418), although 3 and 4 Maccabees were rejected as apocrypha.[1]

For More, the thousand years of ecclesiastical prescription had even greater weight than the decrees of early councils. His souls appeal twice to the authority of Jerome (180/24, 183/16), although that greatest of biblical scholars, in deference to the Jewish canon, had treated the *deuterocanonica* somewhat as second-class. They also twice invoke "other old holy doctours" (180/24–25, 183/16), without using the definite article which, on other issues, presents the church fathers as a solid bloc. They repeatedly single out the giant, Augustine, who for good measure was also Luther's favorite theologian. Before climaxing his argument with Augustine's famous dictum that firmly puts scripture in the gift of the church, More introduces a criterion dear to most reformers: let the Bible bear witness to itself. He makes John's gospel, the holiest book of the New Testament,[2] testify on behalf of the Maccabean

---

[1]*Apocrypha*, in the Protestant tradition, designates all books not in the Hebrew canon, including the whole Maccabean corpus, while both the Greek and Latin churches reserve the epithet for books (such as 3 and 4 Maccabees) rejected from early Christian canons.

[2]The proverbial ascendancy of "saynt Iohans gospell" finds repeated expression here (181/2, 183/5, 184/18) and in other works of More. Translating Pico, he quotes Savonarola's reference to a secret "which is as trew as the gospell of seint Iohn"; *The Workes . . . in the Englysh tonge* (London, 1557; *STC*[2] 18076), sig. a5; cited hereafter as *EW*. When Tyndale, to enhance the written word, cites "storyes" showing that mankind knew

books. It is the New Testament, likewise, that bears witness to Maccabees by showing that at least one fruit of the Maccabean renewal stood the test of time, namely "the grete feste of the dedycacyon of the temple of Hierusalem called festum enceniorum" (181/15–16), which modern Judaism calls Hanukkah, meaning "dedication." The lesson More draws from Christ's celebration of this feast with his fellow Jews is in keeping with his method of using the New Testament to throw light on the Old, a universal method in Christendom.[1] The supporting link is not so much between two texts as between two persons: Christ celebrates the feast of the Dedication in compliance with the decree of Judas Maccabaeus and within the tradition born of it (181/10–27).

More next chooses the Psalter, "the very somme of clere and lyghtesome prophesyes" (182/3–4), to point out that, by returning to the Hebrew canon against the Christian tradition, the reformers rejected what had been the *sensus communis* of the church from its very cradle. No portion of the Old Testament better illustrates how differently Jews and Christians read their shared literature, especially its prophetic portions. Israel had made the Psalms the staple of synagogue prayer, but the New Testament innovated by treating them as a quarry for doctrinal statements, echoing them more than a hundred times. In the Jewish canon, the Psalter, being part of the "Writings," carries less weight than the Pentateuch and the Prophets, whereas Christ, explaining to his disciples all that concerns him "in the law of Moses and the prophets and the psalms" (Luke 24:44), places the religious lyrics on a par with the noblest sections of the Bible. If Jerome translated them three times, it was because he viewed them as a prophetic *summa* about Christ and his mystical body. Medieval monks recited the whole Psalter every day. The only portion of the Latin Bible ever printed by Caxton was the Psalter (1480?; *STC*[2] 16253), which served as a primer in schools. More advanced learners availed themselves of the five versions in Lefèvre d'Etaples's *Quincuplex Psalterium* (1509).[2] Erasmus' only in-

---

how to write before Noah's day, More dismisses them as not being "any thynge sybbe [i.e., akin] to saynt Iohans gospell" (*CW 8*, 274/8–13; see also *CW 6*, 30/9, 151/32–35).

[1]The Reims translators (1582; *STC* 2884), at John 10:22, comment: "This is the feast of the Dedication instituted by Iudas Machabaeus. Christ vouchsafed to honour and keepe that feast instituted by him: & our Heretikes vouchsafe not to pray and sacrifice for the dead, vsed and approued by him" (vol. 2, sig. 2I$_1$v). The Douay Old Testament also links 1 Mac. 4:56 with this chapter of John (vol. 2, sig. 5S$_1$).

[2]More thought highly of this edition; see Rogers, p. 58. See Guy Bedouelle, *Le Quincuplex Psalterium de Lefèvre d'Etaples: Un guide de lecture*, Travaux d'Humanisme et Renaissance 171 (Geneva, 1979); the title of Bedouelle's tenth chapter, "Christus, clauis Dauid," is Lefèvre's allusion to Rev. 3:7.

roads into Old Testament scholarship were his *Enarrationes* of five psalms.[1] Luther's first book was a commentary on the Psalms, and, like Jerome, he made three different versions of them, treating them as a kind of fifth gospel. John Fisher's first book and best-seller was a collection of ten sermons on the penitential psalms. Later he compiled *precationes ex psalmis,* as did Thomas More;[2] the two men's literary debt to the Psalter is statistically greater than to any other book of the Bible. The very phrase "psalter of Dauyd" (182/3) is specifically Christian, rooted as it is in the New Testament. Both Jesus (for example, Matt. 22:44–45, Luke 20:42–44) and his apostles (for example, Acts 1:16, 2:25, 4:25; Rom. 11:9) say "David" whenever they quote a psalm, as if to enhance the status of the text and proclaim its messianic dimension. The gospel sees David as the king par excellence (Matt. 1:6). Jesus is called "son of David" in the very first verse of the New Testament (Matt. 1:1). That David was not the author of every one of the 150 psalms appears clear from the Psalter itself, as More must have known, yet he is apt to lay great stress on the generic ascription: "For that holye kyng and Prophet Dauid speakynge of blyssednesse, putteth in the begynnynge of al hys psalter."[3] An explicit (and reasoned) instance of More's Christocentric exegesis occurs in this very portion of the *Supplication,* when he reads Christ's Passion in Ps. 37:18—"ego in flagella paratus sum" (190/17–18)—while recognizing that the words "may be well applyed & veryfyed of many an other man" (190/19–20), as John Fisher had done in applying them to the penitent soul.[4] Thus, both the New Testament and Christian literature throughout the ages abundantly prove the "authoryte" of "the hole psalter" (182/3–5) to be such that it makes it a new message, part of the *euangelion.*

What More has said about the Psalter, that its "force and strength" (182/6) depend on the assumptions of the reader, applies *a fortiori* to the relative weight of the two Testaments. Even though the "playn and open wordys" of 2 Maccabees so "manyfestely" (183/19–21) demonstrate the soundness of praying for the dead that any other text may

---

[1] They took the forms of commentary, paraphrase, and sermon. Erasmus also edited older commentaries on the Psalter, one of them (dedicated to Pope Adrian VI) with a revealing preface (Allen, 5, 100–12).

[2] More's *Imploratio diuini auxilij,* a chain of verses from the Latin Psalter, was included both in his *English Works* (1557) and in his *Opera Latina* (1565). It is reproduced in *CW 13,* 214–25. See "Proemial Annotations vpon the Book of Psalmes," in Marc'hadour, *The Bible, 1,* 101–3.

[3] *CW 13,* 74/3–5.

[4] Fisher, *English Works,* p. 84.

appear feeble in comparison, a Christian author addressing a Christian
audience knows he is going up the scale as he proceeds from the Old to
the New Testament. By praising John's gospel (181/1–2, 183/4–6) and
using it to put the seal of Christ on a Maccabean institution, More
fosters in the reader a reverent posture toward the other writings of
that "blessyd apostle and euangelyst" (184/3–4), whose testimony the
enemies of purgatory cannot ignore "excepte they deny saynt Iohan"
(184/18).

The souls are at their vaguest when they quote 1 John 5:16 in Latin
(184/4–5), with a modicum of departure from the Vulgate, without
telling us where to find it among John's five canonical writings. More
would cite the verse again in 1533 in a chapter of the *Confutation* that is
full of quotations from 1 John:[1] no wonder, since Tyndale had published in 1531 *The exposition of the fyrste Epistle of seynt Ihon*[2] with a
preface in which "he denyeth not onely purgatory but also all
punysshement."[3] How natural More's reasoning here is to a Catholic
appears from the note in the Reims New Testament: "the praier which
he speaketh of, must needes be praier for the dead"; the Calvinists
refused to apply it to reprobates "onely to auoid the sequele of praying
for the dead" (sig. 4R$_4$).

For his next Johannine quotation (Rev. 5:13) More gives a clear
reference (184/19–25) but not the Latin text, which his translation
closely follows. The analysis of the psychology of hell (184/28–32) will
reappear, with greater elaboration, in his spiritual writings, especially
in *A Treatise on the Passion:* the opening chapters on the fall of the
proud-hearted angels.[4]

From John, the disciple whom Jesus loved most, the souls move to
Peter, the disciple who loved Jesus most.[5] More quotes the Vulgate
correctly and does not translate it, expecting his public to guess at the
overall meaning of the Latin or else wait until he has elucidated the
meaning of the last three words, which alone concern his purpose:

---

[1]*CW 8,* 439/2–5.

[2]*STC*^{2} 24443; Anthea Hume, "English Protestant Books Printed Abroad, 1525–1535:
An Annotated Bibliography," in *CW 8,* Appendix B, pp. 1063–91 (cited hereafter as
"Hume"), no. 26.

[3]*CW 8,* 426/36–37.

[4]*CW 13,* 3/31–25/7.

[5]See *CW 13,* 94/2–5. More repeats Peter's name at 185/30, 186/32, 187/2–3. Peter
figures even in More's *History of Richard III,* as patron of Westminster Abbey and its
sanctuary (*CW 2,* 28/2–6 [= 115/14–16], 31/20 [Latin only; = 118/10], 32/33–33/2 [=
119/12–14], 38/1–3 [Latin only =123/24–26], 194–95).

"solutis doloribus inferni" (Acts 2:24; 185/32). Peter's Pentecostal discourse was familiar to the man in the pew because it was read at mass on Easter Monday, a holy day of obligation then. More may have responded personally to this page of Acts because Psalm 15, which Peter cites to buttress his testimony (Acts 2:25–28; cf. Ps. 15:8–11), had been included in his *Life of Picus* with Pico's commentary.[1] Just as More had previously translated "in inferno" of Ps. 15:10 by "in hell,"[2] he now renders "doloribus inferni" by "payns of hell" (185/32–33). Writing for a nonscholarly public, he does not bother to echo Erasmus when he points out that the Greek θανάτου does not mean hell, but death.[3] Erasmus' annotation adds that the Greek λύσας makes it "necessary to understand that God did the loosening."[4] More, however, makes Christ, not God, the subject: "cryste at hys resurreccyon dyd lose and vnbynd paynys in hell" (186/32–33). Presumably the sentence in his mind conjured up the harrowing of hell.

More moves on to the much weightier passage in 1 Cor. 3:12–15 (187/10–17). These are an undoubted peak in More's range of New Testament texts. They are, with 2 Maccabees, the one passage never left out of systematic treatments of purgatory, whatever the level, whether it be the deliberations of a council or the exhortations of a popular treatise. His reference to the dissenters' partiality for the difficult prose of the apostle is a refrain of Catholic apologetics (187/3–6).[5] The passage More exploits here begins in a way that appealed to the reformers. He had quoted 1 Cor. 3:11 more fully in the *Responsio* because Luther had cited the verse in favor of scripture by equating *fundamentum* with *scriptura*.[6] The *Supplication* begins its quotation at the next verse (v. 12). Catholic tradition has never limited the words "quasi per ignem" to the fire of purgatory; it has applied them quasi-proverbially to any narrow escape. Yet, given the other places in the New Testament where damned souls find punishment in the everlasting fire created for the devils (Matt. 3:12, 25:41; Mark 9:43; 2 Pet. 3:7; Jude 7),

[1]*EW*, sigs. b₁–b₂v.

[2]*EW*, sig. b₂v.

[3]In Erasmus' *Novum Instrumentum*, 1516; *Opera omnia*, ed. J. Clericus (Leclerc), 10 vols. (Leiden, 1703–06; reprint, Hildesheim, 1961), 6, 444 (cited hereafter as "*Opera omnia*"), the Vulgate *inferni* is criticized for reflecting ᾅδου, less well attested than θανάτου.

[4]*Opera omnia*, 6, 444.

[5]See *CW 6*, 497–98.

[6]*CW 5*, 234/7–236/3. Cf. *Confutation:* "no man can laye any other foundacyon then that that is all redy layed, that is to wyt Iesus Cryste hym selfe" (*CW 8*, 931/26–27). Here again, More shows that the foundation is Christ's person, and not a written document.

it was inevitable that this transitory fire through which other human souls passed on their way to eternal bliss should be seen as purgatorial. In the *Confutation,* More quotes Augustine to the effect that "venyall synnys . . . must be purged wyth that fyre, of whyche the apostle sayth, that the worke shall appere by the fyre."[1] The Pauline echo is amplified further down the page: "we shal so longe abyde in that fyre of purgatory, tyll the venyall synnys aboue named be consumed vp as wode, hey, and stubblys" (968/31–33). Whether authentic or spurious, Augustine's sermon well expresses a reading of 1 Cor. 3:12–15 which had been traditional in Western Christianity "thys thowsande yere and more" (190/26, 191/6).

The image of God as a purging, rather than punishing, fire comes from the prophet Malachi (3:2–3); "Ipse enim quasi ignis conflans . . . purgabit filios Levi." The metaphor of the crucible, which Paul's mention of gold and silver brings forcibly to mind, easily leads to all the sufferings which test and refine and temper man's spiritual mettle during his earthly pilgrimage. English reformers used the passage in a similar sense even outside their polemical writings; thus, George Joye in 1533 writes to Hugh Latimer: "I was full sory when I hard of that fyer that ye sufferyd whereof Paule spekythe 1 cor. 3. to see your worke burnyd befor your face."[2] Some Catholic exegetes agree with the majority of Protestant theologians that Paul's fire "is not the fire of purgatory, for this purifies but does not try."[3] A very influential commentary on 1 Corinthians by H. L. Goudge sums up the Anglican tradition as follows: "There can be no reference to any purgatorial fire between death and judgment. S. Paul is not speaking either of the purification of character, or of the temporal punishment of sin; it is the testing of work that is in question."[4]

The souls' emphasis here, even more than in other stretches of the *Supplication,* is not on punishment but on purification. They speak endlessly of spots (188/19, 22, 35; 189/31, 33, 36), repeat the words *clean/unclean, cleansed/uncleansed* (188/18–19; 189/13, 30, 35), and echo the very name of purgatory with *purged* (188/21, 28, 33) and

---

[1]*CW 8,* 968/9–12.

[2]Letter of April 29, 1533, quoted by Charles C. Butterworth and Allan G. Chester, *George Joye* (Philadelphia and Oxford, 1962), pp. 95–96; see also pp. 94–95.

[3]Fernand Prat, *The Theology of Saint Paul,* trans. John L. Stoddard, 2 vols. (London, 1926–27), *1,* 96; quoted by W. G. H. Simon, *The First Epistle to the Corinthians: Introduction and Commentary,* Torch Bible Commentaries (London, 1959), p. 71.

[4]H. L. Goudge, *The First Epistle to the Corinthians,* 3rd ed., Westminster Commentaries (London, 1911), p. 25.

unpurgeable (188/33–34). How deep the spot can be, how deep the cleansing must reach to remove it, appears in a phrase from More's seasickness parable: "clene from all euyll humours" (189/13). It is not enough for rusty patches and superficial stains to be rubbed off; purgatory probes the soul to revivify its lifeblood and restore the subtle balance of its humors.

What is in question in Paul's fire metaphor, objects Goudge, "is the testing of work."[1] The last word would not bother More, whose purgatory destroys or refashions "such ... workes as can neuer enter heuen" (187/27–28). Unwittingly, perhaps, he echoes Rev. 21:27, which many Catholic apologists or preachers have quoted among the proofs of purgatory. St. John's guide about the heavenly Jerusalem says: "there shall entre into it none vnclene thynge" (Tyndale's version). It is one of the verses More may allude to when he claims "many an other playne texte" (194/23) besides the ten he is exploiting.

More's last two scriptural passages are sayings of Christ's that haunted him throughout his life (Matt. 12:32, 36), judging by the frequency with which he returned to them. Matt. 12:32 concerns the much debated sinning "against the Holy Spirit." In *A Dialogue of Comfort*, More provides another reference, Mark 3:29, for "the abomynable synne of blasphamye/ agaynst the holy goost."[2] Here (191/9–14), he gives no reference, but in both works the terms of his quotation reflect only Matthew. The words "in aeternum" in Mark 3:29 have been alleged to counter Catholic inferences from the two worlds mentioned by Matthew; some Protestants argue that the dichotomy "neyther in thys worlde nor in the world to cum" (191/13–14) is devoid of theological significance.

More ends his biblical round with the most venial of venial sins: idle words. Writing to Dorp in 1515, he had quoted Jerome's argument from Matt. 12:36 that if idle words would be punished, how much more would contumelious ones.[3] The key phrase here is "euery ydle word" (193/32). Since hell is unthinkable for such mild offenses, More reasons in the wake of a long tradition, and since "in to heuen shall neyther synne nor payn enter" (193/14–15, an echo of Rev. 21:27, already found at 187/26–28), God's merciful justice must have made provision for a temporary purging. More's argument in favor of purgatory seems almost to be arranged in a *diminuendo*, with this least

---

[1]Goudge, p. 25.
[2]*CW 12*, 299/19–27.
[3]*CW 15*, 40/4–6.

important detail of idle words mentioned last, as if to emphasize the unquestioning assumption that purgatory must exist, and to undercut the sense that some sort of rational argument is necessary to justify Christian beliefs. Yet, as his attention to the scriptural passages shows, More has carefully mustered and arranged every detail in order to counter Fish's attack on its own, seemingly rational, grounds.

The Dogma of Purgatory

PLACE OR STATE?

J ACQUES LE GOFF, in *The Birth of Purgatory*, points out that "in modern Catholic theology, Purgatory is not a place but a state. . . . Accordingly, Church dogma specifies neither the location of Purgatory nor the penalties to which souls are there subjected, these being matters left up to individual opinion."[1] But Le Goff also points out that this rigorous view of the concept was not an integral part of the birth and development of purgatory; in fact, he insists, the belief in a "geography" of purgatory and in actual physical suffering as a means of expiating one's sins was crucial to the general acceptance of the idea. The dogma of purgatory, then, is sharply divided between pre-Tridentine insistence upon the physical reality of the place, and post-Tridentine belief in purgatory as a state of being rather than as a specific location. More's descriptions of purgatory often evoke the more naturalistic view of medieval Latinity.

A. Michel follows the development of the doctrine from its biblical sources through its formulation by three general councils: Lyons (1274), Florence (1439), and Trent (1563).[2] Throughout the Middle Ages, tradition expanded upon the two most relevant texts of scripture, 2 Macc. 12 and 1 Cor. 3:11–15.[3] In the first passage, Judas Maccabaeus is not portrayed as an innovator: his idea of praying for the dead does not seem unusual to his army or to the priests. Nor does any variant in the manuscripts, whether Greek, Latin, or Syriac, cast any doubt on the authenticity of the text or show any scribal attempt to tone down the basic assertion that it is good to pray for the dead. But this notion of prayers

---

[1] Jacques Le Goff, *The Birth of Purgatory*, trans. Arthur Goldhammer (Chicago, 1984), p. 13 (first published as *La Naissance du Purgatoire*, Paris, Gallimard, 1981); cited hereafter as "Le Goff, *Purgatory*."

[2] A. Michel, "Purgatoire," *Dictionnaire de théologie catholique*, 15 vols. (Paris, 1908–50), *13*, 1163–1326 (1936); cited hereafter as *DTC*.

[3] One might wish to add to this list Matt. 12:31–32 and Luke 16:19–26; see Le Goff, *Purgatory*, pp. 42–43.

being used to help the dead is not yet linked to any concept of separation
of worthy souls from those of unredeemable sinners in the afterlife;
according to Judaic tradition, all souls are assigned to the same place, the
sheol, until the day of judgment.[1] Paul's fire, as described in the first letter
to the Corinthians, adds the potential for the dimension of purification
and of separation of worthy from unworthy to the biblical portrayal of
the afterlife, although its purpose is more to test than to purge. But this
distinction was not clear in the Middle Ages, as Le Goff points out:
"Modern Catholic theology distinguishes between the fire of Hell, which
is punitive, the fire of Purgatory, which is expiatory and purifying, and
the fire of judgment, which is probative. But this is a late rationalization.
In the Middle Ages, all three were more or less confounded."[2] Furthermore, if one believes in venial sin and in the possibility of its remission
after death, this fire, through the symbolic opposition of combustible
hay, straw, and wood to the more durable gold, silver, and precious
stones, seems to express, as it did to Augustine, the idea of purging all
that is worthless away from the soul.[3] This view is supported by the
"baptism of fire" predicted by John the Baptist in Luke 3:16 and interpreted by Origen.[4] An echo of this baptism by fire is to be found in
Origen's commentary on the thirty-sixth psalm, in which he mentions
Paul's first epistle to the Corinthians. Origen also elaborated upon the
nature of those destined for purgatory, whose sins were an unavoidable
part of human nature, as opposed to those "who bear the extra burden
of sins that in theory are mortal."[5] Le Goff reiterates the importance of
Augustine for the development of the dogma of purgatory: his prayers
for Monica reinforced the effect of 2 Macc. 12; and his discussion of
purgatory in book 21 of the *City of God* adds significant vocabulary to the
lexicon of the life hereafter, in particular the adjectives *purgatorius*,
temporarius, and *transitorius*.[6]

Robert Ombres, who studied law before specializing in philosophy
and theology, presents purgatory as "a test case for revealing much

---

[1]See Le Goff, *Purgatory*, p. 42: "medieval Christians looked upon the text as confirming two things: that sins can be redeemed after death and that the prayers of the living are
an effective way of accomplishing this."

[2]Le Goff, *Purgatory*, pp. 43–44. The twenty-first book of *De civitate Dei* is a good
example of this confusion.

[3]Augustine, *De civitate Dei* 21.26.

[4]Le Goff, *Purgatory*, pp. 53–54.

[5]Le Goff, *Purgatory*, p. 55.

[6]Le Goff, *Purgatory*, pp. 63–68. For a detailed study of Augustine's influence on the
doctrine of purgatory, see Joseph Ntedika, *Evolution de la doctrine du Purgatoire chez Saint
Augustin* (Paris, 1966).

larger concatenations of beliefs, practices, ideologies," which include "the relationship of Scripture to Tradition, the nature of the Church, sin and forgiveness, prayer."[1] He notes that the existence of "an intermediate state of cleansing" is clearly indicated in the influential report *The Martyrdom of Perpetua and Felicitas.* Perpetua has two visions of her brother Dinocrates. The first is apparently a solicitation of her aid: she sees her brother "coming out of a dark hole, very hot, thirsty, pale and dirty." After she has prayed fervently for his soul, she sees him "clean and refreshed."[2] Already in this account, purgatory has certain concrete aspects: the punishment includes darkness, heat, and thirst. The location of purgatory was also defined slowly, over the years, in the accounts of various church fathers and medieval monks. There is already something spatial in Origen's "Paradise,"[3] a training place for souls on their way home to their creator, with a river of fire fueled by the wood and hay and stubble of 1 Cor. 3. This vision of a physically real purgatory is rounded out by other, more threatening visions such as that of the monk Wetti and of Charles the Fat, descriptions that pave the way for the very concrete and appropriate torments of Dante's *Purgatorio.*[4] In the valley described by Bede,[5] the western topography of purgatory has become fairly concrete. Peter Comestor makes no major breakthrough by using the noun *purgatorium* (if he was indeed the first to do so).[6]

Still, the twelfth century did see significant progress in the establishment of a geography of purgatory, as Le Goff makes clear in his chapter on the "Locus Purgatorius."[7] St. Bernard of Clairvaux and the Cistercians were responsible for preaching the reality of purgatory and

---

[1] Robert Ombres, O.P., *The Theology of Purgatory,* Theology Today, no. 24 (Butler, Wis., 1978), p. 11.

[2] This account dates from about A.D. 203; Ombres, *Theology,* p. 27. Cf. Psalm 65, and see Le Goff, *Purgatory,* pp. 181–86, for a later but similar vision invoking aid from the living.

[3] For Origen's view of the hereafter, see Le Goff, *Purgatory,* pp. 52–57.

[4] Le Goff, *Purgatory,* pp. 116–22; Dante apparently did read the text of the vision of Charles the Fat.

[5] See below, p. cxv.

[6] In a sermon *In dedicatione Ecclesiae,* attributed in the nineteenth century to Hildebert of Lavardin (*PL 171,* 741): "Nos vero secundum minorem . . . partem loquimur, qui cum ligno, feno et stipula transeunt, et in purgatorio poliuntur." According to Michel (col. 1248), the noun was also used in a letter by Innocent IV in 1254. Le Goff, *Purgatory,* pp. 154–68, 362–66, gives considerable evidence that the noun *purgatorium* was first used in the decade 1170–1180.

[7] Le Goff, *Purgatory,* pp. 154–76.

for further popularizing devotional practices related to alleviating the torments of the dead. The school of Notre Dame, following the lead of Hugh of St. Victor and Peter Lombard, refined the concepts and the lexicon of purgatory.[1] But, to a large extent, it was the defense of the notion of purgatory against attacks by Waldensian and Cathar heretics that encouraged clearer definition of the nature of the place; "penitential bookkeeping," the effort to fit the punishment to the crime in specific temporal terms, was extended to the life hereafter. Still, canon law and most of the leading church authorities refused to locate purgatory and emphasized instead the efficacy of prayers for the dead, even though Innocent III discussed the "middle place" in a sermon.[2] St. Thomas Aquinas and St. Catherine of Genoa (d. 1510) set new milestones in the process of distancing purgatory from hell, and of identifying its flames with "the glowing love of God."[3] The Greeks expressed difficulties "over the application of fire to disembodied souls"[4] and tended to pray for all the dead, including the saints.

Vatican II linked purgatory not with justification but with the church: "all christians are united by the ecclesial bonds of charity. . . . The union of the wayfarers with those who sleep in the peace of Christ . . . is reinforced by an exchange of spiritual goods."[5] Ombres finds this spirit already in Dante's *Purgatorio*. The reciprocity whereby the souls help us is the clear conviction of Thomas More, and a common one in his time.[6] Deprecating all division between clergy and laity, More says we pray "for those that of both partes are passed into purgatorye, and there pray for vs as we pray here for them."[7]

Drawing on the Greek Orthodox tradition, which views "sin as dislocation, discord, unreality, ailment," Ombres describes the cleansing and paying processes with a gamut of metaphors: maturing, rectification, fulfillment, reordering, removal of a blockage, "birth pangs rather than death throes."[8] Peter Comestor's "poliuntur" itself can be

---

[1]Le Goff, *Purgatory*, pp. 167–68.

[2]Le Goff, *Purgatory*, pp. 168–76.

[3]Ombres, *Theology*, p. 43. See pp. 41–44 for discussion of St. Thomas and St. Catherine. See also Ombres's article, "The Doctrine of Purgatory according to St. Thomas Aquinas," *The Downside Review*, 99 (1981), 279–87.

[4]Ombres, *Theology*, p. 45.

[5]Ombres, *Theology*, p. 49.

[6]For More, "the thre estates of holy chyrche, that is to wytte the spyrytualty, the temporalty and the sowles that be in purgatory," are "viagers and pylgrymmes in the same pylgrymage . . . towarde the same place of rest" (*CW 8*, 578).

[7]*EW*, sig. U₁v.

[8]Ombres, *Theology*, pp. 75, 83.

read as an aesthetic term, related to the vocabulary of masonry and construction.[1] When the adjective *purgatorius* was used, the noun it qualified was usually *ignis*—either a real fire or an image of fire. Erasmus firmly upholds the view that this fire is metaphorical, and wishes to wean his readers away from the physical interpretation.[2] More's souls know they speak in parables. They will not apologize for clothing their appeal in bodily "symylytudes"; there is no other way to make "mortall man" perceive "in what manner wyse we bodylesse soulys do suffer" (226/3–4). Yet they do not want their pain to be considered less real for being different. For a popular audience, More fears that too much refining may take away the sense of reality. He sees that the sacramentarians, through a spiritual interpretation of "This is my body," have emptied the eucharist of its substance. So, he takes the gospel's unquenchable fire literally. If material fire, he writes, is empowered by the creator to torture those pure spirits, the devils, why should it be incapable of affecting disembodied souls?[3] The *Debellation* closes with an evocation of "the very fyre of purgatorye," which "verylye burneth soules." In his last polemical work, confuting the "poisoned book" that tried to explain away the reality of Christ's presence in the sacrament, More again refuses to accept that this fire may be only a metaphorical image.[4] More has chosen this "materialism" as the safer bet, partly because he found it already prevalent in his culture and partly in order to counter the allegorizing trend from Basel and Zürich that had already reached England and pushed Tyndale and Frith beyond the teachings of their first master, Luther. In large part, More chose to emphasize purgatory as a place to counter the strong denial of its existence by Luther and his followers, but he also recognized its significance as a state of being or of mind.

Conciliar Definitions

T HAT oriental Christians refused the image of purgatory as a fiery prison was held against them by such polemicists as Fisher and Cochlaeus; next to their schism, this was considered their worst fault, one reason that God scourged them through the Turks. Nevertheless, on the essential point—praying for the dead—the Greek church was at

---

[1]Le Goff, *Purgatory*, p. 155.
[2]Not without alarming Nicholas Beda of the Sorbonne; see Allen, *6*, 105, line 768; *Enchiridion*, canon 20 (*Opera omnia*, *5*, 56); cf. *Novum Testamentum*, Erasmus' commentary on Paul's first epistle to the Corinthians (*Opera omnia*, *6*, 671C–F).
[3]See *Confutation*, *CW 8*, 102–3, in the context of an argument about baptism.
[4]*CW*, *10*, 231/12–13 and *CW 11*, 187/3–23.

one with her Latin sister. In addition to a special commemoration in each liturgy, the Orthodox church still celebrates two "Saturdays of the Souls"—one at the inception of Lent (*Apocreos*), another on the eve of Pentecost—which, as it were, balance the feast of All Souls. Eastern reluctance to follow the West in drawing from those prayers the corollary of a purging place—or at least stage—was an obstacle on the path to full unity; thus it was also the occasion for an official stocktaking of the *status quaestionis* and for an examination of the issue at the highest level, in order to prepare a binding formulation.

The first dogmatic definition stemmed from the Second Ecumenical Council of Lyons, held in 1274,[1] the oriental church being represented by a delegation that included the emperor, Michael Palaeologus. The text agreed upon by the Greek and Latin fathers served as a basis for the discussions at Florence 164 years later and was reproduced almost verbatim by that council. More need not have consulted the proceedings of Lyons, since the last word was the Florentine decree. The Council of Union is richly documented, and the Latin definition of purgatory here reproduced comes from a critical edition with facing Greek text:

> Item, si vere penitentes in dei caritate decesserint, antequam dignis penitentie fructibus de commissis satisfecerint et omissis, eorum animas penis purgatoriis post mortem purgari, et, ut a poenis huiusmodi releventur, prodesse eis fidelium vivorum suffragia, missarum scilicet sacrificia, orationes et elemosynas et alia pietatis officia, que a fidelibus pro aliis fidelibus fieri consueverunt, secundum ecclesie instituta.
>
> Illorumque animas, qui post baptisma susceptum nullam omnino peccati maculam incurrerunt; illas etiam, que post contractam peccati maculam, vel in suis corporibus, vel eisdem exute corporibus, prout superius dictum est, sunt purgate, in celum mox recipi, et intueri clare ipsum deum trinum et unum, sicuti est, pro meritorum tamen diversitate alium alio perfectius: illorum autem animas, qui in actuali mortali peccato vel solo originali decedunt, mox in infernum descendere, penis tamen disparibus puniendas.[2]

---

[1]See *DTC* 9, 1385. For a general discussion of the Greek/Latin controversies see Robert Ombres, "Latins and Greeks in Debate over Purgatory, 1230–1439," *Journal of Ecclesiastical History,* 35 (1984), 1–14.

[2]Joseph Gill, S. J., ed., *Quae supersunt actorum graecorum concilii Florentini necnon descriptionis ejus. Concilium Florentinum,* ser. B, V (Rome, 1953), pp. 463–64; cited hereafter as *AG.* Given the circumstances and the concessions made to the Oriental partners, one may

The following translation keeps to the Latin as closely as English syntax allows; it also pays attention to the Greek, especially for definite articles.

> If people have died truly penitent in the love of God before having satisfied through worthy fruits of penance for what they have done or failed to do, their souls are purged after death by purgatorial pains. Toward relieving them of these pains, the petitions of the living faithful are useful to them, namely the sacrifice of the mass and prayer and alms and the other works of piety, which are done customarily by the faithful for each other according to the traditions of the Church.
>
> The souls of those who, after being baptized, have incurred no stain of sin at all, and also of those who, after contracting the stain of sin, have been purified, either in their bodies or after putting off their bodies (as was stated above), are received straightway into heaven and have the pure vision[1] of God himself, one in three persons, as he is, although they see him more or less perfectly, according to the worth of their merits. As for the souls of those who die in mortal sin, or indeed in original sin alone, they descend straightway into hell, to be punished, however, by unequal pains.

Such then was the profession of faith by the emperor and the Greek experts and hierarchy on July 6, 1439. A summary of the six weeks of discussion throws light on the development of the doctrine in the West. The spokesmen of Greek Orthodoxy and of Roman Catholicism met at Ferrara, where the council began, until the plague drove them to Florence. Purgatory, one of the four points on which the two traditions diverged, headed the agenda. Cardinal Guiliano Cesarini opened the debate on June 4, 1438, by handing the Greeks a statement of the Latin tradition. It based belief in purgatory on three of the biblical texts

---

well consider the Greek text the more authoritative. It probably was not available to More. See also Joseph Gill, *Constance et Bâle-Florence, Histoire des conciles oecuméniques*, no. 9 (Paris, 1965). Father Gill's lifelong labors, including biographical sketches of the protagonists, have not rendered useless some earlier studies. See Adhémar d'Alès, "La question du purgatoire au concile de Florence en 1438," *Gregorianum, 3* (1922), 9–50 (cited hereafter as "d'Alès"); based on the best material available, this article evinces a firm grasp of the text's antecedents and its context. See also Georg Hofmann, "Concilium Florentinum: I. Erstes Gutachten der Lateiner über das Fegfeuer," *Orientalia Christiana, 16*, 3, no. 57 (December 1929), 259–302.

[1] I say "the pure," not "the clear" (vision of God), because καθαρός has the same root as καθαρθείσας in the same sentence.

More was to use (2 Macc. 12:46, Matt. 12:32, and 1 Cor. 3:13–15), on sentences drawn from a number of church fathers, both Greek and Latin, and on theological reasoning that infers purgatory from the demands of God's justice as expressed in Deut. 25:2, Ezek. 33:14–15, and Sap. 7:25.[1] The answers, drafted separately by Markos Eugenikos, metropolitan of Ephesus—whose mind was set against purgatory—and by Bessarion, metropolitan of Nicaea and future cardinal, confirmed that Eastern and Western churches had, from time immemorial, agreed on a posthumous remission of sin, and hence shared the practice of praying for the dead, especially during the eucharist. They only disagreed on how this remission was effected: the Greek tradition included no purgatorial fire.[2]

The key text in this respect was 1 Cor. 3:15: "he will be saved . . . as through fire."[3] The Greeks resorted to St. John Chrysostom, as the surest interpreter of St. Paul's mind, to explain away not the fire but the salvation it achieved: σωθήσεται does not apply to the soul, but to the whole person of the bad workman, who will be preserved body and soul for punishment in everlasting fire, while his works are burnt. What of St. Gregory of Nyssa? the Latins replied. Does he not express unqualified belief in a temporary purgation by fire? The Greeks said he was conditioned by Origen's denial of eternal damnation. As for Gregory the Great's anecdotes of souls appearing to seek release from their fiery prison, the Greeks saw them as allegories. Nor were they convinced by the theological inference of an intermediary place or state premised on the justice of God. Moreover, they said, the prospect of atoning for sin after death can only weaken the determination of the faithful to do penance in this life.

The Dominican Johannes de Turrecremata (Torquemada) retorted that, far from slackening the fervor of the living, belief in remission in an afterlife encourages them to pray, give alms, and perform good deeds both for themselves and for the departed souls. He asked the Greeks: "Where do you locate the souls for whom you pray?" He invoked inspired texts (Ps. 33:22, Deut. 25:2, 2 Kings 12:13)[4] in favor of distinguishing between *culpa* (guilt) and *poena* (pain), between the sin which God's mercy has indeed fully pardoned and its sequels of debt to pay, or blot to purge, or scar to heal. Given the various senses of

---

[1]See d'Alès, pp. 11–13.

[2]*AG*, 25–26; d'Alès, pp. 13–21.

[3]σωθήσεται. . . ὡςδιὰ πυρός. Every one of the words was bandied about and carefully weighed.

[4]D'Alès, p. 26. None of these is exploited in More's *Supplication*.

scripture, he argued, Chrysostom's exegesis of 1 Cor. 3:13–15 need
not exclude that of doctors such as Augustine and Gregory, whose
authority and orthodoxy the oriental church has fully accepted. Besides, Paul speaks to the Corinthians of the Last Judgment, but it is
immediately after their death that all men are judged by God, whether
they are good (John 14:3) or bad (Rev. 2:5). It is at that private judgment that such as are neither wicked nor perfect will be *saved*—the
normal meaning of σωτηρία[1] in scriptural Greek—while the preposi-
tion διά clearly shows that they pass *through* fire and are not consigned
to it forever.

Markos, reluctant to yield, did less than justice to his own tradition
by resorting to a variant of the souls' sleep theory: all the souls, he said,
wait for the resurrection of all the bodies; pending God's final sentence, they receive some remuneration in provisional abodes, like the
paradise Jesus promised to the repentant thief—an antechamber of
heaven—or the deep dark dungeon described in Ps. 87:6 and Job
10:22—an antechamber of hell. Meanwhile, these souls can be delivered from what St. Peter calls a captivity (2 Pet. 2:4); that is why the
church prays indiscriminately for "all who have gone to sleep in the
faith," to relieve their pain or increase their joy as the case may be. As
for the "refreshing" that St. Basil spoke of, it does not allude to fire any
more than David does in Ps. 28:7: fire is an allegory, like the gnawing
worm, which represents the remorse of conscience. Markos clung to
Chrysostom's interpretation of 1 Cor. 3:13–15: the bad workmen are
the unfaithful teachers who, on the foundation of Christ, build worthless material fit only to be consumed by fire. He acknowledged that
imperfect souls have a debt of pain to pay in proportion to the guilt of
each one.[2]

At the concluding session on July 6 the union of East and West was
proclaimed in the bull *Laetentur coeli*.[3] Their shared eschatology was
couched in the text quoted above. The Latins gave up the fire which
they had discovered to be no essential part of their faith. The Greeks
bowed to the evidence that their church had always implicitly believed
in two truths more explicitly formulated by the West: (1) the departed
souls who need expiation accomplish it in a condition intermediary

---

[1]Torquemada's references are Acts 16:30–31 and 1 Cor. 1:18, 5:5, 9:22. See d'Alès,
pp. 29–30.
[2]D'Alès, pp. 32–35.
[3]The patriarch died at Florence on June 10, having acknowledged the primacy of the
pope. Eugenius IV was, of course, head of the whole council and promulgator of the bull.
See Gill, *Constance et Bâle-Florence*, pp. 251–52, 257–59.

between heaven and hell; (2) reward and punishment and purgation begin immediately after death. They obtained, at the final session, a clause stating the varying degrees of reward and punishment.[1] The Decree of Union was the only infallible pronouncement of a council that was undoubtedly ecumenical, although England, among other nations, was not represented, and although Constantinople yielded to considerable pressure so as not to jeopardize the Western aid it needed against the advancing Turks.[2] Finally, in 1563, the Council of Trent reaffirmed the dogma without any significant change; it took account of the reformers' criticism by warning preachers against unsound accretions to the dogma, unedifying subtleties, and any trace of simony in the matter of indulgences.[3]

JEAN GERSON ON PURGATORY

JEAN GERSON, "the Chancellor of Paris," as he was often called, was one of the "discreet" masters concerned with the discernment of spirits. His book on the subject, prompted by the *Revelations* of St. Bridget and recommended by Antony in More's *Dialogue of Comfort*, is but one of several books by "that good godly Doctour" that we know More studied.[4] The same Antony ascribes to "master Gerson" the commonplace wisdom of bearing one's purgatory on earth, but he is probably echoing *The Imitation of Christ*, which More, like most of his contemporaries, attributed to Gerson.[5]

Gerson's years (d. 1429) roughly span the interval between St. Bridget's *Revelations*,[6] which he perused with the critical eye of a sober moralist, and the Council of Florence. His teaching was accepted throughout Europe; some of his writings were printed before 1470, and his collected *Opera* were published at Cologne as early as 1483.[7]

---

[1]See Gill, *Constance et Bâle-Florence*, p. 257.

[2]For a summary of the contents of the bull, see Gill, *Constance et Bâle-Florence*, p. 260. It should be mentioned that all but eight of the Greek delegates, on failing to secure approval at home, withdrew their signatures.

[3]Concilium Tridentinum, 1545–63, Sessio XXV (December 3–4, 1563), "Decretum de purgatorio," in Giuseppe Alberigo et al., eds., *Conciliorum oecumenicorum decreta*, 2nd ed. (Basel, 1962), p. 750; cited hereafter as "Alberigo."

[4]See *CW 12*, 133/7–8, and Indices to *CW 9*, *CW 13*, *CW 14*.

[5]See text and Commentary of *CW 12*, 153/28–30 and *CW 8*, 37/30.

[6]See note on 209/24, below.

[7]The Cologne *Opera* of 1483–84, printed by Johann Koelhoff, was followed by others in 1488 (Strassburg: Johann Grüninger[?]) and 1489 (Basel: Nicolaus Kesler; Nürnberg: Georg Stuchs). The edition nearest to More's polemical years was that prepared by Jacob Wimpheling (Paris: P. Gromorsus for J. Petit and Fr. Regnault, 1521). Because of its accessibility, *Opera omnia novo ordine digesta*, ed. M. L. Ellies Du Pin, 5 vols. (Antwerp, 1706), has been used here.

Five of his works are important to the doctrine of purgatory: a "Complaint," dated October 1427, which is rather like Book 2 of More's *Supplication* in style as well as in content; three All Souls sermons; and a treatise of consolation for the death of friends.[1] The sermons, though preached in French, have come down to us in Latin.

Querela defunctorum in igne purgatorio detentorum ad superstites in terra amicos would be a fitting title for a Latin version of More's own plea "from the prisoners to the earthly survivors." Each paragraph of Gerson's appeal begins with "Orate pro nobis" and adds some new reason why the faithful on earth should pray for the souls in purgatory:

> We are in the harsh prison of purgatorial fire and we cannot help ourselves. Help us that we be delivered from the torments we suffer by the just sentence of the Supreme Judge. You who are sons and daughters of the church living on earth are in a position to assist both us and likewise yourselves if you wish.[2] Pray for us, looking at us devoutly in the light of the true faith, for pity's sake and compassion. Pray for us, your spiritual profit will be greater than if each prayed for his own self: charity wishes for communication and sharing. When we have gone up to paradise with God and the saintly souls, we shall reciprocate in kind, by interceding for those who have helped us with prayers and good works: he who has been merciful will receive mercy. Pray for us, you at least who have known us on earth, who have loved us: let each one in this extreme need prove himself a friend indeed, according to the proverb. Do not turn a deaf ear to our petition: "the hard heart," says scripture, "will come to a sorry end."[3] Pray for us, you at least who live off the goods we have left you, whether by way of alms or some ecclesiastical foundation, or by testament or other donations prompted by love, so that you should pray for us. Do your duty: if you fail, the torments of a just and most cruel condemnation are in store for you; it is a debt which you are under obligation to pay, as heirs to our goods or executors of our last will. The debts which we failed to pay, leaving it for you to pay them on our behalf, are your strict responsibility—would God we had cleared them in our

---

[1] All five works are in *Opera omnia, 3: Querela defunctorum in igne purgatorio detentorum ad superstites in terra amicos*, sigs. Xx₄v–Yy₁ (cols. 703–5); *Sermones III de defunctis:* "Sermo I ad populum Parisiensem, in ecclesia Sancti Severini," sigs. Eeeee₄–Fffff₂ (cols. 1551–58); "Sermo II de die mortuorum," sigs. Fffff₂–₄v (cols. 1558–67); "Sermo III de mortuis vtilissimus ad cogitandum de fine," sigs. Fffff₄–Ggggg₂ (cols. 1567–73); *Tractatus de consolatione in mortem amicorum*, sigs. Y₃–Z₁ (cols. 345–53).

[2] "Vos estis in statu nobis auxiliandi, similiter, si volueritis, & vobis."

[3] See Ecclus. 3:27: "Cor durum habebit male in novissimo."

lifetime. Pray for us, especially you who are our kin. Have the
compassion which children should have toward parents, brothers
and sisters toward each other, or cousins, or husbands and wives,
or parents toward their children. Consider how we would support
each other when we were on earth: if a mother saw her daughter
or a father his son burning in the fire and were unable to deliver
them, how diligently and promptly they would do all in their
power! Pray for us by virtue of that charity which bids man to love
his neighbor as himself. Let every one of you help us according to
his state and possiblities: either by praying, or fasting, or almsgiving, and most of all by offering the blessed sacrament of the altar,
in which he is present who has discharged all our debts; "who
takes away the sins of the world;"[1] "who," according to the apostle, "was made for us wisdom, justice, sanctification and redemption."[2] This offering is made daily at mass; each Christian can and
should make it in the temple of his heart, remembering the passion of our savior Jesus Christ, and begging him to extend to us
the virtue of his passion, so that we may be worthy to reach the
glory of his paradise with all the saints, there to praise him without
end. If you pray, or procure prayer, for us, we shall pray for you
in that glory which we expect with full assurance. First and foremost, pardon all offenses and evil turns done to you, seek no
revenge: nothing is so conducive to our deliverance as charity,
pity, and pardon. Beseech often and devoutly your good angels to
visit, greet, and console us on your behalf; obtain that they may
notify us, to our great joy and comfort, that you pray to God and
his saints for us; that you make alms, oblations, restitutions, and
satisfactions for us; that you keep some fasts or abstinence and do
some penance for us; that for our sake you avoid sinning and
offending God, seek no revenge; that you teach and exhort each
other, especially innocent children, to say the Lord's Prayer and
the Angel's Salutation [Ave, Maria] and other good words for us;
that you procure masses and other suffrages of the church for us;
in brief, that you labor diligently for us, that we may be comforted
and purged and set free from all the pains and bitter torments of
this prison, and the sooner come to the glory of paradise, which
we so love and not without cause do desire. God be of aid to you in
all your deeds and needs, and grant you the grace to live on earth

[1]See John 1:29: "qui tollit peccatum mundi."
[2]See 1 Cor. 1:30: "qui factus est nobis sapientia a Deo, et iustitia, et sanctificatio, &
redemptio."

in such a way that we may see you in everlasting glory, where God
reigns, one in three, Father, Son, and Holy Spirit, Amen.[1]

There follows a response from the living to the dead—"vivi ad
mortuos"—beginning with an Our Father, a pledge to say a number of
prayers "in persona Ecclesiae," to say them by request, as commissioned by the souls themselves, so that their angel may let them know of
it; "to pray specially through the virtue of the holy mystery of thy
blessed incarnation and passion, our redeemer and savior of the whole
world."[2] Liturgical prayers are listed, including Psalm 85, "Inclina,
Domine, aurem tuam," and Psalm 129, "De profundis."

The first of the *Sermones de defunctis*,[3] preached in the Church of St.
Severin, Paris, draws its theme from 2 Macc. 12:46: "It is a holy and
wholesome thought to pray for the dead." Gerson asks that his listeners
first consider the place where the dead are—a fiery prison—and then
compare it with earth, from which they came, and with heaven, where
they will pray for the living. Prayer, he says, has two wings: hope and
fear.[4] The second part of the sermon points out that one should pray
not for those in heaven or in hell, but for those "in medio statu:"
purgatory is the place where our prayer is needed.[5] The manifold
excellences of that prayer are then enumerated: it is infallibly efficacious; it requires a greater act of faith; it increases solidarity by binding
the souls to pray for the living; it brooks no delay, especially if the living
are the executors; it earns for the living the prayers of others after their
deaths; it evinces greater charity since the prayers are offered for souls
other than those of relatives; it discharges various debts toward the
dead; it gladdens the souls' guardian angels; it prompts the avoidance
of sin and the doing of penance, and thus the eschewing of purgatory;
when done publicly, it helps others to believe in the life to come; it is a
marvelous investment, for God's mercy repays with interest; it fosters a
wholesome contempt for this transitory world and a holy ambition to

---

[1] *Querela*, sigs. Xx₄–Yy₁. My translation somewhat condenses the original Latin.

[2] *Querela*, sig. Yy₁.

[3] It is unnecessary to summarize the three sermons and the tract on the same generous
scale as the *Querela*, but I have singled out such threads as are strikingly similar or
dissimilar to those used by More without trying to ascertain either a debt or a conscious
distancing on More's part.

[4] "Sermo I," sig. Eeeee₄v. More adopted another metaphor from Pico: "With these
twayn, as with two spurres, that one of feare, that other of loue: spurre forth thine hors
thorow the short waie of this momentary life, to the reward of eternall felicitie." See *EW*,
sig. a₇. Cf. Fisher, *English Works*, 114/6–7: "saynt Gregory compareth hope & drede vnto
two myll stones wherwith mele is made."

[5] "Sermo I," sig. Fffff₁.

be happy in the next.[1] The third part, which answers miscellaneous questions, explains that God's largesse is boundless, so that praying for many has no less efficacy than praying for oneself or some definite person: one candle can light several persons; further, the purchasing power of a given prayer may be determined by the pope or holy church; the value of each mass is infinite, yet God apportions it as he will.[2] The final prayer begs "the sweetest Jesus" to have mercy on the dead and to grant that those who live in the world may attain the glory of paradise.[3]

The second sermon, preached on All Souls' Day, begins with texts that More's Antony exploits in *A Dialogue of Comfort:* "Blessid be they that wepe & wayle" (Matt. 5:5), and "by many tribulacions must we go into the kyngdome of god" (Acts 14:21).[4] Gerson speaks of the first excellent fruit of grief and sorrow, the liberation of "friends from their harsh prison," foremost among them dead relatives.[5] God's justice, as all peoples—including Saracens, Jews, and pagans—believe, rewards and punishes everyone according to his deeds: the good with heaven, the bad with hell (after some reward here below), while "the intermediary are placed, as it were, in a prison which we call purgatory, because the souls there are purged and purified."[6] "Such is the mercy of our supreme judge," he points out, "that one person can pay another's debt."[7] Gerson develops a dead mother's appeal to her child for relief: "Can you refuse a drop of water to your afflicted mother? one tear that can achieve so much in assuaging her pain?"[8] He then raises a number of questions basic to the doctrine of purgatory and answers them as follows. Purgatory is situated near the limbo of the fathers; its pains are worse than any earthly pain; they are proportionate to the punishment each soul has deserved and to the amount of praying done for each. The souls in purgatory know of our prayers through their guardian angels, who go down fairly often ("saepius") to comfort them. The

---

[1]"Sermo I," sig. Fffff$_1$–Fffff$_1$v.

[2]"Sermo I," sig. Fffff$_1$v.

[3]"Sermo I," sig. Fffff$_2$.

[4]*CW 12*, 70/24–25 and 43/1–2.

[5]"Sermo II," sig. Fffff$_2$v; "parentes nostri" is an obvious gallicism: the context shows that not parents alone, but all kinsmen are involved.

[6]"Propterea hi ponuntur veluti in carcerem, quem nos Purgatorium appellamus, quoniam ibi animae purgantur & purificantur" (sig. Fffff$_2$v). Gerson's diction emphasizes cleansing versus punishment.

[7]"Sermo II," sig. Fffff$_2$v.

[8]"Sermo II," sig. Fffff$_3$.

suffrages of holy church profit more those who have deserved more, and have efficacy even if the minister is in mortal sin. Whether or not it may harm the testator, the executors' negligence is great guilt. Can indulgences be acquired for the dead? Gerson thinks not. The means to help a soul are listed again in the traditional order: the eucharist, which cannot fail; almsgiving, which binds the receiver to pray and requires taking some pains for the love of God; praying; fasting. The souls do feel that they are being relieved, even as those on earth do when mysteriously freed from temptation or despondency. Such souls do appear to the living on occasion.[1] Having dealt with the questions, Gerson reminds his listeners that if Dives even in hell thought of his surviving brothers, how much more would those in purgatory care for the spiritual well-being of living friends. Listen to them, he says, as they urge those on earth to choose the rod instead of death and to say with Augustine, "hic ure, hic seca."[2] Let man appeal from God's court of justice to his court of mercy, in which Our Lady is mistress. After this mention of the Virgin's role as minister of grace, Gerson returns to the broader theme of sorrowing, with sentences also used by More in the *Dialogue of Comfort*,[3] and then ends with a short prayer.

In Gerson's *Sermo tertius de mortuis*, the clamor rising from purgatory is not "Save our souls," but "Remember your end": "memento finis,"[4] a shorter and less biblical equivalent to "memorare novissima" (Ecclus. 7:40), the theme of More's treatise on *The Four Last Things*.[5] Deep and sustained consideration of death and eternity, Gerson preaches, inculcates in man the truth of the paradox that an ordered life—virtuous, reasonable, and godly—is the most pleasurable even in worldly terms. Not everyone attains to it here below; hence the rescue provided by purgatory. But why should man bargain for the second best? Instead, he should complete his purgation now by drastic penance[6] and by

---

[1]"Sermo II," sigs. Fffff$_{3-4}$.

[2]"Sermo II," sig. Fffff$_4$. John Fisher quotes this brief prayer and also ascribes it to Augustine (*English Works*, 41/13); More does not. God is seen as a surgeon who applies the hot iron or the lancet "here," whether "on this sore spot" or rather "here on earth," so we "bear our purgatory here" (*CW 13*, 226/26).

[3]"Sermo II," sig. Fffff$_4$–Fffff$_4$v: "Doleat poenitens, & de dolore gaudeat," ascribed by Gerson to Augustine; and Job 21:13. Cf. *CW 12*, 42/26–28, 168/5–6. "Ad infernum," though understood by Gerson as "to hell," is sometimes regarded more generally by More as "to the grave."

[4]"Sermo III," sig. Fffff$_4$v. The refrain is repeated at least fifty times like the tolling of a knell.

[5]*EW*, sigs. e$_4$v–fg$_8$.

[6]Gerson repeats "Hic vre: hic seca" at sig. Ggggg$_1$v.

making a virtue of necessity, that is, by graciously accepting such adversity as man has to bear. The self-indulgent waste on food, drink, and clothing the money that could ransom souls in purgatory and relieve the poor. They are the worst enemies not only of the suffering church but of the church *tout court,* for the accumulation of individual faults is responsible for the monstrous schism that devastates Christendom. That a general council may heal that gaping wound, Gerson urges prayer to him who is alpha and omega, beginning and end.[1]

The fifth item in this eschatological sequence, *Tractatus de consolatione in morte amicorum,* belongs to a genre that both pagan and Christian authors have practiced. Gerson quotes Seneca in the first of his nine considerations, which has to do with the will of God.[2] The Stoic's wisdom is not far from that of Job (Job 1:21). Death is unavoidable. Life on earth is held on lease, not as a freehold. Man is an exile and wayfarer. A spirit of confidence in God's fatherly care rids man of sterile sadness, fills him with a sober joy which marks the very act of dying. Gerson's only *exemplum* is of a mother to whom her son appears saying: "I am at last in paradise, but your tears, by drenching my tunic, have delayed my arrival here."[3] Christian man must not weep as do the pagans, who have no hope. True, even Augustine wept after burying Monica, but Christian tears are mingled with prayers and with the certainty that the living and the dead shall meet again and be merry together. Meanwhile the living seek the peaceful joy of a pure conscience and train themselves to say, as Christ did thrice during his agony in the garden, "Fiat voluntas tua."[4]

Thus Gerson is the discreet spiritual guide, the circumspect educator; he knows all the sheep of his flock and is readier to nurse than to curse. He belongs with Gerhard de Groote and John Colet and Lefèvre d'Etaples rather than with Ruysbroeck and St. Bridget and Richard Rolle. His ascetic moralizing is never divorced from a vision of faith, but there is little glow of mysticism: no nuptial imagery, no love affair with the person of Christ. Our Lady is the advocate at her son's tribunal but is not seen, as in More, paying frequent visits to her children in purgatory. Surprisingly, he makes no use of the poignant "Miseremini, miseremini mei, saltem vos amici mei" (Job 19:21), which is part of the

---

[1] "Sermo III,", sig. Gggggg₂. "Principium et finis" echoes the theme "memento finis."
[2] *Tractatus,* sig. Y₃. *Epistulae ad Lucilium* 74. 20: "Placeat homini, quicquid deo placuit." Seneca is quoted again as a preacher of detachment along with Tobit at *Tractatus,* sig. Y₄.
[3] *Tractatus,* sig. Y₄v.
[4] *Tractatus,* sig. Z₁.

dirge and has provided the text for many an All Souls sermon both
before and after his time: is it because of this very banality that both he
and More have left it out of their respective supplications *in persona
defunctorum?* The main difference between the two writers is that Gerson takes purgatory for granted and is content to exhort, while More is
called upon to prove that it is not "labour loste to pray for all crysten
sowlys" (114/22–23); he makes his readers understand the scandal and
shock felt by the souls "that eny man shulde nede nowe to proue
purgatory to crysten men" (170/13–14).

JOHN FISHER ON PURGATORY

"MASTER MORE . . . hath in a maner nothynge but that he toke out of
my lorde of Rochester / althoughe he handle it more suttellye," writes
John Frith in his *Disputation of Purgatory*.[1] To Fisher, he continues,
More owes "the chefest of his scryptures,"[2] and yet, because the two
men use different Old Testament verses, Frith opposes the *Supplication*
to Fisher's much broader *Assertionis Lutheranae confutatio*.[3] As early as
1519, More perused the writings of the bishop whom he considered
without a match "in wisdome, learning and long approued vertue
together."[4] He drew on the *Confutatio* within months of its appearance;
and it is the only work by a modern ally that is again quoted in his
Dialogue Concerning Heresies (1529).[5] Fisher's systematic treatment of all
the forty-one articles "asserted" by Luther, after they had been singled
out by the Roman censors to accompany the papal bull asking Luther

---

[1]John Frith, *A disputation of Purgatorye* (London, 1533; *STC* 11387), sig. F₇; cited
hereafter as "*A Disputation*."

[2]*A Disputation*, sig. K₃.

[3]Fisher's *Assertionis Lutheranae confutatio* (cited hereafter as "*Confutatio*") was first published at Antwerp in 1523. Frith points out disagreements between More and Fisher in *A
Disputation*, sigs. A₅v–A₆, G₄v–G₅, and L₂. In citing Fisher's *Confutatio* I will give the
signatures of the Antwerp edition of 1523 followed by those of the Würzburg *Opera
omnia* of 1597 within parentheses or square brackets. The Würzburg edition has been
reprinted (Farnborough, Hants., 1967).

[4]Thus he told his daughter Margaret when she visited him in the Tower (Rogers, p.
520, lines 243–44); see also pp. 136–37 (Ep. 74), More's letter congratulating Fisher on
the Erasmian elegance of his *De unica Magdalena*.

[5]See *Responsio ad Lutherum*, CW 5, 138/23. In 1529 Fisher's "erudyte boke" against
Luther was ascribed, in keeping with the *Dialogue*'s policy of anonymity, to "an honour-
able prelate of this realme" (*CW* 6, 430/3–4). In his *Confutation of Tyndale's Answer*,
although by now Fisher was *persona non grata* at court, More repeatedly mentioned "the
good bysshoppe" of Rochester (*CW* 8, 153/14, 325/15, 331/20, 368/10) and praised him
as "very cunnyng and yet more vertuouse" (153/14), in terms which contrast with Tyndale's plain "Rochester" (324/20).

to revoke them,[1] constitutes a kind of *summa*, the most reasoned and seasoned discussion of Luther's early theology ever to come from a Catholic pen. It was frequently reprinted,[2] and Fisher himself confidently referred his readers to it, as did More in his *Dialogue Concerning Heresies*. Professional divines and other learned men used it as a storehouse, and Cochlaeus translated large portions of it into German.[3] Prevented from representing England at the Fifth Lateran Council, the bishop was influentially present through the *Confutatio* at the much more epoch-making Council of Trent.

Frith, who could have found Fisher's teaching in his sermons,[4] chose the *Confutatio* as the fullest expression of his mind. The pages on purgatory there amount to quite a lengthy treatise, which begins in the "Prooemium" with a retrospective on Luther's earlier pronouncements. The subject reemerges in articles 4, 17, and 18, concerning indulgences; it is the sole theme of articles 37, 38, 39, and 40. More probably felt more at ease dealing with a body of work so rife with heresy under the guidance of a divine who had reconnoitered its every avenue and who had even read Luther's seminal commentary on the epistle to the Galatians (1519). In terms of Luther's early thought, Fisher played in England the role that Cochlaeus was to play on the Continent in tracing its developments.

Fisher begins his confutation by establishing ten preliminary truths. His "fourth truth" may have provided More with his quotations from Luther's fifteenth conclusion: "I am most certain that purgatory exists, nor am I much moved by the blabber of heretics. . . . Must we believe a

---

[1]Following Leo X's bull *Exsurge Domine* of June 1520, Luther published first *Adversus execrabilem Antichristi bvllam, Mar. Lvthervs* (Wittenberg, 1520), covering the first six articles cited in the bull, and then *Assertio omnium articulorum M. Lutheri, per Bullam Leonis. X. nouissimam damnatorum* (Wittenberg, 1521; cited hereafter as "*Assertio*"), which reiterated all forty-one articles.

[2]Fisher's *Confutatio* appeared simultaneously in Paris and in Antwerp (January 1523), and then in Cologne, Dresden, and Venice. It was printed at least fifteen times during the next forty years. See Edward Surtz, *The Works and Days of John Fisher* (Cambridge, Mass., 1967), p. 10.

[3]The Cochlaeus translation, in the two German versions (Strassburg, 1523 and 1524), calls the book "gross und nützlich"; his preface quotes Erasmus in praise of Fisher (Surtz, *Works and Days of Fisher*, p. 11). Polydore Virgil incorporated into his own *De rerum inventoribus* a section of the *Confutatio* dealing with the origin, growth, and abuse of indulgences. See *Polydori Vergilii Vrbinatis De rervm inuentoribus libri octo. . .* (Basel: Michael Isingrin, 1540), sig. F5.

[4]Frith was hardly born when they were preached or first published, but they were still being reprinted: the eighth recorded edition is dated August 13, 1529 (*STC* 10907).

heretic who is hardly fifty years old, and contend that the faith of so
many centuries has been false?"[1] Fisher immediately rebukes Luther
for inconsistency: Luther places purgatory outside the scope of scripture, grounding his belief in it on the testimony of tradition, and yet he
proceeds to cite biblical texts that seem to disprove it. Arius, Elvidius,
and other heretics make it clear that there is no end to a merely scriptural argumentation. The final arbiter of Christian doctrine is the
magisterium of the church, whose authority rests on six pillars:
the pledged assistance of God's spirit; the learning and holiness of the
early fathers; the unity of the mystical body in belief across the fron-
tiers and the centuries; the decrees of general councils; the "apostolic"
traditions, handed down orally from the apostles' time; the ways and
customs that embody the faith in forms of prayer and behavior.[2] Fisher
links Luther's growing disaffection toward purgatory with the money
which flows from Germany to Rome for the purchase of indulgences[3]—a diagnosis the bishop will return to repeatedly. The practice of
issuing pardons, Fisher adds, grew little by little out of the growing
awareness of a common repository of merit. The keys promised by
Christ to Peter (Matt. 16:19) empower his vicar to draw on this treas-
ury, and the oneness of the mystical body, extending beyond the grave,
makes the treasure available even to the souls in purgatory.[4] John
Frith's first quotation from Fisher is a passage acknowledging this
development to be recent, occurring after the schism between Rome
and Constantinople: "There is no man now a dayes that douteth of
purgatory / sayeth he / and yet amonge the olde auncient fathers was
there eyther none or els verye seldome mencyon made of it. And also
amonge the grecyans euen vnto this daye is not purgatorye beleued."[5]

---

[1]*Confutatio*, sig. C₂ (sig. N₁v): "Mihi (inquis) certissimum est purgatorium esse, nec
multum me mouet, quid blaterent haeretici. Et paulo post. Nunquid ideo credendum est
haeretico, vix quinquaginta annos nuper nato, & fidem tot seculorum falsam fuisse
contendendum?"
[2]*Confutatio*, sigs. C₂–C₃ (sigs. N₁v–N₂). In his sermon on Ps. 50 ("Miserere") Fisher
writes: "No meane may be founde so spedefull and redy to proue the certaynte of ony
thynge concernynge our fayth as that the chyrche hath so affermed and ordeyned. The
chyrche of god may in no wyse begyle in those thynges that longeth to our fayth and to
the vndoutefull helth of the soule"; *English Works*, 108/29–34.
[3]*Confutatio*, sig. O₂ (sig. R₁v).
[4]*Confutatio*, sigs. D₂–D₂v (sigs. X₄v–X₅).
[5]*A Disputation*, sig. K₃v. Fisher's Latin from the *Confutatio* (sig. E₁ [sig. X₆v]) reads:
"Nemo certe . . . iam dubitat orthodoxus, an purgatorium sit, de quo tamen apud priscos
illos, nulla, vel quam rarissima fiebat mentio. Sed & Graecis ad hunc vsque diem non est
creditum purgatorium esse."

Fisher ascribes the slow development of the doctrine to the fervor of the early faithful, who sought the rigors of canonical penance more eagerly than any relief from them, and thus completed in this life the expiation of their sins: "indulgences began after the torments of purgatory had been for a certain while a source of trembling."[1]

If More, as is likely, had already perused Fisher's full survey of the forty-one theses condemned in the papal bull, one can imagine him rereading the four articles on purgatory, articles 37–40, to prepare his own defense of that dogma. Luther's article 37 is brief and well known: "Purgatory cannot be proved by any canonical scripture."[2] The Catholic answer, here articulated by Fisher, is no less familiar: "Even if there were no scriptural proofs, its truth must be believed by all Christians, the more so because the church has from antiquity prayed for the departed souls and especially commemorated them at mass."[3] Augustine, says Fisher, while appealing to the Bible for evidence, laid even more stress on this universal practice. Other early witnesses are Chrysostom; Gregory, with the many stories in his *Dialogue* and the use he made of Matt. 12:32 and 1 Cor. 3:12–15; and Jerome and Ambrose, who also interpreted Paul's "quasi per ignem" as a reference to purgatory.[4] Is it likely, Fisher argues, that so many great men have spoken without any proofs? Nor is it credible that holy writ should be totally silent about a doctrine that fosters charity toward the souls in need, fear to commit even venial sins, and hope to be purged of one's weaknesses in that blessed crucible and thus to avoid hell. Indeed, "since the sacred scripture is a kind of repository of all the truths which it is necessary for Christians to know, nobody can doubt that the truth of purgatory is contained in it."[5] The bishop urges that the samples he

---

[1] "Coeperunt igitur indulgentiae, postquam ad purgatorii cruciatus aliquandiu trepidatum erat"; *Confutatio,* sig. E₁v (sig. X₆v). Indulgences were justified in Henry VIII's *Assertio septem sacramentorum,* sigs. b₁–b₃; and consequently not only by Fisher but also by More in the *Responsio ad Lutherum (CW* 5, 324–33, 338–41), written in defense of Henry's book.

[2] "Purgatorium non potest probari ex sacra scriptura, quae sit in canone"; *Confutatio,* sig. ii₃v (sig. Hh₁v); *Assertio,* sig. h₅.

[3] *Confutatio,* sig ii₃v (sig. Hh₁v).

[4] See the notes on 187/10–17, 190/32–34, 190/34–191/2, 193/4–8, 202/31–32, 203/6, 204/9–13, 204/20–22, 210/6, 210/6–7, 210/7.

[5] "Et quoniam scriptura sacra, conclaue quoddam est omnium veritatum, quae Christianis scitu necessarie sunt, nemini potest ambiguum esse, quin purgatorii veritas in ipsa contineatur"; *Confutatio,* sig. ii₄ (sig. Hh₂). Surtz, *Works and Days of Fisher,* pp. 106–7, gives a slightly different translation of this "startling declaration," as he calls it.

will produce be read "secundum orthodoxorum interpretationem."
The threat of Matt. 12:32—"neither in this world nor in the next"—
"subinfert," he cautiously says, "suggests and supports the inference"
of purgatory, as does 1 John 5:16 with its two categories of sin, one "not
leading to [eternal] death." He links Phil. 2:20 and Rev. 5:13, because
they both refer to creatures in an underworld that cannot be hell, since
God is honored there, "subtus terram." These four texts, he says,
clearly assume the existence of purgatory, and many others confirm its
reality by their interweaving evidence. One is the parable of Dives and
Lazarus (Luke 16:19–31), three times exploited in the *Supplication*
(179/5–9, 196/9–10, 226/29–30). Fisher's last proof is a sentence
(Matt. 12:36) already used in his sermons: "Also of euery worde spoken vnprofytably and in vayne we shall gyue accounte before god."[1]
This group of scriptures puts the existence of purgatory beyond all
doubt, he concludes, for anyone who is not contumacious.[2]

Frith's jeer at evidence drawn from Ps. 65:12—"we haue gone thorow fyre and water & thou hast brought vs in to colenesse"[3]—echoes the
taunt of Luther himself, who applied the verse to the trials of the
martyrs on earth. Agreed, replied Fisher, but it also fits the less heroic
disciples of Christ, both here and hereafter; as Origen says, "Certain
things are tested by fire, others by water."[4] The psalm leads Luther to
"illud 1 Cor. 3."[5] Paul's famous warning, Luther says, obviously refers
to Judgment Day. To counter this exclusive interpretation, Fisher invokes one patristic giant from each tradition: Origen and Augustine.
The Greek exegete shows the Lord using that fire to "purge the sons of
Judah" of their stains and base alloys.[6] The Latin father speaks of
Paul's fire as "transitorio igne," where "non capitalia, sed minuta peccata purgantur," and urges his flock to rid themselves of their sinful
dross now and so avoid that posthumous fire, more cruel than any pain

---

[1]Fisher, *English Works*, 75/26 and 359/6.

[2]*Confutatio*, sigs. ii$_4$v–kk$_1$v (sigs. Hh$_2$–Hh$_2$v).

[3]Quoted in the English of Frith, who proceeds to refute the proof (*A Disputation*, sig.
L$_2$).

[4]Fisher (*Confutatio*, sig. kk$_1$v) cites Origen's homily 25 on Numbers; see the note on
190/28–31. For Luther's rejection of Ps. 65, see *Assertio*, sig. h$_5$. The psalm is there
mistakenly numbered as 76, an error reproduced in the quotation of Luther in Fisher's
Confutatio.

[5]Quoted in *Confutatio*, sig. kk$_2$ (sig. Hh$_3$); *Assertio*, sig. h$_5$.

[6]*Confutatio*, sig. kk2 (sig. Hh$_3$). The reference is to Origen's homily 6 on Exodus; see
the note on 190/28–31.

they can feel or even imagine on earth.[1] And when Luther's next
objection limits the flames in 1 Thess. 1:8 to the conflagration marking
Christ's return in glory, Fisher replies that they can at the same time
designate the fire, perpetual or temporary, to which souls are consigned immediately after their particular judgment.[2]

Predictably, Luther climaxes his demolition of purgatory with
2 Macc. 12; in his view the passage "carries no authority because we
read nothing like it in either the New or the Old Testament."[3] Fisher
retorts that both Jerome and Augustine approve and use the Maccabean books as part of the Christian canon.[4] Transcending the scholastic arena in which he is Dr. Fisher wrestling with Dr. Luther, the bishop
of Rochester becomes for a while the All Souls preacher he has often
been and quotes from Augustine a long appeal which rings very like
the most moving passages in the *Supplication:*

> The souls lying in torments call every day, and few are those who
> answer their clamor; they weep and wail, and there are none who
> comfort them. Oh, what great cruelty, my brethren! What great
> inhumanity! . . . But remember that it is a holy and wholesome, a
> pious and blessed thought, pleasing to God and the angels, to pray
> for the dead, so that they be delivered from the pains they suffer
> for their sins.[5]

When Luther says that the Roman church fears for its profits,[6] Fisher

---

[1]"Durioremque futurum illum ignem affirmat, quam quicquid in hoc seculo
poenarum, aut videri, aut sentiri, aut cogitari potest;" from Augustine's sermon 4, "De
commemoratione animarum" (quoted in *Confutatio,* sig. kk₂v [sig. Hh₃]). Fisher echoes
and Englishes Augustine's almost proverbial dictum in his sermons on the penitential
psalms: "Ille ignis grauior est quam quicquid homo pati potest in hac vita. The fyre of
purgatory is more greuous than ony payne man may suffre in this lyfe" (Fisher, *English
Works,* 54/28).

[2]*Confutatio,* sig. kk₂v (sig. Hh₃).

[3]"quum nihil simile, neque in nouo, neque in veteri testamento legatur"; *Confutatio,*
sig. kk₂v (sig. Hh₃); *Assertio,* sig. h₅.

[4]Fisher quotes Jerome's second prologue to Maccabees and three writings of Augustine's: *De ciuitate Dei* 18.36, *De cura pro mortuis gerenda,* and *Admonitio in sermones ad
fratres in eremo* 44 (*Confutatio,* sig. kk₃ [sigs. Hh₃–Hh₃v]). See notes on 180/24, 203/26,
and *PL 40,* 1320.

[5]*Admonitio* 44 (see previous note), quoted in *Confutatio,* sigs. kk₃–kk₃v (sig. Hh₃v). This
passage contains an echo of 2 Macc. 12:46. The phrase "weep and wail" is used by both
Fisher and More in connection with the departed; More's "pewlyng" (136/31) might
even be more apt, and his "vnkyndenes" (192/8) renders Augustine's "inhumanitas"
excellently.

[6]*Confutatio,* sig. kk₃ (sig. Hh₃v); *Assertio,* sig. h₅.

replies that his assault will inflict a worse loss on the souls than on the pope, and that the faithful who *bona fide* purchase pardons for themselves or others benefit more than the pope does.[1]

One is not a heretic for not believing in purgatory, says Luther, pointing to the Greek Orthodox church.[2] But the Greek fathers do share that belief with us, says Fisher, who enumerates writings by Origen, Athanasius, Dionysius, and Chrysostom, not to mention many other Greek authors quoted in a document drawn up at the Council of Basel and used to impress the Greek delegation at the Council of Florence.[3]

"Anyway," Luther continues, "I personally believe in purgatory, and I counsel others to believe in it, but I want nobody compelled."[4] Fisher, however, sees Christ's "compelle intrare" (Luke 14:23) as justifying some pressure on the ignorant.[5] As for the nature of purgatory, the two theologians agree to infer it from that of hell—purgatorial pain differs only in not lasting forever.[6] The essential pain, Luther contends, is dread and horror. Fisher, however, insists on fire: the gospel's own image for hell can safely be posited also for that impermanent hell, purgatory.[7]

Luther's article 38 reasserts and fleshes out two statements condemned by the papal bull: (1) the souls of purgatory do not know for sure where they are, at least not all of them; (2) it is not proved that they are incapable of acquiring merit or of growing in charity.[8] Following the consensus of Catholic tradition, Fisher answers that all souls, at their particular private judgment, know of their sentence; their punishment follows that sentence. They also use their wits in the after-

---

[1] *Confutatio*, sigs. kk$_3$–kk$_3$v (sig. Hh$_3$v).

[2] *Confutatio*, sigs. kk$_3$v and kk$_4$ (sig. Hh$_3$v); *Assertio*, sig.h$_5$.

[3] *Confutatio*, sig. kk$_4$ (sigs. Hh$_3$v–Hh$_4$). For Origen see p. lxxxviii, n. 4, and p. cvii, n. 6, above; pseudo-Athanasius, *Quaestiones ad Antiochum ducem* 34 (*Patrologiae Cursus Completus: Series Graeca*, ed. J-P. Migne, 161 vols., Paris, 1857–66, *28*, 618; cited hereafter as *PG*); Dionysius, *Ecclesiastica hierarchia*, chap. 7 (*PG 3*, 559–62); Chrysostom, *In Epistolam primam ad Corinthios*, homily 9 (*PG 61*, 75–82).

[4] *Confutatio*, sig. kk$_4$v (sig. Hh$_4$); *Assertio*, sigs. h$_5$–h$_5$v.

[5] *Confutatio*, sig. kk$_4$v (sig. Hh$_4$).

[6] Fisher refers to the vision recounted by Bede, whereby it appears that purgatory is adjacent to hell; "confine gehennae" (*Confutatio*, sig. ll$_2$ [sig. Hh$_4$v]); see p. cxv, n. 3, below. In his first sermon on the Psalms, Fisher says, "Of a trouth in that place is so grete acerbite of paynes that no dyfference is bytwene the paynes of hell and them, but onely eternyte" (Fisher, *English Works*, 10/22–24).

[7] *Confutatio*, sig. ll$_1$v (sig. Hh$_4$v).

[8] *Confutatio*, sig. ll$_2$ (sig. Hh$_4$v); *Assertio*, sig. h$_5$v.

life, as appears from the dialogue between Abraham and Dives in Luke
16:23–31. The angels undoubtedly comfort them, especially each
guardian angel, who reminds his beloved charge of heaven forthcoming. And finally the Holy Spirit, dwelling in these blessed souls, comforts them more now than when they were in the prison of the body; he
prompts them to say "Abba, Father!" and makes them feel secure.[1]

As Luther's next thesis involves the whole theology of grace, Fisher
devotes much space to proving that the disembodied souls cannot
merit: he quotes John 9:4, Gal. 6:10, 2 Cor. 5:10, and several fathers on
this point. Nor do the souls, for all their love of God, love their pain
insofar as it is pain, any more than Christ, the supreme lover, found his
passion pleasing. Since the charity of the souls is already perfect, they
cannot grow in grace, but they acquire "fulgorem," a radiance im-
parted by their cleansing. Their "punitorium" is even more truly a
"purgatorium."[2]

Luther's article 39 is too paradoxical to engage Fisher at length:
"The souls in purgatory sin continually as long as they seek rest and
recoil from pain."[3] Did Christ then sin, Fisher asks, when he confessed
his terror and anguish in the garden? He did not, and they do not;
otherwise there would never be an end to their purgation.[4] To the
proposition of article 40—"The souls delivered from purgatory by the
suffrages of the living enjoy less bliss than if they had made satisfaction
by themselves"[5]—the bishop answers, yes, if they had made atonement
in their lifetime. But all they can do in purgatory is to get rid of their
stains.[6] In article 41 Luther vents his animosity toward the mendicant
orders; that he wishes them all abolished indicates how inseparable the
image of the friars was from that of pardons and purgatory.[7]

More than a decade before Luther's challenge reached England,
Fisher had published a sequence of ten sermons on "the fruitful sayings of David," that is, on the penitential psalms.[8] Why purgatory? he

---

[1]*Confutatio*, sigs. ll$_2$–ll$_2$v (sig. Hh$_5$).

[2]*Confutatio*, sigs. ll$_2$v–mm$_2$ (sigs. Hh$_5$–Hh$_6$v).

[3]*Confutatio*, sig. mm$_2$ (sig. Hh$_6$v); *Assertio*, sig. h$_5$v; Luther's articles 40 and 41, also
discussed in this paragraph, are likewise found on sig. h$_5$v.

[4]*Confutatio*, sig. mm$_2$ (sig. Ii$_1$).

[5]*Confutatio*, sig. mm$_3$ (sig. Ii$_1$); *Assertio*, sig. h$_5$v.

[6]*Confutatio*, sig. mm$_3$v (sig. Ii$_1$v).

[7]*Confutatio*, sig. mm$_4$ (sig. Ii$_1$v); *Assertio*, sig. h$_5$v.

[8]John Fisher, *This treatise concernynge the fruytfull saynges of Dauyd the kynge & prophete in
the seuen penytencyall psalmes* . . . (London, 1508; *STC* 10902); for convenience, references
to this work are cited from Fisher, *English Works*.

asks in his first sermon. Because "there abydeth in the soule a certayne
taxacion or duty whiche . . . must nedes be content & satysfyed eyther
here in this lyf by temporal payne or elles after this lyfe in purgatory."[1]
The cost is greater if payment is postponed; hence the prayer of Augustine: "Hic vre, hic seca [Burn here, cut here]. Good lorde punysshe
me in this lyfe."[2] Sinners should use these psalms "as lettres of supplycacyon."[3] Moreover, Fisher comments on Ps. 37:17 (a verse also
analyzed by More): "Quoniam ego in flagella paratus sum. I am redy
good lorde to do all maner penaunce for my synnes."[4] Rather than
breed desperation by stressing the rigor of God's justice, he fosters
confidence by stressing God's mercy.[5] Hell is "the depe dungeon of
dyspayre";[6] purgatory is a jail too, yet from its depths there rises the
trusting call of saved souls: "De profundis clamavi ad te Domine" (Ps.
129:1). Fisher urges, "let vs ofte repete this sayd verse for them that be
in the paynes of purgatory."[7] Fisher, like More, alternates "poor soule"
with "sely soule."[8]

Fisher's funeral orations for Henry VII (May 1509) and his mother,
the Lady Margaret (July 1509), were occasions that he seized upon
eagerly to seek prayer not for them alone but for "all crysten soules."[9]
The life of the countess of Richmond, however, had been so edifying
that a "lamentable mornynge" was out of place; her dirge was to be
"gladde & ioyous," given the "euydent lyklyhode & coniecture" that
her soul "was borne vp in to the countre aboue with the blessyd
aungelles."[10]

No statement of Catholic eschatology in early Tudor English carries
more weight than the *Two fruytfull Sermons, made & compyled by the ryght
Reuerende father in god Iohan Fyssher / Doctour of Dyuynyte and Bysshop of*

---

[1] Fisher, *English Works*, 24/27–31.

[2] Fisher, *English Works*, 41/14–15.

[3] Fisher, *English Works*, 70/24 and 73/5. John Fen, who translated these sermons into Latin for the 1597 *Opera*, renders "lettres of supplycacyon" as "libelli supplices" (sigs. Vvv₃v, Vvv₄).

[4] Fisher, *English Works*, 84/21–23.

[5] Fisher, *English Works*, pp. 81–88, 207–9.

[6] Fisher, *English Works*, 213/32, 233/30.

[7] Fisher, *English Works*, 209/5–6.

[8] See Fisher's last penitential sermon on the Psalms, *English Works*, 243/22; 253/12, 18. In the Latin of 1597, "sely soul" becomes "animula" (sig. BBbb₃) or simply "anima" or "animus" (sig. BBbb₄v).

[9] Fisher, funeral sermon for Henry VII, *English Works*, 281/21.

[10] Fisher, funeral sermon for the countess of Richmond, *English Works*, 309/15,19–21; 310/1,4.

Rochester. The only extant edition of these sermons on Matt. 5:20 was printed on June 28, 1532, by More's nephew William Rastell.[1] At this time More, freed from the burden of public office, was still envisaging a response to John Frith on purgatory. Meanwhile he must have welcomed, if he did not actually sponsor, the publication of these model pieces of pastoral teaching by a professional divine whose episcopal authority and academic prestige were enhanced by a reputation for sanctity. The sermons were preached for the twin feasts of All Saints and All Souls, November 1 and 2, most probably in 1520, when the public still had vivid images "of many goodly syghtes whiche were shewed of late beyonde the see,"[2] at the Field of Cloth of Gold. Fisher exhorts his flock, as he did "in other yeres past,"[3] to draw the corollaries of a belief that the majority of them take for granted.

There is some contrast between the two panels of this diptych. The first sermon portrays purgatory as a prison where the blessed souls "for theyr dettes lye now deteyned . . . tyll tyme they haue payd the vttermost ferthyng of theyr dettys."[4] In the second sermon, purgatory, true to its name, is a place (or state) not of punishment but of cleansing: venial sins are likened to dust or to "the rust of a knyfe" removable "with a lytle rubbynge and scourynge."[5] All in all, however, the carceral image dominates. The term *prison* occurs more than a dozen times, with epithets such as "myserable," "ferefull," "greuous," and, of course, "paynfull."[6] Even *limbus patrum* is a "pryson of darkenes."[7] Fisher acknowledges the grimness of the situation and uses it as an

---

[1]John Fisher, *Here after ensueth two fruytfull Sermons . . .* (London, 1532; *STC* 10909). These sermons are not included in Fisher's *English Works.* A Latin translation of the second sermon, by John Fen, is found in the 1597 *Opera* (sigs. DDdd$_4$–EEee$_1$). The first sermon is, however, generously sampled in E. E. Reynolds' *Saint John Fisher,* rev. ed. (Wheathampstead, Herts., 1972), pp. 85–90, and portions of it are reprinted in Joyce-lyne G. Russell, *The Field of Cloth of Gold* (London, 1969), pp. 216–19. In addition there is Sister Marie Denis Sullivan's *A Critical Edition of "Two fruytfull sermons" of Saint John Fisher, Bishop of Rochester* (Ann Arbor: University Microfilms, 1961).

[2]Fisher, *Two fruytfull Sermons,* sig. [A$_3$] (missigned A$_2$). Reynolds favors the date of 1520 for these sermons (*Saint John Fisher,* p. 85), as does Jean Rouschausse in *John Fisher, évêque de Rochester; sa vie et son oeuvre* (Lille, 1971), pp. LV, 56. See Marc'hadour, *L'Univers de Thomas More* (Paris, 1963), pp. 15–16. Rastell's "Newly Enprynted" (sig. [H$_2$]) seems to imply an earlier edition.

[3]Fisher, *Two fruytfull Sermons,* sig. C$_3$.

[4]Fisher, *Two fruytfull Sermons,* sigs. B$_4$, C$_2$. This is an echo of Matt. 5:26 and is repeated at sigs. D$_1$v and D$_2$.

[5]Fisher, *Two fruytfull Sermons,* sigs. C$_4$v, G$_4$.

[6]Fisher, *Two fruytfull Sermons,* sigs. C$_4$, C$_4$v, D$_2$; "paynfull" at sigs. D$_1$v, D$_2$v, D$_3$, D$_4$v.

[7]Fisher, *Two fruytfull Sermons,* sig. F$_3$v.

incentive to a strenuous discipline on earth, so that humankind shall
not "be arested for [their] dettes, and so be cast into that paynfull
pryson."[1] He reinforces the biblical tenor of the cleansing by connect-
ing the metaphor with the flaming "two edged swerde" wielded by the
cherubim stationed east of Eden to bar man's access to the tree of life.[2]
All sinners, which means practically everyone, "must haue a scouryng /
either in this worlde, or else in the fyre of purgatory."[3] To stir devotion
to the departed souls, the bishop lists five considerations which "shold
moue vs effectually to remember them": (1) the "manyfold bondes" of
nature and the spirit which tie the living and the dead; (2) the special
application of such a bond where friends and kinsmen are concerned;
(3) the extreme need and grievous plight of the souls cut off from both
the pleasures of life and the joys of heaven; (4) their piteous cries,
appealing for help through masses, prayers, fastings, and alms or
other charitable deeds; (5) the reward from God for pitying his prisoners, from the souls themselves when they are delivered, and from
the good angels "appoynted there to gyue theyr attendaunce vpon
these blessyd soules."[4] Wisdom invites man to "eschew that paynefull
pryson" by trying hard to avoid even peccadillos, since "many lytels
makyth a moche,"[5] and by paying one's debts to God's justice now,
scouring the soul now, rather than waiting till after death.

The purging flame, like a sharp tooth, represents also "the frettynge
and gnawynges of theyr troubled conscyence."[6] But the "silly souls"
undergo duller forms of punishment too: they feel something like the
"werynesse," "lothsomnes," and "fastydyousnes" (that is, disgust) that
attend "at length of tyme" even pleasures as splendid as those of the
Field of Cloth of Gold.[7] The price mortals pay for their folly is not,
however, beyond human endurance as long as they do not cut themselves off from Christ, their "moste gracyous & louynge prynce."[8] The

---

[1]Fisher, *Two fruytfull Sermons*, sig. D_1v.
[2]Fisher, *Two fruytfull Sermons*, sig. G_1v; cf. Gen. 3:24.
[3]Fisher, *Two fruytfull Sermons*, sig. G_4v. The image of the two-edged sword wielded by
the cherubim is given a lengthy explanation (sigs. G_2–G_4v): its slaying blade administers
death to body and soul and thus represents "euerlastynge ponyshment" (sig. G_3), while
its "brennynge flambe [which] shall swynge away . . . venyall synnes" (sig. G_4v) is the fire
of purgatory. For other references to "scouring," see sigs. G_1v, G_3, G_3v; cf. "purged from
venyall synne" (sig. $[H_1]$).
[4]Fisher, *Two fruytfull Sermons*, sigs. B_4–B_4v, C_1–C_4.
[5]Fisher, *Two fruytfull Sermons*, sigs. D_4v, G_4.
[6]Fisher, *Two fruytfull Sermons*, sig. F_3v.
[7]Fisher, *Two fruytfull Sermons*, sigs. A_3v–A_4, C_4v.
[8]Fisher, *Two fruytfull Sermons*, sig. F_4v.

way Fisher uses *gracious* again and again to qualify heaven and purgatory and the good life on earth[1] prepares us to catch the resonance of *gracious* and *ungracious* in More's *Supplication*.

Closer to the *Supplication* in date, and notable for being Fisher's only antiheretical writings in the English language, are the two official sermons he preached against Luther at Paul's Cross on May 12, 1521, and February 11, 1526.[2] A few excerpts will show the influence they may have had on More when he gave a voice in the *Supplication* to the souls in purgatory: "Yf all these so many testymonyes bothe of grekes and latyns shall not counterpease agaynst one frere. what reason is this?"; "all be it that for fere of the temporall lawes they [the disciples of Wyclif] durst slee no man. yet put they vp a byll of artycles vnto the temporall lordes in the parlyament season mouynge them to slee theyr aduersaryes"; "the gospelles be in the psalter: and the psalter is in the gospelles: and the spirite of Christe maketh one roundell of them all"; "a frere and a nounne together, can this be any good mariage?"; "the couplyng of hym [Luther] & of his mate to gydere is a veray brothelry."[3]

In the *Spiritual Consolation*, which Fisher composed in prison, the dogma of purgatory and its practical consequences are gathered in a nutshell:

> Recounte your selfe as dead, & thinke that your soules were in pryson of Purgatorie, & that there they must abyde till that the Raunsom[4] for them be truly payde, eyther by long sufferance of payne there, or els by suffrages done heere in earth by some of your speciall friendes. Be you your owne friend, doe you these suffrages for your owne soule, whether they be praiers or almes deedes, or any other penitentiall paynefulnesse.[5]

---

[1]For example, "a new gracyouse lyfe in chryste" (sig. D₂), "the gracyouse water of teares" (sig. D₄), "good and gracyouse workes" (sig. D₄), "thys moost gracyouse tree [of life]" (sig. E₄).

[2]*The sermon of Johan the bysshop of Rochester made agayn the pernicyous doctryn of M. luuther* (London, 1521?; STC 10893) and *A sermon had at Paulis, vpon quinquagesom sonday concernynge certayne heretickes* (London, 1528?; STC 10892). In the second of these, forgetting that the *Responsio ad Lutherum* is pseudonymous, Fisher praises "the boke of maister More;" see Fisher, *English Works*, 455/35.

[3]Fisher, *English Works*, 321/6–8, 344/29–32, 457/14–17, 472/11–12, 474/33–4.

[4]It is rather surprising that "ransom," which comes from "redemption," never occurs in the mouths of More's "poor prisoners," nor elsewhere in Fisher's writings on purgatory.

[5]Fisher, *English Works*, 362/24–31.

Fisher's aim to arouse and mobilize soft and slumbering souls explains his stress on debt and pain rather than on the purging of stains.

The crudest objection from Frith[1] against England's apologists of purgatory was that More represented it, in the words of Zech. 9:11, as a pit of fire with no water (178/26–30, 179/13–14), whereas Fisher, drawing on Job 24:19 as well as Ps. 65:12, combined the two incompatible elements: "Euen as in the forge of a Smith, the colde water when it is cast into the Fyer, causeth the Fyer to be much more fearse and violent."[2] The heat and cold are reminiscent of the passage in Bede's *History of the English Church and People,* a book familiar to both Fisher and More in its Latin original. Perhaps in emulation of his beloved St. Gregory, whose involvement with England's conversion fills many chapters of his Book 1, Bede reports a number of miracles. In Book 5, chapter 12, a Northumbrian who has returned from the dead recounts his experience of the various places where souls are either rewarded, punished, or purged in preparation for bliss. Purgatory had no name yet at the time Bede was writing his *History* (A.D. 731), but the theology of it is not far different from that of More's time. Bede's Northumbrian describes

> a very broad and deep valley of infinite length. The side to our left was dreadful with burning flames, while the opposite side was equally horrible, with raging hail and bitter snow. . . . Both sides were filled with men's souls, which seemed to be hurled from one side to the other by the fury of the tempest. When these wretches could no longer endure the blast of the terrible heat, they leaped into the heart of the terrible cold; and finding no refuge there, they leaped back again to be burned in the middle of the unquenchable flames.[3]

The Northumbrian thought this was hell, but his guide told him, "The valley that you saw, with its horrible burning flames and icy cold, is the place where souls are tried and punished. . . . they will all be admitted

---

[1]Frith, *A Disputation,* sigs. A5v, G4v.

[2]Fisher, *English Works,* 424/7–10. The purgatorial juxtaposition of heat and cold would later be vividly expressed by Shakespeare's Claudio in *Measure for Measure* (III, i, 122–23): "To bathe in fiery floods, or to reside/ In thrilling regions of thick-ribbed ice." Mayor notes this passage in his introduction to Fisher's *English Works,* p. xxviii.

[3]Bede, *Historia ecclesiastica* 5.12, *PL* 95, 248. The English translation is that of Leo Sherley-Price, *Bede: A History of the English Church and People* (Harmondsworth, 1955), p. 285. Mayor, in his introduction to Fisher, *English Works,* p. xxviii, gives this passage in the Elizabethan translation of Thomas Stapleton.

into the Kingdom of Heaven on the Day of Judgment. But many are helped by the prayers, alms, and fasting of the living, and especially by the offering of Masses, and are therefore set free before the Day of Judgment."[1]

Luther, as we have seen, rejected Ps. 65:12 as evocative of purgatory, not because the two elements were joined—the metaphor is the psalmist's responsibility—but because for him the fire and water evoked the various tribulations of the pilgrim church on earth, and especially of the martyrs.[2] Fisher, in a Good Friday sermon, applied Job 24:19 to the damned—"they shall be shyfted out of the colde snow brought into the outragious heates":—and links "the coldenesse of the snow" with the gnashing of teeth, which is part of the gospel image of hell (Matt. 8:12; Luke 13:28).[3]

Fisher readily granted to Luther that indulgences—like God's own indulgent mercy—had led to gross abuses, had been granted from impure motives, and had been sought in a mercenary spirit. He was not in favor of multiplying them any more than he approved of the proletariat of chantry-priests. Those who suspect Erasmus of heterodoxy because his last will left bequests for poor scholars and none for obits should remember that, three decades earlier, John Fisher had prevailed upon the Lady Margaret to give up the magnificent chantry she had planned for herself and her son, Henry VII, in Westminster Abbey, persuading her instead to devote the money to the foundation of Christ's College. He was convinced that the formation of a learned clergy would benefit her soul's health no less than the multiplying of masses. And the bishop added to her legacy for the foundation of St. John's College, Cambridge, as much as he could from his own revenues, "for the good of [his own] soul." Of course, the souls in purgatory were not neglected: specific sums were earmarked for trentals to be celebrated by fellows of the college.[4]

---

[1]Bede, *Historia ecclesiastica, PL* 95, 250; Sherley-Price, pp. 287–88. Bede maintains that this valley of flame and ice is for those souls who were in fact penitent at the hour of their death. It is for this penitence, however belated, that they will all be admitted to heaven on Judgment Day.

[2]*Confutatio*, sig. kk₁v (sig. Hh₂v); *Assertio*, sig. h₅.

[3]Fisher, *English Works*, 423/10–11, 424/2–3. In *The Confutation of Tyndale's Answer*, as if to demonstrate the elasticity of an elemental metaphor, More applies the snow and heat sentence to the extreme "chaunges of the soule, whom the deuyll dryueth out of one vice into his contrary" rather "as ye body in an agew chaungeth from colde to hete, and from hete some tyme into colde agayne" (*CW 8*, 488/25–8).

[4]T. E. Bridgett, *Life of Blessed John Fisher*, 3rd ed. (London, 1902), pp. 21–22, 33; see also Surtz, *Works and Days of Fisher*, pp. 181–82, 480, n. 4.

As for Frith and his judgment of Fisher's arguments, it was perhaps unfair of him to treat the purgatory section of Fisher's *Confutatio* as an exposition or assertion of that dogma. The fire and water passage that the young reformer seized on with special zest is not a proof of Fisher's own choosing; the bishop's business was to refute Luther's contention that Ps. 65:12 is totally irrelevant, inapplicable, and absurd. Had Fisher been writing a treatise rather than a response, he probably would not have used it. Even here, however, his pastoral and educational concerns prompted him to go beyond mere polemics and to offer enough elements of a positive construction for us to get a rounded view of his doctrine if we also consider the pulpit works. Something stern in his temperament, together with the need he felt to arouse a flock less than vigilant for its own spiritual well-being, accounts for the darker strokes of his brush, for a certain shrillness in his tone. His purgatory seems closer to hell than Gerson's or More's. Its "innumerable paynes" are so great "that the soules there may scante haue remembraunce of ony thynge elles," neither presumably of their friends on earth nor of their greater Friend in heaven; "therefore the prophete sayth, Quoniam non est in morte qui memor sit tui. No creature beynge in purgatorye may haue the in remembraunce as he sholde."[1]

More, although he was a judge and fond of carceral images to describe man's life on earth, does not use the words *prison* and *prisoners* in his *Supplication* as repeatedly as Fisher does in his All Saints sermon, nor does More ever conjure up the jail of Matt. 5:25–26 where "thou wilt lie till thou hast paid the last farthing." More's souls echo only once Augustine's deterring superlatives about purgatory's fire. Fisher quotes them in his sermon on Ps. 37,[2] in his *Confutatio*, and twice in the short compass of the All Saints sermon: "more greuous than any paynes thou canst see, fele or thynke in this world."[3] Modern readers who object to More's somber hues may well pause and consider the even starker insistence of John Fisher. Both men had in mind the salvation of their readers and hence neither shrank from painting the picture he believed likely to prove most effective.

---

[1]Fisher, *English Works*, 15/26–27, 16/1–3, with quotation of Ps. 6:6.
[2]Fisher, *English Works*, 54/28–29; see *CCSL 38*, 384.
[3]Fisher, *Two fruytfull Sermons*, sig. D₁v; cf. sig. C₂: "more greuouse than any maner of payne that can be sene in this worlde, or felte, or yet thought."

LETTER AGAINST FRITH

T HOMAS MORE'S short *Letter* against John Frith's doctrine of the "blessed sacrament of the aultare" is the mildest of all his polemical works. Written late in 1532 while Frith was a prisoner in the Tower of London, it is addressed to an unnamed recipient,[1] assumed to share with More a commitment to Catholic doctrine and loyalty to Henry VIII—lauded throughout the treatise as a virtuous and orthodox monarch protecting his people from the virus of heresy. The recipient is also assumed to share with More the wish that Frith, whom More continually mentions as a "yong man," return to the orthodoxy that he has lately attacked. More's tone implies that Frith may be redeemed and that the great hopes that others have placed in him and his precocious learning may be fulfilled.

Yet the purpose of More's *Letter* is clear throughout: to show how Frith has erred from orthodoxy and to refute all the young man's errors. He directs his remarks against a short statement in which Frith had outlined his views of the eucharist, a statement that had been delivered to More in three handwritten copies. More speaks in the beginning of the success of the government's campaign against forbidden books—a campaign that he had vigorously prosecuted as lord chancellor—but points out that the heretics have not stopped circulating their works. Instead they have begun sending around handwritten copies (233/1–23). And so heresy creeps forth like a cancer, secretly corrupting the good common people. Shifting his metaphor, he likens this secret spreading of heresy to a smoldering fire, eating its way through "some olde roten tymber vnder cellers & celynges"; if not discovered, it will break out into open flames (233/33–234/16).

Having laid a rhetorical foundation, More builds upon it by pointing out a little treatise by Frith on the sacrament that has been closely held among the "brethren," as More liked to call the heretics. Frith's heresy goes far beyond that of Luther and even that of Tyndale, More says, for the young man denies the real presence of the body and blood of Christ in the eucharist, though Frith admits that Christ made many statements that make this radical sort of heresy untenable. More

---

[1] See *CW* 3/2, Commentary at 280/1–6.

grieves, he says, "very sore, to see thys yonge man so cyrcumuented and begyled by certayn old lymmes of the deuyll" such as Wycliff, Oecolampadius, Tyndale, and Zwingli (236/21–32). Thus More sets the course he will follow throughout the work, acknowledging that, though Frith is a bright young man worthy of personal affection, his doctrines place him among the most hated of the English and continental heretics, men whose doctrines no English government could espouse and be afterward confident of the loyalty of the English people. Englishmen were willing to tolerate attacks on the pope, but were not yet ready to accept a revolution in the forms and beliefs of daily religious practice.

More always believed, probably rightly, that Tyndale was a Zwinglian in his eucharistic doctrine. But as he correctly implies here, Tyndale never wrote openly about the doctrine of the eucharist in such a way as to evoke more controversy among English evangelicals when they desperately needed unity to withstand the counterattacks of Catholic polemicists like More and a government unwilling to be tarred with the brush of heresy as it made its precarious way into schism with Rome.

Tyndale's perceptions were correct. The eucharistic controversy divided English evangelicals for years, and Frith would have been better served if he had followed Tyndale's advice and kept silent about his views. But he had written his little treatise, called *A Christian Sentence*, and it was against this work that More wrote his measured reply, which may very well have been responsible for bringing Frith to the stake in July 1533. We may leave the details of More's work to a later place. It seems best first to set them in context by discussing the evolution of Frith's career to the moment when he was seized and imprisoned in 1532.

The Early Career of John Frith

JOHN FRITH was by all accounts one of the most attractive of the early English Protestants. Writing a generation after Frith died at the stake on July 4, 1533, John Foxe, the martyrologist, grieved at the death of "so learned and excellent a young man."[1] Foxe claimed that Frith knew Latin and Greek so well that he could converse fluently in both. According to the testimony of his evangelical colleagues, who sought to make him a saint of superhuman intellect and virtue, he lived

---

[1]Foxe, 5, 3.

in the abstemious simplicity that they took for godliness. He was also sweet-tempered and courageous, a bold writer, much less vindictive than others in his camp, a good organizer, a sociable man.

Frith was born in 1503 in Kent and grew up there. Like most early English Protestants, he came from a comfortable but nonprofessional family (his father kept an inn). Lacking important connections, he made his way up in the world through the church, which recognized and nourished his intelligence and sponsored him first at Eton and later at Cambridge.

He has traditionally been associated with the group that met at the White Horse Tavern to discuss the new theology drifting like smoke across the Channel from the Continent, where Martin Luther was setting the world ablaze. The group at the White Horse included many future Protestants, among them the later martyrs Thomas Bilney, Robert Barnes, Hugh Latimer, Nicholas Ridley, and John Lambert. But the group also included conservatives like Stephen Gardiner and Edward Fox, and these early discussions were probably an effort to discover what Luther meant rather than a campaign to introduce his dogmas into Cambridge. The common bond was not an affection for Lutheranism but rather the yearning that Lutheranism represented, a yearning to reform the Catholic church and Christian life and to restore to Christianity a power many thought it had lost.

The group began meeting about 1521, and if Frith was indeed a member, he was much younger than most of the others. His precocity, especially in the study of languages, may have granted him a place among men influenced not only by Luther but also by Erasmus and by the Erasmian conviction that the study of scripture in its original tongues might open the way to piety and reform. Frith could have been introduced to the group, ironically enough, by Stephen Gardiner, later bishop of Winchester and one of the prelates responsible for the examinations that resulted in Frith's execution over a decade later. Gardiner was Frith's tutor at Cambridge, and he was the most obvious person to recognize his intelligence and his inclinations and to draw him to the informal sessions at the White Horse. But it seems unlikely that Frith went over immediately to heretical doctrine. These talks with men of such interest and conviction might have planted seeds that germinated later on when he came to a more mature understanding of himself and his mission. But they did not convert him on the spot.

Foxe says nothing about Frith and the White Horse. Rather, he says, Frith "fell into knowledge and acquaintance with William Tyndale, through whose instructions he first received into his heart the seed of the gospel and sincere godliness."[1] The reference is maddeningly vague. Frith might have met Tyndale at Cambridge, where the future translator of the Bible lived from about 1519 until 1522.[2] But since Tyndale left Cambridge at about the time Frith arrived, it seems more likely that they became friends later on, probably when Tyndale was in London about 1524, vainly hoping that London's new bishop, Cuthbert Tunstal, might finance his translation of the New Testament. Tyndale is not known to have shared in the conversations at the White Horse. He was not a convivial sort; he drank only small beer, and it is hard to imagine him participating in theological discussions that went on in a tavern, even in the sixteenth century.

Thus Frith was probably converted to heresy in London not in Cambridge.[3] Whatever the place, he was converted, and he and Tyndale entered into a friendship that would endure until Frith's death by fire. Perhaps the best testimony of Frith's good temper is the fact that he was the only one of Tyndale's known close associates with whom Tyndale did not finally quarrel. Tyndale was the man with whom Frith's mind and heart were most closely attuned. Both of them preserved something of the old Lollard sentiment against the papacy and against the high clergy who lived in luxury while the poor languished without food or the true gospel of Christ. Both of them exalted the simple life. Both came to their understanding of the faith by a journey that took them through the Greek New Testament of Erasmus, whose annotations not only condemned corruptions in church practice but also suggested that church doctrines had been corrupted by the accretions of ceremonial tradition.

Frith took his B.A. from King's College, Cambridge, in January 1526.[4] He had already been appointed fellow at Wolsey's new endowment, then called Cardinal College, Oxford, now Christ Church.[5] Wolsey meant the buildings to be grand and his scholars glorious, and it is a sign of Frith's reputation that he was in the first group of young

---

[1]Foxe, 5, 4.

[2]Clebsch, p. 139.

[3]Mozley presents the difficulties of just where the two men met and concludes that it is impossible to know. J. F. Mozley, *William Tyndale* (London, 1937; reprint, Westport, Conn., 1971), p. 20; cited hereafter as "Mozley."

[4]Robert E. Fulop, "John Frith and His Relation to the Origin of the Reformation in England" (Ph.D. dissertation, University of Edinburgh, 1956), p. 44; cited hereafter as "Fulop."

[5]Fulop, p. 45.

fellows to be called to the college Wolsey meant as a monument to himself. In his letter to Oxford of 1518 condemning those students and dons opposed to Greek studies, More held up Cambridge as an example. There, he said, Greek flourished; it was a shame for Oxford to lag behind. "But their present enthusiasm for you will undoubtedly wane if they find that their pious intentions are mocked there in Oxford, particularly since in Cambridge, which you have always been wont to outshine, even those who are not learning Greek are each moved by a common devotion to their school to make a handsome personal contribution for the salary of a lecturer to teach others Greek."[1] In bringing Frith and other bright young men over from Cambridge, Wolsey was probably planning to modernize Oxford along lines suggested by More—though as a patron of Greek studies himself, he did not have to read More's letter to be moved to encourage the new learning at the university where he had taken his own degree.

But with Greek came a penchant for novelty of many kinds, and the stress that Erasmus laid on the sufficiency of scripture could become heresy in hands less cautious and less Catholic than his. As we have seen, Cambridge was receptive not only to Greek but also to open discussion of Luther's ideas. Now with the transfer of Frith and several other Cambridge scholars to Oxford, heresy—or at least a certain open-mindedness about heresy—came to the quiet old university town on the upper Thames. In March 1528, William Warham, archbishop of Canterbury, wrote an anguished letter to Wolsey announcing that some members of Oxford had been "infected with the heresies of Luther and others of that sort."[2] Warham—something of a habitual lamenter—grieved that now both the universities in England were infected with the "pestilent doctrines" of the heretics. He begged Wolsey to punish the leaders but to be merciful to "the novices which be not yet thoroughly cankered in the said errors, and to put them to such correction as the quality of their transgression shall require." Warham also recommended that the matter be kept as quiet as possible lest the university be shamed and heretics gladdened in England and beyond the sea.[3]

Wolsey evidently made the authorities at Oxford get busy. Foxe tells

[1]CW 15, 144/17–23.
[2]Fulop, p. 48; see Sir Henry Ellis, ed., *Original Letters Illustrative of English History*, 4 vols. (London, 1846), *1*, 239; cited hereafter as "Ellis." Fulop dates the letter 1525 or 1526, but it seems more probable, from internal evidence, that the letter should be dated 1528.
[3]Ellis, *1*, 241–42.

of a seemingly sudden and unexpected search in 1528 that turned up a great number of heretical books from abroad. He says that those found with the forbidden books were imprisoned in a deep cellar used to store salt fish under the college, so that some of the men died "through the filthy stench thereof" and some of them died in their own rooms from the effects of their imprisonment.[1] Foxe lists Frith among those who suffered this incarceration. Eventually Wolsey sent word to release the prisoners because, Foxe says, "he would not have them so straightly handled."[2] Frith was ordered to keep himself within ten miles of Oxford. But he heard that the leaders of the conventicle were being interrogated and forced to recant and bear a faggot testifying to their worthiness to be burned, and so he fled to the Continent. By escaping before his turn came, Frith avoided formal condemnation for heresy and left open the possibility of recantation later on when he became a pawn in Henry VIII's elaborate game against the Catholic church. Had Frith recanted in 1528 and returned to his heresies later on, the laws of both church and state would have required that he be burned after the second conviction. Since Frith was not immediately examined, he may have been one of "the novices which be not yet thoroughly cankered in the said errors" mentioned by Warham in his letter. Evidently the authorities did not consider him a serious menace. His imprisonment might have been intended as a rough admonition to stop short on the way he had so dangerously begun.

Frith's travels on the Continent remain a mystery. R. E. Fulop, his only modern biographer, speculates that Frith went directly to Antwerp, where Tyndale now lived in busy hiding, writing books and pamphlets, studying Hebrew, preparing to translate the Pentateuch and other parts of the Hebrew scriptures, and ultimately to revise his English New Testament. Frith may have accompanied Tyndale on a journey to Hamburg that Foxe says Tyndale made early in 1529.[3] Some have supposed that Frith may have attended the Marburg Colloquy, where in 1529 Luther and Zwingli tried unsuccessfully to reconcile their differences over the eucharist. We know that he married a woman as fervent in the evangelical cause as he was himself and that

---

[1]Foxe, 5, 4–5. The real killer was probably not the stench but scurvy, a supposition made plausible by Foxe's statement that those who died ate nothing but salt fish from February to the middle of August.

[2]Foxe, 5, 5.

[3]Fulop, p. 63; Foxe, 4, 563.

cxxiv   INTRODUCTION

they had at least one child and perhaps more than one.[1] By his own testimony, Frith helped Tyndale translate scripture, perhaps from Hebrew into English. George Joye put out the story that Frith wrote Tyndale's *Answer* to Thomas More's *Dialogue Concerning Heresies* and had it printed in Amsterdam.[2] But as in so many things about the relations between the two men, we are ignorant of the exact role Frith played in Tyndale's work. William A. Clebsch, having studied the problem carefully and having compared the literary style of the two men, concludes that Frith wrote the point-by-point refutation of More's four books of the *Dialogue Concerning Heresies*, a part of the *Answer* that is tacked on somewhat like an appendix.[3] Clebsch's supposition seems reasonable, especially since this material contains a reference to Tyndale in the third person.[4]

We know that Tyndale loved Frith and was loved by him in return. In part their affection for one another grew from the beliefs they shared. But in part it was something else, something intangible born of their common exile, their common dreams, and their mutual dependence. When Frith lay in the Tower awaiting death and knowing full well that he could escape the fire by recanting, Tyndale wrote him three letters that were preserved by John Foxe.[5] In them he begged his young friend to hold fast and to die bravely. The letters are fervent, their passion partly fueled by Tyndale's sense of how valuable Frith's martyrdom would be to the progress of the faith in England, how damaging to that faith any recantation would be by one hitherto so staunch and so admired. "Let not your body faint," Tyndale says. "He that endureth to the end shall be saved. If the pain be above your strength, remember, 'whatsoever ye shall ask in my name, I will give it you.' And pray to your Father in that name, and he shall ease your pain, or shorten it."[6]

But the human affection in these letters is far stronger than any sentiment of mere human expediency. Tyndale writes, "Brother Jacob" (a pseudonym Tyndale used for Frith, perhaps a sign that Frith

---

[1]We may assume her fervor by the letter preserved by Foxe and written by Tyndale while Frith was in prison, a letter with the comment "Sir, your wife is well content with the will of God and would not, for her sake, have the glory of God hindered" (Foxe, 5, 132).

[2]Mozley, p. 200; *CW 8*, 1234; George Joye, *An Apologye made by George Joye to satisfye (if it may be) w. Tyndale* (London, 1535; *STC*² 14820), sigs. E₁–E₁v.

[3]Clebsch, pp. 96–97.

[4]See Louis Schuster in *CW 8*, 1234, note 3.

[5]Foxe, 5, 130–34.

[6]Foxe, 5, 132.

should be progenitor of the people of God to come in England), "beloved in my heart! There liveth not in whom I have so good hope and trust, and in whom my heart rejoiceth, and my soul comforteth herself, as in you."[1] As is not uncommon among close friends, Tyndale cherished those qualities in Frith that Tyndale found lacking in himself. "God hath made me evil-favoured in this world, . . . speechless and rude, dull and slow witted." Frith's part, Tyndale writes, "shall be to supply what lacketh in me."[2] All the testimony we have about Frith shows him to have been charming and well beloved, qualities that Tyndale here acknowledges sadly were not his own, and the evidence shows that Tyndale was not being falsely modest.

What Tyndale found especially admirable and useful in Frith was the ability to smooth over differences among the evangelicals and to help them hold a united front before the Catholic church. By 1528, when Frith began his exile, evangelical unity had been irretrievably shattered, much to the dismay of the evangelicals themselves and much to the savage delight of Catholic apologists. In his *Dialogue Concerning Heresies* of 1529, More not only mocked these divisions but claimed them as evidence for the Satanic origin of the heretical doctrine.[3] The comparison of the unity of the Catholic church with the chaotic divisions of heretics was an old tactic in Catholic polemic; Irenaeus of Lyons had used it in the second century.[4] The presence of Protestant warring factions in the sixteenth century gave the tactic new life, and the existence of the printing press magnified its power. God could not be Lord of anarchy; he was unity himself, and his one, united church was the reflection of his being.

Frith and Tyndale shared the impulse to compromise—at least to a point. Deeply troubled by the divisions within the evangelical ranks, they believed that some semblance of unity was necessary if their convictions were to win the battle for Christian Europe. They hoped that once Protestantism had won the religious field from the papacy, the differences among the competing sects would be reconciled and a united Christendom based on scripture and warmhearted communion would replace the hierarchical church based on papal primacy and held together by force.

Frith picked up some themes from Tyndale and asserted the doc-

---

[1]Foxe, 5, 133.
[2]Foxe, 5, 134.
[3]*CW 6*, 192; *CW 8*, 428.
[4]See *DTC* 7/2, 2426–77; *PG* 7, cols. 966–67, 1177, 1178.

trine now called "double justification," justification before God and
vindication before the human community. He spoke of faith as a fountain and said, "Out of this fountain spring those good works which
justify us before men, that is to say, declare us to be very righteous."
This doctrine had all the more importance to the evangelicals since
Catholics such as Thomas More were accusing them of championing
licence and depravity, and they had to prove themselves fit to become
the moral and religious directors of an orderly society. They also had to
appeal to kings since, before kings would support the evangelical reformation, they had to be sure that the new doctrines would not create
a social revolution. But Frith knew that good works were not an infallible sign of justification, for men could be deceived by hypocrisy.[1]

So he always stressed the free, divine graciousness of salvation and
usually let it go at that, not plunging into long disquisitions on the
necessity of good works to prove salvation. Yet the doctrine of double
justification does crop up here and there in his writing. Why do we do
good works? Because God has commanded them, Frith says. Why has
God commanded them? "Because thou art living in this world, and
must needs have conversation with men, therefore hath God appointed thee what thou shalt do to the profit of thy neighbor and the taming
of thy flesh. . . . These works God would have us do, that the unfaithful
might see the godly and virtuous conversation of his faithful, and
thereby be compelled to glorify our Father which is in heaven."[2] We
can hardly ask for a more succint statement of the doctrine of double
justification, and yet such statements are relatively infrequent in his
works.

Frith varied from orthodox Catholic faith in several particulars, but
it was his doctrine of the eucharist that brought him into literary conflict with Thomas More, and here Frith was truly radical. He rejected
both the Catholic teaching of transubstantiation and the Lutheran
doctrine of the real presence, often called "consubstantiation."[3] Here
he followed Zwingli and Oecolampadius, who taught that the elements
in the eucharist only symbolized the body and blood of Christ and that

---

[1] "A Letter which John Frith wrote unto the Faithful Followers of Christ's Gospel," in
The Works of the English Reformers William Tyndale and John Frith, ed. Thomas Russell, 3
vols. (London, 1831), *3*, 253; cited hereafter as "Russell."

[2] Russell, *3*, 137.

[3] For a detailed discussion of the controversy over the eucharist during the Reformation and particularly for More's contribution to the debate, see the Introduction to *The
Answer to a Poisoned Book, CW 11*, xvii–xxxvii.

the bread and wine were neither transformed into body and blood, as Catholics taught, nor joined with the body and blood, as Luther taught.

The Zwinglian view of the eucharist which Frith espoused, a view generally called "sacramentarianism," was radical. It went with a proto-puritanical desire to reduce the importance of ceremonies in religion as much as possible, and it seemed to go also with a profound antagonism toward popular piety. As we know from More's *Dialogue Concerning Heresies* and from the *Colloquies* of Erasmus, this antagonism toward popular piety was in part a hostility to the rampant superstition, the open fraud, and the magical elements in the religion of the common people, and it was not manifested solely by the evangelicals; to some extent this antagonism was shared by Christian intellectuals of various sorts, including those who had no intention of deserting the old church for the new gospel. More and Erasmus both mocked the excesses—especially the miracle-mongering—of the people's religion, and they both scorned the begging friars who ministered and often pandered to popular taste.[1]

But More at least recognized that different kinds of people require different kinds of ministry. So he defended many kinds of religious devotion that he did not practice himself in any noteworthy way. We do not, for example, know that he ever went on a pilgrimage, and he seems to have had little personal preoccupation with relics or with images of the saints. The Holbein drawing of his household shows a strikingly middle-class home with a clock hanging in the upper center but devoid of religious images on the walls. And in More's own devotional works (as distinguished from his polemical works), neither images nor relics nor pilgrimages nor prayers to saints play any conspicuous role. His personal piety was as Christ-centered as that of any of the Protestants. But he defended with adamantine tenacity the place of such things in the piety of the common people, for whom images were books and pilgrimages and relics were devices that lifted coarse and heavy hearts toward God. Erasmus was much less tolerant of popular piety than More, and the evangelicals who took his views to extremes set out to eradicate those parts of popular piety that led, in their view, to ungodly superstition.

Frith and other evangelicals like him were resolved to eliminate from the faith what they regarded as materialistic crudity, that is, the

---

[1]*CW 3/1*, 4–7; *CW 15*, 286–88.

common religious expressions of ordinary people, and to elevate all piety to a decorous, warmhearted spiritual unity which was sustained by emotional ties to God and neighbor and reduced the sensual to a minimum. In this campaign, the doctrines of purgatory and the real presence assumed a particular importance: purgatory because it produced a superstitious reliance on indulgences and meritorious works, and the real presence (whether in the Lutheran doctrine or in the Catholic faith in transubstantiation) because it seemed to center worship on something physical. Tyndale, and we may presume Frith too, rejected the notion that any miracles had taken place after the time of the apostles. Since transubstantiation required a miracle during each consecration of the sacrament of the altar, English Protestants of Tyndale's persuasion had yet another reason to make the eucharist a bare symbolic exercise. Nothing happened to the substance of the elements. To venerate them was "idolatry" in English Protestant parlance because to worship bread and wine was to worship a created thing rather than the Creator.

HENRY VIII's APPROACH TO FRITH

DESPITE his radical views on the eucharist and his short writings on various topics while he was in exile, Frith did not become notorious as a heretic. In July 1529 he published a book called *The Revelation of Antichrist* (largely a translation of Luther's *Offenbarung des Endchrists*) and together with it a little work called *Antithesis wherin are compared to geder Christes actes and oure holye father the Popes*. These works were published under the pseudonym "Richard Brightwell," leaving Frith's own name untainted by public heresy.[1] He worked with Tyndale in a quiet way. He wrote the treatise against purgatory that eventually was printed and banned about June 1531.[2] But he did not write openly of his beliefs concerning the eucharist. Zwingli and Luther tried unsuccessfully at Marburg to reconcile their differences in 1529. Tyndale and Frith both recognized that in following Zwingli they held a minority position, and, as we have noted, Tyndale was reluctant to stir up more dissension within the evangelical ranks by writing about the eucharist. Frith himself might never have written anything on the subject had it not been for the sudden importance he assumed for the government of Henry VIII in its floundering about for a solution to the King's "great matter"—his divorce from Catherine of Aragon.

---

[1]See Hume, no. 11; J. B. Trapp, *CW 9*, 351.
[2]*LP 5*, app., no. 18, p. 768.

After Campeggio adjourned the hearings he held with Wolsey on the divorce in the summer of 1529, the king increasingly understood that he would get no satisfaction from Rome. Sometime in 1530 he began a flirtation with heresy that was to wax and wane for the rest of his life.[1] Exactly what he intended in this early flirtation we cannot know; perhaps he did not quite know himself. He may have hoped to use heresy and heretics only as a threat to make the pope move in his favor. He may have been misled by councillors—especially Thomas Cromwell—who leaned toward the new doctrines and allowed the king to suppose that the heretics were much less radical than they really were. Henry, whose religious temper was fundamentally conservative, may have been unable to comprehend just how radical some Englishmen could be.

Whatever his thoughts, he first made a tentative approach to William Tyndale, and when that failed, partly because his reading of Tyndale's work showed him just how heretical Tyndale was, he began to court John Frith.[2] Frith had published nothing to attract passionate hostility to his beliefs. His sentiments about purgatory were recognized, but in the murky religious waters of those days his opinion might be interpreted as simple anticlericalism rather than as outright heresy. More construed Simon Fish's *Supplication of Beggars* of 1529 as an attack on the doctrine of purgatory itself, and many others have held that More drew the correct inferences, although Fish's virulent little work can be read as an assault only on the abuses connected with the doctrine. If John Foxe is to be believed, Henry took Fish under his protection and even took him on a hunt![3] Frith had gone further than Fish, but he had done nothing as yet to create an unbridgeable gulf between himself and the king. In early 1531 the king—or at least his agents—believed that the young man could be won over, made to forsake his radical beliefs, and persuaded to take up the king's side in the divorce.[4]

It is difficult to follow events during these months because the evidence is so fragmentary. But sometime during Lent of 1531 Frith returned secretly to England, apparently without a safe conduct and without the prior knowledge of any of the government officials trying

---

[1] For an account of Henry's dealings with Tyndale and Frith, see Mozley, pp. 187–211; Richard Marius, *Thomas More* (New York, 1984), pp. 386–96; cited hereafter as "Marius."

[2] Marius, pp. 387–90.

[3] Foxe, *4*, 658.

[4] Mozley, p. 197.

to reach him. It has been surmised that More's warfare against heretics and heretical books had so demoralized the evangelicals in England that Frith returned to encourage and reorganize them.[1] Why did he come secretly when Henry's agents were seeking him, presumably with a safe conduct? He may have supposed, as Tyndale did, that the safe conduct could not protect him from the clergy and from More, then waging a fierce war against heresy from his high office as lord chancellor.

However that may be, he made his way to Reading, where he hoped to make contact with the prior of Reading, a man sympathetic to the evangelical cause. But there he was arrested, so Foxe tells us, as a vagabond, put in the stocks, and released only when he spoke to the local schoolmaster in both Latin and Greek. Fulop suggests, probably correctly, that the subject of the polyglot conversation between the prisoner and the teacher was evangelical doctrine, and that the schoolmaster arranged for Frith's release out of sympathy for the young man's beliefs.[2] By then, Foxe says, More had learned of Frith's presence in England and had begun to scour the country for him, so that the young man was quickly taken and imprisoned.[3]

On March 22, 1531—a date that fell in Lent of that year—Eustace Chapuys, the imperial ambassador in London, wrote to the Emperor Charles V of a conversation he had had shortly before with the duke of Norfolk. Norfolk had mentioned that on the previous day "the finest and most learned preacher" among the Lutherans in England "had been arrested and was in danger of being publicly burnt alive." The duke was quite sorry at this prospect, "for he said the king had no fitter or better qualified man to send abroad on an embassy to a great prince."[4]

Chapuys reported that the Lutheran preacher was brought before Archbishop Warham and refused to answer questions unless lay members of the Privy Council might be in attendance. Accordingly, Norfolk along with Thomas Boleyn, Earl of Wiltshire, and other noblemen were assigned to the case, and before them, said Chapuys, "the said priest proceeded to make his declaration and propounded heresy

---

[1]Clebsch, p. 100. The evidence for Frith's trip is found in Stokesley's register and is reported by Fulop, p. 29.

[2]Fulop, pp. 94–95.

[3]Foxe, 5, 6.

[4]*Calendar of Letters, Despatches, and State Papers, relating to the Negotiations between England and Spain*, ed. G. A. Bergenroth et al., 13 vols. (London, 1862–1954), *4*, pt. 1, no. 664, p. 96; cited hereafter as *CSPS*.

enough." Two days afterward the man appealed to the king and was
conducted into the royal presence by several bishops who argued with
him. The king picked up a parchment roll containing a list of the
preacher's heresies and saw written first the claim that the pope was not
the sovereign chief of the Christian church. And, so Chapuys had
heard, Henry said, "This proposition cannot be counted on as heretical, for it is both true and certain." Afterward Henry sent the preacher
"back to his own dwelling on condition of preaching one of these days a
sermon, and retracting some of his doctrines which the King does not
consider as thoroughly orthodox."[1]

Who was this "Lutheran"? (Norfolk's ability to tell the difference
between a Lutheran and a Zwinglian is open to question; the duke was
not noted for his capacity to make subtle theological distinctions.)
Robert Barnes was in Wittenberg throughout 1531, and so this mysterious "Lutheran" could not have been he. Only Frith seems to stand
out as important enough for the notice of the duke of Norfolk and for
an intervention by the king himself. Since Henry had been seeking
Frith, he would have been eager to see the young man from whom his
councillors hoped for so much. The idea of sending Frith on an embassy, surely to support the king's divorce in foreign lands, would naturally have occurred to those who had experienced his charm and knew
of his gift for languages.

Indeed almost everything about the story fits with what we know of
the young and brilliant Frith, and the interview with the king and the
subsequent liberation of the preacher fit with what we know of Henry's
desire to win Frith over during 1531. (We cannot know exactly what
Chapuys meant by reporting that the "Lutheran" had been sent back to
"his own dwelling.") The incident would have been a crushing humiliation for More and reason enough for him to have passed it over in
silence in his later writing about Frith. It would also help explain the
relatively mild remarks about Frith, whom More often called simply
"the yong man" in his subsequent *Letter* impugning Frith's doctrines.
Since Frith was later burned as a heretic, those around Henry had little
motive for perpetuating the story of how the king had earlier released
him from custody. No later historian whom I have found identifies this
"Lutheran" or even dwells on the incident. Foxe knows nothing of it,
and we may be sure that had he heard of it, he would have reproduced
it in some fashion, however garbled, since it is exactly the sort of tale he
loves to tell. (Neither does Foxe know anything about the government's

---

[1]*CSPS 4*, no. 664, p. 96.

efforts to win Tyndale over.) So it may be that there was a later, successful campaign by the government to hush the matter up. Obviously we cannot be sure that this "Lutheran" was Frith, but no one else fits the evidence so well.

Whatever the agency, Frith did get free and returned to the Continent after this visit in 1531, remaining there until after More had resigned as lord chancellor. But within a few weeks after he had been apprehended, Cromwell was instructing his agent Vaughan[1] to find him, to offer him a safe conduct to come back to England, and to convey warm feelings from the king which might plausibly be supposed to have resulted from an earlier meeting. The king felt hopeful, Cromwell said, that the grace of God and the exhortations of good people might lead the young man away from the evil doctrines of Tyndale; but Cromwell did not say what doctrines those were, and since Henry's acquaintance with Tyndale's work was slight and Tyndale did not express himself unequivocally about the real presence, Henry might well have been uninformed about all the doctrines Tyndale and Frith agreed upon.[2] Vaughan reported at first that he could not locate Frith,[3] but then they did make contact, and it seems likely that they did meet, for on June 28, 1531, Vaughan wrote that he expected Frith to arrive soon in Antwerp, apparently for a conference.[4]

In July 1532 Frith came back to England for the last time. His biographer supposes that Frith returned for the same reasons that brought him back in 1531, because the evangelical congregations at home had been shattered by the burning or abjuration of many of their preachers and needed strong leadership.[5] Frith may have supposed that with More out of the way and, so rumor had it, suspected heretics being released, he might now have an access to the dissidents in England that had been previously denied him. If he was indeed the "Lutheran" in the story Chapuys tells, he would have had all the greater reason to suppose that he might be left unmolested if he returned to his homeland.

But in October 1532 he was arrested and confined to the Tower of London. Here he quickly impressed Edmund Walsyngham, lieutenant

---

[1] On Stephen Vaughan see Marius, pp. 387–89.
[2] LP 5, no. 248, pp. 113–14.
[3] LP 5, no. 246, p. 112.
[4] LP 5, no. 311, p. 146.
[5] Fulop, pp. 99–100.

of the Tower, who wrote Cromwell that it would be a great pity to lose
such a man as Frith if he could be reconciled. Lose him for what cause?
Obviously the king's divorce.[1] Cromwell himself visited Frith shortly
afterward, probably to win the young man over.[2] And Frith's arrest
may have been deliberately staged by the government to force the
young man to change his views and to come into the field in support of
the divorce.

FRITH'S *CHRISTIAN SENTENCE*

FRITH's imprisonment was not hard—at least not for a while. According to one tale, he was allowed out of the Tower at night to visit
other evangelicals.[3] This tale, though implausible, may be true. Henry's attitude toward Frith and other evangelicals must have thoroughly
confused some of his servants not privy to his thoughts, and Walsyngham may have let Frith roam in the belief that Henry would not
object. Even if the story is untrue, Frith did share imprisonment with
friends, and so he had companionship.[4] He was able to write, though
furtively, and one of several short works he produced was *A Christian
Sentence,* a small pamphlet intended to reconcile the warring evangelical factions.[5] The issue was dividing Protestant Englishmen just at
the moment when they required unity to survive, and the irenic Frith
hoped to make others irenic as well; yet he was not so irenic as to
forsake his efforts to convert them to his own view that the body and
blood of Christ were only symbolized in the eucharist and that the
bread remained only bread and the wine only wine.

Eventually English Protestants were to adopt a somewhat subtler
and more ambiguous version of Frith's view, but in 1532 no issue
created more dissension among them. Tyndale managed to get several
letters to Frith during Frith's imprisonment. Tyndale, whose metaphors suggest that he, too, rejected the doctrine of the real presence,
warned Frith to avoid as much as possible any discussion of the issue,
for "Barnes will be hot against you."[6] Barnes, a Lutheran who was
being assiduously and successfully courted by Henry and Henry's
agents during 1532, had fled to Wittenberg, where he had become a

---

[1]*LP* 5, no. 1458, pp. 615–16.
[2]*LP* 5, no. 1467, pp. 618–19.
[3]Fulop, p. 104.
[4]Fulop, p. 102; *LP* 5, no. 1467, pp. 618–19.
[5]Reprinted in this volume as Appendix C, pp. 427–33.
[6]Foxe, 5, 133.

great favorite of Luther's.[1] He held strong Lutheran sentiments in favor of the real presence of the body and blood of Christ in the bread and wine of the sacrament, and Tyndale knew he would fiercely oppose any sign of Zwinglianism, however mildly presented. Tyndale's caution was justified; later on Barnes was instrumental in procuring death by fire for the Zwinglian John Lambert, an incident that shamed John Foxe so much that the martyrologist could scarcely bear to write about it, and in what he did write he glossed over Barnes's role in the miserable affair.[2] It seemed clear to everyone that for Frith to speak or write openly about his convictions concerning the eucharist was to run terrible risks.

Yet Frith could not leave the subject alone. For one thing, he believed passionately in the mass as sign and symbol and not as vehicle for some real presence in the elements. For another, the evangelicals in England needed direction, and many of them looked to him for help in understanding what they were supposed to believe. According to Foxe, the young man entered into communication "with a certain old familiar friend of his" on the subject of the eucharist. We may infer from Foxe's account that the friend was allowed to visit Frith in prison and that the two men talked about the eucharist, for the friend asked Frith to set down his arguments so the friend could better remember them. Frith did not want to write anything, Foxe says, but at last "he, being overcome by the entreaty of his friend, rather followed his will, than looked to his own safeguard."[3]

The friend was thereupon convinced by a traitorous tailor, once William Holt, to lend the work. Holt carried the manuscript straight to More, "being then chancellor: which thing, afterwards, was occasion of great trouble, and also of death, unto the said Frith; for More, having not only gotten a copy of his book of this sycophant, but also two other copies, which at the same time, in a manner, were sent him by other promoters, he whetted his wits, and called his spirits together as much as he might, meaning to refute his opinion by a contrary book."[4] This account shows how confusing and inaccurate Foxe can sometimes be. More had resigned two months before Frith returned to England in 1532, and he had been out of office for months before Frith wrote the little book that More answered. But it is not at all surprising that copies

---

[1]See James P. Lusardi in *CW 8*, 1387.
[2]Foxe, 5, 227–28, 234.
[3]Foxe, 5, 6.
[4]Foxe, 5, 6–7.

of such heretical treatises were sent to More, who was well known from his previous writings as a defender of orthodoxy.

Frith's little book was entitled *A christen sentence and true judgement of the moste honorable Sacrament of Christes boddy & bloude declared both by the auctorite of the holy Scriptures and the auncient Doctores. Very necessary to be redde in this tyme of all the faythful.* The work was not printed until it appeared anonymously about 1545, and it has only recently been recognized as the pamphlet to which More replied in his *Letter against Frith.*[1]

Frith begins by pleading with his fellow evangelicals to put aside all strife over the doctrine of the physical presence of Christ in the eucharist until such time as God will make his will clear on the subject. Whatever we may believe about the real presence will neither damn us nor save us, he says.[2] In Frith's view, we are damned or saved according to what is in our hearts and not according to what we believe about the elements of the eucharist. But having made this declaration, he attacks the Catholic doctrine of transubstantiation with arguments similar to those used by Zwingli and Oecolampadius in their disputation with Luther over the real presence. The body of Christ "was natural and not phantasticall, but had the qualyties of an other body in all thynges saue synne." A body cannot be in two places at the same time, and since the body of Christ is in heaven, it cannot be in many places here on earth.[3] Frith manages to present this teaching with a condescending and ironic tone that belies the tolerance often claimed for him. At the end of his earthly ministry, Frith says, Jesus was taken up into heaven, and the angel testified that from thence he will come to judge the quick and the dead. "Nowe yf ye can perswade your owne consciences and vnderstande the Scriptures yᵗ he playde boo pype with his Disciples, and dyd but make hym selfe inuisible onely, than may ye take your pleasures, for Christe teacheth vs not to be contentious."[4]

But what did Christ mean when he said at the Last Supper, "This is my body"? Both Catholics and Lutherans in their different ways took him literally. Frith argued for a symbolic understanding of these words. Christ uses other figures to refer to himself, Frith says, and we do not take him literally. He called himself a door and a true vine; why

---

[1]Germain Marc'hadour, *Thomas More et la Bible* (Pairs, 1969), pp. 298, 302; cited hereafter as "Marc'hadour, *La Bible.*"

[2]Appendix C, 428/1–42.

[3]Appendix C, 429/8–30.

[4]Appendix C, 429/42–430/2.

should we suppose that he intended anything more than a similar figure when he said, "This is my body"?

To illustrate, Frith gives the example (common among the sacramentarians) of a hypothetical bridegroom required to make a long journey that would take him away from his bride for a long time. In parting, he might give her a ring as a reminder of his love.[1] So Christ gave the supper as a reminder of his love for his own bride, the church. Frith means that the bread and wine are only tokens of the presence of Christ, who has departed from this world. As the ring is not the bridegroom but a symbol of the bridegroom, so are the bread and the wine only symbols of the body and blood of Christ. The analogy was not original with Frith; it originated in Cornelius Hoen's sacramentarian pamphlet, which Zwingli printed in 1525.[2]

It naturally follows that if the elements in the eucharist are only symbols, no special priesthood is required to make those symbols efficacious. The priest has no effect on the sacrament, Frith says. Even if the priest should refuse to give the sacrament in both kinds, it does not matter. The true Christian can take what is offered with thanksgiving to God and will receive the full benefit of the sign. No matter what the priest says over the elements, they work as God intended so long as the heart of the recipient is faithful.[3] Frith ends his little treatise with a meek prayer: "But commytte you to God desyrynge hym to open his lyght more abundauntly vnto vs all that we may walke therin praysynge hym eternally."[4] The apparent meekness does not hide his conviction that when God does enlighten all Christians, they will agree with Frith.

For More the sacrament of the altar was the center of religious practice, and he was devoted to it throughout his life. He was vehemently hostile to the Zwinglian (and Frithian) teaching that the bread and the wine were mere signs. The issue was amazingly complex. In his *De captivitate Babylonica*, Luther maintained that the bread and the wine are not changed in the consecration of the mass but that the body and blood of Christ are added to the elements much as heat may be added to iron.[5] (Luther's doctrine is commonly called "consubstantiation" though he himself did not call it that.) Although More attacked Luther's view, he recognized that this doctrine, heretical though it

---

[1]Appendix C, 431/38–432/13.
[2]See *CW 11*, xx.
[3]Appendix C, 432/22–37.
[4]Appendix C, 433/24–26.
[5]*WA 6*, 510.

might be, was still closer to orthodoxy than the symbolic view of Zwingli, Tyndale, and Frith.[1] On this point he was apparently aware of the history of the formulation of the orthodox teaching about the eucharist.

In the eleventh century, Berengarius had taught a doctrine similar to that of the later sacramentarians, and he had been forced to recant, for that view was always regarded as outrageously heretical by the medieval church. The church taught that Christ was physically present in the eucharist. But how was that presence to be understood? The doctrines of transubstantiation and consubstantiation both affirmed the real presence, and it was only by a long historical evolution that transubstantiation won out. Modern scholars have set as the benchmark of the doctrine the Fourth Lateran Council of 1215, when, under the leadership of Pope Innocent III, transubstantiation was defined as the proper understanding of the eucharist. But for several decades after Fourth Lateran, writers on the subject regularly listed what came to be called consubstantiation as a view held by some Christians, and these writers did not call the doctrine heretical, though they generally disapproved of it. Thomas Aquinas was the first to call consubstantiation a heresy.[2]

The point at issue, as James F. McCue has called it, was always the real, that is to say a *physical,* presence in the eucharist, and this doctrine was no mere philosophical quibble, as Tyndale, Frith, and their mentor Zwingli held it to be. It was the central article of the faith that God never deserts his creation, that he is continuously present in the physical world where we live daily by the five senses, and that we are not cut off from him by our bodies and by our bodily existence in a bodily universe.

The doctrine of the real presence, whether it is expressed by consubstantiation or transubstantiation, is a firm pronouncement against the Manichaean dualism that in one form or another plagued Christianity from the time of the New Testament itself. It was a daily affirmation in the Catholic liturgy of the doctrine of the goodness of physical creation, the incarnation, the resurrection of the body, and the belief in monotheism that underlay the historical Christian faith. And it is no accident that the church gradually consolidated its faith around

---

[1] *CW 8*, 608.

[2] I have here summarized the splendid discussion by James F. McCue, "The Doctrine of Transubstantiation from Berengar through Trent: The Point at Issue," *Harvard Theological Review, 61* (1968), 385–430.

transubstantiation partly in reaction to the Cathar heresy of the twelfth and thirteenth centuries; for that heresy again injected into European religion a radical dualism of matter and spirit that threatened the historic Christian understanding of creation and redemption, the incarnation of Christ, and monotheism itself. The doctrine of the real presence is one way of affirming that the material creation is good and that the same God who created the world also acted in a human and physical Christ to redeem the world.[1]

It may be argued that those most likely to reject any doctrine of the real presence, whether transubstantiation or consubstantiation, were also likely to express their religion in terms reminiscent of the ancient dualistic heresy. Tyndale and Frith as well as Zwingli seemed to regard sin as *carnality*, by which they seemed to mean attention to the body. Most Catholic and Protestant interpreters of the apostle Paul have taken "flesh" in Paul's epistles as a principle within human beings warring against the spirit so that we are always at war within ourselves. "Flesh" does not mean "body" according to this standard Christian interpretation. God created the physical world, and though it may be corrupt, it cannot be evil by nature, although Cathars in the Middle Ages and Gnostics in the earlier centuries preferred to think of a god of pure spirit at war against the devil god of physicality.

Mainline Protestants, including Zwingli, could not become out-and-out dualists. Zwingli and Tyndale had to preserve some place for the notion of the earthly state as a divinely ordained institution that Christians might freely serve, doing the will of God. But much of Zwingli's rhetoric has a dualist tone, and the stark purgation from the Zwinglian liturgy of any expression that might smack of sensuous beauty—including instrumental music and songs not found in the book of Psalms—lends credence to the view that Zwingli found the physical unworthy to bear the divine. In 1525, the same year that Tyndale published his English New Testament, Zwingli published his *De vera et falsa religione commentarius,* an influential compendium of his theology.[2] Here he

---

[1] For some insight into how important the doctrine of transubstantiation was in the battle against the Cathar or Albigensian heresy, see Eckbertos Schoneugiensis, "Sermones contra catharos," *PL 195,* 15, 84–97. The famous formulation of the doctrine of transubstantiation at the Fourth Lateran Council of 1215 appears as a kind of introduction to the constitutions of the council within a list of Catholic affirmations of dogma directed against heretical beliefs held by the Cathars. It does not occupy a singular rhetorical position in the list of received doctrines here affirmed, and that is probably why Fourth Lateran was not recognized as a landmark in the debate over transubstantiation until several decades had passed. See Alberigo, pp. 206–7.

[2] *CRZ 3,* 590–912.

speaks much of the warfare of "flesh" and the soul, and in his eucharistic doctrine in particular he seems to teach that body *qua* body is unworthy of containing Christ.[1] Again and again he seems to equate "flesh" with "body"; over and over he quotes the phrase "caro non prodest quicquam" (John 6:63) as proof that the "body" in Christ's words of the institution of the eucharist cannot possibly be meant literally as the body of Christ, the real presence in the eucharist. In a ringing sentence he declares: "Et, quod quicquid corpus est, quicquid sensibile, fidei obiectum esse nulla via potest."[2] Religious beliefs are rarely systematic or carried to their logical conclusions. But it is not surprising that such beliefs, expressed as vehemently as Zwingli and then Frith expressed them, seemed to undermine not only a Catholic doctrine but the entire orthodox Christian conception of God's relation to creation. Such doctrines would naturally undermine all the sacraments, depending as they did (and do) on the faith that God's spirit can regularly use a physical vehicle to communicate with us—creatures as we are of spirit and body.

The eucharistic controversy also raised the question of whether human social and civic life is possible and whether there can be any optimism about the daily life in the world. As it was, Zwingli and his English disciples saw the godly prince or council as the divine instrument for reformation, and so they were prohibited by their political hopes from falling into the radical dualism of the Cathars. But some of the Anabaptist and spiritualist sects that separated from the Zwinglian movement did go all the way in the journey toward heretical dualism, and it is altogether consistent with their theology that they rejected not only the sacraments but also the religious value of the secular world.

MORE'S DEFENSE OF THE REAL PRESENCE
AGAINST FRITH

MORE followed the progress of Frith's case carefully and, we may imagine, with dismay. In his *Apology*, published in April 1533, when Frith had lost the king's favor and was well along his way to the stake, he defends himself against the charge that he had eagerly wished for Frith's death. He says that someone told him "that Fryth labored so sore that he swette agayne, in studyeng and wrytyng agaynst the blessed sacrament." The news, More says, made him sad, and he wished that "the yonge folysshe felowe" had a good Christian friend who might draw him away from "that frantyke heresye," which was

---

[1]*CRZ 3*, 792.
[2]*CRZ 3*, 798.

enough to make him "perysshe bothe body and soule." If Frith should write against the sacrament, More said, it would all be in vain, since neither Frith nor all his fellows in heresy could destroy this faith of all Christian men. More recalls that he told his informant "that yf Fryth laboure aboute the quenchynge therof tyll he swete / I wolde some good frend of hys shold shew hym, that I fere me sore that Cryst wyll kyndle a fyre of fagottes for hym, & make hym therin swete the bloude out of hys body here, and strayte frome hense send hys soule for euer into the fyre of hell."[1]

More's account in *The Apology* of how he came to write against Frith reveals a certain anxiety. He says, "For ye shall vnderstand, that after that Fryth had wryten a false folysshe treatyce agaynste the blessed sacrament of ye aulter / I hauyng a copy therof sent vnto me, made shortely an answere therto."[2] More's reply was finished at Chelsea on December 7, 1532, and was in print before the end of the year. But More comments that Frith's work "was not put abrode in prent." Consequently, he says, he did not want his reply to be indiscriminately distributed, "For as I haue often sayde, I wolde wysshe that the comon people sholde of suche heresyes neuer here so myche as the name."[3] He had his own work printed, he says, "vnder myne own name, to thentent I myghte as in dede I haue, gyue oute some to suche as I perceyued had sene hys boke before."[4] The words "vnder myne own name" may be set in contrast to the works of heretics published anonymously or under pseudonyms. Or it may mean that More had his little book against Frith printed at his own expense and delivered to him rather than spread around in bookshops, and the remark may offer us some clue as to how More managed to keep on publishing his work throughout 1533, when the mood of the government was against him and booksellers were probably not willing to take his work on speculation. But the most important inference we can draw from this passage is that More wanted to avoid spreading the controversy among the volatile English people, where firebrands might use it to widen the circle of damage already inflicted on the Catholic church.

Until December 1533, when he released it to be sold together with his *Answer to a Poisoned Book* (a much more elaborate defense of the real presence),[5] More distributed his reply to Frith only to those he thought

---

[1]*CW 9*, 122/16–21.
[2]*CW 9*, 123/25–28.
[3]*CW 9*, 123/28–31.
[4]*CW 9*, 124/10–12.
[5]See *CW 11*, xxxi–xxxii.

should see it. He titled it *A letter of syr Tho. More kynght impugnynge the erronyouse wrytyng of Iohan Fryth agaynst the blessed sacrament of the aultare*. More's tone in this small work is surprisingly gentle. We find none of the furious invective that marks and mars his other polemical works. Frith is throughout "the yong man," and More seems to take him as one led astray by a vainglorious trust in his own wit, a young man who may be led back to the way.

Why did More treat Frith so kindly, especially since Frith espoused a heresy that More and centuries of church tradition before him regarded as particularly heinous? We have already touched upon one plausible explanation: Frith was at this time a counter in Henry's game against the pope. If Frith was indeed the "Lutheran" released by Henry in March 1531, More had run head-on against the king's will and had suffered a humiliating defeat.

All the evidence shows that the government's efforts to win Frith over were continuing vigorously late in 1532. We know that Frith first saw More's reply to him in the London home of Stephen Gardiner, his old teacher, now bishop of Winchester. It was the day after Christmas, and Gardiner had evidently removed Frith from the Tower for the holidays. In his *Apology* More put the best face he could on Gardiner's kindness, saying that the bishop was only exercising a "fatherly favor" toward one who had once waited on him and been his student.[1] It seems true that even to the last Gardiner hoped for Frith's redemption from a heresy which the bishop abhorred. His kindness in having Frith to his home during the holidays was extraordinary. But even here More mentions "other causes" prompting Gardiner's interest in Frith.

Chief among these "other causes" was surely the divorce. Gardiner was conservative about priesthood and the liberties of the church from the secular authority, but he supported the divorce.[2] He and others advising Henry on religious matters wanted Frith's brilliance on their side. All the arguments for the divorce turned on studious and complex inquiries into the writings of the fathers of the church to see how they had interpreted the fatal text of Leviticus that Henry claimed as the source of his scruples of conscience. Frith knew the fathers so well that Gardiner and others may have supposed him able to fit both the royal supremacy and the divorce into an argument based on the ancient doctors, whose writings on both marriage and the papacy were nebulous and contradictory and hence capable of yielding proof texts

---

[1] *CW* 9, 124.

[2] See the standard biography by J. A. Muller, *Stephen Gardiner and the Tudor Reaction* (New York, 1926).

that might testify against Henry's union with Catherine of Aragon. Gardiner, and later Thomas Cranmer, who would become archbishop of Canterbury on Warham's death, apparently strove to get Frith to moderate his view on the eucharist so that he could be useful in other ways.

In the last month of 1532, More faced a terrible dilemma. He had to refute a heretic, but the heretic had attracted the benign interest of Henry VIII and his government. It was not politic to attack such a man with the usual invective. For one thing, if the "Lutheran preacher" released on Henry's command in 1531 was indeed Frith, More would be placing Henry in a most embarrassing position by calling vehement, public attention to Frith's heresies on the eucharist. And yet More knew that Henry detested the sacramentarian view that Frith espoused. Henry had defended transubstantiation stridently in his *Assertio septem sacramentorum,* and he believed in transubstantiation until he died. In 1538 he presided in person over the trial of John Lambert for holding the same sacramentarian views that Frith held. He bullied Lambert unmercifully during the hearing and sat by in majestic satisfaction while Thomas Cromwell read the sentence of death to the unresisting victim.[1] It is entirely possible that Henry's closest religious advisers had hidden from him the extent of Frith's heresies, hoping that they could get the young man to return to the orthodox faith before Henry found out how far he had deviated from it.

In *The Apology,* published when Henry's flirtation with Frith was over, More wrote that Frith did not want the "brotherhood" to know his true sentiments about the eucharist,[2] and this comment probably reflects the reluctance we have noted in Tyndale (and in Frith as well) to shift the theological debate from what they regarded as more important issues to the doctrine of the eucharist. It is quite unlikely that Henry—never a great reader of books—had read anything Frith had written or even suspected how radical the man was. More's tactic, then, seems to have been to inform his sovereign, in a mild and somewhat indirect way, about the man the king's advisers were trying to bring over to his side. He could explain his own reluctance to bring his work into print because Frith's own little pamphlet had not been printed: "I wolde not therefore lette myne runne abrode in mennes handes" since he always wished "that the comon people sholde of suche heresyes neuer here so mych as the name."[3] It is an explanation that rings

[1]Foxe, 5, 234.
[2]*CW 9,* 124–25.
[3]*CW 9,* 126.

hollow, given More's enormous printed production of polemical works
against heresy, though there can be no doubt that the general sentiment expressed here was true enough. But it was a truth that probably
covered other truths: that More's little book, distributed where it
would do the most good, would have served to make it impossible to
keep from Henry Frith's views of the eucharist; that it would have
revealed to others just what it was that Frith believed; and that it would
have made the government's dealings with the young man publicly
embarrassing or even dangerous.

Seen in this light, the book is an exercise of considerable rhetorical
merit. His tactic of not addressing the work to Frith himself but to a
third party who has asked for advice both provides a rhetorical justification for writing the book and removes More a step from the center of
the stage, making him appear to be a minor player commenting on the
main drama rather than taking part directly in it—a part befitting a
retired lord chancellor.

His praise for Henry, who "lyke a most faythfull catholyke prynce"
has by royal proclamation forbade "suche pestylente bokes as sowe
suche poysened heresyes among his people" and interdicted the im-
portation of all books printed in English beyond the sea (233/8–12),
both guards More's little tractate from the accusation that it is written
against the government and announces the course that good Catholic
Englishmen approve in their king. With skillful understanding of a
government always worried about disorder, he shifts immediately to
his old saw that heresy leads to sedition so "that it burneth vp whole
townes, and wasteth whole countrees, ere euer it can be maystered"
(234/10–11).

It is a powerful image, and one fully in keeping with the Thomas
More whose Utopians considered private gatherings of people to discuss things in secret as a threat to society at large.[1] The general theme,
that heresy and sedition go hand in hand, runs throughout More's
polemical works and is expressed with special vehemence in the introduction to The Confutation.[2] At a time when the government was acutely
worried about public opinion and when the imperial ambassador was
speculating hopefully about the increasing popularity of Catherine of
Aragon, More's shots about sedition must have found a mark here and
there, especially when they were tied to a doctrine of such importance.

Against Frith's arguments, More brings his own favorite argument
—the venerable and sacred tradition of the Catholic church, the

[1]CW 4, 124–25.
[2]CW 8, 29–34.

consensus fidelium. Christ clearly said in John 6, "My flesh is veryly mete, and my blode is verily drynke" (235/11–12). The sacred doctors of the church took Christ literally, and so has the church done for fifteen hundred years (236/28–30). We do not take literally the sayings of Christ that he is a door and that he is the true vine, because context shows that these statements are not to be taken literally. Zwingli and his disciples regularly argued that Christ's words of institution at the eucharist were nothing more than allegories, like so many other allegories in the gospels.[1] But this will not do for More. Writing of Christ's statements about the eucharist on the one hand and of those about doors and vines on the other, More says, "And thcrfore it appereth well, that ye maner of speaking was nat lyke. For if it had / than wolde nat the old exposytours haue vsed suche so far vnlyke fashyon in ye expounyng of them" (240/21–23). To decide that because allegories appear in one place in scripture they must appear everywhere is nonsense, "Whyche yf it may be suffered, muste nedes make all the scrypture as towchyng any poynt of our fayth, of none effecte or force at all" (238/1–3). Frith aligns himself, says More, not with the constant church tradition but with the perversions of heretics going back to Arius, the greatest heretic of all (239/1–9). The Arians, More says, tried to take from Christ his "omnipotent godhed" (238/19–20) by misinterpreting plain texts of scripture that affirm the equality of Christ with God. More points out that the church has always agreed that Christ was the son of God. But the Arians took other texts where the term *god* or *son of god* was used in a clearly metaphorical way, and they argued from these texts that such terms applied to Christ must also be understood metaphorically or—as More says—allegorically. He was evidently thinking of the Arian use of such texts as Exodus 7:1, where God tells Moses, "Behold, I shall make you the god of Pharaoh," or Exodus 22:28, where God commands Israel, "Do not slander the gods" in a passage that clearly intends "gods" to refer to mortal leaders of the people. The Arians, as More points out, fell avidly on such texts to argue that Christ was not the son of God in any unique way. They believed that Christ was a creature, something made, and their doctrine became a threat to the church just because it did seem to have so many texts of scripture to support it.[2] More's point was that the Arians took the obvious allegorical sense of some passages of scripture and

---

[1]For example, *CRZ 3,* 796.

[2]For a summary of Arian proof texts, see J. N. D. Kelly, *Early Christian Doctrines,* 2nd ed. (New York, 1960), pp. 229–31.

tried to use it to corrupt the obvious literal sense of other passages that
declared Christ to be the son of God. Allegory has no standard except
the tradition of the church, and throughout the Middle Ages theologians were reluctant to allow disputation that depended on allegory.
Allegory, like metaphor, might illustrate doctrines established in other
ways, but allegory could not establish doctrine by itself. If scripture
were to be interpreted in such a fashion, no Christian doctrine, not
even those professed by Protestants and Catholics alike, could long
endure. The point has a special irony, for More's Protestant opponents
claimed always to renounce allegory and to depend on the plain, literal
meaning of the text of scripture.

More then turns to Frith's claim that the body of Christ can be in only
one place at once and that it is therefore impossible for that body to be
present in the eucharist. Here once again More discusses the relation
of reason and faith, a principal issue of scholastic thought and one that
became acute in the religious thought of the sixteenth century, when
confidence that both reason and faith led to God, though by different
routes, was breaking down.

More holds against Frith that it is impossible for human reason to
understand how God can make the body of Christ be in several places
at once—in heaven and in the eucharist as the mass is said throughout
Christendom every day. But nothing is impossible for God, and reason
set against God's revelation cannot be heard (243/19–24). Frith has
argued that Christ's body was natural like our own and that Christ
could no more be in many places at once than Frith can be, and he has
claimed the authority of a dubious text from Augustine to support his
view. But More replies with a thundering pronouncement: "But yf
Chryste wolde telle me that he wolde make eche of bothe theyr bodyes
too be in fyftene places at ones, I wolde byleue hym I, that he were able
to make hys worde trewe in the bodyes of bothe twayne / and neuer
wolde I soo myche as aske hym whyther he wolde gloryfye them bothe
fyrste or not. But I am sure gloryfyed or vngloryfyed, yf he sayde it he
is able to do it" (246/10–16). Christ told his disciples that it was as
impossible for a rich man to be saved as it was for a camel to go through
the eye of a needle, but he also said that all things were possible to God,
and, in More's view, God can make the camel pass through the eye of a
needle, save a rich man, and make both Christ's body and Frith's body
be in two places at once. The right question for the Christian is always
this: What has God said? For whatever God has said, that God will do.
The wrong question is always this: How can I understand how what
God says is reasonable or not?

The dubious text Frith adduces from Augustine costs More a lot of effort in this argument. According to Frith, Augustine declared: "Corpus in quo resurrexit in vno loco esse oportet."[1] It happens to be the only patristic text cited in *A Christian Sentence,* but Frith does not tell where it is located.[2] More accepts the authenticity of the text merely for the sake of argument though he protests that to find one line out of all the saint's books was like seeking a needle in a meadow (243/27–28). Even if the text is genuine, More says, it does not mean that Christ's body must be in heaven and nowhere else. It may mean that Christ "muste haue one place for hys specyall place, and that place must be heuen / as we say god must be in heuen, and angels muste be in heuen" (244/7–10). The point is that when we say Christ in his physical body is in heaven, we do not mean that that same physical Christ cannot be on earth at the same time. In effect More is making a Trinitarian argument and an incarnational statement with almost the same stroke of his pen, making Christ have all the attributes of God and holding that while "heaven" is a name for the special place of God, the name does not imply that God is in one place and that we are in another. God's place is special, but it embraces our place just as the unseen world— always so near in More's works (including the *Utopia,* where the dead are believed to be "present when they are talked about, though invisible to the dull sight of mortals")[3]—is never in some remote and isolated place away from this world but includes our world although our mortal senses do not take it in. More's argument from this dubious text reaches out, then, spontaneously to incarnational theology as the principal significance of the doctrine of transubstantiation. Christ is not *there* and we are not *here* as if *there* and *here* were two different countries; God and Christ his son exist in a special realm (we are tempted, in today's jargon, to say a "special dimension") which transcends but is not cut off from creation, and Christ can be in that special realm and be present also here with us in the sacrament that we perceive with our senses.

From the theological argument which he so effortlessly adduces, More turns quickly to a simple grammatical statement. The Latin word *oportet* used in Frith's citation of Augustine means "it is necessary." But More quotes Christ in Luke 24:26, "Nonne haec oportuit pati Christum, et ita intrare in gloriam suam?" (The words were spoken by

---

[1] Appendix C, 429/20–21.

[2] It comes from a collection of Augustinian texts hashed together by Gratian. Melanchthon had already placed this sentence in its true Augustinian context and showed that it applied to Christ's *visible* presence on earth as a preacher. See *CW 11,* lv.

[3] *CW 4,* 225.

the risen Christ to two of his followers on the road to Emmaus on the day of the Resurrection.) In John 10:18, More points out, Jesus claims that he gives up his life of his own free will, and the messianic prophecy of Isaiah 53 foretells the same choice (244/17–27). So clearly, More holds, *oportet* does not imply the necessity that negates any choice of alternatives; the word can refer to convenience or expediency. And Augustine's words mean only that the body of Christ must be in one place but not that it can be in no more than one.

All these arguments, so carefully woven from an Augustinian text that More cannot identify, support his most fundamental argument that God can do what he wishes and that our natural reason cannot comprehend his ways. We may choose to believe God; we cannot choose to understand him or to match our reason with his will. God can do whatever he says he will do, for if there were anything that God could not do, "than were god not almyghty" (247/28).

As people nearly always do when they attempt to reconcile faith and reason, More turns to some common experiences and uses some analogies familiar in the long debate over the nature of the real presence. His underlying point about reason is that true reason always recognizes its own limitations. He always believed that unfathomable mysteries run through the "comon course of nature here in erthe," as he says in his *Letter against Frith* (248/18–19). Frith holds that the body of Christ cannot be in several places at once, but More says that one face may be seen in several mirrors at once and that if one mirror is broken into twenty, the face is duplicated twenty times (248/20–21). Turning from this analogy (a standard illustration of transubstantiation), he takes up one of his favorite examples of how reason might declare something to be impossible unless the eyes testified that it was indeed so—here glassmaking. He comments on the marvel of making glass itself from "suche mater as it is made of" (248/22–23), doubtless wondering at how molten sand and ashes from ferns can produce a substance so unlike them both.[1] And if Frith and others are driven to turn into allegory those literal texts which they believe make impossible claims, no article of our faith can finally stand (249/7–16).

In concluding his brief arguments against the real presence, Frith

---

[1]More's fascination with glass is constant; his Utopians have glass windows in their houses (*CW 4*, 123), and in his *Dialogue Concerning Heresies* he mentions glass manufacture to make the same point that he makes here, that many things that seem impossible to natural reason when considered in the abstract are not only possible but are parts of daily life (*CW 6*, 66).

says: "Besydes that ye can shewe no reason why he shulde be in many places at once, and not in all, but in all places at once he can not be, wherfore we must conclude that he can not be in many places at once."[1] Although the argument is brief, its vocabulary reflects some traditional preoccupations of Christian theology (nor is the argument original with Frith). Frith has begun by declaring that the body of Christ was "natural and not phantasticall."[2] He has thereby made an incarnational statement in an effort to guard himself against the charge of Manichaean dualism that threatened the Christian doctrine of creation for centuries. Christ has a real body; it is not a mere illusion, not a disguise, not a fantasy. It is a body like all other human bodies except that it is without sin. And therefore it cannot be everywhere at once.

But Frith's argument calls forth More's deepest scorn and makes him condescend to teach Frith a lesson in logic. He traces out Frith's line of reasoning. Frith's argument has been first to say that it is not physically possible for a body to be in two places at once. Then he holds that it is not possible for God to make his body occupy two places at once unless we could tell how and why and whereby and show the reason (249/29–32). More, always the lawyer and ever the lover of disputations in universities, reduces Frith's argument to a syllogism (250/4–10):

Major premise:	If the body of Christ can be in many places at once, then it can be in all places at once.
Minor premise:	But in all places at once it cannot be.
Conclusion:	Therefore, it cannot be in many places at once.

More argues that the form of the major premise leads to a bad argument. It would be an absolute argument to say the following: He may be in all places; therefore, he may be in many. But to state the argument as Frith states it, "He may be in many places; therefore, he may be in all," is as fallacious as this statement: "Many men run; therefore, all men run"; or this one: "Men run in many places; therefore, men run in all places." As More shows, the syllogism is not valid according to the ancient laws of logic that govern the making of syllogisms. It begins with a fallacy and can lead only to a fallacious conclusion.

Having demonstrated that Frith's way of stating an argument is baldly deficient, More turns to the minor premise, which, as he says, contains the substance of Frith's case: The body of Christ cannot be in

---

[1]Appendix C, 429/27–30.
[2]Appendix C, 429/8–9.

all places at the same time. How, asks More, does Frith prove such a proposition (250/20–23)? More is content to declare that since God is almighty, he can do anything he wants, and if he wishes to make the body of Christ be all places at once, he can do that. If Frith says otherwise, he limits the power of God (251/9–10). And More enjoys himself by commenting on the foolishness Frith exhibits by doing such a thing: "I am in good fayth sory to se thys yong man presume so farre vpon hys wytte, so soone ere it be full rype. For surely suche lykynge of theym selfe maketh many wyttes waxe roten ere they waxe rype" (251/28–31). More very carefully does not say that Christ's body *is* everywhere in the universe; he says merely that God could make it so if God so willed.

He attacks Frith for saying "that euery man may in thys mater wythout parell byleue whych waye he lyst" (252/21–22). More claims that the correct doctrine of the eucharist is taught in scripture and in the writings of "the olde holy fathers interpretours of the scrypture" (252/31). It cannot, therefore, be a matter of indifference in faith. Henry VIII, says More, has written in response to Luther on this same point after Luther, in *De captivitate Babylonica,* had declared that Christians may believe in either consubstantiation or transubstantiation without peril to their souls. The king responded that if Luther granted that the orthodox belief was no peril and that if all the church thought that Luther's belief was peril indeed, Luther condemned his belief out of his own mouth and provided an excellent argument that might allow Christians to persevere in the old faith (253/21–39). In More's view, to dispute a doctrine agreed upon by the consensus of the church was to substitute private judgment for divine revelation and thereby to commit a blasphemy unforgivable if unrepented.

More seems to take note, however obliquely, of the efforts to win Frith back to the old faith, but he does not do so gently. With heretics he was always more likely to flail than entice.

> Lo thys reason of the kynges grace clerely concludeth thys yonge man vppon hys owne confessyon / and playnely proueth that excepte he leue hys bylyefe whyche all good chrysten folke holde for dampnable, and come home agayne to hys olde fayth yᵉ comon fayth of all the chyrch / in whych as hym selfe agreeth there is no perell: I wyll not for courtesye saye he is starke madde / but surely I wyll say that for his owne soule, the yong man playeth a very yonge wanton pageaunt. [253/34–254/2]

As for Frith's concluding remarks about priesthood and its unimportance to the sacrament, More returns to the traditional view of the church formulated against the Donatists in the time of Augustine.[1] The priest is necessary to the sacrament, but his malice or his oversight cannot damage our participation in the mass, since the mercy of God supplements the failings of the priest "yf there be no faute vpon our owne part" (254/12–14). But if we take the sacrament when we know that it is unblessed and unconsecrated and "care not whyther Crystes instytucyon be kepte and obserued or no, but reken it is as good wythout it as wyth it / than make we our selfe parteners of the faute, and lese the profyte of the sacrament, and receyue it with dampnacyon / not for the prestes faute but for our own" (254/21–25).

In concluding, More makes some remarks to show how isolated Frith is in his sacramentarian doctrine. He says that Berengarius was the first to fall into Frith's error but that he freely recanted the error when he had better considered the doctrine "and for bycause he had ones holden it, the good man dyd of hys owne good minde vncompelled grete penaunce wyllyngly all his lyfe after" (255/22–24). Berengarius must not have recanted as freely as More claims he did, since he was forced to make a second confession some two decades after his first. Still the fundamental point is sound, since it is clear that Berengarius held a view similar to that of Frith and Zwingli and his opinion was universally execrated.

More also points out that Robert Barnes abhorred Frith's heresy and makes a startling revelation:

> For at hys laste beynge here, he wrote a letter to me of hys own hand / wherin he wryteth that I lay that heresye wrongfully to his charge / and therin he taketh wytnesse of god and hys conscyence / and sheweth hym self so sore greued therwyth, that any man shold so repute hym by my wrytyng, that he sayth he wyll in my reproche make a boke agaynst me, wherin he wyll professe and proteste hys faythe concernyng thys blessed sacrament. [255/28–35]

It may be that Barnes was alarmed by More's accusation because he thought that Henry might believe it and that he wanted at all costs to purge that suspicion from the royal mind. We do not know. But More was able in a remarkable way to demonstrate the divisions of the heretics and Frith's relative isolation even in the ranks of the evangelicals. (The later role of Barnes in bringing Lambert to the stake shows how

---

[1]Jaroslav Pelikan, *The Emergence of the Catholic Tradition (100–600)*, vol. 1 of *The Christian Tradition: A History of the Development of Doctrine* (Chicago, 1971), pp. 309–13.

passionately Barnes felt about the matter, and his letter to More demonstrates his concern that he isolate himself from such a manifest heresy as Frith's.) Enjoying his advantage, More took a condescending swipe at Frith's youth and inexperience:

> It well contenteth me that frere Barns beynge a man of more age, and more rype dyscressyon and a doctour of diuinyte, & in these thynges better lerned than thys yonge man is / abhorreth thys yonge mannes heresy in this poynt, as well as he lyketh hym in many other. [256/8–12]

At the end More composes a prayer for the reception of the sacrament in response to Frith's concluding prayer, for which, More says, "I wold not gyue ye paryng of a pere for his prayour though it were better than it is, pullynge a waye the trewe fayth therfore as he doth" (257/13–15). Every good Christian woman could make a better prayer, he says, giving then a moving confession of what it was for simple people to share in the eternal life of Christ by partaking of the host at the mass (257/15–258/2).

More's prayer provides as well as anything might the theological and devotional rationale for the doctrine of the real presence. It is the joining of two worlds, the spiritual and the physical, under God, one creator. The body of Christ will endure eternally in heaven, and so More sees the mass as a communion that joins time and eternity and all the created order.

More's position is consistent not only with the tradition of the Catholic church but also with his own religious sentiments. He argued always that religion and religious truth unfolded in a world compatible with the daily life of Christians. He was a thoroughly incarnational thinker, seeing the divine union of a secret mystery with a bodily presence that the entire Christian community could know in the same way that we know houses and hills, the earth under our feet, the sky above, the whole created world of space and time, the world made by God and preserved by God and in the end to be redeemed by God at the great day of doom and the resurrection of the dead.

For Thomas More religion was never compelling merely because it satisfied the requirements of abstract reason, formal logic, or what might pass for common sense. He interpreted his faith in such a way that it harmonized with experience and sanctified the common perceptions of ordinary people at worship. His religious vision embraced those toiling Christians who took comfort from the sacrament of the altar and their faith in the physical presence of Christ that came to them in their physical world where they had to make their way. For

More the religious experience was an experience also of generations, of centuries, that had taken a similar comfort in similar worlds of time.

His argument against Frith comes down to this: simple Christians have trusted for centuries that they receive Christ physically in the mass; you cannot rob them and future generations of that experience merely because you decide that it does not make sense. More's God never made himself a tyrant over that experience; instead he dealt with his creation with a sense of measure appropriate to a divine father stooping to consider the nature of his children. One of More's favorite scriptural texts was 1 Corinthians 10:13: "God is faythfull whiche shall not suffre you to be tempted aboue y^t ye may bere / but with the temptacyon shall also make you a way to get out, so that ye may well welde it."[1] God does not ignore our being; he preserves the right measure for all parts of our human condition.

FRITH'S COUNTERATTACK AND DEATH

MORE sent his little book around to people who, he thought, might profit from it. Foxe gives us to understand that More's answer to Frith's attack on the eucharist helped drive Frith to his death, and although we have seen how confused Foxe is about Frith's comings and goings, it may be that here he preserves the substance of truth. More himself reports in his *Apology* that Gardiner had perceived that Frith did not want his views on the eucharist to become general knowledge beyond the "brotherhood." While Frith was at Gardiner's house during Christmas of 1532, the bishop told him that it was too late for secrecy, saying (so More reports), "For your bokes of this mater haue ben sene abrode in many mennes handes / and that so longe, that lo here is an answere allredy made vnto yt."[2] Thereupon the bishop showed Frith More's *Letter* "in prent" as proof that Frith's heresy was widely known. (The bishop's motive for showing Frith More's book was almost certainly to put greater pressure on the young man to recant his beliefs about the sacrament. Now that those beliefs were known, Frith would have lost much support from among evangelicals and he would have been in much greater danger of burning.) At the time he wrote his *Apology*, More knew that Frith was hard at work on a reply and knew also—doubtless from his informants—that some of Frith's friends had smuggled books in to him to help the young man with his writing and that Frith had "begonne and gone on a great way in a newe boke agaynste

---

[1]More's translation appears in *CW 8,* 553–54, and in many other places in his works.
[2]*CW 9,* 125.

the sacrament."[1] More also knew, by the time he wrote his *Apology,* that Tyndale and George Joye had got letters to Frith, urging him to stand fast.[2]

Gardiner would not let Frith have the book, More says, but Frith obtained a copy anyway and began to reply to More's work under the pretense that the *Letter* had really been written by Gardiner. This pretense, More said, arose "of a solempne pryde that he wolde haue his boke seme a dysputacyon betwene the boy and the byshoppe."[3] More wrote that when Frith had finished the book and the work "happeth to come to myne handes, I trust to make almost euery boy able to perceyue the false foly thereof, though he couer hys roten frute as close and as comely as euer any costerdmonger couered hys basket."[4] He never wrote this second answer, though he was still speaking of it in *The Answer to a Poisoned Book.*[5]

This detailed information that More gives in his *Apology* about Frith's activities must have been disconcerting to evangelicals, who were thus able to see how well informed More was, and it must have also been disconcerting to the government to have it noised abroad that Frith's friends were able to communicate with him so readily and to deliver books to aid him in his writing. Above all, More's knowledge of his activities must have created some anxiety in Frith himself and, rather than making him recant, gave him the boldness of desperation. If his beliefs were no longer secret, he could see that he was now in a battle for his life that he might well lose, and if he was indeed headed for the stake, he might as well express himself fully and clearly. When he did reply, he wrote of being "bounde at the bushopes pleasures / euer lokynge for the day of my dethe."[6]

And reply he did, obviously stung by More's arguments and driven to defend himself and his doctrines. The reply was printed shortly after his death under the title *A boke . . . answeringe vnto M mores lettur.* It was well over three times as large as More's *Letter* and represents altogether an aggressive restatement of all the arguments made in *A Christian Sentence.*

---

[1]*CW* 9, 125.
[2]*CW* 9, 91.
[3]*CW* 9, 125.
[4]*CW* 9, 125–26.
[5]*CW* 11, 10.
[6]*A boke made by Iohn Frith prisoner in the tower of London / answeringe vnto M mores lettur* . . . (n.p., 1533; STC 11381; Hume, no. 30), sig. B₄; cited hereafter as "*A boke . . . answeringe vnto M mores lettur.*"

From the first he acknowledges More's authorship and does not try to use the ploy of boy versus bishop that More claimed the young man was planning to use in the work. (More's announcement of this intention in *The Apology* would have been enough to deter Frith from such a course if ever he had contemplated it.) He puzzled over the secrecy in which More had written and circulated the *Letter* against his doctrines. He had seen the work in print "in my lorde of wynchesters howse / vppon S. Stephyns day [December 26] last paste," he says. "But neither I nether all the fryndes I cowd make / mighte attayne any copie / but only one wrytyn copie which as yt semed was drawyn oute in great haste."[1] He suggests that More may have been ashamed of the book and thus sought to keep it from circulating—a suggestion that may reveal how ignorant he was of the masterly way in which More was maneuvering him and the government at once.

Having mocked More, he plunges into a point-by-point refutation of More's work, and by the time he is done, his treatise is as good as a death warrant. His arguments, carefully spelled out, are not without interest, especially as they reflect some of the fundamental concerns of people like himself and of the times in general. He makes a list of things that God cannot do: he cannot save the unfaithful; he cannot restore lost virginity; he cannot sin. These remarks, however plausible, went sharply against the theological spirit of the age, in which thinkers began with the assumption that God, through his absolute power, could do anything he chose but that, through his ordained power, he chose to do only what he had promised. His reply is much more learned than his original statement, particularly in his use of patristic sources.

He brings up the old stercorian argument, complaining that if we accept the doctrine that we eat the physical body of Christ in the sacrament, it follows that the body of Christ must be defecated, "ẃ thinge is abominable."[2] He steadfastly maintains that Augustine supports his position in the interpretation of the eucharist. And he holds that the honor and worship shown the eucharist among Catholics "is plaine Idolatrye."[3] His work seems to confirm More's accusation that he had books smuggled into his cell, for he quotes the fathers frequently—especially Augustine—and he argues more sharply and in much greater detail than in *A Christian Sentence*. But his clarity was his undoing, for

---

[1] *A boke . . . answeringe vnto M mores lettur*, sig. A₃.
[2] *A boke . . . answeringe vnto M mores lettur*, sig. F₇.
[3] *A boke . . . answeringe vnto M mores lettur*, sig. H₃.

LETTER AGAINST FRITH   clv

now the government could not use him for its own purposes without
testifying to all the world and above all to the fundamentally conservative and Catholic English people that the cost of Henry's divorce
would be heresy, and heresy of a most hated and abhorrent sort.

Anne Boleyn was pregnant by early 1533. Throughout the winter and
spring of 1533, Henry was in a hurry to get papal approval of Thomas
Cranmer as archbishop of Canterbury, and Eustace Chapuys was in-
forming the emperor of the Catholic sentiment in the country and
urging invasion. Cranmer was confirmed; he dissolved Henry's marriage with Catherine; and on June 1, Anne Boleyn paraded through
the streets to her coronation as queen of England. If Chapuys is to be
believed, she was regarded by the populace as the queen of whores
rather than as queen of the realm.

Henry's public policy was then to prove that he was as Catholic as
anyone else in Christendom and that his quarrel with the papacy was
only another of those frequent altercations that had taken place between popes and princes throughout the centuries. If he should nur-
ture such an open heretic as Frith, he might expose himself to a
crusade from abroad abetted by rebellion at home. So the government
turned from wooing Frith to making an example of him. In an appendix to *Acts and Monuments,* John Foxe tells the story of Frith's death and
of Henry's part in it. A Dr. Currein, Henry's "ordinary chaplain,"
preached a sermon against sacramentarianism and, as Foxe has it,
cried, "It is no marvel though this abominable heresy do much prevail
amongst us; for there is one now, in the Tower of London so bold as to
write in the defence of that heresy, and yet no man goeth about his
reformation."[1]

Foxe ties Currein's alarm and wrath directly to the treatise Frith had
written in reply to More's *Letter.* The sermon, Foxe says, was part of a
plot by Stephen Gardiner to make Henry recall that Frith was in the
Tower—suggesting that Henry had forgotten about Frith and that
perhaps he had never thought enough about him to know much about
his beliefs. Foxe gives the further information, all plausible, that the
accusation against Frith was part of a plot against Cromwell, who
favored the reformers.[2] And it may be that Gardiner and the conservatives he represented, once convinced that Frith could not be won
over, were bringing pressure to bear on the king himself. They had as
much interest as anyone in doing what they could to keep Henry from

---

[1]Foxe, *8,* 695.
[2]Foxe, *8,* 695–96.

going so far along the way to heresy that neither he nor the realm could be pulled back, and Gardiner always looks like a man doing his best to save what he could until, as he did under Mary, he might help England back to full participation in the old Catholic faith.[1]

The sermon was evidently preached in June, shortly after Anne's coronation, when public opinion was running high against the king and his consort. Henry immediately sent Cranmer and Cromwell to examine Frith to see exactly what the man believed. Frith had been in the Tower since at least October 21, 1532.[2] In the ordinary course of ecclesiastical and secular law, a man accused of heresy would have been subjected almost immediately to a formal examination before the proper church officials. Foxe represents Henry as furious because Frith had been in the Tower for so long without such an examination.

A panel was quickly put together to examine the prisoner. The judges included John Stokesley, bishop of London, and Cranmer, as well as others whom Foxe does not name. Cranmer, afraid of public outcry, moved the hearing out to Croydon. Foxe claims that Cranmer sent two gentlemen to bring Frith from the Tower to Croydon. On the way the gentlemen begged him to recant his beliefs about the sacrament so that he might save his life. Foxe implies that the gentlemen believed that Frith's view of the sacrament was correct but "untimely." They were, in effect, begging him to dissemble and to wait for a more convenient season.[3]

But Frith refused to budge. He had made much of conscience in his reply to More, and now he resolved to stand on his. Besides, he believed that scripture, the ancient doctors, and some of the schoolmen stood on his side and that even "the very bishops of Rome of the oldest sort shall also say for me and defend my cause." He seems to have believed that in a free disputation he might win, converting the bishops and perhaps the king himself! Perhaps he remembered an earlier meeting when the king had released him from custody though the clerics had been against him. The gentlemen thought otherwise and pointed out that Christ had not had an impartial hearing in his time and that Frith was unlikely to get one now. Even Christ might have a hard time getting a hearing for "this your opinion, the same being so odious unto the world, and we so far off from the true knowledge thereof."

---

[1] For a fine summary of Gardiner's career, see the note by J. B. Trapp, *CW 9*, 368–69.
[2] *LP* 5, 1458.
[3] Foxe, *8*, 696.

Frith admitted that his doctrine was "contrary to the opinion of this realm" and "very hard meat to be digested both of the clergy and the laity." But, said he, within twenty-five years the entire realm would accept his opinion about the Lord's Supper. In such an expectation, he was willing and almost happy to die. Or such at least is Foxe's story, and Foxe was writing three decades later and always painted the lily when he could.

The gentlemen offered Frith an opportunity to escape, but he refused it. According to Foxe, Frith responded to their overtures with a gallant statement: "For if you should both leave me here, and go to Croydon, declaring to the bishops, that you had lost Frith, I would surely follow after as fast as I might, and bring them news that I had found and brought Frith again."[1] He would, he said (doubtless remembering Jonah), be running from God if he fled the opportunity to bear witness to the bishops.

But if Frith did expect to convert Nineveh, he was not to do so on that day, although, by Foxe's account, Cranmer and his counsellor Dr. Heath were almost convinced on the spot. As Fulop points out, Cranmer himself visited with Frith several times in private, pleading with the young man to desist and to recant.[2] But the king's will was working behind all this talk, and the king's will was as implacable as Thomas Cranmer was pliable.

On June 20 Frith stood accused and unyielding before Stokesley, Gardiner, and John Longland, bishop of Lincoln, who held an ecclesiastical court in St. Paul's Cathedral. Among the charges against him were his denial of the real presence in the eucharist and his having written and published a book denying the existence of purgatory. According to Stokesley's Register, Frith signed the list of charges against him and wrote his own short statement saying he had indeed held such opinions and had published them in books. The bishops argued with him, but to no avail. Gardiner may have had another private interview with him. But Frith was unyielding. Stokesley then, "cum dolore cordis," pronounced sentence against him.[3] Frith was duly handed over to Stephen Peacock, mayor of London, and to John Martin the sheriff. He was burned at Smithfield on July 4 in the company of another heretic, Andrew Huett, who, though apparently unable to express his own views, told the authorities that he agreed with

---

[1]Foxe, *8*, 698.
[2]Fulop, pp. 121–22.
[3]Foxe, *5*, appendix, no. 22.

Frith about the sacrament and so shared his death.[1] Before he died Frith had the opportunity to write a fairly long letter to his friends, describing the questions put to him at the hearing at Croydon and the answers he had made.[2] Obviously to the last he had friends able to keep up his communications with the outside world and the loyal band of his sympathizers.

In *The Apology,* written before Frith's death, and in *The Answer to a Poisoned Book,* written afterward, More's attitude toward Frith was far harsher than it was in the *Letter.* He did not gloat over Frith's death as he did over that of some other heretics, since to do so would have been to call attention to the government's flirtation with the young man. But the depth of his feeling about the matter is revealed in *De Tristitia,* his moving work on the sadness of Christ, written in the Tower in the very shadow of death. For here he discusses the two heresies about the eucharist (consubstantiation and sacramentarianism), and although he does not mention Frith by name, his loathing for Frith's heresy and for those who hold it remains unabated. Twice within only a few lines he calls it by far the worse of the two, and he says of those who reject the Catholic teaching,

> How little difference is there, I ask you, between them and those who took Christ captive that night? How little difference between them and those troops of Pilate who in jest bent their knees before Christ as if they were honoring Him while they insulted Him and called Him the king of the Jews, just as these people kneel before the eucharist and call it the body of Christ—which according to their own profession they no more believe than the soldiers of Pilate believed Christ was a king.[3]

And echoing in a remarkable way the sentiments of his opening in the *Letter against Frith* he says:

> Therefore, whenever we hear that such evils have befallen other peoples, no matter how distant, let us immediately imagine that Christ is urgently addressing us: "Why are you sleeping? Get up and pray that you may not enter into temptation." For the fact is that wherever this plague rages today most fiercely, everyone did not catch the disease in a single day. Rather the contagion

---

[1]Foxe, 5, 16–18.
[2]Foxe, 5, 11–14.
[3]*CW 14,* 357.

spreads gradually and imperceptibly while those persons who
despise it at first, afterwards can stand to hear it and respond to it
with less than full scorn, then come to tolerate wicked discussions, and afterwards are carried away into error, until like a
cancer (as the apostle says) the creeping disease finally takes over
the whole country. Therefore let us stay awake . . .[1]

He had small reason to be pleased with Frith's fate, for by the end of
1533 England was already launched into schism, and he was only
months away from the Tower. Yet in some respects the *Letter against
Frith* was More's most effective polemical work. He exposed a heresy
that had been relatively hidden, and he thereby helped to provoke a
series of events that led Frith to his death.

[1]*CW 14,* 359.

THE TEXTS

LETTER TO BUGENHAGEN

M ORE's *Letter to Bugenhagen,* though most probably written within a
year after the publication of Bugenhagen's *Letter,*[1] was not published
until 1568, in Louvain by John Fowler (designated *1568* in the variants). On his title page Fowler claimed that he set the work from an
autograph manuscript which More had corrected, and there is no
reason not to believe him. His wife Alice was the daughter of John
Harris, More's secretary, who took with him from England a large
collection of More's letters and papers.[2] The copy-text for the present
edition is the copy of Fowler's edition at the Henry E. Huntington
Library, San Marino, California. Copies at Princeton University Library and at Oscott College (Sutton Coldfield, West Midlands)[3] have
also been completely collated and reveal no stop-press corrections in
either the text or the sidenotes. We have reproduced the copy-text
exactly except that long ſ has been replaced by *s,* all abbreviations
except & and those indicated by a final period have been expanded,
and the sidenotes, which appear in roman type in the copy-text, are
here in italic and inset. The first and the third sidenotes cannot have
been written by More, and it is likely that most or all of the sidenotes
were provided by Fowler or an assistant. The copy-text uses diacritical
marks to distinguish forms with the same spelling; for example, *quàm*
for the adverb, *quam* for the relative pronoun, *hîc* for the adverb, *hic* for
the demonstrative pronoun. Such marks have been silently omitted
except where the syntax may leave some doubt. Enclitics separated
from the preceding word in the copy-text have been joined to it: thus
"sit ne" is silently changed to "sitne." Question marks used to indicate
an exclamation rather than a question have been retained. Ligatures
such as œ and æ have been printed as separate letters. Periods at the
end of sidenotes have been uniformly omitted.

---

[1]Rogers, "Sir Thomas More's Letter to Bugenhagen," in *Essential Articles,* pp. 448–49,
and *CW 6,* 457.

[2]See *CW 2,* xlix–l, and *CW 12,* xxii.

[3]The Oscott copy contains marginalia by Thomas Stapleton (see Charles W. Crawford,
"Thomas Stapleton and More's *Letter to Bugenhagen,*" *Moreana, 19–20* [1968], 101–7, *26*
[1970], 5–13).

More's quotations from Bugenhagen are not always identical with the printed text of Bugenhagen's *Letter*, perhaps because the copy to which he replied seems to have been a manuscript given to one of his servants, a manuscript that may not have agreed perfectly with the printed editions of Bugenhagen's *Letter*.[1]

SUPPLICATION OF SOULS

More's *Supplication of Souls* was printed twice in 1529 by William Rastell (*STC*[2] 18092, Gibson, no. 72, hereafter designated *1529*[1]; and *STC*[2] 18093, Gibson, no. 71, *1529*[2]). William Rastell also reprinted it from *1529*[2] as part of More's *English Workes* of 1557 (Gibson, no. 73, sigs. t$_4$v–y$_6$, *1557*).[2] It was reprinted in 1950, 1970, and 1971.[3]

External evidence allows us to assign the first two editions, which are undated, to 1529. In *1557* William Rastell added the phrase "Anno .1529." in the title ("made, Anno .1529. by syr Thomas More," sig. t$_4$v), which suggests that the work was not only printed but also written in 1529. In the *Supplication* (161/34–162/14), More himself implies that the book he is answering, Fish's *Supplication for the Beggars*, was issued later than Tyndale's *Obedience*, which is dated October 2, 1528. John Foxe suggested that Fish's book was sent from the Continent to England "in the yeare (as I suppose) 1528."[4] On the other hand, the title pages of the first two editions of More's *Supplication* identify him only as chancellor of the duchy of Lancaster and hence were printed before October 25, 1529, when he became chancellor of England.[5]

---

[1] The text More quotes cannot be linked to any of the printed editions we have examined (Geisenhof, nos. 181–84). See Appendix A, p. 395, n. 1.

[2] Ballard MS. 72 in the Bodleian Library contains the second book of the *Supplication of Souls*, the preface of *The Confutation*, and some Tower letters (see *CW 8*, 1420, note 4). The second book of the *Supplication* in this manuscript was copied from *1557*: all the sidenotes in the manuscript appear in *1557* and in at least ten places it reproduces readings peculiar to *1557* (173/23, 175/7, 175/26, 177/4, 179/10, 182/3, 194/7, 195/5–7, 196/11, 199/4). Its variants, which are merely scribal errors or orthographical alternatives, have not been recorded among the variants in this edition.

[3] The modernized edition by Sr. Mary Thecla, S.C. (Westminster, Md., 1950) contains some useful notes. An inaccurate and unreliable transcription by Eileen Morris was printed by Primary Publications (London, 1970); see Germain Marc'hadour's review in *Moreana*, 26 (1970), 69–72. A photographic facsimile of *1529*[2] was published as No. 353 of The English Experience series of Theatrum Orbis Terrarum (Amsterdam, 1971).

[4] Appendix D, 439/34.

[5] In the 1529 edition of *A Dialogue Concerning Heresies*, John Rastell identified More on the title page as chancellor of the duchy of Lancaster, but when William Rastell printed a second edition in 1531 he added "Newly ouersene by the sayd syr Thomas More chauncellour of England" (*CW 6*, 549 and frontispiece of Part 1).

Since the two folio editions of 1529 contain no place, date, or printer and closely resemble each other, they have frequently been confused.[1] The typography of *1529*[1] is sufficient to establish its priority, since its title page is not part of the sequence of unequal signatures[2] and contains the errata list on its verso, whereas *1529*[2] includes the title page in a sequence of equal signatures and prints its errata list at the end of the text.[3] Moreover, two errors in *1529*[1] suggest that it was set from a manuscript with interlined corrections. One of these errors occurs at 173/10–15:

> or ellys that nature and reason haue tought men euery where to perceyue yt that they haue such bylefe. For surely not onely by such as haue bene trauayled in many cuntrees among sondry sectys / but also by the olde and auncyent wryters that haue bene among theym: we maye well & euydentely perceyue.

The errata of *1529*[1] and *1529*[2] have:

> or ellys that nature and reason haue tought men euery where to perceyue yt. For surely that they haue such bylefe not onely by such as haue bene trauayled in many cuntrees among sondry sectys / but also by y[e] olde and auncyent wryters that haue bene among theym: we maye well & euydentely perceyue.

The clause "that they haue such bylefe" was probably interlined in the manuscript above "perceyue yt. For surely not onely" and the compositor of *1529*[1] inserted it in the wrong place. The other error in *1529*[1] suggesting that it was set from a manuscript occurs at 199/9–10:

> For as for the pope who so consyder ytt well / goeth farther from the sample of god that hath set for crystys vycar in hys church. . . .

1529[2] has:

> For as for the pope who so consyder yt well /goeth farther from the sample of god that ys set for crystes vycar in hys church. . . .

---

[1]Both Gibson and *STC*[1] believed that *1529*[2] preceded *1529*[1] and numbered them in the wrong order. Gibson also wrongly described no. 72 as a quarto instead of a folio, and in his collation of it he said that the text begins on a_1v instead of a_1.

[2]After the unsigned title page the signatures are a^2 b–i^4 k–l^4 m^2. The text begins at the top of a_1, which is also the first numbered leaf. The first book ends in the middle of f_4, and the second begins at the top of g_1. There is nothing in the text or format to indicate why the first gathering contains only two leaves instead of the usual four.

[3]The signatures are A–I^4 K–L^4. The text begins on the verso of the title page (A_1) and ends near the bottom of L_4, which is filled out with the errata. L_4v is blank. The first book ends in the middle of F_2v, where it is immediately followed by the second book.

It seems that the manuscript from which 1529^1 was set originally read "sample that god hath set" and that the compositor set the correction imperfectly.[1] That 1529^2 derives from 1529^1 is shown by at least seven errors found in both editions.[2] In fact 1529^2 is a line-for-line (not page-for-page) resetting of the first edition.[3]

Both 1529^1 and 1529^2 were almost certainly printed by William Rastell, since the main body of the text in both editions is set in Bastard 102, a typeface that appears in books printed by him.[4] But he may well have been working in conjunction with his father, John Rastell, to whom some of the type in both editions seems to have belonged.[5]

The first edition was set and proofread rather carefully.[6] Most of the forty-one items in the list of errata correct obvious misprints. Only six or

---

[1]The errors "Snuskyn" for "Huskyn" at 211/1–2 and "relyese" for "relyefe" at 111/25 are probably misreadings of a manuscript. There is a hint that the manuscript not only was not a fair copy but also was in More's hand: the spelling "necligence" in 1529^1 at 219/1 (where 1529^2 has "neglygence"). Though the spelling with c was not uncommon in More's time and though "neglygence" also occurs in 1529^1, the Valencia autograph of More's *De Tristitia Christi* shows that he regularly preferred the spelling with c in words derived from *negligo* (*CW 14*, 115/5, 119/7, 125/6, 131/4, 133/5, 145/1, 203/1, 327/6, 597/7, 691/11–17).

[2]See the variants at 120/23, 144/35, 161/30, 168/7, 181/1, 183/29, and 226/29.

[3]1529^1 normally has 42 lines to a page; 1529^2 normally has 43, so that it gains two whole pages in the course of the book. It gains another half page by beginning the second book immediately after the first in the middle of a verso page, whereas 1529^1 leaves half a page blank at the end of the first book and begins the second at the top of the following recto. The line-for-line correspondence is usually very close, except where the compositor of 1529^2 made slight adjustments to allow for the different sizes of the block initials at the beginning of each book, to shift the beginning of paragraphs from midline to the left margin, or to obtain a better distribution of type.

[4]See Frank Isaac, *English & Scottish Printing Types 1501–35*1508–41* (Oxford, 1930), fig. 74. The block letter "W" which begins the second book of 1529^2 belonged to William Rastell (Isaac, fig. 75), as did the block letter "I" (supported by two unicorns) which begins the first book. In William Rastell's 1530 edition of *A Dialogue Concerning Heresies*, the "I" appears on sigs. b$_1$, k$_6$v, r$_5$, r$_5$v, v$_1$, and z$_2$; the "W" appears on sigs. d$_3$v, h$_6$, i$_2$, and z$_6$. In 1529^1 the books open with large squares containing at the middle an uppercase "I" and a lowercase "s" from the Bastard 102 font.

[5]"The fawtys escapyd in the pryntyng" on the verso of the title page of 1529^1 is set in the same type as the errata sheet of John Rastell's 1529 edition of *A Dialogue Concerning Heresies* (Isaac, fig. 39). The first line of the title page and the heading "The seconde boke" in both 1529 editions of the *Supplication* are set in John Rastell's Textura 220 (Isaac, figs. 40b and 43). On the cooperation of John and William Rastell, see Arthur W. Reed, *Early Tudor Drama* (London, 1926), pp. 74–77.

[6]In addition to the seven uncorrected misprints listed in note 2 on this page, there are only about a dozen misprints not caught by the proofreader (see the variants at 113/34, 116/30, 126/1, 131/3, 133/21, 135/21, 142/36, 171/23, 176/8–19, 181/12).

not neuer shall by goddys grace happen/eny such rebellyon as the beg
gars proctour & hys felowes what so euer they say long full sore to se.
¶ But thys man agaynste þ clergye fetcheth forth old farne yeres/&
reneth vp to kyng Jhans days/spedyng mych labour about the prayse
& commendacyon of þ good gracyous kyng/& cryeng out vppon þ pope
þ then was and the clergye of Englande/and all the lordys and all þ
comens of the realm/because kynge Jhan as he sayth made the realm
trybutary to the pope/wherin he meaneth peraduenture the peter pense
But surely therin ys all hys hote accusacyon a very colde tale when þ
trouth ys knowen. For so ys yt in dede þ albe yt there be wryters þ say
the peter pence were grauntyd by kynge Jhan for the release of the in
terdyccyon: yet were they payed in dede ere euer kynge Jhans greate
graundfather was borne/and therof is there profe inough. Now yf he
say as in dede some wryters say/that kyng Jhan made England and
Irland trybutary to the pope and the see apostolyque by the graunt of
a thousand markys: we dare surely say agayn that yt ys vntrew/and
that all Rome neyther can shew suche a graunt nor neuer could/and yf
they could yt were ryght nought worth. For neuer coulde eny kynge of
England geue away the realm to þ pope/or make the lande trybutary
though he wolde/nor no such money ys there payed nor neuer was.
And as for the peter pense yf he meane the/neyther was þ realme trybutary by the/nor kyng Jhan neuer grauntyd the. For they were payed
before the conquest to the apostolyk see toward the mayntenance therof but onely by way of gratytude and almes. Now as for the archBysshop Stephen/whom he sayth beyng a traytour to the kynge/the pope
made archebyshop of Canturbury agaynst the kyngys wyll/therin be
there as we suppose ii lyes at onys. For neyther was þ Stephen euer
traytour agaynst the kyng as farre as euer we haue herd/nor the pope
none other wyse made hym archebyshop then he made all other at that
tyme: but þ same Stephen was well & canonycally chose archebyshop
of Canturbury by þ couet of þ monkys at Crystis church in Canturbury/
to whom as þ kyng well knew & denyed yt not/þ eleccyd of þ archebys
hop at þ tyme beloged. Nor þ kyng respytyd not hys eleccyon bycause
of any treasó þ was layd agaynst hym: but was dyscotétyd therwyth/
& after þ hys eleccyd was passyd & cofyrmed by þ pope: he wold not of
long seasó suffer hym to enioy þ byshoprych/because hym selfe had re-
comédyd a nother vnto þ monkys/whó they reiectyd & preferryd Ste-
phé. And that thys ys as we tell you/and not as the beggars proctour
wryteth for a false foudacyon of his raylyng: ye shall mow parcepue/
not onely by dyuers cronycles/but also by dyuers monumentys yet re
maynynge as well of the eleccyon and confyrmacyon of the sayd arche
byshop/as of the long sute and proces that after folowed theruppon.
　　　¶ Nowe sheweth he hym selfe very wrothe wyth the spyrytuall iuryspdiccyon/whyche he wolde in any wyse were clene taken
away.

away / sayng that yt muste nedys dystroy the iurysdyccyon temporall: where as the good prynces passed haue graunted / and þ nobles
in theyre tymes / and the people / to haue by playne parlyamentes confermed them / and yet hytherto blessyd be good they agre better to gyther / then to fall at varyaunce for the wylde wordes of suche a malycyouse make bate: whyche for to brynge the spyrytualtye in to hate
red / sayth that they call theyr iurysdyccyon a kyngdome. In whyche
word he may say hys pleasure / but of treuth he seldom seeth eny spyrytuall man at thys daye that so calleth eny spyrytuall iurysdyccyon þ
he vseth.

Nowe where thys man vseth as a profe therof / that the spyrytualte nameth therm selfe alwaye byfore the temporaltye: thys maner
of namyng cometh not of them / but of the good mynde and deuocyon
of the temporaltye: so farre forthe that at the parlyament when that
eny actes be conceyued / the wordes be comenly so couched / that the
byll sayth yt ys enacted fyrste by our soueraygne lorde þ kyng and by þ
lordes spyrytuall a temporall and þ comens in that present parlyament
assembled. And these byllys be often drawen put forth a passed fyrste
in the comen howse / where there ys not one spyrytuall man present.

But suche treuth as the man vseth in thys poynte / suche vseth he
where he calleth the pore freres almoyse an axaccyon: surmysynge
that yt ys exacted by force and the people compelled to pay yt / where
euery man well wytteth that they haue pore men no way to compelle
no man to gyue the aught not though they shulde dy for defaut. But
thys good honest true man sayth that who so wyll not pay the freres
theyre quarterage they wyll make hym be taken as an heretyque.
We be well contente that ye take thys for no lye / as manye as euer
haue knowen yt treu. But who herd euer yet that eny man taken for
an heretyque / dyd so myche as ones saye that he thought yt conuayd
by the malyce of any frere for refusyng to pay þ freres quarterage.
Thys lye so ys a lytle to lowde / for eny man that were not waxen
shameles.

Lyke a treuth ys there in thys that he sayeth / yf any man trouble a
preeste for any temporall suyte: the clergye forth wyth wyll make hym
an heretyque and burne hym / but yf he be content to bere a fagotte for
theyre pleasure. The falsehed of thys can not be vnknowen / for me
know well in many a shyre how often that many folk endyght preest
of rape at the sessyons. And as there ys somtyme a rape commyttyd
in dede / so ys there euer a rape surmysed were the women neuer so
vpstyrnge / and oftentyme where there was nothynge done at all.
And yet of eny suche that so procured preestes to be indyghted: howe
many haue men herd taken and accused for heretyques.

c.ii.   ye

Supplication of Souls, 1529[1], sig. c₂ (reduced)

seven might have required recourse to the manuscript,[1] and there is no evidence that More himself read proof. But anomalies on three pages in gathering c suggest that More added three or four lines to c_1v after the gathering had been completely set. The errata list corrects two places on c_1v (128/36, 129/25) and one place on c_4 (136/13) where the correct readings are already present in the text. Moreover, the places to be corrected on c_1v are in different lines from the ones given in the errata list: the first is in line 14 rather than 15 and the second in line 35 rather than line 33. All the other line numbers in the errata list are correct. Finally, c_1 and c_1v contain 44 lines rather than the usual 42.[2]

This evidence suggests that c_1 and c_1v were originally set with the usual 42 lines. The proofreader found the errors in lines 15 and 33 and corrected them on the errata sheet. If he had also discovered a passage the compositor had missed in the manuscript, he would not have placed the errors in the errata list but would have corrected them when the passage was added. Then More decided to add a few lines to c_1v somewhere between lines 15 and 33. The printer moved the top two lines of c_1v back to the bottom of c_1, leaving himself four extra lines on c_1v. (At the same time he corrected the error on c_4, which was in the same form as c_1v, but did not bother to remove it from the errata list.) An extraordinary proliferation of abbreviated forms in lines 30–38 of c_1v ("but y^e . . . preferryd Stephen," 129/18–27) suggests that More added some details here about the election of Stephen Langton to the see of Canterbury. In the 1529 edition of *A Dialogue Concerning Heresies,* he made a similar addition to gathering O, so that eight pages of it were reset with three extra lines in each column.[3]

Unlike *1529¹*, *1529²* contains dozens of uncorrected misprints, more than enough to fill the last page of the book (L_4v), which was probably left blank for the errata list. But only eleven "fawtys escapyd in the pryntyng" were listed at the bottom of the preceding page (L_4), including only one from the last four gatherings, which contain more than thirty misprints. The compositor of *1529²* also omitted one phrase and three words of the text.[4] In about forty places he carelessly and wrongly changed the punctuation of *1529¹*. Nevertheless, some-

---

[1]See, for example, the variants at 122/1, 150/8, 162/16, 165/2, 169/1, 173/11–12, 177/18.

[2]The only exceptions are a_1 and a_1v (which have 41) and d_1, f_1v, and $l_4v–m_2$ (which have 43). The first book ends in the middle of f_4v (which has only 20 lines), and the first page of the second book (g_1) has only 37 lines because of the large heading at the top.

[3]See *CW 6*, 553–54.

[4]See the variants at 132/31, 141/21, 150/18 and 184/36.

one did correct the copy of *1529*[1] from which *1529*[2] was set. He incorporated all the corrections in the errata list of *1529*[1] and corrected
about seventeen fairly obvious misprints.[1] But several of his corrections required very close attention to the sense and immediate context,
such as the following emendations:

> Whervppon forthwyth at yᵉ parlyment holden yᵉ same yere / lyke
> wyse as that ryall prynce / his vertuouse and hys good chrysten
> communes / deuysed good lawes agaynst heretyques. *1529*[1].
> *1529*[2] *has* vertuouse nobles & *for* vertuouse and (143/28–31)

> some other Iohan goose bygan to bere that byll a brode agayn / &
> made some bablyng a whyle but yt auayled hym not. And now
> bycause some heretyques haue bene of late abiured / thys gos-
> elyng therfore hath made thys beggers byll / and gageleth agayn
> vppon the same mater *1529*[1]. *1529*[2] *has* gagling *for* bablyng
> (144/12–16)

> But yᵗ ys the thyng yᵗ thys begger complayneth vppon. *1529*[1].
> *1529*[2] *has* thys beggers proctor *for* thys begger (148/17–18)

> Now yf they will say no / and wyll contend that yt can not be
> accountyd holy scrypture though the chyrche of Cryste so take
> take yt / but yf the Iewes to take [*1529*[1] *corr. err.* so take] yt
> too: then go they nere to put oute saynt Iohans gospell out
> of scrypture too / for the Iewes neuer toke yt for none.
> *1529*[1]. *1529*[2] *has* the Iewes so toke yt too *for* the Iewes so take yt too
> (180/32–181/3)

> Doth not the blessyd apostle saynt Peter as appereth in yᵉ secund
> boke of the apostles actes *1529*[1]. *1529*[2] *has* chapiter *for* boke
> (185/29–31)[2]

The following emendations are even less obvious and seem to require
the hand of More himself:

> albe yt that the people were (as the Affrycanys be) very barba-
> rouse / fyerce & boystuouse *1529*[1]. *1529*[2] *has* these Affrycanis
> *for* the Affrycanys (144/33–35)

---

[1]See the variants at 113/34, 116/30, 124/26, 126/1, 130/4, 133/21, 135/30, 138/1,
150/27, 153/27, 171/23, 176/14, 181/12, 181/24, 199/10, 207/31, and 220/12.
[2]For similar examples, see the variants at 125/18, 131/3, 137/4, 150/8, 157/14, 178/22,
193/18, 212/11, 216/9, 219/21.

> and syth . . . the churche of cryste receyueth and taketh and . . . hath approued and fermely byleued the godly boke of the Machabeys to be one of the volumes of holy scrypture   *1529*[1]. *1529*[2] *has* holy boke *for* godly boke (183/14–18)

> and beyng not fully fyfty / began to gaynsay the fayth of almost .xv. hundred yere afore hys days in the churche of Cryste / besydys fyue tymes .xv. C. yere among other faythfull folk before. *1529*[1]. *1529*[2] *has* fyfty yere old *for* fyfty *and* .xv. C. yere thre tymys told *for* fyue tymes .xv. C. yere (212/17–18)

The last emendation depends on an awareness that the usual length of time assigned to the period between Adam and Christ is closer to 4,500 years than to 7,500.[1]

That More was not the only corrector is suggested by a corrupt passage in *1529*[1] that was unsuccessfully emended in *1529*[2] (212/15–18). And there are eight places where it might be plausibly argued that the changes in *1529*[2] are due either to a careless compositor, or to an overzealous corrector, or even to More himself.[2] In these places it seemed best to follow the copy-text, *1529*[2]. On the whole, the evidence shows that *1529*[2] was produced from a copy of *1529*[1] that had been corrected by a careful reader and, at least partly, by More himself; the text was then set by a careless compositor and hastily proofread to produce the brief and inadequate list of errata.

It is clear that *1557* was set from a copy of *1529*[2]. In fact the copy of *1529*[2] that William Rastell used to set the *Supplication of Souls* is now preserved in the Beinecke Library at Yale University.[3] This copy, in which the errata had already been entered in the text, was corrected rather perfunctorily and provided with sidenotes, probably by William Rastell himself. It was cast off and set by three compositors, who corrected about forty obvious misprints but also overlooked two corrections[4] from the errata of *1529*[2] and made a number of errors or false corrections of their own.[5] The compositor of the x gathering of *1557* omitted a line[6] of *1529*[2] and neglected one of Rastell's corrections.[7]

---

[1]See note on 212/17–18.
[2]See the variants at 139/20, 168/21, 175/7, 182/3, 182/30, 214/26, 222/1, 225/22.
[3]For a fuller discussion, see Appendix F.
[4]See the variants at 131/28 and 167/8.
[5]See the variants at 112/30, 118/16, 126/6, 130/19, 147/27, 160/21, 179/10, 196/11, 199/4, 202/31, 209/16, 211/24, and 213/27.
[6]See the variants at 195/5–7.
[7]See the variants at 177/6. But it is possible that the "t" was added before "here" not by Rastell but by a later hand.

But some of Rastell's own corrections are more inventive than percep-
tive, and on the whole it is fortunate that we do not have to rely on *1557*
for the text.

The copy-text of this edition is *1529*[2], the last edition produced
during More's lifetime. A complete collation of the two copies in the
Beinecke Library at Yale revealed no stop-press corrections.[1] The
copy-text has been printed and the variants in *1529*[1] and *1557* have
been recorded in accordance with the norms set forth in *CW 8*, 1447–
50.[2] The symbol *1529* in the variants indicates the agreement of both
1529[1] and *1529*[2]. Information about *1529*[1] is based on microfilms of
the copies in the libraries of the Union Theological Seminary in New
York and of Queen's College, Oxford; a complete collation of both
revealed no stop-press corrections.[3] The Klein and Larned Fund copies of *1557* at Yale have also been completely collated and reveal no
stop-press corrections or shifted sidenotes. Nevertheless, other copies
of *1557* show that sigs v$_4$–v$_5$v were set twice; apart from a few typographical errors, which are recorded in the variants as *1557*[a] and
1557[b], there are no substantive differences between the settings.[4] Paragraphs, which are indicated by pilcrows in *1529*[1] and *1529*[2] and which
are almost entirely ignored in *1557*,[5] are here marked by indentation.
The pilcrows on the title page and in the headings of the two books
have been omitted. The 1529 editions contain no sidenotes; those in
1557 are here given with the variants. Lowercase *w* at the beginning of
three sidenotes (112/19–20, 118/8–10, 208/1–2) has been changed to
the uppercase form, and a few obvious misprints have been silently
corrected. Periods at the end of sidenotes, except where they indicate

---

[1]In addition to the two Yale copies, there are copies of *1529*[2] in the following collec-
tions: at Cambridge in Kings, Pembroke, Sidney Sussex, and Trinity Colleges; at Oxford
in All Souls, Balliol, and Lincoln Colleges and two copies in the Bodleian; in London in
the British Library, Guildhall, and the University; Tollerton Hall near Nottingham;
Ampleforth Abbey; John Rylands Library in Manchester; Gloucester Cathedral; St.
Andrews University; Trinity College Dublin; Bibliothèque Nationale. In the United
States there are copies at the Boston Public Library, College of New Rochelle, Folger
Shakespeare Library, Newberry Library, University of Illinois, St. Louis University,
University of San Francisco, and Henry E. Huntington Library (Constance Smith,
Updating of R. W. Gibson's St. Thomas More, St. Louis, 1981, p. 34).

[2]The spelling of a reading listed as in two or more editions is that of the first edition
listed.

[3]Copies of *1529*[1] are in Guildhall in London, John Rylands Library, Union Theological Seminary, College of New Rochelle, and Queen's College, Oxford; there is a
fragment in the University Library at Cambridge (R. Keen, "A Correction by Hand in
More's *Supplication*, 1529," *Moreana*, 77 [1983], 100, n. 1).

[4]See Appendix F, p. 466, below.

[5]*1557* retains the pilcrows of *1529*[2] only at 112/26 and 133/10.

an abbreviation, have been silently removed. The abbreviated form "Ihān" in *1529*[1] and *1529*[2], which regularly appears as "Iohn" in *1557*, has been expanded to "Iohan." The line above *a* is not intended to represent a second *n* but is the printer's equivalent of a line through the ascender of *h*.[1] In *1529*[1] and *1529*[2] passages quoted or closely paraphrased from Fish's *A Supplication for the Beggers* are in the same type as the rest of the book but are marked off by a vertical series of colons in the outer margin. In *1557* they are not set off typographically in any way. In this edition they are placed within double quotation marks; whenever the colons begin a little too soon or too late, the discrepancy is noted in the Commentary.

LETTER AGAINST FRITH

THE textual history of More's *Letter against Frith* is comparatively simple and straightforward. No manuscript copies of it are known, and the text given here is based on the first edition of December 1532 (*STC*[2] 18090; Gibson, no. 66; hereafter designated *1532*), which was reprinted in the *English Works* of 1557 (Gibson, no. 73, sigs. G₅–H₂v; *1557*). The first edition was also reprinted as no. 190 in Elizabeth Rogers' edition of More's correspondence (Princeton, 1947). Fortunately the two sixteenth-century editions were carefully printed.

More dated *A Letter against Frith* from Chelsea on December 7. The first edition (*1532*) was dated 1533 by William Rastell in its colophon, but it was actually printed in December 1532, as More himself informs us in *The Answer to a Poisoned Book* (December 1533).[2] He also tells us there why he prevented the printed copies of the *Letter* from being sold at that time: Frith's first treatise on the eucharist (against which the *Letter* was directed) had not yet been printed and was still circulating only in manuscript. But since printed copies of *The Souper of the Lorde* (Hume, no. 29; *CW 11*, Appendix A) and Frith's reply to the *Letter* (Hume, no. 30) had been smuggled into England during 1533, More

---

[1]Rastell's 1533 edition of More's *Answer to a Poisoned Book* uses the abbreviation "Iohñ," which appears as "Iohan" in the two places where the name is given in full. In his 1557 reprint of *The Answer*, Rastell regularly printed "Iohn." In the Valencia autograph of *De Tristitia Christi*, More normally writes the name in full ("Ioannes") but once he abbreviates it with a line through the *h* (*CW 14*, 41/3).

[2]*CW 11*, 222/6–18 and Commentary. See also *CW 9*, 123/25–29. In *A Boke . . . answeringe vnto M mores lettur* (July 4, 1533; Hume, no. 30), sig. A₃, Frith said he had seen a printed copy of More's *Letter against Frith* "vppon S. Stephyns day last paste," that is, on December 26, 1532.

arranged to have the *Letter* offered for sale together with *The Answer to a Poisoned Book* in December 1533.[1]

The first edition of the *Letter* (*1532*) was set rather carefully and contains no errata sheet. Because the work is brief and contains no subdivisions, the edition provides no running heads. All the marginal glosses except one identify scriptural passages with less accuracy[2] than we would expect from More, but one gloss identifying a passage in Jerome's *Aduersus Luciferianos* (239/27–29) might well derive from More himself. The body of the text is set in textura, with a few Latin words in corresponding italic typeface.[3] Rastell used the title-page border of the *Letter* in his edition of More's *Apology*.[4]

There is no ironclad evidence that *1557* was set from *1532*, but Rastell's usual practice and the very close correspondence between the two editions make it all but certain that it was. By sixteenth-century standards, *1557* is a very careful reprint.[5] It offers no evidence that a manuscript or any other source except *1532* was used to produce it. It reprints all the sidenotes of *1532* and adds thirty-five new ones (ten of them identifying scriptural passages).

The copy-text of this edition is *1532*, of which three copies have been completely collated.[6] Collation of these copies revealed no stop-press corrections or shifted sidenotes. The Larned Fund copy of *1557* at Yale has been completely collated and the substantive variants from it recorded in the apparatus criticus according to the norms given in *CW 8*, 1450.[7] Sidenotes in the margins of *1532* and *1557* have been inset, and sidenotes present only in *1557* are marked with an asterisk.[8] The

---

[1]See *CW 11*, lxxxvii.

[2]See the glosses at 226/1, 4; 247/7–8; 251/18–19.

[3]For the typefaces of *1532* see Isaac, *English and Scottish Printing Types, 1501–35*1508–41* (Oxford, 1930), fig. 75. The textura and italic of *1532* are Isaac's 92, except for the first two words on the title page, which are Textura 220. The sidenotes are Bastard 68. The body of the text opens with a block-letter "I."

[4]R. B. McKerrow and F. S. Ferguson, *Title-Page Borders Used in England & Scotland 1485–1640* (London, 1932), no. 17. See also *CW 9*, xci.

[5]It contains very few misprints, a few careless errors (see variants at 239/1, 245/22, 247/17, 256/30, 257/15), and some minor corrections (233/36, 244/17, 244/29, 245/18, 249/36, 254/14–15). It omits two words (243/21, 256/11).

[6]Microfilms of the copies at the Bodleian Library, Oscott College (Sutton Coldfield, West Midlands), and the Folger Shakespeare Library. The only other known copy, which we have not seen, is in the possession of George Goyder (Rotherfield Greys, Oxon.).

[7]Whenever there seemed to be a difficulty, the other two Yale copies of *1557* were also examined.

[8]In some sidenotes on *1557* commas appear where periods were intended; they have silently been changed to periods. For example, "Actes,1," appears here as "Actes.1"

pilcrow on the title page and the printer's ornament in the colophon
have been omitted. In our text we have silently expanded most abbreviations and made certain typographical adjustments in accordance with
the norms presented in *CW 8*, 1447–50. Ligatures such as æ have been
printed as separate letters. The typeface Textura 92 in *1532* appears
here as roman; Italic 92, as italic; and Bastard 68 (in the sidenotes), as
smaller italic.

LETTER TO BUGENHAGEN

DOCTISSIMA
D. THOMAE MO-
RI CLARISSIMI AC DI-
sertissimi Viri Epistola, in qua non minus
facete quam pie, respondet Literis
Ioannis Pomerani, hominis
inter Protestantes nomi-
nis non obscuri.

*Opusculum certe Sacrarum literarum studiosis
tum vtile, tum iucundum : ex Authoris quidem autographo emendato, dum viueret, ex-
emplari desumptum, nunquam vero antehac
in lucem editum.*

LOVANII,
Ex officina Ioannis Fouleri,
M. D. LXVIII.
CVM PRIVILEGIO.

DOCTISSIMA
D. THOMÆ MO-
RI CLARISSIMI AC DI-
serti ss. Viri Epistola, in qua non minus
facetè quàm piè, respondet Literis
Ioannis Pomerani, hominis
inter Protestantes nomi-
nis non obscuri.

*Opusculum certè Sacrarum literarum studiosis
tùm vtile, tùm iucundum : ex Authoris quidem autographo emendato, dum viueret, ex-
emplari desumptum, nunq̃ verò antehac in lucem editum.*

LOVANII,
Ex officina Ioannis Fouleri,
M. D. LXVIII.
CVM PRIVILEGIO.

1

Title page, *Letter to Bugenhagen,* 1568

A LEARNED EPISTLE
BY SIR THOMAS MORE,
THAT FAMOUS AND
ELOQUENT MAN,
In which he replies
With no less wit than piety
To the Letter of John Pomeranus,
A man of no small reputation
Among Protestants

*A short book designed to instruct and delight
students of theology. Edited from the author's
own autograph copy, corrected while he was
still alive, and never before brought to light.*

LOUVAIN
From the Shop of John Fowler
1568
WITH THE PRIVILEGE OF
EXCLUSIVE PRINTING RIGHTS

D. Thomae Mori Tetrastichon ab ipso conscriptum, triennio antequam mortem oppeteret.

Môraris, si sit spes hic tibi longa morandi:
Hoc te vel môrus, More, monere potest.
Desine môrari, & coelo meditare morari:
Hoc te vel morus, More, monere potest.

Aliud eiusdem Distichon eodem
conscriptum tempore.

Qui memor es Mori, longae tibi tempora vitae
Sint, & ad aeternam peruia porta, mori. [*₂]

Ioan. Fouleri Bristoliensis in D. Th. Mori
effigiem Hexastichon.

Effigiem quamcunque tui sic fingimus, at non
Tam facile est mores fingere, More, tuos.
Quam vellem Pictor mihi tam perfectus adesset,
Pingere qui vere posset vtrumque simul.
Tum quoque qui vitam totam, mortemque referret,
Ille magis multo doctus Apelle foret.

Aliud Eiusdem.

Talis erat Morus perfunctus honoribus hîc, at
Nunc alio fungens munere qualis erit?
Scilicet haud illi est quicquam splendoris ademptum,
Sed noua, pro fragili, gloria summa data est.
At neque qui coelo viuit, famaque per orbem
Clarus vbique viget, mortuus esse potest.
O quanto splendore tui dignantur amici
Christe Deus, quanta gloria, honore, bonis!
Viue igitur duplici & vita, & cumulatus honore.
Te fecit vere viuere, More, mori.

18 referret,] referret. *1568*   26 viget,] viget; *1568*

A Quatrain by Sir Thomas More
Written Three Years before
He Met His Death

You are playing the fool if you hope to linger long on earth. Even a fool, More, can tell you that. Stop playing the fool and be mindful of remaining in heaven. Even a fool, More, can tell you that.

Another Couplet by the Same Author
Written at the Same Time

You who remember More, may your lifetime be long and your death an open gate to eternal life.

A Six-Line Poem by John Fowler of Bristol,
on a Portrait of Sir Thomas More

In such a picture as this we show what you looked like, but it is not so easy to portray your character, More. I wish I had a painter so skillful that he could portray both your appearance and your character together. But then a painter who could also represent your whole life and your death would be far more expert than Apelles ever was.

Another, by the Same Author

This is what More looked like when honored here on earth. Now that he enjoys another position elsewhere, what is he like? To be sure he has lost none of his splendor. Rather he has exchanged a brittle glory for a glory which is new and everlasting. But a man who lives on in heaven and grows in fame throughout the world cannot be dead. O the splendor, the glory, honor, and blessings with which your friends, O Christ my God, have been worthily endowed! Live doubly, then, alive in heaven and full of honor. Death, More, has made you truly alive.

Gentianus Heruetus Aurelian. in Th. Mori
caput stipiti infixum in Ponte Londinensi.

Quod capiti quondam Ciceronis rostra fuere,
Hoc est pons capiti, More diserte, tuo.
5 *Ducentes Angli suspiria pectore dicunt:*
Doctior & melior nullus in orbe fuit. [*₂v]

Alani Copi Londinensis Distichon.

Quis viuente velit Thoma non viuere Moro?
Quis Moro nolit sic moriente mori?

10 Eiusdem Tetrastichon.

Mortuus an Morus, qui sic in mortis agone
Vixerat, vt mors sit victa coacta mori?
Imo pijs morum meritis nunc viuit & orbi,
Et pura mentis relligione, Deo.

15 Aliud.

Mortuus hic viuus, viuus quoque mortuus idem
Dissimili constans in ratione fuit.
Vixit in hac vita sic, mundo vt mortuus esset,
Sic obijt mortem, viuat vt ipse Deo.

20 Ioan. Vultei Remensis ex lib. Epigram. 2.
Epitaphium Mori.

Hîc situs est Thomas Morus, tuus, Anglia, vates,
Turba Poetarum, quem cecidisse, gemit.
Dum Regum docte metuendos admonet enses,
25 *Illum carnificis Rex iubet ense mori.*
Illum Amor & Charites deflent, deflentque Camoenae,
Nec damnum credit, qui sapit, esse leue.
Gallia, quid posset, testisque Britannia, testis
Italia, & semper Graecia testis erit. [*₃]

---

4 tuo.] tuo, *1568*

On Thomas More's Head Attached to a Pole on London Bridge,
by Gentien Hervet of Orléans

What the rostrum once was to Cicero's head, the bridge is now to
your head, eloquent More. Englishmen say, with heartfelt sighs,
there was never a wiser or better man in the whole world.

A Couplet by Alan Cope of London

Who would not want to live while Thomas More was still living?
Who would not want to die with More dying as he did?

A Quatrain by the Same Author

Do you think More is dead when he lived even in the toils of
death so that death was beaten and forced to die? No, he is still
alive to the world by virtue of his pious deeds, and he is still alive
to God in the pure bond of the spirit.

Another

Here he is dead but he lives, he lives though he is dead, always
unchanging, but with a difference: he lived in this life so as to be
dead to the world and passed through death so as to live truly
himself in God.

More's Epitaph, from Book Two of the Epigrams of
Jean Visaigier of Reims

Here lies Thomas More—your poet, England, whose fall a host
of poets lament. He taught us wisely to fear the swords of kings,
and the king ordered him to die by the executioner's sword.
Love and the Graces weep for him. The Muses also weep for
him. No one who is wise can think the loss is light. How great he
was France will testify. Britain and Italy will testify too, and the
testimony of Greece will last forever.

PHILIPPO,
Potentissimo Hispaniarum, &c.
Regi Catholico.

*S*I LIBELLVS iste (Rex potentissime & non vno tantum nomine
5 Catholice) quanta eruditione ac lepore sermonis conscriptus est, tanta
etiam praestaret operis magnitudine: nec mihi sane vlla foret excusatione
opus, quod tantillum volumen Maiestati tuae offerre auderem, nec ita
parum dignum hoc qualecunque munus videretur, quo minus tanto
Principi posset merito dedicari. Sed obscurum non est singulare illud
10 animi tui stu[*₃v]dium, quod tum in omnes Catholicos (perinde ac si non
tam cognomine, quam cognatione quapiam coniuncti tibi essent) tum
maxime in eos, qui pro fide Catholica quicquam aduersi sunt passi, multis
modis clarissime innotuit. Igitur non tam me deterruit huius opusculi
exiguitas, quo minus illud Maiestati exhiberem tuae: quam incitauit &
15 tuum istud, quod dixi, in Catholicos studium, & ipsius Thomae Mori
nomen et virtus, qui & pro fide Catholica defendenda, tuaeque simul
magnae Materterae pientissimae foeminae causa propugnanda, ex-
tremum passus est supplicium. Qui vir cum pro eadem causa, pro qua tu
iam diu pugnas, non dubitarit vt fortissimus vere miles sanguinem suum
20 fundere, cumque probe sciamus, te illum etiam mor[*₄]tuum ob eandem
causam summa prosequi beneuolentia: non immerito hoc opusculum
(quod ex Authoris nomine ac praestantia summum videatur mereri pretium) vel iure deberi tibi quodammodo videbatur, quo tanquam altero
gladio acutissimo confundi queant ac penitus conuinci ij, qui tuis armis
25 ita debellati non sunt, vt ab erroribus deficerent suis, ac Catholicae
rursus subijcerentur Ecclesiae. Ita enim dilucide ac neruose tum in genere plaerasque nostri temporis haereses, tum imprimis Lutheranam, quae
in his Belgicis regionibus nuper coepit repullulascere, in hoc Epistolio
proterit prosternitque, vt vix quicquam putem tam paucis verbis conscribi
30 potuisse accuratius, elegantius, ac festiuius. Suscipe ergo, Rex Catholice,

8

To Philip
The Most Powerful,
Catholic King of Spain, Etc.

O KING most powerful and (for more than one reason) Catholic, if this small book were as large in size as it is learned and elegantly written, I would need no excuse to be bold enough to offer such a slight volume to your Majesty, nor would it seem to be an unsuitable gift to dedicate to so great a prince. But everyone knows that you are extremely zealous in behalf of all Catholics, as if they were joined to you not so much by that title "Catholic" as by a certain blood relationship. And it is even more apparent that you are particularly concerned for those who have suffered adversity for the Catholic faith. And so I am not deterred by the small size of this volume from presenting it to your Majesty. Instead, I am encouraged by that zeal you have, as I said, for all Catholics everywhere, and I am also encouraged by the name and virtue of Thomas More himself, who suffered the extreme punishment in defense of the Catholic faith, fighting for the cause of that saintly woman, your great-aunt. Like a brave and true soldier, he shed his blood for the same cause you have been fighting for all these years. We are also well aware that after his death you have been more favorably disposed toward him for the same reason. In a sense, then, it seems only proper that this small book, valuable because of the author's name and distinction, should belong to you. It is as though it were another sharp sword capable of confounding and completely defeating those who are not conquered by your armies and forced to abandon their error and submit to the Catholic church. In this brief Epistle More clearly and forcefully overthrows and crushes under foot most of the heresies prevalent in our time, particularly the Lutheran heresy, which recently began to sprout up once again here in the Low Countries. I can hardly imagine a work so concise that is more accurate, more elegant in style, and more amusing.

9

hoc quale[*₄v]cunque tandem sit, ac illud puta ab ipso Thoma Moro
deferri tibi, qui si nunc viueret (et viuit certe Christo) omne suum obse-
quium, quo quicquam posset efficere, tanto ac tam Catholico Principi
meritissime praestari debere existimaret. Catholici sane omnes nunquam
5 *desistent Deum Opt. Max. comprecari, vt Sacram, Catholicam, Regiam-*
que Maiestatem tuam diutissime nobis, ac toti Orbi Christiano sanam &
incolumem conseruet, ac bonis omnibus ornatam cumulatamque in terris
reddat, tandemque in coelo cum Sanctis suis remuneret gloria sempiter-
na. Louanij, 14. Decemb. 1568.

10   Qui totus Maiestati tuae
                                inseruit animo ac voluntate,
                                    Ioannes Foulerus Anglus. [A₁]

---

2 tibi,] tibi. *1568*

For whatever it is worth, therefore, accept this work, O Catholic King, and think that it is presented to you by Thomas More himself. For if he lives (and he surely lives in Christ), he would consider that he justly owed to so great and so Catholic a prince as yourself all his obedience and all the fruit of his obedience. In truth all Catholics will never cease to pray that almighty God will preserve whole and unharmed for years to come your Holy, Catholic, Royal Majesty both for us and for the whole Christian world. We pray that he may shower all good things upon you on earth and that he may at last reward you with eternal glory in heaven with his saints. Louvain, 14 December 1568.

> John Fowler, Englishman,
> who serves your Majesty
> with his whole heart and soul.

DOCTISSIMA SIMVL AC *Elegantiss. D. THOMAE MORI*
Clariss.^{mi} Viri EPISTOLA, in qua non minus pie quam facete
respondet Literis cuiusdam Pomerani,
hominis inter Protestantes
nominis non obscuri.

5

Redevnti domum ex itinere tradidit e ministris quidam literas mihi, quas accepisse se dicebat ab ig-
Barlous is erat,   noto quopiam. Vbi resignaui, reperio,
pseudoepiscopus   Pomerane, haud scio cuius manu, sed
Cicistrensis
10   nomine scriptas tuo: verum ita scriptas
tamen, vt neque nominatim, neque in genere missae viderentur
ad me. Inscripseras enim: *Sanctis qui sunt in Anglia.* At ego quam
procul inuitus ab illis disto, in quos ve[A₁v]re tantus competat
titulus: tam longe libens absum ab ijs, qui soli sancti sunt,
15 Pomerane, tibi: cui nihil sanctum esse, praeter Lutherani sectam, video.
    Itaque primum demirabar mecum, quid ei, quicquid erat
hominis, venisset in mentem: vt epistolam talem potissimum
curaret obtrudendam mihi, qui me Lutherano negotio nun-
20 quam immiscueram. Verum pressius expendenti rem subijt du-
bitatio: ne, quod in ea re nihil hactenus me commouissem, id
ipsum fortassis in causa fuerit, vt idoneus existimatus sim, qui
tali tentarer epistola. Nam quum omnes hic mortales passim
aduersus execrabiles eius haereses clamarent, nec ego ea de re
25 quicquam fere loquerer, quod neque Theologus eram, nec vllam
personam gererem, ad quam eius vlceris cura pertineret:
Lutheranum quempiam spem concepisse reor, fore, vt ae-
quitatem meam facile talis Epistola, tam in speciem [A₂] pia,
pelliceret in partes suas.
30   Haec ego mecum reputans, tametsi nihil responsi tuae re-
quirebant literae, & ego plane decreueram ab eiusmodi pestis
attactu noxio semper abstinere: tamen quia mihi res obtrusa est,

12

A LEARNED AND GRACEFULLY WRITTEN *EPISTLE*
BY *SIR THOMAS MORE,* THAT FAMOUS MAN,
In which he replies with no less piety than wit
To the letter of someone named Pomeranus,
A person of no small reputation
among Protestants

As I WAS RETURNING home from a trip, one of my servants gave me a letter which he said he had gotten from someone he had never seen before. When I opened it, Pomeranus, I found that it was written in your name, but whose hand it was in I do not know. And it was written in such a way as to seem addressed to me neither personally nor generally. For you addressed it, *To the Saints in England.* I am, against my will, as far removed from those who truly deserve such a noble title as I am glad to remove myself from the only ones you regard as saints, Pomeranus. For I see that nothing is sacred to you except the Lutheran sect.

This was Barlow, the pseudo-bishop of Chichester

And so I was puzzled at first as to how it had come into his head—whoever he was—to want to force such a letter on me, especially me, for I had never got mixed up in the Lutheran business. But when I thought about it more carefully, I began to suspect that maybe that was it: someone thought I was the right person to try such a letter on precisely because I had not really become involved in the controversy up to that point. When everyone here was crying out everywhere against Luther's foul heresies, I said almost nothing about it. I was not a theologian, and the part I played in the world did not require me to deal with corruption of that kind. I suspect some Lutheran hoped that such a letter—one that seemed on the surface so devout—would easily lure me from my impartial stand and make me take sides with him.

I turned these things over in my mind. Although your letter needed no reply and although I had firmly resolved to avoid all contact with that dangerous disease of yours, I nevertheless decided that it was forced on me against my will. And besides, by

& fors tacendo forem spem improbam porrigentis aucturus:
statui potius ad literas tuas rescribere, quo testatum reddam
omnibus, me quantumuis rudem rei Theologicae, constantius
tamen esse Christianum, quam vt sustineam esse Lutheranus.

5 Respondebo igitur singulis Epistolae tuae partibus, quo facilius
scire possis, quantum quaque parte profeceris. Hunc ergo in
modum incipis:

    Gratia vobis & pax a Deo Patre nostro, & Domino nostro Iesu Christo.

Nihil est his in verbis mali, sed fecisse modestius uidereris, si
10 mores Apostoli potius esses imitatus, quam si tibi arrogasses
Apostolicum stylum. Nam Apostolicum est propemodum & illud: [A₂v]

*Non potuimus non gaudere, quando audiuimus & in Anglia Eu-
angelium gloriae Dei apud quosdam bene audire.*

15 An non haec dum legit, interim lectori subit Apostolus Ecclesiae quondam in cunis adhuc lactenti congratulans? Quem tu,
Pomerane, demum quam concinne nunc imitaris, scilicet? Quasi
velut olim, tempore Apostolorum, Corinthijs Euangelium
praedicari coepit, aut Galatis: ita nunc tandem, praedicantibus
20 vobis, Euangelium audiri coeperit & placere Britannis: atque id
tamen tam nuper, & parce, vt ne adhuc quidem in Britannia
bene audiat Euangelium Dei, nisi apud quosdam.

Quid tu appelles Euangelium, nescio: verum id scio, si id
fateris esse Euangelium, quod in mun-
25   *Verum Christi*   dum protulit Christus, quod quatuor
   Euangelium, ac eius   olim Euangelistae scripserunt, Mat-
   pulchra quaedam   thaeus, Marcus, Lucas & Ioannes, sic
   descriptio   intellectum, quomodo veteres omnes
Ecclesiae Proceres in[A₃]terpretati sunt, & totus Christianus
30 orbis annos iam plus quam mille & quingentos & intellexit, &
docuit: istud, inquam, Euangelium annos plus minus mille perpetuo bene audijt in Anglia, vsqueadeo vt illis etiam passim hic
placeret ac probaretur Euangelica fides, quorum fragilitas erat
infirmior, quam vt mores praestarent Euangelio dignos. Sin
35 Euangelium videri postulas noua ista, perniciosa & perabsurda
dogmata, quae velut Antichristus, nuper Lutherus inuexit in
Saxones, quae Carolostadius, Lambertus, Oecolampadius, ac
tute, non aliter ac Lutheri Cacangelistae promouetis, ac per

keeping quiet, I might perhaps increase the misplaced hope of the person who gave it to me. So I decided to reply to your letter and make it clear to everyone that no matter how ignorant I am of theology I am still too loyal a Christian ever to be a Lutheran. And so I will answer the parts of your epistle one by one, and let you see readily enough what you have accomplished in each. You begin, then, like this:

Grace be to you and peace from God our Father and our Lord Jesus Christ.

There is nothing wrong with that, but you would have seemed more modest if you had imitated the conduct of the apostle rather than the apostolic style. For this is almost apostolic too:

We could not but rejoice when we heard that in England, too, the gospel of the glory of God has been well received by certain persons.

On reading these words are we not reminded of the apostle congratulating the church when it was still a suckling babe in the cradle? How cleverly you imitate him! Just as the gospel was first preached to the Corinthians or Galatians in the time of the apostles, so too, now that you are preaching, you would have us believe, the gospel finally begins to be heard and welcomed by the British. But this is all so new, you say, and occurs so infrequently that the gospel of God is still not well received in Britain except among a few people.

I do not know what you call the gospel. But I know this: if you agree that the gospel is what Christ revealed to the world, and what the four Evangelists—Matthew, Mark, Luke, and John—wrote in the past, and what all the ancient leaders of the church interpreted as the gospel, and what the whole Christian world for more than fifteen hundred years has understood and taught as the gospel—this gospel, I say, has been well received in England continuously for a thousand years, more or less. In fact the faith of the gospels was welcomed everywhere in this nation and accepted even by those who were too weak and frail to act in a way that was worthy of the gospels. But if you want us to take as gospel those new, destructive, absurd doctrines that Luther, like another Antichrist, recently introduced among the Saxons—those doctrines that you, Karlstadt, Lambert, and Oecolampadius (Luther's cacangelists) foment and scatter

The true gospel of Christ, and a fine definition of it

orbem spargitis: sunt in Anglia profecto, id quod nos non
gaudere non possumus, vix quidam
Vtinam & hoc quoque
nunc tam vere dici liceat
apud quos adhuc bene audiat istud
Euangelium vestrum.

5   *CAETERVM & illud nobis annuntiatum est, multos infirmiores ad-*
huc auerti, propter rumores nescio quos [A₃v] *qui istic feruntur ab illis,*
qui Euangelio Dei aduersantur, de nobis. Haec est gloria nostra: tantum
abest, vt mendacia in Euangelij professores iactata refellenda duxerim:
alioqui in quo videretur illa beatitudo? Beati eritis, quum maledixerunt
10 *vobis homines.*

Auertuntur a vobis haud dubie non infirmiores, sed multo
firmiores in fide: non propter vlla mendacia, quae iactantur in
Euangelij professores (sic enim vocas Lutheranos) sed propter
assidua scelera, quae nimium vere designatis vos Euangelij per-
15 uersores. Nam quaeso te, quae mendacia feruntur de vobis? Aut
quomodo Euangelium profitemini? An mendacium esse con-
tendes, si quis factionem vestram dicat bonam Germaniae partem tumultu, caede, rapinis, incendio deuastasse? Audebis eos
mendaces dicere, qui vestram doctrinam impiam, tot scelerum,
20 tot damnorum, tot vastitatum causam esse testantur? [A₄] An
seditiones mouere, laicos in Clerum concitare, plebem in Magistratus armare, populos aduersus
Fructus doctrinae
Lutheranicae
Principes incendere, pugnas, ruinas,
bella, strages procurare, idem esse
25 probabis, quod Euangelium profiteri? Dic, obsecro, nobis
egregie professor Euangelij, destruere Sacramenta Christi,
Sanctos Christi spernere, Matrem Christi blasphemare, Crucem
Christi contemnere, vota Christo facta
Pietas ac religio quam
nouum Lutheri
Euangelium peperit
vilipendere, dicatum Christo caelibatum soluere, virginitatem Christo
30
consecratam polluere, Monachos ac
velatas Christo virgines ad coniugium, hoc est, ad perpetuum
stuprum hortari, nec hortari solum verbis improbis, sed exemplo quoque foedissimo prouocare: Dic, inquam, praeclare
35 professor Euangelij, vel tu Euangelista Lutheri, vel Christus tuus
Lutherus ipse, an haec flagitia facere & docere, id demum sit
Euangelium profiteri? [A₄v]

throughout the world—if that is what
you mean by the gospel, then there is
hardly anyone in England who wel-
comes that gospel of yours. And for
that we are very glad indeed.

Would that the same could be said as truthfully now

But we have also been told that many weaklings still reject us because of vague rumors reported of us there by those who oppose the gospel of God. This is our glory. I consider it unnecessary to refute the lies told about those who proclaim the gospel. How else could we experience in our own lives the beatitude, Blessed shall you be when men have reviled you?

As a matter of fact it is not the weaklings who turn away from you, but those who are much firmer in faith. They turn away not because of any lies told against those who profess the gospel (as you call the Lutherans), but because of the unending sins which you perverters of the gospel all too truly perpetrate. I ask you, what lies are you talking about? Or how do you profess the gospel? Would you call it a lie if someone says your sect has destroyed a good part of Germany in riots, murder, looting, and arson? Do you dare call people liars who testify that your unholy doctrine is the cause of so many crimes, so many injuries, so much desolation? Inciting riots, setting laymen against clergy, arming the people against magistrates, inflaming the people against princes, plotting battles, disasters, wars, massacres—do you call that preaching the gospel? Since you are a distinguished preacher of the gospel, tell us, I beg of you, whether one who destroys the sacraments of Christ, rejects the saints of Christ, blasphemes the mother of Christ, scorns the cross of Christ, makes

The fruits of Lutheran teaching

The piety and religion brought forth by the new gospel of Luther

light of vows made to Christ, renounces celibacy dedicated to Christ, defiles virginity consecrated to Christ, urges marriage (that is to say, everlasting defilement) on monks and virgins veiled for Christ—and who urges these things not just with words, foul as they may be, but who provokes them as well with his filthy example—tell us, I say, you famous preacher of the gospel—or evangelist of Luther, if you like, for Luther himself is your Christ—tell us whether doing and teaching these shameful things is what you call preaching the gospel.

Auertuntur igitur a vobis haud dubie (quod dixi) non infirmiores, sed multo firmiores in fide: non propter ea tantum, quae
vere narrantur de vobis, id est, ob ea quae tam scelerate passim
vestra designat factio, propter quae Deus vltione manifesta fac-
5 inorosam sectam persequitur: verum etiam quod talia vident
esse vestra dogmata, quae pugnent exitialiter aduersus doctrinam Christi.

Qua in re quanquam habeant contra conatus vestros in pleris-
que omnibus aperta Scripturae verba: tamen quo minus dubi-
10 tent in scripturae sensu non hallucinari se, habent aduersus in-
conditos clamores vestros (quibus nimirum solis probata vultis
haberi, quae dicitis) primum sanctissimos quosque Patres, quotquot olim illustrati diuinitus, & Scripturas elucidarunt, & op-
timorum exemplo morum, Chri[A₅]stiani populi promouerunt
15 pietatem. Habent deinde totius Orbis Christiani per tot aetates,
quot a Christo passo fluxerunt adusque vestra tempora, perpetuum consensum: quem si contenditis absque Sancto Spiritu
conspirasse, qui facit vnanimes in domo, si videri vultis Ecclesiam totam per tot secula (seducente Diabolo) in vnum consen-
20 sum potuisse coalescere aduersus Euangelium Christi: quid aliud agitis, quam vt funditus omnem adimatis Christi Euangelio
fidem? Quippe quod (vt ipsi fatemini) nec agnosci quidem posset, nisi commonstraret Ecclesia.

Habent aduersus vos & illud, quod ea quae iam docetis vos,
25 pleraque omnia docuerunt ij, quorum errores iam olim dam-
narunt Patres, quorum conuictum semper explosit Ecclesia,
quorum impietatem [A₅v] supplicio detexit Deus; quum vos e
diuerso nihil habeatis omnino, quod aduersus beatorum Patrum
vitas (quorum memorias tot aetates Ecclesia veneratur) prorsus
30 possitis hiscere. Illi ergo quum vniuersi nostram fidem propug-
nent, vestraque prosternant dogmata: quis non se declaret insanum, qui vestros velit authores eo sequi, quo suus eos demersit

There is no doubt, then, just as I said: it is not the weaklings who turn away from you, but those who are much firmer in faith. They turn away from you not only because of the truth told about you—I mean the vicious evils your faction is responsible for, which is why God pursues your vicious sect with manifest vengeance—they also turn away from you because they see that your doctrines are opposed to the teaching of Christ in a fight to the finish.

And speaking of doctrines—in almost every instance they have clear scriptural evidence to oppose to your efforts. Still, to be certain they are not deceived about the meaning of scripture, they have first of all every one of the Fathers to set against your wild yawps. (But of course that is all you want, to prove your points by yelling.) They have all the ancient Fathers who were enlightened by God and not only interpreted scripture, but also provided an example of noble behavior and thus increased the piety of the Christian people. They also have the support of an unshaken consensus of the whole Christian world through all the ages, from the passion of Christ down to your own time. But perhaps you object that this consensus came about without the help of the Holy Spirit, who makes all men of one mind in his house. Or you may want to pretend that the devil deceived the whole church through all those centuries and brought it to-gether in a consensus against Christ's gospel. If that is the case, you are simply denying the possibility of any faith in the gospel of Christ whatsoever. For unless the church had shown you the gospel in the first place, you would have had no way of knowing what it is. You admit that yourselves.

They also score this against you, that almost everything you currently teach was previously taught by men whose errors have long since been condemned by the Fathers of the church. When-ever heretics gather together, the church has always driven them out, and God has revealed their wickedness by the punishment inflicted on them. But you, on the other hand, have nothing whatsoever to insinuate against the lives of the blessed Fathers, whose memory the church has venerated for so many ages past. All of them fight for our faith and overthrow yours. A person, therefore, would have to be mad to follow the founders of your faith down where their errors have drowned them. Anyone

error, ac non ijs malit adiungi, quos cum Christo regnare, nec
vos dubitatis, qui, quoad potestis, per odium illis atque inuidiam
detrahitis? Nam initio quum falso vobis esset persuasum, vos
omnia solos scire, orthodoxae fidei stu-

Luterus eiusque sectatores diosis nihil vsquam legi praeter concer-
5 *noui Gnostici & omniscij*
tationes scholasticas: tum freti (vt videbatur vobis) aliena ignorantia, profitebamini sanctorum
Patrum sententijs vos staturos. At posteaquam vos vidistis vestra
spe atque opinione falli, & iam decreta vestra passim sanctis-
10 simorum virorum testimonijs redargui: [A₆] tum vero vobis e
superbia tam immanis natus est liuor, vt dum Superis pudet
cedere, statueritis inferis omnia deuouere. Sic ea demum nata
est apud vos & impia simul & insanis-

Ipsius Lutheri verba sima blasphemia: *Non curo decem Hiero-*
15 *nymos, non curo centum Cyprianos, non curo mille Augustinos, non*
decies mille Chrysostomos.

Denique ne quid officeret luminibus vestris Sanctorum cum
Christo regnantium gloriosa maiestas & splendor: aggressi estis
conceptam de illis opinionem reuellere, dignationem lacessere,
20 autoritatem detrahere, cultum omnem atque honorem, quoad
potuistis, auferre. Sed illi, Pomerane, fortes & inuulnerabiles, &
iam in sublimi petra collocati, conatus vestros inualidos, vt par-
uulorum sagittas, irrident. Honorantur

Psal. 63 enim, & honorabuntur semper amici
25 Dei, & viuet eorum memoria in secu-
Psal. 138
lum seculi: quum eorum interim [A₆v]
omnium, quos vester error tam multiplex, ab haeretico quisquis
erat primo, per tot aetates habet auto-

Psal. 9 res, memoria perierit cum sonitu. Nam
30 cum tot orthodoxi libri, per tot saecula sic seruati sint, vt pretium
cum tempore creuerit: haereticorum omnium, paulo post suam
cuiusque mortem, sic interierunt opera, vt hodie nullius antiqui
quicquam prorsus extet vsquam. Nec tamen olim, quum peri-
bant illa, legibus adhuc erat cautum, vt addicerentur ignibus: vt

would prefer to join himself to those who reign with Christ, and you have no doubt that they do reign with him, even though out of hatred and envy you do whatever you can to disparage them. At first you wrongly persuaded yourselves somehow that you were the only ones who knew anything and that learned men among orthodox Christians never read anything except scholastic controversies. And so, rely-

Luther and his followers are the new Gnostics and omniscients

ing on the ignorance of others (as it seemed to you), you stated that you would take your stand on the opinions of the holy Fathers. Afterward, however, you saw that your hope and expectations were all wrong. The testimony of those saintly men refuted all your basic principles. Then in truth your pride led you to such monstrous hatred that, since you are ashamed to submit to heaven, you have decided to damn everything to hell. And so, you gave birth to this ungodly and completely insane blasphemy: *I care not for ten Jeromes, I care not for a hundred Cyprians, I care not*

Luther's own words

for a thousand Augustines, nor for ten thousand Chrysostoms.

And finally, for fear the glorious majesty and splendor of the saints who reign with Christ will dim your lights, you have begun to destroy the received opinion about them. You attack their reputation, disparage their authority, and take away as much of their veneration and honor as you possibly can. But they are powerful and invulnerable, Pomeranus. They stand at this moment on a lofty rock and laugh at your feeble attacks as at the arrows of children. For the friends of God are accorded honor and they always will be. Their memory will live forever. But the memory of all those will perish together with the sound of their words, all those who created the labyrinths of your deceptions, from the time of the very first heretic,

Psalm 63

Psalm 138

Psalm 9

whoever that was, through all the ages. Although thousands of orthodox books have been preserved over the centuries, increasing in value with age, the works of all the heretics have disappeared shortly after their deaths. No work of any ancient heretic exists today. And yet when those heretical works disappeared in ages past, there was no law that said they had to be consigned to

plane testatum sit, ipsius Dei manu factum, vt haereticorum
telae velut aranearum casses deciderent, & per se neglectae sordibus & situ funditus exolescerent. Nec dubium est, quin vestris
quoque laboribus (qui multo maiorem moliuntur Christianae
5 pietati perniciem) haud minus pernix instet atque incumbat interitus: quum sanctorum interim Patrum (quantumuis ringatur
inuidia) & venerabilis erit memoria, & in manibus flo[A₇]rescent
opera: e quibus aduersus vestra venena (quibus almum Scripturae fontem inficitis) assidue sugat populus fidelis antidotum.
10 Quorum consensus Patrum vt fortiter aduersus vos consistit: ita
non minus fortiter vestra vos oppugnat dissensio, qua non sin-
guli solum pugnant inter se, verum etiam quisque passim dissentit sibi. Verum vt ista, quae dixi, multaque itidem alia Catholicos
auertunt a vobis: ita procul dubio cordatos viros abstrahunt &
15 illa factionis vestrae plusquam scelerata facinora.

   Qua in re rursus ac rursus miror, ita me amet Deus, qua fronte
possis scribere mendacia confingi de vobis, & eam esse omnem
gloriam vestram. Adeo tibi fugit pudor omnis, vt sustineas dicere, ea falso factionis vestrae sicarijs impingi, quae nec ipse
20 nescis, nimium vere passim magno cum Germaniae tumultu, &
tot millium internecione [A₇v] patrari? Et quum tam immania
sint sacrilega illa facinora, quibus grassatur in praeceps
effraenata licentia, praetextu libertatis Euangelicae, vt vix vlla sit
vrbs in bona parte Germaniae, vix oppidum vllum, villa, domus,
25 rusculum, vbi non ista vestra factio rapinae, stuprorum, sanguinis, sacrilegij, caedis, incendij, ruinae ac vastitatis tristissima
monumenta reliquerit: tu nobis interim, Pomerane, quam Eu-
angelice succinis? *Haec est gloria nostra.* Nec dignaris refellere,
sed beatos praedicas esse vos, quum vobis maledicunt homines.
30 Recte ista, si mendacia in vos confingerentur. Recte, si ideo vobis
maledicerent homines, quia vos bene faceretis. At nunc quid
dicere possis ineptius, quum vos vere tanta mala & facitis, &
docetis, vt maiora de vobis ne fingere quidem quisquam possit?
Et quam praeclare gloriaris, quasi beati sitis, scilicet, quod vobis

---

17 scribere] scribere: *1568*

the flames. It was thus clearly demonstrated that God destroyed them himself by his own hand so that the snares of heretics might give way like spiderwebs and disappear completely, neglected like dirt and filth. No doubt just as quick a destruction threatens and overhangs your labors, for they constitute a far greater danger to Christian piety. Envy may well bare its teeth and snarl, but the memory of those holy Fathers will be revered, their works will grow in popularity, and the faithful will ever draw from them an antidote against the poisons with which you infect the life-giving wellspring of scripture. The Fathers of the church stand firmly in consensus against you, but you also stand just as firmly in opposition to yourselves because of your own internal dissension. You not only contend against one another, but each of you also disagrees with himself, over and over again. No doubt Catholics turn away from you because of the things I have mentioned and many others like them. I also have no doubt that you alienate thoughtful people by the unspeakably wicked crimes your faction commits.

God love me, I am amazed, time and again, at this: how you can have the gall to write that people are lying about you and that that is all your glory? Have you no shame? How can you stand yourself when you say that the murderers belonging to your sect are falsely accused when you know yourself they are guilty as charged, witness the uprisings all over Germany and the slaughter of so many thousands. Unbridled license rages to such an extent under pretext of freedom of the gospel that there is hardly a city in most of Germany, hardly a town, countryseat, house, or farm where your sect has not left bitter reminders of looting, rape, bloodshed, sacrilege, slaughter, fire, ruin, and devastation. When your sect commits such monstrous, sacrilegious crimes, Pomeranus, how can you chant to us so evangelically that *this is our glory?* You do not bother to make a rebuttal, you simply proclaim that you are blessed when men curse you. And you would be right if people were making up lies about you. You would be right if you were cursed because you did what was right. But no one could possibly invent anything about you worse than what you already teach and do, and so your argument is completely beside the point. How splendidly you preen yourself! You put it, of course, that you are blessed because men

maledicant homines propter iustitiam: quum [A₈] re vera propter iniquitates vestras, propter scelera, seditiones, caedes,
rapinas, haereses, & perniciosa schismata meritissimo iure vobis
& homines maledicant, & Deus?

5   Sed istud videlicet animos tibi facit, quod ista Wittenbergae
non fiant: nam ita videris tibi praeclare moderari sermonem,
quum statim ista subiungis:

Neque tamen defendimus, si qui alibi praetextu Christianae libertatis
quid designent non Christianum: quandoquidem non omnes Christum
10 *induerunt, qui Christi nomen sibi vendicant.*

Quam modeste, quam parce moderaris istud, Pomerane? Si
qui, Si quid, Si alibi, Si non Christianum: quum intelligas, &
vbique ferme, & omnes, qui quidem vestri sint, & omnia, non
solum non Christiana, verum etiam passim designare plusquam
15 Diabolica. Quod si Wittenberga sibi temperaret ab istorum socie-
tate facinorum, an id satis esse [A₈v] causae censes, vnde vestris
dogmatibus accrescat autoritas: e quibus videamus reliquam
Germaniam totam concuti, periclitari, subuerti? Verum quis
credat integram scelerum Wittenbergam esse, qui videat ex illo
20 fonte profluere totam istam lutulenti coeni colluuiem, quae tam
late terras omnes tetra peste peruasit?

Integra scilicet Wittenberga sit, in qua Lutherus scelerum caput, malorum machinator & artifex, truculenti Dux exercitus
castra sibi fixit: vbi legatis assidentibus vobis in horas initur con-
25   silium, quo non aliud quam de mouen-
       Scopus consilij   da seditione, de subruenda fide, de ex-
       Lutheranorum   tirpanda Religione, de prophanandis
sacris, de corrumpendis moribus, de prostituendis Virginibus,
de populanda virtute tractatur. Vnde velut e Praetorio datur
30 signum, petuntur tesserae, mandata mittuntur, & summittuntur
auxilia. Vos ardentem facem in totam immisistis Germaniam.
[B₁] Vos ingentem flammam, qua nunc ardet orbis, accendistis.
Vos adhuc flatu noxio sceleratum promouetis incendium. Et
quum haec & illustriora sint, quam vt latere, & sparsa latius,
35 quam vt negari, & magis perniciosa, quam vt tolerari queant: tu,
Pomerane, tamen quam sancte nobis ista praescribis?

---

20 colluuiem,] colluuiem: *1568*   25 aliud] aliud, *1568*

curse you for the sake of righteousness, when in fact both man and God curse you with perfect justice because of your iniquities, because of your crimes, your sedition, slaughter, pillaging, heresies, and pernicious schisms.

You are obviously encouraged because such things do not happen at Wittenberg, for it is remarkable how you seem to qualify your language by immediately adding:

But we make no defense if men elsewhere perform unchristian acts under the pretext of Christian liberty, since not everyone who claims for himself the name of Christ has put on Christ.

How discreetly, how cautiously you put all that, Pomeranus— *if anyone . . . if anything . . . if elsewhere . . . if unchristian*—when you are well aware that it is almost everywhere and everything and everyone—everyone, that is, who belongs to your sect. You do things that are not only unchristian, but absolutely diabolic. If Wittenberg refrains from participating in those crimes, do you think that is sufficient reason for people to attribute any authority to your beliefs? After all, we can see that your beliefs stir up, endanger, and destroy all the rest of Germany. Who could believe that Wittenberg is pure and innocent when he sees that it is the fountain from which flows all the sewage and filthy muck that carries foul corruption and broadens out through all the earth?

But of course Wittenberg is innocent. It is simply the place where Luther pitched his camp—Luther, captain of evildoing, architect and artificer of evil, leader of an army of savages. In council with you and his other lieutenants he makes plans hour by hour, devising nothing but how to incite rebellions, subvert the faith, uproot religion, profane holy things, corrupt morals, prostitute virgins, and destroy virtue. Just as if it were a council of war, the signal is given, passwords devised, commands issued, and reinforcements dispatched. You hurled a burning torch on all of Germany. You lit the wildfire that is now consuming the world, and you keep on fanning the wicked flames with your poisonous breath. All this is too well known to be concealed, too widely circulated to be denied, and too destructive to be tolerated. So how can you write so sanctimoniously, Pomeranus, and say:

The aim of the Lutherans' plan

Hoc certe miramur, cur sacrum Christi Euangelium quidam isthic
verentur suscipere: propterea quod de nobis mala dicuntur, ignorantes
quod oportet filium hominis reprobari a mundo, & stultitiam haberi
praedicationem Crucis.

5   Desine, Pomerane, mirari, & omnes vobis desinite tam impen-
se placere, quam falso. Neque sic insaniatis, vt velitis e duobus
aut tribus Apostatis, & a Christi fide transfugis, totam aestimare
Britanniam. Si minus tibi notus est populus (quem si pernosses,
aliter sentias) si minus noti Pontifices, (qui si cuiusmodi sunt,
10   intelligeres, im[B₁v]probam istam spem deposuisses): at vel ex
eruditione notior tibi sit, necesse est, quam vt eius ditionem de-
beas tibi corrumpendam sumere, huius inclyti regni Princeps,
non magis inuictus, quam pius, quum sit inuictissimus. Is quum
iam pridem praeceptorem tuum Sacramenta Christi oppug-
15   nantem clarissimis Scripturis & euidenti ratione prostrauerit:
vnde tibi tandem fiducia creuit, vt eius populum te speres posse
seducere? An quod absque manuum impositione, contra sacras
literas, contra Sanctorum dogmata, contra totius Ecclesiae perpetuam consuetudinem, ausus es Episcopi tibi nomen arrogare
20   Wittenbergae, ibique, velut officij sancti doctrinam salutarem,
praeter inuectas haereses alias, adiuncta tibi, quum Sacerdos
esses, ac vouisses castitatem, libidinis tuae socia, docere sis ausus
homines, Deo dicata vota negligere: idcirco viam tibi factam [B₂]
censuisti, qua Pontificis munus obires apud Anglos, atque id tam
25   valde magnifice? Tanquam apud nos successus omnis Euangelici
negocij prorsus penderet a vobis, velut si vos hic bene audiatis,
prosperet Euangelium: sin laboretis infamia, res Euangelica
simul abeat retro.

Nae vos profecto magnifice fallimini. Nam nec Euangelium
30   hîc tam parui fit, neque vos tam magni, vt propter vos aut recip-
iatur, aut repudietur Euangelium. Sed nec filius hominis re-
probatur a nobis, nec habetur pro stultitia praedicatio Crucis.
Imo (quae scandalum Iudaeis est, & stultitia gentibus) ea Christi

What surprises us is this: why is it that some people there are afraid to receive the holy gospel of Christ because evil is spoken of us, not remembering that it behooves the son of man to be reproved by the world and the preaching of the cross to be esteemed foolishness?

Stop wondering, Pomeranus. All of you, stop being so immensely and mistakenly pleased with yourselves. Do not be so insane as to want to form an opinion of all the people in Britain from two or three apostates and deserters of the faith of Christ. You know little about the common people. If you did, you would think differently. You know little about the bishops. If you understood what sort of men they are, you would abandon your audacious hopes. And because of his learning, you should at least have known that you could not take over and corrupt the authority of the king of this glorious realm. For he is as devout as he is invincible—completely invincible. He defeated your master long ago when Luther was warring against the sacraments. He defeated him by using overt scriptural evidence and irrefutable logic. So how can you be so confident as to hope to seduce his people? Is it because you dare to claim for yourself the title of Bishop of Wittenberg without the laying on of hands—which is contrary to sacred scripture, contrary to the teaching of the saints, contrary to the custom of the entire church through all the ages? Besides bringing in other heresies, you dared to instruct the people of Wittenberg to ignore vows made to God, acting as if your instruction were wholesome and suited to your holy office. For although you were a priest and had taken the vow of chastity, you joined yourself to a female companion in lust. Did you think that opened the door and cleared the way for you to assume the office of Pope of the English, and to do it so grandly too! You speak as though every success the gospels enjoy here depends completely on you. You would have us believe that the gospel prospers when you are well received here, and that when you fall in disgrace, the cause of the gospel is likewise set back.

You certainly are wrong about that! For the gospel is not taken so lightly here, nor are you so highly regarded that it is either accepted or rejected because of you. Nor is the son of man reproved by us and the preaching of the cross esteemed as foolishness. In fact the cross of Christ is glorious to us Christians,

Crux gloria est Christianis nobis. Sed profecto ridiculum est,
quoties audimus Lutheranos magnifice loquentes de Cruce, cum
in Crucem ipsam Christi (quae sacrum & venerabile corpus eius
in sua Passione, nostra vero redemptione gestauit) [B₂v] ip-
5 sorum Christus Lutherus, homo non vna tantum cruce dignus,
tam impias passim blasphemias euomat. Quas ne quis me putet
fingere, legat, qui volet, execrandam eius concionem de Cruce.
Quae scelerata concio, vna cum alijs eiusdem, & aliorum item e
vobis, multo adhuc sceleratioribus libellis, quum nusquam fere
10 non prostent, nusquam non odorem tetrum & tartareum virus
exhalent: tu tamen, perinde ac si codices omnes vestri dilaberen-
tur e coelo, merum nectar, meram redolentes Ambrosiam, non
erubescis hoc pacto scribere:

Quid si verum esset, quod de nobis mentiuntur propter Christum: ipsi
15 *scilicet ideo non susciperent a Deo oblatum Euangelium salutis? Quid*
stultius, quam vt magis curiosus sis ad meam iniquitatem, quam ad tuam
salutem? Ideo tu nolis esse Christianus, quia ego sum peccator? [B₃]

Pape, quam praeclare simul & facete, scilicet? Quasi mentiantur, qui te, cum sacerdos esses, & coelibem castitatem promisisses
20 Deo, nunc duxisse dicant vxorem, id est, quum videri velis Episcopus, publicum & perpetuum esse scortatorem. Aut quasi
mentiantur, qui de Lamberto vestro, qui Franciscanus erat, ac de
multis praeterea Lutheranis alijs idem praedicarent: aut mentiantur denique, qui Lutherum ipsum dicerent, quum Augusti-
25 nianus erat, per stuprum iunxisse sibi, velut coniugem, diu iam
dicatam & Deo direptam Monacham: aut qui vos omnes dicat,
haereses impias & insanas inuehere, aut vestram factionem
clamitet multa passim flagitia designare. Quam rem nimium veram esse, vtinam non tot locorum miserae vastitates, non tot
30 millium doctrina vestra seductorum strages miseranda compro-
baret.

Sed ista tot scelera vestra tamen [B₃v] obstare non debent, quo
minus recipiamus a vobis Euangelium salutis: quasi nunc primum per vos offerat nobis Deus Euangelium salutis. Eu-
35 angelium ergo Christi, quod Euangelistae scripserunt, quod
praedicarunt Apostoli, quod Sanctissimi Patres interpretati
sunt, non erat Euangelium salutis? Nec hactenus a Christo passo

though a stumbling block to the Jews and foolishness to the Gentiles. It is utterly ridiculous to hear the Lutherans speak so highly of the cross when their Christ (that is, Luther—a man deserving a few crosses himself) vomits such ungodly blasphemies against the cross of Christ, which bore his holy and venerable body during his passion—or rather, our redemption. If anyone thinks I am inventing all this, he has only to read Luther's detestable sermon on the cross, which is on sale almost everywhere, along with other still more sinful tracts by the same author and others, exuding their foul odor and hellish stench. But you act as if all your books fluttered down from heaven smelling of pure nectar, pure ambrosia, and so you are not ashamed to write:

What if the lies that men tell about us for Christ's sake were true? Would they therefore not accept the gospel of salvation offered to them by God? What could be more foolish than to be more concerned with my wickedness than with your own salvation! Will you therefore be no Christian because I am a sinner?

Wonderful! You put that so well and so cleverly! Is it a lie to say that although you were a priest and had vowed to God never to marry, you have nevertheless taken a wife? Or to say that, although you want to be regarded as a bishop, you are a common fornicator every day of your life? Or is it a lie to say the same thing about your friend Lambert, who was a Franciscan, and many other Lutherans as well? Or is it a lie to say that Luther himself, when he was an Augustinian monk, engaged in whoredom, not marriage, with a nun dedicated to God for many years and then stolen from him? Or is it a lie to say that all of you introduce wicked, crazy heresies or to proclaim that your sect commits many disgraceful things throughout the world? Would that the miserable devastation of so many places and the pitiful destruction of so many thousands of people seduced by your teaching did not prove how true all these statements are.

But these manifold sins of yours should not be an obstacle to our receiving the gospel of salvation from you. Would you have us believe that through you God first offered us the gospel of salvation? The gospel of Christ, the gospel that the evangelists wrote, the apostles preached, and the holy Fathers of the church interpreted, was not that the gospel of salvation? Was no one

quisquam seruatus est, quoad nunc demum vos elegit Deus, per
quos seruaret mundum, ac miseris, & hactenus per Apostolos &
Euangelistas, perditis & seductis mortalibus, offerret Euangelium salutis? Certe, Pomerane, si vera sunt ista (vt sunt pro-
5 fecto verissima) quae tu mentiris, nos mentiri de vobis: haberi
non debet absurdum, si respicientes impietatem vestram, non
satis fidamus vobis, nec satis credamus idoneos, qui (quum tam
foedis vlceribus laboretis ipsi) salutem [B₄] afferatis alijs. Nam si
hactenus per tot saecula non habuissent Christiani verum Eu-
10 angelium Christi, sed in fide Christi tota tot aetates errasset Ecclesia: non esset dubitandum, quin bonos & pios esset electurus
Deus, quibus hoc demandaret negotij, vt in nouitatem spiritus a
carne reuocarent mundum: additurus haud dubie tantae rei,
quae fidem facerent praedicationi, miracula. Nec tantam rem
15 tam negligenter ageret, vt quos olim suam fidem praedicare
vetuit (quum per Prophetam peccatori
Psal. 49 dixit Deus: Quare tu enarras iustitias
meas, & assumis testamentum meum per os tuum?) eos nunc
demum solos, per quos praedicaretur, eligeret. Et cum eis credi
20 vellet ab omnibus, nihil tamen omnino faceret, cur eis credere
quisquam aut deberet, aut posset.

Nam quod Lutherus haberi postulat pro miraculo, quod tantum Chri[B₄v]stiani populi tam breui tempore a Christi fide in
ipsius desciscat haereses: facit certe absurditas earum & insania,
25 vt nonnihil monstri simile videatur, quenquam cui scintilla sit
vlla sensus humani, tantum vnquam posse furiosae persuasionis
admittere. Caeterum ad propositam vitae libidinosae licentiam
populum praecipitem ruere, id habet tantam miraculi speciem,
quam saxa deorsum cadere.

30 Iam quod ita, Pomerane, quaeris, cur non sequuntur Pauli
regulam: Omnia probate, quod bonum
1 Thess. 5 est tenete: Hoc vnum Pauli verbum
vestra subuertit omnia. Nam quum omnia probando, vestra
comperimus pessima, tenemus quod bonum est: nempe quod
35 eos docuisse legimus, quorum sibi placuisse Deus & vitam testa-

saved from the time of Christ's passion until this present moment, when God finally chose you to save the world and preach the gospel of salvation to wretched mortals, corrupted and led astray until now by the apostles and evangelists? You lie, Pomeranus, when you say that we lie about you and that the things we say are not true, for they are true indeed. Is it so odd, then, considering your wickedness, that we do not trust you enough or think you are the right sort of people to bring others health and salvation when you yourselves suffer from such horrible running sores? For if after all these years Christians still did not possess the true gospel of Christ and if the whole church were mistaken about the faith of Christ for so many generations, God would have undoubtedly chosen some good, holy men for his work of recalling the world from the flesh to a renewal of the spirit. In something as important as that God would undoubtedly also have performed miracles to encourage belief in what was being preached. He would not have been so careless as to choose to preach his faith those very men, and only those men, to whom he had already forbidden that right. For through the prophet God spoke to the sinner: "What right have you to speak of my laws and take *Psalm 49* my covenant upon your lips?" Since God wanted all men to believe his holy preachers, why would he be so careless as not to do anything whereby people could or should believe them?

Luther claims it is a miracle that in such a short time so many Christians deserted the faith of Christ and went over to his heresies. To be sure, his heresies are absurd and crazy enough to make it seem like a portent of some sort that anyone with a spark of human intelligence would entertain such wild beliefs. As for people rushing headfirst into the life of freedom and sensual gratification he offers them—that seems about as much like a miracle as rocks falling downhill.

Now as for that question of yours, Pomeranus, why people do not follow Paul's rule: "Test all things, and hold fast to what is good." That one *1 Thessalonians 5* sentence of Paul's subverts everything you say. When we test all things, we discover that what you write is the worst, and we hold fast to the good. And the good we hold fast to is the writings of those men whose life and faith God indicates were pleasing to

tur, & fidem. Respuimus vestra, quoniam sanctorum Patrum sunt & moribus, & doctrinae contraria, &, quod est adhuc amplius, [B₅] aduersa publicae fidei tot aetatum, totius Ecclesiae.

Matt. vlt.

Cuius fidem nisi regat Deus, & Euangelij vacillat authoritas, & non est verax in verbis veritas, quae se promisit cum ea futuram vsque ad consummationem seculi.

Sed iam operae pretium fuerit, considerare paululum: quam tecte, quam timide doctrinae vestrae vlcus attingis.

Verum aiunt, inquis, rudiores: quis ista tam varia capere poterit? Disputatur enim de libero arbitrio, de votis & sectis monasticis, de satisfactionibus, de abusu venerandae Eucharistiae, de cultu Sanctorum, de statu defunctorum, de purgatorio. Alij aiunt: veremur, ne sub ista varietate lateat venenum.

Non recte rem accipis, Pomerane. Neque enim veretur quisquam, ne sub ista varietate lateat venenum. Imo videmus & scimus, verissimum esse et manifestum toxicum, quod vos his de rebus omnibus, non sobrie quidem disse[B₅v]ritis, sed impie atque arroganter decernitis. Nam quum eo nomine soleatis insectari Theologiam scholasticam, quod illic cum periculo veritas trahatur in dubium: a vobis falsitas pro indubio aduersus verum asseritur, & quod illic pro argumento proponitur, id vnum apud vos pro veritate concluditur.

Quaeritur in scholis, sitne aliqua libertas arbitrij, an omnia temere agantur, an regantur fato: An

Theologia scholastica a calumnijs vindicata & eiusdem vtilitas

diuinae maiestatis voluntas indeclinabilis ab aeterno sic decreuit omnia, vt in tota rerum natura nihil admittat omnino, quod in vtramlibet partem sese possit conuertere: An pugnent inter se humani arbitrij libertas, & Dei praescientia: Nostrae voluntatis libertatem an Adae peccatum peremerit, an perimat Christi gratia. Haec atque huiusmodi talia quum proponuntur in scholis, si sobrie disserantur & proposito pio: non [B₆] exiguum certe fructum affert disputatio. Conueniunt enim in

2 contraria,] contraria. *1568*

him. We reject your writings because they are contrary to the
deeds and teaching of the holy Fathers and, what is even more
important, because they are contrary to the faith of the people of
the whole church through so many centuries. If God did not
guide the faith of his church, the authority of the gospel would
waver, and there would truly be no
truth in the words whereby Truth *The last chapter of*
promises he will be with her even to the *Matthew*
end of the world.

It would be useful now to consider a bit how carefully and
tenderly you touch the sore spot in your teaching.

But, the less educated will say, you assert, *Who is able to understand
all these different arguments? Men dispute about free will, about vows
and monastic orders, about works of satisfaction, abuse of the holy eucharist, the worship of saints, the whereabouts of the dead, and purgatory.
Others say, We are afraid that poison is hidden under all this
disagreement.*

You do not have it right, Pomeranus. No one is afraid that
poison is hidden under all this disagreement. On the contrary,
we see and we know that the poison is there, very real and apparent. You do not bother to discuss it soberly and rationally. You
simply pontificate about it impudently and arrogantly. You always mock scholastic theology on the pretext that it is dangerous
because it brings truth into doubt. But you assert that falsehood
is absolutely true, even against the truth. The only thing you
accept as truth is what theology proposes in the schools merely
for the sake of argument.

In the schools men raise such questions as whether the will has
any freedom, whether all things occur
at random, whether they are ruled by *Scholastic theology*
fate, whether the unchanging will of *defended against false*
the divine majesty has decreed all *accusations, and its*
things from eternity in such a way that *usefulness*
in the whole natural order he allows no possibility for anything
to follow one alternative rather than the other, whether man's
free will and God's foreknowledge contradict one another,
whether Adam's sin removed our free will, or whether it is removed by Christ's grace. When these questions and others like
them are proposed in the schools and are discussed calmly and

In disputatione de rebus
sacris quae sint
obseruanda

disceptationem nihil de fine dubij:
quippe qui conclusiones earum rerum
omnium firmas & inconcussas semper
circumferunt secum: impressas vi-
5 delicet cordibus Fidelium omnium ex fidei Christianae dogmatibus, plerasque etiam publico quodam communis sensus
proloquio. Nam quotusquisque est, qui quidem sensum aliquem
habet rationis humanae, qui non sibi persuadeat, & Deum, qui
facit omnia praescire omnia, & sese tamen experimento sentiat,
10 actiones suas non aliena vi, sed sua voluntate peragere? Iam
quum rationes aut Scripturae proferuntur aduersus eam partem, quam illi veram habent atque infallibilem: vtiliter exercent
ingenia, & adspirante Deo, qui pios conatus promouet, multa
perspicue soluunt: de quibus & Deo gratias agunt, & non ipsi
15 modo iucundissimam atque honestissimam, [B₆v] addo etiam
sanctissimam, animi voluptatem capiunt, verum alijs etiam doctrinae scitu dignae salubres fructus afferunt. Scripturas enim in
speciem veritati contrarias clariorum collatione scripturarum di-
lucidant. Quod si quis in sacris literis textum alicunde quempiam
20 ita durum arbitretur ac difficilem, vt ipsi nullius, neque veteris
cuiusquam, neque recentioris interpretatio satisfaciat, quo
minus publico alicui fidei Catholicae articulo videatur occurrere:
statim succurrit illi, quod beatissimus pater Augustinus ad-
monuit, aut aliquam librorum mendam impedire, aut eius loci
25 sensum se non satis assequi. Neque enim quisquam sacrarum
literarum locus adeo me commouere debet, vt si quid aduersus
ea dicere videatur, quae pro certis & indubitatis articulis am-
plexa est Ecclesia Christi Catholica, a gnisiis & germanis fidei
Christianae dogmatibus dimouear atque [B₇] depellar. Quippe
30 quae certo persuasum habeam, eundem Spiritum cordibus in-
scripsisse fidelium, qui affuit scribentibus Euangelia: atque ideo
quicquid illi scripserunt, Ecclesiae fidei esse consentaneum: si
quale scriptum est, tale perseueret, & quo sensu scriptum est,
eodem queat intelligi. Quod si aut vitium literis obuenerit, aut

9 omnia,] omnia: *1568*   11 rationes] rationes, *1568*

for a pious purpose, the debate pro-
duces results that are quite useful. For *What must be observed in*
theologians enter into debate together *disputes about sacred*
with no doubt as to the final outcome. *things*
They always carry around in their heads firm and unshakable
conclusions about everything they discuss—the same conclusions that are impressed on the hearts of all the faithful by the
teachings of the Christian faith, and many of them also by some
public pronouncement of the the ordinary belief. Take people
who have some shred of human intelligence. They are convinced that God, who makes all things, foresees all things. At the
same time they also know from experience that they do what
they do by their own free will and not from some external compulsion. Now when theologians bring reason or scripture to bear
on what they hold to be true and infallible, then they use their
talents to advantage. They solve many problems by the inspiration of God, who assists devout endeavors, for which they give
him thanks. They not only take an intellectual pleasure in this—
one that is most pleasant, most honest, and I might even add
most holy—they also give others the fruits of their teachings,
which are not only sound, but well worth knowing. They shed
light on passages of scripture by comparing those that seem
contrary to truth with other passages that are more easily understood. But suppose someone thinks a particular text in sacred
scripture is so hard and difficult that no one, neither ancient nor
modern, can interpret it satisfactorily so as to make it seem not
contradictory to some common article of the Catholic faith.
Then all of a sudden he recalls the advice of the holy Father
Augustine that there is either a mistake in the text or he has not
followed the sense of the passage well enough. For no passage in
sacred scripture ought to disturb me like that. If it seems to
contradict what the Catholic church of Christ has embraced as
sure and undoubted articles of faith, I should not allow it to
separate me and drive me away from the genuine, legitimate
teachings of the Christian faith, since I am convinced that these
teachings were written in the hearts of the faithful by the same
Spirit who was present to the evangelists as they wrote. And so
whatever they wrote is consistent with the faith of the church so
long as it remains as it was written and can be understood in the
same sense in which it was written. Even if there is a corrupt

textus ex se sit obscurior: non est cur quisquam debeat minus
habere pro certis, quae Christus docuit Ecclesiam suam, quam
per Spiritum sanctum docuit omnem veritatem, & se cum ea
promisit ad finem vsque seculi futu-
5   *Ioan. 16*   rum: curaturum nimirum (quod pre-
         Matt. 28   cibus impetrauit a patre) ne vllis libro-
rum mendis (quas per studiosorum
hominum laborem sanctum repurgat indies) nullis literarum
ambagibus (quas, quibus ipsi temporibus visum est, per erudi-
10 torum calamos virorum explicat) nullis tyrannorum persecu-
tionibus (quos Martyrum suorum [B₇v] victorijs subiugauit) nullis haereticorum conatibus (quorum ora per orthodoxorum
Patrum libros obstruit) nullis denique machinamentis Diaboli
(quem ipse prostrauit in cruce) fides Ecclesiae possit deficere.
15   Quod si quid humanae rationis inter disputandum videatur
oppugnare veritatem, nihil ex ea re deperit pietati: quando ea
quae fidei sunt, certum sit atque exploratum, vt diuina reuela-
tione fulciri, sic rationem omnem mortalium longissime super-
are. Itaque sicut quaedam tanto spectamus iucundius, quanto
20 minus eorum causam rationemque possumus deprehendere:
Sic eo magis in suauissimam diuinae maiestatis admirationem
subuehimur, quo magis ea dissidere videntur & inter se pugnare, quae simul tamen consistere & consentire sit indubitatissimum. Sic & sine noxa, Pomerane, & non absque fructu,
25 talia disputari possunt in scho[B₈]lis: quum vos interim, qui
Scholasticas disputationes tanquam veritatis altercatrices, &
mysteriorum temeratrices inuaditis, conclusiones absurdissi-
mas, & haereses insanissimas aduersus homines omnes, aduersus Deum ipsum credendas omnibus absque seria vlla discepta-
30 tione praescribitis. Et quicquid vanitatis asserit Lutherus, illud
irrefragabile, & quod Graeci dicunt ἀκίνητον, haberi postulatis:
vt rationem poscentibus impij atque insani dogmatis, satis haberi
debeat, quod αὐτὸς ἔφα: nimirum, quia se certum clamat ipse,
dogmata sua se habere de coelo. Et quum praeter ipsius com-
35 menta stolidissima, contra perpetuam totius Ecclesiae senten-

---

9–10 ambagibus (quas, quibus . . . est, . . . explicat)] ambagibus, quas (quibus . . . est) . . .
explicat, *1568*

reading in the text or if the text itself is somewhat obscure, there is no reason to believe less firmly in what Christ taught his church. Through the Holy Spirit he instructed the church in all truth and promised that he would be with her even to the end of time. Christ will certainly see to it that the faith of the church will not falter. This was a promise he obtained from the Father through prayer. It will not falter through errors in the text, for he corrects these day after day through the devout labor of dedicated men; nor through ambiguities in the literal sense, for he explains these, at such times as he finds appropriate, through the pens of learned men; nor through the persecutions of tyrants, for he has subdued them through the victories of his martyrs; nor through the endeavors of heretics, for he has stopped their mouths through the books of the orthodox Fathers; nor from the machinations of the devil, for on the cross he laid him low.

John 16

Matthew 28

Reverence is not lost if in the course of a dispute reason seems to run counter to truth, for it is absolutely certain that since faith is sustained by divine revelation, it far surpasses the reason of mortal men. The less we are able to understand the nature and causes of things, the more pleasure we take in observing them. And so it is with the divine majesty: we are all the more caught up in sweet wonder at it, the more some things seem to disagree and conflict with one another, at the same time as we realize that they undoubtedly agree with one another and come together in harmony. So you see, Pomeranus, the schools are capable of examining these things harmlessly and not without profitable results. But you attack scholastic disputation as something that opposes truth and violates mystery. At the same time, however, you command everyone to believe without any serious discussion your own absurd conclusions and crazy heresies in opposition to all men and to God himself. And you demand that whatever foolishness Luther chooses to utter be considered irrefutable, and as the Greeks say, ἀκίνητον. If anyone asks why you believe the dogmas of this crazy, impious man, he has to be satisfied with the answer αὐτὸς ἔφα, and no wonder either, since Luther proclaims he is certain he got his dogmas from heaven. And though you have nothing to bring to bear against the judgment of the

tiam nihil habeatis: tu tamen, Pomerane, vt conclusiones istas pulchre videaris adstruere, omnia fingis vobis apertissimis sacrarum literarum testimonijs esse comprobata.

Quasi vero nos agamus, inquis, *persuasibilibus humanae sapientiae* 5 *verbis, & non* [B₈r] *manifestissimis scripturis, quibus ne portae quidem inferorum hactenus praeualere potuerunt: aut quasi aduersarij nostri aliud contra nos producant, quam statuta & traditiones humanas, quas damnat Dominus, Esaiae. 20. & Christus, Matthaei. 15. Quid ergo veneni hic timebis, dum in occulto agimus nihil, & omnia nostra toti* 10 *mundo proponimus iudicanda?*

Dixti, Pomerane, pulchre: quasi non Dei traditiones sint, quibus Ecclesia Dei nititur in Sacramentis & Articulis fidei. Quasique non istud vobis & alij praeterea viri docti, & Rex illustrissimus Angliae, ratione, scripturis & concordibus ortho-
15 doxorum Patrum sententijs probasset apertissime: ad quae nemo vestrum hactenus verbum respondit vllum. Aut quasi vos Scripturis probetis omnia, ac non potius glossematum vestrorum somnijs, aduersus veterum omnium doctissimorum & sanctissimorum sententias, sacrarum lite[C₁]rarum Authori-
20 tatem ad sacrilega dogmata vestra detorquentibus. Aut quasi non omnes haeretici semper idem fecerint, quod nunc facitis vos: nempe vt venena sua toti propina-

Vide Hilar. lib[.] 4. de rent orbi, & poculum circumferrent
Trinitate, & item lib. ad palam Scripturarum melle circumli-
Constantium Augustum
25 tum, quas ipsas non minus fidenter, quam vos, clamabant esse clarissimas. Nam quid aliud olim clamabant Ariani, quam quod nunc clamatis Lutherani: Scripturas esse pro se manifestissimas, aduersarios humanis tantum statutis inniti, quae damnaret Dominus? Quid aliud clamabant & haere-
30 tici omnes reliqui, & ipsi cum primis Pelagiani? Quorum vos Lutherani tam stulte Scyllam fugitis, vt recta vos auferat error in Charybdim. Quanquam sicuti vos intelligere non vultis, Dei traditiones esse, non hominum, quibus Ecclesia nititur in rebus fidei: ita nescio an ipse satis intelligam, quod tu scribis, nempe
35 [C₁v] vos manifestissimis Scripturis agere, quibus ne portae quidem inferorum hactenus praeualere potuerunt. Nam quod

12 Ecclesia] Eccclesia *1568*

entire church through all the ages except Luther's own inane inventions, nevertheless, Pomeranus, to make it seem that you have neatly built up your conclusions, you pretend that you have proved them all by the indisputable evidence of sacred scripture.

As if, you say, we deal in the enticing words of human wisdom and not the palpable evidence of scripture, against which even the gates of hell have not yet been able to prevail. Or as if our adversaries brought forth anything against us except human statutes and traditions, which the Lord condemns in Isaiah 20 and Christ in Matthew 15. What poison, then, are you afraid of, since we do nothing in secret and set all our works before the whole world to be judged?

You put that very nicely, Pomeranus. As if there were no traditions of God, on which the church of God relies in the sacraments and articles of faith. Or as if the most illustrious king of England and other learned men as well had not proved this clearly to you by reason, scripture, and the universal opinion of the orthodox Fathers, to which no man among you as yet has uttered one word of reply. Or as if you proved everything by scripture and not by your own fantastic glosses, twisting the authority of sacred scripture into your own sacrilegious dogmas against the opinions of all the most learned and most holy ancients. Or as if all heretics had not always done the same thing you do now: they administered their poison to the whole world and openly handed around the cup anointed with the honey of scripture, which they proclaimed, just as boldly as you do now, to be perfectly clear. For the Arians once proclaimed the same thing the Lutherans do now: that scripture was clearly with them, while their opponents depended only on human statutes which the Lord condemned. And all the other heretics proclaimed the same thing, especially the Pelagians. You Lutherans are so stupid that when you try to avoid their Scylla, your error snatches you straight off to Charybdis. You do not even try to understand that the church relies in matters of faith on the traditions of God, not on the traditions of men. And so I am not certain I understand you well enough when you write that you deal in the palpable evidence of scripture against which the gates of hell have not yet been able to prevail. When you say that you

See Hilary, De Trinitate, IV, and also Liber ad Constantium Augustum

non agitis admodum persuasibilibus humanae sapientiae verbis,
id vero & intelligo satis, & verissimum esse confiteor. Caeterum
illud alterum vtram in partem sumi velis, addubito. Vtrumne sic
accipias, vt aduersus Scripturas ipsas non potuerint hactenus
5 inferorum portae praeualere: an aduersus positiones vestras,
quas adornatas & Scripturis palliatas a vobis, haberi vultis Euangelium salutis, quod nunc primum per vos oblatum coelitus,
gaudetis apud quosdam bene audire etiam in Britannia.

Quanquam non admodum magni refert, in vtram partem
10 sumpseris. Vtrobique certe tantundem profeceris. Nam si dogmata vestra vera sunt, & apertis firmata scripturis, quum ea
nunquam hactenus Ecclesia Christi credi[C₂]derit, quum ea
semper exploserit, damnarit, exusserit: necesse est fatearis, portas inferorum aduersus Scripturas Dei, hactenus praeualuisse
15 perpetuo. Sin e diuerso verum est quod dixisti, portas inferorum
nunquam praeualuisse contra Scripturas Dei: tum tu fateris,
Ecclesiae fidem semper fuisse consonam Scripturis Dei.

Quam ob rem quum eadem semper fuerit dogmatibus vestris
aduersa: nonne vides, Pomerane, consequi, vestra ista praeclara
20 dogmata Scripturis esse contraria? Alioqui si contendas Ecclesiam hactenus eadem sensisse, eadem credidisse semper, quae
iam creditis vos (imo, quae iam praedicatis vos: nam credere
quae praedicatis, ita me amet Deus, nec vos opinor) ostende
quaeso, quae fuit illa Ecclesia? Dic ante vos quando fuit? Dic
25 quibus in terris, & eris mihi magnus Apollo. Nam etsi vestrarum
Haeresum alios aliae, [C₂v] diuersis locis ac temporibus
habuerunt authores, tamen qui tam multa simul & tam absurda
crediderit, vt vobiscum in fide consenserit, non modo nullus
vnquam populus, sed nec vllus vsquam homo, aut tam impius,
30 aut tam stolidus ante Lutherum fuit.

Quod si contendas fuisse quidem semper aliquos, quanquam
tam paucos, vt orbem latuerint, tam dispersos, vt coetum nullum
fecerint, tam illiteratos, vt nihil scripserint, tam infantes, vt nihil
dixerint, quorum tamen dispersio, vera semper Ecclesia fuerit:
35 necesse est tamen fatearis, aduersus istam Ecclesiam tuam, eos

---

10 Vtrobique] vtrobique *1568*   22 creditis vos] creditis vos, *1568*

do not deal in the enticing words of human wisdom, that I understand quite well and confess it is absolutely true. But I am not certain how you want the rest of the statement to be taken. Do you mean that the gates of hell have not yet been able to prevail against the scriptures themselves? Or do you mean that they have not yet been able to prevail against your propositions, which you trick out and clothe in scripture so that they will be regarded as the gospel of salvation, which is now first offered by you from on high, rejoicing that it is well received by some people even in Britain?

Actually it does not matter a great deal which one you mean, since it amounts to the same thing either way. The church of Christ has never yet believed what you teach. It has always rejected it, cursed it, destroyed it by fire. If, then, your doctrines are true and confirmed by clear texts in scripture, you have to admit that the gates of hell have continuously prevailed against God's scripture. But if, on the other hand, what you say is true, that the gates of hell have never prevailed against the scripture of God, then you admit that the faith of the church has always been in agreement with God's scripture.

But the faith of the church has always been opposed to the sort of things you teach. And so, Pomeranus, you see, do you not, it follows that your famous beliefs are contrary to scripture. Moreover, if you argue that the church has always thought and believed the same thing you now believe (or rather what you now preach, for so help me God, I cannot imagine you believe what you preach)—tell me, I beg of you, what church are you talking about? When did it exist before you came along? Where on earth was it located? Tell me that, and I will take you for great Apollo himself. For although some of your heresies had various champions at different times and different places, no one—no one people and no one individual—was ever so fundamentally irreligious and so stupid as to believe so many different, completely absurd heresies as you do. No one, that is, until Luther.

But perhaps you argue that there was always a scattered remnant who, though dispersed, nevertheless constituted the true church even though they were so few as to be hidden from the world, so scattered as never to meet, so illiterate as never to write, and so dumb as never to speak. If so, you have to admit that the

perpetuo scripsisse Patres, quos Ecclesia Christi veneratur in
Sanctis.

An tu igitur, Pomerane, speras, adeo stipites esse Christianos
omnes, vt eis persuadere possis, quum Deus in Synagoga
5 Iudaeorum curarit, vt sanctissimi aliqui viri post mortem
haberentur [C₃] in pretio, ne populo suo redderetur ambiguum,
quos sibi proponerent imitandos: nunc in Ecclesia filij sui permitteret, sanctos & fideles omnes inhonoratos iacere, coli vero
pro Sanctis impios & haereticos curaret, qui suis scriptis orbem
10 totum seduxerint, atque ab Euangelij vero sensu praedicatione
falsa distraxerint, eorum aliquot etiam decoraret Martyrio,
omnes insigniret integritate vitae, nullos non illustraret mira-
culis, ne quis dubitare posset, eorum fidem placuisse Deo,
quorum pietatem prodigijs salutaribus orbi declararit. Quid is-
15 tud, obsecro, fuisset aliud, quam id egisse Deum, vt ipsius opera
sua falleretur Ecclesia? Necesse est ergo, Pomerane, velis nolis,
eam fatearis Ecclesiam, cuius pars erant & Doctores illi, quos
veneramur, sanctissimi patres: quos si contendas in fide cunctos
errasse, necesse est id concedas etiam, quod ante negasti,
20 ad[C₃v]uersus scripturas inferorum portas annos plus mille
praeualuisse. Quamobrem si tibi perstandum censes in eo quod
ante dixisti, portas inferorum hactenus aduersus Euangelium
praeualere non potuisse: omnino fatearis oportet, sanctissimos
illos Patres recte sensisse de fide: quod vbi semel concesseris,
25 quum & illud negare non possis, illos ista damnasse quae vos
docetis, quantumuis tergiuerseris, tandem tibi fatendum est, ista
quae tam obstinate velut Euangelium obtruditis, esse falsissima
dogmata.

Sed quam varietate doctrinae belle dogmatum vestrorum late
30 confusam colluuiem cogas & constringas in arctum, operaepretium est cognoscere. Ais enim.

Et ne varietatem doctrinae excuses, breuiter dico: vnum tantum Arti-
culum a nobis doceri, vtcunque quotidie multa praedicemus, multa
scribamus contra aduersarios nostros, vt & ipsi salui fiant. Est [C₄]

---

31 Ais] ais *1568*   34 Est] est *1568*

Fathers, whom the church of Christ venerates among the saints, always wrote against this church of yours.

Or do you hope, Pomeranus, that all Christians are such clods that you can convince them of anything? In the Jewish synagogue God saw to it that the holiest men among them were held in esteem after their death so that the people would not be left in doubt about what models to imitate. That being so, would you have us believe that now, in the church of his Son, God would allow all his holy and faithful people to lie in dishonor while he saw to it that those who were worshiped as saints should be men who were heretics and fundamentally irreligious, who had seduced the whole world with their writings, who had drawn it away from the true meaning of the gospel by their false preaching? Would you have us believe that he adorned some of these men with martyrdom, distinguished them all with integrity of life, and never failed to render them illustrious through miracles, demonstrating their piety to the world through wholesome signs and tokens so that no one could doubt that their faith was pleasing to God? Tell me, do you really think God purposely did all this to deceive his own church? Like it or not, Pomeranus, you have to admit that this is God's church and that it had within it and as its teachers the holy Fathers whom we venerate. If you argue that they were all mistaken in matters of faith, then you have to admit what you denied before, that the gates of hell have prevailed against the scriptures for more than a thousand years. But if you think you have to stick with what you said before, that the gates of hell have never been able to prevail against the gospel, then you must also admit that the holy Fathers were right in matters of faith. Once you have granted that, then no matter how much you squirm about, you are going to have to admit that what you bullheadedly force on us as the gospel is completely wrong. For you are unable to deny that the Fathers of the church have already condemned what you teach.

It may be worth our while to learn how you rake up the diverse and far flung rubbish of your teachings in a neat little pile. For you go on to say:

And lest you plead as an excuse the variety of our teaching, let me say briefly that we teach but one article of faith no matter how much we preach every day, no matter how much we write against our opponents so that

autem Articulus ille: Christus est Iusticia nostra. Nam is factus est nobis
a Deo sapientia, iusticia, satisfactio, redemptio. Quisquis hoc non dederit
nobis, non est Christianus: quisquis fatebitur nobiscum, apud eum statim
cadit omnis iustitia humana.

5   O compendium! Nihil igitur omnino scribitis, nihil omnino
docetis, nisi Christus est iusticia nostra? Hoc vnum Pronun-
tiatum tam sanctum, omnia dogmata vestra tam varia, tam inter
se dissona, tam absurda, tam impia complectitur? Sic vt si quis
istud concedat vobis, quod Christus est Iustitia nostra, idem sit
10   necessario concessurus, in Eucharistia restare panem? nihil cuiquam prodesse Missam? Ecclesiam totam hactenus perperam
sacrificasse, hactenus vsam impio et sacrilego Canone, & Ordinem inane esse figmentum? Et haec erit bona consequutio,
Christus est iusticia nostra, ergo mulier idonea est cui fiat pec-
15   catorum sacramentalis Confessio? [C₄v] Et mulier potest con-
ficere corpus Christi? Et item haec, Christus est iustitia nostra,
ergo nullum est Purgatorium? Et nullum est liberum arbitrium?
Et nulla lex humana Christianum quenquam obligat? Et,
Christus est iustitia nostra, ergo sola fides sufficit ad salutem, &
20   non est opus bonis operibus? Et nihil damnare potest Christianum, nisi sola incredulitas? Et Christus est iustitia nostra, ergo
Monachus ducere debet vxorem? Haec omnia dogmata, & multa
itidem alia, nihilo minus absurda, necessario scilicet consequun-
       tur istam, Christus est iustitia nostra?
25   *Quam apte & apposite*   Quid ni? Nam si is factus est vobis a Deo
       haec singula totidem   iustitia, quid opus est vobis iustitiam
       Scripturae locis refellit   quaerere & persequi eam? Si factus est
                                      vobis sapientia, quid opus est vobis esse
       Matt. 10   prudentes sicut serpentes? Si satisfac-
30   *Rom. 6*   tio, quid opus est vobis, sicut exhibuistis
                                      membra vestra seruire immunditiae &
       Prouer. 13   iniquitati ad iniquitatem, ita nunc [C₅]
                                      exhibere membra vestra seruire iusti-
tiae in sanctificationem? Si redemptio, quid opus est animam
35   redimant viri diuitiae suae? Et tam perspicue rem explicasti,
postquam hunc articulum protulisti, vt illico, velut re dilucide
probata quibus oportuit iudicibus, subiungas.

_____

36 protulisti,] protulisti: *1568*

they too may be saved. And this is that one article: Christ is our right-eousness. For God made him our wisdom, righteousness, satisfaction, redemption. Whoever does not grant us this is no Christian; whoever agrees with us in this will soon give over all righteousness of man.

The soul of brevity! You do not write anything, then, you do not teach anything except that Christ is our righteousness? Does this one holy pronouncement encompass all your dogmas, varied as they are, discordant with one another, absurd, and impious? If one were to grant you this, that Christ is our right-eousness, does he also have to admit that the bread in the eucharist remains bread? That the mass is of no use to anyone? That the whole church has performed the sacrifice incorrectly up till now? That up to now it has used an impious and sacrile-gious canon, and that the sacrament of ordination is an empty lie? And will this follow logically: Christ is our righteousness, therefore a woman is fit to hear sins in the sacrament of confes-sion? And a woman can consecrate the body of Christ? And this: Christ is our righteousness, therefore there is no purgatory? And no free will? And no human law a Christian has to obey? Christ is our righteousness, therefore faith alone is sufficient for salvation, and there is no need for good works? And nothing can damn a Christian except his lack of faith alone? Christ is our righteousness, therefore a monk ought to take a wife? Do all these beliefs and many others just as absurd necessarily follow from the fact that Christ is our righteousness? Why not? For if God made Christ your righteousness, what need have you to seek out and fol-low righteousness? If he was made your wisdom, what need have you to be as cunning as a serpent? If he was made your satisfaction, what need have you to deliver your limbs as servants to righ-teousness unto holiness as you deliv-ered your limbs as servants to un-cleanliness unto iniquity? If he was made your redemption, what need

How aptly and justly he refutes each of these points with corresponding passages from scripture

Matthew 10

Romans 6

Proverbs 13

have men to ransom their souls by using their wealth? After mentioning this article of faith, you explained it so well, believ-ing you had proved it to the judges' satisfaction, that you imme-diately add:

Quisquis autem fatebitur nobiscum, apud eum statim cadit quaecun-
que alia iustitia humana. Nihil erit hic Pelagianae haeresis, qua, licet
mutatis verbis, infecti sunt, qui vel solos se gloriantur Christianos: nihil
valebit omnis sectarum, quae hodie sunt, & operum fidutia, quam (ab-
5 *negato Crucis Christi scandalo) nostri iustitiarij nobis inuexerunt, dum*
opera pro Christo venditarunt, contra quos, & contra totius Sathanae
regnum hoc argumentum fortissimum cum Paulo producimus: Si ex
operibus & nostro arbitrio iustificamur, ergo gratis Christus mortuus est.
Iustitia haec quae Christus est, testimoni[C₅v]*um habet in lege & Pro-*
10 *phetis, ad Rom. 3. Qui autem suam iustitiam sequuntur, ad veram*
iustitiam, vt Iudaei, non perueniunt. ad Rom. 9. Iustitiae Dei subijci non
possunt. ad Rom. 10. Haec iustitia Dei tua est, dum per fidem suscipis
Christum. Non enim pro se mortuus est, aut pro suis delictis, sed pro te, &
tuis delictis. Igitur quicquid aliud tentaueris ad iustitiam, id est, vnde
15 *iustificeris, & liber sis a Dei Iudicio, peccatis, morte, & inferis: hypocrisis*
erit, mendacium, & impietas, quacunque pietatis specie fulgeat. Pug-
nabit enim contra Dei gratiam, & Christi erit abnegatio.

NON dubito, Pomerane, quin tibi videaris oppido quam
praeclare dixisse: sed interim non aduertis, quod totus hic spec-
20 iosus sermo duobus mendacijs mendacissimis innititur, quibus
impudenter aspergis Ecclesiam, vt sacrosancta ista praedicatio
vestra verum videatur [C₆] Euangelium. Nam primo falsis-
simum est, quod nos fingis haeresi Pelagiana, mutatis verbis,
infectos.

25 Deinde, quod nos mentiris, abnegato Crucis Christi scandalo,
operum & sectarum inuexisse fiduciam, & opera venditare pro
Christo, nos interim nunc appellans pro tua libidine Iustitiarios,
nunc eos qui se solos esse Christianos gloriantur. Et profecto
quanquam nihil magis abhorret ab Ecclesiae doctrina, quam vt
30 quisquam sibi quicquam tribuat: tamen communi totius Ecclesiae nomine Catholicis Christianis licet verissime sancta quadam
superbia gloriari, se solos esse iustos, se solos esse Christianos.
Inter mortales enim extra Ecclesiam neque sancti quicquam est,
neque Christianus quisquam.

35 Sed ad rem reuertar: Ecclesia quemadmodum non credit Pe-

---

6 venditarunt,] venditarunt. *1568*   12 Dei] Dei, *1568*   13 sed] Sed *1568*

Whoever agrees with us in this will soon give over all righteousness of man. There will be no trace left here of the Pelagian heresy, by which (although the words are changed) they have been infected who boast that they are the only ones who are Christians. The sects that exist today will count for nothing, nor will all their trust in good works, which our self-justifiers have thrust upon us, rejecting the stumbling block of Christ's cross, peddling works instead of Christ. Against them and against the entire kingdom of Satan we bring forth with Paul this most powerful argument: If we are made righteous by works and by our own free will, then Christ died in vain. This righteousness which is Christ is testified to by the law and the prophets (Romans 3). A man who follows his own righteousness, will, like the Jews, not arrive at true righteousness (Romans 9). They are not able to submit to God's righteousness (Romans 10). This righteousness of God is yours when you receive Christ through faith. For he did not die for his own sake or for his own sins, but for your sake and for your sins. Whatever else, therefore, you have tried in order to arrive at righteousness—that is, to become righteous and free from the judgment of God, from sin, death, and hell—will be hypocrisy, lies, and wickedness, no matter how it shines with a semblance of piety. For it will strive against the grace of God and deny Christ.

I have no doubt, Pomeranus, that you think you put that extremely well. But you fail to see that all this brilliant discussion of yours is based on two fundamental lies. You use them shamelessly to slander the church and make that sacrosanct preaching of yours seem like the true gospel. In the first place you are absolutely incorrect to imply that we are infected by the Pelagian heresy, though our terminology is different.

You also lie when you say that we refused the stumbling block of Christ's cross, introduced a reliance on works and sects, and peddle works instead of Christ. To amuse yourself you call us at times self-justifiers and at other times braggarts who boast that they alone are Christians. Although nothing is more opposed to the teaching of the church than to attribute anything to oneself, nevertheless Catholic Christians are permitted in the name of the whole church in general to claim justifiably with a kind of holy pride that they are the only ones who are righteous, that they are the only ones who are Christian. For among men there is no holiness outside the church, nor any Christian either.

But let me return to the subject at hand. The church does not

lagio, ad bene faciendum naturae vim ac faculta[C₆v]tem sufficere cum generali quodam influxu gratiae, sed opus esse
fatetur ad actum quenque bonum gratia quadam peculiari: sic
vel magis dissentit vobis, qui gratiam Dei subdole studetis at-
5 tollere, vt penitus auferatis humanae voluntatis arbitrium, dum
eius libertatem nihil aliud asseritis, quam (vt vestris verbis vtar)
rem esse de solo titulo, & nihil agere prorsus, sed duntaxat pati, nec
aliter a Deo formari, quam ceram a manu
artificis. Qua in re admodum errarunt
Pelagiani: sed multo tamen perniciosius erratis Lutherani. Nam illi, quum
nimium tribuebant naturae, honorem
tamen inde tribuebant Deo, quem ag-
noscebant naturae conditorem. Prae-

Lutheri sunt verba in
10 *Assertionibus suis. Artic.*
36

Lutherani perniciosius
errant quam Pelagiani

15 terea quum faterentur difficulter admodum operari naturam
relictam sibi, facilius vero suffultam gratia, necessitatem etiam
relinquebant implorandae gratiae. At vos contra nihil relin-
quitis, quur habeatur Deo gra[C₇]tiae quicquam naturae nostrae
gratia: quam, si vobis credimus, habemus talem, vt etiam post
20 Baptismi gratiam satius esset ea caruisse, quippe quae quum hoc
habeat, vt assidue labatur & concidat: ad resurgendum por-
rigenti gratiam Deo nec surgere contra sese, nec conniti possit.
Deinde dum pati tantum voluntatem nostram, & nihil omnino
facere praedicatis: an non humanam omnem industriam, & co-
25 natum omnem ad virtutem tollitis? An non omnia manifeste
trahitis ad fatum? Quum voluntas per se secundum sectam vestram non solum sit malefica, verum etiam vertere non possit ad
bonum, sed mera voluntate Dei alius fingatur ad bonum, alius
relinquatur ad malum, non alio quam naturae merito, quam
30 citra peccatum suum talem sortitus est homo, & is qui ad bonum
sumitur, ita fingatur ac formetur a gratia, vt nihil interea faciat
aut cooperetur ipse, sed [C₇v] velut arbor folia producit & fructus, sic peragente in electis Deo, in reprobis natura, cuius etiam
author Deus est, illi bona, hi mala proferant. Iam quis non videt

---

20 caruisse,] caruisse. *1568*

hold with Pelagius when he says that the strength and power of nature, along with some general influx of grace, are enough to enable a man to do good. The church holds instead that special grace is needed for every good act. Similarly, the church disagrees with you even more when you cunningly try to exalt the grace of God in order to destroy completely the force of man's free will. You say nothing about the freedom of the will except that *it exists only in name,* to use your own words, that it accomplishes nothing, but is simply passive, that it is shaped by God in the same way wax is shaped by the hand of an artist. The Pelagians were completely wrong about all this, but you Lutherans are even

Luther's words in his Assertions, Article 36

The Lutherans are more perniciously mistaken than the Pelagians

more perniciously mistaken. Although the Pelagians attributed too much to nature, they nevertheless attributed the ultimate honor to God since they recognized him as the creator of nature. Moreover, they kept the need to pray for grace since they admitted that it is extremely difficult for nature to function alone and that it works more smoothly supported by grace. But you, on the contrary, leave no reason why we should give thanks to God for the gift of our nature. Our nature is such (if we were to believe you) that we would be better off without it, even after the gift of grace in baptism. For although our nature is such that we constantly slip and fall, it is not capable of rousing itself sufficiently to rise to God's offer of grace. It is not even able to make the effort. Then too, since you preach that our will is merely passive and does nothing whatsoever on its own, do you not destroy the possibility of all human endeavor and all attempts at virtue? Are you not obviously ascribing everything to fate? According to your sect, the will is not only evil in itself, it is not even able to turn toward the good. It is simply God's will that fashions one person for good while another remains evil. There is no reason other than that of one's nature, which one receives through no fault of his own. One who is elected to be good is so shaped and formed by grace that he does not do anything himself, not even cooperate. Just as a tree produces leaves and fruit, so when God works within the elect and nature, which is also his creation, works within the reprobates, the elect bring forth good and the repro-

consequi, vt hac ratione vestra neque voluntas voluntas sit: sed
electione sublata homo nihil distet ab arbore, neque scelerum
quicquam homini possit imputari, sed vt bonorum, ita malorum
quoque omnium causae necessario referantur in Deum, & cle-
5   mentissima illa natura Dei punire credatur flagitia quae fecit.
Quae opinio tam impia est & sacrilega de Deo, vt dispeream, ni
malim decies esse Pelagius, quam semel ista credere, quae docet
Lutherus. Sed Ecclesia quam improbatis, vtriusque vitans errorem & vicissim improbans, voluntatem bene facere non credit
10 absque gratia, sed gratiam credit omnibus non aliter ac lumen
solis esse propositam, malos oblatam negligere, bonos amplecti:
vtrosque vero suae voluntatis arbitrio. Sic & per [C₈] gratiam
seruatur, quisquis seruatur, nec tamen otiosum est interim liberum voluntatis arbitrium. Nec enim video quicquam, nisi per
15 lumen. Et tamen aliquid ad id adiuto, dum oculos aperio &
intendo aciem. Si quis in puteum demisso fune extrahat eum,
qui per se non posset emergere, an non vere dicetur suis viribus
non ascendisse de puteo? nec tamen ad id nihil ipsius vires con-
tulerunt, cum & amplexus est funem, & non est passus elabi. Ad
20 hunc se habet modum libertas arbitrij. Nihil enim potest absque
gratia, sed cum eam liberaliter offerat Diuina benificentia: in
bonis viris arbitrium voluntatis amplectitur, & bene cooperatur
cum ea, in malis respuit voluntas, & marcescit in malitia. Hoc est,
Pomerane, quod credimus, neque, vt tu mentitus es, Pelagio
25 credentes, nec Pelagio deterioribus vobis: sed & diuinae gratiae
debitum seruamus honorem, & facinorosis hominibus ampu-
tamus ansam, quam vos porri[C₈v]gitis, qua suae voluntatis
obstinatam maliciam in Diuinae voluntatis reiiciant ineluctabi-
lem necessitatem.
30   IAM de operibus agemus paululum, in quibus quam impie
erras ipse, tam improbe falso sugillas Ecclesiam: quam docere
mentiris, abdicato Crucis Christi scandalo, fiduciam in sectis &
operibus esse collocandam, & opera venditare pro Christo. Primum quod ad Religiones attinet, quas
35   *Religionum institutio &*   vos sectas vocatis & schismata: non
        vita defensa   opinor magnum esse flagitium, si sub

---

14 Nec] nec *1568*

bates evil. Now anyone can see that it follows according to your line of reasoning that free will is not free will. With no freedom of choice a man is no different from a tree. No evil can be imputed to man but rather God is necessarily the cause of all deeds, evil as well as good. God's most merciful nature is thought to punish the very sins it has committed. This concept of God is so wicked and so sacrilegious that I'll be damned if I would not rather be Pelagius ten times over than believe for a moment what Luther teaches. But the church you condemn avoids the errors of both these heresies and condemns them both in turn. The church believes that without grace man's will is incapable of performing good acts, but that grace is available to all like the light of the sun. Evil men neglect it when it is offered, good men embrace it, and both do what they do according to their own free will. Thus a man who is saved is saved by grace, and yet free will is not inoperative. I do not see anything except by light, and yet I assist the light to some extent when I open my eyes and focus them. If someone lowers a rope in a well and pulls out a man who could not get out by himself, would it not be true that the man in the well did not get out through his own power? And yet he contributed something of his own by hanging onto the rope and not letting it get away. The freedom of the will is similar to that. It can do nothing without grace. But when the divine goodness bestows grace liberally, the free will of a good man clings to it and cooperates with it properly. The free will of an evil man does not accept it and wears itself out in malice. This is what we believe, Pomeranus, and not the lie you tell of us, that we believe Pelagius, nor do we believe you, who are worse than Pelagius. We preserve the respect owed to divine grace and cut off the opportunity you afford vicious men to blame the stubborn malice of their own will on the unavoidable necessity of the divine will.

Now we will treat good works for a while. You are wicked and wrong on this point, and you wantonly, falsely slander the church. You lie and say that she has given up the stumbling block of Christ crucified and teaches that one should have confidence in sects and good works, peddling works instead of Christ. First, concerning the religious orders, which you call sects and schisms, I do *Defense of the foundation* not think it a major crime if under *and way of life of* Christ, as under a single general, differ- *religious orders*

vno duce Christo alij sub alijs diuersis veluti Tribunis militent, &
dum omnes bene atque ad Euangelicam normam ex praescripto
Euangelico viuant, alius tamen aliter tempus transigat, & diuersis virtutum generibus vnusquisque in suo sensu abundet,
5   praesertim quum satis constet, & a sanctissimis viris inuenta &
tradita, quae vos improbatis, instituta viuendi; & non solum plu-
rimos insigni [D₁] sanctitate viros inde prouenisse, verum etiam
quantumuis aut aliquot Monachorum suo non satisfecerint Or-
dini, aut aliquot degenerarent Ordines ad mores circumfusi sibi
10 seculi, tamen purissimam populi Christiani partem perpetuo
fuisse apud Religiosos. Qui tantum abest, vt alium sequantur pro
Christo, vt ij sint potissimum, qui vendentes quicquid habebant
& erogantes pauperibus, Crucem tollunt, & sequuntur Christum, dum vigilijs, ieiunijs & orationibus totam dedicantes vitam,
15 & Agnum in castitate sequentes, carnem suam crucifigunt cum
vitijs & concupiscentijs.

Quod vitae genus si est, vt vos videri vultis, aduersus Euangelium: oportet Euangelicam vitam huic esse contrariam: hoc
est, esse talem, vt se curet molliter, bene comedat, bene bibat,
20 bene dormiat, libidinetur, & voluptate diffluat. Quod vitae
genus si sit [D₁v] Euangelicum, negare profecto non possumus,
quin vestri vitam viuant Euangelicissimam: nisi quod ad virtutes
istas tam praeclaras addunt vim tyrannicam, & plusquam feri-
nam feritatem, qua contra Christianos & Deo deditos Fratres
25 ferocius fere quam vlli vnquam Gentium Tyranni saeuiunt.

Sed iam, vt dixi, veniamus ad opera, quae tu nos fingis venditare pro Christo: nec id te pudet scribere, cum nos & credere
scias, & docere, opera nostra neque bona fieri sine misericordia
Dei, neque merere quicquam sine fide Christi: at ne sic qui-
30 dem coeli esse capacia de natura sua (Neque enim condignae
sunt passiones huius temporis ad fu-
Rom. 8   turam gloriam quae reuelabitur in
nobis) sed immensae benignitati Creatoris ita placuisse, vt operibus nostris, suapte natura tam vilibus, tantum strueret pretij,
35 & ope[D₂]ras nostras, qui quum omnia fecimus, serui tamen
inutiles sumus, neque quicquam supra
Luc. 17   quam debuimus facere, fecimus, tam
pretiosa mercede conduceret.

---

4 abundet,] abundet. *1568*   12 habebant] habebant, *1568*

ent men serve under different leaders—military tribunes, as it were. While all of them lead a good life according to the rule and precepts of the gospel, different religious orders nevertheless spend their time differently. Each in its own way is rich in various kinds of virtue, especially when one realizes that those rules of life which you condemn were discovered and handed down by saintly men. Religious orders have produced a great many men of extraordinary sanctity. Although some monks have not always lived up to their order and some orders have degenerated to the behavior of the world around them, nevertheless the purest segment of the Christian people have always been found in religious orders. The members of these orders are far from following anyone other than Christ, for they are the ones primarily who sell what they have and give it to the poor and take up the cross and follow Christ. Dedicating their entire lives to vigils, fasts, and prayer, and following the Lamb in chastity, they crucify the vices and desires of the flesh.

If this kind of life is contrary to the gospel, as you would have it, then the life according to the gospel would have to be contrary to it—a life, that is, in which one tenderly takes care of himself, eats well, drinks well, sleeps well, satisfies his lust, and melts with pleasure. If that is living the life of the gospel, we certainly agree that your people lead a most gospel-like life, except that they add to those splendid virtues a tyrannical violence and brutality worse than that of a wild beast. They rage against Christian friars dedicated to God more ferociously than any pagan tyrant ever did.

But now, as I said, let us come to good works. You put it that we peddle them instead of Christ. You are not embarrassed to write such things even when you know that we believe and teach that our works are not made good without God's mercy and bring no merit without the faith of Christ. And even then they are not in themselves deserving of heaven. (For the sufferings of this present time are not worth comparing with the glory that is to be *Romans 8* revealed to us.) It pleased the great kindness of the creator, however, to place such a high value on our good works, which are cheap in themselves. Even when we have done everything, we are still unprofitable servants and have not done anything other than *Luke 17* what we ought to do. And yet he hires our labors at a high salary.

Alioqui si nihil omnino valent opera nostra, quantumuis in
fide facta, quantumuis imbuta charitate, quantumuis adiuuante
gratia (nam alioqui nihil esse, tute scis nos fateri) verum si ne sic
quidem valent quicquam: cur paterfamilias denario diurno otio-
5 sorum hominum operas conducit in vineam? Si nihil valent ad

homines liberandos ab ira, iudicio, pec-
Matt. 20   catis, morte, & inferis: quorsum illud
Baptistae? genimina viperarum, quis
Luc. 3   ostendit vobis fugere a ventura ira? Fac-
10   ite fructus dignos poenitentiae. Quor-
Eccles. 3   sum illud Sapientis? Sicut aqua extinguit ignem, ita eleemosyna extinguit
1 Cor. 11   peccatum. Quorsum illud Apostoli? Si
nosmetipsos dijudicaremus, non vtique
Rom. 6   iudi[D₂v]caremur. Quorsum illud eius-
15   dem? Sicut exhibuistis membra vestra
Luc. 10   seruire immunditiae & iniquitati, ita
nunc exhibete membra vestra seruire
Matt. 25   iustitiae. Quorsum illud Christi? Fac
20 hoc, & viues. Quorsum illud denique, quod in finali iuditio coelum daturus est operibus misericordiae, & eorundem omis-
sionem ac neglectum reprobis exprobraturus?

Si non sunt ista, Pomerane, mendacia (nec sunt opinor, si
verum sit Euangelium) nunquam potes effugere, quin istud sit
25 mendacium, quod ipse scribis: hypocrisim esse, mendacium, &
impietatem, pugnam contra gratiam Dei, & esse prorsus abnega-
tionem Christi, quacunque sanctitatis specie fulgeat, si quis
praeter fidem tentarit aliud: hoc est, si fidei iungat charitatis
opera, sine quibus fides mortua est, si per fidem simul & opera
30 conetur ad iustitiam. Neque per opera pugnat contra gratiam,
qui se fatetur absque gratia bene operari non [D₃] posse: neque
velut Pharisaeus confidit in operibus, qui & ea nouit nihil absque
fide valere, nec aliunde pretium quam ex mera Dei largitate
sumere. Sed illi plane pugnant contra gratiam, & Christum pror-
35 sus abnegant, qui in hoc duntaxat extollunt gratiam, & fidem
Christi commendant, vt ablato bonorum operum (non damnosa

---

30 Neque] neque *1568*

If, moreover, our works have no value at all—no matter if performed in faith, imbued with charity, aided by grace (for you know full well we admit that otherwise they are nothing)— if even so our works have no value, then why does the owner of the estate hire idle men to work in the vineyard for one denarius a day? If works are of no help in freeing man from wrath, judgment, sin, death, and hell, why did the Baptist say, "Generation of vipers, who showed you how to flee the wrath to come? Bring forth fruits worthy of repentance"? Why did the wise man say, "As water puts out fire, almsgiving puts out sin"? Why did the apostle say, "If we judge ourselves, surely we would not be judged"? And again, "As you have yielded your limbs to serve uncleanliness and iniquity. so now yield your limbs to serve justice"? Why did Christ say, "Do this and you will live"? And finally, at the Last Judgment why will he reward those who performed works of mercy with heaven and reproach the wicked for omitting and neglecting them?

Matthew 20

Luke 3

Ecclesiastes 3

1 Corinthians 11

Romans 6

Luke 10

Matthew 25

If these things are not lies, Pomeranus (and I do not think they are if the gospel is true), then you cannot escape the fact that what you write is a lie: you call it hypocrisy, untruth, impiety, a struggle against the grace of God, and an utter denial of Christ, no matter how it shines with the semblance of sanctity, if anyone makes any effort beyond faith—that is, if he joins to faith the works of charity, without which faith is dead, and if through both faith and works together he attempts to live a life of righteousness. A person who acknowledges that he cannot do good works without grace does not struggle against grace in trying to do good works. He does not, like the Pharisee, rely on works, for he knows they are worthless without faith and purchase no reward except through God's sheer generosity. Those who are clearly opposed to grace and utterly deny Christ are the ones who exalt grace and trust in the faith of Christ only to

fidutia, quam nos abunde tollimus, sed) bonitate prorsus &
fructu, reddunt homines ad bene faciendum tepidos. Ex qua
segnitie & fidem breui perdunt & gratiam: praesertim quum (vt
nunc mores sunt) magis propemodum inhortandi sint homines
5   ad bonorum operum frugem, quam ad ipsam, sine qua nihil
valent opera, fidem, quando non paulo plures inuenias, qui ma-
lint bene credere, quam bene facere.

Sed hac in parte quam malam causam foueatis, vel illud in-
dicat, quod tam nihil omnino constatis vobis, sed ita [D₃v] per-
10 plexe loquimini, vt cauere de industria videamini, ne quis vos
intelligat: ita posterius quodque verbum pugnat priori. Nam
paulo post ita subiungis.

At hoc forte interrogabis: Quid de moribus, cultu Dei, Sacramentis, &
huiusmodi sentiamus, & docemus. Respondeo, Christus est iustitia
15 *nostra, factus est & Doctor noster: quicquid is suo ore nobis prodidit, hoc*
docemus, quemadmodum & praecepit. Matthaei vltimo.

Et nos idem, Pomerane, fatemur, & docemus idem. Sed tu,
obsecro, nihil docebis aliud, imo dedocebis omnia, quaecunque
Christus non docuit ore suo? Ergo quicquid ante Christum
20 natum per Moisen & Prophetas docuit Deus, ea dedocebis omnia: nisi quicquid eorum Christus docuit rursus ore suo? Ergo
dedocebis rursus, quae Christus Ecclesiam docuit per tot sanctos
Patres, Euangelistas, Martyres, & Apo[D₄]stolos, nisi quicquid
docuit ore suo?
25 Dic igitur, vbi te docuit istud ore suo, nihil aliud esse credendum, quam quod docuit ore suo? Dic, vbi docuit ore suo, dogmata ista, quae vos docetis orbem? Dic vbi docuit ore suo, homini
non esse liberam voluntatem? Vbi docuit ore suo, ei ducendam
vxorem, qui ante vouerat castitatem? Vbi docuit ore suo, amicam
30 Lutheri aequalem esse Matri Christi? Vbi docuit ore suo, Missam
nihil prodesse defunctis? Vbi docuit ore suo, nullum esse Purgatorium, sed animas etiam mortuorum dormire vsque ad diem
extremi iudicij? Vbi docuit ore suo, abijciendam Crucem suam,

---

6 fidem,] fidem. *1568*

make men lukewarm in doing good. They completely deny that good works have any goodness or merit in them whatsoever, whereas we condemn only the sinful reliance on works. When men are slow to do good, they quickly lose both faith and grace, especially in the present state of the world, when men have to be urged to see the value in good works almost more than in faith, without which works are of no avail. For you find far more who would rather believe well than do well.

But your complete inconsistency is enough to indicate what an evil cause you support. You speak in such confusion that you seem intentionally to guard against anyone's understanding you. Each succeeding word contradicts the one before. For after a bit you go on to say:

But perhaps you will ask what we think and teach about morals, the worship of God, the sacraments, and things of that sort. I answer that Christ is our righteousness and also became our teacher. Whatever he has revealed to us with his own mouth, this we teach, even as he commanded. The last chapter of Matthew.

So do we, Pomeranus. We profess that and teach it too. But tell me, is that all you will teach? I mean, will you unteach everything except what Christ taught with his own mouth? Will you unteach whatever God taught before the birth of Christ through Moses and the prophets except for those portions Christ taught again with his own mouth? Will you unteach whatever Christ taught the church through so many holy Fathers, evangelists, martyrs, and apostles unless he taught it with his own mouth?

But tell me, where did Christ with his own mouth teach you that we should believe only what he taught with his own mouth? Tell me, where did he teach with his own mouth the beliefs you teach to the whole world? Tell me where he taught with his own mouth that man has no free will. Where did he teach with his own mouth that one who has sworn a vow of chastity has to take a wife? Where did he teach with his own mouth that Luther's girlfriend is equal to the mother of Christ? Where did he teach with his own mouth that the mass is of no use to the dead? Where did he teach with his own mouth that there is no purgatory, but that the souls of the dead sleep until the day of the Last Judgment? Where did he teach with his own mouth that

& in tenebras quolibet abstrudendam: ne videlicet in suum
cultum absumat aurum, quod alioqui recta ad pauperes isset,
scilicet?

Haec, opinor, Christus Lutherum non docuit ore suo, cum
5   *Matt. 26 & Ioan. 12*   dixit: pauperes sem[D₄v]per habetis
vobiscum. Sed ore suo docuit Frater
Lutheri Iudas, quum dixit: vt quid perditio haec? Potuit venun-
dari multo, & dari pauperibus.

Ecce, Pomerane, qui tantum ea credi postulatis, quae Christus
10   docuit ore suo, caetera tollitis omnia, quae Deus Ecclesiam docuit per Spiritum Sanctum: tamen ea docetis interea, quae neque
Christus docuit, neque bonus quisquam homo possit tolerare.

Nam quod subiungis: *Primum autem docuit Christus, hoc esse opus
Dei, vt credamus in illum quem pater nobis misit:* fatemur esse veris-
15   simum. Sed illud non fatemur esse verum, cuius vnius causa tu
istud allegas in medium. Allegas enim, vt occulte persuadeas,
solam fidem sufficere: verum timide tamen rem attingis, pleraque subticens mysticae doctrinae vestrae, quae frustra subtices
Magistri vestri libellis totum vulgata per orbem. Lutherus hoc
20   scholae vestrae [D₅] placitum declarat apertius, & rem definit
aliquanto fortius. Nam is aperte scribit, quod nullum peccatum
damnare potest hominem Christianum, praeter solam incredulitatem. Caetera omnia, si stet aut redeat fides qua salui
erimus per promissum Dei, protinus in momento prorsus ab-
25   sorberi a fide: ne quis necesse putet aut peccata confiteri, aut de
commissis dolere, aut malefacta benefaciendo rependere, quae
omnia manifeste tollit. Tu, quod dixi, timidius attingis rem, &
quam callidissime potes, declinas eius assertionis inuidiam: dis-
simulans, quod ita praedices fidem, vt homines interim animes
30   ad vitia, virtutem dedoceas: sed tanquam sic intelligas, quod ais
solam fidem sufficere, quasi qui fidem habeat, is necessario
fugiat vitia, & amplectatur virtutes.

Quae res si sic se haberet, tamen stultissimus esset hic tumultus his cross should be taken down and hidden away in the shadows somewhere lest gold be wasted in adorning it—gold which otherwise, of course, would go directly to the poor?

I think Christ did not teach these things to Luther with his own mouth when he said, "The poor you will always have with you." But Brother Judas, Luther's brother, taught it with his own mouth when he said, "What is the sense in all this waste? It could have been sold for a lot of money and given to the poor."

Matthew 26 and John 12

See here, Pomeranus, when you insist that people believe only what Christ taught with his own mouth, you take away everything else God taught the church through the Holy Spirit and you end up teaching things Christ never taught, things no decent man can tolerate.

For you go on to say, *First of all Christ taught that this is the work of God, that we believe in him whom the Father sent us.* We allow that that is perfectly true. But we do not allow the truth of the conclusion which you draw from it and which is the only reason you bring it up. For you mention it in order to persuade people covertly that faith alone is sufficient. You touch it timidly, concealing the greater part of your mystic teaching. You conceal it in vain, however, since it has been spread abroad through the whole world in the books of your master. Luther treats this opinion of your school more openly and explains it somewhat more boldly. He writes plainly that no sin can damn a Christian except the sin of unbelief. According to the promise of God, we will be saved by faith, and if faith remains or if faith returns, all sins are immediately swallowed up by faith. It is not necessary to confess one's sins or be sorry for one's transgressions or compensate for evil by doing good, for Luther has obviously done away with all these things. As I said, you touch on this more timidly than Luther and shrewdly try to avoid the odium of such an assertion. You hide the fact that you preach the doctrine of faith so as to lure people to vice and unteach virtue. When you say that faith alone is sufficient, you want it to seem as though you mean that if one has faith he will naturally shun vice and embrace virtue.

Even if that were the case, this uproar of yours and this rag-

vester, quo [D₅v] aduersus opera bona tumultuamini. Nam si
bona sunt opera, quae necessario producat fides: quid aliud facitis, disputantes aduersus opera bona, quam deblateratis aduersus fructum fidei? Quod si nullum est bonum opus omnino, id
5 quod plane vestra contendit factio, quomodo consistis tecum,
quum dicis eum qui fidem habet, arborem esse bonam, quae non
poterit suo tempore non ferre fructum bonum?

Quanquam istud si ita praecise verum est, vt qui fidem habet,
is necessario proferat opera bona: quur ait Apostolus? Si ha-
10 buero omnem fidem, ita vt montes transferam, charitatem autem non habuero, nihil sum. Quur illud
1 Cor. 13   ait? si fidem habeam sic, vt dem corpus
meum vt ardeam, Charitatem autem non habuero: nihil mihi
prodest. [D₆]
15 Frustra dicerentur ista, si fides absque charitate non esset.
Quod fides absque operibus mortua est,
Iacobi 2   quod daemones credunt & contremiscunt: frustra vobis allegem Epistolam Iacobi, quae quoniam
vobis incommoda est, desijt esse vobis Apostolica. At Adam,
20 opinor, Deo credidit. Nam, vt ait Apostolus, Adam non est seductus, & tamen peccauit. Quod si cum
1 Tim. 2   fide potest consistere operari male, potest haud dubie cum fide consistere non operari bene.

Sed tu fortasse non credis Apostolo, qui nihil credis aliud,
25 quam quod prodidit ore suo Christus. Age igitur, an non hoc
prodidit ore suo Christus, quod aliquando venturi forent multi,
qui dicerent ei: Domine, Domine, non-
Matt. 7   ne in nomine tuo prophetauimus, & in
nomine tuo daemonia eiecimus, & in nomine tuo virtutes multas
30 fecimus? Et tunc confitebor illis, inquit, [D₆v] quia nunquam
noui vos. Discedite a me, omnes qui operamini iniquitatem. An
non hic locus aperte docet, fidem, etiam tam ingentem, vt sufficiat ad edenda miracula, tamen in quibusdam hominibus
bonum fructum non ferre, nec eos homines propter immensam
35 fidem arbores esse bonas, sed ficus prorsus aridas, radicitus ex-
cidendas, & conijciendas in ignem? Non est ergo, Pomerane,
verum, fidem solam sufficere, & quicumque fidem habet, eum

---

5 factio,] factio: *1568*   20 Nam] nam *1568*   27–28 Domine, nonne] Domine nonne
1568   31 me,] me *1568*

ing against good works would still be extremely stupid. If faith necessarily produces works that are good, what do you think you are doing when you argue against good works? Are you not running on at the mouth against the product of faith? But if there is no possibility of good works—a position your faction obviously holds—then you are not consistent when you say that one who has faith is like a good tree that necessarily bears good fruit in its season.

But if it is so true that one who has faith will necessarily produce good works, why does the apostle say, "If I have such faith as will move mountains but have not charity, I am as nothing"? Why did he *1 Corinthians 13* say, "If I have such faith as to deliver my body to be burned but have not charity, I gain nothing"?

All that would have been said in vain if faith did not exist apart from charity. Thus, "Faith without works is dead" and "Demons be- *James 2* lieve, and shudder" . . . but there is no sense in my quoting from the Epistle of James. Since it inconveniences you, you no longer consider it to be apostolic. But Adam, I suppose, believed in God, for as the apostle said, "Adam was not deceived," and yet he *1 Timothy 2* sinned. If it is consistent with faith to do evil, it is no doubt consistent with faith not to do good.

But perhaps you do not believe the apostle, since you believe only what Christ said with his own mouth. Very well then. Did Christ not say with his own mouth that many people would come to him someday and say, "Lord, Lord, did we not prophesy in your *Matthew 7* name and in your name cast out demons and do many mighty deeds in your name?" "And then I will declare to them," he said, "I never knew you. Depart from me, all you evildoers." Is it not clear from this passage that faith—even a faith great enough to perform miracles—does not bring forth good fruit in certain people? Such people are not through their great faith good trees. They are fig trees, utterly dry, ready to be cut down to the root and cast in the fire. Thus, Pomeranus, it is not true that faith alone is sufficient and that whoever has faith will nec-

necessario producere fructum bonorum operum.

At quid ego tibi allego Christum? Quin allego potius Lutherano Lutherum? Audi igitur quid ille dicit, cuius apud te irre-
fragabilis est authoritas. *Nihil,* inquit, *damnare potest hominem*
5 *praeter solam incredulitatem. Nam caetera omnia, si stet aut redeat fides,*
absorbentur, inquit, *a fide.*

Si decennium totum meditatus esset, [D₇] quonam pacto clarissime posset explicare, non aliud sentire se, quam scelerum
genus omne patrari posse, salua atque incolumi fide: non video
10 profecto, quibus istud verbis potuisset enunciare lucidius. Nam
verba illa, *si stet fides,* alio torquere non potes, quam vt manere
fidem sentiat, dum fiunt scelera. Qua ex re facile vides consequi,
non eam necessario bonum opus producere, quae potest cum
malo consistere.

15 Apage igitur, Pomerane, fucos istos, quibus impium dogma sic
adornare studes, vt, dum solam fidem praecipis, bona simul omnia videaris imperare, tanquam habeatis persuasum, fide non
arceri solum peccata necessario, sed etiam produci virtutes.
Apertissime siquidem docet, vt audisti, Lutherus, peccata omnia
20 non illaesa tantum fide patrari, sed patranti quoque propter
insitum fidei meritum non officere. *Nam si stet,* inquit, *fides, pec-*
cata omnia ab[D₇v]*sorbentur a fide.*

Quanquam si te fortasse nunc praeceptoris tui pudeat, cuius
impiam sententiam tam aperte vides omnibus renudatam in-
25 uolucris, & videri velis ipse sentire sanctius: verba tua profecto,
Pomerane, non adeo concinnasti callide, quin omni luce clarius
elucescat, illius impietatem te vel aequare certe, vel vincere. Nam
primum aliquot scripturae propositionibus aduersus bona opera
deblateras, nempe illo: *Si ex operibus & nostro arbitrio iustificamur,*
30 *Christus pro nobis gratis mortuus est.* Quo in versu illud de libero
arbitrio addidisti ex arbitrio tuo, ne sacris in literis non ageres
sacrilegum falsarium. Quem Scripturae textum nemo non videt,
nihil derogare meritis bonorum operum: quum nihil velit aliud,
quam Christum gratis mortuum, si ex operibus absque fide iusti

---

11 fides,] fides: *1568*   17 imperare,] imperare. *1568*   23 pudeat,] pudeat,, *1568*.

essarily bring forth the fruit of good works.

But why do I quote Christ to you? Why not quote Luther to a Lutheran? Since you think his authority is infallible, listen to what he says: *Nothing can condemn a man to hell except the sin of unbelief. If faith remains or if faith returns, all other sins,* he says, *will be swallowed up by faith.*

If he had thought about it for ten years, I do not see how he could have explained it more clearly. He believes that as long as faith remains whole and unharmed, one can commit any sort of sin he wants to. I certainly do not see what words he could have used to explain this more clearly. For you cannot twist these words—if faith remains—to mean anything other than that he thinks a man can commit sins and still have faith. And you can easily see how it follows that faith does not necessarily produce good works, since it is capable of existing side by side with evil.

Get out of here, then, with your pretexts, Pomeranus, trying to trick out your ungodly beliefs so that it seems as though when you command faith alone you are issuing a command to perform all the good in the world, as though you believed that faith necessarily not only prevents sin but also produces virtue. As you heard, Luther quite openly teaches that a person can commit sin and still have his faith remain unharmed. Not only that, but he himself remains unharmed because of the inherent merit of his faith. *For if faith remains,* Luther says, *all sins will be swallowed up by faith.*

Perhaps now you are embarrassed by your teacher when you see his evil belief stripped bare of its cover and revealed for what it is. Perhaps you want to appear to believe something more pious than that. If so, Pomeranus, you have certainly not expressed it cleverly enough, for it is clear as day that you are at least equal to him in impiety, if you do not surpass him. For first you run on at the mouth against good works, using some statements from scripture, such as: *If we are made righteous by works and by our own free will, Christ died for us in vain.* You used a little free will of your own in that verse when you added the business about free will. After all, you had to keep up your role as a sacrilegious forger of sacred scripture. Anyone can see that that particular passage does not denigrate the value of good works. It simply means that Christ would have died in vain if we were made

redderemur. Neque enim gratis mortuus est Christus, [D₈] si
nihil valent opera sine fide, etiam si fidei copulata valeant plu-
rimum: vt ne adijciam id dictum ab Apostolo de operibus legis
Mosaicae.

5   Tum illud adiecisti: quod *qui suam iustitiam sequuntur, ad veram
iustitiam, vt Iudaei, non perueniunt.* Et illud: *Iusticiae Dei subijci non
possunt.* Vbi illud, *vt Iudaei,* de tuo rursus, ne quam Scripturam
videri possis Iudaeo citare syncerius, admiscuisti. Porro Pauli
verba quum in his locum habeant, qui aut sola putent opera legis
10   iustitiam conferre sine fide Christi, aut qui de suis operibus inani
efferantur gloria: quid faciunt ad Christianos, qui nulla credunt
opera quantumlibet bona, quantumlibet multa, compotem
quenquam coeli reddere, nisi fiant in fide? Sed ne sic quidem aut
fieri posse sine gratia, aut sui natura mereri beatitudinem: sed
15   tam immensum ac supra meritum meritorum humanorum pretium [D₈v] a mera Dei gratuitate largientis & paciscentis
proficisci.

Igitur vbi bona opera tam fabrefactis machinis oppugnasti,
iam (tanquam expugnaris quae non attigisti) transis ad iustitiam
20   Dei, qui Christus est: cui, tanquam id quisquam neget, testi-
monia corrogas ex Lege & Prophetis. Sed quorsum tandem af-
fers ista? nempe, vt reiectis atque explosis operibus, mortales
vniuersos inuitares ad solam fidem.

Haec, inquis, *iustitia Dei tua est, dum per fidem suscipis Christum.*
25   Verum quidem istud est, neque mali haberet quicquam, nisi
quod quam solicite commendas fidem, tam solicite repulisses
opera.

Iam quod statim subdis: *Non enim pro se, aut suis delictis mortuus
est Christus, sed pro te, & delictis tuis:* fatemur esse verissimum. Sed
30   de te veremur, ne in hoc afferas, vt ex eius fidei fidu[E₁]cia
confirmes peccandi licentiam, libidinemque reijciendi seuerioris
vitae sanctimoniam. Non recuso quin curiosus videar ad calum-
niam, nisi tua ipsius verba quae sequuntur, non tenuem quidem
aliquam suspicionis eius coniecturam insinuent, sed apertissima

righteous by works without faith. For Christ did not die in vain if works avail nothing without faith, even if they are worth a great deal when united with faith. I need not mention that the apostle said this about the works of the Mosaic Law.

Then you went on to add that *a man who follows his own right-eousness, will, like the Jews, not arrive at true righteousness.* And this: *they are not able to submit to God's righteousness.* You added the phrase *like the Jews* on your own hook once again for fear of quoting scripture more truthfully than a Jew. Now, the words of Paul apply to those who believe that righteousness comes only from the works of the law without the faith of Christ, or to those who are lifted up by vain pride in their own works. But what do these words matter to Christians, who believe that no works, no matter how good or how many, can make a person partaker of heaven unless those works are performed in faith? Even so, good works cannot be performed without grace, and they cannot earn eternal happiness in and of themselves. It is God's generosity alone that grants the immense reward of heaven, which is so far beyond what men deserve. He freely agrees to give it and he bestows it on us.

Now that you have attacked good works with such skillful weapons, thinking you have overwhelmed what you have not even touched, you pass on to the righteousness of God, which is Christ. You collect testimony from the law and the prophets, as if anyone ever denied it. And why do you do that? Just to get rid of and destroy the concept of good works and lure everyone over to your doctrine of faith alone.

This righteousness of God, you say, *is yours when you receive Christ through faith.* Very true. There is nothing wrong with what you say except that you reject good works just as earnestly as you commend faith.

Now we admit that what you set down after that is absolutely true: *For he did not die for his own sake or for his own sins, but for your sake and for your sins.* In your case, though, we are afraid that you bring it up only to encourage, by reliance on faith alone, man's freedom to sin and the desire to avoid the sanctity of a more disciplined life. I do not deny that I would seem eager to in-terpret you incorrectly, were it not that what you write immedi-ately following suggests something more than a slight hint of this

documenta proponant. Sic enim subijcis: *Igitur quicquid aliud tentaueris ad iusticiam, id est, vnde iustificeris, & liber sis a Dei iudicio, peccatis, morte, & inferis: hypocrisis erit, mendacium & impietas, quacunque pietatis specie fulgeat. Pugnabit enim contra Dei iustitiam,*
5   *& Christi erit abnegatio.*

Haec tua verba perspicue te declarant, in hoc fidem docere, vt opera bona dedoceas. Qua in re perspicuum faciam, Lutherum, qui impietate caeteros omnes vnus antecellit, abs te tamen vno longe lateque superari. Nam is (quod
10   *Luthero ipso magis impius*   ante recensui) ne quis putaret quicquam
         Pomeranus   sibi curandum quam flagi[E₁v]tiose viueret, fidem scripsit omnia absorbere peccata.

Cui tu sententiae vt calculo tuo suffragareris, vbi quasdam commemorasti virtutes, quas vos docere praedicas, (quam rem
15   paulo post efficiam, vt intelligant omnes, quam falso praedicas) ita protinus adiunxisti: *Et quia in carne sumus, quicquid ex ijs non fit, aut non satisfit, & quicquid adhuc peccatur, docemus cum Christo, vt iugiter oretur delicti venia, quemadmodum orare praecepit: Dimitte nobis debita nostra, & propter istam fiduciam in Deum docemus, non*
20   *imputari peccatum quod est in carne reliquum. Non enim inuenio in me, id est, in carne mea, bonum, sed gratia Deo, quod Christus venit, non propter iustos, sed propter peccatores, & publicani & meretrices praecedent iusticiarios pharisaeos in regnum coelorum.*

His tu, Pomerane, verbis, quod Lutherus ait, nihil hominem
25   damnare pos[E₂]se praeter solam incredulitatem (nam fidem solam caetera absorbere peccata) eandem rem aliter explicas: nempe non imputari peccata, si quis eam habeat fiduciam in Deum, vt credat propter solam fidem suam peccata sua sibi non imputari. Ais tamen vos docere, vt fidei iungatur oratio, videlicet
30   ista: Dimitte nobis debita nostra.

In his ergo duabus, nempe sola fide cum oratione breuissima, tota vobis vel non imputandorum, vel absorbendorum peccatorum omnium summa consistit, vt mortalibus per vos pateat per vitam in terra licentissimam mirum ad coelos compendium:
35   quippe quibus deflendi peccati lachrymas, confitendi taedium,

---

4 Pugnabit] pugnabit *1568*   19 nostra,] nostra. *1568*   21 mea,] mea *1568*
22 peccatores,] peccatores. *1568*   33 constitit,] constitit. *1568*   34 licentissimam]
licentissimum *1568*

suspicion. You make it perfectly obvious. For you say: *Whatever else, therefore, you have tried in order to arrive at righteousness—that is, to become righteous and free from the judgment of God, from sin, death, and hell—will be hypocrisy, lies, and wickedness, no matter how much it shines with a semblance of piety. For it will strive against the justice of God and deny Christ.*

Those words make it obvious that you teach faith in order to unteach good works. On this point I shall make it perfectly clear that although Luther alone exceeds everyone else in impiety, you alone surpass him by far. As I said before, for *Pomeranus more ungodly than Luther himself* fear that people would think there was anything to care about except lustful living, he wrote that faith swallows up all sins.

You vote for that notion by mentioning some virtues you claim to teach (which I will deal with a little later on and show how false your claim really is), and then immediately adding: *And because we are still in the flesh, whatever good we do not do or do not do well enough, whatever sins we still commit, we teach with Christ that one should pray constantly that his sins will be forgiven, just as he taught us to pray: forgive us our trespasses. And because of this trust in God, we teach that whatever sin still remains in the flesh will not be imputed to us. For I discover in me—that is, in my flesh—no good thing. But I give thanks to God that Christ came not for the righteous, but for sinners. And publicans and prostitutes will enter into the kingdom of heaven before self-righteous Pharisees.*

You say the same thing Luther did, Pomeranus: that a man cannot be damned except through unbelief, since faith alone swallows up all other sins. You explain the same thing another way by saying that a person's sins are not imputed to him if he has such trust in God that he believes that because of his faith alone his sins will not be imputed to him. But you also say you teach that prayer is united with faith, namely this prayer: Forgive us our trespasses.

And so by these two things, by faith alone along with the briefest possible prayer, you have established that the sum total of all sin will either not be imputed to you or else will be absolved. And so you have opened up for mortals a wonderful shortcut to heaven by means of a completely debauched life on earth. In fact you are such compassionate people that you take away all need

satisfaciendi fastidium, homines perquam benigni sustulistis. Atque in hac re nihil me narrando deprauare, nihil interpretando calumniari, tum verba tua testantur, tum ea, quae de poenitentiae Sacramento scribit magister [E₂v] tuus in Captiuitate
5 Babilonica, liquidius omni luce demonstrant.

Nemini igitur potest obscurum esse, eam esse non Lutheri modo sententiam, sed etiam, Pomerane, tuam: quod non solum absque bonis operibus, sed etiam cum flagitijs & sceleribus, sola fides sufficiat ad salutem. Caeterum, vt coepi paulo ante dicere,
10 tu non hac impietate contentus, vlterius tibi procurrendum statuisti, nec ante desistendum, quam docuisses, bona opera non floccifacienda modo, verumetiam velut nocitura nobis & auersura Deum, sedulo cauteque fugienda. Tua enim verba, sicuti commemoraui, sunt ista.

15 *Haec iusticia Dei tua est, dum per fidem suscipis Christum. Non enim pro se mortuus est, aut pro delictis suis: sed pro te, & delictis tuis. Quicquid aliud igitur tentaueris ad iustitiam, id est, vnde iustificeris, et liber sis a Dei iudicio, peccatis, morte, & inferis, hypochrisis erit, mendacium [E₃] & impietas, quacunque pietatis specie fulgebit. Pugnabit*
20 *enim contra Dei gratiam, & Christi erit abnegatio.*

Non vtar hic oratorio more, vt in istorum tuorum verborum impietatem inuehar. Neque enim oratione cuiusquam opus est, vt bono cuiquam viro reddatur inuisus, qui tanto spiritu, tanto Serpentis antiqui sibilo, tanto cum tartareo fremitu caeteras vir-
25 tutes omnes, praeter solam fidem, tam aperte, tam impudenter, tam odiose blasphemat, vt eas vocare atque appellare non dubitet Hypochrisin, & impietatem, quacunque pietatis specie fulgeant: & eas omnes non modo pugnare contendat aduersus gratiam Christi, sed ipsum etiam Christum prorsus abnegare.
30 Quum ista, Pomerane, dicis: quaeso te, quid dicis aliud, quam Deum Patrem, vnigenitum suum non ob aliud in terram destinasse, quam vt doceret mortales, in hoc venisse se, vt eos om[E₃v]nes ab omni virtutum cura, & labore liberaret, atque in omne flagitiorum genus indulgeret impunem atque irre-
35 frenatam licentiam? & tandem post vitam talem in terris actam, aeternam daret in coelo beatitudinem: tantum illud contra

---

3 columniari,] columniari: *1568*   18 inferis,] inferis: *1568*

for men to weep with sorrow for their sins or endure the irksomeness of confession and the unpleasantness of satisfaction. I am not distorting any of this or twisting its interpretation. That is clear from your own words and the words of your master when he writes about the sacrament of penance in his *Babylonian Captivity*. You both prove what I say plainer than day.

It is clear to everyone, then, that in Luther's opinion and in yours also, Pomeranus, faith alone is sufficient for salvation not only without good works, but even when accompanied by immorality and sin. But as I began to say a little before, you were not satisfied with that amount of impiety. You decided you had to go on and not stop until you taught not only that good works were completely negligible, but also that they should be carefully avoided because they would be harmful and would alienate us from God. Here are your words, which I have already referred to:

This righteousness of God is yours when you receive Christ through faith. For he did not die for his own sake or for his own sins, but for your sake and for your sins. Whatever else, therefore, you have tried in order to arrive at righteousness—that is, to become righteous and free from the judgment of God, from sin, death, and hell—will be hypocrisy, lies, and wickedness, no matter how it shines with a semblance of piety. For it will strive against the grace of God and deny Christ.

I will not use rhetoric to attack the wickedness of your words. For there is no need for rhetoric to make a good man hate someone who is so full of the breath, so full of the hissing of the ancient serpent, so full of the raging fury of hell that he would not hesitate to blaspheme openly, shamelessly, and maliciously against all other virtues except faith alone by designating and calling them hypocrisy and wickedness, no matter how much they shine like piety, and by contending that they not only oppose Christ's grace but completely deny Christ himself.

I ask you, Pomeranus, when you say these things, are you not simply telling us that God the Father sent his only begotten son to earth to teach men that he came to free them from all work and worry about virtue? That he came to grant them permission and complete freedom to give themselves up to all kinds of debauchery? And then, after they had led that sort of life on earth, he would give them eternal happiness in heaven, only

poscere, ne dubitaret ei quisquam hac in promissione fidere: ne
forte si minus fideret, aut magis bonus, aut minus malus esset?

Quum haec, Pomerane, non solum tam impia sint, sed etiam
tam absurda, quae sentis, vt nisi clarissimis verbis istam animi tui
5 sententiam declarasses, nemo futurus esset, cui videri posses,
quum esses homo, tam plane belluina sentire: adhibui profecto
cogitationem & studium, si quid forte possem reperire, quod
colorem saltem aliquem reciperet, quo putari queas, aliud quip-
piam sensisse, quod tametsi nihil boni haberet aut honesti,
10 at minus tamen ali[E₄]quanto perniciosum ac sacrilegum videretur.

Quam in rem & tui causa simul & mea, quum memet dili-
genter darem (tua, quod me vehementer puderet tui, ac mi-
sereret: mea, quod cupiebam omnibus reddere testatissimum,
15 illo me animo esse quo semper fui, vt aliorum scripta, quantum
possem, omnia in meliorem partem cupiam & benigniorem flectere) nihil tamen profecto nec inuenire quiui, nec comminisci
quicquam, quod impietatis tam absurdae non opinionem
quidem aliquam de te conceptam, sed certissimam hominum ex
20 apertissimis verbis tuis natam scientiam leniret.

Etenim dum tento omnia, dum nullum non saxum moueo,
succurrebat istud: Quid si fingamus illum sensisse sic: Quum
dicit, *hypochrisin esse, si quis aliud quaerat praeter fidem*, non id
quidem velle, quod sit hy[E₄v]pochrisis, aliam virtutem vllam
25 cum fide coniungere, sed si quis aliam sibi sumat loco fidei, in
qua sibi fidat ac spem reponat absque Christi fide.

Sed haec interpretatio statim apparuit impudentior, quam vt
eam pudor meus vnquam sustineret defendere. Videbam illico
vniuersos mihi reclamaturos, improbissimum ac nugacissimum
30 effugij genus frustra me esse commentum. Nam quaesituros
protinus, quî fieri possit, vt ita, Pomerane, senseris: quum eos
omnes quos reprehendis, idem sentire non nescias.

Siquidem quis est eorum, inquient, omnium, aduersus quos
ille scribit, quos Iustitiarios appellat, quos pro Pharisaeis insec-
35 tatur, qui virtutem vllam credit sine fide prodesse? Itaque vel

---

2 esset?] esset. *1568*   9 sensisse,] sensisse: *1568*   13 darem (tua] darem: tua
1568   16–17 flectere)] flectere: *1568*   23 dicit,] dicit: *1568*

demanding in return that no one hesitate to trust that promise of his, for fear perhaps that if anyone trusted less, he might become either a better or a less bad person?

These beliefs of yours, Pomeranus, are not only wicked, they are absurd. If you had not expressed your opinion explicitly, no one would believe you could be so beastly, since you are, after all, a man, not a beast. I actually put in a good bit of thought and effort trying to find anything that would make it at least seem as though you believe something different, something neither good nor honest but still a good deal less destructive and sacrilegious.

I applied myself to it diligently, for your sake as well as my own: for your sake, because I was extremely ashamed for you and because I pitied you; for mine, because I wanted to make it perfectly clear to everyone that I still have the same disposition I have always had—I would like to interpret everyone's writings in the best and kindest light possible. But I could neither discover nor imagine anything to mitigate what is not in fact merely an opinion about your absurd impiety but rather positive knowledge of it fixed in men's minds by your own explicit language.

While I was trying everything I could, leaving no stone unturned, I thought to myself, what about this? When Pomeranus says, *it is hypocrisy to seek anything other than faith,* suppose he does not mean that it is hypocrisy to possess other virtues besides faith. Suppose he means it is hypocrisy to put some other virtue in the place of faith, some virtue in which an individual places his trust and reposes his hope without the faith of Christ.

But right away this interpretation seemed to me so shameless that I could never bear the shame of defending it. I saw that everyone would immediately contradict me and say that I had wasted my time in thinking up a dishonest and ridiculous way of explaining it. They would want to know right away, Pomeranus, how you could mean that when you know that everyone you criticize believes the same thing.

For they would say, of all the people he writes against, whom he calls self-justifiers, whom he criticizes as Pharisees, is there anyone who believes that virtue is of value without faith? And so,

inuiti cogamur oportet fateri, nihil te minus quam illud,
Pomerane, sensisse.

At fortasse tandem simulabis, hoc voluisse te: non vetuisse
videlicet, nequis [E₅] praeter fidem solam alias praeterea virtutes
5   persequatur. Sed istud monuisse tantum, ne vllam quis
caeterarum virtutum omnium, ne quod opus hominis, quantumuis bene factum, quantumuis praeditum & formatum fide,
persuadeat sibi, vel ad salutem consequendam, vel ad vitandum
gehennae supplicium, vllius omnino momenti fore: imo si quis
10 eo animo bene statuat facere, quod illud sibi credat vel ad obti-
nendum coelum, vel ad declinandam gehennae flammam quicquam profuturum: eum non modo sese frustrari prorsus & fal-
lere, verum etiam ob id ipsum, quod ita credat, & foelicitatem
perditurum, & ad inferos praecipitem, velut abnegato Christo,
15 ruiturum.

Si sic te, Pomerane, velis intelligi, quid aliud quam e fumo
(quod aiunt) in flammam incidisti? Nam
Expedi te, si vir es,   ego statim, Pomerane, abs te quaeram:
Pomerane   si quis bona opera negligat, & commit-
20 tat mala, [E₅v] vtrum ea res ei coelum claudat, vel aperiat inferos? Si negas istud: nemini relinquis ambiguum, quod valde
cupias tegere, eum esse te, qui mundum totum in vitia, proposita
scelerum impunitate, prouoces. Sin illud, sicut est necesse, concesseris: nunquam negare poteris, quin si operum nostrorum
25 malitia demergat ad inferos, eorum bonitas, quae diuino oper-
amur auxilio, ab inferis nos adiutet, atque aliquatenus reddat
idoneos ad coeli promissum praemium. Etenim perquam absurdum fuerit, ita tibi persuadere de Deo, tanquam natura tam
clemens, quum vitijs decernat supplicia, nullo virtutes praemio
30 remuneret.

Verum quam absurda sit haeresis ista, quam aperte repugnet
Scripturae sacrae locis aliquot, supra demonstrauimus. Etenim
tametsi fatemur, neminem debere de sua virtute superbire, sed
agnoscere bonorum operum preti[E₆]um, non ex operum natu-
35 ra, sed liberalissima Dei aestimatione manare, nec ad ea ipsa
facienda potuisse quenquam solis naturae suae viribus absque
peculiari gratia sufficere, denique merito quenque posse de suo

---

18 *sidenote*: si] se *1568*

whether we want to or not, we have to admit, Pomeranus, that that is the last thing you believe.

But perhaps you will want it to seem as though this is what you meant: you did not forbid anyone to pursue any virtues other than faith alone. You simply wanted to warn people against convincing themselves that any of all the other virtues or any work of man, however well performed, however shaped and formed by faith, will be of any importance at all in attaining salvation or avoiding the punishment of hell. On the contrary, if someone decides to do good with the idea that it will help him either obtain heaven or avoid the flames of hell, he not only undoes himself and deceives himself completely, but he will also lose felicity and fling himself headlong into hell precisely because of that belief. For it is as though he had denied Christ.

If that is what you want us to think, Pomeranus, are you not leaping, as they say, from the frying pan into the fire? For I ask you straight off, Pomeranus, if someone fails to do good works and commits sin, does that *Get out of this, Pomeranus, if you are man enough* not close the gates of heaven and open to him the gates of hell? If you deny this, you leave no one in doubt (though you would very much like to conceal it) that you are the one who beckons the whole world to vice by leaving sins unpunished. If you grant that, as you must, then you will never be able to deny that if the wickedness of our actions plunges us down into hell, then the goodness of our actions, which we perform with the assistance of God, helps us out of hell and makes us more or less suitable for the reward of heaven promised to us. For it would be completely absurd to persuade yourself that God, whose nature is so merciful, would punish sin but offer no reward for virtue.

But we have already shown how foolish this heresy is and how it overtly contradicts several passages of holy scripture. We admit that no one should be proud of his virtue. He should recognize that good works are rewarded not in and of themselves because of their own nature, but because of the value God generously places on them. For no one is able to perform good works through his own nature alone without a special gift of grace.

facto metuere, ne forte latente quopiam vitio sit infectum: tamen
de bene factis nostris & bene sperare possumus, & semper conari
debemus, non vt sola fide seruemur, sed etiam declinando mala,
& bona faciendo, ad vitam veniamus aeternam.

5   Nam infinitum illud & incogitabile praemium, quanquam
nemini promisit infideli Deus: adeo non promisit tamen soli
fidei, vt non vno loco non vnus fateatur Apostolus, fidem solam
quantumcumque magnam nihil omnino proficere, sed absque
bonis operibus prorsus haberi pro mortua.

10   Porro quod operibus ipsis in fide [E₆v] factis, tribuatur praemium aeternum, an non illud aperte testatur quod ait Scriptura:
                                  Redemptio animae viri diuitiae suae?
            Prouer. 13   Non illud Euangelicum: Date eleemo-
                                  synam, & omnia munda sunt vobis?
            Luc. 11   Non illud iudicaturi quondam Christi,
15
            Matt. 25   quo se daturum praedicat aeternam
                                  beatitudinem, velut mercedem prae-
miumque praestitae liberalitatis in pauperes?

       Vides ista, Pomerane, tam aperta esse Scripturae sacrae testi-
20 monia, vt quantumcunque te torseris, nihil vnquam inuenturus
sis, quod contra possis opponere. At tu fortassis homo sanctus
ferre non potes nomen mercedis, & praemij, sed ita gratis hominem iubes seruire Deo, vt nihil inde prorsus retribuendae mercedis expectet: tanquam mercenarij sit ac non filij, non inseruire
25 gratis & libere, sed stipe seruire conductum.

       Quis terram coelo non misceat, & mare [E₇] coelo, quum
Lutheranus Episcopus, qui votum rupit, qui fidem fregit, qui
sacerdotalem castitatem violauit, qui coniugij nomine perpetuo
volutatur incestu, qui de virtute loquutus clunem agitat, subito
30 nobis velut e coelo demissus grauem istam ac seueram de colen-
do Deo normam edictumque proponat, ne quis bene factorum
suorum vllum expetat aut expectet praemium? Si quis id optet ac
speret, eum Christo non habendum pro Christiano: nempe mer-

---

18 praestitae] praestitiae *1568*

Even then one should fear that what he does may be infected by some secret vice. We can, however, be hopeful about our good works, and we ought always to try not to be saved by faith alone, but to avoid evil and do good and in that way to come to life eternal.

God did not promise that infinite and inconceivable reward to anyone lacking faith, and by the same token he did not promise it to anyone who has faith alone. There are more places than one where more than one apostle states that faith alone (no matter how great) is of no use, and that without good works it must be considered completely dead.

Moreover, does not the following passage of scripture show clearly that when good works are performed in faith they receive an eternal reward? For it is written, "the ransom of a man's soul is his wealth." And what about this passage from the gospels, "Give alms and all things are clean unto you"? What about Christ's words concerning the judgment to come, where he says he will give the wages and reward of eternal bliss for acts of generosity to the poor? *Proverbs 13* *Luke 11* *Matthew 25*

You see, Pomeranus, the witness of holy scripture is so self-evident that no matter how you twist it, you will never be able to find anything to contradict it. But perhaps you are such a holy person that you cannot bear to hear the words *wages* and *reward*. You would prefer man to serve God freely and expect no reward in return. Otherwise one would be a hireling and not a son. For hirelings do not willingly work for nothing. They render service only for a price.

Who would not confound heaven and earth, sea and sky when he sees a Lutheran bishop—a man who has broken his vow, shattered his faith, violated the chastity of his priesthood, who wallows in continual incest, which he prefers to call marriage, who shakes his ass as he preaches about virtue—suddenly pontificate about the grave and weighty rules and regulations concerning the worship of God as if he were sent down to us from heaven? No one, he says, should expect or look for any reward for his good deeds. If anyone desires or hopes for reward, he should not be regarded by Christ as a Christian because he is a

cenarium esse, non filium.

Pudet, vt video, Pomeranum virum supra communem sancti-
moniae sortem sanctulum inter eos
connumerari mercenarios, quos pa-

Matt. 20

5 terfamilias denario conducit in vineam. Hic vero tam gene-
roso est animo, vt potius quam in vineam sese conduci sinat
denario, extra vineam velit perire suspendio. Quis non videt,
quam ille sit e sublimi velut illiberalem seruum despecturus
con[E₇v]tempturusque Prophetam, quem non puduerit aperte
10 profiteri, Deo se seruire propter retributionem?

Psal. 118

At non videt interea prudentissimus pater, in quas se conijcit
& compingit angustias. Nam aut nihil praemij sperat atque ex-
pectat retribuendum fidei, & fidem iam non minus inutilem
15 infructuosamque praedicat, quam ante praedicauit opera: aut
fidei praestolatur mercedem, & in idem iam discrimen incidit,
propter quod ab operum bonorum praemio abhorruit, nempe
vt fidem sibi faciat mercenariam.

Quod si respondeat non deberi, ne fidei quidem, beati-
20 tudinem ex natura fidei, sed Dei benignitate sola sequuturam,
nec sequuturam dubitandum quicquam, quum ita pepigit ac
promisit Deus: & tamen haud ideo credendum esse Deo, vt
praemium quod credenti promisit consequamur, sed eo
ani[E₈]mo & cogitatione accedendum, vt etiam si nihil vnquam
25 commodi reportandum esset, nihilo tamen minus & eius dicto
fidem haberemus, & ineffabilem eius Maiestatem coleremus:
haec si mihi respondeat Pomeranus, fatebor illum tam vere sanc-
teque dicere, quam rem nihil attingere.

Siquidem non est, opinor, tam stupidus, vt non intelligat, nihil
30 hoc sermone se de fide loqui, quod non ex aequo competat in
opera. Nam nec illa dicimus suapte natura talia, quae coelum sibi
possint arrogare: sed liberaliter idem promisisse operibus
nostris Deum, quod nostrae promisit fidei: nempe ita demum
vtrisque se daturum coelum, si in amborum capacibus ambo
35 coniungerentur.

16–17 incidit, propter] incidit. Propter *1568*   27 haec] Haec *1568*   29 intelligat,]
intelligat: *1568*

hireling and not a son.

Pomeranus is such a holy little saint, far beyond the ordinary measure of saintliness! I see that he is ashamed to be included among those hired hands the house-holder pays a denarius to work in his *Matthew 20* vineyard. His spirit is so truly highborn that he would rather die on the gallows outside the vineyard than work inside it for one denarius. See how he looks down from his perch and despises the prophet for having the ignoble mentality of a slave because he was not ashamed to say in public that *Psalm 118* he served God for what he hoped to receive in return.

Meanwhile our foresighted father does not see what a tight place he has squeezed himself into and gotten himself stuck. For he either hopes for no reward and expects no return for his faith, thus proclaiming that faith is just as unprofitable and unre-warding as the good works he spoke about earlier, or else he expects a reward for his faith and thus falls into the same danger that made him shudder at the idea of a reward for good works—the fear, that is, of putting his faith out to hire.

Pomeranus, perhaps, would reply that the reward of heaven is not granted even to faith in its own nature, but proceeds entirely from the generosity of God: since God has so ordained and promised, there is no doubt that heaven awaits us. Nevertheless one should not believe in God merely to seek the reward he has promised to those who believe in him. We should approach him with the idea that even if we were to obtain no advantage we would still have faith in his word and worship his ineffable majesty. If this is what Pomeranus were to answer, I would have to admit that his reply was as truthful and reverent as it was completely beside the point.

I imagine, however, he is not such a fool as not to understand that nothing he said in this discourse about faith would not apply equally as well to works. For we do not say that works are capable of laying claim to heaven in and of themselves, but rather that God has generously promised the same thing for our works that he has promised for our faith. That is to say, he will give the gift of heaven to those who have the capacity for both faith and good works and in whom both are joined together.

Alioqui qui ipsius adiuti gratia vtrumque possent, altero tantum niterentur, nempe qui vel sola fide, vel solis ingrederentur
operibus: eos non in vitae [E₈v] via progredi, sed errore deceptos
regredi.

5   Neque tamen quicquam impedit, si quis ieiunio, castitate, pre-
catione & caeteris se virtutibus exerceat, quas tu, Pomerane, cum
Luthero tuo destruere atque demoliri contenditis: quin eo
pietatis euadat aliquando, vt sibi videatur ea facturus omnia,
etiam si Deum sciret nihil mercedis omnino perpetuis eius la-
10 boribus redditurum.

Atque ego quidem vt animum istum pium, & cogitationes
eiusmodi sanctas esse confiteor, & exoptandas: ita non solum
fidei atque operibus communes esse contendo, verum etiam
plane confirmo, quisquis id quod tu, Pomerane, facis, operibus
15 bonis praedicat nihil inesse boni, nihil opera bona sequuturum
praemij, nihil aduersus inferos opera bona prodesse, sed per ea
oppugnari gratiam, & Christum prorsus abnegari: eum non id
conari modo, vt populum [F₁] ad opera bona, velut rem inutilem
atque infrugiferam, frigidum reddat ac segnem, verum etiam vt
20 tanquam pestem aliquam noxiam ac laethiferam, mortalium
omnium pectoribus bene faciendi studium reuellat atque re-
ijciat, &, quo dogmata sua magis adblandiantur plebi, libidinis &
licentiae lenocinio, facillimam illis in omne flagitij genus facultatem securitatemque indulgeat.

25 Igitur quum ea quae tu proponis tibi, manifeste, Pomerane,
sint eiusmodi, quumque videres istud ex verbis tuis, quae supra
commemoraui, tam aperte clarescere, vt vereri coeperis, ne nimium id liquidum esset, ac foret fortasse tam inuidiosum, vt ne
malis quidem atque improbis hominibus ferendum videretur,
30 exoriri quenquam tandem tam absurde nebulonem nequam, vt
contra communem omnium tot seculorum sensum audeat, tam
acerbe vir[F₁v]tutes inuadere, & promouere flagitia: coactus es
ipse dissidere tecum, &, quo venenatum spiculum, exertum iam
plus satis & conspicuum, aliquo fuco tegeres, tam apertis
35 vitiorum suasionibus & virtutum dehortamentis adiungere vos
etiam virtutes, docere.

Quod tu quàm falso dicis, quanquam & ex sectae vestrae dog-

---

34 conspicuum,] conspicuum *1568*

On the other hand, those who are assisted by God's grace and have the capacity for both, but rely on only one or the other—that is, either faith alone or works alone—do not proceed on the path of life. They have lost their way and go backward.

Besides, Pomeranus, it does not hurt someone to busy himself with fasting, chastity, prayer, and the other virtues which you and your friend Luther try to demolish and destroy. There is no reason why that should prevent him from reaching, at times, such piety that it seems as though he would do all those things even if he knew God would not reward his constant efforts.

That is certainly a pious attitude. I confess that such thoughts are holy and greatly to be desired. And I not only contend that they apply both to faith and good works, I also claim that anyone who preaches as you do, Pomeranus, that good works are of no avail, that good works are not rewarded, that good works are of no help in avoiding hell, and that they obstruct grace and utterly deny Christ—anyone who preaches that, I say, not only tries to make people cold and slack toward good works, regarding them as useless and sterile. He also cuts the desire to do good out of men's hearts and casts it away as if it were deadly, diseased tissue. And in order to seduce the common people to his beliefs, he panders to them with lust and licentiousness, allowing them a safe berth and easy opportunity to perform all sorts of shameful things.

That is evidently what you have in mind, Pomeranus. But since you saw yourself bringing it out in the open by the language you use, quoted above, you began to be afraid. Your intentions were becoming too transparent and perhaps too odious. You were afraid that even the wicked and evil might think it unbearable that an absurd, good-for-nothing wretch like you has finally appeared on the scene and has dared, against the common understanding of all these many centuries, to promote vice and assault virtue so violently. So you have been forced to contradict yourself by teaching that, in addition to your obvious persuasions to vice and dissuasions from virtue, you Lutherans have some virtues of your own. You do this to hide your poisoned sting, though it sticks out now clearly enough for everyone to see.

Your falsehoods will become even more obvious as soon as we

matibus appareat, nec verba tua, quae supra nunc excussimus,
ambiguum esse permittant: statim tamen quum ea ipsa verba
ventilabimus, magis adhuc euidens atque illustre reddetur. Interim operaepretium est videre, quam pulchro & spetioso
5 putamine fructuum vestrorum marcidam plane putridamque
carnem conuestias. Ais enim hoc pacto.

Quisquis in illum crediderit, arbor bona est, & non poterit suo tempore
non ferre fructum bonum: non quem fructum hypocrisis fingit, sed quem
Spiritus Christi illic sua sponte producit. Qui enim [F2] *Spiritu Christi*
10 *aguntur, hi sunt Filij Dei. Sobrie, atque pie, & iuste adorabit Deum in*
spiritu & veritate, non in elementis mundi, cibis & vestitu, aut alia
hypocrisi. Sentiet de Sacramentis quod Christus docuit & instituit, for-
mabit proximos doctrina, consilio, oratione, rebus, etiam cum dispendio
vitae, nec solum amicos, sed etiam inimicos. Haec docuit Christus, ad
15 *haec trahit natura spiritus corda credentium, & nos haec omnia docemus*
facienda. Et quia in carne adhuc sumus, quicquid ex his non fit, aut non
satisfit, & quicquid adhuc peccatur, docemus cum Christo, vt iugiter
oretur delicti venia, quemadmodum orare praecepit: Dimitte nobis debita
nostra. Et propter istam fiduciam in Deum non imputari peccatum, quod
20 *est in carne reliquum. Non enim inuenio in me, id est, in carne mea*
bonum, sed gratia Deo, quod Christus venit, non propter iustos, sed
propter peccatores. & Publicani, & meretrices praecedent Iustiti-
[F2v]*arios Pharisaeos in regnum coelorum, quicquid hic obganniet os*
iniquum, quod nos alia docemus. Deus per Moysen dicit: Quisquis
25 *Prophetam illum, id est, Christum non audierit, ego vltor existam. Au-*
diant hoc contra se Dei iudicium Euangelij hostes. Et pater clamat super
Christum: Hunc audite. Et Christus: Oues, inquit, meae vocem meam
audient, & non alienorum.

Paulo post excutiemus ista, quae sunt in speciem tam sancta,
30 an tam vere sancta sint, quam videntur esse. Nam quod orandum sit pro peccatis, miror id afferre te, tanquam partem huius
nouae Doctrinae vestrae: quasi nos, qui vobis per contumeliam,
tam falso, quam saepe Pharisaei vocamur & Iustitiarij, non di-
camus orationem Dominicam, neque nos fateamur esse pec-
35 catores. Illud certe magis adhuc miror, quod tu vel orare suades,
vel eorum quicquam facere, de quibus ais, [F3] *Nos haec omnia do-*

---

30 videntur] videnter *1568*

have had a chance to winnow your words, but they are clear enough from the doctrines of your sect. Your own words, which we have examined above, permit no ambiguity. At the moment it may be worthwhile to see how you clothe with a handsome, beautiful rind the rotten, totally decayed flesh of your fruit. For you speak thus:

Whoever believes in him is a good tree, and cannot fail to bear good fruit in its season: not the fruit imagined by hypocrisy, but the fruit which the spirit of Christ produces there of its own accord. For those who are moved by the spirit of Christ are the sons of God. Such a one will adore God soberly, piously, and justly, in spirit and truth, not in the elements of this world, in food, clothing, and other hypocrisy. About the sacraments he will believe what Christ taught and established. He will influence his neighbors with instruction, advice, prayer, material possessions, even at the cost of his life. And this not only for friends, but also for enemies. Such are the things Christ taught us; the nature of the spirit draws the hearts of believers to these things; and these are the things we teach must be performed. And because we are still in the flesh, whatever of these we do not do or do not do well enough, and whatever sins we still commit, we teach with Christ that one should pray constantly that his sins will be forgiven, just as he taught us to pray: forgive us our trespasses. And because of this trust in God, we teach that whatever sin still remains in the flesh will not be imputed to us. For I discover in me—that is, in my flesh—no good thing. But I give thanks to God that Christ came not for the righteous, but for sinners. And publicans and prostitutes will enter into the kingdom of heaven before self-righteous Pharisees, despite the fact that wicked backbiters grumble that we teach otherwise. God says through Moses, "Whoever will not hear that prophet (meaning Christ), I will take vengeance on him." Let the enemies of the gospel hear this judgment of God against them. And the Father cries aloud over Christ, "Hear him." And Christ, "My sheep will hear my voice and not the voices of strangers."

We will see a little further on whether these words that seem so saintly are in fact as saintly as they seem. That one must pray for forgiveness for his sins—it amazes me that you bring that up as part of this new teaching of yours. You insult us quite often by calling us Pharisees and self-justifiers. You sound as though we never said the Lord's prayer or admitted that we are sinners. But it amazes me even more that you advise people to pray and do the sort of things you mention when you say, *And these are the*

cemus facienda.

Nam cur suades quicquam, si nulla est libertas arbitrij? Cur hortaris, vt orem, vt proximos consilio formem, doctrina promoueam, rebus adiutem, nec vitae meae parcam dum alijs pro-
5 sim: si mihi nullo modo sit in manu, vt horum quicquam faciam? Deum duntaxat orare debes, vt haec in me peragat omnia, non etiam adhortari me, vt in istorum quicquam connitar, si nec adiutus gratia quicquam cooperor, sed omnia duntaxat patior.

Quis hortatur lapidem, vt sese formet in statuam? Quis aerem
10 hortatur, vt pluat? Terram quis hortatur, vt germinet? Si fato

Contra fati patronos   procedunt omnia, neque quicquam prorsus libere fit ab hominibus, id quod mordicus tenetis Lutherani: nihil profecto causae reliquisti tibi, quur aut quenquam ad virtutem commoueas, aut castiges nox-
15 ium. Nec habes omnino quicquam quod obijcias [F₃v] aduersarijs, si nihil libere faciunt, sed omnia coacti fato: nisi te fortasse

Facete   respondeas, nec ista quidem, quae scribis ipse, tua te sponte scribere, sed instinctu fati.

20 Sed & hoc, Pomerane, miror, quum ista quae tu facienda suades, si modo suades, vt dicis, eadem pleraque sint, quae suademus & nos, & quae bona sunt opera: cur nominatim toties

Dic colorem Pomerane   aduersus bona opera deblateras? Nam si contemnis, cur suades? Si suades,
25 quur contemnis?

An fieri quidem talia permiseris, sed eadem vetabis opera bona vocari? At quur tu sic vocari prohibeas, quum sic appellet

Marc. 14   & Deus? Haec, inquit, mulier bonum opus operata est in me. An ideo dis-
30 plicet, quia quum bonum sit, vocatur opus hominis? At hoc ipsum ipse testatur Christus, cui vni te scribis credere. Nonne dixit: Bonum opus operata est mulier? An non idem dixit [F₄]

Ioan. 8   similibus vestri Iudaeis: Si filij Abrahae estis, opera Abrahae facite?

---

32 dixit: . . . mulier?] dixit? . . . mulier. *1568*

things we teach must be performed.

Why do you persuade people to do anything if there is no free will? Why do you urge me to pray, to give my neighbor good advice, enlarge his mind with learning, assist him with material goods, and not spare my own life if I can be of help to others? Why recommend all this if I am not able to do any of it? You simply ought to pray to God to perform all this in me. You should not even ask me to try to do these things, for according to you, even with the help of grace, I do not cooperate. I simply accept it all passively.

Who urges a stone to shape itself into a statue, the clouds to rain, or the earth to bear crops? If everything is caused by fate and noth- *Against those who defend* *belief in fate* ing accomplished by man himself, as you Lutherans firmly hold, then there is no reason at all for you to rouse men to virtue and castigate wrongdoing. You also have no grounds for objecting to your opponents, since they have no free will and are driven by fate to do what they have to do. But perhaps you would reply that what you write is not voluntary but dictated by *Cleverly put* the promptings of fate.

I am also amazed, Pomeranus, that you urge people to do so many of the same things that we urge them to do. If you really do what you claim to, you recommend that they perform good works. So why pick out good works as your specific target to babble on about? If you despise them, why recommend them? If you recom- *State your position,* *Pomeranus* mend them, why despise them?

But perhaps you permit people to do good works, but forbid them to call them that. If so, why disallow the term when even God uses it? "This woman," he says, "has performed a good work for me." *Mark 14* Or perhaps you object because it is called the work of man, even though it is good. Let us call Christ to witness, since you write that you believe only what he says. Did he not say, "the woman has done a good work"? Did he not say the same to the Jews, whom you resemble: "If you are the children of Abraham, do the works *John 8* of Abraham"?

Iam vos qui omnibus in rebus exigitis manifestas Scripturas,
quur hic tergiuersamini in locis Scripturae manifestis? Quam
multis in locis & iubet, & vetat Christus? Quorsum ista, si nihil
facimus? Esuriui, inquit, & dedistis
5   *Mat. 25*   mihi manducare. Sitiui, & dedistis mihi
bibere. Hospes eram, & collegistis me.
      Christus eos dedisse dicit, & collegisse: vos vtrunque negatis.
Deum enim fecisse dicitis omnia: ipsos nihil omnino, sed tantum
passos in se facientem Deum. Ille crudelitatem exprobrat immi-
10 tibus, imputans quod esurientem non cibarint, sitientem negle-
xerint, hospitem sub dio contempserint. Quam inclementer im-
putabit omnia, si aut nihil horum facere, ne adiuti quidem gratia
queant: aut, ne valeant, citra demeritum suum subtrahatur
gratia? [F₄v]
15   Quid vos ad haec Lutherani? Quid aliud quam loca quaedam
contra congeritis e Scriptura sacra, quaecunque libertatis humanae vires videntur adimere, & referre peccatorum nostrorum
causas in Deum? Deinde vel citatis illis perperam, vel intellectis
nequiter, triumphum buccinatis aduersus Pharisaeos &
20 Iustitiarios: dissimulantes interim tot loca turpiter, quae vestras
acies obruunt atque prosternunt, & vestra subinde succinentes:
ad ea quae vel soluunt vestra, vel proferuntur contra, nihil re-
spondetis omnino. Nisi quis forte sic insaniat, vt ab Luthero belle
putet esse responsum ad Scripturas illas, quas eruditissimi viri, &
25 de Christi Ecclesia bene meriti *Diatribe pro Arbitrij Libertate* protulit. Quibus sic omnino respondit Lutherus, in eo libro quem
inscripsit de *Seruo Arbitrio,* vt interim plane declararit, quam
furioso daemoni, dum illa [F₅] scriberet, ipsius seruiebat
arbitrium.
30   Quid enim affert aliud aduersus clarissima illa verba Scripturae: Si vis ad vitam ingredi, serua
        Matt. 19   mandata, & alia eiusdem generis innu-
mera, quibus tam aperte, quam passim arbitrij nostri libertatem
sacrum testatur Eloquium: quam quod illa ironice dicta sint om-

---

25 *Diatribe pro Arbitrij Libertate*] Diatribe pro Arbitrij libertate *1568*

You require clear evidence from the scripture for all your beliefs; so why do you keep shifting ground in the face of these perfectly plain passages of scripture? How often does Christ command and forbid? What good are these passages if we do nothing? "I was hungry," he says, "and you gave me to eat. I was thirsty, and *Matthew 25* you gave me to drink. I was a stranger, and you welcomed me."

Christ says people gave him these things and welcomed him. But you deny it. You say God did it all, and the people simply permitted God to work in them. Christ reproached cruel people for their harshness, saying they did not feed the hungry, disregarded the thirsty, and despised the stranger under the open sky. How stern Christ is to make those charges if they are not able to do any of these things even when assisted by grace or when, through no fault of their own, grace is withheld.

What do you Lutherans say to that? Nothing at all. You simply collect certain passages of scripture, whatever seems to strip man of freedom and imply that God is the source of our sins! Then, either misquoting the verses or misunderstanding them, you trumpet your victory over the Pharisees and the self-justifiers. At the same time, you dishonestly ignore all the other passages of scripture that overwhelm your order of battle and destroy it, constantly chanting about the places that support what you believe. You have nothing at all to say about the scriptural quotations that either explain the ones you gathered or are cited in opposition to them. A person would have to be crazy to think that Luther did a good job in responding to the passages cited by the author of the *Treatise in Favor of Free Will*—an extremely learned man who deserves much thanks from the church of Christ. Luther's reply, in the book entitled *The Slavery of the Will*, did no more than reveal clearly how his own will was enslaved to a raving demon when he wrote that book.

For what does Luther say in reply to this perfectly obvious passage in scripture, "If you would enter into life, keep the commandments"? *Matthew 19* Or what does he say about other passages everywhere in scripture, perfectly transparent in meaning, that testify to

nia? Quod Deus ideo scilicet hominem
O vocem Lutheri impiam, iussit facere, quia sciebat hominem fa-
& blasphemam cere, quod iussit, non posse, commentum tam insanum, vt (si hos excipias, qui libenter in istud dogma
5 velut perniciosae licentiae viam discedunt, & necessitatis istius
opinionem cupide amplectuntur in scelerum suorum patro-
cinium) neminem sis inuenturus alium, qui non stolidissimum
istud responsi genus irrideat, detestans & subsannans interim
vanissimi viri glorias insanissimas, quibus tam assidue Sardonio
10 cum risu gestiens, victorias, trophaea, triumphos buccinat, & se
tam praeclare praedicat [F₅v] respondisse, vt nec Diabolus, nec
Angelus possit euincere. Quasi vero difficile sit nebuloni, vbi
meras eblterauit insanias, illico furiose clamare, tam egregia
disseruisse sese, vt nemo possit dissoluere.
15 Quin Luthero ipsi quam absurda videantur ista, quae respondet Diatribae, & ipsius praedamnata conscientiae, tum quam
indigna censeat, quae aliud quam risum aut stomachum cuiquam moueant alij quam haeresis suae fautoribus: lucidissime
declarat ipse, quum aperte fatetur responso suo, neminem capi
20 posse, nemini persuaderi quicquam, nisi qui legendis ipsius libris
hausisset spiritum. Quod quid aliud est, quam ea quae respondet
omnia, caeteris, qualia sunt, vniuersis fore conspicua, nempe
absurda, insana, sacrilega: eis duntaxat visum iri formosula,
quorum oculis caliginem haeresis Lutheranae studium & fauor
25 offuderit, quosque ex lectione Luthe[F₆]ranorum librorum,
spiritus idem, qui Lutherum furijs agitat, reiecta fide Christi,
dementauerit?
Ita vides, Pomerane, quam pulchre soluitis eas Scripturas,
quae pro arbitrij libertate proferuntur aduersus vos. Quibus aut
30 dissimulatis omnino, aut insanissime refutatis, aliquot vicissim
loca pro vobis aduersus Ecclesiam proponitis. Quorum quum
quaedam efferantur per hyperbolen, omnia vero (quod ex con-
stanti sanctorum Patrum interpretatione constat liquidissime)
nihil aliud velint, quam & quosdam immani voluntatis prauitate
35 meritos, tandem destitui gratia, (quos obdurare dicitur Deus,

---

3 posse,] posse. *1568*   8 irrideat,] irrideat. *1568*   27 dementauerit?] dementauerit.
1568

the freedom of the will? Only that they were all said ironically. That God commanded man to do something precisely because he knew man could not do it is such a crazy idea that you would be hard put to find

Oh the ungodly and blasphemous language of Luther

someone who would not laugh at a stupid answer like that. The only ones who could possibly take it seriously are those who want to be free to seek their own destruction, gladly embracing the idea of fate to defend their sinfulness. Anyone else would mock and scorn that vain man's insane boasting. And all the while he runs around with a sardonian laugh trumpeting victory, trophies, triumphs, claiming his reply is so perfect that neither devil nor angel could talk him down. It is easy for a wretch who babbles insane nonsense to shout in his madness that he has argued so brilliantly that no one could possibly refute him.

What he replies to the *Treatise* seems absurd even to Luther himself. He knows ahead of time that it will be condemned. He knows it is capable of provoking only laughter or anger in anyone other than the partisans of his own heresy. He demonstrates this most clearly when he admits in his reply to the *Treatise* that no one can be won over or persuaded of anything unless he has drunk in the spirit by reading his books. What is that if not admitting that to all others his reply will clearly appear to be what it is in fact, namely absurd, insane, sacrilegious? Only those who have had the wool pulled over their eyes by their love and affection for the Lutheran heresy will find anything very pretty about it. By reading Luther's books they become possessed by the same spirit that makes him tremble with raging madness and, once they have rejected the faith of Christ, drives them mad too.

So you see, Pomeranus, how well you handle the passages of scripture cited against you in favor of free will. You either dissemble completely or reply to them in the craziest way, while citing other passages that support you against the church. Some of these are hyperbolical, but all of them taken together (as the holy Fathers of the church persistently attest in their interpretation) simply indicate that certain people are finally deprived of grace because of some enormous depravity of the will. God is said to make these people hard because he has de-

quod eis omnino decreuerit gratiam suam nunquam offerre de-
nuo, quae saxea corda remolliat) & neminem prorsus esse mortalium, qui quicquam possit sine Deo; id quod nos plane
fatemur.

5   Quis enim neget quod affirmat ve[F₆v]ritas, quae dicit: Sine
me nihil potestis facere, &, Nemo potest
Ioan. 15   venire ad me, nisi pater, qui misit me,
traxerit eum? At vos eo vesaniae pro-
Ioan. 6   gredimini, vt hominem contendatis ni-
10 hil omnino facere, ne cum Deo quidem, nec ad patrem venire
cum tractu, sed trahi duntaxat inuitum, non connitentem cum
trahente conscendere: quum Christus contra manifeste mon-
stret, se paratum semper trahere, sed non trahere, si quis nolit
trahi. Quoties, inquit, volui congregare
Luc. 23   filios tuos, quemadmodum gallina con-
15 gregat pullos suos sub alas, & noluisti?
Quin, quo in loco maxime videtur opera nostra deprimere, vt
humanam retundat arrogantiam: tamen ibi quoque vires & libertatem nostrae voluntatis ostendit.
Luc. 17   Quum feceritis omnia, inquit, quae
20 praecepta sunt vobis, dicite: serui inutiles sumus. Quod debuimus facere, fecimus. Ecce, qui soli [F₇] Christo credere vos
iactatis, iam nec illi creditis. Ille nos ait facere, vos contra, quod
dicit ille, negatis, & vos asseritis duntaxat pati.
25 I nunc & iacta, Pomerane, vos docere quaecunque prodidit
ore suo Christus. Quin & hoc demiror, si formare proximos
oratione, consilio, & rebus adiuuare, etiam cum vitae dispendio
docetis, quo id consilio docetis: Si non modo nihil valent ista
aduersus Iudicium, peccatum, mortem, & inferos, sed etiam
30 recta deducunt illuc. Sic enim paulo supra scripsisti: *hypocrisin
esse, mendacium, & impietatem, & impugnationem gratiae, & abnega-*

---

5 neget] neget, *1568*   6 facere,] facere. *1568*   8 eum?] eum. *1568*   10 quidem,]
quidem. *1568*

cided never again to offer them grace, which softens hearts of stone. The scripture you cite also means that no mortal is capable of anything without God—all of which we obviously agree with.

For who would deny what truth itself affirms when it says, "Without me you can do nothing," and "No one can come to me unless the Father who sent me draws him." But you are so far gone into madness that you *John 15*

John 6

contend that man is capable of absolutely nothing, even with God's help. You contend that man does not come to the Father by being drawn to him, but only by being dragged involuntarily. You say that man does not even make an effort to rise up with the one who draws him. Christ, on the other hand, clearly states that he is always ready to draw men to him, but not someone who is not willing to be drawn. "How often would I have gathered your children together," he says, "as a hen gathers her chicks under her wings, and you would not." *Luke 23*

But even where Christ seems to make the least of human activity, so as to put a check on human arrogance—even there he indicates the strength and freedom of our will. "When," he says, "you have done all that is commanded of you, then say, 'We are unworthy servants. We have done only what was our duty.'" See, *Luke 17*

you brag that you believe in Christ alone, and now you do not even believe in him. He tells us that we act, and you on the contrary deny what he says and assert that we are merely passive.

Go and brag now, Pomeranus, that you teach whatever Christ said with his own mouth. But this is what really puzzles me. You teach that a person should influence his neighbors with prayer and advice, that he should assist them with material possessions and even at the cost of his own life. But what do you mean by this teaching if everything you mention is not only completely worthless so far as judgment, sin, death, and hell are concerned, but leads straight down to hell? For that is what you wrote a little above: *It is hypocrisy, lying, and wickedness, and a striving against grace, and a denial of Christ for a man to attempt*

tionem Christi, si quis aliud tentet, quo liberetur a peccatis, morte, &
inferis, praeter solam fidem.

Quae res si sic se habet, quur non solam doces fidem? Quur
ista simul doces opera, si aut sola per se sufficit fides, aut haec
5   necessario fidem sequun[F₇v]tur? Nam quis eum hortatur, qui
stat in sole, quis hortatur, inquam, vt edat vmbram? quam, velit
nolit, est editurus, quam diu perstat in sole.

Vides ergo, Pomerane, haec doctrina vestra (quam vos tam
constantem videri vultis, & nouum prorsus haberi Euangelium)
10 quam multis modis tam faede secum pugnat, vt alia pars con-
ficiat aliam. Quae res non alia de causa vobis accidit, quam quod
aliud docetis ex animo, aliud videri vultis docuisse.

Nam cum serio praedicatis, & quanta potestis vehementia contenditis, vt mortales cuncti solius fidei fiducia liberos sese persua-
15 deant ab omni cura & solicitudine caeterarum virtutum omnium, tutos item & coeli certos in omni flagitiorum licentia:
tamen quo declinetis aliquantulum tam insani dogmatis inuidiam, quaedam interdum obiter interseritis, his quae scrip-
sistis ante, contraria, quibus controuersum [F₈] reddatis, an tam
20 insane, quam sunt illa vobis scripta, senseritis. Quam rem tamen
non ita callide tractasti, Pomerane, quin fucus istarum virtutum,
quem tibi cura fuit allinere, facillime possit abstergi. Quod quo
dicto citius factum videas, expendemus illico, cuiusmodi fructus
isti sint: quos vestrae factionis homines, arbores videlicet tam
25 bonae, non proferre non possunt.

Quisquis, inquis, *in Christum crediderit, arbor bona est, & non po-*
terit suo tempore non ferre fructum bonum. Non quem hypocrisis fingit,
sed quem Spiritus Christi illic sua sponte producit. Qui enim Spiritu
Christi aguntur, hi sunt Filij Dei.

30 Haec tametsi, Pomerane, pleraque verba sint Christi, & quae si
quis afferret Orthodoxus, nihil non haberent salubre: tamen
quoniam tuis intermixta sunt, qui omnia trahis & detorques ad
Lutherana dogmata, merito nos ipsa res excitat, vt ipsum etiam
mel habea[F₈v]mus, offerente Lutherano, suspectum, ne quod
35 sub melle venenum lateat: veluti id quod ais, fructum bonum in

---

1 Christi,] Christi: *1568*

anything to free himself from sin, death, and hell except faith alone.

If that is how things are, why not teach the doctrine of faith alone? If faith alone is sufficient or if good works necessarily proceed from faith, why bother to teach good works at all? Take a man standing in the sunlight. Who would urge him to cast a shadow, since he will cast one whether he wants to or not as long as he stands in the sun?

So you see, Pomeranus, this teaching of yours is in many ways so horribly at odds with itself that one part contradicts the other. But you want it to seem harmonious so as to be accepted unconditionally as the new gospel. The problem is you are teaching one thing from the heart while wanting to seem as though you are really saying something else.

You seriously preach and contend as strongly as you can that everyone should be convinced the only true freedom is in reliance on faith alone—freedom from every care and worry about all the other virtues, safe and sure of heaven despite a life of license and sin. Still, in order to deflect a little of the hatred inspired by such insane teaching, you insert in passing now and then something contrary to what you wrote before, thus raising the question of whether your true beliefs are as crazy as what you write. But you have not handled it all that cleverly, Pomeranus. The cosmetic coating of virtue you carefully applied can easily be wiped off. To let you see that this is no sooner said than done, we will consider right now what kind of fruit the people of your faction cannot but bring forth, for they are, as you say, such good trees.

Whoever believes in Christ, you say, *is a good tree and cannot fail to bear good fruit in its season. Not the fruit imagined by hypocrisy, but the fruit which the spirit of Christ produces there of its own accord. For those who are moved by the spirit of Christ are the sons of God.*

Many of these are Christ's own words, Pomeranus, and if they were published by someone of orthodox faith, they would be wholesome enough. But since you mix them all up with your own opinions and turn everything to your own advantage by twisting them into Lutheran doctrine, we are properly led to suspect even honey itself when offered by a Lutheran for fear it is poisoned. Take, for example, what you say about the spirit of Christ producing good fruit of its own accord in those who

credentibus, Christi spiritum sua sponte producere.

Quod quanquam verum fatemur esse, tamen non fatemur esse verum in eo sensu, quo tu videris accipere. Neque enim in homine credente, bonorum operum fructum sua sponte sic pro-
5   ducit Christus, vt eum producat absque sponte & voluntate hominis. Quod vnum sentire te, declarat haeresis, qua prorsus aufers arbitrij libertatem.

Iam illud quod sequitur satis ostendit, quem fructum sentias. *Sobrie,* inquis, *pie & iuste adorabit Deum in spiritu & veritate.* Recte
10 istud quidem. Sed perge paulo quid amplius. *Non in elementis mundi, cibis & vestitu, aut alia hypocrisi. Sentiet de Sacramentis, quod Christus docuit & instituit.*

At hoc illud est, hinc illae lachrymae. [G₁] Nam vos homines spirituales, consilio, quod Christus pro-
Ioan. 4
15   didit, (qui Deum adorare velit, in spi-ritu & veritate oportet adorare) sic decreuistis obtemperare, vt Deo prorsus auferatis omne carnis obsequium. Sed hoc est, Pomerane, sic adorare spiritu, vt non adores in veritate. Neque enim vere adorat Deum, qui sic sibi blanditur oratione spiritus,
20 vt interim carnem negligat lasciuientem subdere & domare ieiunijs.

Vobis omne corporis obsequium, quod Deo praestatur, hy-pocrisis est. At Mariae non erat, quae
Luc. 6   lachrymis lauit pedes Christi, & capitis
25   capillis extersit. Vobis omnis vestitus
Ioan. 12   horridior est hypocrisis: at idem Bap-tistae non fuit, qui pilis cameli vestitus
Mar. 1   est. Hypocrisis est vobis omnis abstinen-tia ciborum: at illi non erat, qui tantum
Matt. 3
30   vescebatur locustis. Sed nec Paulo quidem, qui se optabat omnem diem posse ieiu[G₁v]nare. Vobis sunt hypocrisis omnia, per quae vota sua Deo pietas Fidelium effundit in templis. At non idem sensit Propheta, quem regia celsitudo non vetuit coram archa
2. Reg. 6
35   foederis & psallere, & saltare cum pop-ulo. Nec impune tulit stulta & superba mulier, quae genus id

---

18 Neque] neque *1568*   26 horridior] horridior, *1568*

believe.

Although we agree that what you say is true, we do not agree that it is true in the sense in which you seem to take it. For Christ does not of his own accord produce good fruit in a man of faith without the individual's own will and volition. But that is precisely what you think, as is clear from your heretical denial of free will.

Now what you say next shows what fruit you are thinking about. *He will adore God,* you say, *soberly, piously, and justly, in spirit and truth.* That much is perfectly all right. But go on a little farther, and see what happens. *Not in the elements of this world, in food, clothing, and other hypocrisy. About the sacraments he will believe what Christ taught and established.*

That is the place; that is where it really hurts. For you spiritual men have decided to obey the counsel Christ set forth when he said, "One who desires to worship God must worship him in spirit and in truth," in such a way as to destroy completely the obedience of the flesh to God. But this, Pomeranus, is to worship in spirit and not in truth. One who fools himself with talk of the spirit and fails to subdue and tame the wantonness of the flesh with fasting does not truly worship God.

John 4

You think all obedience of the body offered to God is hypocrisy. But it was not hypocrisy to Mary, who washed Christ's feet with her tears and dried them with the hair of her head. Coarse clothing is hypocrisy to you, but it was not hypocrisy to John the Baptist, who dressed in the skin of camels. Abstinence from food is hypocrisy to you, but it was not hypocrisy to John, who ate only locusts. And it was not hypocrisy even to Paul, who wanted to be able to fast all day. It is hypocrisy to you when the faithful pour out their devotion to God in the churches. But the prophet did not believe it was. The dignity of his kingship did not keep him from singing and dancing with the people before the ark of the covenant. And that proud and foolish woman did not go unpunished when she reproached him for worshiping God in that

Luke 6

John 12

Mark 1

Matthew 3

2 Kings 6

cultus tunc reprehendit in illo, quod vos Lutherani nunc, nec
minus stulti, & magis superbi, sugillatis in grege Christiano.

Profecto, Pomerane, si cuius ita pietas tepet, vt caro eius non
efferuescat in cultu Dei: is verissimus erit hypocrita, si sese dicat
5 feruenter adorare spiritu.

De Sacramentis, inquis, *credet quod Christus docuit & instituit.* Satis
profecto breuiter, verum haud satis dilucide. Nam vos in quaes-
tionem trahitis, quid docuerit Christus. Nos non dubitamus
Christum docuisse, quicquid Ecclesia Christi credit, in quo sine
10 Christi contumelia non posset errare: alio[G₂]qui frustratus es-

Matt. 28

set promissum Christus, quo se cum ea
promisit futurum vsque ad consummationem seculi.

Vos omnia negatis praeter manifestas Scripturas, & quae sunt
15 manifestae, vocatis obscuras: aut, quod est impudentius, quod
clarum est aduersum vos, id clarum clamatis esse pro vobis. Ecclesia demum ipsa quaenam sit, altercamini, & ita redditis am-
biguam, vt in terra statuatis omnino nullam. Denique sic tractatis, vt nisi, quod magis verisimile est, ipsi sitis impij, impios
20 fuisse necesse sit, quicunque hactenus a Christo passo habiti sunt
vsquam pij.

Nam quis vnquam bonus Ordinem habuit pro figmento? Quis
vnquam blaterauit aduersus Contritionem? Imo quis non hor-
tatus est ad dolorem pro peccatis? Quis mulieres permisit audire
25 Confessionem? Quis aduersus opera bona contendit? Quis floccifecit ieiunia? Quis contempsit preces Ec[G₂v]clesiae? Quis templis detraxit ornatum? Quis inuidit Sanctorum cultui? Quis
negauit ignem Purgatorium? Quis Eucharistiam in Missa non
habuit pro Sacrificio? Quis panem restare sensit cum carne
30 Christi?

Quanquam hoc aliquot e primarijs vestrae factionis hominibus
Lutherano more iam recantauerunt. Nam vt is dogmata sua
semper mutare solet in peius, quod & de Venijs fecit, & potestate
Pontificis, & ipsa item Eucharistia: sic Carolostadius & Suinglius,

fashion. But now you Lutherans—no less foolish and more proud than she—jeer at the Christian flock for doing the same thing.

Actually, Pomeranus, the true hypocrite is one whose piety is so lukewarm that he does not feel his flesh grow warm when he worships God, and yet he says that he still adores God ardently in spirit.

About the sacraments he will think, you say, *what Christ taught and established.* Short enough, certainly, but not very clear. For you bring into question what Christ taught. We do not doubt that Christ taught whatever the church of Christ believes, since it cannot err without injury to Christ. Otherwise Christ would have deceived us in promising that he would be with the church even to the end of time.   *Matthew 28*

You deny everything except what is clearly mentioned in scripture, and what is clearly mentioned there you call obscure, or, more boldly, you shout that what is obviously against you is obviously for you. And then you wrangle about what constitutes the church, and you make it so ambiguous that you come to the conclusion that there is no church at all on earth. Finally, you manage it so that either you would have to be fundamentally irreligious (which is most likely) or else all those would have to be so, who from the time of Christ's passion until this very day were believed to be devout.

What good man ever believed that the sacrament of orders is a mere fiction? Who ever babbled against contrition? Who, in fact, ever urged us not to feel sorrow for our sins? Who allowed women to hear confession? Who argued against good works? Who belittled fasting? Who held the prayers of the church in contempt? Who pulled down the decorations in churches? Who has envied the saints their worship? Who denied the fire of purgatory? Who failed to believe that in the mass the eucharist is a sacrifice? Who believed that bread remains bread along with Christ's flesh?

Some of the important leaders of your faction, however, have recanted that last statement—Lutheran fashion. For Luther always changes his beliefs for the worse, as he did with indulgences, the power of the pope, and the eucharist itself. And now

quibus se tandem iunxit OEcolampadius, carnem Christi penitus abstulerunt, merum linquentes panem. Quod ipsum plane
moliebatur olim Lutherus, fecissetque procul dubio, nisi Carolostadius eum praeuenisset & Suinglius.

5   Nam quorsum tendebant illa, quod prius liberum permisit
omnibus, vt citra periculum crederent panem cum corpore simul esse in Eucharistia, nihil [G₃] tamen damnans, si quis panem
mutari credat in carnem. Deinde pro haeretico habebat, si quis
panem crederet in carnem verti.

10   Quorsum illud, quod Missae mutauit Canonem, Sacrificium
aut oblationem vetuit appellari, ceremonias & cultum detraxit,
contrectandum permisit Laicis, conficiendum foeminis, in templis honorandam seruari Eucharistiam prohibuit: asserens eam
non institutam, vt honoraretur, sed vt reciperetur tantum. Imo
15 ne reciperetur quidem, nisi cuique semel voluit in Babilonica,

Luther in Capt. Babil.   videlicet e vita migranti, sicut Bap-
                            tismus duntaxat semel confertur
ingredienti.

An non haec eo pedetentim se ferebant omnia, vt Christi cor-
20 pus ex Eucharistia prorsus aliquando tolleret? Et ita sibi viam
struxerat, vt aperte statim rem esset aggressurus: nisi iam iam
facturientem scelus auocasset a scelere. Nam ab haereseos impiae propera & a[G₃v]perta praedicatione sola retraxit inuidia.
Carolostadio enim & Zuinglio eum inuidit honorem, quod al-
25 teruter ipso magis haberetur impius. Nec minus id honoris post
inuidit Oecolampadio. Ita quam rem eum vident omnes olim
vehementer molitum, eam contra demoliri maluit, quam vt alium quenquam praeter se permitteret impiae cuiusquam sectae
Haeresiarcham esse.

30   Verum quid refert, quem is animum habeat de Eucharistia,
cuius libri satis ostendunt, quam sacrilegum habeat animum de
Christo? Quis enim dubitet, quam impie de Christo sentiat, qui &
Sanctos eius blasphemat, & Crucem eius conspurcat, & vene-
rabilem eius Matrem suae meretrici coaequat? At quid refert
35 adeo, quid ei videatur de Christo, cuius animum spurcissimum

Karlstadt, Zwingli, and Oecolampadius, who finally joined the
rest, have completely removed Christ's flesh from the host and
left only bread. Luther was already working on the idea and no
doubt would have carried it off himself if Karlstadt and Zwingli
had not beaten him to it.

That is where it was tending when he permitted people to
believe without danger that the eucharist consists of both, bread
and Christ's body. At that point Luther did not condemn those
who believed that the bread was turned into flesh. But after a
while he considered anyone who held that belief a heretic .

Where do you think Luther was heading when he changed the
canon of the mass, forbiding it to be termed a sacrifice or offering? Or when he pulled down ritual and ceremony, allowed
laymen to handle the host, permitted women to consecrate it,
and refused to allow it to be kept in the tabernacle and venerated
in the church? He said that Christ did not institute the eucharist
for it to be venerated, but only for it to be received. In fact, it
should not even be received, as Luther
says in the *Babylonian Captivity*, except   *Luther in* The
once, when a person is leaving this life,   Babylonian Captivity
just as he receives baptism only once, when he is entering it.

All this proceeded step by step until eventually Luther would
have undoubtedly taken the body of Christ right out of the
eucharist. He had smoothed the way and was obviously about to
proceed with it. But just as he was about to start, one sin kept him
from committing another. It was only envy that restrained him
from going ahead and preaching that ungodly heresy in public.
For he envied Karlstadt and Zwingli the honor of seeming more
irreligious than he. And afterward he envied Oecolampadius
too. He preferred to dismantle what he had formerly built up (as
anyone could see he was doing) rather than allow anyone else to
become the heresiarch of any godless sect.

But what does it really matter what Luther thinks about the
eucharist when his writings show clearly enough the sacrilegious
ideas he has about Christ? How can anyone doubt how he feels
about Christ when he blasphemes Christ's saints, defiles Christ's
cross, and equates Christ's venerable mother with his own
whore? But what does it really matter what he thinks about
Christ when his filthy heresy testifies to the revolting ideas he has

aduersus naturae Diuinae sublimitatem foedissima testatur
haeresis, qua clementissimum atque Optimum DEVM, adempta
[G₄] voluntatis libertate, scelerum omnium non vltorem magis
facit quam authorem? Qua vna haeresi vt nulla potest excogitari
5 magis impia atque sacrilega aduersus sacrosanctam Maiestatem
Dei: sic nulla potest ad animandos in omne flagitij genus mortales excogitari perniciosior. Et cum tam impia & tam absurda
doceatis, non pudeat interim ita loqui, quasi Lutherani soli sint
idonei, qui proximos forment doctrina: videlicet, opinor, quia
10 docet Lutherus, Christianos omnes omnibus solutos esse legibus: tum autem consilio, quia sancte & seuere consulit, vt qui
coelibem vouit continentiam, contempto voto prouolet ad vxorem, & maritorum si quis est inualidus ad libidinem, consulit, &
perquam comiter, vt vxori conducat adulterum.
15   Nam quod rebus Lutherani iuuent proximos vsque ad dispen-
dium vitae, idque non amicos modo, sed inimicos [G₄v] quoque:
quis sic audire potest, vt in re atrocissima simul & miserrima
risum tamen queat continere? Quum videat vestrae factionis
facinorosas cohortes passim conglobari, demoliri pulcherrimas
20 domos, sacratissimas aedes incendere, sanctissima templa di-
ripere, miseros & innocentes Fratres bonis & fortunis omnibus
exutos, omni vitae subsidio nudatos, corpore plerosque male
mulctatos eijcere. Hoccine est, Pomerane, rebus adiuuare, etiam
cum dispendio vitae? Idque non solum amicos, sed inimicos quo-
25 que? Sic, opinor, videlicet: quum eos tractatis vbique pessime,
quicunque sunt vbiuis optimi.
   Nam si quis leuis sit & inconstans nebulo, paratus vltro
seueritatem vitae strictioris abijcere: hunc obuijs vlnis amplectimini, hic sanctissimus est in Christo Frater, & sceleratis turmis
30 sceleratus miles adiungitur. At si quis amplexus veram pietatem
constanter in[G₅]sistat proposito, & abominetur facinorosam licentiam: hic statim Pharisaeus vobis, & Iustitiarius, & hypocrita
proscinditur non aliter a Lutheranis, afficitur, exturbatur, af-
fligitur, quam ab Ethnicis olim Tyrannis solent innocentissimi
35 Martyres. Et tamen interim, si superis placet, ita loquimini, quasi
soli sitis Christiani, & grauiter obiurgatis Ecclesiam, tanquam

9 videlicet] Videlicet *1568*

about the sublimity of the divine nature? When he did away with the freedom of the will, Luther made our all-good, all-merciful God not the avenger, but the originator of sin. One can hardly imagine a more impious and sacrilegious heresy against God's holy majesty and a more deadly temptation to commit all sorts of disgraceful acts. At the same time you go about teaching these absurd, ungodly things, you are not embarrassed by speaking as though Lutherans only had a right to influence their neighbors by teaching. The reason you think so, I suppose, is that Luther teaches that all Christians are above all law. And you are well advised to think so, since he advises, in his holy, austere fashion, that one who has taken a vow of celibacy can forget all about it and snatch up a wife. He also very obligingly advises that if a husband is impotent he should hire some man to commit adultery with his wife.

Now as for the Lutherans helping their neighbors at the cost of their own lives, and this not only for friends, but also for enemies—who could listen to that and not burst out laughing, even though the thought of it is very sad and depressing? One sees the savage troops of your sect massing together on every side, destroying beautiful homes, burning sacred buildings, plundering holy churches, casting out the pitiful and innocent friars, stripped of all their goods and fortune, bereft of all means of support, and many of them with serious bodily injuries. Is that what you call helping your neighbors even at the cost of your own life? And this not only for friends, but also for enemies? I suppose so. No doubt you always treat the best people the worst.

For you take in with open arms any flea-brained, shifty wretch who is willing to cast off the rigors of a disciplined life. He is your holy brother in Christ, and thus another godless soldier is added to the godless troop. But take someone who is truly pious and pursues his purpose without wavering and despises the freedom enjoyed by criminals, you immediately regard him as a Pharisee and self-justifier. He is scorned as a hypocrite by the Lutherans. He is abused, driven off, and harassed just as the innocent martyrs were by pagan tyrants. And yet, so help me God, you speak as though you are the only Christians and gravely rebuke the church as if she had never heard of Christ. You yelp like a dog the Father's words about God the Son, "Hear him"—out of

non audiat Christum: obgannientes extra locum verba Dei patris
de Deo filio: Ipsum audite. Sed interim vides, quod non dixit
pater, Pomeranum audite, nec Lutherum audite.

Nam quod ex Mose profers: *Quisquis Prophetam illum non au-*
5   *dierit, ego vltor existam, dicit Dominus,*
            Deut. 18   vobis ipsis minatur exitium. Ecclesia si-
quidem, quia Christum audit in se loquentem, seruat eandem
fidem, quae Christi morte per Apostolos, Martyres, & Confes-
sores sanctissimos ad haec vsque tem[G₅v]pora perpetuo Christi
10 flatu deriuata est: ad finem vsque seculi, inuitis haereticis omnibus atque omnibus haereticorum socijs Daemonibus, dura-
tura.

At vos, qui Ecclesiam Christi contemnitis, quos ob id ipsum
tanquam Ethnicos & Publicanos haberi
15   *Matt. 18*   iubet Christus, vos estis, inquam, qui in
Ecclesia sua Christum spernitis, qui Christum Ecclesiae suae loquentem audire negligitis, atque ideo Deum aliquando sensuri
estis vltorem.

Nam etsi diuina bonitas interdum per tales Daemonum satel-
20 lites, vel bonorum qui sunt in Ecclesia probet patientiam, vel
castiget peccata fidelium: tamen fidelis
            1 Cor. 10   erit, & dabit cum tentatione prouen-
            Apocal. 7   tum, & omnem aliquando lachrymam
absterget ab oculis emendatorum. Sed
25   *1 Thes. 2*   eius ira atque indignatio vos, vos, inquam, impios & truculentos Fidelium
            Psal. 1   carnifices, spiritu oris sui difflabit in
cinerem, ac velut puluerem [G₆] proijciet a facie terrae.

Cuius vindictae nuper, edidit perhorrendum specimen, quum
30 miserrimi nebulones illi rustici doctrina vestra seducti, postquam demoliti sunt tot Religiosorum Coenobia, atque aliquan-
tisper huc illuc caedibus & rapinis impune grassati sunt: quum
iam se fere consequutos crederent improhibitam atque indo-
mabilem scelerum omnium licentiam,
35   *Psal. 28*   ecce autem Deus maiestatis intonuit, &
            1 Thes. 5   subitus superuenit interitus. Inuoluit
eos mare miseriae velut pecora, passim

24 Sed] sed *1568*

context. Note, however, that God did not say, "Hear Pome-ranus" or "Hear Luther."

For the passage you quote from Moses threatens to ruin you: *Whoever will not hear that prophet, I will* *take vengeance on him, says the Lord.* The *Deuteronomy 18* church hears Christ's voice speaking from within itself and thus maintains the same faith that from the time of Christ's death through the apostles, martyrs, and holy confessors even to this present age flowed without interruption from Christ's own breath, and it will endure despite all heretics and all the demons allied to them even to the end of time.

But you condemn the church of Christ, and thus Christ com-mands us to regard you as pagans and *Matthew 18* publicans. At one time or another you will experience the vengeance of God for rejecting Christ in his church and refusing to listen to Christ speaking to his church.

The divine goodness uses at times such agents of demons to test the patience of good men in the church or to punish the sins of the faithful. But God will be true to his word and along with the temptation   *1 Corinthians 10* provide a way out, and eventually he will wipe away every tear from the eyes   *Apocalypse 7* of those who have mended their ways.   *1 Thessalonians 2* But his wrath and indignation, you— you, I say, you ungodly, cruel slayers of   *Psalm 1* the faithful—with the breath of his an-ger he will blow you to ashes and drive you like dust from the face of the earth.

God recently gave a horrifying instance of this vengeance when those pitiful wretches, the peasants who were led astray by your teaching, destroyed so many monasteries and roamed about aimlessly for a while killing and looting wherever they wanted. When they believed they had achieved almost unlimited and unrestricted license to commit all kinds of crime, behold, the God of glory thundered and destruc-tion suddenly came over them. A sea of   *Psalm 28* misery overwhelmed them like sheep.   *1 Thessalonians 5* All told, more than seventy thousand

perempti sunt plusquam septuaginta millia: tum reliqui, quotquot erant, omnes in acerbissimam seruitutem sunt redacti.

Qua in re non vos Lutheri pudet Imperatoris vestri, qui ex
sceleratissimo duce turpissimus factus transfuga, quos prius
5   vnus ad omne nephas accenderat, armauerat, stimularat: eos vbi
vidit fortuna destitui, sceleratis suis [G₆v] scriptis truculenter
proscidit, ac proscripsit, & lacerandos prodidit Nobilibus: vt
nepharius adulator miserorum sanguine, quos & excitauit, &
mactauit ipse, suscitatam in se inuidiam restingueret.

10   Quis, qui vel guttam haberet humani cruoris in pectore, non
decies potius elegisset mori, quam adulatione tam foeda & pal-
patione tam dira vitam Dijs & hominibus inuisam viuere? Et
tamen fieri potest, vt non sit inuenturus tam parum cordatos
Nobiles, vt vnis literis emolliti statim obliuiscantur, per quem
15   effectum est, vt pene in extremam perniciem sint adducti. Nam
rusticis, opinor, omnino nunquam excisurum, per quem bis per-
ierunt. Hic homo impius, & vltione diuina caecus, dum vtram-
que partem studuit demereri: nec alteram lucrifecit, & alteram
plane perdidit.

20   Quanquam ego profecto & Nobiles [G₇] illi, & rusticos optem
ignoscere, modo ita se statuat gerere, maxime vt ignoscat Deus:
id est, si resipiscat ab haeresi, si sine fuco pessima recantet dogmata, si per ignominiam suam quaerat gloriam Christi, nec improbam sinat superbiam obsistere, quo minus in honorem Dei
25   suam fateatur insaniam.

Quod si Lutherus ita de se desperat, vt salutem negligat suam,
tu tuae tamen, Pomerane, consule. Im-
Epilogus
piam istam sectam, & omnium quae
fuerunt vnquam flagitiosissimam, desere. Ecclesiae Catholicae
30   redde ac restitue te. Denique quod tua praedicatione iam diu
corrupisti, quantum potes, omnibus modis corrige. Episcopatum quem per nefas occupas, relinque. Miseram illam puellam,

perished. And the rest, whatever the number, were all reduced to bitter servitude.

Are you not disgraced by the part Luther played in this? He was your general and changed from the wickedest commander in the world to the most dishonorable deserter. He was the one who inflamed the peasants to every crime they committed; he armed them and egged them on. Then, when he saw that fortune had deserted them, he grimly cut them down by writing his vicious pamphlets against them. He outlawed them and turned them over to the nobles to be hacked to pieces. And that unspeakable politician did all this in order to extinguish with the blood of those pitiful wretches the fires of hatred directed against himself. He first stirred them up, and then he sacrificed them.

If Luther had a drop of human blood in his heart, he would have preferred to die ten times over rather than by such filthy maneuvering and horrible cringing live a life loathsome to God and man. But perhaps he will find that the nobles are not stupid enough to be softened up with one letter and forget that he was the one who brought them to the brink of destruction. As for the peasants, I suspect they will never forget the man who destroyed them twice over. Godless and blind as he is to divine vengeance, Luther worked to ingratiate himself with both parties. But he failed to gain the one, and he obviously lost the other.

Yet it is my sincere hope that the nobles and peasants will forgive him, provided that he decides to act in such a way that God above all can forgive him. I mean, if he recovers from heresy, if without deception he recants his evil beliefs, if he seeks Christ's glory through his own disgrace and does not allow his insatiable pride to keep him from confessing his insanity for the honor of God.

But if Luther has fallen into such despair that he pays no attention to his own salvation, you, Pomeranus, must consider yours. *Epilogue* Abandon that ungodly sect, the most shameful that ever existed on earth. Return and rejoin the Catholic church. Then, in every way you can, correct what you corrupted for so many years with your preaching. Give up your illegitimate bishopric. Send away that unfortunate girl you whore with in the name of marriage.

in quam coniugij titulo scortaris, ablega. Et vitae, quod reliquum
dabitur tibi, in ante actae poenitentia consume. [G₇v]

    Haec, Pomerane, si feceris (quae Deum precor vt facias) tum
demum vere gaudebis de nobis, & nos vicissim, qui te perire
5 dolemus, inuentum esse gratulabimur. [G₈]

Haec Epistola insignis et praeclari Martyris Thomae Mori
dignissima mihi videtur, quae imprimatur.

Cunerus Petri, Pastor S. Petri.
10   *7. Aprilis. Anno. 1568.*

And spend the rest of your life in repentance for what you have done.

If you do these things, Pomeranus—and I pray to God you will—then will you truly joy in us, and instead of feeling sorrow that you are lost, we in turn will rejoice that you are found.

This Epistle by the famous and illustrious
Martyr Thomas More seems to me to be
Very worthy of being printed.

Cuner Peeters, Pastor of S. Peter's
7 April 1568

THE SUPPLICATION OF SOULS

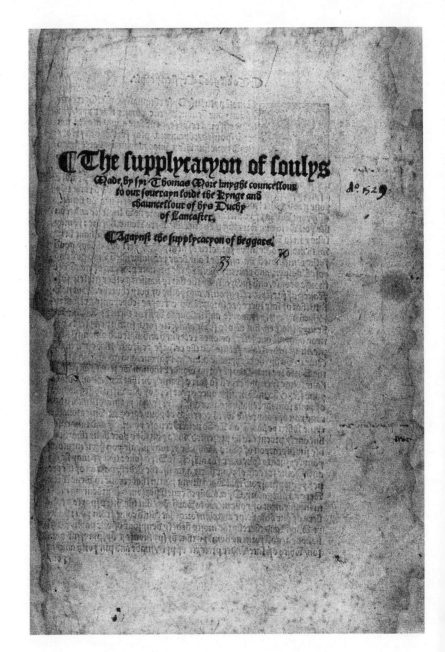

Title page, *Supplication of Souls*, 1529[2] (reduced)

[A₁]

The supplycacyon of soulys
Made by syr Thomas More knyght councellour
to our souerayn lorde the Kynge and
chauncellour of hys Duchy
of Lancaster.
Agaynst the supplycacyon of beggars.

5

---

1 soulys] *1529*², soulys. *1529*¹, soules *1557*   2 Made] *1529*, made, Anno. 1529.
1557   6 beggars.] *1529*² *1557*, beggars *1529*¹

To all good Crysten people.

IN most pytuouse wyse continually calleth & cryeth vppon your
deuout cherite & moste tender pyte / for helpe cumfort & relyefe / your late aquayntaunce / kindred / spouses / companions /
play felowes / & frendes / & now your humble & vnacquaynted & 5
halfe forgoten supplyauntys / pore prysoners of god yᵉ sely
sowlys in purgatory / here abydyng & endurying yᵉ greuouse
paynys & hote clensynge fyre / yᵗ freteth & burneth owte yᵉ
rustye & fylthy spottes of our synne / tyll yᵉ mercy of almighty
god yᵉ rather by your good & cherytable meanes / vowchesaufe 10
to delyuer vs hense.

From whense yf ye meruayll why we more now moleste and
trouble you wyth our wrytyng then euer we were wonte byfore:
yt may lyke you to wyt and understand / that hytherto / though
we have bene wyth many folke mych forgoten of neglygence / 15
yet hath alway good folke remembred vs / and we have bene
recommended vnto god and eased / holpen / and relieued / both
by the pryuate prayers of good vertuouse people / and specyally
by the dayly masses & other gostely suffrages of prestys / relygyouse / and folke of holy churche. But now syth that of late 20
there are sprongen vp certayne sedycyouse persones / whych not
onely trauayle and labour to dystroy them by whome we be mych
holpen / but also to sowe and sette forth such a pestylent opynyon agaynst our selfe / as ones receyued and byleued among yᵉ
people / must nedys take frome vs the relyefe & cumforte that 25
euer shuld come to vs by the cherytable almesse / prayour / and
good wurkes of the world: ye may take yt for no wonder though
we sely sowlys that have longe lyen and cryed so farre frome you

---

2 continually] *1529*¹ *corr. err.*, *1529*², continully *1529*¹, continuallye *1557*   5–7 *Side-*
note 1557: The sely soules in purgatorie call vnto vs for help   19–20 *Sidenote 1557:*
Howe the soules in purgatorie be relieued   25 relyefe] *1529*¹ *corr. err.*, *1529*², relyese
*1529*¹, reliefe *1557*

that we seldome brake your slepe / do now in thys oure great fere
of our vtter losse for euer of your louyng remembraunce and
relyefe / not yet importunatly byreue you of your reste wyth
cryenge at your eares at vnseasonable tyme when ye wold (as we
5 do neuer) repose your self and take ease / but onely procure to
be presented vnto you thys pore boke thys humble supplycacyon
of owrs / whyche yt may please you parcell meale at your leysure
to loke ouer for all sely sowlys sake: that yt may be as an holsome
tryacle at your harte agaynst the dedely poyson of theyre
10 pestylent persuasyon / that wold bryng you in that errour to
wene there were no purgatory. Of all whych cruell persones so
procuring not yᵉ mynysshement of your mercy toward us / but
the vtter spoyle & robbery of our hole helpe and comforte that
shuld come from you: yᵉ very wurste and thereby the moste
15 dedely deuysour of our paynys and heuynes (god forgeue hym)
ys that dyspytuouse & dyspytefull person / which of late vnder
pretexte of pyte / made and put forth among [A₂] you / a boke
that he namyd the supplycacyon for the beggars / a booke in
dede nothynge lesse intendyng / then the pyte that yt preten-
20 deth: nothyng myndyng yᵉ weale of eny man / but as we shall
hereafter shew you / mych harme and myschyefe to all men /
and among other great sorow dyscumfort and heuenysse vnto vs
your euen crysten and nygh kynne / your late neyghbours and
pleasaunt companyons uppon erth / and now pore prysoners
25 here.

And albe yt yᵗ hys vnhappy boke / doth for our owne parte
towche vs very nere: yet we be mych more moued to geue yᵉ
world warnyng of hys venymous wrytynge / for the dere loue &
cheryte that we bere to you / then for the respecte of our awne
30 relyefe. For as for vs / albe yt that the gracyouse helpe of your
prayour / almesse dede / and other good warkis for vs / may be
the meanes of relyeuyng and releasyng of our present paynis /
yet such ys the mercyfull goodnes of god / that though the hole
world wold clene forgete vs / yet wold his mercy so remember vs /

4–5 *Sidenote 1557:* The soules in purgaterie doe neuer rest   19–20 *Sidenote 1557:*
What the supplicacion of beggars pretendeth   30 your] *1529,* oure *1557*
31 prayour] *1529*¹, pryour *1529*², prayoure *1557*

that after temporall punysshement and purgyng here he wyll
not fynally forgete to take vs hense: and wypyng all yᵉ terys owt
of our eyen / translate vs at sondry tymes as hys hygh wysedom
seeth conuenyent / in to that eternal heuenly blesse / to whych
his holy blyssyd blood hath bought vs. But surely to you worldly   5
people lyuynge there vppon erth / not onely for this present
tyme / but also for as longe as thys world shall endure: the
wreched maker of that vngracyouse boke (whome god giue onys
the grace to repente & amend) yf folke were so fonde to folowe
hym / shulde not fayle to worke / as well myche worldely trouble 10
to euery kynde of people / as ouer that (whych most losse were of
all) to brynge many a good symple soule / for lakke of belefe of
purgatory / the very strayght way to hell.

   And the case so standynge / there wold we thynke no man
dowte / but thoughe the man that made the boke were well   15
knowen amonge you and in holde also / whereby hys heyghnouse treason to god and yᵉ world dysclosed & declared by vs /
he myght be in parell of exquysyte paynefull punysshement: yet
we both myght and ought / rather to put hym in the daunger of
hys awne demeanure / then for the sparyng of hys iuste correc- 20
cyon / to suffer hym abuse yᵉ people wyth hys pestylent wrytynge / to the inestymable harme of the hole worlde in goodys /
body / & sowle. And syth we so myght of reason / & so shuld of
cheryte though the man were knowen and taken / how myche
may we nowe more frankely tell you all and nothynge shall nede 25
to spare hym / syth hys boke ys nameles / & so hym self among
you unknowen and therby owte of the parell of eny punysshement for hys vnhappy dede?

   But for that both ye & he shall well perceyue / that we desyre
but your weale and ours by gyuyng you warnynge of hys malyce / 30
and [A₂v] nothyng entend to procure hys punysshement /
whyche we rather beseche our lord of hys mercy to remytte: ye
shall understand that neyther ys his name nor persone
vnknowen among vs / and therfore we might well discouer hym
yf we were so mynded. For there is not onely some of hys ac- 35

12–15 *Sidenote 1557:* The lacke of belief of purgatory, bringeth a man to hell   34 we
might] *1557,* me myght *1529¹,* we-might *1529²*

quayntaunce and counseyll / whome god gaue at theyre deth the
grace to repente / comen hyther to purgatory / nothyng more
now lamentyng among vs / then theyre cruell vnkyndenesse to
ward vs / in geuyng counseyll agaynst vs / to the makyng of that
5 vngracyouse boke / wyth infydelyte and lakke of bylyefe of the
pourgyng fyre whych they now fynde and fele: but he ys also
named and bosted among vs by that euell aungell of hys / owre
and your gostely enemy the deuyll. Whych as sone as he had set
hym a wurke wyth that pernycyouse boke / ceaced not to come
10 hyther and boste yt among vs: but wyth his enmyouse & enuyouse laughter gnasshyng the teeth and grynnynge / he tolde
vs that hys peopyll had by the aduyse and counsayll of hym and
of some heretyques almost as euill as he / made suche a boke for
beggars / that yt shuld make vs begge longe are we gete aught.
15 Wherby he trusted that som of vs shuld not so sone crepe owte of
our payne as we had hoped.

    Wytte ye well these wordes were heuy tidynges to vs. But yet
bycause yᵉ deuyll ys wonte to ly / we toke some comfort in that we
could not belyue hym / specyally tellynge a thynge so farre in-
20 credyble. For who could euer haue thought that eny crysten man
could for very pyte haue founden in hys harte to seke and study
the meanes / whereby a crysten man shuld thynke yt labour loste
to pray for all crysten sowlys? But alakke the whyle we founde
sone after / that the falshed and malyce of the man / preued yᵉ
25 dyuyll trewe. For by some that dyed sone after the boke put forth /
we haue herde & perceyued the wreched contentys therof / well
and playnely declarynge / what euyll spyryte inspyred hym
whyle yt was in makynge. For albe yt that yt ys so contryued / and
the wordys so cowched / that by the secrete inwarde wurkynge of
30 the deuyll that holpe to dyuyse yt / a symple reder myght by
delyte in the redyng be dedely corrupted and venemed: yet yf a
wyse man well warned / aduysedly wyll way the sentence / he
shall fynde the hole boke nothyng elles / but falshed vnder pretext of playnesse / crueltye vnder the cloke of pyte / sedycyon

---

10–11 enuyouse] *1529²* corr. err., *1529¹*, enuoyuse *1529²*, enuious *1557*   17 tidynges]
1529², tydynges *1529¹* corr. err., tydyng *1529¹*, tydinges *1557*   23 sowlys?] *1529¹*,
sowlys. *1529²*, soules. *1557*   33–34 *Sidenote 1557:* The contentes of the boke of
beggars

vnder the colour of counsayle / prowde arrogans vnder ye name of supplycacyon / & vnder ye pretence of fauour vnto pore folke / a deuylyshe desyre of noyaunce both to pore & rich / preste / religiouse / & lay man / prynce / lord / & peple / as well quycke as dede.   5

He deuyseth a pytuouse byll of complaynte and supplycacyon / fayned to be by the pore sykke and sore beggers put vpp to the kyng / lamentyng theryn theyre nomber so sore encreaced / that good folkes [A$_3$] almoyse not half suffysyng to fynde them mete / they be constraynyd heuely to dye for hunger. Then layth he y^e 10 cause of all these pore beggars / both theyr encrese in nomber & theyr defaut in fyndyng / all this he layth to the onely faut of the clergy: namyng them in hys bederoll byshops / abbotes / pry- ours / deacons / archedecons / suffragans / prestes / monkys / chanons / frerys / pardoners / & sommoners. All these he calleth   15 myghty sturdy beggers & ydle holy theuys / whych he sayth hath beggyd so importunatly / that they haue gotten in to theyr handys ye thyrd parte of all the realm of Englond / besyde tythys / preuy tythys / probatys of testamentes & offrynges / wyth masse pens & mortuaryes / blyssyng & cursyng / cytyng / suspendyng &   20 soylyng. Then cummeth he pertyculerly to freres: to whom he maketh as he thynketh a playn & open rekenyng / that they reseyue by beggyng thorow ye realm yerely .xliii. thousand .iii. C. xxxiii. pound .vi. s. viii. d. sterlyng. Then shewyth he that all thys cast to gyther / amounteth yerely farre aboue the half of the   25 hole substaunce of the realme. After this presupposyng as though he had prouyd yt that the clergy hath the half / he then to proue the two hundred parte of that they haue were more then suffycyent for them: taketh for hys ground that yf the number of them be compared wyth the nomber of lay men / the clergy be   30 not ye hundreth parte: & y^t yf they be compared wyth the lay men women & childern / the clergy ys not then the foure hun- dred person of that nomber. And then entendyth he therby to proue & conclude / that syth they haue as he sayth more then the

---

4–5 quycke as dede] _1529^1 corr. err._, _1529^2_, quycke & dede _1529^1_, quick as ded _1557_   13–15 _Sidenote 1557:_ The bederoll of the boke of beggars   28 hundred] _1529^2_, hundreth _1529^1_, .C. _1557_   32–33 hundred] _1529^2 1557_, hundreth _1529^1_

half of all to gether / & be them self not fully the foure hundred
parte: therfore if that better half that they haue were deuyded
into two hundreth partes / then were yet one parte of those two
hundreth partys as he thynketh to mych for them / specyally
5 because they labour not. After thys he gathereth a great hepe of
euyls / wherwyth he belyeth the clergy / to bryng them in dyspleasure of the kynge and hatered of the people. And leste men
shuld eny thyng esteeme the clergye for the suffragys of theyre
prayoure in relyefe of vs sely crysten sowlys in purgatory / to take
10 a way that good mynde oute of good crysten mennys hartes / he
laboreth to make the worlde wene that there were no purgatorye
at all. Wherein when he hathe done what he canne / then laboureth he to the kynge for a lycence to rayle vppon the clergye:
sayeng that there ys none other effectuall remedye agaynste
15 theym / but that yt myght please the kynge to gyue hym and
suche other fre lycense and lyberte / to dyffame the clergye at
theyr pleasure amonge the people. For he sayth that yf any of
them be punyshed any thyng by the temporall lawes / than they
sore troble the laborers therof by the spyrytuall law / and then
20 the heddys of the clergy do so hyghly more than recompence the
losse of theyre felows / that they may be bolde to do the lyke
offence agayn at theyr pleasure. And for to proue that yt ys
alway so / [A$_3$v] he layth that yt hath bene so thryse: and as yt
shall after be shewed he lyeth in all thre. The furste he layth that
25 the byshop of London was in a grete rage for endyghtynge of
certayn curatys of extorcyon and incontynency the last yere in
the wardmote questis. And for the second he laith that doctour
Aleyn after that he was punished by premunire for his contempt
commytted agaynst the kyngys temporall law / was therfore by
30 the byshoppys hyghly recompensed in benefyces. And for y^e
third he layth that Richard Hunne because he had sued a premunire agaynst a preest for suyng hym in ye spyrytuall court in a
mater determynable in the kyngys court / was accused of heresy

---

1 hundred] *1529*^{2} *1557*, hundreth *1529*^{1} 3 hundreth] *1529*, hundred *1557*
4 hundreth] *1529*, hunred *1557*   9 prayoure] *1529*^{1}, prayour *1529*^{2} *corr. err.*, pryoure
1529^2, prayer *1557*   30 hyghly] *1529*^{2}, hygly *1529*^{1}, highly *1557*   31–32 *Sidenote*
1557: What a premunyre is

and commytted to byshoppys pryson: where he sayth that all the
world knowyth that he was murtheryd by doctour Horsey wyth
his complyces then the byshoppys chauncellour. And that y^e
same doctour Horsey he sayth vppon other mennys mouthis
payed .vi. hundred poundes for hym & hys complyces: & after   5
obteyned the kyngys most gracyous pardon. Wheruppon he
sayth the captayns of the spyrytualte because he had faughten so
manfully agaynst the kynges crown and dygnyte / promotyd
hym forth wyth benefyce vppon benefyce to the valew of .iiii.
tymes as myche. And by these ensaumples he concludyth there   10
wyll no such punyshment serue agaynst the spyritualte: and also
who y^t iustly punysh a preest by the temporall law / ys vniustly
trobled agayn in ye spyrytuall law. Wherof he wold conclude that
of necessyte for a specyall remedy / the kyng must nedis graunt a
licence to such lewd felows to rayle vppon them. Than cometh he   15
at laste vnto the deuyce of some remedy for the pore beggars.
Wherin he wold in no wyse haue none hospytals made / because
he sayth that therin the profyte goeth to the prestys. What remedy than for the pore beggars? He deuysyth nor desyreth
nothynge to be geuen them / nor none other almoyse or helpe   20
requyreth for them: but onely that ye kyngis hyghnes would
furst take frome the hole clergye all theyre hole lyuynge / and
then sette theym abrode in the worlde to gette theym wyues / and
to get theyre lyuyng wyth ye labour of theyr handys and in the
swete of theyr facys / as he sayeth yt ys the commaundement of   25
god in the furst chapiter of Genesis: and fynally to tay them to
the cartes to be whyppyd naked about euery market towne tyll
they fall to labour. And then yf these petycions were onys
grauntyd and parformyd / he sheweth many great commodytees
that wold as he sayth ensue theruppon / both to the kynge & the   30
people / and to the pore beggars. Which thyngys we shall ere we
leue / in such wyse repete and ponder / that your wysdoms may
consyder and parceiue in your self / what good frute wold folow
the spede of hys goodly supplycacion / whereof we haue rehersed you the hole some and effect.   35

---

9 forth wyth] *1529*, furthwith, *1557*   13 conclude] *1529*[1], include *1529*[2] *1557*
19 beggars?] *1529*[1] *1557*, beggars. *1529*[2]

Trewthe yt ys y^t many thyngys wherewyth he florysheth hys
[A$_4$] maters to make them seme gay to the reders at a sodayn
shew / we leue out for the while / because we wold ere we come
therto / that ye shuld furst haue the mater self in short set forthe
5   before your eyen. And than shall we peruse hys prouys / and in
such wyse consyder euery thynge aparte / that we nothyng dout
but who so shall rede hys worshypfull wrytyng after / shall sone
parceyue therin / floryshyng without frute / suttelte wythout
substaunce / rethoryk wythout reason / bolde babelyng wythout
10   lernyng / & wylynes wythout wyt. And fynally for ye foundacyon
and ground of all hys prouys: ye shall fynde in hys boke not half
so many leuys as lyes / but almost as many lyes as lynes.

And albe yt we lye here in that case that about thexamynacyon
and answeryng of such a mad malycyouse boke we haue neyther
15   lust nor leysoure to bestow the tyme / wherof mispent in our lyfe
we geue now an hard and a heuy rekenynge: yet not only the
necessyte of our cause dryueth vs to declare vnto you the
feblenes of hys reasons / wherewyth he wold bryng you in the
case to care nothyng for vs / beleuyng y^t there were no purgatory /
20   but also most specyally dothe our charite towarde you / styrre vs
to shew you the myschefe that he myndeth to your self / aswell in
that poynt of infidelyte / as in all the remnaunt of hys sedicyouse
boke. In answeryng wherof we wold gladly let hys foly and lak of
lernyng passe / yf yt were not more than necessary / that all folk
25   shuld parceyue hys lyttell lernyng and lesse wyt / lest symple folk
wenyng hym wyse and well lernyd / myght vnto theyr harm
esteme hys euyll wrytyng the better for theyr wronge opynyon of
hys wyt and lernyng. As for hys malycyouse mynde and vntreuth /
there can no man loke that we shuld leue vntowchyd / but he that
30   wold rather the man were beleued than answeryd / and wold
wysh hys byll sped were yt neuer so malycyouse and false.

For where he so deuyseth hys introduccyon / as all hys purpose shuld haue a great face of charyte / by that he speketh all in
the name of the pore beggars / thys ys nothyng els but the deuyls
35   dryft / alway coueryng hys poyson vnder some tast of suger. As

---

8–10 *Sidenote 1557:* What things are to be found in the boke of beggars   16 an hard
and a heuy] *1529*, a hard & heuy *1557*   32 so] *1529*^{2} *corr. err.*, *1529*^{1} *1557*, to
1529^2 34–35 *Sidenote 1557:* The deuilles drift

for vs we truste there wyll no wyse man doute what fauour we
bere to beggers as folk of theyr own felyshyp and faculte / and of
all whom / there be no where in the world nether so nedy nor so
sore / and so syk nor so impotent / and so sore in paynes as we.
And that so farforth that yf ye myght se them all on the tone syde / 5
and but one of vs on the tother syde / we be very sure that the
world wolde pyte one of vs / more than them all. But although we
be more beggars then your beggers be / as folk dayly beggyng
our almes of you and them both: yet enuy we not them as one of
them dothe a nother / but we pray and require you to gyue them 10
for our sakes / wherby your gyft gretly cumfortyth vs both. And
they be also our proctours and beg in our name / and in our
[A₄v] name receaue your money / wherof we receyue both your
deuocyon and theyr prayours. So yᵗ ye may be well assured /
there coud be put no byll nor supplycacyon forth for theyr 15
aduauntage / whych we wold in eny wyse hynder / but very
gladly forther in all yᵗ euer we myghte. But in good fayth as our
poré brethern the beggars be for many causes greatly to be
pytyed for theyr dysease and syknes / sorow / payn & pouerte: so
do we mych in thys case sorow theyre myshap / that they haue 20
nott had at the leste wyse so muche fortune / as to fall vppon a
wyser scryuener to make theyr supplycacyon: but vppon such a
one as vnder hys great wylynes sheweth so lyttell wyt / that begynnyng wyth a cloke of charyte / doth by and by no lesse dys-
close hys hatered and malice / than yf he nothyng els had en- 25
tended / but to cast of yᵉ cloke and set out hys malyce naked to
the shew. Whyrin lyke a beggars proctour he goeth forth so
nakedly / yᵗ no begger ys there so bare of cloth or money / as he
sheweth hym selfe bare of faythe / lernynge / trouth / wyt or
charite. Whych thyng as it all redy well appereth to wyse men: so 30
wyll we make yt euydent to all men / takyng our bygynnynge at
the declaracyon of hys vntrewth: whych one thyng well perceyued / wyll be suffycyent to answer and ouertorne all hys hole
enterpryse. How be yt we nether shall nede nor do purpose to
cumber you wyth rehersall and reprofe of all hys lyes: for that 35

---

5 ye] *1529*¹ *corr. err.*, *1529*² *1557*, he *1529*¹   9–11 *Sidenote 1557:* The soules in purgatorie praye for beggars

were to long a work / wherof we fere ye shuld be wery to abyde
the heryng. But of so many we shall pray you take pacyence
whyle we shewe you some / and such as for the matter be re-
quysyte to be knowen / for as much as all hys proues be specyally
5 grounded vppon them.

And furst to begyn where he begynneth / when he sayth that
the nomber of such beggars as he pretendeth to speke for / that
is as hym self calleth them "the wretched hyduouse monsters /
on whom he sayth scarcely eny eye dare loke / the foule vnhappy
10 sort of lepers & other sore people / nedy / impotent / blynde /
lame and syk / lyuyng onely of almes: haue theyre numbere
nowe so sore encreased / that all the almoyse of all the well
dysposed people of the realme ys nott halfe inowghe to sustayne
theym / but that for very constraynte they dye for hunger:" vnto
15 all those wordys of hys / were yt not that though we well wyst our
self he sayd vntrew / yet wold we be lothe so to lay as a lye to his
charge eny thyng / wherof the vntrewth were not so playnly
parceyued / but that he myghte fynde some fauourers whych
myghte say he sayd trew: els wold we paraduenture not let to tell
20 hym / that for a bygynnyng in these few wordes he had wrytten
two lyes at onys. If we shuld tell you what nomber ther was of
pore syk folke in days passed long before your tyme: ye were at
lyberte not to beleue vs. How be yt he cannot yet on y^e tother syde
for hys part nether / bryng you forth a bederoll of theyr namys:
25 wherfore we must for bothe our partes [B$_1$] be fayn to remyt you
to your owne tyme / & yet not from your chyldhed (whereof
many thynges men forget when they come to farr greater age)
but vnto the days of your good remembraunce. And so doyng /
we suppose yf the sory syghtys y^t men have sene / had left as gret
30 impressyon styll remaynyng in theyr hartys / as the syght maketh
of the present sorow that they se: men shuld thynk & say y^t they
haue in days passed sene as many sykke beggers as they se now.
For as for other syknes they rayn not god be thanked but after
such rate as they haue done in tymes passed. And then of the
35 french pokkys .xxx. yere a go went there about syk / fyue

---

23 cannot] *1557*, cannot not *1529*

agaynst one y^t beggeth wyth them now. Wherof who so lyst to say that he seeth it otherwyse: we wyll hold no great dyspycyons wyth hym theruppon / because we lakke the namys of both the sydes to make the tryall wyth. But surely who so shall say the contrary: shall as we suppose eyther saye so for his pleasure / or els shall it fare by his sight as folkis fare with theyr felyng / which what they fele they whyne at / but what they haue felt they haue more then half forgotten / though they felt it ryght late. Whych maketh one that hath but a pore boyle vppon hys fynger / thynk the grefe more great / than was the payne of a great boch that greued hys hole hand lyttell more than a moneth a fore. So that in thys poynt of the nomber of syk beggers so sore encreased so late / albeit we wyll forbere so to say to hym as we mighte well say: yet will we be so bolde to denye it hym till he bryng in some better thyng than hys bare word for the profe.

And in good faith if he be put to the profe of the tother poynt also / that is to wyt that for very constraynt those pore syk folk dye for hunger: we verely trust & think he shall seke farr and fynde very few yf he fynde any at all: for albeit that pore house-holders haue these dere yeres made ryght hard shyft for corne: yet our lorde be thanked men haue not bene so farr from all pyte / as to suffer pore impotent parsons dye at theyr doorys for hunger.

Now where as he sayth that the almes of all well disposed peple of thys reame is not half inough to sustayn them / and the well dysposed people he calleth in this matter all them that gyueth them almoyse / & he speketh not of one yere nor twayn but of these many yerys now passed / for neyther be the nomber of the clergy nor theyr possessyons nor the freres almes in whych thynges he layeth the cause why the almes of good people ys not half suffycyent to kepe & sustayn the pore and syk beggers fro famyshyng / any great thynge encreased in these .x. or .xii. or .xx. yeres last passed / & therfore yf that he sayd were trew: then by all these .x. yeres at the lest / the almoyse of good people hath not bene half able to susteyn the pore & syk beggers from famyshynge. And surely yf that were so that in .iiii. or .v. yerys in which was plenty of corne / the pore & syk beggars for lak of mennys almes died so fast [B$_1$v] for hunger: thogh many shuld

fall sik neuer so fast again / yet had they in y^e laste .ii. dere yerys
dyed vp of lyklyhod almost euerychone. And whether thys be
trew or not we purpose not to dyspute: but to referr and report
our self to euery mannys eyen and eares / whether any man here
of so many dede / or se so many the fewer.

When he hath layd these sure stonys to begyn the ground &
foundacyon of hys byldyng wyth / that sore and syk beggars be so
sore encreasyd / that the almesse of all the good people of thys
realme is not half inough to sustayn them / and that therfore by
very constraynt they dayly dye for hunger: vppon them he
layeth a nother stone / that the cause of all thys euyll is the great
possessyons of the spyrytualte / and the great almys gyuen to the
frerys. But herein furst he layth that besydys tythes and all such
other profettes as ryse vnto the chyrch by reason of the
spyrytuall law or of mennys deuocyon / that they haue the thyrd
parte of all the temporall landes of the realme. Whych who so
can tell as mich of the reuenews of the realme as he can tell lytell
that made the booke / doth well know that though they haue
mych: yet is the thyrd part of all farre an other thing / & y^t he
sayth in thys poynt vntrew. Than goeth he to the pore frerys.
And there as we told you he shewyth that ye almes geuen them /
of certeynte amounteth yerely vnto .xliii. thousand .CCC. xxxiii.
li. vi. s. viii. d. sterlyng: paraduenture men wold wene the man
were some apostata / and that he neuer coud be so pryuy to the
frerys reconyng / but if he had bene long their lymytour / and
sene some generall vyew of all theyr hole accountys. But surely
syth the man is bad inough besyde / we wold be loth folk shuld
reken hym for apostata / for surely he was neuer frere for aught
that we know / for we neuer wyst that euer in hys lyfe he was half
so well dysposed. And also when ye here the ground of hys
reconyng: ye wyll your self thynk that he nether knoweth mych
of theyr maters / & of all the realme besyde make as though he
knew many thyngys for trew / which many men know for fals.

For furst he putteth for the grounde of hys rekenyng that
there are in the realme / twoo and fyfty thousande parysh

churches / whych ys one playne lye to begynne with. Then he
putteth y^t euery paryshe one wyth a nother / hath ten howseholdes in yt: meanynge besyde suche pore howses as rather aske
almes then gyue / for of such ye wot well ye frerys get no quarterage. & y^t poynte albe yt the grounde be not sure / yet bycause   5
yt may to many men seme lykely / therfore we lette yt passe. But
then he sheweth ferther for a sure trouth a thynge that all men
knowe surely for a great lye: that ys to say that of euery
howsholde in euery paryshe / euery of y^e fyue ordres of freres
hath euery quarter a peny: for we knowe full well & so do many   10
of you to / fyrst y^t the comen people speke but of .iiii. ordres / the
whyte / the blakke / the austayne / and the grey / and whych [B$_2$]
ys the fyft in many partes of the realme fewe folke can tell you.
For yf the questyone were asked abowte / there wolde be peraduenture founden many mo the more pyte it is / that coulde name   15
you the grene freris then the crowched. Ye know ryght well also
that in many a paryshe in england / of fourty howseholdes ye
shall not fynde fowre pay neyther .v. pense a quarter nor .iiii.
nother / and many a parysshe neuer a peny. And as for the .v. d.
quarterly / we dare boldely say that ye shall fynde yt payed in   20
very fewe paryshes thorow the realme / yf ye fynde yt payed in
any. And yet this thynge beynge suche a starke lye as many men
all redy knoweth / & euery man shortely may fynde it / he putteth as a playne well knowen trouth for a specyall poste to bere
vpp his rekenynge. For vppon these growndes now maketh he a   25
clere rekenynge in this maner ensuynge / whyche is good also to
be known for folke that wyll lern to cast a compt. "Ther be .lii. M.
paryshes: and in eche of them .x. howsholdes. So haue ye the
hole some of the howsholdes .v. hondred thowsand and twenty
thowsande. Euen iust. Go nowe to the money then. Euery order   30
of the .v. orders of freres hathe of euery of these howsholdes a
peny a quarter. Summa for euery howse amonge all the .v. orders euery quarter .v. d. & here by may ye lerne that fyue tymes

---

1 with.] *1557*, with *1529*   4–5 quarterage.] *1529*[1] *1557*, quarterag. *1529*[2]
11 *Sidenote 1557:* Foure orders of freres   17 howseholdes] *1529*[1], howseholders
1529[2], housholders *1557*   27 .lii. M.] *1529*[1] *corr. err.*, *1529*[2] *1557*, .lii. *1529*[1]
28 howsholdes.] howsholdes *1529*, housholdes. *1557*   30 iust.] *1557*, iust *1529*
32 quarter.] *1557*, quarter *1529*

one maketh .v. Nowe this is he sheweth you amonge the .v. orders of euery howse for the hole yere .xx. d. and so lerne ye there
that .iiii. tymes fyue maketh .xx. Summa sayth he .v. hondreth
thowsande and .xx. thousande quarters of angelles." Here we
5   woulde not that bycause the realme hath no coyne called the
quarter aungell / ye shulde therfore so farre mystake the man as
to wene that he ment so many quarter sackes of aungels. For in
dede (as we take hym) by the namynge and comptyng of so many
quarters of aungels / he meneth nothynge elles but to teche you a
10 poynt of rekenyng and to make you perceyue and knowe / that
.xx. d. is the fourth parte of .vi. s. viii. d. For after that rate it
semeth that he valueth the aungell noble. Then goeth he forthe
with his rekenyng & sheweth you that "fyue hundred thowsand
and .xx. thowsand quarters of aungels / maketh .ii. hundred
15 thre score thowsand halfe aungellys." And by thys lo ye may
perceyue clerely / that he ment not quarter sackes of aungels: for
then they woulde haue holden ye wote well many moo pecys of
fourty pence / then fourty tymes thys hole some commeth to.
Then he sheweth you ferther that ".CC. lx. thowsand halfe
20 aungellys / amounte iust vnto .C. xxx. thowsand aungels."
Wheryn euery man may lerne that the halfe of .lx. ys .xxx. and
that the half of twayne ys one. Fynally then he casteth yt all to
gyther and bryngeth yt in to poundes. "Summa totalis .xliii.
thowsand poundes .iii. hundred & .xxxiii. li. vi. s. viii. d." But
25 here to contynewe the playnesse of hys rekenynge / he forgote to
tell you y^t .iii. nobles make .xx. s. & that .xx. s. make a pound.
But who [B$_2$v] can now dowte of thys rekenynge whan yt cometh
so rounde / that of so great a somme he leueth not out y^e odde
noble? But now syth all thys rekenynge ys grounded vppon two
30 false groundes / one vppon .lii. thowsande paryshe churches:
the other that euery of the fyue orders hath euery quarter of
euery howshold a peny: thys rekenyng of .xliii. thowsand .CCC.
xxxiii. li. vi. s. viii. d. semeth to come mych lyke to pas as yf he

---

16 aungels:] *1529*^{1}, aungels *1529*^{2}, angelles, *1557*   22–23 all to gyther] *1529*^{2}, all
togyder *1529*^{1}, altogether *1557*   23 poundes.] *1529*^{1} *1557*, poundes *1529*^{2} 24 d.]
1557, d *1529*   26 that] *1529*^{2} *1557*, the *1529*^{1}; pound.] pound / *1529*^{1}, pound *1529*^{2},
pownde. *1557*   28–29 odde noble?] *1529*^{1}, ode noble *1529*^{2}, odde noble. *1557*

wold make a rekening wyth you y^t euery asse hath .viii. eares.
And for to proue yt wyth / bere you furst in hande that euery
asse hath fowre heddes / and then make summa .iiii. heddes.
Then myght he boldely tell you ferther / that euery asse hed
hathe two eares / for that ys comenly trew excepte any be cutte   5
of. Summa then .ii. eares and so summa totalis eyght eares. At
thys accompte of eyght eares of one asse ye make a lyppe and
thynke yt so madde that no man wold make no suche. Surely yt
were a madde compt yn dede / and yet as mad as yt were / yt were
not so madde by halfe as ys hys sadde and ereneste compt that he   10
maketh you now so solempnely of the frerys quarterage. For
thys shuld he ground but vpon one lye / where he groundeth y^e
tother vpon twayne as open lyes as thys & as greate. Now myght
we (and we wold) say that all hys rekenynge were naught / bycause he rekeneth .xx. d. for the quarter of the aungell / and all   15
the remenaunt of hys rekenyng foloweth forth vpon the same
rate. But we wolde be lothe to put hym in the fawlte that he
deserue not. For surely yt myght be that he was not ware of the
new valuacyon: for he ranne awaye byfore the valuacyon
chaunged. But now vpon thys greate some of .xliii. thow-   20
sand .CCC. xxxiii. li. vi. s. viii. d. vpon these good groundes
heped vp to gether he bryngeth in hys ragmannes roll of his rude
retoryque agaynst the pore freres / begynnyng wyth such a gret
exclamacyon that we herde hym hyther / & sodaynly were all
afrayed when we herd him cry out so loude / "Oh greuous &   25
paynfull exaccyons: thus yerely to be payed / frome the whyche
the people of your noble progenytours auncyent Brytons euer
stode fre." And so goeth he forth agaynst the pore freres wyth
Danes / and Saxons / and noble kyng Arthure / and Lucius the
emperoure / the Romaynes / the Grekys / & the great Turke /   30
shewynge that all these had ben vtterly marred & neuer had ben
able to do nothynge yn the warre / yf theyr people had gyuen
theyre almoyse to freres.

---

1 eares.] *1557*, eares *1529*   4 Then] *1529*[1] *1557*, Thene *1529*[2]   12 groundeth]
1529[1] *1557*, grounddth *1529*[2]   15 rekeneth] *1557*, rekeneh *1529*   18 deserue]
1529[2] *1557*, deserued *1529*[1]   20–21 thowsand] *1529*[1], thusand *1529*[2], thousand
1557   22 ragmannes] *1529*[2] *1557*, ragge mannys *1529*[1]

After hys raylyng retoryque ended agaynst the freres / then thys some of .xliii. thowsand .CCC. xxxiii. li. vi. s. viii. d. he addeth vnto all ye tother that he sayd byfore that all the clergye hath besyde / whych he summeth not but sayth that thys and that
5 to gyther amounte vnto more bytwene theym then halfe of the hole substaunce of the realme. And thys he affermeth as boldely as though he could reken the hole reuenews and substaunce of all england / as redely as make the rekenyng [B₃] of hys beggers purse.
10 Then sheweth he that thys better halfe of the hole substaunce ys shyfted amonge fewer then the fowre hundred parte of the people. Whyche he proueth by that he sayth that all "the clergye compared vnto the remannaunte of the men onely / be not the hundreth persone. And yf they be compared vnto the rema-
15 naunte of men / women / and chyldren / so are they not he saeth the fowre hundreth person." But nowe some folke that haue not very longe a go vppon greate occasyons taken the rekenynge of prestes and relygyous places yn euery diocise / & on the other syde the rekenynge and the nomber of the temporall men yn
20 euery countye: know well y^t thys mannes madde rekenynge goeth very farr wyde / and semeth that he hath herd these wyse rekenyngis at some congregacyon of beggers. And yet as thoughe bycause he hath sayd yt he had therfore proued yt / he runneth forth in his raylyng retoryque agaynst the hole clergye /
25 and that yn suche a sorte and fassyon that very harde yt were to dyscerne whyther yt be more false or more folyshe. For fyrste all the fawtes that any lewde preest or frere doth / all that layeth he to the hole clergye / as well and as wysely as though he wold lay the fawtes of some lewde lay people to ye defaut and blame of all
30 the hole temporaltye. But thys way lyketh hym so well that thus layeng to the hole clergye ye fawtes of suche as be simple & fawty theryn / and yet not onely layeng to theyr charge ye breche of chastyte & abuse in fleshely lyuyng of suche as be nought / but also madly lyke a fonde felow layeng mych more to theyr charge

---

1 retoryque] *1529²*, retorque *1529¹*, rethorique *1557*   4 besyde /] *1529¹*, besyde *1529²*, beside *1557*   6 hole] *1529*, old *1557*; boldely] *1529¹*, boldyly *1529²*, boldelye *1557*   8 hys] *1529¹* *1529² catchword,* thys *1529²*, this *1557*   15 saeth] *1529²*, sayth *1529¹*, sayeth *1557*

& myche more ernestly reprouynge ye good & honest lyuynge of those y^t be good / whome he rebukethe and abhorreth by-cause they kepe theyr vowes & perseuer yn chastyte (for he sayeth that they be the marrars and dysstroyers of the realme / bryngeng the land yn to wyldernesse for lacke of generacyon by theyr abstaynynge from weddyng) then aggreuyth he hys great crymes wyth heynouse wordys / gay repetycyons & greuous ex-clamacyons / callyng them blood suppers & dronken in ye blood of holy marters & sayntes / whyche he meanyth for the condem-nynge of holy heretykes. Gredy golophers he calleth them and ynsacyable whyrlpoolys / because the temporalte hath gyuen theym possessyons / & gyue to the frercs theyr almoyse. And all vertuouse good preestys & relygyous folke he calleth ydle holy theues / because they spend theyr tyme yn prechynge and prayour. And than sayth he / "these be they that make so many syk & sore beggers. These be they that make these horys & baudys. These be they that make these theuys. These be they that make so many ydle parsons: These be they that corrupte ye generacyons. And these be they that wyth the abstaynyng from weddyng hynder so the generacyon of the people / y^t the realme shall at lenght fall yn wyldernes but yf they wed ye soner." And now vpon these hygh[B₃v]nous crymes layed vnto the hole cler-gye / & layd as euery wyse man seeth some very falsely and some very folyshly: after hys goodly repetycyons he falleth to hys great and greuous exclamacyons / cryeng out vppon the great brode botomlesse occean see of yuels / and vppon the greuouse shyp-wrak of the comen welth / the translatynge of the kyngys kyngdome / and the ruyne of the kynges crown. And therwyth rollynge in hys retoryke from fygure to fygure / he falleth to a vehement inuocacyon of the kynge / & gyueth hym warnyng of hys greate losse / askynge hym feruently: where ys your sword / power / crown / and dygnyte bycome? as though the kynges grace had clene loste hys realme / specyally for lacke of people to reygne vppon / bycause that prestes haue no wyuys. And surely

---

the man cannot fayle of suche eloquence: for he hath gathered
these goodly flowres out of Luthers gardyne almost worde for
worde wythout any more laboure but onely the translatynge
owte of the latyn into the englyshe tonge.

5   But to enflame the kyngys hyghnes against the church / he
sayth that the clergye laboureth nothyng elles / but to make the
kynges subgectes fall in to dysobedyence and rebellyon agaynst
hys grace.

Thys tale ys a very lykely thynge / as though the clergye knew
10 not that there ys nothyng erthly y^t so moche kepeth them sclf in
quyet rest and suertye / as doth the dew obedyence of the people
to the vertuouse mynde of the prynce. Whose hygh goodnesse
must nedes haue myche more dyffycultye to defende the clargye
and kepe the churche in peace / yf ye people fell to dysobedyence
15 & rebellyon agaynste theyr prynce. And therfore euery chyld
may se that the clergye woulde neuer be so madde as to be glad to
brynge the people to dysobedyence & rebellyon agaynst the
prynce / by whose goodnes they be preserued in peace / and
were in suche rebellyon of the people lykely to be the fyrst that
20 shold fall in parell. But neyther ys there desyred by the clergye
nor neuer shall by goddes grace happen / any such rebellyon as
ye beggars proctoure & hys felowes what so euer they say long
full sore to se.

But thys man agaynst ye clergye fetcheth forth old farne yeres
25 & ronneth vp to kyng Iohans days / spendyng mych labour about
ye prayse & commendacyon of y^t good gracyous kyng & cryeng
out vppon ye pope y^t then was and the clergye of England / and
all the lordys and all ye comens of the realme / because kynge
Iohan as he sayth made ye realm trybutary to the pope / wherin
30 he meaneth peraduenture the peter pense. But surely therin ys
all hys hote accusacyon a very colde tale when ye trouth ys
knowen. For so ys yt in dede y^t albe yt there be wrytars y^t say y^e
peter pense were grauntyd by kyng Iohan for the release of the
interdyccyon: yet were they payed in dede ere euer kyng
35 Iohans grete graundfather was borne / & therof ys there profe
ynough. Now yf he say as in dede some wryters say / that kynge

---

30 *Sidenote 1557:* Peter pence; pense.] pense *1529*, pence. *1557*

Iohan made Englande & [B₄] Irland trybutary to the pope &
the see apostolyque by the graunt of a thowsand markys: we
dare surely say agayn that yt ys vntrew / & that all Rome
neyther can shew suche a graunt nor neuer could / and if they
could yt were right nought worth. For neuer coulde eny kyng   5
of England geue away the realm to yᵉ pope / or make the lande
tributary though he wolde / nor no such money ys there payed
nor neuer was. And as for the peter pense if he meane them /
neyther was yᵉ realme trybutary by them / nor king Iohan neuer graunted them. For they were payed before the conquest to   10
the apostolyk see toward the mayntenaunce therof but onely by
way of gratytude & almes. Now as for the archbysshop Stephen /
whom he sayth beyng a traytour to the kynge / yᵉ pope made
archebyshop of Canturbury agaynst yᵉ kyngys wyll / therin be
there as we suppose .ii. lyes at onys. For neyther was yᵗ Stephen   15
euer traytour agaynst the kyng as farre as euer we haue herd /
nor yᵉ pope none other wyse made hym archebyshop then he
made all other at that tyme: but yᵉ same Stephen was well &
canonycally chosen archebyshop of Canturbury by yᵉ couent of
yᵉ monkis at Christes church in Canturbury to whom as yᵉ kyng   20
well knew & denyed yt not / yᵉ eleccyon of yᵉ archebysshop at yᵗ
time belonged. Nor yᵉ kyng resystyd not hys eleccyon bycause
of any treason yᵗ was layd agaynst hym: but was discontentyd
therwith / & after yᵗ his eleccyon was passyd & confirmed by yᵉ
pope: he wold not of long season suffer hym to enioy yᵉ by-   25
shoprich / because hym selfe had recommendyd another vnto
yᵉ monkys / whom they reiectyd & preferryd Stephen. And that
thys ys as we tell you / & not as the beggars proctour wryteth for
a false foundacyon of hys raylyng: ye shall mow parceyue not
onely by dyuers cronycles / but also by dyuers monumentis yet   30
remaynynge as well of the eleccyon and confyrmacyon of the
sayd archebyshop / as of the long sute and proces that after
folowed theruppon.

Nowe sheweth he hym selfe very wrothe wyth the spyrytuall

2–5 *Sidenote 1557:* A king cannot make hys land tributary   8 was.] *1529*¹ *1557*, was
*1529*²   10–12 *Sidenote 1557:* Peter pence wer payd before the conquest   29 mow]
1529, nowe *1557*

iurysdyccyon / whyche he wolde in any wyse were clene taken
awaye / saynge that yt muste nedys dystroy the iurysdyccyon
temporall: where as the good prynces passed haue graunted /
and yᵉ nobles in theyre tymes / and the people to / haue by
5   playne parleamentes confermed them / and yet hytherto blessed
be god they agre better to gyther / then to fall at varyaunce for
the wylde wordes of suche a malycyouse make bate: whyche for
to brynge the spyrytualtye in to hatered / sayth that they call
theyr iurysdyccyon a kyngdome. In whyche word he may say his
10 pleasure / but of trewth he seldom seeth eny spyrytuall man at
thys daye that so calleth eny spyrytuall iurysdyccyon yᵗ he vseth.
    Nowe where thys man vseth as a profe therof / that yᵉ
spyrytualte nameth theym selfe alwaye byfore the temporaltye:
thys maner of namyng cometh not of them / but of the good
15 mynde and deuocyon [B₄v] of the temporaltye: so farre forthe
that at the parlyament when that eny actes be conceyued / the
wordes be comenly so cowched / that the byll sayth it ys enacted
fyrste by our souerayne lorde yᵉ kyng and by yᵉ lordes spyrytuall
& temporall & the comens in that present parlyament as-
20 sembled. And these byllys be often drawen put forth & passed
fyrste in the comen howse / where there ys not one spyrytuall
man present.
    But suche trewth as the man vseth in thys poynte / suche vseth
he where he calleth the pore freres almoyse an axaccyon: sur-
25 mysynge that yt ys exacted by force and the people compelled to
pay yt / where euery man well wotteth that they haue pore men
no way to compelle no man to gyue them aught not though they
shulde dy for defawt. But thys good honest true man sayth that
who so wyll not pay the freres theyre quarterage they wyll make
30 hym be taken as an heretyque. We be well contente that ye take
thys for no lye / as manye as euer haue knowen yt trew. But who
herd euer yet that eny man taken for an heretyque / dyd so
myche as ones saye that he thought yt conuayd by the malyce of

---

4 people to /] *1529*², people / to *1529*¹, people too, *1557*   6 god] *1529*¹ *corr. err.*, *1529*²,
good *1529*¹, God *1557*   19 that] *1529*, thys *1557*   24 axaccyon] *1529*, exaccion
1557   26 wotteth] *1529*² *1557*, wytteth *1529*¹   26–27 pore men no way] *1529*, no
power *1557*   30 well] *1529*¹ *1557*, wyll *1529*²

any frere for refusyng to paye ye freres quarterage. Thys lye lo ys
a lytle to lowde / for eny man that were not waxen shameles.
    Lyke treuth ys there in thys that he sayeth / yf any man trouble
a preeste for any temporall suyte: the clergye forthwyth wyll
make hym an heretyque and burne hym / but yf he be content to   5
bere a fagotte for theyre pleasure. The falsehed of thys can not
be vnknowen. For men know well in many a shyre how often that
many folk endyght prestes of rape at the sessyons. And as there
ys somtyme a rape committed in dede / so ys there euer a rape
surmysed were the women neuer so wyllynge / and oftentyme   10
where there was nothynge done at all. And yet of eny suche that
so procured preestes to be indyghted: howe many haue men
herd taken and accused for heretyques? Ye se not very many
sessyons passe / but in one shyre or other thys pageant ys playd:
where as thorow the realme such as be put to penaunce for   15
heresy / be not so many in many yeres as there be prestys en-
dyghtyd in few yerys. And yet of all such so taken for heresye / he
shall not fynde foure this four score yere / peraduenture not
thys four hundreth yere / that euer pretended them selfe so
troubled for endyghtyng of a preste. So that hys lye ys herein to   20
large to get eny cloke to couer yt.
    Nowe where he saith that "the captayns of doctour Aleyns
kyngdome / haue hepyd hym vp benefyce vppon benefyce / &
haue rewardyd hym .x. tymes as mych as the .v. C. poundis
whych he payd for a fyne by the premunire / and that thus hath   25
the spyrytualtye rewarded hym because he fought so manfully
agaynst the kyngys crowne & hys dygnyte": all that know the
matter do well parceyue that the man doth in thys mater as he
doth in other / eyther lyeth for hys pleasure / or els [C₁] lyttell
wotteth how that the matter stode. For it ys well knowen that   30
doctour Aleyn was in the premunire pursued only by spyrytuall
men and had moch lesse fauour & myche more rygour shewed
hym therin by the greatest of the clergy / then by any temporall men.

---

1 refusyng] *1529*, refususing *1557*   3 treuth] *1529*² *1557*, a treuth *1529*¹   8 ses-
syons] *1529*¹ *1557*, sessynos *1529*²   12 heretyques?] *1529*² *1557*, heretyques. *1529*¹
22 doctour] *1529*¹, doctours *1529*², Doctour *1557*   24 poundis] *1529*, ponndes *1557*
28 thys] *1529*² *corr. err.*, *1529*¹, hys *1529*² *1557*

He sayth also to the kynges hyghnes / "your grace may se what
a worke there ys in London / how the byshop rageth for endyghtyng of certayne curates of extorcyon and incontynencye
the laste yere in the warmoll quest." Wolde not vppon these
5   wordes euery straunger wene that there had bene in London
many curates endyghted of extorcyon and rape / and that the
byshop wold labour sore to defend theyr fautes and that there
wer aboute y^t matter a greate commocyon in all the cyte? How
shameles ys he that can tell thys tale in wrytynge to ye kynges
10 hyghnes for a trouth / wherof neyther byshop / nor curate / nor
mayre / nor alderman / nor eny man ellys / euer hard word
spoken? Hyt were harde to say whether we shulde take yt for
wylynes or lacke of wytt / y^t he sayth all thys worke was in the cyte
the last yere: & then hys boke neyther was put vp to the kynge /
15 nor bereth eny date. So y^t a man wold wene he were a fole that so
wryteth of the last yere / y^t the reder cannot wyt whych yere yt
was. But yet wene we he doth yt for a wylynes. For syth he knoweth hys tale false: yt ys wysdome to leue the tyme vnknowen / that
hys lye may be vncontrolled. For he wold that men shulde wene
20 alwaye that yt was in one yere or other.

But fynally for a specyall poynt he bryngeth in Rychard
Hunne and sayth y^t yf he had not commencyd an accyon of
premunire agaynst a preste / he had bene yet alyue and none
heretyke at all. Now ys yt of trewthe well knowen / that he was
25 detectyd of heresye before the premunyre sued or thought vppon. And he began that suyte to helpe to stop the tother wythall /
as in dede yt dyd for the whyle. For all be yt that he that was sued
in the premunire was nothynge bylongynge to the byshop of
London byfore whome Rycharde Hunne was detectyd of
30 herysy: yet lest suche as wolde be glad synysterly to mysseconster
euery thynge towarde the blame of the clergye / myght haue
occasyon to say that the matter were hotely handeled agaynst
hym to force hym to forbere his suyt of the premunire / the
bysshop therefore dyd the more forbere / tyll yt appered clerely
35 to the temporall iudges and all that were eny thyng lerned in the

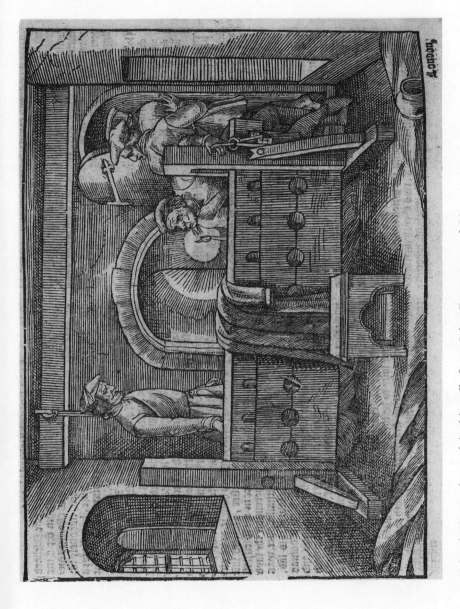

Richard Hunne hanged in his cell, from John Foxe, *Acts and Monuments*, London, 1563, sig. Nn₄v (reduced)

temporall law / that hys suyte of the premunire was nothynge
worthe in the kynges lawe / for as moche as by playne statute the
matter was owt of questyon that the ple to be holden vpon mortuaryes / belonge vnto the spyrytuall courte. After whyche
thynge well aperynge / the matter wente forth afore the byshop /   5
& he there well proued nought / and hys bokes after brought
forth / suche and so noted wyth hys own hande in the margentes /
as euery wyse man well saw what he was / [C₁v] and was full sory
to se that he was suche as they theyre sawe hym preued.

   Now goeth he ferther and asketh the kynge / "dyd not doctor   10
Horsay and hys complyces moost heynously as all the worlde
knoweth / murder in pryson that honest marchaunt Rychard
Hunne / for that he suede your wrytt of premunire agaynst a
prest that wrongfully held hym in ple in a spyrytuall courte / for
a mater wherof the knowlege bylonged vnto your hyghe   15
courtes? And what punyshment hathe he for yt? After that he
had payed as yt ys sayd .vi. hundreth poundes for hym and hys
complyces / as sone as he had obtayned your moost gracyouse
pardon: he was immedyatly promoted by yᵉ captaynes of hys
kyngdome wyth benefyce vpon benefyce to the value of .iiii.   20
tymes as myche. Who ys he of theyr kyngdome that wyll not
rather take corage to commyt lyke offense / seyng the promocyons that fell to suche men for theyr so offendyng / so weke &
blunt ys your swerd to stryke at one of the offenders of thys
croked and paruerse generacyon." We haue here sumwhat com-   25
bred you wyth a pece of hys awn wordes / bycause ye shuld haue
a shew of hys vehement eloquence: wyth whych the bolde beggers proctour so arrogantly presumethe in hys byll to aske the
kynge a questyon / and to bynde hys hyghnes to answere as hys
maystershyp appoyntted hym. For yf hys grace say nay: then he   30
telleth hym byfore / that all the worlde woteth yes. But surely yf
he call all the world all that euer god made: then ys there .iii.
partes that knoweth the contrary. For we dare be bolde to war-
aunt you / that in heuen / hell / and here among vs in purgatory /

---

8 sory] *1529*¹, sore *1529*², sorie *1557*   16 punyshment] *1529*¹, punysment *1529*²,
punishement *1557*   21 kyngdome] *1529*² *1557*, kyndome *1529*¹   28 proctour]
*1529*¹ *1557*, proctours *1529*²

of all that thys man so boldely affermeth / the contrary ys well
and clerely knowen. And yf he call yᵉ world but onely men
among you ther lyuyng vppon mydle yerth: yet so shall he peraduenture fynde in some parte of the worlde yf he seke yt well /
5   mo than .iiii. or .v. good honest men / that neuer hard speke of
the mater. And of suche as haue hard of the mater & knowen yt
well: he shall fynde inow and specyally we thynk the kynges
grace hym self (whose hyghnes he ys so homly to aske the questyon and appoynt hym hys answer hym selfe) that of all fyue
10 thynges whych he hathe herc in so fewe lynes affyrmed / there ys
not one trew but lyes euery one. For fyrst to begyn where he
leueth / when he sayth that the clergy haue syns the deth of
Rychard Hunne / promoted doctor Horsay wyth benefyce vpon
benefyce .iiii. tymes as mych as .vi. C. poundes / the playn
15 vntreuth of thys poynt may euery man sone know yᵗ wyll sone
enquyre. For he lyueth yet at exester / and theyr lyueth vpon
suche as he had before / wythout that new hepe of benefyce
gyuen hym by yᵉ captaynes of hys kyngdom for kyllyng of
Rychard Hunne / or thank ether saue onely of god for hys long
20 pacyence in hys vndeserued trouble. But to thend yᵗ ye may se
how lyttell thys man forceth how lowd [C₂] he lye: consyder yᵗ he
sayth that the clergye gaue vnto doctor Horsay after he cam out
of pryson benefyce vppon benefyce to the valew of .iiii. tymes as
much as .vi. C. poundes. Now yf thys be trew / then hath doc-
25 toure Horsay had in benefyces besydes all such as he had before
hys troble / the valew of .ii. thousand .iiii. C. pounde. We truste
that the man hys substaunce and hys lyuelod ys so well known /
that we nede not to tell that the beggers proctor in thys poynt
hath made one lowd lye. Another ys that he sayth that Hunne
30 was kept in ple in the spyrytuall law for a matter determynable in
the kynges court: for the mater was for a mortuary / whych by
playn statute ys declared to pertayne to the spyrytuall law. The
thyrd ys that Hunne was honest / except heresy be honeste. The
fourth ys that doctour Horsey and hys complyces murdred hym

---

7 specyally] *1529*, speciallly *1557*   8 homly] *1529²*, homely *1529¹* *1557*
14 poundes /] poundes *1529*, poundes: *1557*; the] *1529² corr. err.*, *1529¹* *1557*, he
1529²   16 exester] *1529*, Excester *1557*

in pryson: for therof ys ye contrary well knowen / and that the
man hanged hym selfe for dyspayre / dyspyte / and for lak of
grace. We myght and we wold lay for the fyft / the payment
whych he speketh of the .vi. C. poundes / wyth whyche money he
wolde men shuld wene that he bought hys pardon. Wherin he ⁵
layeth a good great some / to thend that folk well wyttyng that
doctour Horsay was not lyke to haue so mych money of hys awn /
shuld wene therwyth that ye clergye layed out the money among
them / & then gaue hym benefyces wherof he myght pay them
ageyn. But thys layeth he from hym self / and shewyth not to ₁₀
whom / for he sayth yt ys sayd so. And yet were yt no wrong that
yt were accounted hys owne / tyll he put yt better from hym / and
proue of whome he herde yt. How be yt syth there ys other store
ynough: we shall leue thys lye in questyon betwene hym and we
wote nere whom ellys / and we shall for the fyfte laye you that lye ₁₅
y^t he layeth forth hym selfe / that ys to wytte / where he sayeth
that the chaunceller purchased the kynges mooste gracyouse
pardon for the murderyng of Hunne. For thys ys the trouthe
that he neuer sued eny pardon therfore. But after that the matter had ben by longe tyme & great dylygence so ferre forth ₂₀
examyned / that the kynges hyghnes at length (as tyme alwaye
tryeth owte the trouth) well perceyuyd hys innocency & theyrs
also that were accused and endyghted with hym: hys noble grace
when they were arraygned vppon that endyghtment and therto
pleded that they were not gyltye / commaunded hys attornay ₂₅
generall to confesse theyr ple to be true / whyche is the thyng
that hys hyghnes as a moost vertuouse prynce vseth for to do /
when the mater ys not onely iuste / but also knowen for iust
vppon the parte of the partye defendaunte. Bycause that lyke as
where the mater appereth dowtefull he doth as reason ys / suffer ₃₀
yt to go forth and letteth ye trouth be tryed / so where he seeth
and perceyueth the ryght to be on ye other syde / hys hyghnes
wyll in no wyse haue the wrong sette forth or mayntayned in hys

8 layed] 1529¹ corr. err., 1529², lyed 1529¹, laid 1557   10 layeth] 1529¹ 1557, layeh
1529²   18 trouthe] 1529¹ 1557, trouhe 1529²   21 length] 1529² 1557, lenght
1529¹   21–22 Sidenote 1557: Time trieth out the trouth   24 endyghtment] 1529¹,
endyghment 1529², endightment 1557   30 ys /] 1529², ys 1529¹ 1557   31 letteth]
1529¹ 1557, letteh 1529²

name. Now when yt was then thus in dede / that [C₂v] neyther
the chaunceller nor eny man elles euer suede eny charter of
pardon for yᵉ mater: thys ys then yᵉ fyft lye that thys man hath
made in so few lynes. Whych thynges who so well consyder / can
5 not but meruayle of the sore pyththy poynt wherewyth he knytteth vppe all hys heuy matter / saynge to the kyng: "who ys there
of theyr kyngdome yᵗ wyll not take corage to commyt lyke offence seynge the promocyons that fall to suche menne for theyre
offendyng: so weke and so blunte ys your sworde to stryke at one
10 of the offenders of thys croked and peruerse gcneracyon." Loo
how thys greate zelator of the commen welthe cryeth owte vppon
the kynge / that hys swerd ys not stronge & sharpe to stryke of
innocentys heddis. He hath of lykelyhed ransaked vppe all dame
retoryques rolles to fynd owte thys goodly fygure / to call vppon
15 the kynge and aske hys hyghnes where ys youre swerde / and tell
hym hys swerde ys to dull: as though he wolde byd hym bere yt to
the cutlers to grynde / that he myghte stryke of doctor Horsayes
hed whome hys grace had founde fawtelesse / and testyfyed hym
hym selfe for an innocente. If thys man were here matched wyth
20 some suche as he ys hym selfe / that hathe the eloquence that he
hath / that coulde fynde out suche comely fygures of retoryque
as he fyndeth / sette forthe and furnyshed wyth suche vehement
wordes as he thundreth owte lyke thunder blastys / that hathe no
lesse maters in hys mouth than the greate brode botomlesse
25 occean see full of euyls / the wekenes and dulnes of the kynges
swerde / the translacyon of yᵉ kyngys kyngdome / the ruyne of
the kynges crowne / wyth greate exclamacyons / Oh greuouse
and paynfull exaccyons / oh case most horryble / oh greuouse
shyp wracke of the comen welth: what myght one that had suche
30 lyke eloquence saye here to hym? surely so myche and in suche
wyse as we sely poore pewlyng sowles neyther can deuyse nor
vtter. But verely two or thre thynges we se and maye well saye
that neyther be these greate maters mete for the mouthe of the

---

5 pyththy] *1529*, pythye *1557*   12 swerd] *1529*² *1557*, sworde *1529*¹
15–16 swerde . . . swerde] *1529*² *1557*, sworde . . . sworde *1529*¹   26 swerde] *1529*²
1557, sworde *1529*¹   28 case] *1529*¹, cause *1529*² *1557*   30 hym?] *1529*² *1557*,
hym / *1529*¹

beggers proctour / nor suche prechyng of reformacyon and
amendement of the world mete maters for hym to medle wyth /
whych wyth open heresyes and playne pestylent errors / besely
goeth aboute to poyson and infecte the worlde: nor very conuenyent for hym to take vppon hym to gyue counsayle to a kynge /   5
when he sheweth hym self to haue so moche presumpcyon and
so lytell wytt / as to aske the kyng a questyon and appoynte hym
hys answer: and therin to tell hym that all yᵉ worlde knoweth that
thynge to be trew / whych the kynge hathe hym selfe all redy by
hys atturney and hys iudges in open iugement / and in hys hygh   10
courte of recorde testefyed & confessed for false. If that man
were not for malyce as mad not as marche hare / but as a madde
dogge that runneth forth and snatcheth he seeth not at whome:
the felowe could neuer elles wyth suche open foly so sodenly
ouer se hym [C₃] selfe. But yt were wrong wyth the worlde yf   15
malyce had as myche wytte / cyrcumspeccyon and prouydence in
the pursute of an vngracyouse purpose / as yt hath hast / yuell
wyll and wylynesse in the fyrst interprysynge. For as an ape hath
some symylytude of a man / and as a fox hath a certayne wylynesse somewhat resemblyng an vnperfayte wytte: so fareth   20
thys felowe / that begynneth as one wolde wene at good zeale and
cheryte borne towarde the poore beggers. But forthewyth he
sheweth hym selfe that he nothyng ellys entendeth: but openly
to dystroy the clergye fyrst / & after that couertly as many as
haue aught aboue the state of beggers. And where as he wold in   25
yᵉ begynnynge by yᵉ towchyng of great maters / fayne seme very
wyse: wythin a whyle in the progresse he proueth hymself a very
stark fole. And where he wolde seme to shewe many notable
thynges whych no man had marked but he / he prouydeth wysely that no man may beleue hym / he maketh so many lyes / and all   30
that euer he dothe ferther / he buyldeth vppon the same.

He layeth that the lyuynge whych the clergye hathe ys the
onely cause that there be so many beggers that be syk and sore.
Very well and wysely / as though the clergye by theyre substaunce made men blynde and lame. The clergye also ys the   35

4 infecte] *1529*² *1557*, effecte *1529*¹   12 marche] *1529*, a march *1557*   30 hym /]
hym *1529*, him *1557*

cause he sayth why they dye for hunger / as thoughe euery lay man gaue to beggers all that euer he coulde / and the clergye gyue them neuer a grote: & as though there wolde not mo beggers walke a brode yf the clergye lefte of suche lay men as they
5 fynde.

But he proueth you that the clergy must nedys be the cause why there be so many poore men and beggers. For he sayth that before the clergy came in theyr were but few pore people: and yet they beggyd not neyther / but men he sayth gaue them
10 ynough vnasked. But now where sat he when he saw the people gyue pore folke so fast theyr allmes vnasked y^t no man neded to beg before the clergy began. Thys man of lyklyhod ys of grete age / & or ere ye clergy began was wonte to syt at saynt Sauours wyth a sore leg: but he beggyd not men gaue hym so mych
15 vnasked. For where as he alledgyth the byble for hym in the actes of the appostles / verely we meruayll mych what the man meneth. For there he may se that the apostels and the deacons whych were then the clergy / had all to gyther in there own handys / & dystrybuted to euery man as them self thought good. And ther-
20 fore we wonder what he meaneth to speke of that boke. For we thynke that he meneth not to hurt the clergy so now / as to put all in to theyr handes. And surely but yf he meane so / els ys thys place nothing for hys purpose.

Now herein he sheweth also an hygh poynt of hys wyt / where
25 he sayth that the greate lyuyng that the clergy hath / whyche he layeth and lyeth to be more then half of the hole reuenews and substaunce of the [C$_3$v] realme: ys shyfted among fewer then the foure hundreth part of the people. As though y^t of the clergyes parte there had no lay people theyr lyuyng / no seruaunt eny
30 wagys / none artyfycer eny money for workyng / no carpenter no masyn eny money for byldyng: but all the money that euer cummeth in theyr handes / they put yt by & by in theyre own belyes / and no lay man hath eny relyef therof. And therfor thys poynt was wysely wrytten ye se as well as we. Now for the trouthe ther-
35 of / yf yt were trew that he sayth / that the clergy compared to the

1 they] *1529*^{2} *1557*, the *1529*^{1} 17 *Sidenote 1557:* Ca. 4. and .6.   19 dystrybuted]
1529^1 *corr. err.*, *1529*^{2} *1557*, dystrytuted *1529*^{1}

resydew of the men onely / be not one to an .C: then shall ye not
nede to fere yᵉ greate Turke and he cam to morow / except ye
suffer among you to grow in great nomber these Lutherans that
fauoure hym. For we dare make you the warantyse that yf hys lye
be true / there be mo men a greate meany in London and wythin   5
.iiii. shyres next adioynyng / than the great Turk bryngeth in to
Hungary. But in thys ye must hold him excused / for he medleth
not mych wyth augrym to se to what summe the number of men
aryseth that ys multyplyed by an .C. All hys practyse in
multyplycacyon medleth wyth nothyng but lyes: & therein   10
mache hym wyth whom ye wyll / he wyll gyue you a .C. for one.
Wherof yf ye lack let thys be the sample yᵗ he sayth / yf thabbot of
westmynster shuld syng euery day as many masses for hys
founders as he ys bounden to do by hys foundacyon / a .M.
monkes were to few. Ye dout not we think but he can tell you who   15
hath bound them to how many / & so can make ye yᵉ playn
rekeninge yᵗ thabbot ys bound in the yere to no fewer masses
than .iii. C. lxv. M. He knoweth what ys euery mannes dutye saue
hys owne. He ys mete to be a beggers proctour / that can soo proll
aboute and can tell all thynge.   20

But now were all his payntyd proces ye wot well nothing worth /
but yf he deuysed agaynste all these myscheues some good and
holsom help. It ys therfore a world to se what polytyke deuyces
he fyndeth agaynst yᵉ great brode botomlesse occean see of
euyls: what remedyes to repayre the ruyne of the kyngys crown: 25
to restore and vphold hys honour and dygnyte: to make hys
swerd sharp and strong: & fynally to saue all the shypwrak of the
comen welth. Ye wolde peraduenture wene yᵗ the man wolde
now deuyse som good holsome lawes for helpe of all these maters. Nay he wyll none therof. For he sayth he douteth that the   30
kyng ys not able to make any law agaynst them. For he sayth that
the clergy ys stronger in the parliament than the kyng hym self.
For in the hygher house / he rekenyth that the spyrytualte ys
more in nomber and stronger than the temporalte. And in the

1 .C:] *1529*[1], .C. *1529*[2] *1557*   14 foundacyon /] foundacion / *1529*[1], foundacyon
1529[2] *1557*; a .M.] *1529*[1], .M. *1529*[2] *1557*   15 few.] *1529*[1], few / *1529*[2], few,
1557   20 can tell] *1529*[2] *1557*, tell *1529*[1]

comen house he sayth that all the lerned men of the realme
except the kynges lerned councell / be feed wyth the church to
speke agaynst the kynges crown and dygnyte in the parlyament
for theym: and therfore he thynketh the kynge vnable to make
5 eny law agaynst the fawtys of the clergye. [C₄]

Thys beggars proctour wold fayn shew hym self a man of great
experyence / and one that had great knowlege of the maner &
order vsed in the kyngys parlyamentys. But than he speketh so
sauourly therof: that yt well apperyth of hys wyse wordes he
10 neyther canneth eny skyll therof / nor neucr cam in the house.
For as for yᵉ hygher house furst yᵉ kynges own ryall parson alone
more than counterpaysyth all yᵉ lordys spyrytuall present wyth
hym and the temporyll to. And ouer thys the spyrytual lordys
can neuer in nomber excede the lordys temporall / but must
15 nedys be farre vnderneth them yf yt please the kyng. For hys
hyghnes may call thyder by hys wryt many mo temporall lordys
at hys own pleasure. And beyng as they be / there was neuer yet
sene that the spyrytuall lordes bendyd them selfe there as a
partye agaynst the temporall lordes. But yt hath bene sene that
20 the thynge whych the spyrytuall lordes haue moued and thought
resonable / the temporall lordes haue denyed & refused: as
appereth vppon the mocyon made for legytymacyon of the
chyldren borne before the maryage of theyr parentys. Wherin
albe yt yᵗ the reformacyon whych the lordes spyrytuall moued /
25 was a thyng that nothyng partayned to ther awn commodyte /
and albe yt that they layed also for theyr parte the constytucyon
and ordynaunce of the church and the lawes of other crysten
cuntrees: yet could they not obtayne agaynst the lordes temporall that nothynge alleged to the contrary but theyre owne
30 wylles. And therfor in the hygher house the spyrytuall parte
neuer apperyd yet so strong / that they myght ouer matche the
temporall lordes. And then how mych ar they to feble for them
and the kyng to / whose hyghnes alone ys ouer strong for them
both / & may by hys wryt call to hys parlyament mo temporall
lordes whan he wyll. Now where he sayth yᵗ in the comen house

10 therof] *1529¹*, herof *1529²*, hereof *1557*   21 the temporall] *1529*, the the temporall *1557*   23–25 *Sidenote 1557: Ca. tanta est vis matrimonii qui fil. sunt legi.*

all the lerned men of the realme ar feed to speke for the clergy
except the kynges lerned counsell: there be .ii. folyes at ones. For
neyther be all the lernyd men of the realme knyghtes or burgeyses in the comen house / and the kyngys lerned councell ys
not there at all. And therfore yt semeth that he hath hard sum-   5
what of sum men that had sene as lytell as hym self. And surely yf
he had bene in the comen house as some of vs haue bene: he
shuld haue sene the spyrytualte nat gladly spoken for. And we
lytell dout but that ye remember actes and statutes passyd at
sondry parlyamentes / suche and in such wyse & some of them so   10
late / as your self may se that eyther yᵉ clergy ys not the strenger
parte in the kynges parlyement / or elles haue no mynd to stryue.
And for the ferther profe that the kynges hyghnes ys not so weke
& vnable in hys owne parlyament as thys beggers proctour so
presumptuously telleth hym / hys grace well knowyth and all hys   15
people to / yᵗ in theyr own conuocacyons hys grace neuer deuysed nor desyred any thyng in hys lyfe / yᵗ euer was denyed
hym. And therfore thys gay inuencyon of thys beggers proctour / yᵗ he fayneth the kynges [C₄v] hyghnes to be in hys hygh
courte of parlyament more weke and feble then the clergye / ys a   20
very feble deuyce.

But now syth he wyll haue no law deuysed for the remedy of
his greate complayntes / what helpe hath he deuysed els? The
helpe of all thys gere ys he sayth none other thing / but to lett
hym & suche ryall raylers / rayle & gest vppon the church / and   25
tell the people yᵉ prestes fawtes: and for the lewdnes of parte /
brynge yᵉ hole clergy in contempt and hatered amonge all the
temporall folke. Whych thyng he sayth yᵉ kyng must nedes suffer / yf he wyll eschew the ruyne of hys crowne & dygnyte. And
thys thyng he sayth shalbe more spedefull & effectuall in the   30
matter / than all the lawes that euer can be made be they neuer so
strong. Lo good lordys & masters then shall ye nede no mo
parlyamentys. For here ys god be thankyd an easye way wysely
founden to remedye wythe raylynge the greate brode botom-

---

11 strenger] *1529*, stronger *1557*   21 very feble] *1529*¹, feble *1529*² *1557*   23 els?]
*1529*¹ *1557*, els. *1529*²   29 dygnyte.] *1529*¹ *1557*, dygnyte / *1529*²   31 so] *1529*¹
1557, to *1529*²

lesse occean se of yuels / and to saue the comen weale frome
shypwracke / & the kynges crowne from ruyne.

But now to the poore beggers. What remedy fyndeth theyr
proctour for them? to make hospytals? Nay ware of y^t / therof he
5 wyll none in no wyse. For therof he sayth the mo ye worse /
because they be profytable to prestes. What remedy than? Gyue
them any money? Nay nay not a grote. What other thyng then?
Nothyng in ye world wyll serue but this: that yf ye kynges grace
wyll byld a sure hospytall y^t neuer shall fayle to releue all the
10 sycke beggers for euer / let hym gyue nothynge to them / but
loke what the clergye hath & take all that from them. Is nott here
a goodly myschef for a remedy? Is not thys a ryall fest to leue
these beggers meteles / and then send mo to dyner to theym? Oh
the wyse. Here want we voyce and eloquence to set out an ex-
15 clamacyon in the prayse and commendacyon of thys specyall
hygh prouysyon. Thys byll putteth he forth in the poore beggers
name. But we verely thynk yf them self haue as myche wyt as
their proctour lacketh / they had leuer see theyr byll maker
burned / then theyr supplycacyon sped. For they may sone per-
20 ceyue that he myndeth not theyr almoyse / but onely the spoyle
of the clergye. For so that the clergye lese yt: he neyther deuyseth ferther / nor ferther forcyth who haue yt.

But yt ys ethe to se wherof spryngeth all hys dyspleasure. He ys
angry & fretyth at the spyrytuall iurysdyccyon for the ponysh-
25 ment of heretykes and burnyng of theyr erronyouse bokes: for
euer vppon that stryng he harpeth : very angry wyth the burnyng of Tyndals testament. For these matters he calleth them
blood suppers dronken in the blood of holy sayntes and marters.
Ye merueyll paraduenture which holy sayntes & martyrs he
30 menyth. Surely by hys holy sayntes and marters he meanyth
theyr holy scysmatykes and heretykes / for whose iust ponyshment these folk that ar of y^e same sect / fume / frete / [D$_1$] frote
and fome / as fyerce and as angerly as a new huntyd sow. And for
the rancour conceyuyd vppon this dysplesure / cometh vp all hys
35 complaynt of the possessyons of the clergye. Wheryn he spareth
& forbereth the nunnys yet / because they haue no iurisdyccyon

8 this:] _1529_^{1}, this _1529_^{2} _1557_   22 who] _1529_^{1} _corr. err._, _1529_^{2} _1557_, why _1529_^{1}
36 they] _1529_^{2} _1557_, the _1529_^{1}

vppon heretykes: for els he wold haue cryed out vppon theyr
possessyons to. But thys ys now no new thyng nor ye furste tyme
y^t heretykes haue bene in hand wyth the mater. For furste was
there in the .xi. yere of kynge Henry the fourth / one Iohan
Badby burned for heresy. And forthwyth theruppon was there   5
at the next parlyment holden ye same yere / a byll put in /
declaryng how mych temporall land was in the church / which
rekenyng the maker therof gessyd at by ye nomber of knyghtis
fees / of whych he had went he had made a very iuste account.
And in thys byll was yt deuysed to take theyr possessyons out   10
agayn. How be yt by the byll yt appered well vnto them whych
well vnderstode ye mater / that the maker of the byll neither wyst
what land there was / nor how many knyghtes fees there was in
the church / nor well what thyng a knyghtes fee ys: but the byll
deuysed of rancour & yuell will by some such as fauoured Bad-   15
by that was burned / and wolde haue hys heresyes fayne go
forward.

     And so y^t byll suche as yt was / such was yt estemed and set a
syde for nought. So happed yt then sone after that in ye first yere
of ye kynges mooste noble progenytour kynge Henry the fyfte   20
those heresyes secretely crepyng on styll among the people: a
great nomber of theym had fyrst couertely conspyred and after
openly gathred and assembled theym selfe / purposyng by open
warre and batayle to destroy ye kyng and hys nobles and subuerte the realme. Whose traytorouse malyce that good catho-   25
lyque kynge preuented / wythstode / overthrew / and punyshed:
by many of them taken in the feld / and after for theyr
traytorouse heresyes bothe hanged and burned. Whervppon
forthwyth at ye parlyment holden ye same yere / lyke wyse as that
ryall prynce / his vertuouse nobles & his good crysten communes /   30
deuysed good lawes agaynst heretyques: so dyd some of suche as
fauored theym / efte sonys put in the byll agaynst the spyrytuall-
tye. Whyche efte sonys consydered for suche as it was and cum-
mynge of suche malyciouse purpose as yt cam: was agayne
reiected and set a syde for nought. Then was there longe after   35

---

7 church /] *1529*², church. *1529*¹, church, *1557*   21–22 *Sidenote 1557:* The veri propertie of heretiques   30 prynce /] prynce *1529 1557*; vertuouse nobles &] *1529*² *1557*,
vertuouse and *1529*¹

that / one Rycharde howndon burned for heresye. And then forthewyth were there a rable of heretyques gatheryd theym self to gyther at Abyndon: whych not entendyd to lese eny more labour by puttynge vp of byllys in the parlementes / but to make
5 an open insurreccyon and subuerte all the realme / and then to kyll vp ye clergye and sell preestes heddes as good chepe as shepys heddes thre for a peny bye who wold. But god saued ye chyrch & ye realm both & tourned theyre malyce vppon theyre awne heddes. And yet after theyr [D₁v] punyshment then were
10 there some that renewed the byll agayn. And yet long after this was ther one Iohan Goose rosted at ye towre hyll. And theruppon forth wyth some other Iohan goose bygan to bere that byll a brode agayn / & made some gagling a whyle but yt auayled hym not. And now bycause some heretyques haue bene of late
15 abiured / thys goselyng therfore hath made thys beggers byll / and gageleth agayn vppon the same mater / and that as he thynketh by a proper inuencyon lykely to spede now / bycause he maketh his byll in the name of the beggers / and hys byll cowched as full of lyes as any begger swarmeth full of lyce.
20 We neyther wyll nor shall nede to make myche busynes abowte thys mater. We truste myche better in the goodnesse of good men / then that we shuld nede for thys thyng to reason agaynst an vnresonable body. We be sure ynoughe that good men were they y^t gaue this gere in to the churche: and therfore nought
25 shuld they be of lykelyhed that wold pull yt out thense agayn. To whych rauyne and sacrylege our lorde we trust shall neuer suffer thys realme to fall.

Holy saynte Austeyn in his dayes when he parceyuyd that some euyll people murmured at the possessyons that then were
30 geuen in to hys church: dyd in an open sermon amonge all the people offer them theyre landys agayne / and that hys church and he wold forsake them / and bad theym take theym who wolde. And yet was there not founden in all the towne / albe yt that the people were (as these Affrycanis be) very barbarouse /
35 fyerce & boystuouse / yet was there none as we say fownden eny

---

13 gagling] *1529² 1557*, bablyng *1529¹*   18 cowched] *1529¹*, cowhed *1529²*, couched
1557   34 these] *1529² 1557*, the *1529¹*   35 fownden] fowden *1529*, founden *1557*

one so badde / that his harte wold serue hym to entre in to one
fote.

When Pharao the kynge of Egypte bought vp in the dere yeres
all the landys that were in euery mannes hande / so that all the
people were fayne to sell theyre enherytaunce for hunger: yet
ydolater as he was he wold neuer suffer for eny nede the possessyons of ye prestes to be solde / but made prouysyon for theym
beside / and suffred theym to kepe theyre landys styll / as the
byble bereth wytnesse. And we verely truste that the good
chrysten pryncesof the chrysten realme of Englonde shall neuer
fayle of more fauour towarde the clergye of Cryste / then had
that prynce Idolatre to the preestes of hys ydolles. Yet ys yt not
ynough to the cruell mynde of thys man to take frome the hole
clergy all that euer they haue / but that he wold ferther haue
theym bounden vnto cartes and whypped to dryue theym to
labour.

Of all theues ys thys one of the wurste and moste cruell kynde.
For of all theues men most abhorre them that whan they haue
taken a mannes money frome hym / then take and bynde hym
and bete hym to. But yet ys this wretche mych wurse. For he
fareth as a cruell thefe that wolde wythout respecte of hys awne
commodyte / take a mannes [D$_2$] money frome hym and caste yt
he care not where / and then bynde the man to a tree and bete
hym for hys pleasure. Oh the cheryte.

But he sayeth he wolde haue theym whypped to compell them
to laboure and gette theyre lyuynge in the swete of theyre faces.
And thys wold he not good man but for fulfullyng of goddys
commaundement. For he sayeth that yt ys commaunded them in
the fyrst chapter of Genesys. And therfore ys he theryn so indifferent that he excepteth none / but calleth the beste but ydle holy
theues / and so wold haue them all robbed and spoyled / bound-
en and beten to compell them to wurk wyth theyre handes / to
gete theyre lyuyng in the swete of theyr faces for the fulfullyng
of goddys commaundement. Amonge thys company that he
wolde sodaynely sende forthe newe robbed wyth ryght naught
lefte theym: ys there many a good man that hath lyued full godly

5

10

15

20

25

30

35

---

3 *Sidenote 1557:* Gene, 47

many a fayre day / and duely serued god & prayd for vs / which
we haue well founden: many an olde man: many a sore syk man:
and many blynde and many lame to. All whyche as sone as they
be dreuen owte of theyre awne dores / this cherytable man wolde
5   be very well content to see them bounden and beten to / bycause
they be of ye clergy. For excepcyon maketh he none / in thys
world.

He layeth vnto the charge of the clergy that they lyue ydle all /
& that they be all bounde to labour and gette theyre lyuyng in the
10   swete of theyre faces / by the precepte y^t god gaue to Adam in the
fyrste chapiter of Genesys. Here this man sheweth hys connyng.
For yf thys be so: then were the preestes in the olde lawe bound-
en therto as well as ys ye clergy now. And then howe happed yt
that of thys poynte there was no mencyon made by Moyses?
15   howe happed yt that god in that lawe prouyded theym myche
larger lyuynge then he dyd the lay people? & that such kynde of
lyuynge as declared that hys pleasure was that they shuld lyue
owt of labour and vppon ye labour of other mennes handes? The
holy apostle saynt Powle / all though hym self in some places
20   forbare to take hys lyuinge frely / but rather chose to lyue of hys
owne labour then to be in theyre daungeour whych wolde happely haue sayd y^t he preched because he wold lyue at ease therby / and thys dyd he specyally to put suche false apostles to
sylence / as for suche desyre of ydle lyuynge fell some where to
25   false prechynge: yet neyther dyd he so in euery place / and also
confessed and sayed that he myght well and lawfully haue done
the contrary / affyrmynge yt for good reason y^t he that serueth
the awter shuld lyue of the awter & sayng also: yf we sow vnto
you spirituall thynges / ys yt a great thing yf we repe your carnall
30   thynges? Now chryst hys awne mouth sayd vnto the people / that
they shulde not leue theyr dutyes vnpayed vnto the preests. And
thys good chrysten man wold haue theym all clene taken frome
theym and yet the preestes well beten to. [D₂v]

He rekeneth all the clergye ydle / bycause they labour not wyth
35   theyre handes tyll theyre faces swete. But our sauyour chryst

---

6 clergy.] *1529*¹ *1557*, clergy *1529*²   20 of hys] *1529 1557*ᵃ, of of hys *1557*ᵇ
23 *Sidenote 1557:* Corin. I. ca. 9   32 haue theym] *1529*, haue thē *1557*ᵃ, haue then
*1557*ᵇ

rekened farre other wyse in blessyd Mary Magdalene. Whose
ydle syttyng at her ease and herkenyng / he accounted and declared for better busynes then the busy styryng & walkyng abowt
of his good hostesse Martha whyche was yet of all worldly busynes occupyed abowte the beste: for she was busye abowte almoyse and hospetalyte / and ye gestynge of the beste pore man
and moste gracyouse geste that euer was gested in thys worlde.

Now yf thys can not yet content thys good man bycause of
goddes commaundement geuen vnto Adam / that he shuld eate
hys brede in ye swete of hys face: then wold we fayne wyt whyther
hym self neuer go to mete / tyll he haue wrought so sore wyth hys
handes that hys face sweteth. Surely we beleue he laboureth not
so sore before euery meale. But yet yt were not good to truste hys
answere / for he wyll happely say yes / and not lette for one lye
amonge so manye. How be yt he thynketh yt peraduenture
inough for hym / y^t he sytteth and studyeth tyll he swete in
sekynge owte olde heresyes / & deuysyng newe. And verely yf he
loke y^t suche busynes shulde serue hym for a dyscharge of hande
labour / moche better may we thynk dyscharged therof / many
good men whome he wold haue beten therto / lyuyng theyr lyues
in fastyng / prayer & prechyng / and studyeng abowt the trouth.

But yt ys good to loke bytyme what this beggers proctour
meaneth by thys commaundement of hand labour that he
speketh of. For yf he confesse that yt byndeth not euery man:
then ys yt layed to no purpose agaynste the clergye. For there
was a small clergye when that word was sayed to our first fader
Adam. But now yf he call yt a precepte as he doth / and then wyll
that yt extend vnto all the hole kynd of man / as a thynge by god
commaunded vnto Adam and all hys ofspryng / then thogh he
say litle now / he meneth to go ferther here after then he speketh
of yet. For yf he myght fyrst haue the clergy put owt of theyre
lyuynge / and all that they haue clene taken frome theym / &
myght haue theym ioyned to these beggers that be now / and

---

1 Magdalene.] *1529*[1] *1557*, Magdalene / *1529*[2]   4 *Sidenote 1557:* Iohn. ca. 11
5 beste] *1529 1557*[b], beast *1557*[a]   6 gestynge] *1529 1557*[a], gestinst *1557*[b]
12 sweteth.] *1529*[1] *1557*, sweteth *1529*[2]   15 thynketh yt] *1529*, thinketh it *1557*[a],
thinketh yet *1557*[b]   17 newe.] *1529*[1] *1557*, newe *1529*[2]   27 yf he] *1529*, if ye
1557   30 here after] *1529*[2], hereafter *1529*[1] *1557*

ouer yᵗ added vnto them and send a beggyng to / all those yᵗ the
clergye fynd now full honestly: thys pageaunt ones played / and
hys beggers byll so well spedde / then whan the beggers should
haue so mych lesse lyuynge and be so many moo in multytude:
5 surely lyke wyse as for the beggers he now maketh hys byll to the
kyngys hyghnesse agaynste bysshops / abbottys / pryours / prelatys / and preestys: so wold he then wythyn a whyle after make a
nother byll to the people agaynst merchauntys / gentylmen /
kyngys / lordys / and prynces / and complayne that they haue
10 all / and saye that they do nothyng for yt but lyue ydle / and that
they be commaunded in Genesys to lyue by yᵉ labour of theyr
[D₃] handys in the swete of theyre facys / as he sayth by the
clergye now. Wherein yf they wene that they shall stande in
other case then the clergye doth now: they may peraduenture
15 sore deceyue theym selfe. For yf they wyll thynk that theyre case
shall not be called all one bycause they haue landys and goodys to
lyue vppon / they must consyder so hath the clergye to. But yᵗ ys
the thyng yᵗ thys beggers proctor complayneth vppon / and wold
haue theym taken away. Now yf the landed men suppose that
20 theyre case shall not seme one wyth the case of the clergye /
bycause they shall happely thynk that the church hath theyre
possessyons gyuen theym for causes whych they fulfyll not / and
that yf theyre possessyons happen to be taken frome theym yt
shalbe done vppon that grounde / and so the lay landed men
25 owte of that fere bycause they thynke that suche lyke occasyon
and ground and consyderacyon fayleth and can not be founden
in them & theyre enherytaunce: surely yf any man clerk or lay
haue landis in yᵉ gyft wherof hath bene eny condycyon adioynyd
whych he fulfylleth not / the geuer may well with reson vse
30 theryn such aduauntage as yᵉ law geueth him. But on yᵉ tother
syde who so wyll aduyse pryncys or lay people to take from yᵉ
clergy theyr possessyons / allegyng maters at large / as layng to
theyr charge that they liue not as they shuld / nor vse not well
theyr possessions / and that therfore yt were well done to take
35 them from theym by force and dyspose them beter: we dare
boldly say who so gyueth this deuyce as now doth this beggars

---

18 beggers proctor] *1529²* *1557*, begger *1529*¹   35 from] *1529*¹ *1557*, fom *1529²*

proctour / we wolde gyue you counsell to loke well what wyll folow. For he shall not fayle as we sayd before yf thys byll of his were sped / to fynde you sone after in a new supplicacyon new balde reasons ynow y^t shuld please the peoples eares / where-wyth he wold labour to haue lordys landis and all honest mennys goodys to be pulled from them by force & dystrybuted among beggars. Of whych there shuld in thys wyse y^t he deuyseth en-creace and grow so many / that they shuld be able for a sodayn shyft to make a strong parte. And surely as the fyre euer krepeth forward and laboreth to turn all into fyre: so wyll such bold beggars as thys is / neuer cease to solycyte and procure all that they can / the spoyle and robbery of all that ought hauc / and to make all beggars as they be them self.

We be content y^t ye beleue vs not / but yf yt haue so prouyd all redy by those vplandysh Lutherans that rose vp in Almaygne. Whych beyng onys raysed by such sedycyose bokes as ys thys beggars supplycacyon / & such sedycyouse heretykys as ys he that made yt: set furste vppon spyrytuall prelatys. But shortly theruppon they so strechyd vnto the temporall pryncys / that they were fayne to ioyne in ayde of them self with those whom they laughed at furst to se them put in the paryll / hopynge to haue had the profyte of theyr losse / tyll they saw y^t they were lykly to lese theyr owne wyth them. And for all the ponysh-[D$_3$v]ment y^t they pursued vppon those rebellyouse parsons / of whom ther were in one somer slayn aboue .lx. M: yet ys that fyre rather couered than quenchyd / because they suffered yt crepe forth so farre at furst / y^t dyscencyon grew therby among the lordys them self / as there can neuer lak some nedy rauenouse landed men / that shalbe redy to be captayns in all such re-bellyons: as was the lord Cobham called Oldecastell somtyme a captayn of heretykes in Englande in the dayes of kynge Henry the fyft. And surely there would sone folow some sore chaunge in the temporalte / yf thys beggers proctour haue hys mal-ycyouse supplycacyon spedde agaynst the spyrytualte.

---

11 procure] _1529_^{1} _1557_^{b}, precure _1529_^{2} _1557_^{a} 25 .M:] _1529_^{1}, .M. _1529_^{2} _1557_
26 couered] _1529_^{1} _1557_, couored _1529_^{2} 30 _Sidenote 1557:_ Lord Cobham; somtyme]
_1529_^{2}, sometyme _1529_^{1} _corr. err._, sometome _1529_^{1}, sometime _1557_

But yet lest folk shulde abhorre hys hard harte and cruelte: ye man temperyth hys mater wyth a goodly vysage of the sore inwarde sorow y^t he taketh for the mynyshment of mankynd / and wyth the greate zele that he bereth to generacyon for the good
5 encreace of crysten people in the land. For he wold for that cause in eny wyse that all ye clergy shuld haue wyues. For he asketh ye kynges hyghnes (as the man hath caught a great pleasure to appose the kyng / wherin he vseth a fygure of rethoryk that men call sawce malaperte) what an infynyte number of people myght
10 haue bene encreased to haue peopled your realme / yf thys sort of folk had ben maried lyke other men. This mater that prestes must nedys haue wyues he bryngethe in dyuersly in .iii. or .iiii. placys. And amonge other he hathe one / wherin he sheweth in raylynge agaynst the clergy a princypall parte of hys excellente
15 eloquence. For there he vseth hys ryall fygure of rethoryke called repetycyon / repetyng often by ye hole clergy: these be they in ye beginnyng of hys clause: "These be they y^t haue made an .C. M. idle hores in your realme. These be they y^t corrupt the generacyon of mankynd in your realm. These be they that draw
20 mennys wyues in to incontynency in your realme." And after dyuers of such these be these / he concludeth & knytteth vp the mater wyth his accustomyd vehemence fet out of Luthers volumys / askyng who is able to nomber the great brode botomlesse occean see full of yuels / that thys myscheuouse and synfull
25 generacyon bryngeth vp vppon vs? As though all the hole clergy were of thys condycion and no man els but they. But among all hys these be thays / this ys one whych as the sorest and the most vehemente / he setteth in the fore front of them all: "These be they that by theyr abstaynyng fro maryage / do let the genera-
30 cyon of the people / wherby all the realme at lenght yf yt shuld be contynued shalbe made desert and inhabytable."

Lo the depe insyght that thys beggars proctour hathe in the brode botomlesse occean see full of yuels to saue the greuouse

6 clergy] _1529_^1 _corr. err._, _1529_^2 _1557_, cergy _1529_^1   8 appose] _1529_^2 _1557_, oppose _1529_^1   8–9 _Sidenote 1557:_ A figure cald sawce malepert   17 clause:] _1529_^1, clause _1529_^2, clause. _1557_   18 an .C. M.] _1529_^1 _corr. err._, an .C. _1529_^1, .C. M. _1529_^2 _1557_   26–27 all hys these] _1529_ _1557_^a, al these _1557_^b   27 thays] _1529_^2, these _1529_^1, thei _1557_   29–30 generacyon] _1529_, generacion _1557_^b, generaciin _1557_^a

shypwrak of the comen welth. He seeth farre farther than euer
Cryst was ware of / or eny of hys blyssed apostles / or eny of y^e old
holy fathers of crystys fayth and religyon syns hys holy assencyon
hetherto / tyll now y^t [D$_4$] Luther cam of late and Tyndale after
hym / & spyed out thys great secrete mystery that neyther god   5
nor good man coud espye. If theyr abstaynyng fro maryage
shuld make all the land desart and inhabytable / how happeth yt
that habytacyon endureth theryn so long: for the lande hathe
lasted syth the begynnynge of theyre absteynynge frome maryage ye wot well many a fayre day. And now yf theyr abstayning   10
from maryage not wythstandyng / the land hath bene vpholden
with the generacyon of you y^t ar the temporalte so long: ye shall
lyke wyse hereafter by goddes grace and the helpe of good
prayours for kepyng the land from wyldernes / be able to get
chyldern styll your self / and shall not nede to call neyther   15
monkys nor freres to help you.

Now yf yt be so that ye clergy be as he sayth but the hundred
part of the men / and yet not so mych nether: there ys not then so
great parell of the land to fall to wyldernes / but y^t the .lxxxxix.
partes may mayntayn yt populouse / though the hundred part   20
abstayn. But he for to shew that he hath not left hys anxyouse
fauour toward his natyue contrey though he be ronne away from
yt for heresy: fereth sore lest ye hundred parte forberyng maryage / all the .lxxxxix. partes shall not be able so to preserue yt
with generacyon / but that yt shall wax not onely desert / but also 25
(wherof we most wonder) inhabitable / y^t is to say suche as of yt
self shall not be able for mannys habytacyon. But he paraduenture taketh inhabytable for desart / desolate and not inhabyted /
because men shuld se that he can so roll in hys rethoryk / that he
wotteth not what hys owne wordys meane.   30

And sumwhat yet ys yt to be consydered / that in such parte of
his boke that he wold haue yt appere that theyr lyuyng is to
mych: there he wold make yt seme that they were very few. And
where he wold haue them take wyuys: he wold haue them seme
so many / that theyr abstaynyng from maryage were able to   35
bryng all the land into desolacyon and wildernes. And thus he

handleth eyther parte so wysely: y^t there lakketh hym nothyng
yerthly theryn / but euen a peny weyght of wyt. For fawt wherof /
hys wyly foly foreseeth not that one parte of his proces euer
impugneth a nother. For they that were right now so small a
5 parte of people that a littell wold suffyse for theyr lyuyng: be
now sodenly so many that yf they were maryed / infynyte
nomber of people he sayth to ye kyng wold increase to people his
realm wyth. Now yf that be trew that of them alone yf they were
maryed / so infynyte nomber of people wold encrease / that yt
10 wold make ye realm populouse: then eyther ar they contrary to
hys count mo then the hundreth part (for one out of a .C. is no
very parceyuable mysse / nor one added to an .C. no very par-
ceuable encrease) or els yf they be but the hundred parte as he
made hys rekenyng ryght now / yet yf yt be then trew that he
15 sayth syns / that of the hundred parte maryed so infynyte [D$_4$v]
nomber of people myght yncrease to people the realme: then
can he not deny but that of the .lxxxxix. partys there may grow
.lxxxxix. tymes infinite nomber of people. And then that beyng
so / thoughe y^e clergye beyng as he sayth but y^e hundred part
20 neuer mary: yet shall y^e pore fole not nede to wake & wax lene
for fere of the realm fallynge to wyldernes. In whych he seeth y^t
there maye of the .lxxxxix. partis resydew / grow and encrease
.lxxxxix. tymes infynyte nomber of people to make ye land
populouse.
25   Yet maruayle we mych of one thyng y^t in all his fere y^t generacyon shuld fayle because ye clergye maryeth not: he seeth
no man vnmaried in all the realme but them. How many
seruauntys? How many tall seruynge men are there in the
realm that myght yf men saw such a sodayn necessyte / rather
30 mary then the clergy y^t haue vowed to god the contrary? But he
forceth nott so mych for the mater that he maketh hys pretext /
as he doth in dede to haue all vowes voyd / that he myght get
Luther sum lewd companyons in Englond.

---

2 yerthly] *1529 1557*^{a}, earthly *1557*^{b} 8 wyth.] *1529*^{1}, wyth *1529*^{2}, w^t. *1557*
13 the] *1529*^{1} *corr. err.*, *1529*^{2} *1557*, thy *1529*^{1} 18 tymes] *1529*^{2}, tymys *1529*^{1} *corr. err.*,
times *1557*, ty- *(at end of line) 1529*^{1}; that] y^t *1529*^{1}, they *1529*^{2} *1557*   21 to] *1529*^{1} *corr.*
err., *1529*^{2} *1557*, to to *1529*^{1} 27 them.] *1557*, them *1529*

But now what yf thys good man had the rule of this mater /
and wold put out all the clergy and byd them go wed? He shuld
paraduenture fynde some that wold not mych styk therat: but
they shuld be of the worst sort / and such as now be sklaunder of
theyr order / & whom yt were most nede to kepe fro genera-   5
cyon / leste yuell crowes bringe you forthe yuel byrdys. But as for
the good prestys & good relygyouse whose chylderne were like
to be best and to be best brought vp: they wolde not mary for
breche of theyr vowes. And thus shulde ye haue the naughty
generacyons encrease wherof there be to many all redy: and of   10
the better neuer the mo.

What wold thys good man do now wyth good folk of the clergy
y^t wold not mary? He wold of lyklyhod bynde them to cartes and
bete them / and make them wed in the wanyand. But now what
yf women wyll not wed them / namely syth he sendith them out   15
wyth ryght noght / sauynge slaunder / shame and vylanye? what
remedy wyll he fynde therfore? He wyll of lyklyhod compell the
women to wed theym: & yf the wench be nyce and play the
wanton and make the mater strange: then wyll he bete her to
bed to.   20

Surely we can not but here confesse the trouth / these nyce and
wanton wordis do not very well with vs: but we must pray god
and you to pardon vs. For in good fayth hys mater of monkys
maryagys ys so mery and so mad / that yt were able to make one
laugh that lieth in the fyre: & so mych the more / in how mych he   25
more ernestly preacyth vppon the kyng in thys poynt / to haue in
any wyse the clergy robbed / spoyled / bounden / beten and
weddyd. Wherby what oppynyon he hath of weddyng / ye may
sone parceyue: for ye se well that yf he thought yt good / he
woulde not wyssh yt theym.   30

Many that rede hys [E$_1$] wordys / wene that he were some mery
mad geste: but he seemeth vs farre otherwyse. For excepte he
were a wonderouse sad man of hym selfe / he coud neuer speke
so ernestely in so mad a mater.

3–4 *Sidenote 1557:* The worste sort of pristes do mary   16 slaunder] *1529*, sklaunder
1557   19 strange:] *1529*^{1}, strange *1529*^{2} *1557*   27 robbed /] *1529*^{1}, robbed *1529*^{2},
robbed, *1557;* spoyled] *1529*^{2} *1557*, spolyd *1529*^{1}

Yet one thing wold we very fayn wyt of hym. When he had
robbed / spoyled / bounden / beten and wedded all the clergy /
what wold he then? Shuld eny of them be curatys of mennys
soules and preche and mynyster the sacramentys to the people
5 or nat?

If they shuld: yt were a very strange fassyon to robb hym /
bynde hym / and bete hym on the tone daye: and then knele to
hym / and confesse to hym / and receyue the sacrament of hys
hande on ye tother day: reuerently here hym preche in the
10 pulpytte / and then bydde hym go gette hym home and clowte
shone. Eyther he muste mene to haue yt thus / whyche none
honeste man coulde endure to se: or ellys of whych twayne we
wote nere well whyther is the wurse / he entendeth to haue all
holy orders accompted as nothynge / and to haue no mo sacra-
15 mentys mynystred at all: but where as sone after crystes ascencyon hys church buryed the ceremonyes of the iewes synagoge
wyth honour and reuerence / so wold he now that crysten people
shuld kyll & cast owte on a donge hyll the blessyd sacramentys of
cryste wyth vylany rebuke and shame. And surely to tell you y^e
20 trouth / thys ys hys very fynall intent and purpose / and the very
marke that he shoteth at / as a specyall poynt and foundacyon of
all Luthers heresyes wherof thys man ys one of the baner berers.
And therfore here wold his awne hygh sore wordys haue good
place agaynst hym selfe. For this myscheuouse deuyse of hys / ys
25 in dede a great brode botomelesse occean see full of euyllys /
wheryn wold not fayle the greuouse shypwrake of the comen
welth whych god wold sone forsake yf ye people ones forsake hys
fayth / and contempned hys holy sacramentys / as thys beggers
proctour laboureth to brynge abowte. Whyche thynge hys de-
30 uyce and conueyaunce well declareth / all though he forbere
expressly to saye so farre / bycause of the good & gracyous
catholyke mynde that he well knoweth and by hys gracys excellent wrytynge perceyueth to be borne by the kynges hyghnes / to
the catholyk fayth. For whyche he couereth hys malycyouse en-

---

2 robbed /] *1529*[1], robbed *1529*[2], robbed, *1557*   9 day:] *1529*[1], day / *1529*[2], day, *1557*;
reuerently] *1529*, reuerenly *1557*   31 expressly] *1529*[1] *1557*, expressy *1529*[2]; so
farre /] *1529*[1] *corr. err.*, *1529*[2], so / farre *1529*[1], so farre, *1557*

tent and purpose toward the fayth / vnder ye cloke of many temporall benefytes / that he sayth shuld succede and folow to the kyngys hyghnes and hys realme / yf these hys hygh polytyque deuyces were ones by hys grace agreed.

For in ye ende of all hys byll: he gathereth hys hygh com-   5
moditees to gether / saynge that yf the kynge take all frome the clergye / sette them abrode at the wyde world wyth ryght nought to wed & take wyues / and make theym labour for theyre lyuynge tyll they swete / bynde theym to cartes and bete theym well / he saythe to the kynge in y^e beggers names: "then shall as well the   10
nombre of our forsayd monstru[E$_1$v]ouse sort / as of the bawdes / hores / theuys / and idle people decreace. Then shall these great yerely exaccyons ceace. Then shall not your sworde / power / crowne / dygnyte and obedyence of your people be translated frome you. Then shall you haue full obedyence of your people.   15
Then shall the ydle people be set awork. Then shall matrymony be myche better kepte. Then shall the generacyon of your peo-ple be encreased. Then shall your comens encrease in ryches. Then shall none take owre almoyse frome vs. Then shall the gospell be preached. Then shall we haue inough and more.   20
Then shalbe ye beste hospytall that euer was founded for vs. Then shall we pray to god for your noble estate longe to en-dure."

Lo here here ye heped vp many great commodytees / yf they were all trew. But we shewed you byfore and haue also proued   25
you / that hys byll ys myche grounded vppon many great lyes / wherof he by and by byganne wyth some and after went forth wyth mo. And now to thentent that thende shuld be somewhat sutely to the remanaunte as he byganne wyth lyes and went forth wyth lyes / so wyll he with lyes lyke wyse make an ende: sauyng   30
that in the bygynnyng he gaue theym oute by tale / and in the ende he bryngeth theym in by hepes. For fyrst he sayth y^t then shall the nomber of sore and syke beggers decreace. How so? shall there by the robbyng / weddynge / byndynge and betynge of the clergye / blynde beggers gette theyre syght agayn or lame   35

---

8 labour] *1529*, layour *1557*   13 ceace.] *1529*^{1} *1557*, ceace / *1529*^{2} 24 ye] *1529*, he *1557*

beggers theyre legges? ys there no man in all the clergy syk and
sore that shalbe by thys way sent vnto them? shold there not
many that now be in good helthe waxe shortely syk and sore /
and sytte and begge wyth theym? were thys a mynyshement of
5 syk and sore beggers to make mo and send to them?
    Then shall (he sayth) bawdes / & hores / theues / & ydle peple
decrece. Thys man weneth he were cosyn to god / & coud do as
he dyd: Dixit & facta sunt. For as sone as he hath dyuysed yt /
nowe weneth he y^t yf they were all put owte & so serued by & by /
10 then were all forthwith in good order. As sone as he sayth lette
theym wedde / nowe he weneth y^t forthwyth euery preeste
monke & frere hath a wyfe. As sone as he hath sayd bind theym
& bete them to wurke / forthwyth he weneth euery man ys at hys
wurke. And all thys he rekeneth sure ere euer he prouyde wurke
15 for theym / or where they shall dwell / or who shall take so many
to wurk at onys y^t neuer were wonte to wurke byfore / and thys
where he seeth many walke ydle all redy / that eyther no betyng
can dryue to wurke / or ellys no man wyll take to wurke. Fyrste
we trust that among the clergye there be many men of that
20 goodnes and vertue / that scante a deuyll could fynde in hys
harte to handle them in suche dyspytuouse and dyspyghtfull
maner. But go to lette theyre honest lyuyng and vertue lye styll in
questyon / yet at the leste [E$_2$] wyse he wyll graunte they be good
or nought. Nowe then yf they be good: he ys to very a vylayn y^t
25 wold sarue good men so. And on y^e tother syde yf they be all as
he wolde haue them all seme / vnthryfty / lewde / and nought:
howe can yt be that by the reason of so many so noughty / so
sodaynly sette owte at large / ye shuld haue bawdes / harlottys /
theuys / & ydle people decreace? excepte he thynke that those
30 whome he calleth nought all redy beynge as they nowe be kepte
in / and in honest fassyon refrayned / & many kepte vp in
cloysters / wylbe better ruled abrode runnyng at ye wyld world as
bukkys broken owt of a parke. Over thys howe can there by the
maryagys of preestys / monkys / & fryres / be fewer hores and
35 bawdys / when by the very maryage yt self beynge as yt were

---

7 *Sidenote 1557:* Psal. 148   27 the] *1529*^{1}, that *1529*^{2} *1557*   32 cloysters /] *1529*^{2},
cloysters *1529*^{1}, cloisters, *1557*   35–157/1 *Sidenote 1557:* The mariage of priestes is
incestuouse

incestuouse & abhomynable / all were starke harlottys that maryed them / and all stark bawdys that shuld helpe to bryng them to
gether.

Then shall he sayth / these great yerely exaccyons ceace. How
can such thyngys ceace as neuer yet byganne. Ye remember what 5
thyngys he called exaccyons / the freres quarterage / whych he
sayd that they exacte of euery household / and compell theym to
pay yt vppon payn of heresye / beryng of a fagot or burnyng.
Can he among so many as payeth yt not / lay you one sample y^t
euer any sayd he was so serued thys seuen yere / thys .vii. score 10
yere / thys .vii. C. yere? Can he saye y^t euer yt was exacted of hym
selfe? We knowe where he dwelled / and that yf he had had none
other cause to runne away / surely for eny fere of freres y^t euer
exacted of hym quarterage / he wold not haue bene afrayed to
dwell by the beste of theyre berdes.   15

Then shall ydle folke he sayeth be sette a wurke. By what
meanys? Whom hath he deuysed mo to sette ydle men a wurke?
but yf he loke that ydle men shalbe sette a wurke by theym
whome he sendeth owte of theyre awne housys wythout money
or ware / neyther he nor they wote whyther.   20

Then shall matrymony be myche better kepte. Why so? bycause there be mo men vnmaryed sent owt abrode to brek yt?
Who (yf they be suche as he calleth theym) were (yf they wente all
abrode) well lykely to breke many a nother mannys maryage ere
they made all theyre awne.   25

Then shall the generacyon of your people be encreaced. Is
that the greateste fawte he fyndeth / the lak of generacyon? If he
saw as farr as he wold seme to se / then shuld he spye y^t it were
first more nede to prouyde houses to dwell in / wyth lande layde
therto for tyllage: or ellys experyence techeth that there is gener- 30
acyon ynough for y^e corne that the grounde bereth. And that
thynge ones well prouyded for / there wyll ynowe be founden to
multyply more generacyon of suche as may laufully wedde and
wold wedde / yf they wyste where after wed[E$_2$v]dynge theyre
wyfe and theyre chyldren shuld dwell.   35

Then shall not your swerde / power / crowne / and dygnyte / and obedyence of your people / be taken frome you. Who hath taken yt away nowe? who hath hys sworde borne but hys hyghnes hym selfe or suche hys deputyes as he appoynteth yt vnto? his crowne no man wereth but hym selfe / as farre as euer any of vs
5   herde. And yet yf hys hyghnes haue any crowned kynges vnder hym / his swerd / power / crown & dignyte / ys nothyng defaced nor mynysshed: but honowred & enhaunced by that. But all the myschefe ys that the spyrytuall court hath examynacyon of here- tyques / thys ys all the gryefe. For as for obedyence of the kyngys
10 people / hys hyghnes fyndeth none taken from hym. Was there euer kynge in thys realm better obayd then he? Hath his hyghnes of eny part of hys realm bene better obayd or more humbly serued then of hys clergy? Was there euer eny kynge in the realm that had hys crowne translated frome hym / bycause the clergye
15 had landys geuen them / or bycause men gaue almoyse to the pore freres? in good fayth ye may truste vs we neuer knewe none suche. Whan ye beggers proctour preueth any suche ye may then byleue hym: and in the meane tyme ye may well byleue he lyeth.
      Then shall ye haue obedyence of your people. Yet agayn? Tyll
20 he fynde in the kyngys realm some that dare dysobay hym / yt were not myche agaynst reason that harpynge so myche vppon that strynge / y^t euery mannys eare perceyueth so false and so farre owte of tune: he shulde confesse hym selfe a fole.
      Then shall your people encreace in rychesse. Wherefore y^e
25 rather? Not one halfepeny for aught that he hath spoken yet / except he mean when he taketh the lande frome the clergye / then to dyuyde yt among the people and make a dole of the freres almoyse to. And yf he mean so: when he sayeth yt owte playnely then wyll we tell you what he meaneth more. But in the
30 meane season to proue hym both false and folysshe / yt ys ynough to tell hym / that the people can not waxe rych by theyr commyng to them that are sent owte naked and bryng naught wyth theym.
      Then shall none begge our almoyse frome vs. No parde / none
35 but all they that ye wyll haue sent owte naked to you / whyche

---

6 power /] *1529*[1], power *1529*[2], power, *1557*

wolde be mo then ye wolde be gladde to se sytte and begge wyth
you / and se them ask your almoyse from you y^t were wonte to
gyue almoyse to you.

Then shall the gospell be preched. Ye mary that that. There is
ye great mater that all thys gapyng ys for. For vndowtedly all the   5
gapynge ys for a new gospell. Men haue bene wonte thys many
yeres to preche the gospell of criste in suche wyse as saynt
Mathew / saynt Mark / saynt Luke / and saynt Iohan hath wryten
yt / and in such wyse as y^e old holy doctours saynt Hyerom / saynt
Austyn / saint Ambrose [E$_3$] saynt Gregory / saynt Chrysostome /   10
saynt Basyle / saynt Cypryan / saynt Barnerd / saynt Thomas /
and all the olde holy faders synnis crystys dayes vntyll your awne
dayes haue vnderstande yt. Thys gospell hath bene as we say
alway thus preched. Why sayeth he now that yf y^e clergy were
caste owte for nought / that then ye gospell shold be prechyd.   15
Who shuld then be these prechours? He meaneth not y^t ye clergy
shall / ye may se that well. Who than? Who but some ley Luther-
anes? And what gospell shall they preche? Not your old gospell
of Cryste: for y^t is yt whych was wonte to be preched vnto you.
And he wold ye shuld now thynk that the gospell shall begyn to   20
be prechyd: and yet not begyn to be prechyd among you / tyll the
clergy be cast out. What gospell shall that be than that shall then
be prechyd? What gospell but Luthers gospell and Tyndals gospell? tellyng you y^t onely fayth suffyseth you for saluacyon: and
that there nedyth no good workys / but y^t yt were sacrylege and   25
abhomynacyon to go about to please god wyth eny good workys:
and that there ys no purgatory / nor that the sacramentys be
nothyng worth / nor y^t no law can be made by man to bynde you:
but that by your onely fayth ye may do what ye wyll: & y^t yf ye
obey any law or gouernour / all ys of your owne curtesye & not of   30
eny duty at all: fayth hath set you in such a lewd lyberte.

Thys & many a mad frantyke foly shalbe the gospell y^t then
shall be prechyd / wherof he bosteth now as of one of the moste
specyall commodytees / that shall succede vppon hys goodly and
godly deuyces.   35

23–24 *Sidenote 1557:* Luthers and Tindals gospell   24 saluacyon] *1529*[1] *1557,* salua-
cayn *1529*[2]

Wyll ye playnly parceyue yᵗ he meaneth thus? After all hys
myscheuys rehersyd agaynst the church: he hathe an other matter in hys mynde / whych he dare not yet speke of / but he
maketh therof a secret ouerture leuyng yt in such wyse at large /
as he wold that men shulde gesse what he ment / & yet he re-
seruyth hym self some refuge to flytte therfro when he lyst. For
yf he shuld se that men shuld myslyke yt / he wold in such case
say that he ment some other thyng. And therfore he purposeth
yt vnder these wordys: "Here leue we out yᵉ greatyst mater of
all / lest we declaring such an horrible carrayn of euyll agaynst
the mynysters of iniquyte / shuld seme to declare the one onely
fawte or rather yᵉ ignoraunce of our best belouyd mynyster of
ryghtuousnes. Whych ys to be hyd tyll he may be lerned by these
small enormytees yᵗ we haue spoken of / to know yt playnly hym
selfe."

Thys thyng put forth lyke a rydle / harde to rede what yt
shulde sygnyfye: we haue had synnys / by suche as we byfore
shewed you yᵗ dyed and cam hyther / playnly declared vnto vs.
And surely who so well aduyseth hys wordes / and well pon-
dereth hys hole purpose / and the summary effecte of his boke:
shall mowe sone perceyue what he meaneth in that place. For
what shuld that thyng be that he leueth out / that shuld be the
greatest of all / and that shuld be layed agaynste the [E₃v] mynysters of inyquyte whych he meaneth and calleth yᵉ hole clergye /
and that shuld be such an horryble carayne of euyll / yᵗ yt shud
passe & excede any myscheuouse matter that he had all redy
spoken agaynste byfore? What maner of myscheuouse mater
shuld thys be? Thys horryble carrayn of yuell that he leuyth out /
syth yt ys as he sayth the greatest mater of all / must nedys ye wot
well be greater agaynst the clergy / than all that great brode
botomelesse occean see of yuels: more than all hys These be
theys: more than the makyng of such great nomber of beggars /
of ydle men / bawdys / hoorys and theuys: more than the

1 thus?] *1529*¹ *1557*, thus: *1529*²   5 ment] *1529*¹ *1557*, men *1529*²   21 mowe]
1529, now *1557*   22 out /] *1529*¹, out *1529*² *1557*   24 clergye /] *1529*¹, clergye
*1529*² *1557*   25 shud] *1529*², shuld *1529*¹, should *1557*   27 myscheuouse] *1529*¹
1557, mycheuouse *1529*²   33 bawdys] *1529*¹, bawdy *1529*² *1557*

hyndryng of matrymony / corruptyng of generacion: more than translatyng the kyngys kyngdom: more than bryngyng the kyngys crown to ruyne: more than bryngyng the comen weale to shyp wrak / and all the realm to wyldernes. What thyng can thys horrible carrayn be that the clergy dothe / that he leueth out for 5 yᵉ whyle / that so farre excedyth these myscheuouse maters before remembryd / that in comparyson of yt he calleth them all small enormytees / & as a man wold say lytle prety peccadulyans? Verely by thys thyng meaneth he none other / but the prechyng of the very hole corps and body of the blessed fayth of Cryste / 10 & the mynystryng of the blyssed sacramentis of our sauyour Cryste / and of all those in especyall the consecratyng of the sacred body the flesh and blood of our sauyour Cryst. For the techyng & prechyng of all whych thyngys / thys beggers proc- tour or rather the dyuels proctour wyth other beggers that lak 15 grace and nether beg nor loke for none: bere all thys theyr malyce & wrathe to the churche of Cryste. And seynge there ys no way for attaynyng theyr entent but one of the twayn / yᵗ ys to wyt eyther playnly to wryte agaynst the fayth and the sacra- mentys (wheryn yf they gat them credence and obtaynyd / they 20 then se well the church must nedys fall therwyth) or els to labour agaynst the church alone / & get the clergye dystroyd / wherup- pon they parceyue well that the fayth and sacramentes wold not fayle to decay: they parceyuyng thys / haue therfor furste as- sayd the furst way all redy / sendyng forth Tyndals translacyon 25 of the new testament in such wyse handled as yt shuld haue bene the fountayn and well spryng of all theyr hole heresyes. For he had corrupted and purposely changed in many placys the text / wyth such wordys as he myght make yt seme to the vnlerned people / that the scrypture affyrmed theyr heresyes it selfe. 30 Then cam sone after out in prynt the dyaloge of frere Roy & frere Hyerome / betwene yᵉ father & yᵉ sonne agaynst yᵉ sacra- ment of yᵉ aulter: & the blasphemouse boke entytled the beryeng of the masse. Then cam forth after Tyndals wykkyd

---

6 yᵉ] *1529*¹, a *1529*² *1557*; myscheuouse] *1529*¹ *1557*, mycheuouse *1529*²   14 tech- yng] *1529*¹ *1557*, techynh *1529*²   30 scrypture] *1557*, scryputre *1529*   30–32 *Side- note 1557:* Tindals translation of the new testament purposely corrupted

boke of Mammona / & after that his more wykkyd boke of obydyence. In whych bokys afore specyfyed they go forth playnly
agaynst the fayth and holy sacramentis of Crystys church / and
most especyally [E₄] agaynst the blyssed sacrament of yᵉ aulter /
5   wyth as vylanous wordes as the wreches coud deuyse. But when
they haue perceuyd by experyence yᵗ good people abhorred
theyr abomynable bokes: then they beyng therby lernyd yᵗ the
furst way was not yᵉ best for yᵉ furtherance of theyr purpose /
haue now determined them selfe to assay the secunde way / that
10 ys to wytte yᵗ forberynge to wryte so openly and dyrectely
agaynste all the fayth & the sacramentys as good crysten men
coulde not abyde the redyng / they wolde / wyth lyttell towchyng
of theyre other heresyes / make one boke specially agaynst yᵉ
church & loke how that wold proue. Whyche yf yt succede after
15 theyre appetytys that they myght wyth false crymes layd vnto
some / or wyth the very fawtis of some / brynge the hole churche
in hatered and haue the clergye dystroyed: then shuld they more
esely wynne theyre purpose that waye. For when the prechours
of the fayth and very gospell were dystroyed or farre owte of
20 credence wyth yᵉ people / then shulde they haue theyre awne
false gospellys preched / as ye may perceyue that thys man
meaneth where he sayth yᵗ then shall the gospell be preched.
And therfore thys ys the thynge whych thys man as yet leueth
owt agaynst them / that is to wytte the prechyng of the ryght
25 fayth and the sacramentys / whych thynge he rekeneth in the
clergye a more horryble carayn / then all the crymes wheryn he
hath bylyed them byfore. And therfore sayth he yᵗ he leueth yt
owte / leste he shulde seme to declare the one and only fawt of
the kyngis hyghnes. Whych one onely fawte he meaneth his
30 gracys moste famouse and moste gracyouse boke / that hys
hyghnes as a prynce of excellent erudycyon / vertue / and deuocyon toward yᵉ catholyke fayth of cryst / made of thassercyon of
the sacramentys agaynst yᵉ furyouse boke of Marthin Luther.
Thys godly dede done by hys hyghnes / wyth thacceptacyon of
35 hys godly well deserued tytle of defensoure of the fayth gyuen

---

16 some /] *1529¹*, some *1529² 1557;* hole] *1529¹ corr. err.,* *1529² 1557,* holy *1529¹*
27 byfore.] *1529¹*, byfore: *1529² 1557*   32–34 *Sidenote 1557:* Kinge Henries most
gracyouse booke against Luther

his grace by the see apostolyque / thys calleth thys beggers proctoure the kyngys one and onely fawt and ignorance of theyre
false fayth in estymacyon of these heretyques / whych this beggers proctour sayth that he wyll for the whyle hyde and couer
vnder hys cloke of sylence / tyll the kynge may by these enor- 5
mytyes wherewyth he bylyeth the churche in hys beggers byll
(whyche enormytyes he calleth smale enormyties in comparyson
of the prechyng of the catholyke fayth and the sacramentys) be
lerned. What lesson trow ye? None other surely / but that they
hope that as well hys hyghnes as hys peple / may by suche beg- 10
gers byllys be fyrste alured and brought in / to contemne / hate
and dystroye yᵉ church: and then therby lerne the tother lesson
whych he now leueth owte for the whyle / that ys to wytte to sette
at nought the catholyque fayth and all the blessyd sacramentys /
after the techyng of Luthers and Tyndallys gospell. And ther- 15
fore sayth he as we tolde you by[E₄v]for / that then shall the
gospell be preched.

And in the mene tyme yᵉ man vseth as he weneth hym self
toward yᵉ kyngys grace a very wyse fassyon of flatery / callynge
hym theyre best belouyd mynyster of ryghtuousnes: yet be they 20
not onely ronne away for fere of the ryghtuousnes of theyr best
belouyd mynister of ryghtuousnes / but also wold yt shuld seme
yᵗ his hyghnes were such a mynyster of ryghtuousnes / as eyther
set so lyttel by ryghtuousnes that he wold wyttyngly suffer / or els
had so lytyll insyght in ryghtuousnes that he coud not parceyue / 25
so great a mater and such an horryble carrayn of yuell commyttyd by the church / as were so heynouse / so houge and so great:
that in comparyson therof / the translatyng of hys kyngdome /
the ruyne of hys crown / the shypwrak of hys comen weale / the
dyspeplyng of hys realm / and bryngyng all hys land in to desola- 30
cyon and wyldernes: were but sleyght maters and small enormytees. And that hys hyghenes shuld towarde thys great horrible & intollerable myscheuouse demeanure of the church / be
ayding and assystent eyther of yuell mynde or of ygnoraunce /
tyll that by theyr beggarly byll beyng torned into the hatred & the 35
dystruccyon of yᵉ church / he myght thereby be illumynyd to
lerne and parceyue that the faythe whych hys grace had before

36 church /] 1529¹, church 1529² 1557

both lernyd & taughte / and wherof hym self ys the deffensor / ys
false and faynyd: and that the sacramentes be but mennys inuencyons / and that theruppon he shuld be contente to lern the
gospel of Luther and the testament of Tyndale. And thus ye may
5   se what the beggars proctour ment by his proper inuentyd rydle /
by whych as ye se vnder a fond face of flatery he vseth towarde
his prince and souerayn lord (whose maieste both by the law of
god & the dutye of hys allegyaunce he were hyghely bounden to
reuerence) and open playn dyspyte and contumely.
10   Now to thentent yᵗ ye may yet farther parceyue and se yᵗ they
by the dystruccyon of the clergy / meane the clere abolycyon of
Crystys fayth: yt may lyke you to conferre and compare to gether .ii. placis of hys beggars byll. In one place after that he hath
heped vp to gether all hys lyes agaynst the hole clergy / & therto
15   adioyned hys greuouse exclamacyon: Oh yᵉ greuouse shypwrak
of the comen weale: he sayth that in auncyent tyme before the
comyng of the clergy / there were but few pore people & yet they
dyd not beg / but there was gyuen them ynogh vnasked / because
at yᵗ tyme he sayth there was no clergy (whom he calleth alway
20   rauenouse woluys) to ask yt fro them: and thys sayth he appereth
in yᵉ boke of the actys of yᵉ apostles. In this place we let passe hys
threfold foly. One that he wold by that there were no beggars in
one place / proue therby that there were none in all yᵉ worlde
besyde. For as he for lakke of wyt and vnderstandyng mystaketh
25   the booke / he weneth that there were none that beggyd in
Hyerusalem. [F₁] Whych yf yt were trew / yet myghte there be
ynow in other placys. Another of his folyes is in that he alledgeth
a boke for hym that no thyng proueth hys purpose. For in all that
hole boke shall he neyther fynde that there was at that tyme few
30   pore peple / nor yᵗ pore peple at that tyme begged not. For of
trouthe there were pore people and beggers / ydle people / and
theues to / good plenty bothe then and all way byfore / synnes
almoste as longe as Noes flode / and yet peraduenture seuen
yere afore that to. And so were there in dede in Hyerusalem also

1 deffensor /] *1529²*, deffensor: *1529¹*, defensour, *1557*   2 faynyd:] *1529² 1557*,
faynyd / *1529¹*   30 For] *1529¹ 1557*, Far *1529²*   34 dede] *1529¹ corr. err.*, *1529²*
1557, dyd *1529¹*; Hyerusalem] Hierusalem *1529¹ 1557*, Heyrusalem *1529²*

amonge theym all / tyll crystendome came in / and yet remayned
then amonge such peple there as tourned not to the fayth of
Cryst. The thyrde foly ys / he layeth that boke for hym whyche in
dede preueth playne agaynst hym. For where he sayeth yt appereth there that the clergy was not then come / we can not in y^e   5
worlde deuyse of what people he speketh Paynyms / Iewes / or
crysten men. If he meane amonge Paynyms / hys folye and hys
falsehed both ys to euydent. For who knoweth not that amonge
the Paynyms they had alway theyre preestys / whose lyuynge was
well and plentuously prouyded for / as ye may perceyue not   10
onely by many other storyes / but also by many places in the
byble / and specyally in the .xlvii. chapyter of genesys. If he
speke of the Iewes / euery man woteth well that they had a clergy
thousandes of yeres bifore the boke that he alledgeth / & theyr
lyuynge farre more largely prouyded for / then eny parte of y^e   15
people bysyde / and that by goddys awne ordynaunce. Now yf he
speke of ye crysten people that was at that tyme in Hierusalem
where ye fayeth byganne / hys boke maketh sore agaynst hym.
For there was a clergy as sone as there was eny chrysten peple.
For the clergy byganne then. And that clergye had not a parte of   20
the crysten peples substaunce / but had yt all to gether / and dyd
dystrybute yt as they sawe nede / whych no man dowteth but that
the partyes shewed theym / or ellys in some nedys they must
nedys haue laked. So that here were many pore men yf they be
pore that haue naught left / & all they beggers / yf they be   25
beggers that be fayne to shew theyr nede and aske / and ye clergy
had all to gyther. And yet layeth this wyse man thys boke for hym /
beyng suche as yf he shulde haue sytten and studyed therfore /
he could not haue founden a boke that made more agaynst hym.
    But as we sayed byfore / we shall lette hys false foly passe / and   30
praye you to consyder what he wold haue you byleue. He sayeth
and wold ye shuld wene that there were few pore folke / and no
beggers no where byfore ye clergy of crystendom cam in / but
that all ye pouerte & beggary cam in to ye world wyth the cristen
clergy. Now knoweth euery man y^t the crysten clergy & the   35

---

2 then] *1529*[1] *corr. err.*, *1529*[2] *1557*, nowe *1529*[1]   20–21 *Sidenote 1557*: Acta. 4
21 and] *1529*[1] *1557*, anh *1529*[2]

crysten fayth / cam in to the crysten people to gether / so that in
effecte hys wordys way to thys y^t all pouerte and beggary came in
to the worlde wyth the crysten fayth. [F$_1$v]

Sette nowe to thys place the tother place of hys in the ende and
conclusyon of hys boke / where he sayth that after the clergy
spoylyd onys and cast out / then shall the gospell be preched /
and then shall we beggars haue ynough & more: lo lyke as in the
tone place he sheweth that all begary cam in wyth ye clergy y^t
brought in ye fayth / so sheweth he in the tother that there shuld
wyth the clergy all beggary go forth agayn / yf they were so clene
cast out that Cristys gospell beyng cast out wyth them / and the
fayth whych cam in wyth them / they myghte haue that gospell
prechyd as they say they shulde and as in dede they shuld whych
they call the gospell / that is to wit Luthers gospell and Tyndallys
testament / prechynge the dystruccyon of Crystys very fayth &
hys holy sacramentes / auauncyng & settyng forth all boldenes of
synne & wrechydnes / and vnder the false name of crysten fredome / spurryng forward the dyuylysh vnbrydeled appetyte of
lewd / sedycyouse and rebellyouse lyberte / that slew in one
somer as we shewed you before aboue .lx. M. of ye pore vplandysh Lutheranis in Almayn. And thys ys all that these heretykys
loke for as the frute of theyr sedycyouse bokys and beggars
byllys / trustyng by some such ways to be eased of theyr beggary /
whych they now sustayn beyng ronne oute of the realm for
heresy. For yf they might (as they fayn wold) haue ye clergy cast
out / and Crystys gospell cast of / and theyr owne gospell
preched: then hope they to fynde that word trew where he sayth:
then shall we haue ynough and more.

For of all that euer he hath sayd / he hath not almost sayd one
trew word saue thys. And surely this word wold after theyr gospell onys prechyd & receyuyd be founden ouer trew. For then
shuld the beggers / nat such beggars as he semeth to speke for
that be syk sore and lame / but such bold presumptuouse beggars as he ys in dede / hole & strong in body but weke & syk in
soule / y^t haue theyr bodys clene fro skabbys and theyr soulys

---

foule infect wyth vgly great pokkys & leprye: these beggars wold
hope to haue & except good men take good hede wolde not fayle
to haue ynough and a great deale more. For after that they
myght (the clergy furst dystroyd) bryng in onys after y^t the
prechyng of Luthers gospell and Tyndals testament / and myght   5
wyth theyr herysyes and fals fayth infect and corrupt the people / causying them to set the blyssyd sacramentes asyde / to set
holy days and fastyng days at nought / to contemne all good
workys / to gest & rayle agaynst holy vowed chastyte / to blaspheme the olde holy fathers and doctours of Cristys church: to   10
mok and scorne the blyssed sayntys and martyrs y^t dyed for
Crystys fayth / to reiect and refuse ye fayth that those holy mar-
tyrys lyued / and dyed for / and in the stede of ye true fayth of
cryst contynued thys .xv. C. yeres / to take nowe the false fayth of
a fond frere / of olde condemnyd and of new reforgyd wythyn so   15
few days [F₂] wyth contempte of god and all good men / and
obstynate rebellyouse mynde agaynst all lawes / rule and gouer-
naunce / wyth arrogante presumpcyon to medle wyth euery
mannys substaunce / wyth euery mannys lande / and euery mannys mater nothynge partaynynge to them: yt ys we say no dowte /   20
but that suche bolde presumptuouse beggers wyll / yf ye loke not
well to theyre handes / not fayle to haue as he wryteth ynough
and more to. For they shall gather to gyder at laste / and assem-
ble theym selfes in plumpes and in great rowtes / and from
askynge fall to the takynge of theyre almoyse theym selfe / and   25
vnder pretexte of reformacyon (berynge euery man that aught
hath / in hande that he hath to myche) shall assay to make newe
dyuysyon of euery mannys lande and substaunce: neuer
ceacynge yf ye suffer theym / tyll they make all beggers as they be
theym selfe / and at laste bryng all the realme to ruyne / and thys   30
not wythout bochery and fowle blody handys.

   And therfore this beggers proctour or rather the proctour of
hell / shuld haue concluded hys supplycacyon not vnder the
maner that he hath done / that after the clergye caste owte / than

---

5–6 *Sidenote 1557:* The effectes of Luthers gospel   8 nought] *1529² corr. err., 1529¹,*
yought 1529², ynought 1557   9 chastyte] *1529¹ 1557,* castyte *1529²*   17 lawes /]
lawes *1529,* lawes, *1557*   33 hell /] *1529¹,* hell *1529²,* hel, *1557*

shall the gospell be preched: then shall beggers and bawdys
decreace: then shall ydle folk and theuys be fewer: then shall the
realme encreace in rychesse and so forth. But he shuld haue
sayed: After that the clergye ys thus destroyed and caste owt /
5 then shall Luthers gospell come in / then shall Tyndallys testament be taken vp: Then shall false heresyes be preched: Then
shall yᵉ sacramentes be sett ate nought: Then shall fastyng &
prayour be neglected: Then shall holy sayntes be blasphemed:
Then shall almyghty god be dyspleased: Then shall he wyth-
10 drawe hys grace and lette all runne to ruyne: Then shall all
vertue be hadde in derysyon: Then shall all vyce reygne and
runne forth vnbrydeled: Then shall youth leue labour and
all occupacyon: Then shall folk waxe ydle and fall to vnthryftynesse: Then shall horys and theuys / beggers and bawdys en-
15 creace: Then shall vnthryftys flok togyder and swarme abowte
and eche bere hym bolde of other: Then shall all lawes be
laughed to scorne: Then shall the seruauntes set nought by
theyre maysters / and vnruly people rebelle agaynst theyr rulers:
Then wyll ryse vp ryflyng and robbery / murder and myscheyfe /
20 & playn insurreccyon / wherof what wold be thende or when you
shuld se yt / onely god knoweth. All whych myschyefe may yet be
wythstanden easely and wyth goddes grace so shall yt / yf ye
suffer no such bold beggers to seduce you wyth sedycyouse
byllys. But well perceyuyng that theyre malycyouse purpose ys to
25 brynge you to destruccyon / ye lyke good crysten people
auoydyng theyre false traynes and grynnes / geue none eare to
theyre heynowse heresyes / nor walke theyr sedycyouse wayes.
But perseueryng in your olde fayth of criste / and ob-
ser[F₂v]uyng hys lawes wyth good and godly warkis and obe-
30 dyence of your moste gracyouse kyng and gouernour / go forth
in goodnesse and vertue / whereby ye can not fayle to flowre and
prospere in ryches and worldely substaunce: whyche well employed wyth helpe of goddys grace abowte cherytable dedes to
the nedy / and the rather in remembraunce and relyefe of vs /

---

7 nought] *1557*, nough *1529*   7–9 *Sidenote 1557:* Behold the sequele of Luthers
gospell   9–10 wythdrawe] *1529*¹, *1529*² *corr. err.*, *1557*, wythdrade *1529*²
14 theuys /] *1529*¹, theuys *1529*², theues, *1557*   21 se] *1529*² *1557*, set *1529*¹

whose nede ys relyued by your charyte shewed for our sake to
your neyghboure / be able to purchace you myche pardon of the
bytter payn of thys paynfull place / and bryng you to yᵉ ioyefull
blesse / to whyche god hath wyth hys blessyd blode bought you
and wyth hys holy sacramentys enseygned you. And thus wyll we   5
leue the mannys malycyouse foly / tendyng to the dystruccyon
fyrst of the clergye and after of your selfe / wheryn hys madde
rekenynge hath constrayned vs to trouble you with meny tryfles
god wote full vnmete for vs: and nowe wyll we tourne vs to the
treatyng of that one poynte / whyche thoughe yt specyally per-   10
teyneth to our selfe / yet mych more specyally perteyneth yt vnto
you: yᵗ ys to wytte the impugnacyon of that vncherytable heresye
wherwyth he wolde make you to owre great harme and mych
more your awne / byleue that we nede none helpe and that there
were no purgatory.   15

The ende of the
fyrst boke

---

1 your] *1529*¹ *1557*, you *1529*²; charyte] *1529*¹ *corr. err.*, *1529*² *1557*, prayour *1529*¹
13 wherwyth] *1529*¹, wherwhyth *1529*², wherwith *1557*

The seconde boke.

W<small>HEN</small> we consyder in our self dere brothern & systern in
our sauyour Cryste / yᵉ present paynfull panges yᵗ we fele / &
therwyth ponder vppon the tother parte / yᵉ parylouse estate of
5 you yᵗ ar our frendys there lyuyng in yᵗ wrechyd world: wyt you
very surely that thys pestylent oppynyon begon agaynst purgatory / not so mych greuyth vs for yᵉ lak yᵗ we shuld fynde therby in
yᵉ relyefe of our own intollerable tormentes / as doth for the loue
yᵗ we bere you / the fere & heuynes yᵗ we take for yᵗ parell &
10 ieopardy yᵗ shuld euerlastyngly fall to youre owne sowlys therby.
Nor of all the heuy tydyngys yᵗ euer we hard here / was there
neuer none so sore smote vs to yᵉ hart / as to here the world wax
so faynt in the fayth of Criste / that eny man [F₃] shulde nede
nowe to proue purgatory to crysten men / or that any man could
15 be founden / whych wold in so great a thyng so fully and fastly
beleuyd for an vndowted artycle thys .xv. C. yere / begynne now
to staggar and stand in dowt / for the vnwyse wordys of eny such
malycyouse parson / as ys he yᵗ made the beggars supplicacyon.
For whose answere & full confutacyon yt semeth vs suffycient /
20 that ye may clere parceyue hys wordys to be of lytle weyght /
whyle ye se that the man hath neyther lernyng / wysdome nor
good entent: but all hys byll vtterly grounded vppon errour /
euyll wyll & vntrouth. And surely thys were to vs greate wonder
yf crysten men shulden nede eny other profe in thys world to
25 reproue such sedycyouse folk wythall / then the onely token of
the dyuels badge whych theym selfe bere euer about them: the
badge we mene of malyce and of a very dedely dyuelyshe hate.

    For where as oure sauyoure Cryste hathe so lefte loue & char-
yte for the badge of his crysten people / that he commaundeth
30 euery man so largely to loue other / that hys loue shold extend

---

10 euerlastyngly] *1529² corr. err., 1529¹ 1557,* euerlystyngly *1529²*   21 lernyng] *1529,*
learuing *1557*   27 *Sidenote 1557:* The badge of the sedicious   28–29 *Sidenote 1557:*
Math. 5

and strech vnto hys enmy / nor there ys no naturall man nether
Paynym / Iew / Turk nor Saracene / but he wyll rather spare his
foo than hurt his frende: thys kynde of folk ys so farre fallen not
onely from all crysten charyte but also from all humanite and
felyng of eny good affeccyon naturall / and so chaungede into a   5
wylde fyerce cruell appetyte more than brutysh and bestyall /
that they furste wythout grounde or cause take theyre frendys
for theyre foes / hatynge the churche dedely because yt wylleth
theyr weale and laboureth to amend them: and after to do the
chirch hurt whom they take for theyr enmyes / they labour to do 10
vs mich more hurt whom they call styll for theyr frendys. For
they to get pulled from the clergy the frayle commodytees of a
lytle worldy lyuyng / labour to haue vs theyr fathers / theyr
mothers / theyr frendes and all theyr kynne left lyeng in the fyre
here helplesse & forgotten / they lytle force how long. And in   15
thys they shew theyr affeccyon mych more vnnaturall &
abomynable / than he y^t wold wyth his swerd thrust his frend
thorow the hole body to the hard haft / to gyue hys enmy behynd
hym a lytle pryk with the poynt. Thys ways of theyrs were very
noght & detestable / although they truly ment in dede / as mych   20
good as they falsly pretend. For where as they cloke theyr cruell
purpose & intent / vnder colour of a gret zele toward ye comen
welth / which they lay to be sore empayryd by gret pomp &
inordynate lyuyng vsed in ye church: we be so farre fro the
mynde of defending eny such spyrytuall vyce / carnall vnclen-   25
nes / or worldly pomp & vanyte vsed in ye clergy / y^t we wold to
god yt were mych lesse than yt is / not in them only but also in y^e
temporalte. And there is none of nether sort but yf he were here
with vs but one half houre / he wold set lytle by all such worldly
vanitees all his life after / & lytle wold he force or rek whether he 30
ware sylk or sak cloth. [F$_3$v]

    But surely thys man yf he ment well: the fautys of yuell folk he
wold lay to them self / & not vnto y^e hole clergy. He wold also
labour for amendment & betteryng / not for dystruccyon &

---

5 affeccyon] 1529^1 1557, effeccyon 1529^2 9 to do] 1529^1 corr. err., 1529^2 1557, to
1529^1 14 the] 1557, thy 1529 23 they] 1529^2 1557, the 1529^1 24 lyuyng]
1529^1 1557, lynyng 1529^2

vndoyng fynally. He wold hold hym self wythyn hys boundes /
onely deuysyng agaynst mennys vyces / & not start owt therwith
in to playn & open heresyes. But surely so hath yt euer hetherto
prouyd / that neuer was there any that shewed hym self an enmy
to the church / but though he couered it neuer so close for the
whyle / yet at the last alway he prouyd hym self in some parte of
hys workes so very an enmy to the catholyk faythe of Cryste / that
men myght well parceyue that hys malyce towarde the clergy
grew furst & sprang of infydelyte & lak of ryghte belyefe. And of
thys poynt was there neuer a clerer ensample than thys beggars
proctour: whych was so farforth farsed / stuffed & swollen with
such venamouse heresys / that albe yt he longed sore to kepe
them in for the season / and onely to rayle agaynst the clergy &
hyde hys enmyouse intent toward the fayth: yet was he not able
to conteyn and hold / but was fayn for brastyng to puffe out one
blast of his poysonyd sect agaynst vs sely sowlys: yᵉ goodnes of
god dryuyng hym to yᵉ dysclosyng and dyscoueryng of hys malycyouse heresy / to thentent ye shuld therby parceyue out of
what vngracyouse ground hys enmyte sprang that he bare
agaynste the churche. Whyche thyngys ones parceyuyd and consyderyd: muste nedys mynyshe and byreue hym hys credence
among all such as ar not affeccyonate toward hys errours and
infect and venomed wyth hys mortall heresyes / and of suche
folk we trust he shall fynde very few.

For surely not onely among crysten peple and Iewys / of
whome the tone hath / the tother hath had / the perceyuyng and
lyght of fayth / but also amonge the very myscreaunt and
ydolaters / Turkys / Saracens / and Paynyms / excepte onely
suche as haue so farre fallen from the nature of man in to a
brutyshe bestely persuasyon as to byleue yᵗ soule & body dye
both at onys: ellys hath allwaye yᵉ remanaunt comenly thought &
byleued / yᵗ after the bodyes dede and deceaced / the soulys of
such as were neyther dedely dampned wreches for euer / nor on
the tother syde / so good but that theyre offences done in this

5–7 Sidenote 1557: Enmitie to yᵉ church springeth of infidelitie   13 agaynst] 1529¹
1557, aganst 1529²   28 ydolaters /] ydolaters 1529, idolaters, 1557   30–32 Sidenote
1557: The painims belieued that there was a purgatorye

world hath deserued more punyshement then they had suffred
and sustayned there / were punyshed and pourged by payn after
ye deth ere euer they were admytted vnto theyre welth and reste.

Thys fayth hath allwey not onely faythfull peple had: but also
as we say very myscreauntes and ydolaters haue euer had a
certayne opynyon and persuasyon of y^e same: whyther that of
the fyrste lyght and reuelacyon gyuen of suche thyngys to our
formar fathers / there hath allway remayned a glymerynge that
hath gone forth fro man to man / fro one generacyon to a nother / and so contynued and kepte a[F_4]monge all peple: or ellys
that nature and reason haue tought men euery where to perceyue yt. For surely that they haue such bylefe not onely by such
as haue bene trauayled in many cuntrees among sondry sectys /
but also by y^e olde and auncyent wryters that haue bene among
theym: we maye well & euydentely perceyue. And in good fayth
yf neuer had there bene reuelacyon gyuen therof / nor other
lyght then reason: yet presupposed the immortalyte of mannys
soule whych no resonable man dystrusted / and therto agreed
the ryghtuousenes of god & hys goodnes whyche scant the deuyll
hym selfe denyeth / purgatory must nedes appere: For syth that
god of hys ryghtuousenesse wyll not leue synne vnpunyshed /
nor hys goodnes wyll perpetually punysh the fawt after ye mannys conuersyon: yt foloweth that ye punyshement shall be temporall. And now syth the man often dyeth byfore suche
punyshement had / eyther at goddys hand by some afflyccyon
sent hym or at hys awne by due penaunce done / whych ye moste
parte of people wantonely doth forslouth: a very chylde almost
may se the consequent y^t the punyshement at ye deth remaynyng
due & vndone / ys to be endured & sustayned after. Whych / syth
hys maiestye ys so excellent whom we haue offended / can not of
ryght & iustyce be but heuy and sore.

Now yf they wolde peraduenture as in magnyfyenge of
goddys hygh goodnes saye / that after a mannys conuersyon
onys to god agayn / not onely all hys synne ys forgyuen but all the

5

10

15

20

25

30

11–12 perceyue yt. For surely that they haue such bylefe not] *1529²*, *1529¹ corr. err.*,
1557, perceyue yt that they haue such bylefe. For surely not *1529¹*   20–22 *Sidenote*
1557: The probacion of purgatorye   23 y^e]*1529¹*, y^t *1529²*, the *1557*

hole payn also / or that they wyll vnder colour of enhauncing the
merite and goodnes of Crystes passyon tell vs y^t hys payn suffred
for vs / standeth in stede of all our payn & penaunce / so that
neyther purgatory can haue place nor eny penaunce nede to be
5   done by our self for our own synne: these folk that so shall say /
shall vnder pretext of magnyfyeng hys marcy / not onely sore
mynyshe his vertewe of iustyce / but also mych hinder the opynyon and parsuasyon that men haue of hys goodnes. For albe yt y^t
god of his great marcy may forthwith forgyue some folke frely
10 theyr synne and payn both wythout preiudyce of hys ryghtuousnes / eyther of hys lyberall bounte or for some respect had vnto
the feruent sorowfull harte that fere and loue wyth helpe of
specyall grace haue brought into the penytente at the tyme of his
retorne to god / and also that the bytter passyon of our sauyour
15 besyde the remyssyon of the perpetuyte of our payn do also
lessen our purgatory and stand vs here in maruelouse hygh
stede: yet yf he shuld vse thys poynt for a generall rule / that at
euery conuersyon fro synne with purpose of amendement and
recourse to confessyon / he shall forthwyth fully forgyue wyth-
20 out the partyes payn or eny other recompence for the synnys
commyttyd saue onely Crystys passyon payd for them all: then
shuld he gyue gret occasyon of lyghtnes and bold corage to
synne.

    For when men were onys parsuaded that be theyr synnys neu-
25 er so [F$_4$v] sore / neuer so many / neuer so myscheuouse / neuer
so long contynued / yet thay shall neuer bere payn therfore: but
by theyr onely fayth and theyr baptysm wyth a short returne
agayn to god / shall haue all theyr synne & payn also clene
forgeuen and forgotten / nothyng els but onely to cry hym marcy
30 as one woman wold y^t tredyth on a nothers trayne: thys way
wolde as we sayd gyue the worlde great occasyon & corage not
onely to fall boldly to synne and wrechednes / but also carelesse
to contynew theryn / presumyng vppon that thyng that suche
heretykes haue parsuaded vnto some men all redy / that .iii.
35 or .iiii. wordys ere they dye shall suffycyently sarue them to
bringe them strayghte to heuen. Where as besydys the fere that

---

12 *Sidenote 1557:* No[te]   26 so long] *1529*^{2} *corr. err., 1529*^{1} *1557,* long so *1529*^{2}

they shulde haue lest they shall lak at last the grace to turne at
all / and so for faut of those .iii. or .iiii. wordys fall to the fyre of
hell: yf they beleue therwyth the thyng y^t trewth is bysyde / that
ys to wyt that though they happe to haue the grace to repent & be
forgeuen the synne & so to be delyueryd of the endlesse payn of   5
hell / yet they shall not so frely be deliuered of purgatory / but
that besyde the generall relyefe of Crystys hole passyon extended vnto euery man not after the valure therof but after the
stynt and rate appoyntyd by goddis wysdom / great and long
payn abydyth them here amonge vs / wherof theyre wyllyngly   10
taken penaunce in the world / & afflyccyon there put vnto them
by god / & there pacyently borne and suffred wyth other good
dedys there in theyr lyfe done by theym / & fynally the merytes
and preyours of other good folkys for them / may mynyshe and
abbredge the payne / whyche wyll ellys hold them here wyth vs in   15
fyre and turmentys intollerable onely god knowyth how long:
thys thyng we say as yt ys trew in dede / so yf the world well &
fyrmely for a sure trewth beleue yt / can not fayle to be to many
folke a good brydle and a sharpe bytte to refrayne theym from
synne. And on ye tother syde ye contrary belyefe wolde sende   20
many folke forward to synne / & therby in stede of purgatory in
to euerlastynge payne.

  And therfore ys thys place of our temporall payne of purgatory not onely consonaunt vnto hys ryghtuouse iustyce / but also
the thyng that hyghly declareth hys greate mercy and goodnes /   25
not onely for that the payn therof / houge and sore as yt ys / ys yet
lesse then owr synne deserueth: but also moste especyally in that
by the fere of payn to be suffred and susteyned here / hys goodnes refrayneth men from the boldenes of synne and neclygence
of penaunce / & therby kepeth and preserueth theym from   30
payne euerlastynge: where as the lyght forgeuenes of all to gether / wold geue occasyon by boldenes of synne and presumpsyon
of easy remyssyon / myche people to runne downe hedlynge
thyther. And therfore were as we sayed that way very far con-

---

7 hole] _1529²_, holy _1529¹_, whole _1557_   13–15 _Sidenote 1557:_ Good folkes prayers
abbredge ye payn of purgatorye   26 therof / houge and sore as yt ys / ys] therof hough
and sore as yt / ys _1529¹_, therof hough and sore ys yt / is _1529²_, thereof though great &
sore it is, is _1557_; houge] _1529¹ corr. err._, hough _1529_

trary not onely to goddys iustyce & ryghtuousenes / but also to
hys goodnesse & mercy. Wheruppon as we sayd byfore it must
nedes folow [G₁] that syth the payne ys allway due to synne / and
is not allwaye clene forgeuen wythout conuenyent penaunce
5 done or other recompence made / nor payne ys not allwey done /
nor eny recompence made in the mannes lyfe / and yet the man
dyscharged of hell by hys conuersyon: all yᵉ payn yᵗ remayneth
muste nedys be sustayned here wyth vs in purgatory.

But nowe yf these heretyques as they be very selfe wylled and
10 wyllefull / wyll sette at nought the comen opynyon and beleyfe
and persuasyon of almoste all the world: and as they be very
vnresonable make lyttel force of reason and euer aske for scripture / as though they beleued holy scrypture / and yet when yt
maketh agaynst them / they then wyth false and fonde glosys of
15 theyre owne makynge / do but mok and shyfte ouer in suche a
tryflynge maner that yt may well appere they byleue not scrypture neyther: yet syth they make as they byleued scripture &
nothyng els / let vs therfore se whether that purgatory do not
appere opened and reueled vnto crysten people in holy scryp-
20 ture selfe.

And fyrste yt semeth very probable and lykely / that yᵉ good
kyng Ezechias for none other cause wepte at the warnyng of hys
deth geuen hym by the prophete / but onely for the fere of
purgatory. For albe yt that dyuers doctours alledge dyuers
25 causes of hys heuynes and lothenes at that tyme to depart and
dye: yet semeth there none so lykly as the cause that auncyent
doctours alledge / that ys to wyt yᵗ he was lothe to dye for the fere
of hys estate after hys deth / for as mych as he had offendyd god
by ouermych lykyng of hym self: wherwyth he wyst yᵗ god was
30 dysplesyd wyth hym & gaue hym warnyng by the prophete / that
he shuld lyue no lenger. Now consyderyd he so the weyght of hys
offence / yᵗ he thought and estemyd the onely losse of thys
present lyfe farre vnder the iust & condygne ponyshment therof / and therfore fell in gret drede of farre sorer ponyshment
35 after. But beyng as he was a good faythfull kyng / he coud not lak

8 sustayned] *1529*² *1557*, substayned *1529*¹   9–10 *Sidenote 1557:* Heretikes are self-
willed and wilfull   14 fonde] *1529*² *1557*, founde *1529*¹   19 reueled] *1529*² *1557*,
reuelled *1529*¹   21 *Sidenote 1557:* Esai. 38

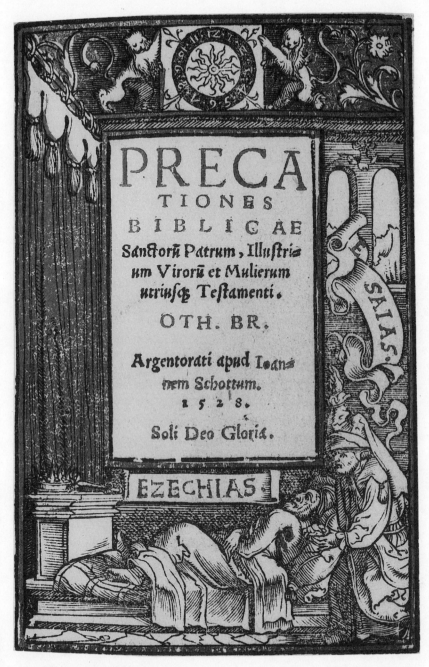

Title page, Otto Brunfels, *Precationes Biblicae*, Strasbourg, 1528 (enlarged)

sure hope thorow hys repentaunce of such forgyuenes / as shold
presarue hym from hell. But syth his time shuld be so short y^t he
shuld haue no laysour to do penance for hys faut: he therfore
fered y^t the remnaunte of hys ryghtuouse ponyshment shuld be
parformyd in purgatory. And therfore wept he tenderly & long- 5
yd to lyue lenger / that hys satysfaccyon done there in the world
in prayour & other good vertuouse dedes / might abolish & were
out all the payn y^t els were toward hym here among vs. To whych
hys feruent boone & desyre at the contemplacyon of his penitent
hart / our lord of his hygh pyte condyscended & grauntyd hym 10
the lengthyng of hys lyfe for .xv. yeres / makyng hym for his
farther cumfort sure therof by y^e shew of a manyfest myracle.
But wherto grauntid our lord y^t lenger lyfe / to be bestowed
vppon worldy delite and pleasure? Nay nay verely. But to thentent yt myght appere that it was of goddys great [G$_1$v] marcy 15
grauntyd for the redemyng of his purgatory by good workys for
hys satysfaccyon: he was promysed by the prophete not onely y^t
he shuld wythin .iii. days be recouered and hole / but also that he
shuld go in to the temple to pray. So that yt may therby appere
for what end and entent he longed so sore for a lenger lyfe. 20

Now yf the beggars proctour or Tyndale or Luther eyther /
lyst to say y^t in thys poynt we do but gesse at that good kynges
mynde / and therfore purgatory therby rather sumwhat resoned
than well & surely prouyd: therto may we well answer and say /
that the cyrcumstaunce of the mater consyderyd / wyth the ver- 25
tuouse holynes and connyng of such as so longe ago haue taken
the scrypture thus: y^t place alone is a farr better profe for purgatory / than euer eny of them coud hetherto lay agaynst yt yet.
For albeyt thys beggars proctour sayth y^t ryght wyse & connynge
men wyll say y^t there ys no purgatory at all / by which wyse men 30
he menyth Luther and Tyndall & him self: yet was there neuer
any of theym all that yet layed anye substancyall thynge eyther
reason or authorytye for theym / but onely geste and rayle / and
saye that purgatory ys a thyng of the popes awne makynge /
and that soulys do nothyng tyll domis day but lye styll and slepe. 35

1 forgyuenes] *1529*^{1}, forgeuenes *1557*, forgyneues *1529*^{2} 4 remnaunte] *1529*^{1}, re-
maunte *1529*^{2}, remenant *1557*   6 there] *1529*, here *1557*   worldy]*1529*, worldly
1557   18 .iii.] *1529*^{1} corr. err., *1529*^{2} *1557*, .iiii. *1529*^{1}

And thus tellyng such wyse talys for theyre owne parte / and
makyng mokkys and mowes at euery thyng that maketh agaynst
theyr foly for our parte: they go forth in theyre euyll wyll and ob-
stynacy / and with murmur & grudge of theyre owne consyence /
5 content theym selfe wyth ye onely feding of theyre malycyouse
myndis by the encreace of theyre faccyon / of such as fall in to
theyre felyshype rather of a lyght mynde and lewde pleasure to
take a parte / then of eny greate credence that they gyue vnto
theym or greately force whyche way they byleue. For surely yf
10 these folke were resonable and indyfferent as yt ys not well
possyble for them to be / after that they refuse onys to byleue y^e
catholyque church & in ye vnderstandyng of scripture lene onely
to theyre awne wyttys / but ellys as we say yf they could wyth an
equall & indyfferent mynd consyder and way what they here:
15 they shulde sone se theyre heresye reproued and purgatory
surely confermed / not onely by probable reason taken of the
scrypture as in ye place that we rehersed you of Ezechyas / but
also by playne and euydent textys.

For haue ye not the wordys of scrypture wryten in the boke of
20 the kyngys: Dominus deducit ad inferos et reducit: our lord
bryngeth folke downe in to hell and bryngeth theym thense
agayne? But they y^t be in that hell where the dampned sowles be:
they be neuer delyuered thense agayne. Wherfore yt appereth
well that they whom god delyuereth and bryngeth thense
25 agayn / be in that part of hell that ys callyd purgatory.

What say they to the wordys of the prophete zachary: Tu
quoque [G_2] in sanguine testamenti tui eduxisti vinctos tuos de
lacu in quo non erat aqua: Thou hast in the blode of thy testament brought out thy bounden prysoners owte of the pyt or lake
30 in whych there was no water? In that they whom the prophete
there speketh of were bounden / we may well perceyue that they
were in a pryson of punyshement. And in that he calleth theym
the prysoners of god: yt ys eth to perceyue that he meaneth not
eny that were taken and emprysoned by eny other than the

20–21 *Sidenote 1557:* 1. Reg. 2   22 that hell] 1529^2 1557, that 1529^1 27 *Sidenote*
1557: zacha. 9; sanguine] 1529^1 1557, saguine 1529^2 30 water?] 1529^1, water. 1529^2
1557

dampned spyrytys the very gaolers of god. And in that he sayth
that there ys in that lake no water: we may well perceyue that he
spake yt in descrypcyon of that drye pyt of fyre / where in there
ys no refreshyng: For as hote are we here as they are in hell. And
what hete ys in the pyt where there lakketh water: our sauyour   5
hym selfe declareth by the wordys of the rych gloton lyeng in
such a lake from whense at syght of pore Lazarus in Abrahams
bosom / he desyred heuely to haue hym sent vnto hym wyth one
droppe of water to refreshe hys tonge / that after all the delycates that yt had tasted in his lyfe / lay there then sore burnyng /   10
& neuer set half so mych by twenty tonne of wyne / as he set by
one pore drop of water. So that as we shewe you / these wordys of
ye prophete zachary. Thou haste brought owte thy bounden
presoners owte of the lake where in ys no water: do ryght well
appere to be spoken of these pore empresoned sowlys whom   15
cryst after hys bytter passyon by hys precyouse blode wherwyth
he consecrated hys church in hys newe testament / delyuered
owt of the lake of fyre wherin they lay bounden for theyre
synnys. But nowe ys there no man y^t dowteth whyther cryste
delyuered the dampned sowlis owt of hell or not. For in y^t hell ys   20
there no redempcyon / & in limbo patrum the sowlys were in
reste. Wherfore it appereth clerely that those presoners whom
he brought owte of theyre payne / he brought onely owte of
purgatory: And so se these heretyques purgatory clerly proued
by the playn wordys of thys holy prophete.   25

   Another place ys there also in the olde testament that putteth
purgatory quyte owt of questyon. For what ys playnner then the
places whych in the boke of the Machabees make mencyon / of
the deuowt remembraunce / prayoure / almoyse / & sacryfyce /
to be done for sowlys when the good and holy man Iudas Ma-   30
chabeus gathered money among the peple to by sacryfyce wythall to be offred vp for ye sowlys of theym that were dede in the
batayle. Doth not thys place of scrypture so openly declare the
nede that we sowlys haue in purgatorye / & the relyefe that we

---

7–8 *Sidenote 1557:* Luke. 16   10 yt] *1529,* he *1557*   14 where] *1529¹ corr. err., 1529²*
1557, were *1529¹*   26 putteth] *1529¹ 1557,* putteh *1529²*   30–31 *Sidenote 1557:*
2. Machab. 12

fynd by the prayour and suffragys of good peple vppon erthe /
that all the heretyques that barke so faste agaynst vs / can fynd
neyther glose nor colour to the contrary?

What shyfte fynde they here? surely a very shamelesse shyfte /
and are fayne to take theym to that takelynge that ys theyre shote
anker [G₂v] allway / when they fynde the storme so great that
they se theyr shyp goth all to wrekk. For first they vse to set some
false glose to the text that ys layed agaynst theym / and deny the
ryght sense.

But now yf the texte be so plaync that they can haue no suche
colour: then when they can haue no more holde but se that
theyre parte goth all to naught / they fall to a shamelesse boldnes
& let not to deny the scrypture and all / & say yᵉ holy scrypture
whych ys layd agaynste them ys none holy scrypture at all / as
Luther playth wyth the godly epystle of Crystys blyssed apostle
saynt Iamys. And euyn the same do those heretykes wyth the
authoryte of this holy boke of Machabees: they be not ashamed
to say that yt ys not scrypture. But vppon what grownd do they
deny yt for scrypture / because yt is not founden and accompted
for holy scrypture among yᵉ Iewys? They neyther do nor can
deny but that yt ys taken for holy scripture by the churche of
Cryste. For yf they wold denye that / both the hole chyrche
bereth wytnes agaynst them at this day / & it also appereth playnly by saynt Hyerome / saynt Austayn / & other old holy doctours / that the church so toke yt also in theyr days & before: then
wold we gladly wit of these new men these enmyes we mean of
ours / whyther the chyrch of crist be not of as great authoryte
and as mych to be beleuyd in the choyse & eleccyon of holy
scrypture as the Iewes. If they wyll say yes: then answere they
them self: for then ys the boke of the Machabees by yᵉ choyce of
the chyrch prouyd holy scrypture though the Iewes neuer accounted yt so. Now yf they will say no / and wyll contend that yt
can not be accountyd holy scrypture though the chyrch of Cryste

so take yt / but yf the Iewes so toke yt too: then go they nere to
put out saynt Iohans gospell out of scrypture too / for the Iewes
neuer toke yt for none. And surely yf they admyt for scripture
that book that the Iewes admytted / & deny that boke to be
scrypture whych the church of Cryste receyueth for scrypture: 5
then do they say that the spyryte of god was more effectually
present and assystent vnto the synagoge of the Iewys in the law
of hys prophete Moyses / then vnto the church of hys awne onely
bygoten sonne in the law of crystys gospell.

If they consyder well the bokes of ye Machabeys / they shall   10
fynd suche thynge therin as maye geue theym good occasyon to
put lyttell dowte but that yt shuld be of great and vndenyable
authoryte. For they shall fynde there that the greate good and
godly valyaunt capytayne of goddys people dyd instytute and
ordayne the great feste of the dedycacyon of the temple of   15
Hierusalem called festum enceniorum of the annuall instytucyon / of whyche feste we rede no where ellys but in y^e boke of
the Machabeys. And yet fynde we that feste euer after contynued and had in honour vntyll crystes awne dayes / and our
sauyour hym selfe went to the celebracyon of that same feste / as 20
appe[G_3]reth in the gospell of saynt Iohan. So that yt may well
appere that y^e bokys of that noble hystory wherof remeaneth so
noble a monument and remembraunce / contynually kepte and
reserued so longe after / and honowred by crystes awne precyouse person and testyfyed by hys holy Euangelyste in the boke 25
of hys holy gospell: can not be but vndowted trewth and of
dyuyne authoryte.

And surely yf they deny ye boke of the Machabeys for holy
scripture bycause the Iewys accompte yt not for suche: then shall
they by the same reason refuse the authoryte of the boke of   30
Sapyence / and proue theym selfe insypyentys. And lykewyse yf

---

1 take] *1557*, take take *1529*; so toke] *1529*^2 *1557*, to take *1529*^1, so take *1529*^1 *corr.*
err.   12 vndenyable] *1529*^2 *1557*, vndeuyable *1529*^1   15–16 *Sidenote 1557:* The
feaste of the dedicacion   21 *Sidenote 1557:* Iohn. 10   24 crystes] *1529*^2, cryste
1529^1, Christes *1557*   27 authoryte.] anthoryte. *1529*^2, authoryte: *1529*^1, authoritie.
1557

they take all scrypture bysyde the newe testament to be of none
other force and authoryte then yt ys accomptyd in the rule and
canon of the Iewes: then shall the hole psalter of Dauyd the very
somme of clere and lyghtesome prophesyes / leese amonge
5   theym greate parte of his authoryte / syth yt ys not taken in lyke
force and strength among the Iewes as yt ys in Crystys church.

Fynally for the boke of the Machabees / syth the church of
Cryste accounteth yt for holy scrypture: there can no man dout
therof but he that wyll take awaye all credence and authoryte
10 from the hole scrypture of god the very gospellys and all. For yf
these heretykys deny for holy scrypture eny boke that the
chyrche of Cryste accounteth for holy scrypture: then deny they
one of the grettyst foundacyons of all crysten fayth / and the
thyng whych theyr master Marten Luther hym self hath all redy
15 confessed for trew. For he affyrmyth hym selfe that god hath
gyuen vnto the church of Cryste that gyfte / that the church
cannot fayle surely and certeynly to discerne betwene the wordys
of god and the wordys of men: & y^t yt cannot be desceyuyd in the
choyse of holy scrypture and reiectyng of the contrary: so far-
20 forth that he confessyth as he nedys must of necessyte / that the
noble doctour and gloryouse confessour saynt Austeyne sayd
very well / when he sayd that he shuld not haue beleuyd the
gospell but for ye authorite of ye church. For he had not knowen
whych had bene the very boke of the gospels and whych not
25 among so many as were wryten / but by the authoryte of the
church / whom the spyryte of god assysted as yt euer dothe and
euer shall / in the choyse and receyuyng of holy scripture and
reieccyon of the counterfete and false. Wherby yt apperyth
clerely not onely by that holy doctour saynt Austeyn / but also by
30 the confessyon of ye archeheretyke Luther hym selfe / that the
church cannot be dysseyuyd in the choyce of holy scrypture and
reieccyon of the contrary: so farforthe y^t yt neyther can receyue
as holy scrypture eny booke that ys none / nor reiect for other

---

3 the hole] *1529*^{2}, that holy *1529*^{1}, the whole *1557*   6 strength] *1529*^{1} *1557*, strenght
1529^2 7 Fynally] *1529*^{1}, Fynall *1529*^{2} *1557*   12 accounteth] *1529*^{1} *1557*, ac-
counteh *1529*^{2} 13 grettyst] *1529* greatest *1557*   16–18 *Sidenote 1557:* The
churche cannot fayl in the choyse of scripture   21 sayd] *1529*^{1} sayth *1529*^{2}
1557   30 y^e] *1529*^{2} *1557*, y^t *1529*^{1}; archeheretyke *1529*, archereretike *1557*

then holy scrypture eny boke that is holy scrypture in dede. And
surely yf the churche myghte so be deceyuyd in the choyse of
holy scripture / that they myghte take & approue for holy scrypture [G₃v] eny boke that were none: then stode all crystendome
in dout and vnsurety / whether saynt Iohans gospell were holy   5
scripture or not / and so forth of all the new testament.

And therfore syth as we haue shewed you by the heretykes
owne confessyons / the church of Cryste cannot be deceyuyd in
the choyse & eleccyon of holye scrypture / by whyche theyre
confessyon they muste nedys abyde and not flyt therfro / as they   10
dayly do chaunge and vary from theyr owne wordes in many
other thyngis / except that they wyll in the fallyng from that
poynte refuse the strengthe and authoryte of the newe testament of cryste: and syth as your selfe well perceyueth also the
churche of cryste receyueth and taketh and (as ye se by saynt   15
Hyerome and other olde holy doctours thys thowsande yere)
hath approued and fermely byleued the holy boke of the Machabeys to be one of the volumes of holy scrypture: and then in that
boke ye se so manyfestely purgatory proued / that none heretyque as shamelesse as they be can yet for shame say the contrary /   20
but are by the playn and open wordys of that holy boke so dreu-
en vp to yᵉ hard wall / that they can no ferther but are fayne to
say that the boke ys no parte of scrypture / whyche shyfte they
must nedys forsake agayne or ellys reuoke theyre awne wordys
and therwyth also thauthoryte of all crystes gospell: there shall yf   25
eyther reason or shame can holde / neuer nede eny ferther
thyng for the profe of purgatory to stoppe yᵉ mowthys of all the
heretyques that are or shalbe to the worldys ende.

But yet syth they be so shamelesse and vnresonable that the
thyng whyche they can in no wyse defende / they can not yet   30
fynde in theyre prowde harte to gyue ouer / but when yt ys
prouyd by dyuers playne textis of yᵉ olde testament / then
hauyng no probable reason for theyre parte they neuer the more
gyue place to trewth / but stykke to theyre obstynate nay: let vs se

---

13 strengthe] *1529*¹ *1557*, strenghte *1529*²   17 holy] *1529*² *1557*, godly *1529*¹
29 shamelesse] shameles *1557*, hamelesse *1529*; vnresonable] *1529*¹ *1557*, vnresonabse
*1529*²

whyther our purpose be not preued by good and substancyall
authoryte in the newe testament also.

   And fyrste let vs consyder the wordys of the blessyd apostle
and euangelyst saynt Iohan / where he sayth: Est peccatum
5 vsque ad mortem / non dico vt pro eo roget quis. There ys sayth
he some synne that ys vnto the deth / I bydde not that eny man
shall praye for that. Thys synne as the interpreters agre / ys
vnderstanden of desperacyon and impenytens: as though saynt
Iohan wolde say / y\(^t\) who so depart owt of thys world impenitent
10 or in dispayre / eny prayour after made can neuer stande hym in
stede. Then appereth yt clerely that saynt Iohan meaneth that
there be other whyche dye not in such case for whom he wolde
men shuld pray / bycause y\(^t\) prayour to suche sowlys may be
profytable. But that profyte can no man take neyther beyng in
15 heuen where yt nedeth not / nor beyng in hell where yt boteth
not. Wherfore it appereth plaine y\(^t\) such prayour helpeth onely
for purgatory: whych [G\(_4\)] they muste therfore nedys graunte /
excepte they deny saynt Iohan.

   What saye they to the wordys of saynte Iohan in the fyfte
20 chapyter of the Apocalyps: I haue harde saythe he euery creature that ys in heuen and vppon the yerth and vnder the yerthe
and that be in the see and all thyngys that be in them / all these
haue I harde say: benedyccyon and honoure and glorye and
power for euer / be to hym that ys syttyng in the trone / and vnto
25 the lamb.

   Now wotteth euery man well / that in hell among damnyd
soulys ys there none that gyueth glory to Criste for the redempcyon of man. For they for anger that by theyr owne defaut they
haue lost theyr parte therof / and cannot for prowd hart take
30 theyr faut to them self / fall to blasphemy as the deuyll doth hym
self / and impute theyr synne to the faut of goddys grace / and
theyr damnacyon to the blame of hys creacyon. So that the
prayse and glory that ys geuen by creatures in hell vnto the lamb
for mannys redempcyon / ys onely by the sowlys in purgatory /
35 that be and shalbe partyners of that redempcyon: as the creaturys walkyng vppon yerth or saylynge in the se / that gyue the

4 Sidenote 1557: 1. Iohn. 5   36 yerth or] 1529\(^1\), yerth 1529\(^2\), earth 1557

honour to Cryste for mannys redempcyon / be onely the crysten
people whyche loke and hope to be parteners therof / and not
infydels that beleue yt not. But the blessyd creaturis in heuen
geue honour to Criste for mannys redempcyon / for that ioy and
pleasure that theyre charyte taketh in the socyete and felyshyp of
saued soules. And in thys place yt ys a worlde to se the foly of
some heretykys / what euasyon they seke to voyd from thys place
of scrypture. They sey that yt ys no more to be vnderstanden by
sowlys here in purgatory nor crysten men lyuyng vppon erth /
then by fyshes in the see and the dyuell and damnyd soulys in
hell: because the text sayth that euery creature in the se and in
hell spake that laud and honour to the lamb. But by this wyse way
myght they preue / that when ye pray for all crysten sowlys / ye
mean to pray for our Ladyes soule and for Iudas too: and that
our sauyour when he sent hys apostles and bad them preche his
gospell to euery creature / thay may bere you in hand that he bad
them preche to oxen and keene and theyre caluys to / because all
they be creaturis. But as they were sente to none other creature /
then suche as he ment of thoughe he spake of all / nor ye meane
to pray for no soulys but such as haue nede and may haue help
though ye speke of all: so though saynt Iohan spake of euery
creature in hell geuyng honour to Cryste for mannys redempcyon / yet ment he but such as be in that hell in whych they
reioyce therin and shalbe parteners therof / whych be onely we
in purgatorye / and not the dyuels and damnyd soulys yᵗ blaspheme hym though theyr iust ponishmente redownd agaynst
theyr wyll to the glory of goddys ryghtuousnes.

   If all thys wyll not satysfye theym / wyll ye se yet a nother clere
[G₄v] place and suche as none heretyque can auoyde? Doth not
the blessyd apostle saynt Peter as appereth in yᵉ secund chapiter
of yᵉ apostles actes / say of our sauyour cryste in this wyse: Quem
deus suscitavit solutis doloribus inferni: In these wordes he
sheweth that paynys of hell were losed. But these paynys were
neyther paynys of that hell in whych the dampned sowlys be
payned / whych nether were losed then nor neuer be losed / but

be to hym that ys syttyng in the trone/and Into the lamb.

¶Now wotteth euery man well/that in hell among damnyd soulys ys there none that gyueth glory to Cryste for the redempcyon of māī, for they for anger that by theyr owne defaut they haue lost theyr pte therof/and cannot for prowd hart take theyr faut to them self: fall to blasphemy as the deuyll doth hym self/and impute theyr synne to the faut of goddys grace/and theyr damnacyon to the blame of hys creacyon. So that the prayse and glory that ys geuen by creatures in hell Into the lamb for mannys redempcyon/ys onely by the soulys in purgatory/that be and shalbe partyners of that redempcyon: as the creaturys waskyng vppon erth or saylyng in þ se/that gyue þ honour to Cryste for mannys redempcyon/be onely the crysten people whyche loke and hope to be partyners therof/and not infydels that beleue yt not. But þ blessyd creaturys in heuen geue honour to Cryste for mānys redempcion/for that ioy and pleasure that theyre cheryte taketh in the socyete and felyshyp of saued soules. And in thys place yt ys a world to se þ foly of some heretykys/what euasion they seke to voyd from thys place of scrypture. They say that yt ys no more to be vnderstanden by soulys here in purgatory nor cristen men lyuyng vppd erth/then by fysshes in the see ɫ the dyuell and damnyd soulys in hell: Because the text sayth that euery creature in the se and in hell spake þ laud ɫ honour to the lamb. But by thys wyse way myght they preue/that when ye pray for all crysten soulys/ye mean to pray for our Ladyes soule and for Judas too: and that our sauyour whē he sent hys apostlys and bad them preche hys gospell to euery creature/they may bere you in hand that he bad them preche to oxen and kene and theyr calues too/Because all they be creaturys. But as they were sente to none other creature/thē such as be mente of thoughe he spake of all / nor ye meane to pray for no soulys but such as haue nede ɫ may haue help though ye speke of all: so though saynt Jhān spake of euery creature in hell geuyng honour to Cryste for mannys redempcyon / yet ment he but such as be in þ hell in whych they reioyce therin ɫ shalbe partyners therof/whych be onely we in purgatyre/ɫ not þ dyuels ɫ dampned soulys that blaspheme hym though theyr iust ponyshmenie ys so wnd agaynst theyr wyll to the glory of goddys ryghtuousnes.

¶If all thys wyll not satysfye theym/wyll ye se yet another clere place and suche as none heretyque can auorde. Doth not the blessyd apostle saynt Peter as appereth in þ secund boke of the apostles acꞇ/say of our sauyour cryste in thys wyse: Que deus suscitauit solutie doloribus inferni: In these wordꝭ he sheweth that paynys of hell were losed. But these paynys were neyther paynys of that hell in whych the dāpned soulys be payned / whych nether were losed then

not

noz neuer be losed/but be and shalbe as oure sauyour sayth hym selfe
euerlastyng: noz these paynys þ were than losed were not þ paynys
in lymbo patrum/for there were none to be losed/for the good soulys
were there as our sauyour sheweth hym selfe in quyete cumforte and
reste. And so appereth yt euydently/that the paynys of hell that were
losed/were onely the paynys of purgatorp whych ys also called hell
by occasyon of the latyn word and the greke worde both . for in these
tongys (for as mych as byfore the resurreccyon of our sauyour cryst
there was neuer none þ ascended vp in to heuen) there was no peple
that otherwyse spake of soulys/then that they were gone down
byneth in to the lowe place. And therfore in the wordys of the comen
crede ys yt sayed of our sauyour cryste after hys passyon: descendit
ad inferna: that ys to say he descended downe byneth in to the lowe
placys. In stede of whyche low placys the englyshe tonge hath euer
vsed thys worde hell. And certayne ys yt and very sure/that cryste
descended not in to all these low placys/nor in to euery place of hell/
but onely in to lymbus patrum and purgatorp. Whych two placys by=
cause they be partys of habytacyons of soulys byneth (all whych ha
bytacyons byneth haue in englyshe bene allway called hell) therfore
are these two placys amonge other taken and comprehended vnder þ
name of hell. Whych word hell nothynge ellys sygnyfyeth vnto vs
in hys generall sygnyfycacyon / but the habytacyons of soulys byneth
or vnder vs in the low placys vnder þ ground. Albe yt bycause lymbus
patrum and purgatorp be called in englyshe also by theyre specyall
namys besyde: therfore ys moste comenly thys word hell restrayned
to the specyall sygnyfycacyon of that low place byneth in whych the
dampned soulys be punysshed. Thys mych haue we shewed you of thys
word hell/bycause we wold not that the comen takyng therof mygat
bryng you in to eny errour. So that by thys place ye se preued by the
playne wordys of saynt Peter/that cryste at hys resurreccyon dyde
lese and vnbynd paynys in hell/whych as we haue shewed you coud
be no where there but in purgatorp. For in the specyall hell of damned
soulys þ paynys were not losed. And in lymbus patrum was no paynys
to be losyd. And therfore except they denye saynt Peter/they cannot
deny purgatorp.

And yet yf they deny saynt Peter: we shall then alledge the saynt
Poule/whom they be best content to here of/bycause that of the dyf=
fyculte of hys wrytyng/they cach sumtyme some mater of contencyon
for the defence of theyr false exposycyon. Thys blyssed apostle in hys
furst epystle to the Corynthyes the thyrd chapyter spekyng of oure
sauyoure Cryste the very foundacyon and the onely foundacyon of
all our fayth & saluacyon: sayth/If any man bylde vppon thys foun
cyon

be and shalbe as oure sauyour sayth hym self euerlastyng: nor
these paynys y^t were than losed were not ye paynys in limbo
patrum / for there were none to be losed / for the good soulys
were there as our sauyour sheweth hym selfe in quiete cumforte
5 and reste. And so appereth yt euydently / that the paynys of hell
that were losed / were onely the paynys of purgatory whych ys
also called hell by occasyon of the latyn word and the greke
worde both. For in these tongys (for as mych as byfore the resurreccyon of our sauyour cryst there was neuer none y^t ascended
10 vp in to heuen) there was no peple that ony otherwyse spake of
sowlys / then that they were gone down byneth in to the lowe
place. And therfore in the wordys of the comen crede ys yt sayed
of our sauyour cryste after hys passyon: descendit ad inferna:
that ys to say he descended downe byneth in to the lowe placys.
15 In stede of whyche low placys the englyshe tonge hath euer vsed
thys worde hell. And certayne ys yt and very sure / that cryste
descended not in to all these low placys / nor in to euery place of
hell / but onely in to lymbus patrum and purgatory. Whych two
placys because they be partys of habytacyons of sowlys byneth
20 (all whych habytacyons byneth haue in englyshe bene allway
called hell) therfore are these two placys amonge other taken
and comprehended vnder ye name of hell. Whych word hell
nothynge ellys sygnyfyeth vnto vs in hys generall sygnyfycacyon / but ye habytacyons of sowlys byneth or vnder vs in ye low
25 placys vnder ye ground. Albe yt bycause limbus patrum and
purgatory be called in englyshe also by theyre specyall namys
besyde: therfore ys moste comenly thys word hell restrayned to
the specyall sygnyfycacyon of that low place byneth in whych the
dampned soules be punyshed. Thys mych haue we shewed you
30 of this word hell / bycause we wold not that the comen takyng
therof myght bryng you in to eny errour. So that by thys place ye
se preued by the playne wordys of saynt Peter / that cryste at hys
resurreccyon dyd lose and vnbynd paynys in hell / whych as we
haue shewed you coud be no where there but in purgatory. For
35 in the speciall hell of damned sowlys y^e paynes were not losed.

Christ in Limbo, by Albrecht Dürer, from *Passio Domini Nostri*, Nürnberg, 1511, plate xi (reduced)

And in lymbus patrum was no paynes to be losyd. And therfore
except they denye saynt Peter / they cannot deny purgatory.

And yet yf they deny saynt Peter: we shall then alledge them
saynt Poule / whom they be best content to here of / because that
of the dyf[H₁]fyculte of his wrytyng / they cach sumtyme some   5
mater of contencyon for the deffence of theyr false exposycyon.
Thys blyssed apostle in his furst epystle to the Corynthyes the
thyrd chapyter spekynge of oure sauyoure Cryste the very foundacyon and the onely foundacyon of all our fayth & saluacyon:
sayth: If any man bylde vppon thys foundacyon gold / syluer /   10
precyouse stonys / wood / hay / or straw: euery mannys work
shalbe made open / for the day of our lorde shall declare yt / for
in the fyre yt shalbe shewed / & the fyre shall proue what maner
of thyng euery mannys work ys. If any mannys work yᵗ he hath
bylded theron do abyde: he shall haue a reward. If eny mannys   15
work burne: he shall suffer harme / but he shalbe safe / but yet as
by fyre. In these wordes yᵉ apostle shewith yᵗ lykewyse as sum
men abydyng vppon criste & hys very lyuely fayth / bylde vp
theruppon such good workes as are so good & so pure yᵗ they be
lyke fyne gold / fyne siluer / or such fyne precyous stonys / as   20
when they be caste in the fyre yt can fynde no fylth to fech out of
them / and therefore they remayn in the fyre safe and vnmynyshed: so ar there sum on the tother syde / whych thogh they do
not as many other do / wyth mortall synnys & lak of good workes /
wound theyr fayth vnto yᵉ deth & fall fro criste the fundacyon   25
that they must byld vppon: yet do they abydyng vppon yᵗ fundacyon / byld vp theruppon many such symple & frayle and cor-
ruptyble workes as can neuer enter heuen. And such be veniall
synnys / as ydle wordys / vayne & wanton myrth / & such other
thyngys lyke: whych be but lyke wood / hay / or straw. Whych   30
workes when the soule after hys departyng out of the world
bryngeth hether into purgatory: he cannot so gette thorow yt as
dothe the soule whose wurkes were wrought clene or fully purged by penaunce ere he dyed. For yᵗ soule in the fyre can fele no
harm / lyke as fyne gold can in yᵉ fyre nothyng lese of hys   35

14–15 *Sidenote 1557:* Euery mans worke shalbe proued by fire

weyght. But this soule y^t bryngeth wyth hym such frayle workys
eyther wrought by them self or insertyd paraduenture & myxyd
a myddys of sum good & vertuouse wurk / as for ensample sum
lak paraduenture suffyciente attencyon & hede taken by sum
5   sodayn waueryng of the mynde in tyme of prayoure / or some
surrepcyon & krepyng in of vayne glory & lykyng of theyr owne
prayse in theyr almes geuen or other good dede done / not
forthewith resysted & caste oute / but kepte and fedde vppon to
longe / and yet neyther so longe paraduenture nor so greate as
10 oure lorde wyll for that thought depryue hym the meryte and
reward of hys work: lo in such casys as the apostle sayth the day
of oure lorde whych ys to the hole world the day of the generall
iugement and to euery man particuler / the day of hys owne
iugement after hys dethe / shall shew hys work what maner
15 thynge yt ys: the fyre shall proue and declare. For here in purgatory lyke as the fyre can in the clene sowlys take none holde /
but they shalbe theryn wythoute any maner payne or gryefe: so
shall [H$_1$v] yt in the sowlys that are vnclensyd and haue theyr
wurkes imperfyte / vnclene and spottyd: hastely catch / holde
20 and kepe them fast & burne them wyth incessaunt payn: tyll the
fylthynes of theyre synne be clene purged & gone / & y^t shalbe in
sum soner in sum later / as theyr synnys or the spottes remaynyng therof be more easy or more hard to get owt. And y^t ys
the thyng y^t Poule sygnyfyeth by ye wood / haye / & strawe of
25 whych the tone ys a lyght flame sone endede / ye tother
smowdreth mych lenger / and the thyrd ys hoteste and endureth
lengest. But yet hath yt an ende / and so shall haue at lenght all
the paynys of theym y^t shalbe purged here. But what so euer
soule misshappe to dy in dedely synne and impenytent: syth he
30 ys therby fallen of for euer frome our sauyour cryste y^t was hys
fundacyon / & hath byelded vp wreched wurkys vppon your
goostely enemy the deuyll / wherwhyth he hath so thorowly
poysened hym self / that he can neuer be purged: the fyre shall
therfore lye burnyng vppon hym for euer / and his payne neuer
35 lessed / nor hys fylthy spottys neuer the more mynyshed.
    And for as mych as ye neuer can conceyue a very ryght imag-

19 imperfyte /] *1529*^{1}, imperfyte *1529*^{2} *1557*

ynacyon of these thyngys whych ye neuer felte / nor yt ys not possyble to fynde you eny example in the world very lyke vnto the paynys that sely sowlys fele when they be departed thense: we shall therfore put you in remembraunce of one kynde of payne / whych though yt be nothynge lyke for the quantyte of the mater / yet may yt somwhat be resembled by reason of the fassyon and maner. If there were enbarked many peple at onys to be by shyppe conuayed a long iourney by se of such as neuer cam theron byfore / and shuld happe all the way to haue the sees ryse hygh & sore wrought / and somtyme sone vppon a storme to lye long after walowyng at an anker: there shuld ye fynd dyuerse fassyons of folke. Some peraduenture (but of theym very fewe) so clene from all euyll humours and so well attempred of theym selfe / that they shalbe all that long vyage by see as lusty and as iocunde as yf they were on lande. But farre the most parte shall ye se sore syk / & yet in many sondry maner some more / some lesse / some lenger tyme dyseased / and some myche soner amended. And dyuers that a whyle had went they shulde haue dyed for payne / yet after one vomyte or twayne so clene rydde of theyre gryefe / that they neuer fele dyspleasure of yt after. And thys happeth after as the body ys more or lesse dysposed in yt selfe therto. But then shall ye somtyme se there some other whose body ys so incurably corrupted / that they shall walter & tolter / and wryng theyre handys / and gnash the teeth / and theyr eyen water / theyr hed ake / theyre body frete / theyr stomake wamble / and all theyre body shyuer for payne / and yet shall neuer vomete at all: or yf they vomyte / yet shall they vomyte styll and neuer fynde ease therof. Lo thus fareth yt as a small thyng may be resembled to a great [H$_2$] by the soulys deceaced and departed the world: that such as be clene and vnspotted can in the fyre feele no dysease at all / and on the tother syde such as come thense so dedely poysoned wyth synne / that theyre spottys bene indelyble and theyre fylthynes vn- pourgeable / lye fretynge and fryenge in the fyre for euer. And onely suche as neyther be fully clensed nor yet sore defyled but that the fyre may frete owt the spottys of theyre synne: of thys

---

6 by] *1529*[1] *1557*, be *1529*[2]   19 one] *1529*[1], ons *1529*[2], once *1557*

sorte onely be we y^t here lye in purgatory / whych these cruell
heretyques wolde make you byleue that we fele none harme at
all: wherof the blessyd apostle as we haue shewed you wryteth
vnto the Corynthyes the contrary.

5   Now yf they wolde bere you in hande that bycause some doctours do conster those wordys of thappostle in dyuerse other
sensys / as they do conster in dyuerse sensys allmost euery texte
in scrypture / sometyme after the letter / somtyme morall and
somtyme otherwyse / and all to the profyte & edyfyeng of the
10 herers: yf these herctyques wold therfore pretend that saynt
Poule in that place ment nothyng of purgatory / but the fyre that
shalbe sent byfore the dome / or worldely trybulacyon / or some
suche other thynge: ye shall well vnderstand that though hys
wordys may be veryfyed and well and profytably applyed vnto
15 suche thyngys also / yet letteth that nothyng these wordys to be
proprely by saynt Poule spoken of purgatory / no more then yt
letteth these wordes to be proprely spoken by cryste: Ego in
flagella paratus sum: & many an other verse in ye psalter also /
though ye same wordys may be well applyed & veryfyed of many
20 an other man offrynge hym selfe pacyently to the sufferaunce of
vniust punyshement. And therfore leste these heretyques shold
wyth eny such inuencyons bygyle you & make you beleue / y^t we
for the furtheraunce of oure awne cause expoune ye apostles
wordes wrong & so make theym seme to say for our parte: ye
25 shall vnderstande that those wordys haue bene expowned and
vnderstanden of purgatory thys thowsande yere and more by y^e
auncyent holy doctours of crystys churche as well grekys as
latyns. And among other the great clerke Orygene in mo placys
of hys wurkys then one / declareth playnely that the afore re-
30 membred wordes of the apostle / are spoken by ye paynis of
purgatory. The holy confessour and great pyller of cristys
church saynt Austayne / in dyuerse of hys godly and erudite
bokys / expowneth that place of saynt Poule to be clerely spoken
of purgatory. And ouer thys the blessyd Pope saynt Gregory in

---

3 wryteth] *1529*[1], wryteh *1529*[2], writeth *1557*   4 Corynthyes] *1529*, Corinthians
1557   17–18 *Sidenote 1557:* Psal. 37   23 expoune] *1529*, expounde *1557*
25 that] *om. 1557*; expowned] *1529*, expownded *1557*   33 expowneth] *1529*, expoundeth *1557*

the fourth boke of hys godly dyalogys / bereth wytnesse that the apostle in the place aforesayd wrote those wordys of purgatory. So that ye may playnely perceyue that thys exposycyon ys neyther our deuyce nor eny newe founden fantesy / but a very trewth well perceyued and wytnessed by great conyng men & 5 holy blessyd sayntes more then a thowsand yere ago. [H₂v]

Now yf these heretyques wyll be so madde to flyt in thys case from saynt Poule / and say they be bounden to beleue nothynge but onely yᵉ gospell: let vs then yet see ferther whyther we may not playnly proue you purgatory by yᵉ very wordys of the gospell 10 selfe. Doth not our blyssed sauyoure hym selfe say that there ys a certayne synne whych a man may so commyt agaynst the holy goste / yᵗ yt shall neuer be remyttyd nor forgyuen neyther in thys worlde nor in the world to cum? Now as for to dyspute what maner synne that shuld be / both yᵉ mater were very hard / and 15 also we shall here nothing nede to touche yt. But of one thing both ye & we may make vs very sure / that there ys nor can be eny synne commytted in the world so sore / so greuouse / nor so abomynable / but that yf a man wurk wyth goddys grace by contrycyon and heuynes of hart / wyth humble confessyon of 20 mouth & good endeuour of penaunce and satysfaccyon in dede / agaynst hys thought word and dede by whych god was offended / he shall obtayn of goddes goodnes remyssyon / forgyuenes / and pardon.

But yt may paraduenture so befall that by sum kinde of 25 vnkyndnes vsyd toward god extendyng to the blasphemy of his holy spiryte / the commytter of yᵗ synne may so farr offend / that he shall for hys desert & demeryte haue yᵉ grace of almyghty god so clerely wythdrawn from hym / that our lorde shall neuer offer hys grace after / nor neuer more call vppon hym. And then hys 30 grace onys clerely wythdrawen from a man: he can neuer be able to repent and returne agayn to god. For grace ys yᵉ lyght wherwyth men se yᵉ way to walk out of synne: and grace ys the staf wythout help wherof no man is able to ryse out of synne: accordyng to the wordys of holy wrytt spoken to man in the parson of 35

---

4 nor] *1529*[1] *1557*, no *1529*[2]   11 *Sidenote 1557:* Math. 12   18 *Sidenote 1557:* Note   32 *Sidenote 1557:* Grace

our lord god: Ex te perditio tua / ex me saluatio tua: Thy perdy-
cyon cummeth of thy self / but thy saluacyon cummeth of me by
yᵉ ayd and help of my grace. Which grace as we tell you beyng fro
sum man vtterly wythdrawn for sum maner vnkynd behauour
5   towarde god and blasphemy agaynst the holy goste / that synne
for lak of repentaunce whych can neuer cum where grace ys
clene gone / shall neuer be forgeuen in thys world nor in yᵉ
world to cum. And in such a maner kynde of vnkyndenes towarde god and blasphemy towarde the holy goste / fall also all
10 such wretchys as haue yᵉ grace of god euer callyng & knokkyng
vppon them for repentaunce all the days of theyr lyfe: and yet all
that notwythstandyng wyll not vse yt nor worke therewyth nor
turne to god: but wyllyngly wyll dye desperate and impenytente
wretchys.
15   Thys kynde of blasphemers of goddys goodnes & hys holy
spyryte / haue in yᵉ myserable passyng of theyr synfull soule out
of theyr sensuall bodys the grace of god so fully and so fynally
wythdrawen from theym for euer: that they be thereby fyxed
and confyrmed in an [H₃] vnchaungeable malyce / whyche eter-
20 nally dwellyng wyth theym / is the very specyall cause of theyre
euerlastynge turment. But in thys mater as we sayed we wade
owte of our purpose / sauynge that yt semed vs yet necessary /
syth our sauyour in the place that we speke of doth hym selfe
shew that there ys a certayne synne so towchynge the holy gooste
25 that it shall neuer be forgyuen neyther in thys world nor in the
world to come: yt semed as we say somewhat necessary to saye
sumwhat theryn / leste sum that rede yt myght conceyue a wrong
opynion and a false fere drawyng theym towarde dyspayre / that
yf they myshappenyd (whych our lorde forbede) to fall in to
30 blasphemy agaynst the holy gooste / they coud neuer after be
forgeuen how sore so euer they repentyd / or how hartely and
how bysely so euer they shuld pray therfore. In whyche thynge
syth we haue shewed you what we take for trouth: we shall leue

2 *Sidenote 1557:* Ose. 13   4 behauour] *1529*, behauiour *1557*   12 notwythstand-
ynge] *1529*¹, notwyhstandynge *1529*², notwithstandyng *1557*   18 wythdrawen] *1529*¹
1557, wytdrawen *1529*²   25 be] *1529*¹ *1557*, by *1529*²

that mater and shew you how those wordys of Cryste proue you
our pryncypall purpose / that ys to say that there ys a purgatory.
How be yt we shall scantly nede to shew you that: for the very
wordys be playn and euydent of them self. For when our lorde
sayth that the blasphemy agaynste the holy goste shall not be   5
forgeuen nether in thys world nor in the worlde to come / he
geueth vs clere knowlege that of other synnys sum shalbe forgeuen in thys world and sum in the world to come.

Now ar there in this world euery synne forgeuen in such as
shall be saued sowles / except such venyall synnys and such   10
temporall payn as yet due to the dedely synnys / rest and remayn
to be purged here in purgatory. For none other place ys there
then thys in the worlde to cum after mannys lyfe / in whych
eyther synne or payne dew to eny synne shalbe remitted. For in
to heuen shall neyther synne nor payn enter: and in hell shall   15
neuer none be releasyd. And therefore when Cryste by shewynge that sum kynde of synne shall not be remyttyd in the worlde
to cum: doth geue men knowlege that on the tother syde sum
synnys shall in the worlde to come be remytted and forgeuen.
And then syth no man douteth but that neyther in hell shall eny   20
synnys be forgeuen nor in heuen: very reson techyth that the
place in whych some synnys shalbe forgeuen after thys lyfe / can
be none other but purgatory.

There is as we suppose no crysten man lyuyng / but he wyll
thynk that eny one place of holye scrypture ys ynoughe to the   25
profe of eny trouthe. Now haue we prouyd you purgatory by the
playne textis of mo places than one two or thre. And yet shall we
geue you a nother so playn as we suppose & so euydent for the
profe of purgatory / as none heretyke shall fynde eny good
coloure of escape. For oure sauyoure Cryste sayeth as yt ys re-   30
hersyd in the .xii. chapyter of Mathew / that men shall yelde a
rekenyng of euery ydle word / and that shalbe after [H₃v] thys
present lyfe. Then woteth euery man that by that rekenyng ys

---

2 purgatory] _1529_¹ _1557_, purgarory _1529_²   5 blasphemy] _1529_¹, blaphemy _1529_²,
blasphemi _1557_; be] _1529_¹ _1557_, by _1529_²   18 on] _1529_² _1557_, vnto _1529_¹   21 be]
_1529_¹ _1557_, by _1529_²

vnderstanden a punyshement therfore: whyche shall not be in
hell / & mych lesse in heuen. And therfore can yt be no where
ellys but in purgatory.

    Lo thus may ye se purgatory clerely proued by the very scrip-
5 ture self / by the boke of the kynges / by yᵉ prophete zachary / by
the holy boke of yᵉ Machabees / by yᵉ wordes of saynt Iohan / by
thapostle saynt Peter / by the writyng of our sauyour cryst hym
self: so yᵗ we not a lytell meruayle eyther of the ignoraunce or
shamelesse boldnes of all suche as hauynge eny lernynge / dare
10 call theym selfe crysten men and yet deny purgatory. For yf they
haue lernynge & perceyue not these clere & open textes / we
meruayle of theyre ignoraunce. Wyth whych whyle they ioyne a
prowde pretence of lernynge / they fall in to the reprofe yᵗ saynt
Poule spake of the paynym phylosophers: dicentes se esse sa-
15 pientes / stulti facti sunt: whyle they called theym selfe wyse they
proued starke folys. Now yf they perceyue well these textys of
holy scrypture so playnely prouyng purgatory / and yet them
selfe stykke styf in the denyeng: we then meruayle mych more
that they dare for shame call theym selfe crysten men / and then
20 deny the thynge whych the blessyd apostles of cryste / yᵉ sacred
maiestye of our sauyour cryst hym selfe / in the holy scrypture /
in hys holy gospellys / so manefestely and so playnele affyrmeth.

    And yet many an other playne texte ys there in holy scryp-
ture / yᵗ as the olde holy doctours bere witnesse well proueth our
25 purpose for purgatory / whych we speke here nothyng of / syth
fewer textys then we haue all redy shewed you / both myght and
ought to suffyce you. For eny one playne texte of scrypture
suffyseth for the profe of eny trouth / excepte eny man be of the
mynde / that he wyll haue god tell hys tale twyse ere he byleue
30 hym.

    Now yf these heretyques fall to theyr accustumed froward-
nesse / and as they be wont to do wyll rather deny that the
swanne ys whyte and the crow blakke / then agre that eny texte in
holy scrypture hath eny other sense then theym selfe lyste to say /
35 and wyll in thys poynte for the meyntenaunce of theyre heresye

---

7 Peter] *1529*, Paule *1557*   10 purgatory] *1529*¹ *1557*, pargatory *1529*²
13–14 *Sidenote 1557:* Roma. 1

set at nought saynt Austayn / saynt Hyerome / saynt Ambrose /
saynt Gregory / saynt Chrysosteme / saynt Basyle / saynt
Cypryane / and fynally all the olde holy fathers and blessyd
sayntys that eny thynge say agaynst theym: yet can they neyther
deny that the catholyque churche of cryste hath allwaye byleued   5
purgatory / condempnyng for heretyques all suche as wolde
holde the contrary. Nor yf they graunt that: can they then by eny
maner meane auoyde yt / but that the thynge ys trew that all the
churche so full and hole so longe hath in suche wyse byleued / all
though there were not founden in all holy scrypture one texte y^t 10
so playnely proued [H$_4$] yt: as they myght fynde many that
semed to saye the contrary / except they wyll not onely say that
our blessyd lady lost her vyrginite after the byrth of cryst / but
ouer y^t be dreuen ferther to mynyshe the strenght and authoryte of the very gospell self: whych yf the church may erre in   15
the ryght fayth / had clerely lost hys credence.

And therfore as we say / where as we by playn scripture haue
prouyd you purgatory: yet yf there were theryn not one text y^t
eny thyng semed to say for yt / but dyuerse and many textys
whyche as farre semed vnto the mysse vnderstanders to speke   20
agaynste purgatory / as many dyuerse textys of ye gospell appered vnto the greate heretyque Eluidius to speke agaynst the
perpetuall vyrgynyte of crystys blessyd mother: yet syth the catholyque churche of cryste hath allway so fermely byleued yt for a
playne trowthe / that they haue allway taken the obstynate   25
affermers of ye contrary for playne erronyouse heretyques / yt ys
a profe full and suffycyent for purgatory to eny man that wyll be
taken for a member of crystys church / and ys alone a thyng
suffycyent in eny good crysten audyence to stoppe the mowthys
of all the prowde hygh harted malycyouse heretykes / that eny   30
thynge wold barke agaynst vs.

But when they be so confuted and concluded / that they haue
nothyng to say: yet can they not hold theyre peace / but fall to
blasphemy and aske why there cometh none of vs owte of pur-

3–5 *Sidenote 1557:* The churche hath alway beleued purgatorye   5–7 byleued purgatory / condempnyng for heretyques all suche as wolde holde] *1529,* holde *1557*
24 *Sidenote 1557:* Note

gatory and speke wyth theym. By whyche blasphemouse questyon they may as well deny hell and heuen to / as they deny
purgatory. For there cometh as many to them owt of purgatory /
as owt of ether of the other twayn. And surely yf there came one
5   owte of eny of theym all thre / vnto folke of suche incredulyte as
those heretyques be: yet wolde they be neuer the better. For yf
they byleue not now them whome they shuld byleue / no more
wold they byleue hym neyther that shold come owte of purgatory to tell yt them: as Abraam answered the rych man that re-
10   quyred the same in hell / and as yt well appered also by the
myscreaunte Iewys whych were so lyttell amended by the comynge agayn of Lazare owte of lymbus patrum / that leste other
shold byleue hym they deuysed to destroye hym. And yet yf the
thyng that they requyre wold content theym: yt hath not lakked.
15   For there hath in euery contrey and in euery age apparycyons
bene had and well knowen and testyfyed / by whyche men haue
had suffycyent reuelacyon and profe of purgatory / excepte
suche as lyste not to byleue theym: & they be such as wolde be
neuer the better yf they saw theym.
20   For who so lysteth to beleue that all to gether ys lyes that he
hereth so mych people speke of & seeth so many good men wryte
of: for no cuntrey ys there in crystendome in whych he shall not
here credably reported of such apparycyons dyuers tymys there
sene & apperyng / [H₄v] and in the bokis of many an holy sayntes
25   wrytyng / shall he fynde such apparycyons in such wyse told and
testyfyed / as no good man coud in any wyse mystrust them: and
ouer thys when the apostles at Crystes apperyng to the .xi. in the
house / toke hym at the furst for a spyryte / yt well apperyth that
apparycyons of spyrytes was no new thyng among yᵉ Iewys:
30   which ye may well parceyue also by yᵗ yᵉ better sorte of them sayd
in excusyng of saynt Poule / what yf some angell or some spyryt
haue spoken to hym as ys mencyoned in the apostles actys: so
that as we say who so lyst to take all thys for lyes / & ys so
faythlesse and so proudly curyouse that he loketh ere he beleue

---

6 heretyques] *1529*¹ *1557*, heretyque *1529*²   8–9 *Sidenote 1557:* Luke. 16   11 by]
1529, for *1557*   12 *Sidenote 1557* Iohn. 11; Lazare] *1529*¹ *1557*, lazare *1529*²
28 *Sidenote 1557:* Luke. 24   31 *Sidenote 1557:* Actes. 23

them to haue such apparycyons specyally shewed vnto hym self
& myracles wrought in hys presens: wold wax yᵉ wurse and he
saw theym / and wold ascrybe yt eyther to some fantasy or to the
dyuels workis / as dyd those Iewes that ascrybyd Crystys myracles to Belzabub.

For surely yf suche people were in the case of saynte Thomas
of Inde / that they were otherwyse very vertuouse and good /
hauynge in that onely poynt some hardnes of belefe as he had in
Cristes resurreccyon: our lord we dout not wold of hys specyall
goodnes prouyde sum specyell way for theyr satysfaccyon to
recouer them wyth. But now syth they be playn carnall hygh
harted and malycyouse / longyng for myracles as dyd these
croked harted Iewes / whych sayde vnto Cryste yᵗ they longed to
se hym shew sum myracle: he dothe therfore wyth these folk as
Cryst dyd with them. For as he answerd them by the sample of
Ionas the prophete / that he wolde none shew byfore yᵗ peruerse
& faythlesse peple tyll he were dede: so answereth he these
peruers & croked malycyous peple / yᵗ he wyll shew them no
suche apparycions tyll they be dede. And then shall he send
them where they shall se it so surely / & to theyr payne se such a
grysly syght as shall so greue theyr hartys to loke theron / that
they shall say as Criste sayd to saynt Thomas of Inde: Beati qui
non viderunt et crediderunt: Blessyd & happy be they that
beleuyd thys gere and neuer saw yt. For surely in thys world yᵉ
goodnes of god so temperyth such apparycyons / as hys hygh
wysedome seeth yt most profytable for help & reliefe of the dede
and instruccyon and amendement of the quyk: kepynge suche
apparycyons of hys great marcy most comenly from yᵉ syght of
such as wold turne hys godnes in to theyre awne harme. And
surely of hys tender fauoure toward you / doth hys great goodnes prouyde: that such apparycyons / reuelacyons / and myracles / shold not be to copyouse and commune: wherby good men
seyng the thynge at eye / shold lese the great parte of that they
now meryte by fayth: and euyll folke when they were onys fa-

6 *Sidenote 1557:* Luke. 11   14 myracle:] *1529*¹, myracle. *1529*², miracle, *1557*
15–16 *Sidenote 1557:* Math. 12   22–23 *Sidenote 1557:* Iohn. 20   33–34 *Sidenote
1557:* Why reuelacions be not comen   34 and] *1529*¹, ayd *1529*², & *1557*

melyer wyth yt / wolde then as lytle regarde yt as they now lytle
beleue yt.

   Now it is a world to see wyth what folye they fortefy theyr false
[I₁] belyefe / and in to what fonde fantesyes they fall / whyle they
5 declyne from the trouth. For whyle they deny purgatory / they
now afferm (& specyally Luther hym self) that soules vnto
doomys day do nothyng els but slepe. Wo wold they be yf they
fell in such a slepe as many a soule slepeth here / & as Iudas hath
all redy slept .xv. C. yere in hell.

10   Then say they that yf there were eny purgatory / oute of
whych the pope myght delyuer eny soule by his pardon: then
were he very cruell in that he delyueryth theym not wythout
mony: & also that he ryddyth them not hense all to gether at
onys. The furst ys a great foly that syth our lord sendyth them
15 thyder for satysfaccyon to be made in sum maner for theyr
synne: the pope shuld rather agaynst goddys purpose delyuer
them fre / then chaunge the maner of theyr satysfaccyon from
payne into prayour / almes dede / or other good workys to be
done by theyr frendes for them in some poynt profytable &
20 necessary for the hole corps of crystendome or some good member of the same.

   Now ys there in the seconde not onely mych more foly / but yt
importeth also playn and open blasphemy. For presupposed
that the pope may delyuer all sowlys out of purgatory: yet yf he
25 were therfore cruell as oft as he leueth any there / thys vnresonable reason layeth cruelte to yᵉ blame of god / which may vndout-
edly delyuer all sowlys thens and yet he leueth them there. Thys
blasphemy shuld also towch hys hygh maieste for kepyng any
soule in hell / from whens no man douteth but that he myght yf
30 he lyst delyuer them all for euer. But as he wyll not delyuer eny
thens: so wyll he not wythout good order delyuer eny soule
hence. For as of hys iustice they be worthy to ly there for euer: so
be we worthy to lye here for the whyle / and in god no cruelte
though he suffer hys mercy to be communely suspendyd and
35 temperyd wyth the balaunce of hys iustyce. And though he take
vs not hence all at onys orderlesse & at aduenture: hys hygh

5–6 *Sidenote 1557:* A fonde oppinion

wysdome ys prayse worthy & not worthy blame. Our lord forbede y^t euer we so shuld (& such ys hys grace y^t we neuer shall for
eny payne possible y^t we can suffer here) hold our self content to
here such folysh wordes as emply so playn blasphemy agaynst
goddys hygh marcyfull maieste. For surely these folk in puttyng 5
forth of thys theyr vnwyse argument / make a countenaunce to
throw yt agaynst the pope / but in very dede they caste yt at
goddys hed.

For as for the pope who so consyder yt well / goeth farther
from the sample of god that ys set for crystes vycar in hys church 10
by geuyng ouer lyberall pardon: than by beyng theryn to scarce
& strayght. For god remytteth not here at aduenture though he
may do hys pleasure / but obserueth ryght good and great respecte / as the prayours & intercessyons made for vs or other
satysfaccyon done for vs by some other men. And thys order 15
vseth and of reason ought to vse hys vy[I$_1$v]car also in the dys-
pensynge toward oure relyefe / the precyouse treasure of our
comforte that cryste hath put in his kepynge. For ellys yf other
the pope or god shold alway forthwith delyuer euery man here /
or rather kepe euery man hense as these heretyques wold make 20
men byleue that god doth in dede / and wolde that the world
sholde so take yt: then shold god or the pope as we somewhat
haue sayd byfore / gyue a greate occasyon to men boldely to fall
in synne / and lytell to care or force how slowly they ryse agayne.
Whych thyng neyther were mete for the popys offyce / nor 25
agreable to the great wysedome of god / and myche lesse mete
for hys marcy. For by that meane shuld he gyue innumerable
folke greate occasyon of damnacyon / whyche presumyng vppon suche easy shorte remissyon / wolde lustely draw to lewde-
nes wyth lytell care of amendement. 30

And so appereth yt that the thynge whyche these wyse men
wolde haue ye take for cruell / ys of treuth moste mercyfull: and
the thynge whych they wold haue to seme very benygne and
pytyouse ys in very dede moste rygorouse and most cruell:
lykewyse as a sharpe mayster that chastyseth hys seruaunt / is in 35

---

4 emply] *1529*, employ *1557*   9–10 *Sidenote 1557:* The Pope Christs vicar   10 ys]
*1529*² *1557*, hath *1529*¹

that poynt more fauorable than ys an easy one that for lakke of
punyshement letteth theym runne on the brydle and gyueth
theym occasyon of hangynge. Whyche thynge hath place also
bytwene the father and the child. And therfore in holy scrypture
5   that father is not accompted for vnlouyng and cruell / that beteth
hys chyld / but rather he that leueth yt vndone. For he that
spareth the rodde sayth holy wrytt hateth the chyld. And god
therfore that ys of all fathers the most tender / louyng / and most
benygne and mercyfull / leueth no chyld of his vncorrected: but
10 scourgeth eucry chyld that he taketh to hym. And therfore
neyther god remytteth at aduenture the paynys of purgatory:
nor no more must the pope nether / but yf that he wyll whyle he
laboureth to do good and be pytuouse to vs that are dede / be
cruell & do mych more harme to theym that be quyk: and whyle
15 he wyll draw vs owte of purgatory / dryue many of them in to
hell. Frome desyre of which kynd of helpe / we so farre abhorre /
that we wold all rather chose to dwell here long in most bytter
payn / than by such way to gete hense as myght gyue occasyon of
eny mannes damnacyon.
20   Now where they lykewyse obiecte in countenaunce agaynste
the clergy / but yet in very dede they stryke the stroke at vs
whome they wolde byreue the suffragys of good people / obiect-
ynge that no man may satysfye for a nother / nor that the
prayour nor almoyse nor other good dede done by one man may
25 stande a nother in stede / but y^t euery man must nedys all thynge
y^t he wyll haue helpe of / do it euery whyt hym selfe / and so that
no mannys good dede done amonge you for vs in relyefe of our
payn could in eny maner serue vs: this oppinyon as [I$_2$] yt ys
toward vs very pestylent and pernycyouse / so ys yt of yt selfe
30 very false and folysshe. For fyrste yf all that euer muste auayle
eny man / muste nedys be done by hym selfe / and no mannys
meryte may be applyed to the helpe of a nother / then were
wyped a way from all men all the merytys of crystys bytter passyon / in whych though yt be trew that god dyed on the crosse

---

3 hangynge.] *1529*^{1} *1557*, hangynge / *1529*^{2} 7–8 *Sidenote 1557:* Prouerb .13.
Hebrues. 12   8 therfore] *1529*^{1} *1557*, thefore *1529*^{2} 22–24 *Sidenote 1557:* False
and folysh opinions

bycause of the vnite of god and man in person / yet had hys
tender manhed all the payne for vs / and hys impassyble godhed
felte no payne at all. Wherof serueth also yᵉ prayours that euery
man prayeth for other? Wherfore dyd saynt Powle pray for all
other cristen men / and desyre them all to pray for hym also and   5
eche of them for other / that they myght be saued?

And why ys there so specyall a mencyon made in the actys of
the apostles / that at the deliuery of saynt Peter owt of pryson / yᵉ
church made contynuall prayour and intercessyon for hym? but
for to shewe that god the rather delyuered hym for other   10
mennys prayours. And thynke ye that yf god haue pyte vppon
one man for an others sake / & delyuereth hym at a nother
mannys petycyon from a lyttell payne or prysonement in the
worlde there vppon erth: he hath not at other mennys humble
and harty prayour myche more pytye vppon suche as lye in   15
myche more heuy payne and turment here in the hote fyre of
purgatory?

Then fynd these folke a nother knotte hard as they thynke to
vndo. For they say yᵗ yf a nother mannys merytys may serue me /
wherto shuld I nede to do eny good my selfe. Thys obieccyon ys   20
mych lyke as yf they wold say yf other men may take me owt of yᵉ
fyre: wherto shulde I labour to ryse my selfe. Very trewth yt ys
that sometyme the good wurkes of one man wrought wyth good
affeccyon / may purchase an other man grace for to mende and
wurke for hym self. But surely of comen course he that wyll not   25
hym selfe wurk wyth theym / geteth lyttell good of other mennys
good dedys. For yf thy selfe do styll drawe bakward whyle other
good men wyth theyre prayour laboure to pull the forward: yt
wyll be longe ere thou make eny good days iourney. And therfore yᵗ holy doctour saynt Austayne / in yᵉ blessyd boke that he   30
made of the cure and care that men shuld haue of vs sely parted
sowlys: towcheth quykly the very poynte that there can none take
profyte of other mennys good dedys / but onely such as haue
deserued by some good thynge in theyre awne dedys / that other

---

3 all.] *1529*¹, all / *1529*², al, *1557*   4 *Sidenote 1557:* Roma. 1   8 *Sidenote 1557:* Actes.
12   32–34 *Sidenote 1557:* Who may take profite of other mennes dedes

mennys dedys shuld helpe them: and that hath euery man done
at the leste wyse by hys fynall repentaunce and purpose of
amendement / that departeth the world in the state of grace.

For he that ys owte of that state / can not take the profyte of
5 other mennys merytys done for hym. And therfore damned
soulys can not by other mennys merytys be delyuered of damnacyon: nor in lyke[I₂v]wyse he that entendeth to perseuer in
synne and do no good for hym selfe. But syth that we be not in yᵗ
case / but haue with helpe of goddes grace deserued to be parte-
10 ners of such good dedys as ye that are our frendes wyll of your
goodnes do for vs: ye may by your merytes hyghly releue vs here
and helpe to gete vs hense. And surely great wonder were yt yf
we shulde not be able to take profyte of your prayours. For there
wyll no wyse man dowte but that the prayour of eny member of
15 cristendom / may profyte eny other that yt ys made for / whych
hath nede and ys a member of the same. But none ys there yet
lyuyng that ys more very member of crystys mystycall body yᵗ ys
hys church then we be / nor no man lyuyng that hath more nede
of helpe then we. For in surety of saluacyon we be felowes wyth
20 angellys: in nede of relyefe we be yet felowes wyth you. And
therfore beyng so sure members of one body wyth angells / holy
sayntys / and you: and hauyng necessyte both of theyre helpe
and yours: there ys no dowte but syth euery member that nede
hath maye take good by other / we stande in the case that both
25 aungells and sayntys intercessyons and your good prayours &
almoyse dede done for vs what so euer these heretyques bable /
may do vs meruaylouse mych good.

How many haue by goddes moste gracyouse fauour appered
vnto theyre frendys after the deth and shewed theym selfe
30 holpen and delyuered hense by pilgrymage / almoyse dede / and
prayour / and specyall by the sacred oblacyon of that holy sacrament offred for theym in the masse. If these heretyques say that
all suche thyngys be lyes: then be they myche wurse yet then

---

1 man] *1529*¹ *1557*, men *1529*²   3 departeth] *1529*¹ *1557*, departeh *1529*²
7 perseuer] *1529*¹, *1557*, perseruer *1529*²   16–18 *Sidenote 1557:* The soules in purgatorie ar members of the churche   28–30 *Sidenote 1557:* The thynges which comforte the soules in purgatory   31 specyall] *1529*, specialli *1557*

theyre mayster was Luther hym selfe / as longe as eny sparke of
shame was in hym. For he confesseth in hys sermons that many
suche apparycyons be trew: and hys hart could not nor for very
shame serue hym / that so many so often told in so many placis /
so faythfully reported by so many honeste folke / and so substan-   5
cyally wrytten by so many blessyd sayntys: shulde be all false.
Wheryn yf these men lyste lyke lusty skolers to passe and ouer go
theyre madde mayster in thys poynt / & deny these thynges all to
gether: yet shall there styk in theyr teeth / ye scrypture of y^e
Machabees wherof we told you that Iudas Machabeus gatheryd   10
& sent a great offryng to Hyerusalem / for to bye sacrifyce to be
offred for theym y^t he found slayne in the felde / and certeyne
thyngys about them taken of the Idollys forbeden them by the
law / whych caused hym to fere leste they were for theyr synne
fallen after theyr deth in to payne / and therfore made that   15
gatheryng / y^t almes & offring as hym selfe sayth / that they
myghte therby be losyd and delyueryd of theyr synnys. So that
there appereth playnly by scrypture / that such suffragys stande
vs sely soulys in stede. Agaynste whych authorite yf they wyll
wyth theyr master labour to breke out & denye that boke for holy   20
scripture / [I₃] we haue stopped them that gap all redy with such
a bush of thornys / as will pryk theyr handys thorow a payre of
hedgyng glouys ere they pull yt out.
    And fynally for thys poynt that the suffragys of the church
and ye prayours of good crysten people / stand vs here in relyef   25
and cumfort / there nedeth in thys world (as saynt Austayn sayth
& saynte Damascene) none other maner profe then that all cristendome hath euer vsed to do so / & haue thought them self
alway so bounden to do / damnynge alway for heretykys all them
that wold afferme the contrary.   30
    And in thys poynt may they haue a maruelose gret thyng
agaynst them in the iugement of euery good man / the gret
antiquyte of the seruyse of Crystys church / by whych the church
hath so long ago customably recommendyd in theyr prayours all

---

3 not nor] *1529*, not *1557*   10 *Sidenote 1557:* 2. Macha. 12   31–33 *Sidenote 1557:*
The antiquitie of the seruice of Christes churche   32 good man /] *1529¹ corr. err.,*
good man *1529² 1557,* good / *1529¹*

204 THE SUPPLICATION OF SOULS, BOOK II

crysten soulys to god. For we trust that though these heretykys
fynde many men bothe glad to here and lyght to beleue euery
lewd tale that can be surmysed agaynst the church that now is:
yet trust we that they shall fynde few or none so farre out of all
5 frame / but that they wyll at the lest beleue y^t there hath bene
sum good and godly men wyse and well lerned too among the
clergy in days passed one tyme or other. Go then to the old tyme
and to the good men that then were / & here what they sayd / &
se what they dyd / and beleue & folow them. There remayneth
10 yet and bokys ynow therof / the very masse in the very forme and
fassyon / as saynt Basyle / & saynt Chrysostheme / and other holy
fathers in that vertuouse tyme sayed yt: in whych ye shall fynd
that in theyr dayly masses they prayd euer for all crysten soules.
Ye shall also parceyue clerely by saynt Chrisostheme in a ser-
15 mon of hys / that in his tyme there were in the funerall seruyce at
the beryeng of the corps / the self same psalmes songen that ye
syng now at ye dirige. Wherby yt well appareth that yt is no new
found thyng: for his tyme was farr aboue a .M. yere ago: and yet
was y^t thyng long vsed afore hys dayes. And because ye shall
20 know that the more surely: he sayth y^t the gyse & custume to
pray for soulys / was instytute and bygone in the church by the
blessyd apostles theym selfe. And so whyle so good men so long a
go bygan yt / and good folke hath euer synnys contynued yt / ye
may sone gesse whyther they be good men or no that now pro-
25 uoke you to breke yt.
Now where they say that yf the masse could do vs eny good /
that then the prestys be very cruell that wyll say none for vs but
they be waged: thys word ys as trew as theyre entent ys fraudu-
lent & false. For theyre purpose ys in those wordys to make the
30 world wene / that the clergy were so couetouse and cruell therwyth / that there wyll no preste pray for vs pore soulys here /
without he be hyred therto: wherof our lorde be thanked we
fynde full well the contrary. For albe yt [I$_3$v] that of Luthers
prestes we can haue none helpe / syth theyr massys offer not vp
35 the sacrament to god neyther for quyk nor dede / nor make no
very prestes among theym syth they take presthed for no sacra-

---

19–21 *Sidenote 1557:* The apostles dyd institute to pray for the dead   34–36 *Sidenote*
1557: Luthers priestes ar no very priestes

ment: yet of good cristen prestys we fynde greate relyefe as well
in theyre dyryges and mych other suffragys by olde instytucyon
of the churche specyally sayed for vs / though no man geue
theym one peny thorow the yere. And so may all the worlde wyt
that thys word of these heretyques hath myche malyce and lyttell 5
effecte theryn.

But nowe thowghe the prestys praye for vs of theyre awne
cheryte: yet when good people desyre theym thereto and gyue
theym theyre almoyse therefore: then are they dowble bounden /
and then ryseth there myche more good and profyt vppon all 10
sydys. For then take we frute both of the prayour of ye tone and
the almoyse of the tother. And then taketh the preste benyfyte of
hys awne prayour made bothe for the geuer and for vs. The
geuer also getteth frute both of hys awne mercyfull almoyse /
and of double prayour also / that ys to wyt bothe the prayour of 15
the preste that prayeth for vs / whyche comenly prayeth for hym
to / and also the prayour of vs / whyche wyth great feruour of
hart pray for our benefactours incessauntly / and are so ferforth
in goddys vndowted fauour / that very few men lyuyng vppon
erth are so well herd as we: bysydys that of all kynd of almoyse 20
that eny man can geue / the moste merytoryouse ys y^t whych ys
bystowed vppon vs / as well for that yt ys vnto the moste nedy and
also to them that are absent / and fynally for that of all maner
almoyse yt is moste grownded vppon the foundacyon of all
crysten vertuose fayth. For as for to pore folke / a naturall man 25
wyll gyue almoyse eyther for pytye of some pytuose syght / or for
werynesse of theyre importune cryenge. But as for vs pore
sowlys passed the world / whome he that gyueth almoyse neyther
seeth nor hereth: wolde neuer bestowe one peny vppon vs but yf
he had a fayth that we lyue styll / and that he fered that we lye in 30
payne / and hopyd of hys reward in heuen. Whych kynde of
fayth and good hope ioyned wyth his gyft and good wurck / must
nedys make it one of the best kynd of almoyse dede that eny man
can do in the world.

And syth that yt so ys as in dede yt ys: what vncharytable & 35

15–18 *Sidenote 1557:* The soules departed doe continually pray for those that be a-
lyue   23 that are] *1529*[1] *1557*, thet are *1529*[2]   23–25 *Sidenote 1557:* A most meritorious almose   25 vertuose] *1529*[2], vertuouse *1529*[1], vertuous *1557*

what vnfaythfull folk ar these / that for hatred whych they ow to prested / wolde make you beleue that there were no purgatory / & wold rather wysh by theyr wyllys that theyr owne fathers shuld lye here in fyre tyll the day of doome / then eny man shulde geue
5 a preste one peny to pray for them?

And yet ys there here one thyng well to be consyderyd / that they rather hate prestys for hatred of Crystes fayth / then speke agaynst purgatory for hatred of prestys. Whych thyng though yt seme you darke [I₄] at the furst heryng: ye shall yet yf ye loke
10 well / very well parceyue. For yf it so were that thys kynde of people dyd speke agaynst purgatory onely for yᵉ hatred of the pope & yᵉ clergy / then wold they graunte that saued soules ar yet purged in the fyre here for theyr synnis vnsatysfyed in the worlde: and yt shulde then suffyce them to say for theyre pur-
15 pose / that neyther prest nor pope nor eny man els nor eny mannys almes or prayour / can in thys place of ponyshment eny thynge releue vs. For thys were ynough ye se well to sarue theyr purpose agaynst yᵉ clergy. But yet because they haue a farre farther purpose agaynst all good crysten fayth: they be not con-
20 tent therfore to leue at thys poynt / but steppe them forthe farther and deny purgatory vtterly / to thende that men shuld take boldnes to care the lesse for theyre synne. And yf they myght onys be beleuyd theryn: then wold they step yet farther & denye hell and all / and after that heuen to. But as for heuen
25 albeyt yᵗ as yet they denye yt not: yet pull they many a symple sowle thence / whych were yt not for theyr myscheuous doctrine were els well lykly to be there a full bryght and gloryouse saynt.

And surely the more that wyse men aduyse them selfe vppon this mater: the more shall they meruayle of the mad mynd of
30 theym that deny purgatory / or say yᵗ the prayours or good workys of men lyuyng in the world can do vs here no good. For euery man that eny wyt hath: wotteth well that the surest way were in euery dowt best to be taken. Now suppose then that purgatory could in no wyse be prouyd / and yᵗ some wold yet say

---

20 thys] *1529²* corr. err., *1529¹ 1557*, hys *1529²*; poynt /] *1529¹*, poynt *1529²*, point, *1557*   31–33 *Sidenote 1557:* In doubtes take the surest waye   33 taken.] *1529¹ 1557*, taken *1529²*

playnly y^t there were one / & some wold say playnly nay: let vs
now see whether sorte of these twayne might take most harm / if
theyr part were the wrong. Furst he that beleued there were
purgatory / & that hys prayour and good wurkes wrought for
hys frendys soule myghte relyeue them theryn / and because   5
therof vsed mych prayour and almoyse for theym: he could not
lese the reward of hys good wyll / all though hys opynyon were
vntrew / & that there were no purgatory at all / no more then he
leseth hys labour now y^t prayeth for one whom he fereth to ly in
purgatory where he ys all redy in heuen. But on the tother syde /   10
he that beleueth there ys none / and therefore prayeth for none:
yf hys opynyon be false / and that there be purgatory in dede as
in dede there ys / he leseth mych good and getteth hym also
myche harme / for he both fereth myche ye lesse to synne and to
ly long in purgatory / sauyng that hys heresye shall saue hym   15
thense and send hym downe depe in to hell.

And yt fareth bytwene these two kynd of folk as yt fared
bytwene a lewde galand & a pore frere. Whom when the galand
saw goynge barefote in a great froste and snowe / he asked hym
why he dyd take suche payne. And he answered y^t yt was very   20
lytell payne yf a man wold remember hell. Ye frere quoth y^e
galant but what & there be none [I₄v] hell / than arte thou a great
fole. Ye mayster quoth the frere but what & there be hell / than
ys your maystershyppe a mych more fole.

More ouer there was neuer yet eny of that sorte / that coulde   25
for shame saye that eny man ys in parell for byleuynge that there
ys purgatory. But they saye onely that there ys none in dede /
and that they may wythout eny synne afferme theyre opynyon
for trouth. But now vpon the tother syde many an hundred
thowsand / that ys to wyt all the hole churche of cryste that ys or   30
euer hath bene / afferme that the affermyng of theyre opynyon
agaynst purgatory / ys a playne dampnable heresy. Wherfore it
well and playnly appereth and euery wyse man well seeth / that
yt ys the farre surer way to belyue in such wyse as both the partys
agree to be owt of all parell / then that way whych so farre the   35
greter parte and myche farther the better parte afferme to be

---

17 *Sidenote 1557:* A merye tale   31 hath] *1529*² *1557*, had *1529*¹

vndowted dedely synne. And now where as euery fole maye se
that eny wyse man wyll take the sureste way / which ys as ye se
dowble proued to belyue that there ys purgatory: yet sayd the
wyse proctour of beggars y^t wyse men wyll saye there ys none.
5 For he sayth y^t many greate letterd men and ryght conynge men /
wyll not let to put them self in ieoperdye of shame & of deth also /
to shewe theyre myndes that there ys no purgatory. He ys loth
to say y^t these be heretyques but he sayeth these be they that men
call heretyques. Wherin he speketh myche lyke as yf he wold
10 poynt wyth hys fynger to a flokke of fat wethers / and say these be
suche bestys as men call shepe.

But now wolde we fayne se whyche be these wyse men and well
lettred / whych shall not fayle vppon theyre awne confessyon to
agre that theyre aduersaryes take the sure way and fertheste
15 owte of parell / and theym selfe the moste daungerouse and
ferthest from all surety. But yet wolde we for ye whyle fayn here
who they be. Surely none other but Luther and Tyndale / and
thys beggars proctoure / & a few such of that sect / men of such
vertew / wysdome and lernyng / as theyre lewd wrytynge and
20 mych more theyre lewd lyuyng shewyth.

But now ar they farre an other maner sorte both in nomber /
wysdome / lernyng / trewth and good lyuyng / whych affyrme
and say the contrary. And surely yf .iii. or .iiii. C. good and
honest men wold faythfully cum forth & tell one y^t sum of hys
25 frendes were in a farre cuntrey for det kept in pryson / & that hys
charyte myght relyeue them thence: yf then .iii. or .iiii. fond
felows wold cum and say the contrary / and tell hym playn there
ys no such prison at all as he ys borne in hand that his frendys ar
prysoned in: yf he wold now be so lyght to beleue those .iii.
30 or .iiii. noughty persons / agaynst those .iii. or .iiii. C. good and
honest men: he then shuld well decypher hym self / and well
declare therby that he wold gladly cach hold of sum small handell to kepe hys money fast / rather then help hys frendys in
theyre necessyte. [K$_1$]
35 Now yf ye consider how late thys lewd sect began / whych
among crysten men barketh agaynst purgatory / and how few

1–2 *Sidenote 1557:* Wyse men wil take the surest waye

alway for very shame of theyr foly hath hetherto fallen in to
them: and then yf ye consyder on the tother syde how full and
hole the gret corps of all crysten cuntreys so many hundred
yerys / haue euer told you the contrary: ye shall we be very sure
for euery person spekyng agaynste purgatory / fynde for the   5
tother parte mo than many an hundred.

Now yf these men wyll peraduenture say that they care not for
such comparyson / neyther of tyme wyth tyme / nomber wyth
nomber / nor cumpany wyth cumpany / but syth sum one man ys
in credence worth sum .vii. score: yf they wyll therfore call vs to   10
sum other rekening & wyll that we compare of the best choyse on
both sydes a certayn / & match them man for man: then haue we
(yf we myght for shame matche such blyssed sayntes wyth a sorte
so farre vnlyke) saynt Austayn agaynst frere Luther / saynt
Hyerom agaynst frere Lambert / saynt Ambrose agaynst frere   15
Husken / saynt Gregory agaynst preeste Pomeran / saynt
Chrisosteme agaynst Tindale / saynt Basyle agaynst ye beggars
proctour.

Now yf our enmyes wyll for lak of other choyse / help forth
theyr owne parte wyth theyre wyuys: then haue they some   20
aduantage in dede / for ye tother holy sayntes had none. But yet
shall we not lack blessyd holy women agaynst these frerys wyuis.
For we shall haue saynt Anastace agaynst frere Luthers wyfe /
saynt Hildegardes agaynst frere Huskyns wyfe / saynt Brygyte
agaynst frere Lambertes wyfe and saynt Katheryn of senys   25
agaynst prest Pomeranys wyfe. Now yf they wyll haue in these
matches ye qualityes of ether syde consyderyd: then haue we
wysdom agaynst foly / cunnyng agaynst ignoraunce / charyte
agaynst malyce / trew fayth agaynst heresyes / humilite agaynst
arrogaunce / reuelacyons agaynst illusyons / inspyracyon of god   30
agaynst inuencyons of ye deuyll / constaunce agaynst waueryng /
abstynence agaynst glotony / contynence agaynst lechery / &
fynally euery kynde of vertue agaynst euery kynde of vyce. And
ouer thys where as we be not yet very sure whyther y^t all these
nawghty persons whome we haue rehersed you of ye worse syde /   35
be fully fall so madde as vterly to deny purgatory / sauynge in y^t

7 not] _1529_^1 _1557_, no _1529_^2   16 preeste] _1529_, frere _1557_

we se theym in many thynges all of one secte: yet yf there were of
theym farre many such mo / they shall not yet fynd of yᵗ symple
sute half so many / as for our parte remayneth holy blessyd
sayntes to matche theym. For lyke wyse as many theyre holy
5 workys eruditely wryten & by the helpe of yᵉ holy goost endyghted: euydentely declare yᵗ not onely saynt Austayne / saynt
Hierome / saynt Ambrose & yᵗ holy pope saynt Gregory / wyth
saynt Chrisostem / & saynt Basyle afore remembred / & those
holy women also yᵗ we haue spoken of / but ouer yᵗ the great
10 solempne doctour Oregene / all yᵉ thre great doctours & holy
[K₁v] sayntys of one name in grece / Gregorius Nasianzenus /
Gregorius Nissenus / Gregorius Emissenus / saynt Cyryllus /
saynt Damascene / yᵉ famouse doctour & holy martyr saynt
Cipryane / saynt Hylary / saynt Bede / & saynt Thomas / &
15 fynally all suche as are of yᵗ suyt & sorte eyther grekes or latyns /
haue euer taught & testyfyed and exhorted yᵉ peple to pray for
all crystyn soulys & preched for purgatory: so doth there no man
dowte but yᵗ all good & deuowte crysten peple from crystys dayes
hytherto / hath ferme & faste bene of yᵉ same bylyefe / & wyth
20 theyr dayly prayours and almoyse dede done for vs haue done vs
great relyefe. So that as we sayed both for nomber of many folke
and goodnes of chosen folke: our enemyes are farre vnder vs.
And yet haue we for the vauntage as we haue byfore declared
you yᵉ fere of Ezechyas / the boke of the kyngys / the wordes of
25 the prophete zachary / the fayth of Machabeus / yᵉ authoryte of
saynt Iohan / the wordys of saynt Peter / the sentence of saynt
Poule / yᵉ testimony of saynt Mathew / and the playne sentence
of our sauyour cryste.
Now yf these heretyques be so styffe & stoborne / that rather
30 then they wyll confesse theym selfe concluded / they wyll holde
on theyre olde wayes and fall frome wurse to wurse / and lyke as
they haue all redy agaynst theyre formar promyse fyrst reiected
reason and after lawe / & then all yᵉ doctours and olde holy
fathers of crystys churche / and fynally the hole churche yt selfe:
35 so yf they wyll at length as we greatly fere they wyll / reiect all
scrypture & cast of Criste & all: now as we say yf they so do / yet

19–21 *Sidenote 1557:* Al good christians haue belieued purgatorie

haue we left at the wurst way Luther agaynst Luther / Huskyn
agaynst Huskyn / Tyndall agaynst Tyndall / & fynally euery
heretyke agaynst hym self. And then when these folk syt in
Almayn vppon theyr bere bench in iugement on vs & our maters: we may as the knyght of kyng Alexander appelyd from   5
Alexander to Alexander / from Alexander the dronk to Alexander the sober: so shall we appele from Luther to Luther / from
Luther the dronken to Luther the sober / from Luther the heretyke to Luther the catholyke / & lykewyse in all the remenaunt.
For thys dothe no man dout but that euery one of them all /   10
before they fell dronk of the dreggys of olde poysonyd heresyes /
in whych they fell a quaftyng wyth the dyuell: they dyd full sadly
& soberly pray for all crysten soulys. But synnys that they be
fallen dronken in wrechyd & synfull heresyes: they neyther care
for other mennys soulys nor for theyr owne neyther. And on the   15
tother syde yf euer they wurk wyth grace to purge them self of
those poysoned heresyes / wherwyth they be now so dronk / they
wyll than geue sentence on our syde as they dyd before. It were
not yuell y^t we shewed you sumwhat for exsample wherby ye
may se what sobernes they were in before / & in what dronk-   20
ennes the dyuels drawghte hath brought them. And in whom
shuld we shew yt better than in Luther [K$_2$] hym self archeheretyke and father abbot of all that dronken felishyp? Furst
thys man was so fast of our syde whyle he was well & sober / that
yet when he began to be well washed / he coulde not fynde in his   25
hart vtterly to fall from vs. But when his hed furste began to dase
of that euyll drynke: he wrote that purgatory coud not be
prouyd by scrypture. And yet that not wythstandyng he wrote in
this wyse therwyth. I am very sure that there ys purgatory / & yt
lytle moueth me what heretykis bable. Shuld I beleue an here-   30
tyke borne of late scant fyfty yerys ago / and say the fayth were
false that hathe bene holden so many hundred yere? Lo here
thys man spake well vppon our syde. But yet sayed he therwith
one thyng or twayne / that coud not stande therwyth: and therby
may ye se that he began to reele. For he both affyrmyd that   35

1–2 Huskyn agaynst Huskyn] *1529*[1] *corr. err.*, *1529*[2] *1557*. Snuskyn agaynst Snuskyn
1529[1]   24 of] *1529*, on *1557*   28–29 *Sidenote 1557:* Luther sayth ther is a
purgatorie

purgatory coud not be prouyd by scripture / and affyrmyd ferther that nothyng coud be taken for a sure & certayn trewth / but
yf yt appered by clere and euydent scrypture. Whych two
thyngys presupposed: how coud eny man be sure of purgatory?
5   But the help ys that both those poyntes be false. For both ys
purgatory prouyd by scrypture / and the chatholyke fayth of
Crystys church were suffycent to make men sure therof / albe yt
there were not in all scrypture one text for yt / and dyuers y^t
semyd agaynst it as we haue shewed you before.

10   But here as we say ye se how shamfully he staggared & began
to reele: howe be it sone after beyng so dowsy dronk y^t he coulde
neyther stand nor reele but fell downe sow dronk in the myre:
then lyke one y^t nothyng remembred what he had sayd / nor
herd not hys awn voyce / he began to be hym self y^t babelynge
15 heretike agaynst whom he had wryten before: & beyng not fully
fyfty yere old / began to gaynsay ye fayth of almost .xv. hundred
yere afore his days in the churche of Criste / besydys .xv. C. yere
thre tymys told among other faythfull folk before. For now in
hys dronken sermon that he wrote vppon the gospell of ye ryche
20 man & Lazare / where as he had in hys other bokys before
framyd of hys owne fantasy / new fond fassyons of purgatory /
and told them forth for as playn matters as though he had bene
here and sene them: now in thys mad sermon of hys he sayth
playnly that there ys none at all / but that all soulys ly still and
25 slepe / and so slepe shall / vntyll the day of dome. O sow dronken
soule drownyd in such an insensyble slepe that he lyeth and
rowghteth / whyle the apostles / the euangelystys / all the doctours of Crystes church / all the hole crysten people / and among
them cryste hym selfe / stande and cry at hys ere / that we sely
30 crysten sowlys lye and burne in purgatory / & he can not here but
lyeth styll in the myre and snorteth and there dremeth that we
lye styll and slepe as he doth.

---

7 suffycent] *1529*[1] *1557*, suffyeyent *1529*[2]   11 after beyng] *1529*[2] *1557*, after
1529[1]   16 fyfty yere old] *1529*[2] *1557*, fyfty *1529*[1]   17–18 besydys .xv. C. yere thre
tymys told] *1529*[2] *1557*, besydys fyue tymes .xv. C. yere *1529*[1]   24–25 *Sidenote 1557:*
Luther sayth there is no purgatory   32 doth] *1529*[1] *corr. err.*, *1529*[2], doeth *1557*, hoth
1529[1]

And thus where the beggars proctour wryteth that wyse men say there ys no purgatory: ye se now your selfe how wyse ys he whome [K₂v] they take for the wyseste of all that sort / as hym that ys now yᵉ very well spryng & archeherytyque of all theyre secte. Of all which wyse men we leue yt to youre wysedome to consyder: whyther ye fynde eny whom your wysedomes wold in wysedom compare wyth eny of those old holy doctours and sayntys whom we haue rehersed you byfore. But thys man we wote well for a nother of these wyse men meaneth Wyllyam Tyndall. Whose wysedom well appereth in yᵗ mater by yᵗ he layeth agaynst yt nothyng but skoffynge: wheryn he sayth that yᵉ pope may be bold in purgatory / bycause yt ys he sayth a thyng of hys awne makyng: where as we haue proued you by scrypture that purgatory was perceyued and taught and dede mennys soulys prayed for / so longe ere euer eny pope bygan.

But for as myche as he sayth that wyse men wyll say there ys no purgatory / among whych wyse men we dowte not but the wyse man accompteth hym selfe (for he layeth for that parte as hym selfe weneth very wise & weyghty resons / yᵉ wysdom wherof we haue all redy prouyd you very playne frantyke foly) we wyll nowe finyshe the dyspycyons of all thys debate and questyon / wyth yᵉ declaracyon of one or twoo poyntys of hys especyall wysdome / and wyth one of whych hym selfe wysely destroyeth all hys hole mater.

Furste ye se well that albe yt in dede he entendeth to go ferther yf hys byll were ones well spedde: yet he pretendyth nothyng in vysage but onely the spoyle / weddynge / and beatynge of the clergye: to whom he layth not all onely such fautys as ye haue hard / and hath prouyd hys purpose wyth such groundys as we haue prouyd false: but also layth one great necessyte to take all from them / because they breke yᵉ statute made of mortmayn / & purchase more landys styll agaynst yᵉ prouysyon therof. And then sayth he yᵗ eny land whych onys cummeth in theyr handys / cummyth neuer out agayn. For he sayth yᵗ they haue such lawes concernyng theyr landes / as they may neyther geue eny nor sell.

---

14 taught] *1529*¹ *corr. err.*, *1529*² *1557*, thaught *1529*¹   24 hole] *1529*¹, holy *1529*²
1557   27 spoyle] *1529*, spoyls *1557*   34 out] *1529*¹ *1557*, ont *1529*²

For whyche cause lest they shuld at length haue all / he deuyseth
to let them haue nothyng.

　　Now furst where he maketh as though there cam yet for all the
statute dayly much land in to them / & y^t there can none at all
5　come from them: neyther ys the tone so much as he wold make yt
seme / & the tother ys very false. For truly there may cum and
doth cum land fro them by eschete / as we be sure many of you
haue had experyence: & also what lawes so euer they haue of
theyr own y^t prohibyte them to sell theyr landys / yet of thys are
10　we very sure y^t not wythstandyng all ye lawes they haue / they
may sell in such wyse yf they wyll all the lande they haue / y^t they
can neuer recouer fote agayn. And besidys all y^t albe it there be
lawes made by the chyrch agaynst such salys as shrewd husbandes wold els boldly make of y^e landes of theyr monestaryes:
15　yet ys there not so precy[K$_3$]se prouysyon made agaynst all salys
of theyr landes / but y^t they may be alienyd for cause resonable
approuid by y^e aduyse & counsell of theyr chefe hed. And many
a man ys there in y^e realm y^t hath landes geuen or sold out of
abbays & out of byshoppriches both: so y^t this parte is a playn lye.
20　　The tother part ys also neyther very certayne nor very mych to
purpose. For truly though that in the cytee of London to whych
there ys grauntyd by authoryte of parliament / that men may
there deuyse theyr landys in to mortemayn by theyr testamentes / there is sumwhat among geuen into the church / and
25　yet not all to them but the great parte vnto the cumpanyes &
felyshyppys of the craftys: in nother placys of the realme there ys
now a days no great thyng geuen / but yf yt be sometyme some
small thynge for the foundacyon of a chauntery. For as for abbays or such other great foundacyons there be not now a days
30　many made nor haue bene of good whyle / excepte somewhat
done in the vnyuersytees. And yet who so consyder those great
foundacyons that haue thys great whyle bene made eny where /
shall well parceyue that the substaunce of them be not all fownd-
en vppon temporall landys new token owte of the temporall
35 ·handys in to the churche / but of suche as the church had longe a

***

26 in nother] *1529*², els in other *1529*¹, In other *1557*

fore / & now the same translated from one place vnto a nother.
And ouer this shall he fynd that many an abbey (whose hole
lyuyng thys man weneth stoode all by temporall landys geuen
them in theyre foundacyon) haue the great parte therof in benefycys gyuen in and empropred vnto theym. So that yf he con-   5
syder the substaunce of all the greate foundacyons made thys
great whyle / and all that hath in to eny suche these many dayes
be gyuen / & then consyder well therwyth how cold the cheryte
of crysten people waxeth by the meanys of suche deuyls proctours as vnder pretexte of beggynge for the pore / entend and   10
labour to quench the feruour of deuocyon to godwarde in symple and sone ledde sowlys: he shall not nede to fere that all the
temporall lande in the realm shall come in to the spyrytualtye.
And yet yf men went nowe so faste to gyue in styll to the church
as they dyd byfore whyle deuocyon was feruent in the people   15
and vertu plentuouse in the church: yet myght yt be and in other
cuntrees ys prouyded for well ynough / both that mennys deuocyon myght be fauored / and yet not the churche haue all.

   But thys wyse man leste they shulde haue all: wolde leue
theym ryght nought. For hys wysedom weneth there were no   20
meane way bytwene euery whyt and neuer a whyt but nothynge
at all. And surely where that he layeth so sore vnto theym / the
newe purchasynge of more temporall landys eyther bought or
gyuen them: yt appereth well he wolde saye sore to theym yf they
pulled the land fro men by force / whyche nowe layeth so hyghly   25
to theyr charge bycause they take yt when men gyue yt theym:
whyche thyng we suppose hym selfe as holy as he ys / wolde not
myche refuse. Nor they be not myche to [K₃v] be blamed yf they
receyue mennys deuocyon / but yf they bestow yt not well. And
yet where he sayth there can no statute holde them / but they   30
purchace styll and breke the statute / where in he wolde seme
connynge bycause he had a lytell smatterynge in the lawe: yt
were good ere he be so bold to put hys ignoraunce in wrytynge /
that he shulde se the statute better. Whyche when he lyste to loke

---

1 nother.] *1529*[1] *1557*, nother: *1529*[2]   8 cold] *1529*[2] *1557*, could *1529*[1]   8–10
Sidenote 1557: Whereby charitie waxeth colde   18 be] *1529*[1] *1557*, be be *1529*[2]

vppon agayne and lette some wyser man loke wyth hym / yf he
consyder well what remedy the statutes prouyde & for whom: he
shall fynd yᵗ the makers of the statute not so mych fered the great
hygh poynt that prykketh hym now leste the hole temporall
5   landys shuld come in to the churche / as they dyd the losse of
theyre wardys and theyr vnlykelyhed of eschetes & sum other
commoditees yᵗ they lakked when theyr landes were alyened in
to the church: & yet not in to the church onely but also in to eny
mortmayn. And for this they prouyded yᵗ yf eny more were
10   alyened in to yᵉ churche or in to eny maner of morte mayne / the
kyng or eny other lord medyate or immedyate that myght take
losse therby myght entre therin to / to thentent yᵗ ere euer the
purchase were made / they shuld be fayn in such wyse to sue to
euery one of them for his lycence & good will / that eche of them
15   shuld be arbyter of hys owne hurte or losse and take hys
amendys at hys own hand. And thys statute ys not made onely
for yᵉ aduauntage of the temporall lordys agaynst the clergy /
but yt ys made indyfferently agaynst all mortmayn: whych ys as
well temporall folk as spyrytuall / and for the benefyte as well of
20   spyrituall men as temporall. For as well shall a byshop or an
abbot haue the aduauntage of that statute yf hys tenaunt alyen
hys landys in to eny mortemayn / as shall an erle or a duke. And
now when the churche pulleth not away yᵉ land from the owner
by force / but hath yt of hys deuocyon and hys gyft geuen of hys
25   owne offer vnasked / & yet not wythout lycence of all such as the
statute lymyteth: where ys thys great faut of theyrs / for whych
lest they shuld take more in yᵉ same maner / he wold they shuld
lese all that they haue all redy? What wysdome ys thys when he
layth agaynst them theyr dede wherin they breke no law? And
30   yet syth they can not take yt wythout the kyng and the lordys /
hys wordys yf they wayd ought / shuld ronne to the reproche and
blame of them whom he wold fayn flater / wythout faut founden
in them whom he so sore accuseth. But now the specyall hygh
poynt of his wysdome for whych we be dryuen to speke of thys
35   matter he specyally declareth in thys. Ye se well that he wold that
the temporall men shuld take fro the clergy / not onely all these

---

9 for] *1529²* *1557*, ouer *1529¹*   16–17 *Sidenote 1557:* The statute of mortmayn

landys purchased synnys the statute of mortemayn / but also all
that euer they had before too / and yet ouer thys all the hole
lyuyng y^t euer they haue by eny maner mean besyde: because he
thynketh that they haue to much by all to gether. And when he
hath gyuen hys aduyse therto and sayd that they haue to much: 5
then sayth [K$_4$] he by and by that yf there were eny purgatorye in
dede / yt were well done to gyue them yet more / and that they
haue then a great dele to lytle. But now so ys yt that purgatory
there ys in dede / nor no good crysten man is there but he wyll
and must beleue & confesse the same. Wherof yt playnly 10
folowyth that hys own agrement added vnto the trouth / that ys
to say that the church hath as he sayth to lytle yf there be a
purgatory / added vnto the trouth that there ys a purgatory / and
that euery trew crysten man doth & must confesse yt: then hath
loo the wyse man brought all hys purpose so substancyally to 15
passe / that by hys own playne agrement added vnto the
vndoutable trouth / no man may do that he wold haue all men
do / spoyle and pyll the church / but he that wyll furste playnly professe hym self a playn and vndowtyd heretyke.

And therfore syth ye now se the wyt of thys wyse man / y^t 20
laboreth to bryng vs owte of your remembraunce / syth ye se
the symple grounde of hys prowde supplycacyon / and ye perceyue the rancour and malyce that hys mater standeth on: for
fulfyllyng wherof he wold by his wyll bryng all the worlde in
trouble: & syth ye se that he hateth ye clergye for the fayth / 25
and vs for the clergy / and in reprouyng purgatory proueth
hym selfe an infydele: syth we haue made yt you clere that your
prayours may do vs good / and haue shewed yt you so playnely
that a chylde may perceyue yt / not onely by the comen opynyon of all people and the faste vnfallyble fayth of all crysten 30
peple from Crystys dayes vntyll your owne tyme / confermed
by the doctryne of all holy doctours / declared by good reason /
and proued by the scrypture of god / both apostles / and euangelystys / and our sauyour Cryste hym self: we wyll encumber
you no ferther wyth dysputyng vppon the mater / nor argue 35
the thynge as dowtefull / that is vndowted and questyonlesse.

---

28 prayours] _1529_^{1}, prayour _1529_^{2} _1557_

But lettyng passe ouer such heretiques as are our malycyouse
mortall enemyes / prayenge god of his grace to gyue theym
better mynde: we shall tourne vs to you that are faythfull folke
and our dere louyng frendys / besechyng your goodnes of your
5 tender pyte that we may be remembred wyth your cherytable
almoyse and prayour. And in thys parte albe yt we stande in
suche case that yt better bycummeth vs to beseeche and praye
euery man / then to fynde eny fawte wyth eny man: yet are we
somwhat constrayned not to make eny mater of quarell or com-
10 playnt agaynst eny mannys vnkindenes / but surely to mourne
& lament our awne harde fortune & chaunce in yᵉ lakke of
relyefe & cumforte / which we misse from our frendis / not of
euyll mynde wythdrawen vs / or of vnfaythfulnes / but of neg-
lygens forslouthed & foded forth of forgetfulnes. If ye yᵗ ar
15 such (for ye be not all such) might loke vppon vs & byhold in
what heuy plyght we ly: your slouth wold sone be quikened &
your oblyuion tourne to freshe remembraunce. [K₄v]
  For yf youre father / youre mother / youre chylde / youre
brother / youre suster / youre husbande / youre wyfe / or a very
20 straunger to / lay in youre syghte some where in fyre / and that
your meanes myght helpe hym: what hart were so hard / what
stomake were so stony / that could syt in reste at supper or slepe
in reste a bedde / and let a man ly and burne? We fynde therefore full trew that olde sayd saw / owte of syght owte of mynde.
25 And yet surely to say the trewth / we can not theryn wyth reason
mych complayne vppon you. For whyle we were wyth you there /
for wantonnes of that wreched world we forgate in lykewyse our
good frendys here. And therfore can we not meruayle myche
though the iustyce of god suffer vs to be forgoten of you as other
30 haue bene before forgoten of vs. But we beseche our lorde for
both our sakys to gyue you the grace to mend for your parte that
comen faut of vs both / lest when ye cum hether here after / god
of lyke iustice suffer you to be forgoten of them that ye leue
there behynde you / as ye forgete vs that ar come hether afore
35 you. But albe yt we can not well as we say for the lyke faut in our

<hr/>

10 eny mannys] *1529*¹ *corr. err.*, *1529*² *1557*, mannis *1529*¹   19 suster] *1529*², syster
*1529*¹ *1557*   35 you.] *1529*¹ *1557*, you *1529*²

selfe greatly rebuke or blame thys neglygence and forgetfulnes
in you: yet wolde we for the better wysh you that ye myght
wythowt your payn / onys at the leste wyse behold / parceyue /
and se / what heuynes of hart & what a sorowfull shame the sely
soule hath at hys furst commyng hyther / to loke his old frendys   5
in the face here / whom he remembryth hym self to haue so foule
forgoten whyle he lyued there. When albe yt that in thys place no
man can be angry / yet theyr pytuouse loke and lamentable
countenaunce casteth hys vnkynd forgetfulnes in to hys mynde:
wyt ye well dere frendes that among the manyfold great and   10
greuouse paynys whych he suffreth here / wherof god send you
ye grace to suffer eyther none or few: the grudge and greefe of
hys conscyence in the consyderacyon of hys vnkynde forgetfulnes / is not of all them the leste. Therfore dere frendys let our
foly lerne you wysdome. Send hether your prayour: sende   15
hether your almoyse before you: so shall we fynde ease therof /
and yet shall ye fynde yt styll. For as he that lyghtyth a nother the
candell hath neuer the lesse lyght hym self / & he that blowyth ye
fyre for a nother to warme hym doth warm hym self also therwyth: so surely good frendys the good that ye send hether before   20
you / both greatly refresheth vs / and yet ys holly reseruyd here
for you with oure prayours added thereto for youre ferther
aduauntage.

Wold god we coud haue done our self as we now counsell you.
And god gyue you ye grace whych many of vs refused / to make   25
better prouysyon whyle ye lyue than many of vs haue done. For
mich haue we left in our executours handes / whych wold god we
had bestowed vppon pore folk for our owne soulys & our
frendys wyth our own han[L₁]dys. Mych haue many of vs be-
stowyd vppon rych men in gold rynges and blak gownys: mych in   30
many tapers & torchys: mych in worldly pomp and hygh solempne ceremonyes about our funerallys / wherof the brotle
glory standeth vs here god wot in very litle stede / but hath on the
tother syde done vs great dyspleasure. For albe yt yᵗ the kynde

---

1 neglygence] *1529*² *1557*, necligence *1529*¹   11 paynys] *1529*¹, payne *1529*²
1557   12–13 *Sidenote 1557:* Grudge of conscience   19 *Sidenote 1557:* Note
21 holly] *1529*², hole *1529*¹, wholy *1557*

solycytude & louyng dylygence of the quyk vsed about the
beryeng of the dede / is well allowed and approuyd afore the
face of god: yet mych superfluouse charge vsed for boste and
ostentacyon / namely deuysed by the dede before hys dethe / ys
5 of god greatly myslyked: and moste especially that kynde &
fassyon therof wherin some of vs haue fallen / and many besydys
vs that now lye damnyd in hell. For some hathe there of vs whyle
we were in helthe / not so mych studyed how we myght dye
penytent and in good crysten plyght / as how we myght be sol-
10 empnely borne owte to beryeng / haue gay & goodly funerallys
wyth herawdys at our hersys / and ofrynge vp oure helmettys /
settyng vp our skouchyn and cote armours on the wall though
there neuer cam harneyse on our bakkys / nor neuer auncestour
of ours euer bare armis byfore. Then deuysed we some doctour
15 to make a sermon at our masse in our monthys mynde / and
there preche to our prayse wyth some fond fantesy deuysed of
our name / and after masse / mych festyng ryotouse and costly /
and fynally lyke madde men made men mery at our dethe / and
take our beryeng for a brydeale. For specyall punyshement
20 whereof / some of vs haue bene by our euyll aungels brought
forth full heuely in full great despyght to beholde our awne
beryeng / and so standen in great payne inuysyble among the
preace / and made to loke on our careyn corps caryed owte wyth
great pompe / wherof our lorde knoweth we haue taken heuy
25 pleasure.

     Yet wolde ye peraduenture wene that we were in one thyng
well eased / in that we were for the tyme taken hense owt of the
fyre of our purgatory. But in thys poynt yf ye so thynke/ ye be
farre deceyued. For lykewyse as good aungels and saued soulys
30 in heuen / neuer lese nor lessen theyre ioy by chaungyng of
theyre placys / but though there be eny specyall place appoynted
for heuen ferthest from the centre of the hole worlde or where
so euer yt be / be yt bodyly or aboue all bodyly space / the blessyd
heuenly spyrytys where so euer they bycum be eyther styll in
35 heuen or in theyr heuenly ioy: nor Gabryell when he cam down

---

to our lady / neuer forbare eny parte of his pleasure / but he had
yt paraduenture wyth some newe degre encreaced by the cumforte of hys ioyfull message / but mynysshed myght yt neuer be /
not and he had an erand in to hell: ryght so fareth it on y^e tother
syde / that neyther dampned wreches at eny tyme / nor we for 5
the space of our clensynge tyme though we haue for the generaltye our comen place of payne appoynted vs here in purgatory:
yet yf it please our lorde that at eny season [L$_1$v] our gardayns
conuay some of vs to be for some consyderacyons eny tyme ellys
where / as some percase to appere to some frend of ours & shew 10
hym how we stand / & by y^e sufferauns of goddys souerayn
goodnes to tell hym wyth what almoyse / prayour / pylgrymage /
or other good dede done for vs he may helpe vs hense / in
whyche thynge the deuyll ys loth to walke wyth vs but he may not
chese and can no ferther wythstand vs then god wyll gyue hym 15
leue / but whyther so euer he cary vs we cary our payne wyth vs:
& lyke as the body that hath an hote feuer as feruently burneth yf
he ryde an horsbake as yf he lay lapped in hys bedde: so cary we
styll about no lesse hete wyth vs / then yf we lay bounden here.
And yet the dyspyghtfull syghtys that our euyll aungellis brynge 20
vs to beholde abrode / so farre augmenteth our turment: that we
wolde wyshe to be drowned in the darkenes that ys here / rather
than se the syghtys that they shew vs there.

For among they conuay vs in to our awne housys / & ther
dowble ys our payne wyth syght sometyme of ye selfe same 25
thyngys whych whyle we lyued was halfe our heuen to behold.
There shew they vs our substaunce and our baggys stuffed wyth
gold: whych when we now se / we sette myche lesse by theym
then wold an old man that found a bag of chery stonys whych he
layd vp when he was a chylde. What a sorow hath it ben to some 30
of vs when ye deuils hath in dispyghtfull mokkage / caste in oure
teeth our old loue borne to our money / & then shewed vs our
executours as bysyly ryfling & ransakyng our housys / as thogh
they were men of warr that had taken a town by force.

Howe heuely hath yt thynke you gone vnto our harte / when 35

16–19 *Sidenote 1557:* The soule, whither soeuer it remoueth, doth cary his payn with him
19 here] *1529*^{1} *1557*, hete *1529*^{2}

our euyll aungellys haue grynned and lawghed and shewed vs
our late wyuys so sone waxen wanton / & forgetyng vs theyre old
husbandys that haue loued theym so tendrely and lefte theym so
ryche / sytte and lawgh & make mery and more to sumtyme /
5   wyth theyr new woars / whyle our kepers in dyspyte kepe vs
there in payne to stande styll / & loke on. Many tymes wold we
then speke yf we coulde be suffred / & sore we long to say to her:
Ah wyfe wyfe ywysse this was not couenaunt wyfe / when ye
wepte and tolde me that yf I lefte you to lyue by / ye wold neuer
10 wedde agayne. We se there our chyldren to / whom we loued so
well / pype syng and dawnce / & no more thynke on theyre
fathers soulys then on theyre olde shone: sauyng that sometyme
cummeth owt god haue mercy on all crysten sowlys. But yt cummeth owt so coldely and wyth so dull affeccyon / that yt lyeth but
15 in the lyppys and neuer cam nere the harte. Yet here we sometyme our wyuis pray for vs more warmely. For in chydynge wyth
her secunde husbande to spyghte hym wyth all / god haue mercy
sayeth she on my fyrst husbandes sowle / for he was ywysse an
honest man farr vnlyke you. And then meruayle we myche when
20 we here theym say so well by vs. For [L₂] they were euer wont to
tell vs otherwyse.

   But when we fynde in thys wyse our wiuys / or chyldren and
frendys / so sone and so clerely forgete vs / and se our executours
rap and rend vnto theym selfe / catche euery man what he can
25 and holde faste that he catcheth and care nothyng for vs: lorde
god what yt greueth vs that we lefte so mych bihynd vs / and had
not sent hyther more of our substaunce byfore vs by our owne
handys. For happy fynde we hym among vs / yᵗ sendeth byfore
all yᵗ may be forborne. And he that ys so loth to parte wyth aught /
30 that hordeth vp his good and had as lyue dye almost as to breke
hys hepe / and then at last when there ys none other remedye but
that he muste nedys leue yt / repenteth hym self sodenly &
lakketh tyme to dyspose yt / & therfore byddeth his frendys to
bestow yt well for hym: our lord ys yet so marcyfull yᵗ of hys
35 goodnes he acceptyd yᵉ good dedys yᵗ hys executours do in per-

---

1 grynned] *1529*² *1557*, gyrned *1529*¹   27 *Sidenote 1557:* Note   30 lyue] *1529*, leue
1557

formyng his deuyce. And syth that late is better then neuer: our
lord somewhat alloweth the mannys mynde / by whych he wold
hys goodys that he hath immoderately gathered and gredily
kepte to gether as longe as he myght / were yet at the leste wyse
well bestowed at laste when he must nedys go fro them. Whych   5
mynde yet more pleaseth god / then that a man cared not what
were done wyth them. And therfor as we say the goodnes of god
somewhat doth accepte yt. But yet surely syth we myght and
ought to haue done yt our self / and of a fylthy affeccyon toward
our goodys could not fynde in our hart to parte from eny parte   10
of them / yf our executours now deceyue vs & do no more for vs
then we dyd for our selfe: our lord dyd vs no wronge though he
neuer gaue vs thanke of all our hole testament / but imputed the
frustracyon and not performynge of our laste wyll vnto our
owne fawte: syth the delay of our good dedys dreuen of to our   15
deth / grew but of our awne slewth and flesshely loue to the
world ward / wyth fayntenesse of deuocyon to god ward / and of
lytle respect and regard vnto our awne soule. And ouer thys yf
our executours do these good thyngys in dede that we do thus at
laste deuyse in our testament: yet our defawte dryuynge all to   20
our deth as we told you byfore / though god as we sayd of hys
hygh goodnes leueth not all vnrewarded / yet thys warnynge wyll
we gyue you / that ye deceyue not your selfe: we that haue so
dyed haue thus founde yt / that the goodys disposed after vs /
gete our executours great thanke / & be toward vs ward ac-   25
compted afore god myche lesse then half our awn / nor our
thanke nothyng lyke to that yt wolde haue bene yf we had in our
helth geuen half as mych for goddys sake wyth our awne handys.
Of whyche we geue you thys frendely warnyng not for that we
wold dyscorage you to dyspose well your goodys when ye dye: 30
but for that we wold aduyse you to dyspose them better whyle ye
lyue. [L₂v]
    And amonge all your almoyse / sumwhat remember vs: Our
wyuys there remember here your husbandys. Our chyldren

---

4 as he] *1529*¹ *corr. err.*, *1529*² *1557*, he *1529*¹   13 imputed] *1529*¹ *corr. err.*, *1529*²
1557, imported *1529*¹   22–24 *Sidenote 1557:* Note thys warning   31 them] *1557*,
thē *1529*¹, then *1529*²,

there remember here your parentys. Our parentys there remember here your chyldren. Our husbandys there remember
here your wyuys. Ah swete husbandys whyle we lyued there in
that wreched world with you / whyle ye were glad to please vs: ye
5   bestowed mych vppon vs & put your selfe to greate coste and dyd
vs great harme therwyth. Wyth gay gownys and gay kyrtels &
mych waste in apparell / rynges & owchis / wyth partelettes &
pastis garneshed wyth perle / wyth whych proude pykynge vp:
both ye toke hurte and we to / many mo ways then one though we
10 told you not so than. But two thyngys were there specyall / of
whych your selfe felt then the tone / and we fele now the tother.
For ye had vs the hygher harted and the more stoburn to you:
and god had vs in lesse fauour: and that alak we fele. For now
that gay gere burneth vppon our bakkys: and those prowd per-
15 led pastys hang hote about our chekis / those partelettys and
those owchis hang heuy abowt our nekkys and cleue fast fyre
hote / that wo be we there and wyshe that whyle we lyued / ye
neuer had folowed our fantasyes / nor neuer had so kokered vs
nor made vs so wanton / nor had geuen vs other ouchys than
20 ynions or gret garlyk heddys / nor other perles for our partelettys
and our pastys then fayre orient peason. But now for as mych as
that ys passed and cannot be called agayn: we besech you syth ye
gaue them vs let vs haue them still let them hurt none other
woman but help to do vs good: sell them for our sakys to set in
25 sayntys copys / and send the money hether by masse pennys & by
pore men that may pray for our soulys.

    Our fathers also whych whyle we lyued fostred vs vp so tend-
erly / & coud not haue endured to se vs suffer payn: now open
your hartes & fatherly affeccyon / & help vs at the leste wyse wyth
30 a pore mannis almes. Ye wold not when we were wyth you haue
letted to lay out mych money for a great mariage. Whych yf ye
ment for our sakes & not for your own worldly wurshyp / gyue vs
now sum parte therof & releue vs here wyth mych lesse cost then
one maryage / & more plesure then .xv. though euery one were
35 a prynce or a pryncesse of a realm.

---

6 therwyth.] *1529*[1], therwyth? *1529*[2], therwith, *1557*   11 the tone] *1557*, y[e] tone
1529[1], that tone *1529*[2]   12 *Sidenote 1557:* Note ye wyues

Fynally all our other frendys & euery good cristen man &
woman open your hartys & haue sum pyte vppon vs. If ye beleue
not y^t we nede your help / alas the lak of fayth. If ye beleue our
nede and care not for vs / alas the lak of pyte. For who so pytyeth
not vs / whom can he pyte? If ye pyte the pore / there ys none so   5
pore as we / y^t haue not a bratte to put on our bakkys. If ye pyte
the blynde / there ys none so blynd as we whych ar here in the
dark sauyng for syghtis vnplesaunt and lothesum tyll sum cumfort cum. If ye pyte the lame / there is none so lame as we / that
nether can crepe one fote out of the fyre / nor haue one hand at   10
lyberte to defend our face fro the flame. Fynally yf ye py[L₃]te
any man in payn / neuer knew ye payn comparable to ours:
whose fyre as farre passeth in hete all the firys that euer burned
vppon erth / as the hotest of all those passeth a feynyd fyre
payntyd on a wall. If euer ye lay syk and thought the nyght long /   15
& longed sore for day whyle euery howre semed longer than
fyue: bethynk you then what a long nyght we sely soulys endure /
that ly slepelesse / restlesse / burnyng / and broylyng in the dark
fyre one long nyght of many days / of many wekys / and sum of
many yeres to gether. You walter peraduenture and tolter in   20
syknes fro syde to syde & fynde lytle rest in eny parte of the bed:
we ly bounden to the brondys and cannot lyft vp our heddys.
You haue your physycyons wyth you that sumtyme cure and hele
you: no phisyk wyll help our payn / nor no plaster cole our hete.
Your kepars do you great ease and put you in good cumfort: our   25
kepars ar such as god kepe you from / cruell damned spyrytes /
odyouse / enuyouse / and hatefull / dyspytuouse enmys and
dyspytefull turmentours / and theyr cumpany more horryble
and greuous to vs / then ys the payn yt self and thintollerable
turment that they do vs wherwyth from top to too they ceace not   30
contynually to tere vs.
  But now yf our other enmys these heretikys almost as cruell as
they / procuryng to theyr power that we shulde be long left in y^e
dyuels handys wyll as theyr vsage ys to rayle in stede of reson-

---

13–15 *Sidenote 1557:* No payne is comparable to the paynes of purgatory   14 hotest]
1529¹ 1557, hostest *1529²*   22 we] *1529² 1557,* but we *1529¹*   25–26 *Sidenote 1557:*
The kepers of the soules in purgatory

yng / make a game and a ieste now of our heuy payn / and paraduenture laugh at our lamentacyon / bycause we speke of our
heddes / our handys / our feete / and suche our other grose
bodyly members as lye beryed in our grauis & of our garmentys
5   that we dyd were whyche come not hether wyth vs: we bysech
you for our dere ladyes loue to let theyre foly go by / and to
consyder in your owne wysdom that yt were impossyble to make
eny mortall man lyuyng perceyue what maner payn & in what
maner wyse we bodylesse soulys do suffer and sustayne: or to
10   make eny man vppon erth perfytely to conceyue in hys ymagynacyon and fantasy / what maner of substaunce we be: mych
more impossyble then to make a borne blynd man to perceyue in
hys mynd the nature and dyfference of colours. And therfore
except we shuld of our painfull state tell you nothynge at all (and
15   there wold they haue yt) we must of necessyte vse you such
wordys as your selfe vnderstand / and vse you the symylytudes of
such thyngys as your self ys in vre with. For syth neyther god /
angell nor soule / ys in such wyse blynd / dome / defe / or lame /
as be those men y^t for lak of eyen / legges / handes / tonge / or
20   ere / be weke & impotent in ye powers y^t procede from them: but
haue in them selfe a farre more excellent syght / heryng / delyuernesse / and spech / by meanys vncogitable to man / then eny
man can haue liuyng there on yerth: therfore doth holy scripture in spekyng of such thinges / vse to represent them to y^e
25   people by y^e namys of suche powers / instrumentes / & members / [L$_3$v] as men in such thyngys vse and occupye them selfe.
Whyche maner of spekynge in such case who so euer haue in
derysyon: declareth very well how lytle fayth he hath in Crystys
awne wordes / in whych our sauyour hym selfe spekyng of the
30   sowlys of the ryche gloton & pore nedy Lazarus / and of the
Patriarch Abraam also speketh in lyke maner as we do / of fynger
and tonge to / wherof they had neyther nother there. And therfore who so maketh a mok at our wordes in this poynt: ye may
sone se what credence ye shuld geue hym / wheryn we be content

---

23 there on yerth] *1529*[1] *corr. err.*, *1529*[2], theron *1529*[1], there on earth *1557*
25 powers /] *1529*[1], powers *1529*[2], powers, *1557*   29 whych] whychy *1529*, which
1557   31 *Sidenote 1557:* Luke. 16

ye gyue hym euen as mych as ye se your selfe that he gyueth to
god: for more ye ought not and surely lesse ye can not. For he
geueth god not a whyt: but taketh in hys harte that story told by
god for a very fantastyke fable.

And therfore as we say passing ouer suche iestyng and raylyng 5
of those vncherytable heretykys mortall enymyes vnto vs and to
themself both: consyder you our paynys / and pyte them in your
hartys / and helpe vs wyth your prayours / pylgrymagys and
other almoyse dedys: & of all thyng in specyall procure vs the
suffragis and blessyd oblacyon of the holy masse / wherof no 10
man lyuyng so well can tell the frute as we that here fele yt.

The cumforte that we haue here except our continuall hope in
our lord god / cummeth at seasons from our Lady / wyth such
gloryouse sayntys as ether our self wyth our own deuocyon
whyle we lyued / or ye wyth yours for vs synnys our decease and 15
departyng haue made intercessours for vs. And among other
ryght especyally be we beholden to the blessyd spyrytys our own
proper good angels. Whom when we behold cummyng wyth
cumfort to vs / albe yt that we take great plesure and gretly
reioyce theryn: yet ys yt not wythout mych confusyon and sham- 20
fastnes / to consyder how lytle we regardyd our good angels &
how seldum we thoght vppon them whyle we lyued. Thay cary
vp our prayers to god & good sayntes for vs: & they bryng down
fro them the cumfort and consolacyon to vs. Wyth whych when
they cum & cumfort vs: only god and we know what ioy yt is to 25
our hartys & how hartely we pray for you. And therfore yf god
accept the prayour after hys own fauour born toward hym that
prayeth & thaffeccyon that he prayeth wyth: our prayer must
nedys be profytable / for we stand sure of hys grace. And our
prayer ys for you so feruent / that ye can no where fynde eny 30
such affeccyon vppon erth. And therfore syth we ly so sore in
paynys & haue in our great necessyte so gret nede of your help &
y^t ye may so well do yt / wherby shall also rebownd vppon your
self an inestymable profyte: let neuer eny slouthfull oblyuyon

7 themself] 1557, thē self 1529¹, then[new line]self 1529²   11 yt.] 1529² 1557, yt
1529¹   24-25 Sidenote 1557: Our good angelles

race vs out of your remembraunce / or malicyouse enmy of ours
cause you to be carelesse of vs / or eny gredy mynde vppon your
good withdraw your gracyouse almes from vs. Thynk how sone
ye shall cum hether to vs: [L₄] thynk what great grefe and rebuke
5 wold then your vnkyndnes be to you: what cumfort on the contrary part when all we shall thank you: what help ye shall haue
here of your good sent hether. Remember what kyn ye and we be
to gether: what familier frendship hath ere this bene betwene vs:
what swete wordys ye haue spoken and what promyse ye haue
10 made vs. Let now your wordis appere and your fayre promyse be
kept. Now dere frendys remember how nature & crystendom
byndeth you to remember vs. If eny poynt of your old fauour /
eny pece of your old loue / eny kindnes of kinred / eny care of
acquayntance / eny fauour of old frendshyp / eny spark of char-
15 yte / eny tender poynt of pyte / eny regard of nature / eny
respect of crystendum / be left in your brestys: let neuer the
malyce of a few fond felows / a few pestylent persons born toward presthod / relygyon / and your crysten fayth: race out
of your hartys the care of your kynred / all force of your old
20 frendys / and all remembraunce of all crysten soulys. Remember
our thurst whyle ye syt & drynk: our honger whyle ye be festing:
our restlesse wach whyle ye be slepyng: our sore and greuouse
payn whyle ye be playing: our hote burnyng fyre whyle ye be in
plesure & sportyng: so mote god make your ofsprynge after
25 remember you: so god kepe you hens or not long here: but
brynge you shortely to that blysse / to whych for our lordys loue
help you to brynge vs / and we shall set hand to help you thyther
to vs

Finis.
Cum priuilegio

---

1 race vs out] *1529*¹ *corr. err.*, *1529*² *1557*, race out *1529*¹   8 frendship] *1529*¹ *1557*,
frendsyp 1529²   17 felows /] *1529*¹, felowes *1529*², felowes, *1557*   29 Finis.] *1529*,
om. 1557   30 Cum priuilegio] *1529*, *om. 1557*

LETTER AGAINST FRITH

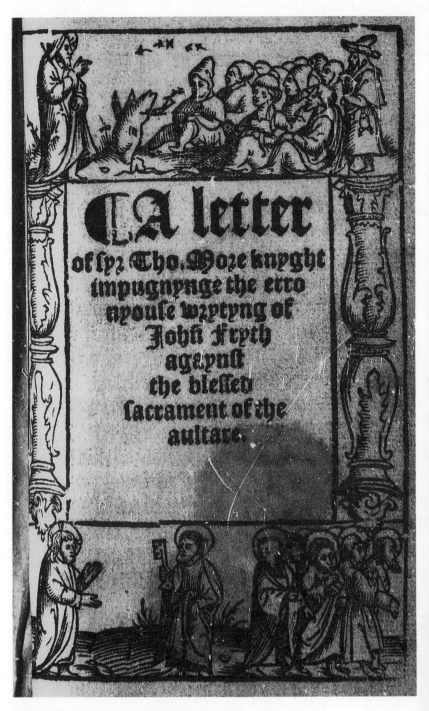

Title page, *A Letter against Frith*, 1533

[a₁]
A letter
of syr Tho. More knyght impugnynge the erro nyouse wrytyng of Iohan Fryth agaynst the blessed sacrament of the aultare.

IN my moste harty wyse I recommend me to you, & sende you by thys brynger the wrytynge agayne whyche I receyued from you / wherof I haue ben offred synnys a couple of copyes mo in the meane whyle, as late as ye wote wel it was. Wherby men maye se how gredyly y^t these newe named bretherne wryte it out, and   5
secretely sprede it abrode. So that

*King Henrye the viii**

where as the kynges gracyouse hyghnes lyke a moste faythfull catholyke prynce, for the auoydynge of suche pestylente bokes as sowe suche poysened heresyes amonge his people, hath by hys open proclamacyons vtterly forboden   10
[a₂v] all englysshe prented bookes to be brought into thys lande from beyonde the see, lest our englysshe heretykes that are lurkynge there myghte there enprent theyr heresyes among other maters, & so sende them hither vnsuspected, & therfore vnperceyued tyll more harme were felte than after were well   15
remedyable: the deuyll hath now taught hys dysciples the dyuysers of these heresyes, to make many shorte treatyses, whereof theyr scolers may shortly write out copyes / but in theyr treatyses to put as mych poyson in one wryten lefe, as they prented before in fyftene / as it well appereth in thys one wrytynge of   20
thys yong mannes makyng, which [a₃] hath I here saye lately made dyuerse other thynges, y^t yet ronne in huker moker so close amonge the brethern, y^t there cometh no copyes abrode.

And wold god for hys mercy that syth there can nothing refrayne theyr study from the deuyse & compassyng of euyll and   25
vngracyouse wrytynge, y^t they coulde and wolde kepe it so secrete, y^t neuer man sholde se it, but suche as are all redy so farre corrupted, as neuer wold be cured of theyr canker. For lesse harme were it yf onely they that are all

Apoca. 22

redy bymyred, were as the scrypture   30
sayth myred on more & more, thanne that they sholde caste theyr dyrt abrode vpon other folkes clene clothys. But [a₃v] alak thys wyll not be. For as saynte Poule sayth, the contagyon of heresye crepeth on lyke a canker. For as

2. Timo. 2
*The nature of a canker**

the canker corrupteth the body ferther   35
and ferther, and turneth the hole

---

36 and ferther] and ferher *1532*, and farther *1557*

233

partes into the same dedely sykenesse: so do these heretykes
crepe forth among good symple soulys / and vnder a vayn hope
of some hygh secrete lernynge, whych other men abrode eyther

5 *The property of heretikes**   wyllyngly dyd kepe from them, or ellys
                                    coulde not teche theym / they dayly
wyth suche abomynable bokes corrupte & destroye in corners
very many before those wrytynges comme vnto lyght, tyll at the
laste ye smoke of that secrete fyre begynneth to reke oute at some
corner / [a₄] and somtyme the whole fyre so flameth oute at onys,
10 that it burneth vp whole townes, and wasteth whole countrees,
ere euer it can be maystred / and yet neuer after so well & clerely
quenched, but y^t it lyeth lurkynge styll in some olde roten tymber
vnder cellers & celynges, that yf it be not wel wayted on and
marked, wyll not fayle at lengthe to fall on an open fyre agayne /
15 as it hath fared in late yeres at mo places then one, bothe the tone
fyre & the tother. And therfore I am bothe sure and sory to, that
those other bokes as wel as this is now of thys yonge mannes, wyll
ones come vnto lyght / and than shall it appere wherfore they be
kept so close. How be it a wors than this is [a₄v] though the
20 wordes be smoth & fayre / the deuyll I trow can not make. For
herein he ronneth a great way beyond Luther / and techeth in
few leuys shortely, all the poyson that wyclyffe, Huyskyn, Tyndale, and zuinglius haue taught in all theyr longe bokes before,
concernynge the blessed sacrament of the aultare / affermyng it
25 to be not onely very brede styll as Luther doth, but also as those
other bestes do, saith it is nothyng els, & that there is neyther the
blessed body of Cryst, nor his blode, but for a remembraunce of
Crystes passyon onely bare brede & wyne. And therin goth he so

30 *O vile heretyke**   farre in conclusyon, y^t he sayth it is all
                                    one vnto vs in a maner whyther it be
consecrated or vnconsecrated. [b₁] And so that blessed sacrament that is and euer hath in all christendom ben holden of all
sacramentes the chyef, & nat onely a sacrament but the very selfe
thynge also whych other sacramentes bytoken, & wherof all

---

16 tother.] *1557*, tother, *1532*   31 vnconsecrated.] *1557*, vnconsecrated *1532*
34 sacramentes bytoken] *1557*, sacramentēs betoken *1532*

other sacramentes take theyr effecte
and strength: he maketh in maner (takyng the consecracyon so sleyghte and so
lyght) no maner sacrament at all.
Wherein he runneth yet beyond Tyndale and all the heretykes 5
that euer I remembre byfore.

All sacramentes take their effect of the sacrament of the aulter*

And now the mater beyng of such a meruelouse wayght it is a
great wonder to se vppon howe lyght and sleyghte occasyons he
is fallen vnto these abominable heyghnouse [b₁v] heresyes.

For he denyeth nat nor can nat say nay, but that our sauyour 10
sayed hym selfe. My flesh is veryly
mete, and my blode is verily drynke.

Iohan. 6

He denyeth nat also that Chryste hym selfe at hys laste sowper
takyng the bred into hys blessed
handes, after that he had blessed hit 15
sayde vnto his disciples, Take you this &
eate it, thys is my body that shalbe gyuen for you. And in
lykewyse gaue them the chalyce after hys blessynge and consecracyon, and sayde vnto them, Thys is the chalyce of my
bloude of the newe testamente, whyche shalbe shedde out for 20
many / do you thys in remembraunce of me. [b₂]

Marci. 14

Luce. 22

The yong man denyeth nat nor can deny, but that our sauyour
here hym selfe sayed yᵗ hit was hys owne body, and sayed that hit
was hys owne bloude / and there ordeyned yᵗ it shulde be in
remembraunce of hym contynually consecrated. So that he must 25
nedes confesse, that all they whyche byleue that it is hys very
body and hys very bloude in dede, haue yᵉ playne wordes of our
sauyour hym selfe vpon theyr syde, for the grounde and fundacyon of theyr fayth.

But now sayth thys yong man against all this, that our sau- 30
youre in other places of scripture,
called hym selfe a very vyne, and his
dyscyples very braunchys. And he
cal[b₂v]leth hym selfe a dore also / nat for that he was eny of
these thynges in dede, but for certayne proprietes for whyche he 35
lykened hym selfe to those thynges. As a man for some propretees sayth of his neyghbours horse, thys horse is myn vppe
and downe / mening that it is in euery thynge so lyke. And lyke as
Iacob byelded an aultare and called it yᵉ god of Israel, and as

Iohan. 15

Iohan. 10

Gene. 35

Gene. 32*

Exod. 13*

Iacob called the place where he wresteled wyth the angell the face of god, and that the pascall lambe was called the passing by of the lorde, wyth

5 infinite such other phrases as he saith natte for that they were so in dede, but for certayne similitudes in the propretees: soo [b₃] sayeth thys yonge man, that Cryste though he sayd by hys playne wordes, Thys is my body, and thys is my blode / yet for all that he ment not yᵗ it was his body and his blode in dede, no more than

10 that he ment that hym selfe was a very dore or a very vine in dede / though for certeyne propertees he called hym selfe bothe. And he sayth yᵗ Cryst ment in lyke wyse here / not that it was or shold be his owne body & hys blode in dede, but yᵗ it shold be to them & vs as a remembraunce of hym in hys absence, as

15 veryly as though it were his very body and his very blode in dede / as yᵉ pascall lambe was a token and a remembraunce of the passynge by of the lord / [b₃v] and as a brydegrome gyueth his bryde a rynge yf he happe to go into a farre countre from her, for a remembraunce of hym in his absence, and as a sure sygne yᵗ

20 he wyll kepe her hys faythe and not breke her hys promyse.

In good fayth it greueth me very sore, to se thys yonge man so cyrcumuented and begyled by certayn olde lymmes of the de-uyll, as we nowe se yᵗ he is / when he is fayne for the defence of thys errour, to flyt in conclusyon fro the fayth of playne and

25 open scrypture & so farre falle to the newe fangled fantasyes of folysshe heretykes, that he wyll for the allegorye dystroye yᵉ trewe sense of the letter, in mayntenaunce [b₄] of a newe false secte, agaynste the hole trew catholyke fayth so fully confyrmed and contynued in Crystes whole catholyke chyrche thys .xv. C.

30 yere togyder. For these dregges hath he dronken of wyclyffe & Ecolampadius, Tindale and zuinglius / and so hath he all that he argueth here besyde. Whiche .iiii. what maner folke they be, is metely well perceyued and knowen / & god hath in parte with his open vengeaunce declared. And euer hath god and euer wyll, by

35   some waye declare his wrathe and indy-
Note*
                                            gnacyon agaynst as many as fall into

suche damnable opynyons agaynst the blessed body and blode of hys onely begotten sonne. From whyche [b₄v] perylous opinyon

he Last Supper, by Albrecht Dürer, from *Passio Domini Nostri*, Nürnberg,
11, plate ii (reduced)

and all his other errours / y^e great mercy of our swet sauiour call
home agayne, and saue thys yonge man in tyme.

As for hys allegoryes I am not offended wyth, nor wyth symylytudes neyther where they maye haue place, though he take
one of his neighbours hors as he doth, and another yf he lyste of   5
hys owne cow. Prouyded alwaye for a thyng whyche he lyste to
call lyke, he mysconstrue not the scrypture, & take awaye the
very thynge in dede as he doth here.

Now his ensample also of hys brydegromys ryng, I very well
How the sacrament is left   allow. For I take the blessed sacrament   10
for a token*   to be lefte wyth vs for a very token and
[c₁] a memoryall, of Cryst in dede. But I
saye that whole substaunce of the same token and memoreall, is
hys owne blessed body / where as thys man wolde make it onely
brede. And so I say that Cryst hath left vs a better token than this   15
man wolde haue vs take it fore / and therin fareth lyke a man to
whom a brydegrome had delyuered a goodly gold rynge with a
ryche ruby therin, to deliuer ouer to his bryde for a token / and
than he wold lyke a false shrew, kepe away that gold rynge, and
gyue the bryde in the stede therof a proper rynge of a rysshe,   20
and tell her that the brydegrome wold sende her no better / or els
lyke one that whan ye brydegrome [c₁v] had gyuen suche a gold
rynge to hys bryde for a token, wold tell her playne and make her
byleue that the ryng were but coper or brasse, to mynysshe y^e
brydegromys thanke.   25

If he sayed that the wordes of Cryste myghte besyde the lytterall sense be vnderstanden in an allegorye / I wolde well agree
wyth hym. For so maye euery worde almoste thorowe the whole
scrypture / callynge an allegorye euery sense, wherby the wordes
be translated vnto some other spyrytuall vnderstandyng, bysyde   30
the trewe playne open sense y^t the letter fyrste entended. But on
the other syde bycause that in some wordes of scrypture is there
none other thynge en[c₂]tended but an allegorye, to go therfore
and in another place of scrypture to take a waye wyth an allegorye, the very trew lytterall sense as he doth here / thys is the   35

---

faute that we fynde in hym. Whyche yf it maye be suffered, muste nedes make all the scrypture as towchyng any poynt of our fayth, of none effecte or force at all. I meruayle me therfore mych y^t he is not aferde to afferme y^t these wordes of Cryste, of
5   hys body and hys blode, must nedes be vnderstanden onely by waye of a symylytude or an allegorye as the wordes be of the vyne and the dore.

Now thys he woteth well, that though som wordes spoken by the mouth of Chryste [c$_2$v] wrytten in scripture, be to be vnder-
10 standen onely by waye of a similitude or an allegory: it foloweth nat therupon that of necessite euery lyke worde of Christ in other places was none other but an allegory. For suche kynde of
          *The shift of the Arrians**   sophisticacion in arguyng, was ye very
                                          cauillacion and shyfte that the wykked
15 Arrians vsed. Whych lyke as thys yong man taketh away now fro the blessed sacrament y^e very body & blood of Christ, by ex- pounynge hys playne wordes wyth an allegory vnder colour of some other places where such allegoryes muste nedes haue place, & were none otherwese ment: so dyd they take from
20 Christes blessed person hys omnipotent [c$_3$] godhed, and wolde
          *The Arrians errour**   nat graunt hym to be equale wyth al-
                                          myghty god hys father / but y^e playne
textes of scrypture whyche proued hys godhed, they expouned wronge and frowardly / nat onely by some other textes that
25 semede to say otherwyse, but also as thys yonge man doth here by some allegories / affermyng that he was called god and the sonne of god in holy scrypture, by suche maner of speking, or as thys yonge man calleth it, by suche a maner of phrase as the scrypture for som propertie calleth certayne other persones
30 goddes and goddes sonnes in other places. As where god sayth to Moyses, I shall make the the god of Pharao. [c$_3$v] And where he
          Exodi. 7   saith, thou shalt nat bakbyte the
                           goddes. And where he sayeth, I saye
          Exodi. 22   you be goddes and y^e sonnes of the
35   *Psal. 81*   hygh god be you all.

---

19 otherwese] otherwise *1557*

And thus agaynste that y^t Cryst was god and the sonne of god /
such cauyllacions these Arrians layed in expownyng the playne
places wyth false allegoryes / resemblyng them to other places in
whych lyke allegoryes muste nedes haue place / as thys yonge
man by the necessary allegoryes of Crystes wordes, vsed in the   5
vyne and in the dore, wolde in lyke wyse wyth lyke cauyllacyons
as the Arryans vsed agaynste Crystes godhed, pull away the
trewe lytterall sense of Crystes wordes, concernyng [c$_4$] the
trouth of hys very body & blode in the blessed sacrament.

And surely yf this maner of handelynge of scrypture may be   10
receyued and broughte in vre, that bycause of allegoryes vsed in
some places euery man maye at hys pleasure draw euery place to
an allegorye, and say the letter meneth no thynge ellys / there is
not any texte in all the scrypture, but a wylfull person may fynde
other textes agaynst it, that maye serue hym to tryfle out the   15
trouth of goddes wordes, wyth cauillacyons grounded vppon
goddes other wordes, in some other place. Wherin yf he maye be
herde as longe as he lyst to talke be it but a woman: yet shall she
fynd chatte [c$_4$v] inough for all an hole yere. And so dyd those
old Arrians / of whome god forbede y^t thys yong man shulde   20
folowe that euyll ensample.

If euery man that can fynd out a new fonde fantasye vpon a
texte of holy scrypture, may haue hys owne mynd taken, and hys
owne exposition byleued, agaynste the exposicions of the old
holy cunnyng doctours and sayntes: than may ye surely se that   25
none article of the christen fayth can stand and endure long. For
as holy saynte Hierom sayth of hym
Hierony. aduersus   selfe, if the exposition of other in-
Luciferianos   terpretours and the consente of the
commune catholyque church, were of no more strenghte, but   30
that euery new man [d$_1$] myght be byleued that coulde bryng
som textes of scrypture for hym expouned as it pleased hym
selfe / than could I sayth thys holy man brynge vp a new secte
also, and saye by scripture that no man were a trew christen man
nor a membre of the church that kep-   35
Luk. 3*   eth two cotes. And in good fayth if that

---

1 y^t] the *1557*   19 inough] Inough *1532*, ynough *1557*

way were allowed / I were able my selfe to fynd out fyften newe
sectes in one fore none, y^t shulde haue as moche probable holde
of scripture as thys heresy hathe. Agaynste which, beside the
comon fayth of all catholyque christen regyons, the expositions
5 of the old holy doctours and saintes be clere agaynste thys yonge
mannes mynd in thys mater, [d$_1$v] as whole as agaynst any heresy
that euer was hytherto herd of. For as for the wordes of Chryst of
whyche we speke touchyng y^e blessed sacrament / though he
may fynd som olde holy men that byside the lytterall sence doth
10 expoune them in an allegory, yet shall he neuer fynde any of
them that dyd as he doth now after wicliffe, Ecolampadius, Tyndale, & zuynglius, deny the lytterall sence / and say that Chryst
ment nat that it was his very body and hys very bloude in dede /
but the olde holy doctours & exposytours byside all suche alle-
15 gories, do playnly declare & expoune, that in those wordes our
sauyour as he expressely spake, so dyd also well & [d$_2$] playnely
mene, that the thing whyche he there gaue to hys dysciples in the
sacramente, were in very dede hys very flesh and bloud. And so
dyd neuer any of the olde exposytours of scripture expowne any
20 of those other places in whych Christ is called a vyne or a dore.
And therfore it appereth well, that ye maner of spekyng was nat
lyke. For if it had / than wolde nat the olde exposytours haue
vsed suche so far vnlyke fashyon in y^e expounyng of them.
    And ouer thys, the very circumstances of the places in y^e gos-
25 pell, in which our sauiour speketh of that sacrament, may well
make open the difference of hys speche in thys mater & [d$_2$v] of
all those other / and that as he spake all those but in an allegory,
so spake he thys playnly menyng that he spake of hys very body
and his very bloud besyde all allegories. For neyther whanne
30 oure lorde sayed he was a very vyne, nor whanne he sayde he was
the dore / there was none that herde hym that any thynge merueyled therof. And why? for bycause they perceyued well that he
ment not that he was a materyall vyne in dede, nor a materyall
                                     dore neyther. But whan he sayed that
            *Iohn. 6**
35   hys flesshe was very mete, & hys blood
was very drynke, and that they sholde not be saued but yf they
dyd eate hys flesh and drynke hys blood / than [d$_3$] were they all
in suche a wonder therof, that they coulde not abyde. And wherfore? but bycause they perceyued well by his wordes and his

maner of crycumstances vsed in y^e spekynge of them, y^t Cryst
spake of hys very flesshe and his very blood in dede. For ellys the
straungenesse of the wordes wold haue made them to haue
taken it as well for an allegorye, as eyther hys wordes of the vyne
or of the dore. And than wold they haue no more merueyled at   5
ye tone than they dyd at the tother. But nowe where as at the
vyne and the dore they merueiled nothing / yet at the eatyng of
his flesshe and drynkynge of hys blood, they so sore merueyled,
and [d₃v] were so sore moued, & thought the mater so harde, &
the wonder so greate, that they asked how coulde that be, and   10
went almoste all theyr waye. Wherby we maye well se, that he
spake these wordes in suche wyse, as the herers perceyued that
he ment it not in a parable nor an allegory / but spake of hys very
flesshe and hys very blood in dede.

Many other playne proues myghte a man gather vppon the   15
cyrcumstances of the very textes, where this thyng is spoken of in
the scrypture / but that it is not my purpose now to stycke in
argumente of thys mater, that is of it self so clere out of all
questyon / but onely a lytle to towche it, [d₄] that ye may se how
lytle pyth and substaunce for hys mater is in all those ensamples   20
of allegorye, whyche wyclyffe, Ecolampadius, Tyndale, & Suinglius haue brought out agaynst the blessed sacrament / & wherwith those old shrewes haue wyth theyr false symylytudes
pytuously deceyued, eyther the symplycyte or the lyghtnesse of
thys sely yonge man / whych myght yf he had not eyther of   25
lyghtnesse ouer ronne hym selfe, or of symplenes ben deceyued,

*Three thinges wherby man is deceued** or of pryde and hygh mynde in puttynge forth heresyes wyllyngly begyled
& blynded / easely haue perceyued hym
selfe, that the mo suche allegoryes that he founde in the scryp-   30
ture in lyke [d₄v] maner of phrases or speche, ye wurse is his
parte / & the more clere is it that these places spekyng of the
blessed sacrament, were playnely ment as they were spoken besyde all suche allegoryes. For ellys hadde neuer bothe the herers
at the tyme, & ye exposytours synnes and all chrysten people   35
besyde thys .xv. C. yere, taken onely in thys one mater the playne

21–22 Suinglius] Zwinglius *1557*

literall sense beyng so straunge & meruelouse that it myghte
seme impossyble, and declyne from the letter for allegoryes in all
suche other thynges, beynge as he sayth & as in dede they be, so
many farre in nomber moo.

5   How be it as for this poynt that an allegory vsed in some [e₁]
place, is not a cause suffycyent to make men leue the proper
sygnyfycacyons of goddes worde in euery other place, & seke an
allegorye and forsake the playne comon sense and vnderstandynge of the letter / thys perceyued yᵉ yonge man well inough
10   hym selfe. For he confesseth that he wolde not so do saue for
necessyte, bycause he seeth as he sayth that the comon lyterall
sense is impossyble. For the thynge he sayth that is ment therby,
can not be trewe / that is to wytte that the very body of Chryste
can not be in the sacrament, bycause the sacrament is in many
15   dyuers places at onys / and was at the maundy, that is to wytte in
the handes of [e₁v] Chryste and in euery of hys apostels mouthes /
and at that tyme it was not glorifyed. And than he sayth that
Chrystes body not beynge gloryfyed, coulde no more be in two
places at onys, than hys own can. And yet he goth after forther,
20   and sayth that no more it can neyther when it is gloryfyed to.
And that he proueth by yᵉ sayeng of saint Austayn / whose
wordes be as he sayth, that the body wyth whyche Chryste rose,
muste be in one place, and that it contynueth in heuen, and shall
do tyll he shall come to iudge bothe quycke and dede. And yet at
25   the laste he proueth that the body of Chryste can not be in many
places at onys. For yf [e₂] it myghte be in many places at onys,
than it myght he sayth be in all places at onys. But in all places at
onys he sayth it can not be / & therof he concludeth that it can not
be in many places at onys. And thus for thys impossybylyte of the
30   thynge that ryseth vppon the comon lytterall sense of Chrystes
wordes, he is he sayeth of necessyte dreuen to fall from it vnto
some allegorye / whyche he confesseth that he wolde not do, yf
the playne lyterall sense were possyble. But alas for the dere
mercy of god, yf we sholde leue the letter and seke an allegorye
35   wyth the destruccyon of the lytterall sense, in euery place where
we fynde a thynge that [e₂v] reason can not reche vnto, nor se
whyche waye it were possyble, and therfore wolde take it for
impossyble: fayne wolde I wytte what one artycle of all our fayth
thys yonge man coulde assygne me spoken of in the scrypture,

from whyche hys reason shall not dreue away the strength of hys
profe in makynge hym leue the lytterall sense / wherin hys profe
sholde stande and sende hym to seke an allegory that maye
stande wyth reason and dreue awaye y^e
Reason should obay vnto   fayth, where he shold byleue the leter   5
fayth*   and make his reason obedyent vnto
fayth.

I meruayle me very mych why the consyderacyon of this impossybylyte, sholde of necessyte dreue this yonge man from [e$_3$]
the playn open lytterall sense of Chrystes wordes spoken of the   10
blessed sacrament / syth so many good and holy men so longe to
gyther thys .xv. C. yere, haue byleued the lyterall sense well &
fermely, & coulde not be dreuen from it for any suche consyderacyon of suche impossybylyte / and yet beyng as naturall
men, as wyse men, as well lerned men, as studyouse in the mater,   15
and men of more age, & more sure, sadde, and substancyall
iudgement, than thys yonge man is yet, and men at the leste as
lykely to se what were possyble and what were impossyble as this
good yonge man is. And therfore as for all his reasons grounded
vpon impossybylyte, syth [e$_3$v] I may be bolde to thynke as all   20
those olde holy men haue thought, and as all wyse men I wene
yet thynke, that no thynge is impossyble
Luk 1*   to god: I esteme all those reasons very
lytle worth.

How be it one thynge he bryngeth in by the waye, that I wolde   25
he hadde shewed in what place we myghte fynde it, that is to
wytte the sayeng of saynt Austayn. For why to seke out one lyne
in all hys bokes, were to go loke a nedle in a medew. But surely yf
we maye se the place where the yonge man found it / we shall I
dowte not make a clere answere to it. And yet euyn as hym selfe   30
hath rehersed it / y^t sayenge maketh nothynge for [e$_4$] the profe
of hys purpose. For saynt Austayne sayth no more but that the
body in whyche Chryste arose, muste be in one place, and that it
contynueth in heuen, and shall do tyll the daye of dome. As
helpe me god excepte thys yonge man in these wordes of saynt   35
Austayn se forther with his yonge syghte, than I can see wyth

---

21 olde] *om. 1557*

myn olde eyen and my spectacles / I merueyle me myche y^t euer
he wolde for his purpose onys brynge them in. For whan saynt
Austayne sayth that the body in whyche Chryst arose, muste
nedes be in one place / he myghte mene by those wordes for any
thynge that here appereth to the contrary, not that hys body
myghte not be [e$_4$v] in two diuers places at onys / but that it muste
be in one place, that is to saye in some place one or other / or that
he muste haue one place for hys specyall place, and that place
must be heuen / as we say god must be in heuen, and angels
muste be in heuen. He speketh no thynge of the sacrament, nor
sayth not hys body wyth whyche he rose must nedes be so in one
place, that it can by no possibilite be in ony mo.

Also thys worde (muste) whyche is in the laten tonge called
Oportet*
oportet, whych word saint Austayne here
vseth as thys yong man reherseth hym /
doth not alwaye sygnyfye suche a necessyte, as excludeth all
possybylyte of the contrary. For [f$_1$] our sauyour sayde hym selfe
Luce. 24
to the two discyples, *Nonne haec oportuit
pati Christum, et ita intrare in gloriam
suam?* was it not so that Chryste muste dye, and so entre into hys
glorye? And yet hym selfe sayde also, that he myghte for all that
Iohan. 10
haue chosen whyther he wolde haue
dyed or no. For hym self sayth that to
departe with his soule and to take hys soule agayn, bothe twayne
were thynges put in hys owne power. And the prophete Esay
Esaie. 53
sayeth of hym, He was offered vppe bycause he so wolde hym selfe. And ther-
fore thys latyn word *oportet,* whyche saynt Austayn hath in that
place / is many tymes in the latyn tonge taken not for full and
precyse neces[f$_1$v]syte, but for expedyent and conuenyent. And
therfore it is translated also into englysshe, not onely by thys
Of this word must*
worde (muste) whyche yet sygnyfyeth
not alwaye an impossybylyte of the con-
It behoueth*
trary / but often tymes by thys worde (it
behoueth) whiche worde sygnyfyeth that it is to be done for our

17 sauyour] sauyours *1532,* sauiour *1557*   29 tymes] *1557,* ty[*new line*]tymes
1532   33 alwaye]al[*new line*]waye *1532,* all way *1557*

behofe & commodyte, & not that it can in no wyse be auoyded
but y^t it must nedes be. And therfore syth all y^t dreueth this
yonge man from the lytterall sense, is as he sayth the impossybylyte of Chrystes body to be at onys in dyuers places, & proueth that thynge impossyble by y^e wordes of saint Austayne / that
sayth no more but that it muste be in one place, & sayth [f$_2$] not y^t
it maye be in no mo but one, nor spheketh not of any such necessyte wherof he putteth the contrary for impossyble, nor spheketh
no worde at all there of the sacramente: syth saynte Austayne I
saye sayth no forther than thys / I meruayle mych in myne hart,
what thynge thys yonge man seeth in hys wordes, worthy y^e
bryngynge in for any profe of hys purpose.

And that ye may the more clerely se that saynt Austayne
speketh here of no necessyte / he not onely sayth that y^e body of
Chryst wyth whych he rose must be in one place / but also he
determineth that one place in whyche he muste be yf thys yonge
man reherse hym ryght, [f$_2$v] that is to saye in heuyn, there to
contynue styll vnto the day of dome.

But now I trow thys yong man thynketh not, that saynt Austayne for all hys determynynge that Chrystes body in whyche he
rose muste be styll in y^e one place, y^t is to wytte in heuyn vntill the
day of dome / he meneth for all that that it is so faste bounden to
abyde onely there, but that he maye whan it pleaseth hym in the
self same body, be byneth here in erth an hundreth tymes before
the daye of dome. And good storyes are there testyfyenge that
he so hath bene dyuerse tymes ere thys, synnys the tyme of hys
ascensyon. And therfore thys yong man [f$_3$] may perceyue
playnely, that saynt Austayne in those wordes, thowgh he say
that Chrystes body wyth whych he rose muste be in one place,
that ys to wyt in heuyn, yet he mente no suche precyse necessyte
as sholde dreue thys yonge man from the lytterall sense of
Crystes wordes vnto y^e allegory. He ment not by thys worde, it
muste be in one place, that is to saye in heuen, that it muste so be
in that one place tyll domes daye, that it myghte in ye meane
whyle be in none other besyde, and that it muste be so of an
immutable necessyte by no powre chaungeable, wherof the con-

5

10

15

20

25

30

35

---

18 vnto] _1557_, vyto _1532_   22 meneth] meaneth not _1557_

trary were by no power possyble. And therfore as for these
wordes of saint Austayne [f₃v] to thys purpose here / I meruayle
mych in good faith / but yf he shewe more hereafter, yᵗ euer thys
yonge man wolde speke of them.

5   Now as for hys naturall reasons be not worth the reasonynge.
For fyrste that the body of Chryste vngloryfyed coulde no more
be in two places at onys thanne hys awne can / bycause he is a
naturall body as Christes was, & Christes body a naturall body as
his is: I wyll not examyne any comparysons bytwene theyr two
10   bodyes. But yf Chryste wolde telle me that he wolde make eche
of bothe theyr bodyes too be in fyftene places at ones, I wolde
byleue hym I, that he were able to [f₄] make hys worde trewe in
the bodyes of bothe twayne / and neuer wolde I soo myche as
aske hym whyther he wolde gloryfye them bothe fyrste or not.
15   But I am sure gloryfyed or vngloryfyed, yf he sayde it he is able
                                               to do it. Whan our sauyour sayde, that it
              Marke 10*
                                               was as possible for a camel or a great
cable rope to entre thorowe a nedles eye, as for a ryche man to
entre into the kyngdome of heuen, and after tolde hys apostles
20   that though those two thinges were both impossyble to men, yet
all thyng was possyble to god: I thynke that he ment that neyther
the sample nor the mater was to god impossyble. Now syth than
at the lest wyse yᵗ it is not impos[f₄v]syble for hym to conuaye the
camel or yᵉ cable rope thorowe the nedels eye / what shall me
25   nede to study now whyther he can brynge them thorow such as
they be, or ellys muste of fyne force be fayne to gloryfye the
camel or the cable fyrste / as thys yong man sayth of hys body, yᵗ
it were impossyble for god to brynge aboute to haue it in two
places at onys suche as it is now, bycause it is yet somwhat groce
30   and vngloryfyed / and than by the comparyson of his owne, he
argueth the lyke of the blessed body of Chryst, beyng lyke his at
his maundye no more gloryfyed than he. But I say yet agayn of
theyr bodyes both twayne, yf he sayed that he wold do it / [g₁] I
wold not dowt but he could do it. And yf he coulde not do it but
35   yf he glorified them fyrst / than were I sure that he wold gloryfye

---

5 Now] *No new para. in* 1557   28 impossyble] impossile *1557*   32 than he] that he *1532*,
then his *1557*

them both. And therfore yf it were trewe, that he coulde not make hys owne body to be in two places at ones at maundy, but yf it were than gloryfyed / than syth I am sure that he there dyde it, I am therby sure also that he than for the tyme glorifyed it. For that thynge was in hys owne power to do as ofte as he wolde, as 5 well before hys deth as at hys resurreccyon / & yet to kepe hys gloryfycacion from perceyuynge, as he dyd from his two dyscyples, whyche for all his gloryfyed body toke hym but for a pylgryme. [g₁v] And therefore as I saye, yf Chryste sayd vnto me that he wolde make 10 bothe hys body and this yong mannes to, ech of them to be in a thousande places at ones / I wolde putte no dowte therin, but that by some maner meanes he were able inough to do it.

Marci. 16

But here wolde thys yong man peraduenture saye, ye say very well yf god so sayed, and by hys so sayenge so mente in dede. But 15 ye wote wel I deny that he so mente though he so sayed. For I saye that in so sayenge he ment but by an allegorye, as he dyd whanne he called hym selfe a vyne and a dore. But nowe muste this yonge man consyder agayne, that hym self confesseth yᵗ the [g₂] cause for which hym self saith that Chryste in so sayeng dyd 20 not so mene, is bycause that if he shold haue ment so, it was impossyble for god to brynge hys menynge aboute / that is to saye yᵗ Crystes body myght be in two places at onys. And therfore but yf he proue that thynge impossyble for god to do, ellys he confesseth that god not onely sayd it, but also ment it in dede. 25

And yet ouer this, yf Cryst had neuer sayde it / yet dowte I no thing but that he is able to do it / or els were there somwhat that he coulde not do, & than were god not almyghty.

Nowe yf thys yonge man wyll saye that to make one body to be in two places, dothe [g₂v] imply repugnaunce, and that god can 30 do no suche thynge: I dare be bolde to tell hym agayne, that many thynges maye seme repugnant both to hym and me, whyche thynges god seeth how to make them stande to gyther well inough.

Suche blynde reasons of repugnaunce induceth many men in 35

---

7 gloryfycacion] gloryfycaciou *1532*, glorificacion *1557*   7–8 *gloss* Marci. 16] Mark. o. *1557*   17 so sayenge] so so sayinge *1557*

*Reasons of repugnaunce** to greate errour, some ascrybynge all thynge to destyny wythout any power of mannys free wyll at all / and some gyuynge all to mannes owne wyll, and no forsyghte at all vnto the prouydence of god / and all
5 bycause the pore blynde reason of man can not se so farre, as to perceyue how goddes prescyence and mannes free wyll can stande and [g₃] agre togyther, but seme to them clerely repugnant.

And surely yf the semyng of our owne feble reason, may dreue
10 vs onys to thynke that one man to be at onys in two places, is a thynge so harde & so repugnaunt, and therfore so impossyble that god hym selfe can neuer brynge it aboute / yᵉ deuyll wyll within a whyle set vs vppon suche a truste vnto our owne reason, that he wyll make vs take it for a thynge repugnaunt and impos-
15 syble, that euer one god sholde be thre persons.

I wote well yᵗ many good folke haue vsed in thys mater many good frutefull examples of goddes other workys, not onely myr- acles wryten in scryp[g₃v]ture, but also done by yᵉ comon course of nature here in erthe, and some thynges made also by mannes
20 hand / as one face beholden in dyuers glassys, & in euery pyece of one glasse broken in to twenty, and the meruayle of the
*Good fruteful examples** makynge of the glasse it selfe suche mater as it is made of, and of one worde comynge whole to an hundred eares at onys, and the syghte of
25 one lytle eye present and beholdyng an whole great countrey at onys, with a thousande suche other meruayles mo, such as those that se them dayly done and therfore meruayle not at them, shall yet neuer be able, no not thys yonge man hym selfe, to gyue suche reason by what meane [g₄] they may be done, but that he
30 maye haue suche repugnaunce layde agaynst it, that he shall be fayne in conclusyon for the chyefe and the moste euydent reason to saye, that yᵉ cause of all those thynges is bycause god that hath caused theym so to be done is almyghty of hym selfe & can do what hym lyste. And also I can not se why it shulde be more
35 repugnaunt that one body maye be by yᵉ power of god in two places at onys, than that two bodyes may be to gether in one place at onys. And that poynt I thynke thys yonge man denyeth not.

16 I wote] *No new para. in 1557*

And I verily thynke there is vnto mannes reason neyther more
semblaunce of difficulty nor of repugnaunce, [g₄v] neyther in
the beynge of one body be it neuer so groce and vnglorified in
twenty dyuers places at onys, than in yᵉ makyng of all that whole
world, in whyche all the bodyes both gloryfyed and vngloryfyed 5
haue all theyr romys and places, to make I saye all that hole
world of ryght nought. Whyche artycle of oure fayth we shall
fynde folke wythin a whyle not greatly force to denye, yf men
fall to this poynt, that for impossibylytees of nature, they thynke
the thynges impossyble also to god that is the mayster and the 10
maker of nature / and that they wyll vppon that ymagynacyon
do as thys yong man doth, flee fro the lytterall sense of the
scrip[h₁]ture, and seke some allegorye in the stede, and saye they
be dreuen therto by necessyte, by cause of the impossybylyte of
yᵉ mater. For thus shall as ye maye wel se, by thys meanes none 15
artycle of oure faythe stande.

Now hys laste argument wyth whych he proueth it impossyble
for one body of Cryst to be in two places at onys is thys. You can
sayeth he shewe no reason, why he sholde be in many places at
onys and not in all. But in all places he can not be / wherfore we 20
muste conclude that he can not be in many places at onys. Thys is
a meruelous concluded argument. I am sure a very chylde maye
sone se that thys conse[h₁v]quent can neuer folowe vpon those
twoo premysses of hys antecedent. For he can no forther conclude vpon them, but that we can shewe no reason why he sholde 25
be in many places at onys. Now yf I sholde graunte hym yᵗ no
man could shewe a reason why he shulde be in many places at
onys / what had he wonne by that? myght he then conclude there
vpon yᵗ he could not be in many places at onys / as though that it
were not possyble for god to make hys body in two places at onys, 30
but if we were able to tell how, and why, and wherby, and shewe
the reason? Now in thys argument he begynneth wyth (shold) in
the maior / and than in the minor [h₂] and the conclusyon turneth in to (can) and so varyeth his extremytes, that the argument
can neuer be good yf it were but for that. If he wolde enduce the 35
conclusyon whych he concludeth here / he must rather haue
argued thus. If it myghte be in many places at ones, than myghte

---

36 rather haue] *1557*, haue rather haue *1532*

it be in all places at onys. But in all places at onys it can not be / &
therfore it can not be in many places at ones. Thus or in some
suche maner must he argue, yf he wyll awghte proue. But here
nowe bothe the partys of hys antecedent be very weke. The
5 fyrste is thys, that yf the body of oure sauyoure maye be in many
places at onys, it may be in all places at [h₂v] onys. Though I wold
graunt thys causale proposycyon for the trouth of the second
part / yet wolde I denye it hym for yᵉ forme. For though I graunt
it to be trewe / yet yᵉ fyrst parte is not the profe of the second /
10 but rather contrary wyse thc seconde inferreth well yᵉ fyrst. For
yᵉ reason is good: he may be in all places, ergo he maye be in
many. But argue the contrary wyse as thys yong man argueth,
and than is yᵉ forme very faynt. For this hath lytle strength: he
maye be in many places, ergo he may be in all, many men ronne,
15 ergo all men ronne, men ronne in many places, ergo men ronne
in all places / but yf the mater maynteyne the argument, eyther
by [h₃] the possybylyte of the antecedent or by the necessyte of
the consequent / as one man is a stone, ergo all men be stones,
one man is a lyuyng creature, ergo all men be lyuyng creaturs.
20 But let thys fyrst proposycyon passe and come now to the seconde, vppon whych all hys argument hangeth / that is, that the
body of Chryste can not be at onys in all places. Thys he sayeth /
but how dothe he proue it? If he wyll byd me proue yᵉ affyr-
matyue / I maye answere that I nede not, for it is not the thynge
25 yᵗ we haue in hande. For we do not saye that he is in all places /
for the sacrament is not at onys in all places. And we be not
bounde for thys mater [h₃v] to go any forther / & yᵗ poynte for so
far I proue by the gospell that sayth it is so. And therfore thys
yonge man that sayeth it can not be / lette hym proue that it may
30 not be. For yf it maye be / he than confesseth that the wordes of
Cryst do proue that it must be. But bycause it can not be sayth
he / therfore he is dreuen to construe these wordes by an allegorye. And now that it can not be in many places / he proueth by
yᵗ that he can not be in all places / and therfore muste he proue
35 that, or ellys gyue ouer thargement.

---

6 Though] *New para. in 1557*   23 it?] *1557*, it. *1532*   32 an] *1557*, ani *1532*,
33 it] *1557*, t *1532*

How be it as for me though I be not bounden to it / I am
content yet to proue that god maye make the body of Cryst [h₄]
to be in all places at onys. And bycause thys yonge man coupleth
yᵗ proposycyon with yᵉ tother / so wyll I do to. And I proue
therfore that god can make hys body be bothe in many places at   5
onys, and in all places at onys / by that yᵗ he is almyghty, and
therfore can do all thynge. And nowe muste thys yong man tell
vs eyther that thys is nothynge, or els denye that god can do all
thynge. And than muste he lymyte goddes power howe farre he
wyll giue god leue to stretch it. But whan this yong man shal   10
come to that poynt / euery wyse man wyll I wene suppose and
thynke in them self that this yonge man hath yet in hys youth
gone to lytell [h₄v] whyle to scole, to knowe all yᵗ god can do / but
yf he brynge good wytnesse yᵗ he hath lerned vppe the vttermoste of all goddes connyng / which thyng the apostle Poule for   15
all that he was rauysshed vp into the thyrde heuyn, rekened yet
so farre aboue hys reche, that he cryed out, Oh the altytude

of the rychesse of the wysdome & the
Roma. 10   connynge of god.

But yet thys yonge man goeth about to proue yᵗ poynt by   20
scrypture. For excepte we graunte hym that poynt to be trewe /

he sayeth that ellys we make the angell a
Mark. 16*   lyar, that sayd he is not here / and also yᵗ
Actes. 1*   ellys we make as though Cristes body in

hys ascencyon dyd not go vp in the cloude in to [i₁] heuen from   25
the erth, but onely hyd hym selfe in the clowde, & played bo pepe
and taryed byneth styll.

I am in good fayth sory to se thys yong man presume so farre
vpon hys wytte, so soone ere it be full rype. For surely suche

lykynge of theym selfe maketh many   30
Note*   wyttes waxe roten ere they waxe rype.

And veryly if it do decreace and go bakwarde in thys fasshyon, it
maye not last longe. For euen here in the ende he forgetteth hym
selfe so fowle, that whan he was a yonge sophyster he wolde I
dare saye haue bene full sore ashamed so to haue ouersene hym   35
selfe at Oxforde at a peruise. For ye wote well that thynge whiche

---

18 rychesse] riches *1557*

[i₁v] he sayth and whiche he muste therfore proue / is that yᵉ
body of Chryste can not be in euery place at onys, by no meane yᵗ
god coulde make. And the textes that he bryngeth in for the
profe, saye no ferther but that he was not in all places at onys /
5 and saye not that by no possyble power of his godhed it coulde
not be in euery place at onys. And therfore thys poynt is as ye se
well of thys yong man very yongely handeled. And therfore
ought euery man abhorre as a playne pestylence, all suche
                        vnreasonable reasons made for nature
10   *Note*   by more then naturall folys, agaynst yᵉ
possybylyte of goddes almyghty power. For we maye knowe it
veryly, that [i₂] agaynst these folyes hath specyally a place yᵉ
                        good gostely counsayle of saynte Poule /
          Collo. 2   where he warneth vs & sayth, Beware
15 that no man begyle you by vayne phylosophy.
    God forbede that any man sholde be the more prone and redy
to beleue this yong man in thys great mater, bycause he sayth in
the begynnynge yᵗ he wyll brynge all men to a concorde and a
quyetenesse of conscyence. For he bryngeth men to the wurste
20 kynde of quyetnesse that can be deuised, whan he telleth vs as he
dothe, that euery man may in thys mater wythout parell byleue
whych waye he lyst. Euery man may in euery mater wythout any
counsayle of his, soone set hym [i₂v] selfe at reste, yf he lyste to
take that waye to byleue as he lyst hym selfe and care not how.
25   But and yf that way had ben sure / saynt
          1 Cor. 11   Poule wold neuer haue shewed that
many were in parell of sykenes and deth to, for lacke of dyscernyng reuerently the body of our lorde in that sacrament, whan
they came to receyue hym.
30   And agaynst thys doctryne of thys yonge brother, is the playne
doctryne of the olde holy fathers interpretours of the scrypture.
And what fasshyon is thys to saye that we maye byleue yf we lyste
that there is the very body of our lorde in dede / and than to tell
vs for a trouth that suche a faith is impossible to be trew / [i₃] for
35 god hym selfe can neuer brynge it aboute to make hys body be
there.
    I am very sure that yᵉ olde holy doctours whyche byleued
Crystes body & his blood to be there, & so taughte other to
byleue, as by theyr bokes playnely doth appere / yf they hadde

thoughte eyther that it coulde not be there, or that it was not
there in dede / they wolde not for all the good in thys worlde
haue wryten as they haue done. For wolde those holy men wene
you haue taught that men be bounden to byleue that the very
body & blood of Chryste is there, yf them selfe thought they were   5
not bounden therto? Or wold they make men honoure and [i₃v]
worshyppe that thynge as the very body and blood of Cryst,
whyche theym selfe thoughte were not it? Thys gere is to
chyldysh to speke of.

Yet one greate pleasure he doth vs, in that he putteth vs all at   10
lybertye, that we maye wythout perell of dampnacyon byleue as
we byleued before / that is to wytte that
And this is the very   in yᵉ blessed sacrament the whole sub-
trueth*   staunce of the brede and the wyne is
transmuted & chaunged into the very body and bloode of   15
Chryste. For yf we may without perell of dampnacyon byleue
thus as hym selfe graunteth that we may / than graunteth he yᵗ
we maye also without any perell of damnacyon byleue that hym
selfe [i₄] lyeth / where he sayth yᵉ trouth of that belyefe is
impossyble.   20

And therfore I shall therin conclude wyth hym, as oure
souerayne lorde the kynges hyghnes in
King Henry the .viii. most   his most famouse boke of assercyon of
famous boke*   the sacrament concludeth in one place
agaynste Luther / whyche in hys Babilonica confessed yᵗ though   25
men in the sacrament of the aulter byleued after the comon
fayth as they dyd before, there was no perell therin. Well than
sayd the kynges grace, ye do your selfe graunte that in our bylief
is no perell. But all the chyrche byleueth that in your waye is
vndowted dampnacyon. And therfore yf ye wyll as wysdome   30
wolde ye sholde, dele surely for your [i₄v] selfe / ye shold rather
leue your vnsure way whych ye byleue, and come your selfe and
counsayle all other whom ye wold dyd well, to byleue as we do.
Lo thys reason of the kynges grace clerely concludeth thys yonge
man vppon hys owne confessyon / and playnely proueth that   35
excepte he leue hys bylyefe whyche all good chrysten folke holde
for dampnable, and come home agayne to hys olde fayth yᵉ
comon fayth of all the chyrch / in whych as hym selfe agreeth
there is no perell: I wyll not for courtesye saye he is starke madde /

but surely I wyll say that for his owne soule, the yong man playeth a very yonge wanton pageaunt. [k₁]

Now where as for an other quyetenes of euery mannes conscyence, thys yonge man byddeth euery man be bolde, and
5 whyther the blessed sacrament be consecrate or vnconsecrate
(For though he moste specially speketh for the wyne yet he
speketh it of bothe) and byddeth care not but take it for all that
vnblessed as it is, bycause the preste he
*A wondreful doctrine**   saith can not deceyue vs nor take from
10 vs the profyte of goddes institucyon, whyther he altre the wordes
or leue theym all vnsayd / is not this a wonderfull doctryne of
thys yonge man? We wote well all that yᵉ preste can not hurte vs
by hys ouer syghte or malyce, yf there be no faute vpon our owne
part. [k₁v] For that perfeccyon that lacketh vppon the prestes
15 parte, the great mercy of god dothe as we trust of hys own
goodnesse supply. And therfore as holy saint Chrysostome saith,
no man can take harme but of hym
*Note**   selfe. But now yf we se the thynge dys-
ordered our owne selfe by the preste, & Crystes instytucion bro-
20 ken / yf we than wyttyngly receyue it vnblessed and vnconsecrated, & care not whyther Crystes instytucyon be kepte and
obserued or no, but reken it is as good wythout it as wyth it / than
make we our selfe parteners of the faute, and lese the profyte of
the sacrament, and receyue it with dampnacyon / not for the
25 prestes faute but [k₂] for our own. How be it as for hys bylyefe
that taketh it no better but for bare brede and wyne, it maketh
hym lytell mater consecrated or not / sauyng yᵗ the better it is
consecrate yᵉ more is it euer noyous vnto hym that receyueth it,
hauyng hys conscyence combred wyth suche an execrable here-
30   sye / by whyche well appereth that he
*I. Cor. II**   putteth no dyfference bytwene the
body of our lord in the blessed sacrament, and the comon brede
that he eateth at his diner / but rather he estemeth it lesse / for yᵉ
tone yet I thynke ere he begynne yf he lacke a preste he wyll
35 blesse it hym selfe, the tother he careth not as he saith whyther it

---

5–6 vnconsecrate (For] vnconsecrate. (For *1557*   12 man? We] *1557*, man. we
1532   14–15 prestes parte, the] prestes, parte the *1532*, priestes part, the *1557*

be blessed or no. Frome [k₂v] whych abomynable heresye & all
hys other, our lorde for his great mercy delyuer hym, and help to
stoppe euery good mannes eares from suche vngracyouse incantacyons as thys mannes reasons be / whyche are vnto such symple
peple as wyll be with yᵉ wynde of euery   5

Ad Ephe. 4*   newe doctryne blowen about lyke a

Gala. 3   wethercok, myche more contagyous a
greate deale, than was that euyll doc-
tryne whyche saynte Poule so sore reproueth, wyth whyche the
false prophetes had bywiched the Galathyes. But as for those   10
that are good and faste faythfull folke, and haue any grace or
any sparke of any reason in theyr heddes / wyl (I veryly thynke)
neuer be so farre [k₃] ouersene as in thys artycle (yᵉ trouth
wherof god hath hym selfe testifyed by as many open myracles as
euer he testyfyed any one) to byleue thys one yonge man vpon   15
his barayne reasons, agaynste the fayth & reason bothe of all olde
holy wryters, and all good christen people thys .xv. C. yeres. All
whyche without any dowt or question, byleued agaynst his doctryne in thys blessed sacrament, vntyll

Berengarius*   Berengarius began to fall fyrst vnto   20
thys errour. Whyche when he better consydered he fell from it
agayn and forsoke it vtterly / and for bycause he had ones holden
it, the good man dyd of hys owne good minde vncompelled grete
penaunce wyllyngly all hys [k₃v] lyfe after, as ye maye rede in
Cronica cronicarum yᵉ .cxc. lefe. And also frere Barns, albe it   25
that as ye wote well he is in many other thinges a brother of thys
yonge mannes secte / yet in thys heresye he sore abhorreth hys
heresye / or ellys he lyeth hym selfe. For at hys laste beynge here,
he wrote a letter to me of hys own hand / wherin he wryteth that I
lay that heresye wrongfully to his charge / and therin he taketh   30
wytnesse of god and hys conscyence / and sheweth hym self so
sore greued therwyth, that any man shold so repute hym by my
wrytyng, that he sayth he wyll in my reproche make a boke
agaynst me, wherin he wyll professe and proteste hys [k₄] fayth
concernyng thys blessed sacrament. By whych boke it shall he   35
saith appere, yᵗ I haue sayd vntrewly of hym, and that he abhor-

---

34 fayth], *printed only as catchword in 1532*, faythe *1557*

reth thys abomynable heresy. Whyche letter of his I forbere to
answere tyll ye boke come. By whyche we maye se syth he for-
saketh thys heresy, what fayth he wyll professe, whyther ye trew
fayth or some other kynde of heresy. For yf he wyll professe the
5   very catholyke fayth / he and I shall in that poynt be very soone
agreed / and I shall than make hym suche answere therin, as he
shall haue cause to be well contented wyth.

But in the meane tyme, it well contenteth me that frere Barns
beynge a man of more [k₄v] age, and more rype dyscressyon and
10 a doctour of diuinyte, & in these thynges better lerned than thys
yonge man is / abhorreth thys yonge mannes heresy in this
poynt, as well as he lyketh hym in many other.

And so I truste wyll euery wyse man / and not be so en-
chaunted wyth such chyldysh reasons as hys be, that they wolde
15 therby do as the herers of Chryste dyd / that for meruayle of thys
                                mater as thys yonge man doth now, re-
          Iohan. 6   fused our sauyour and wente theyr
waye from hym / but wyll rather let them go that wyll go, and
abyde them self with our sauyour stylle / as wyth hym that hath in
20 the stede of thys yong mannes vayne childysh [l₁] folosophy, not
false apparaunt sophystrye, but the very wordes of eternall lyfe.
Whyche wordes I beseche our lord gyue thys yonge man the
grace, agaynste hys owne frowarde fantasyes to byleue / and to y^e
same lyfe brynge hym and vs both / where we shall wythout the
25 vayle or coueryng of any maner sacrament, behold our blessed
sauyour face to face / & in ye bryght myrrour of trouth the very
one godhed of ye thre lyke myghty & eche almyghty persons,
clerely beholde & perceyue both that it may and in dede is, and
also how it maye be, that Cristes one body may be in many places
30 at onys. Whych thyng many that wyll not come there of folysshe
fro[l₁v]wardnes afferme to be playne impossyble.

Lo in stede of a letter haue you almost a boke, longer than I
truste good chrysten folke shall nede in so clere an artycle of the
fayth, and to all fast faythfull peple so farre out of all dowt /
35 sauynge that in sendyng you your copy agayne, me thoughte I
muste nedes wryte you somwhat what I my selfe thoughte of his

---

11 man] *om. 1557*   30 there of] of theyr *1557*

wrytyng. In whych whan I onys began, all be it not very well at ease / y^e abomynacion yet of y^t pestylent heresye & the parell of hys colorable handelynge, drew me forth ferther and ferther / & scant coulde suffer me now to make an end, but that I was half in mynde to haue [l$_2$] towched also the scisme of the Bohemys, whyche he setteth forth here in hys wrytyng / sauynge that it requyreth some length, & that I am in mynde to make answere onys in that mater vnto frere Barns, whiche hath made therin ye wote well an hole treatyce / wherin I wonder yf hym selfe wene he haue sayde well.

And as for that holy prayour y^t thys deuout yong man as a new Cryst, techeth to make at the receyuynge of the blessed sacrament all hys congregacion / I wold not gyue y^e paryng of a pere for his prayour though it were better than it is, pullynge a waye the trewe fayth therfore as he doth. How be it hys prayour there is such de[l$_2$v]uysed, and penned, & paynted with laysour and studye / that I truste euery good chrysten woman maketh a mych better prayour at the tyme of her howsell, by faythfull affeccyon and goddes good inspyracyon sodaynly. For she besyde goddes other goodnes, thanketh hym I thynke for hys hyghe syngulare benefyte there presentely gyuen her, in *A godly prayer** that it lyketh hym to accepte & receyue her so symple and so farre vnworthy of her self, to syt at his owne blessed bord / & there for a remembraunce of his bitter passyon suffred for her synne, to suffer her receyue & eate not brede thoughe it seme brede, but his owne very precyouse body in forme of brede, bothe [l$_3$] hys very flesh blood & bonys, the selfe same with whyche he dyed & wyth whych he rose agayne, & appered agayne to hys apostles, & ete amonge his dyscyples, & with whyche he ascended into heuyn, and wyth which he shall descend agayn to iudgement, and with which he shall reygne in heuyn with his father and theyr holy spyryte in eternall glory, and all hys trewe faythfull byleuyng and louyng peple with hym / whom as the mystycall membres of hys gloryous body he shall than, & from thens forth for euer pleasauntly nurysh & fede and

---

4 now to] nowe. to *1557*   11 And as] *New line not indented after long blank space at end of preceding line in 1532; no new para. in 1557.*   15 therfore] therfro *1557*

sacyate theyr insacyable hunger wyth the beholdynge of hys
gloryous godhed. Whose hunger to heuyn[l₃v]ward he comforteth & fedeth here by hope, and by the sure token and sygne of
saluacyon, the gyuyng of hys owne very blessed body vnder the
5 sygne & lykenesse of brede to be eate & receyued into our bodyes / yᵗ our soulys by the fayth thereof, & our bodyes by the
receyuynge therof, may be spyrytually and bodily ioyned & knyt
vnto hys here in erth / & wyth his holy soule & his blessed body,
and his godhed both with his father & theyr holy spyryt,
10 gloryously lyue after in heuen.

    Thys lo in effecte though not in wordes, can chrysten women
praye, and some of them peraduenture expresse it mych better
to. For god can as the prophete sayth, make not onely [l₄] women
yᵗ haue age, faith, & wit, but the mouthes also of infauntes &
15   yong soukyng chyldren, to pronunce
        Psal. 8   his laude & prayse / so yᵗ we nede not
this yong man now to come teche vs how & what we shall pray, as
Cryste taught his disciples the pater noster. Fryth is an vnmete
                mayster to teche vs what we shold praye
        Frith*
20   at the receyuynge of the blessed sacrament, whan he wyll not knowlege it as it is, but take Crystes
blessed body for nothing but bare bred / and so lytell esteme the
receyuynge of the blessed sacrament, that he forceth lytell
whyther it be blessed or not. I praye god blesse these poysened
25 errours out of hys blynd harte, and make hym hys faythfull [l₄v]
seruaunt / and sende you hartely well to fare. At Chelchith the
.vii. daye of December by the hand of
                            more than all your owne
                            Tho. More knyght.
30   Prentyd at London
               by .w. Rastell.
                 1533

          CVM PRIVILEGIO

COMMENTARY

COMMENTARY

The following bibliography includes works and abbreviations cited frequently in the Introductions and Commentaries. The titles of works referred to only once or occurring only in a brief cluster of references are given in full as they occur. Unless otherwise noted, references to the Bible and Latin quotations from it are from the Clementine Vulgate. In citing and quoting the glosses of de Lyra in the Froben Bible of 1498, we have given modern verse numbers (which are not present in the Froben Bible) instead of volume, page, and column, because the numbered verses can be easily located in the Froben Bible and provide the briefest, most accurate way of referring to the glosses. For quotations from Bugenhagen's *Epistola ad Anglos,* Fish's *Supplicacyon for the Beggers,* and Frith's *A Christen Sentence,* the reader is referred to Appendices A, B, and C, where these works are reprinted.

BIBLIOGRAPHY AND SHORT TITLES

AG. See Gill, Joseph.

A boke . . . answeringe vnto M mores lettur. See Frith, John.

A Christian Sentence. See Frith, John.

A Disputation. See Frith, John.

Alberigo, Giuseppe, et al., eds. *Conciliorum oecumenicorum decreta,* 2nd ed., Basel, 1962. Cited as "Alberigo."

Allen, *See* Erasmus, Desiderius.

Articuli .CCCCC. See Cochlaeus, Johannes.

ASD. See Erasmus, Desiderius.

Assertio. See Luther, Martin.

Barlowe, Jerome. *Rede me and be nott wrothe,* Strassburg, 1528; *STC²* 21427; Hume, no. 5. Cited as "*Rede me.*"

Biblia latina. [Biblia] cum glosa ordinaria et expositione lyre literali et morali: necnon additionibus ac replicis . . . , 6 vols., John Peter and John Froben, Basel, 1498. Bible text interlined with the Gloss of Anselmus Laudunensis, the Glosses of Walafrid Strabo and others, the Postillae and Moralitates of Nicholas de Lyra, the Additiones of Paulus de Santa Maria (bishop of Burgos 1354–1435), with Matthias Döring's replies.

Bugenhagen, Johannes. *Epistola ad Anglos,* Augsburg, Simpertus Ruff, 1525; Geisenhof, no. 181. Cited as "Bugenhagen, *Letter.*"

CCSL. Corpus Christianorum: Series Latina, 111 vols. to date, Turnholt, 1953–.

Chambers, R. W. *Thomas More,* London, 1935; reprint, Ann Arbor, 1958. Cited as "Chambers."

CIC. Corpus Iuris Canonici, ed. Emil L. Richter and Emil A. Friedberg, 2 vols., Leipzig, 1879; reprint, Graz, 1959.

Clebsch, William A. *England's Earliest Protestants, 1520–1535.* New Haven and London, 1964, Cited as "Clebsch."

Cochlaeus, Johannes. *Articuli .CCCCC. Martini Lutheri, ex sermonibus eius sex et triginta,* Cologne, 1525. Cited as "*Articuli .CCCCC.*"

———. *Epistola Iohannis Bugenhagij Pomerani ad Anglos. Responsio Iohannis Cochlaei,* [Cologne], 1526. Cited as "*Responsio Cochlaei.*"

Confutatio. See Fisher, John.

CRZ. See Zwingli, Ulrich.

CSEL. Corpus Scriptorum Ecclesiasticorum Latinorum, 88 vols. to date, Vienna, 1866–.

CSPS. Calendar of Letters, Despatches, and State Papers, relating to the Negotiations between England and Spain, ed. G. A. Bergenroth et al., 13 vols., London, 1862–1954. Cited as *CSPS.*

CW. See More, Thomas.

CWE. See Erasmus, Desiderius.

d'Alès, Ahdémar. "La question du purgatoire au concile de Florence en 1438," *Gregorianum, 3* (1922), 9–50. Cited as "d'Alès."

De genuina . . . expositione. See Oecolampadius, Johannes.

De libero arbitrio. See Erasmus, Desiderius.

Delcourt, Joseph. *Essai sur la langue de Sir Thomas More,* Paris, 1914. Cited as "Delcourt."

Disputatio . . . D. Iohannis Eccij & D. Martini Lutheri Augustani quae cepit .IIII. Iulij, [Erfurt], 1519. Cited as *"Disputatio."*

DNB. Dictionary of National Biography, 63 vols., London, 1885–1900.

Doernberg, Erwin. *Henry VIII and Luther: An Account of Their Personal Relations,* Stanford, 1961.

DTC. Dictionnaire de théologie catholique, 15 vols., Paris, 1908–50.

Eck, John. *See Disputatio.*

Ellis, Sir Henry, ed. *Original Letters Illustrative of English History,* 4 vols., London, 1846. Cited as "Ellis."

Erasmus, Desiderius. *Ausgewählte Werke,* ed. Annemarie Holborn and Hajo Holborn, Munich, 1933. Cited as "Holborn."

———. *The Collected Works of Erasmus,* ed. and trans. R. A. B. Mynors et al., 17 vols to date, Toronto, 1974–. Cited as *CWE.*

———. *The Colloquies of Erasmus,* trans. Craig R. Thompson, Chicago and London, 1965. Cited as "Thompson, *Colloquies.*"

———. *De libero arbitrio* διατριβή *sive collatio,* ed. Johannes von Walter, Quellenschriften zur Geschichte des Protestantismus 8, Leipzig, 1935. Cited as *"De libero arbitrio."*

———. *Opera omnia,* ed. J. Clericus (Leclerc), 10 vols., Leiden, 1703–06; reprint, Hildesheim, 1961. Cited as *"Opera omnia."*

———. *Opera omnia Desiderii Erasmi Roterodami,* ed. J. H. Waszink et al., 11 vols. to date, Amsterdam, 1969–. Cited as *ASD.*

———. *Opus epistolarum Des. Erasmi Roterodami,* ed. P. S. Allen et al., 12 vols., Oxford, 1906–58. Cited as "Allen."

Essential Articles. See Sylvester, Richard S., and Germain P. Marc'hadour.

EW. See More, Thomas.

Fabyan, Robert. *New Chronicles of England and France,* ed. Henry Ellis, London, 1811. Cited as "Fabyan, *Chronicles.*"

Fisher, John. *Assertionis Lutheranae confutatio*, Antwerp, 1523. Cited as *"Confutatio."*

———. *De veritate corporis et sanguinis Christi in eucharistia*, Cologne, Peter Quentel, 1527. Cited as "Fisher, *De veritate*."

———. *The English Works of John Fisher, Bishop of Rochester*, Part 1, ed. John E. B. Mayor, Early English Text Society, Extra Series no. 27, London, 1876. Cited as "Fisher, *English Works*."

Fox, Alistair. *Thomas More, History and Providence*, New Haven and London, 1983. Cited as "Fox, *Thomas More*."

Foxe, John. *Acts and Monuments*, ed. George Townsend, 8 vols., London, 1843–49; reprint, New York, 1965. Cited as "Foxe."

Franck, Sebastian. *Klagbrieff oder Supplication der armen Duerftigen in Engenlandt / an den Koenig dasselbe gestellt / wider die reychen geystlichen Bettler*, Nürnberg?, 1529. Cited as "Franck, *Klagbrieff*."

Frith, John. *A boke made by Iohn Frith prisoner in the tower of London / answeringe vnto M mores lettur . . .* , n.p., 1533; *STC* 11381; Hume, no. 30. Cited as *"A boke . . . answeringe vnto M mores lettur."*

———. *A christen sentence and true iudgement of the moste honorable Sacrament of Christes body & bloude declared both by the auctorite of the holy Scriptures and the auncient Doctores*, London, Richard Wyer, 1548?; *STC* 5190. Cited as *"A Christian Sentence."*

———. *A disputacion of Purgatorye*, London, 1533; *STC* 11387. Cited as *"A Disputation."*

———. *See also* Tyndale, William.

Fulop, Robert E. "John Frith and His Relation to the Origin of the Reformation in England," Ph.D. Dissertation, University of Edinburgh, 1956.

Geisenhof, Georg. *Bibliotheca Bugenhagiana: Bibliographie der Druckschriften des D. Joh. Bugenhagen*, Quellen und Darstellungen aus der Geschichte des Reformationsjahrhunderts 6, Leipzig, 1908. Cited as "Geisenhof."

Gerson, Jean. *Opera omnia novo ordine digesta*, ed. M. L. Ellies du Pin, 5 vols., Antwerp, 1706.

Gibson, R. W., and J. Max Patrick. *St. Thomas More: A Preliminary Bibliography of His Works and of Moreana to the Year 1750*, New Haven and London, 1961. Cited as "Gibson."

Gill, Joseph, S. J., ed. *Quae supersunt actorum graecorum concilii Florentini necnon descriptionis ejus. Concilium florentinum*, ser. B, V, Rome, 1953. Cited as *AG*.

Grafton, Richard. *Chronicle: or, History of England*, 2 vols., London, 1809.

The Great Chronicle of London, ed. A. H. Thomas and I. D. Thornley, London, 1939.

Guy, John A. *The Public Career of Sir Thomas More,* New Haven and London, 1980. Cited as "Guy."

Harpsfield, Nicholas. *The Life and Death of Sr Thomas Moore, knight, sometymes Lord high Chancellor of England,* ed. Elsie Vaughan Hitchcock and R. W. Chambers, Early English Text Society, Original Series no. 186, London, 1932.

Higden, Ranulf. *Polychronicon,* ed. Churchill Babington and Joseph Lumby, 9 vols., London, 1865–82; reprint, 1964. Cited as "Higden, *Polychronicon.*"

Holborn. *See* Erasmus, Desiderius.

Hughes, Paul L., and James F. Larkin, eds. *Tudor Royal Proclamations,* vol. 1: *The Early Tudors (1485–1553),* New Haven and London, 1964. Cited as "Hughes–Larkin."

Hughes, Philip. *The Reformation in England,* 3 vols., London, 1954–56. Cited as "Hughes."

Hume, Anthea. "English Protestant Books Printed Abroad, 1525–1535: An Annotated Bibliography," in *CW 8,* Appendix B, pp. 1065–1091. Cited as "Hume."

The Jerusalem Bible, Garden City, N.Y., 1966. Cited as "Jerusalem Bible."

Lampe, G. W. H. *A Patristic Greek Lexicon,* Oxford, 1968.

Le Goff, Jacques. *The Birth of Purgatory,* trans. Arthur Goldhammer, Chicago, 1984. Cited as "Le Goff, *Purgatory.*"

LP. Letters and Papers, Foreign and Domestic, of the Reign of Henry VIII, ed. J. S. Brewer et al., 21 vols., London, 1862–1932; reprint, Vaduz, 1965.

Luther, Martin. *Assertio omnium articulorum M. Lutheri, per Bullam Leonis .X. nouissimam damnatorum,* Wittenberg, 1521. Cited as "*Assertio.*"

———. *D. Martin Luthers Werke: Schriften,* 94 vols. to date, Weimar, 1883–. Cited as *WA.*

———. *D. Martin Luthers Werke: Briefwechsel,* 16 vols. to date, Weimar, 1930–. Cited as *WABR.*

———. *D. Martin Luthers Werke: Tischreden,* 6 vols., Weimar, 1912–1921. Cited as *WATR.*

———. *The Table-Talk of Martin Luther,* trans. William Hazlitt, Philadelphia, n.d.

———. *See also Disputatio.*

Marc'hadour, Germain. *The Bible in the Works of St. Thomas More,* 5 vols., Nieuwkoop, 1969–72. Cited as "Marc'hadour, *The Bible.*"

———. *Thomas More et la Bible,* Paris, 1969. Cited as "Marc'hadour, *La Bible.*"

————. "Thomas More, les arcanes du nom," *Moreana*, 2 (1964), 60–68; 5 (1965), 73–88.

————. *L'Univers de Thomas More*, Paris, 1963. Cited as "Marc'hadour, *L'Univers.*"

Marius, Richard. *Thomas More*, New York, 1984. Cited as "Marius."

Milan Missal. See Missale Romanum Mediolani, 1474.

Missale ad usum insignis et praeclarae ecclesiae Sarum, ed. F. H. Dickinson, Burntisland, 1861–83. Cited as "*Sarum Missal.*"

Missale Romanum Mediolani, 1474, ed. Robert Lippe, 2 vols., Henry Bradshaw Society 17, 33, London, 1899–1907. Cited as "*Milan Missal.*"

More, Thomas. *The Correspondence of Sir Thomas More*, ed. Elizabeth F. Rogers, Princeton, 1947. Cited as "Rogers."

————. *The Workes . . . in the Englysh tonge*, London, 1557; *STC*² 18076. Cited as *EW.*

————. *The Yale Edition of the Complete Works of St. Thomas More:* Vol. 2, *The History of King Richard III*, ed. R. S. Sylvester; Vol. 3, Part 1, *Translations of Lucian*, ed. C. R. Thompson; Vol. 3, Part 2, *Latin Poems*, ed. C. H. Miller, L. Bradner, C. A. Lynch, and R. P. Oliver; Vol. 4, *Utopia*, ed. Edward Surtz, S.J., and J. H. Hexter; Vol. 5, *Responsio ad Lutherum*, ed. J. M. Headley, trans. Sister Scholastica Mandeville; Vol. 6, *A Dialogue Concerning Heresies*, ed. T. M. C. Lawler, Germain Marc'hadour, and R. C. Marius; Vol. 8, *The Confutation of Tyndale's Answer*, ed. L. A. Schuster, R. C. Marius, J. P. Lusardi, and R. J. Schoeck; Vol. 9, *The Apology*, ed. J. B. Trapp; Vol. 10, *The Debellation of Salem and Bizance*, ed. J. A. Guy, R. Keen, C. H. Miller, and R. McGugan; Vol. 11, *The Answer to a Poisoned Book*, ed. S. M. Foley and C. H. Miller; Vol. 12, *A Dialogue of Comfort against Tribulation*, ed. L. L. Martz and Frank Manley; Vol. 13, *Treatise on the Passion, Treatise on the Blessed Body, Instructions and Prayers*, ed. G. E. Haupt; Vol. 14, *De Tristitia Christi*, ed. C. H. Miller; Vol. 15, *In Defense of Humanism: Letter to Martin Dorp, Letter to the University of Oxford, Letter to Edward Lee, Letter to a Monk, with a New Text and Translation of Historia Richardi Tertii*, ed. D. Kinney; New Haven and London, 1963–. Cited as *CW* followed by volume number.

Mozley, J. F. *William Tyndale*, London, 1937; reprint, Westport, Conn., 1971. Cited as "Mozley."

Oecolampadius, Johannes. *De genuina verborum Domini, Hoc est corpus meum, iuxta vetustissimos authores expositione liber*, Basel [Strassburg], 1525. Cited as "*De genuina . . . expositione.*"

OED. The Oxford English Dictionary, ed. J. A. H. Murray et al., 12 vols. with supplements, Oxford, 1933, 1972–86.

Ombres, Robert. *The Theology of Purgatory,* Theology Today, no. 24. Butler, Wis., 1978.

Opera omnia. See Erasmus, Desiderius.

Otto, August. *Die Sprichwörter und sprichwörtlichen Redensarten der Römer,* Leipzig, 1890. Cited as "Otto."

PG. Patrologiae Cursus Completus: Series Graeca, ed. J.-P. Migne, 161 vols., Paris, 1857–66.

PL. Patrologiae Cursus Completus: Series Latina, ed. J.-P. Migne, 221 vols., Paris, 1844–1903.

Raban, Sandra. *Mortmain Legislation and the English Church 1279–1500,* Cambridge, 1982. Cited as "Raban."

Rede me. See Barlowe, Jerome.

Reed, A. W. *Early Tudor Drama,* London, 1926.

Responsio Cochlaei. See Cochlaeus, Johannes.

Rogers, Elizabeth F. "Sir Thomas More's Letter to Bugenhagen," *The Modern Churchman,* 35 (1945–46), 350–60; reprinted in *Essential Articles,* pp. 447–54.

———. *See also* More, Thomas.

Roper, William. *The Lyfe of Sir Thomas Moore, knighte,* ed. Elsie Vaughan Hitchcock, Early English Text Society, Original Series no. 197, London and Oxford, 1935. Cited as "Roper."

Russell. *See* Tyndale, William.

Sarum Missal. See Missale . . . Sarum.

Stapleton, Thomas. *Tres Thomae,* Douay, 1588. Cited as "*Tres Thomae.*"

———. *The Life and Illustrious Martyrdom of Sir Thomas More* (part 3 of *Tres Thomae*), trans. Philip E. Hallett, London, 1928. Cited as "Stapleton, *Life.*"

The Statutes of the Realm, 11 vols., London, 1810–28.

STC. A Short-Title Catalogue of Books Printed in England, Scotland, & Ireland . . . 1475–1640, compiled by A. W. Pollard and G. R. Redgrave, London, 1926.

STC². Second edition of *STC,* rev. W. A. Jackson, F. S. Ferguson, and Katharine F. Pantzer; 2 vols., London, 1976–1986.

Sylvester, Richard S., and Germain P. Marc'hadour, eds. *Essential Articles for the Study of Thomas More,* Hamden, Conn., 1977. Cited as "*Essential Articles.*"

Thompson, *Colloquies. See* Erasmus, Desiderius.

Thomson, John A. F. *The Later Lollards 1414–1520,* Oxford, 1965.

Tilley, Morris P. *A Dictionary of the Proverbs in England in the Sixteenth and Seventeenth Centuries,* Ann Arbor, 1950. Cited as "Tilley."

TLL. Thesaurus Linguae Latinae, 18 vols. to date, Leipzig, 1900–.

Tres Thomae. See Stapleton, Thomas.

Tyndale, William. *The obedience of a Christen man and how Christen rulers ought to governe* . . . , Marburg [Antwerp] 1528; *STC*² 24446; Hume, no. 7. Cited as "Tyndale, *Obedience.*"

————. *The Works of the English Reformers William Tyndale and John Frith,* ed. Thomas Russell, 3 vols., London, 1831. Cited as "Russell."

Visser, F. T. *A Syntax of the English Language of St. Thomas More,* Materials for the study of the Old English Drama, New Series 19, 24, 26 (Louvain, 1946–56). Cited as "Visser."

WA. See Luther, Martin.

WABR. See Luther, Martin.

WATR. See Luther, Martin.

Whiting, Bartlett J. *Proverbs, Sentences, and Proverbial Phrases from English Writings Mainly before 1500,* Cambridge, Mass., 1968. Cited as "Whiting."

Wilkins, David, ed. *Concilia Magnae Britanniae et Hiberniae,* 4 vols., London, 1737; reprint, Brussels, 1964. Cited as "Wilkins, *Concilia.*"

Wrigley, E. A., and R. S. Schofield. *The Population History of England 1541–1871,* Cambridge, Mass., 1981. Cited as "Wrigley and Schofield."

Zwingli, Ulrich. *Huldreich Zwinglis sämtliche Werke,* ed. Emil Egli et al., 14 vols., Corpus Reformatorum 88–101, Leipzig, 1905–59. Cited as *CRZ.*

2/6 **IOANNIS POMERANI.** Bugenhagen was known as Pomeranus because of his birthplace at Wollin in Pomerania. The 1525 Augsburg edition of the *Epistola ad Anglos,* reprinted below, Appendix A, pp. 398–405, lists the author as Ioannes Bugenhagius Pomeranus. More addresses him solely as Pomeranus. See *CW 11,* Commentary at 128/4.

2/10–12 **ex . . . desumptum.** Fowler is very careful to indicate what sort of manuscript he had to work from. It was written in More's own hand and corrected by the author himself while he was still alive. Fowler probably obtained the manuscript from his wife, Alice Harris. See note on 2/15.

2/15 **Ioannis Fouleri.** John Fowler (1537–1579) was born in Bristol and educated at Winchester School and New College, Oxford. He married Alice Harris, the daughter of John Harris, More's secretary, and Dorothy Colley, Margaret Roper's maid. Harris possessed some of More's letters and papers, which he took with him when he went into exile at Douay (see *CW 2,* xlviii–1), and it was probably through his connection with Harris that Fowler came across the original manuscript of the *Letter to Bugenhagen.* After Harris's death, the More papers he had were inherited by his wife, who loaned them to Thomas Stapleton for use in his biography of More, *Tres Thomae* (Douay, 1588). Having left England at the accession of Elizabeth, Fowler became a publisher at Louvain (1565–1576), Antwerp (1576–1578), and Douay (1578–1579); he was "the most important person connected with the printing of the early Recusant works" on the continent (A. C. Southern, *Elizabethan Recusant Prose 1559–1582,* London and Glasgow, 1950, p. 342). For the works he published, including some of his own translations and editions, see Southern, p. 540; A. F. Allison and D. M. Rogers, *A Catalogue of Catholic Books in English Printed Abroad 1558– 1640* (Bognor Regis: The Arundel Press, 1956), index; and Elly Cockx-Indestege and Geneviève Glorieux, *Belgica Typographica 1541– 1600,* 2 vols. (Nieuwkoop, 1968–1980), indices. Apart from the *Letter to Bugenhagen,* he published the following works by More: *A Dialogue of Comfort* (1573; Gibson, no. 52) and *A Treatise on the Blessed Body,* together with some of More's prayers, in *A Brief Fourme of Confession* (1576; Gibson, no. 96).

4/4–6 **Môraris . . . môrari.** See *CW 3/2,* no. 278. More puns in the second and fourth lines on the Greek meaning of his name: μῶρος, or fool. For a discussion of this and other puns related to the same root, see Germain Marc'hadour, "Thomas More, les arcanes du nom," *Moreana,* 2 (1964), 60–68. "De prime abord, on est tenté de traduire *moraris* par 'tu atermoies,' ou 'tu tergiverses,' voire, par 'tu te demandes, et cela te fait demeurer l'esprit en suspens'. . . . Il vaut mieux trouver ici un oxymoron, où *mōraris* (= tu es fou), est en contraste phonétique et sémantique avec *mŏrandi;* et ce jeu du prémier vers se corse au troisième, dans lequel une seule voyelle distingue *mōrari* de *mŏrari*" (p. 69).

4/10–11 Mori . . . mori. See CW 3/2, no. 278. More puns on his name once again, associating it with the infinitive of *morior* (*mori*), "to die." See Marc'hadour, *Moreana*, 2 (1964), 70 and part II of the same article, *Moreana*, 5 (1965), 78–80.

4/12–19 Ioan. . . . foret. Fowler reprinted this poem, along with an English translation in fourteeners, in the prefatory matter to the 1573 edition of More's *Dialogue of Comfort* (see *CW 12*, 487). In that volume as well as here in the *Letter to Bugenhagen* it appeared on the page opposite a woodcut of More (Stanley Morison and Nicolas Barker, *The Likeness of Thomas More*, New York, 1963, no. 12 and pp. 47–48). The poem was also reprinted in Thomas Stapleton's *Tres Thomae* (sig. s₁v) with the reading "moresque" instead of "mortemque" in the second last line.

4/15 mores . . . More. Fowler plays with the resemblance between More's name and the Latin *mores* ("character, behavior"). For similar puns see Germain Marc'hadour, *Moreana*, 5 (1965), 76–77.

4/19 Apelle. The most renowned painter of antiquity, famous for his portraits of Philip and Alexander. He died on the island of Kos in the third century B.C.

4/30 More, mori. For the pun on *mori*, see note on 4/10–11.

6/1 Gentianus Heruetus. Born near Orléans in 1499, Hervet studied at the University of Orléans. After graduation he moved to Paris, where he served as tutor to Claude de L'Aubespine and joined Thomas Lupset in editing Linacre's translation of Galen. Following Lupset to England, he was appointed tutor to Arthur Pole, the brother of Reginald (later Cardinal) Pole. At the request of Pole's mother, the countess of Salisbury, Hervet translated Erasmus' *De immensa dei misericordia* into English (London, [c. 1526], reprinted 1533, 1547; *STC* 10474–76). He also translated Xenophon's *Oeconomicus* into English (London, 1532, 1537, 1544, c. 1548, 1557, 1573; *STC* 26069–75). When Cardinal Pole went to Rome, Hervet accompanied him, staying in Pole's house and working on various editions and translations of the Greek fathers. After teaching briefly at Bordeaux, he spent some time at Lyons, where two editions of his *Epigrammata*, many of them directed against the reformers, appeared in 1541. Returning to Rome, he became secretary to Cardinal Cervini (later Pope Marcellus II) and served at the Council of Trent in 1545. In 1556 he was ordained to the priesthood, and in 1562 he returned to the Council of Trent with Charles, cardinal of Lorraine and archbishop of Reims. He died at Reims on September 12, 1584. The best account of his life and works is in *DTC* 6, 2315–20.

6/3 **capiti . . . rostra fuere.** After Cicero was murdered by Antony's henchmen in 43 B.C., his head and hands were cut off and sent to Rome, where Antony ordered them to be affixed to the rostra (the public speakers' platform); see Plutarch, *Life of Cicero* 48–49, *Lives* 885ef).

6/4 **pons . . . tuo.** Nicholas Harpsfield made the same comparison in his life of More: "He was executed at the towre, and his head . . . pitifullye cutt off; And the saide head sett vpon London bridge, in the saide Citie where he was borne and brought vp, vpon an high pole, among the heades of traitours: A rufull and a pitifull spectacle for all good Citizens and other good christians, and muche more lamentable to see their christian english Ciceroes head in such sort, then it was to the Romanes to see the head of Marcus Tullius Cicero sett vp in the [same] Citie and place where he had, by his great eloquent orations, preserued many an innocent from imminent daunger and perill, and had preserued the whole Citie, by his great industrie, from the mischieuous conspiracie of Cateline and his seditious complices" (*The life and death of Sr Thomas Moore . . .* , ed. Elsie Vaughan Hitchcock and R. W. Chambers, Early English Text Society, Original Series no. 186, London, 1932, p. 217).

6/7–14 **Alani . . . Deo.** These two poems, both assigned to Alan Cope, were reprinted in Thomas Stapleton's *Tres Thomae* (sig. s₁). Alan Cope (d. 1578), a native of London, studied at Oxford and became a permanent fellow of Magdalen College in 1549. In 1558 he became senior proctor of the university. In 1560 he went to the Low Countries, where he arranged for the publication of Nicholas Harpsfield's *Dialogi sex . . .* (Antwerp, 1566). According to Thomas Tanner, he also wrote *Carminum diversorum lib. i.* He spent his last years at Rome, where he became a canon at St. Peter's and obtained a doctorate in canon law and theology (*DNB*).

6/9–12 **Moro . . . mori?** For the puns on More's name, see note on 4/10–11.

6/20 **Ioan. Vultei.** Born at Reims in the early years of the sixteenth century, Jean Visaigier (or Voulté or Vautier) took a master's degree at Paris and taught at Bordeaux and Toulouse. While still a relatively young man, he was stabbed in the chest during a quarrel and died on December 30, 1542. His first volume of Latin poetry, *Epigrammatum libri II,* written in imitation of Joannes Secundus, was published at Lyons in 1536, one year after More's death, and his second, *Epigrammatum libri IIII, ejusdem xenia,* was published a year later. See the article on Visaigier by Verdun L. Saulnier in *Le seizième siècle,* vol. 2 of *Dictionnaire des lettres françaises* ed. Georges Grente et al. (Paris, 1951), pp. 705–6; and André Blanchard and Jacques Chomarat, "Spicilegium Moreanum," *Moreana,* 74 (1982), 77–79. For Vulteius' relations with Rabelais, see Louis Thuasne, *Etudes sur Rabelais* (Paris, 1969), pp. 315–36.

6/24 Regum . . . enses. For the antiwar sentiments of Christian humanists—Erasmus and Vives as well as More—see R. P. Adams, *The Better Part of Valor: More, Erasmus, Colet and Vives on Humanism, War and Peace* (Seattle, 1962).

8/1–3 PHILIPPO . . . Catholico. The Netherlands, where Fowler and other recusant English Catholics were living in exile, were under direct control of the Spanish crown. Philip II was in effect the king of the realm, and it is only logical that Fowler would have dedicated More's work to him, seeking royal patronage, just as he later dedicated his edition of More's *Dialogue of Comfort* (1573) to Jane Dormer, the duchess of Feria, widow of Don Gomez Suarez de Figueroa y Cordova, an important member of Philip II's council of state (see *CW 12*, 483–91). Philip II was also regarded as the special champion and defender of the Catholic church. Hence it was particularly appropriate to dedicate to him an unpublished defense of the faith written by one who had died for it. See note on 8/26–29.

Philip II ruled Spain from the time of his father Charles V's resignation in January 1556 until his own death from cancer in September 1598. He also ruled over the kingdoms of Naples, Sicily, and Sardinia, the Netherlands, and the Spanish overseas empire. The Hapsburg domains in Germany and the imperial title went to his uncle Ferdinand I. In 1559, three years after inheriting the throne, he returned to Spain and never again left the Iberian peninsula. The atmosphere at court did much to spoil the entire operation of the Spanish government and played an important part in the various rebellions that plagued his reign—the Protestant Netherlands in 1568–1609, and the Spanish themselves in Aragon in 1591–92. "I do not propose nor do I desire to be the ruler of heretics," Philip had said, and he put down religious dissent as quickly as it arose. The major accomplishments of Philip's reign were the defeat of the Turkish navy at the battle of Lepanto (1571), which stopped the last great Ottoman advance and placed the Mediterranean securely under Western control; the unification of the Iberian peninsula; and, most important of all in his eyes, the great victories won for the Catholic faith in preserving the southern Netherlands, preventing the spread of heresy in Spain and Italy, and the Spanish intervention in France, which helped force Henry IV to become Catholic.

8/4–5 Rex . . . Catholice. Catholic (a usual title of Spanish kings) because of his faith and the universal nature of the Spanish empire.

8/17 magnae Materterae. Catherine of Aragon, first wife of Henry VIII, whose divorce—"the King's great matter"—cost More his head, was Philip II's great aunt, the sister of his grandmother.

8/26–29 Ita . . . prosternitque. Fowler seems to speak of a revival of
Lutheranism in the Low Countries around the year 1568, but the
Protestant rebels in the Netherlands were Calvinists. The word "quae"
seems to refer to "Lutheranam" but ought to refer to "haereses."

The difficulties Fowler refers to, which led to open rebellion in the
Netherlands, began with the bull of Pope Paul IV (May 12, 1559),
which created fourteen new episcopal sees where there had formerly
been only four. Led by the count of Egmont and William the Silent,
prince of Orange, the Protestants demanded the recall of Spanish
troops and more moderate language in the public placards against
heresy. When these were not forthcoming, resistance stiffened. Calvinist preachers spilled out from the cities into the towns and countryside. In late August 1566 bands of iconoclastic Protestants, inspired
by the reforms in Geneva, wrecked and pillaged almost four hundred
churches, among them the ancient cathedral of Antwerp. Philip II was
enraged and the following year (1567) dispatched the duke of Alva to
punish the people indiscriminately, Protestant and Catholic alike.
William of Orange and other important Protestant nobles escaped into
exile, and the count of Egmont, who refused to leave, was tried by a
group known popularly as the *Conseil de sang* and sentenced to summary execution in 1567. The turmoil that followed Egmont's execution
made the Spanish government under Margaret of Parma no longer
tenable, and Philip appointed the duke of Alva to succeed her. There
followed eight years of incessant war until the Pacification of Ghent,
November 8, 1576, when the States-General met with representatives
of the rebellious provinces of Holland and Zeeland and agreed to the
principle of toleration for all forms of religion and the removal of the
Spanish troops. Holland and Zeeland under William of Orange still
refused to allow Catholics to practice their religion within their bound-
aries. The accords fell apart, and the war continued, ending finally in
1609 with the separation of north from south.

It is against this background of civil and religious strife—not only in
the Low Countries, but also in England—that Fowler's edition of More
must be viewed. More's *Letter to Bugenhagen* was not only a historical
document to Fowler, a fragment of the More family tradition, inherited by his wife. It was part of the same struggle against the same
fundamental heresy, whether Lutheran or Calvinist, still going on
then. Although More had attacked it a little more than forty years
before, it was still flourishing, and Fowler, like More before him, put all
his talents to work as editor and publisher to combat it. In his translation and edition of Petrus Frarinus' *Oration against the Vnlawfull Insur-
rection of the Protestantes of our time, under pretence to Refourme Religion*
(Antwerp, 1566, *STC* 11333, sig. L₆v), he presents in great detail the
atrocities committed by Calvin and Theodore Beza along with a series
of woodcuts illustrating horrible examples of rape, crucifixion, disem-
bowelment, castration, scalping, and everywhere Protestants crying
"Pilla tout, Pilla tout."

12/6 **ex itinere.** More was returning to his home in Chelsea, outside London. There is no record of a journey of More's outside of England in either 1525 or 1526, but he did travel to various places in England during these years (Rogers, nos. 140, 145, 148, 150). It was not until July 1527 that More accompanied Wolsey to France on an embassy to ratify the treaty of the previous April and arrange for war against Charles V.

12/8–10 **Barlous . . . Cicistrensis.** The marginal notes are Fowler's, not More's. Fowler may be speaking from family tradition in identifying William Barlow as the person who presented More with a copy of Bugenhagen's *Epistola ad Anglos.* The early career of the William Barlow who later became the bishop of Chichester is obscure, and the *DNB* erroneously assigns to him five heretical books of the late 1520s (two of which were almost surely written by Jerome Barlowe); see E. G. Rupp, *Studies in the Making of the English Protestant Tradition* (Cambridge, 1947), p. 62–72, and Anthea Hume, "A Study of the Writings of the English Protestant Exiles 1525–35, (Ph.D. dissertation, University of London, 1961), pp. 100–38. He was probably the member of the canons regular of the order of St. Austin who was successively the prior of a number of small houses between 1509 and 1528 and was prior of Bromehill when it was dissolved by Wolsey in 1528 to assist the foundation of Wolsey's college at Ipswich. In the next two years he seems to have served as a courier between England and Italy during the negotiations with the pope about Henry's divorce. Under the patronage of Anne Boleyn he became prior of Haverfordwest in 1534 and prior of Bisham in 1536. In 1535 he wrote to Cromwell about the clerical corruption and idolatry in the diocese of St. David, and he went to Scotland to try to persuade James V to follow Henry's example of breaking away from Roman jurisdiction (*LP 9*, nos. 730, 1091). In 1536 he became the bishop of St. Asaph and, shortly thereafter, of St. David's in Wales, where he vehemently opposed relics, pilgrimages, the worship of the saints, and other abuses. In 1548 he was translated to the see of Bath and Wells. On Mary's accession, he was imprisoned in the Tower, where he made some sort of recantation and was released or escaped to Germany. He returned to England in Elizabeth's reign and in 1559 became the bishop of Chichester, where he died on December 10, 1569.

In 1531 William Rastell printed *A dyaloge descrybyng the orygynall ground of these Lutheran faccyons, and many of theyr abusys / compyled by syr wyllyam Barlow chanon (STC 1461).* The author of *The Souper of the Lorde* (1533; *STC² 24468; CW 11,* App. A, 332/23–24) claims that More himself wrote this dialogue and put it forth under William Barlow's name (sig. D₂). In *The Answer to the First Part of the Poisoned Book* (1533) More promised to take up the matter in the second part of his answer (*CW 11,* 136, 221), which he never wrote. In the 1553 edition of *A dyalogue descrybyng the orygynall ground (STC 1462),* the work is assigned

to "syr William Barlowe, chanon, late byshop of Bathe." Hence it seems
that the future bishop became more radical between 1531 and 1535.
But Rupp (p. 69) points out that there was another Austin canon
named William Barlowe at St. Bartholomew, Smithfield, during the
1530s, and the 1553 edition may have been wrongly assigned to the
former (and future) bishop. Similarly, the petition to the king renounc-
ing the five heretical books mentioned above (*Letters Relating to the
Supression of the Monasteries,* ed. Thomas Wright, Camden Society, London, 1843, pp. 6–7) was dated "1530" and signed "William Barlo" in a
later hand (Hume, "A Study," p. 100, n. 3). See *CW 8,* 1249–50. In his
edition of *A dyalogue descrybyng the orygynall ground,* Andrew M. McLean
reaffirms William Barlowe's authorship and gives some good reasons
to believe that the William Barlowe who later became bishop of
Chichester brought Bugenhagen's *Letter* to More; see *The Work of
William Barlowe including Bishop Barlowe's Dialogue on the Lutheran Factions,* ed. Andrew M. McLean (Appleford, 1981), pp. 170–72.

In referring to Barlow as "pseudoepiscopus Cicistrensis," Fowler
shows that his information about him is up to date—an indication,
perhaps, that he knew what he was talking about in identifying Barlow
as the one who presented More with a copy of Bugenhagen's *Letter.* See
note on 20/10–12.

12/6–16 **REDEVNTI . . . video.** Cochlaeus also plays briefly with the
notion that Bugenhagen had written a personal letter, not a public
address to the English people. "Ad quid igitur sollicitas sanctos qui sunt
in Anglis? Qui sunt illi sancti? quis Epistolae tuae tabellarius? Si non
agis insidiose, cur non certum transmittis nuncium, qui responsum a
sanctis illis ad te referat, priusquam epistolam tuam euulgaueris?"
(*Responsio Cochlaei,* sig. A₂v).

12/12 **Sanctis . . . Anglia.** Bugenhagen imitates the opening words of
Paul's epistle to the Ephesians: "Paulus Apostolus Jesu Christi per
voluntatem Dei, omnibus sanctis, qui sunt in Ephesi, et fidelibus in
Christo Jesu" (Eph. 1:1). See also Col. 1:2 and note on 14/8.

12/17–29 **Itaque . . . suas.** In fact More had been involved in the
"Lutheran business" ("Lutherano negotio") ever since the time when
he worked with Henry VIII—in whatever capacity—in framing the
king's *Assertio septem sacramentorum* (1521). When Luther replied to the
king's book in an extraordinarily violent, abusive, personal attack entitled *Contra Henricum regem Angliae* (1522), More came to Henry's
defense in the *Responsio ad Lutherum* (1523), attacking Luther as scur-
rilously as Luther had attacked the king. He was careful not to associate
himself with the book, however, pretending that it was written by one
William Ross, who was traveling in Italy and at the request of his host
responded to various arguments of Luther's. The response was later
published without Ross's permission. To lend credence to the story,

More introduces a series of letters to and from Ross, which discuss the origins of the work and help establish his identity (*CW* 5, 1–31, 796–802). The ruse is fairly elaborate, designed to conceal both More and the king. "Indeed," Thomas Stapleton remarked, "during More's lifetime no one had any suspicion that Ross was not the author of the book. Luther was extremely annoyed at finding himself so severely castigated, without knowing whom he might attack in return." But the device was fairly typical. "More was as clever in hiding his virtues as he was in feigning the circumstances in which his books were written . . . ; in artifices of this nature he was resourceful, and indeed a past master" (Stapleton, *Life,* pp. 65–66). Besides the mask of innocence here in the *Letter to Bugenhagen,* which is dependent on the more elaborate disguise of the *Responsio ad Lutherum* for its effect, one need only recollect the elaborate fiction of the discovery of a new country in *Utopia* or the setting of the *Dialogue of Comfort,* to realize that the use of an elaborate literary hoax and the humor and playfulness—the *festivitas*—that arise from it are entirely characteristic of More both as a man and as a writer. See the Introduction, pp. xxxii–xxxiii and xliv–xlv.

12/25–26 **neque . . . pertineret.** At the time of writing the *Letter to Bugenhagen,* More was both undertreasurer and a member of the Royal Council. In July 1525, on the death of Sir Richard Wingfield, he was appointed chancellor of the duchy of Lancaster and high steward of the University of Cambridge. In January 1526 he resigned the undertreasurership but remained at court in attendance on the king. His reputation was primarily that of a courtier, lawyer, diplomat, and humanist—the author of *Utopia* and friend of Erasmus. He was not yet known to have published against the Lutherans. See 12/17–29 and note.

14/5–6 **Respondebo . . . profeceris.** A common method of disputation in the Renaissance used by More in a number of his polemical works and most notoriously in the *Confutation* (*CW 8*), which achieves its inordinate length through extensive quotations from Tyndale followed by even more extensive replies by More. Cochlaeus used the same method in his response to Bugenhagen's letter. As he explains in the dedication, Cochlaeus answers Bugenhagen point by point, reproducing the entire epistle, in order to show the English precisely what they are up against and so forewarn them: "ne Germaniae incommoda sub falso Euangelii praetextu Angliae quoque regnum, quod florentissimum est, inuadant ac perturbent. Quod ut facias lubentius, ipsam epistolam simul cum responsiuncula mea prudentiae tuae expendendam diligentius, mitto" (*Responsio Cochlaei,* sig A₂). See the Introduction, pp. xxxiv–xxxv and xlii–xliii.

14/8 **Gratia . . . Christo.** Eph. 1:2; see 12/12 and note. Hence More's reference immediately below (14/9–11) to Bugenhagen's arrogation of the apostolic style. Cochlaeus also notes the apostolic quality of the language, but to him it sounds apostolically papal: "tanquam e Roma in Vuittenbergam transposita sit sedes Apostolica. . . . Quis te, rogo, Anglis aut Doctorem aut Episcopum constituit?" (*Responsio Cochlaei*, sig. A₂v).

14/15–16 **An . . . congratulans?** Cf. Rom. 16:9, 1 Pet. 2:2, and 1 Cor. 3:1–2.

14/23–34 **Quid . . . dignos.** England had its own priests and bishops, Cochlaeus says, when Wittenberg—that "sordid little town" ("sordidum . . . oppidulum")—was still a desolate solitude: "Habent Angli pastores et episcopos suos, quos a sede apostolica susceperunt ante annos nongentos, e Roma feliciter missos a Gregorio magno, dum sylua adhuc et solitudo esset Vuittenberga vestra" (*Responsio Cochlaei*, sigs. A₂v–A₃).

14/37–38 **Carolostadius . . . Cacangelistae.** Early Protestant reformers and, as More indicates, friends and allies of Luther. The term *cacangelist* is More's own invention, a combination of the Greek κακός (bad, evil) and ἀγγέλλειν (to announce). More reverses the "good news" of the gospels (*evangelium*) and changes it to the "bad news" of the Protestant reformers. Readers in the Renaissance would also have picked up a suggestion of the Latin *cacare*, "to defecate," which goes back to the same Greek root. Besides preaching an upside-down gospel of bad news, the reformers, More implies, are "evangelists of shit." Cf. *Responsio, CW 5*, 228/20–230/2.

Andreas Bodenstein von Karlstadt (c. 1480–1541) was a professor of Thomistic logic and (after 1510) of theology at the University of Wittenberg. After studying law at Rome in 1515, he returned to Wittenberg to become one of Luther's earliest supporters. From 1517 to 1519 he published works expounding Augustine's doctrine on grace and free will, and in 1519 he and Luther debated with Eck at Leipzig. Karlstadt's *De canonicis scripturis* (1520) asserted the doctrine of *sola scriptura*. In 1520 he was mentioned by name in Leo X's *Exsurge Domine*, the bull of excommunication against Luther. He anticipated Luther in rejecting much of the ritual of the mass and was one of the first reformers to marry. Expelled from Wittenberg in 1524 because of his increasing radicalism, Karlstadt associated himself for a time with the Anabaptists in Holstein and Friesland. In 1530 he settled in Zürich and taught at the University of Basel. Despite his early support of Luther, Karlstadt was essentially a divisive force. The iconoclastic disturbances at Wittenberg in the early 1520s can be traced indirectly to his attacks on ritual and ceremony, and he was the originator of the controversy over the eucharist that later divided the reformation. See 94/34–96/4 and notes.

François Lambert (1486?–1530) was a Franciscan friar, the son of a papal official at Avignon. In 1517 Lambert left the Franciscan monastery at Avignon to become an itinerant preacher. By 1522 he had abandoned his order, disputed with Zwingli in Zürich, and made his way to Wittenberg, where he married in 1523. Expelled from Strassburg because he was distrusted by the Germans, Lambert was recommended by Johann Sturm to Landgrave Philip of Hesse, the most liberal of the German princes. Encouraged by Philip, Lambert drew up a scheme for ecclesiastical reform—democratic, congregational—by which the entire church was to be governed by a synod. The scheme was presented by Philip to a synod at Homburg, but Luther opposed it as too democratic and persuaded Philip to withdraw his support. Lambert was later appointed professor of exegesis at Philip of Hesse's new University of Marburg, where he took part in the great Marburg Colloquy in 1529. He died of a disease known locally as *la sueur anglaise* (sweating sickness) on April 18, 1530, and was buried at Marburg. Luther spoke of him as a former general of the order of Franciscans, the son of a nobleman, persecuted and in want, and one whose integrity was not to be questioned. Despite the praise (or perhaps because of the integrity Luther spoke of) Lambert remained independent, identifying himself with neither Luther nor Zwingli. His works include commentaries on the Old Testament prophets, the Apocalypse, the gospel of Luke, Acts of the Apostles, and the book of Kings as well as various controversial tracts beginning with his attack on the Franciscans, *In regulam Minoritarum . . . commentarii vere evangelici* (Wittenberg, 1523; Strassburg, 1525). At the time More was writing his reply to Bugenhagen, Lambert had just published his *De arbitrio hominis vere captivo* (Strassburg, 1525), against Erasmus. For More's interest in the dispute, see 84/23–29 and note. See also *CW 9*, Commentary at 29/10.

Johann Hussgen (*Oecolampadius* is a Hellenization of *Hausschein*, by which he was also known) was born at Weinsberg in the Palatinate in 1482 and died at Basel in 1531. Educated at Bologna, Heidelberg, Stuttgart, and Tübingen, he had an excellent knowledge of Greek, Hebrew, and Latin. As a proofreader for the press of John Froben, he worked on Erasmus' New Testament and his edition of St. Jerome. In 1520, while cathedral preacher at Augsburg, he seems to have experienced a religious conversion as a result of his interest in Luther. He entered the Brigittine monastery at Altenmünster on April 23, 1520, and for the next two years wrote tracts attacking the church and praising Luther. His publications made his future as a monk impossible, and he left the monastery in February 1522, believing that he had at least learned how to be a Christian ("Amisi monachum," he wrote, "inveni Christianum"). In November 1522 he became a professor of holy scripture at the University of Basel and vicar of St. Martin's a year later. Despite the Peasants' Revolt and the excesses of the Anabaptists, he was instrumental in bringing the Reformation to Basel. His best-known work, *De genuina verborum Domini, hoc est corpus meum, iuxta vetustissimos authores expositione liber* (Strassburg, 1525), denied the corporal presence of Christ in the eucharist and was attacked at length by John Fisher in 1527. In 1528 he married Wilibrandis Rosenblatt, a widow who after Oecolampadius' death went on to marry two other reformers, Capito and Bucer. After his marriage he became the pastor of the cathedral and *antistes* over all the Protestant clergy of Basel. While in this position he took a leading part in drawing up the monumental reforming ordinance passed by the city council on April 1, 1529, which established Protestantism and broke the back of Catholic opposition. In the same year he participated in the eucharistic dispute at Marburg between the Lutheran and other branches of the reformed church, supporting the anti-Lutheran position of Zwingli. See *CW 9*, Commentary at 38/33–34, and *CW 11*, xxi–xxvii.

16/1–4 **sunt . . . vestrum.** Cf. Cochlaeus:"Neque haec sine calumnia scribis, quasi minor Anglorum pars a uobis auertatur. Cum satis constet, in toto regno illo neminem Lutheranorum tuto consistere posse. . . . Cum sit manifestum omnibus, Luthericam doctrinam neque publice neque priuatim illic praedicare cuipiam licere, immo capitale sit Lutheri libros illuc importare aut uendere" (*Responsio Cochlaei*, sig. A₃).

16/5–10 **CAETERVM . . . homines.** More's text differs slightly from Bugenhagen's printed letter (see Appendix A, 398/7–12). The word "maledixerunt" may be a misprint for "maledixerint."

16/7–8 **Haec . . . duxerim.** 2 Cor. 1:12: "Nam gloria nostra haec est, testimonium conscientiae."

16/9–10 **Beati . . . homines.** Matt. 5:11: "Beati estis cum maledixerint vobis, et persecuti vos fuerint, et dixerint omne malum adversum vos mentientes propter me."

16/16–37 **An . . . profiteri?** The first of a series of five such catalogues listing what More considered to be Luther's outrageous affronts to orthodox Christianity. See 24/25–29, 44/8–22, 56/26–58/3, and 94/22–98/14. Since Bugenhagen's *Letter* is tied to no particular doctrinal issue but addresses the entire question of reformed faith, it gave More the opportunity, as Germain Marc'hadour notes, "to handle Luther's 'bad tidings' in their globality. Hence the enumeration, at five different points, of the absurd, insane, or impious articles that make up the new gospel" (*Dialogue Concerning Heresies, CW 6*, 457). Similar catalogues appear in the *Responsio* (*CW 5*, 684–92) and *Dialogue Concerning Heresies* (*CW 6*, 348–60), but they are not repeated, as here, in units throughout the work so as to constitute something like a chorus or refrain.

Cochlaeus also falls into the same sort of catalogues in his reply to

Bugenhagen's *Letter,* probably for the same reason as More, but they do not recur with the same regularity, and they are not as long or as vehement. For a typical example, see note on 28/18–28. See also *Responsio Cochlaei,* signs. C_1v, C_4.

The Peasants' Revolt was at its height when Bugenhagen's *Letter* was first published in 1525. See 22/18–24/32 and note; 100/29–102/19. The exact date of More's *Letter to Bugenhagen* is not known, but the nature of the work as a response to something needing an immediate reply and the references here and elsewhere to the recent events of the Peasants' Revolt would seem to suggest that it was written in 1526. By the summer of 1525 the revolt was defeated in Germany although it continued in Salzburg and parts of Austria until the spring of 1526.

16/26 **destruere . . . Christi.** More has in mind *De captivitate Babylonica,* where Luther takes up each of the sacraments in turn and rejects all but three. Cf. "Principio neganda mihi sunt septem sacramenta, et tantum tria pro tempore ponenda, Baptismus, Poenitentia, Panis, et haec omnia esse per Romanam curiam nobis in miserabilem capitvitatem ducta Ecclesiamque sua tota libertate spoliatam" (*WA 6,* 501).

16/27 **Sanctos . . . spernere.** Cf. *Responsio* (*CW 5,* 688/24–690/1 and Commentary) and *Dialogue Concerning Heresies* (*CW 6,* 355/1–2 and Commentary). See also 94/27 and 100/32–33, below. Luther had suggested that all saints' days and holy days be abolished (*WA 6,*445–46), but he continued to believe that images of the saints were of value in assisting the devotion of the ignorant and unlearned. For his belief in the proper use of images, see *WA 10/3,* 30–36. Luther objected to the use of relics, including pieces of the true cross, because of the expense lavished on them, such as encasing them in gold and precious stones. See 56/33–58/3 and note.

16/27 **Matrem . . . blasphemare.** Luther blasphemed the mother of Christ by claiming, More states, that she was equal to his own whore (96/33–34). See note on 56/29–30.

16/27–28 **Crucem . . . contemnere.** See 28/6–10, 56/33–58/3 and note, and 96/33.

16/28–34 **vota . . . prouocare.** See notes on 26/21–22, 28/24–26, and 98/10–14. The phrase "vota Christo facta" refers to vows of chastity, as the context makes clear. Luther argued in the *De captivitate Babylonica* that since marriage is a divine institution, it is superior to any human laws: "ita ut non ipsum propter leges, sed leges propter ipsum debeant merito dirumpi" (*WA 6,* 555). Thus the "impedimentum ordinis," the impediment of ordination, one of the reasons by which the church claimed a marriage null and void, is simply "a lying invention of man": "Impedimentum ordinis quoque merum est hominum commentum, praesertim cum garriant, eo dirimi etiam contractum, semper suas traditiones super dei mandata exaltantes. . . . Est ergo inter sacerdotem et uxorem verum et inseparabile matrimonium, mandatis divinis probatum" (*WA 6*, 557). See *CW 6*, 360/10–13 and Luther's *De votis monasticis* (*WA 8*, 573–669), which appeared a year after the *De captivitate Babylonica* and spelled out what was more or less implicit there: that monastic vows are not binding and that virginity is not a superior state to marriage.

18/3–5 **id est . . . persequitur.** An oblique reference to the Peasants' Revolt. See 22/18–24/32, 24/22–32, 100/29–102/2, and notes.

18/10–17 **habent . . . consensum.** Cf. Cochlaeus: "Audet enim impurus et impius Magister tuus palam scribere. Doctrinam suam (quae prioribus quoque saeculis et aetatibus persaepe damnata est et a sanctis patribus et ab uniuersali ecclesia) non esse suam, sed Dei. . . . Vobis autem et cunctis haereticis maledicit et anathema irrogat Papa et omnis ecclesia Christi iuxta exemplum Petri, qui maledixit Simoni mago, qui in Haereticorum Catalogis primum obtinet locum" (*Responsio Cochlaei*, sig. A₃v).

18/18 **qui . . . domo.** Cf. Ps. 67:7: "Deus qui inhabitare facit unius moris in domo." See Marc'hadour, *The Bible, 1*, 155–56.

18/30–20/3 **Illi . . . detrahitis?** Cf. *Dialogue Concerning Heresies, CW 6*, 422/3–19.

20/7–16 **profitebamini . . . Chrysostomos.** Cf. *Contra Henricum* (1522): "Divina maiestas mecum facit, ut nihil curem, si mille Augustini, mille Cypriani, mille Ecclesiae Henricanae contra me starent" (*WA 10/2*, 215). See also *Responsio, CW 5*, 128/13–15, 572/11–12; *Dialogue Concerning Heresies, CW 6*, 367/20–22. More makes the same point in similar language in the *Confutation, CW 8*, Commentary at 623/30–624/5. For a summary of Luther's attitude toward the fathers, see Bengt Hägglund, "Verständnis und Autorität der altkirchlichen Tradition in der lutherischen Theologie der Reformationszeit bis zum Ende des 17. Jahrhunderts," *Oecumenica*, 1971/72 (Gütersloh, 1972), pp. 35–39.

20/10–11 **e superbia . . . liuor.** More is associating Luther with the pride and envy of Satan (cf. *CW 13*, 14/3–14).

20/10–12 **tum . . . deuouere.** Oscott College possesses a copy of Fowler's edition of the *Letter to Bugenhagen* that was once owned by Thomas Stapleton, the author of *Tres Thomae* and one of More's most important early biographers (see Chambers, pp. 38–39, and Stapleton, *Life*). Stapleton was born in July 1535, the same year and month as More's death. He was educated at Canterbury and New College, Oxford. Sometime after Elizabeth's accession in 1553, Stapleton left England and studied theology at Louvain and Paris. In 1563 he was deprived of his benefice as canon of Chichester by William Barlow, who had been appointed Anglican bishop of Chichester in 1559. This was the same William Barlow who Fowler says was responsible for first sending More a copy of Bugenhagen's *Epistola ad Anglos*. (See the side-note at 12/8–10, above.) Stapleton completed his degree as doctor of divinity in 1571. He joined the Society of Jesus in 1584 but did not finish the novitiate. In 1590 Philip II of Spain appointed him professor of scripture at Louvain, where he remained until his death on October 12, 1598. He was buried in the Church of St. Peter, and his books and manuscripts were given to the English College at Douay, which he had helped found and where he had once served as university professor of divinity. The inscription on the title page of the Oscott College copy, "Thomae Stapletoni / Collegij Anglicani / Soc. Jesu Leodij / Bib. ma.," seems to indicate that Stapleton had the book with him during his brief novitiate with the Jesuits of the Belgian Province at Liège. A similar inscription is found in his copy of Rastell's edition of More's *English Works* (1557). He published his biography of More in *Tres Thomae* in 1588, and it is likely that he had been reading these volumes in 1584 at Liège and collecting material on More with that project already in mind. A full description of the Oscott College volume and its sparse annotations are given by Charles Crawford, "Thomas Stapleton and More's *Letter to Bugenhagen*," *Moreana, 19–20* (1968), 101–7 and *Moreana, 26* (1970), 5–13. Stapleton's notes tend to be one-word exclamations. Opposite this sentence, for example, Stapleton notes in the margin, "Sapienter." Stapleton's marginalia are reproduced in the notes that follow but not the various underlinings. They may be found in Crawford's second article cited above.

20/17–26 **Denique . . . seculi.** See 16/27 and note.

20/22–23 **vt . . . sagittas.** Cf. Ps. 63:8: "Sagittae parvulorum factae sunt plagae eorum."

20/23–25 **Honorantur . . . Dei.** Cf. Ps. 138:17: "Mihi autem nimis honorificati sunt amici tui, Deus; nimis confortatus est principatus eorum."

20/29 **memoria . . . sonitu.** Cf. Ps. 9:7: "Inimici defecerunt frameae in finem: et civitates eorum destruxisti. Periit memoria eorum cum sonitu."

20/29–22/3 **Nam . . . exolescerent.** The works of most heretics do not exist except as fragments embedded in the works of their orthodox opponents. A few of Pelagius' letters are reprinted in the *Patrologia Latina* (*PL 69*, 393–422), for example, but the bulk of his works are no longer extant. What remain are the long quotations used by Augustine in his *Liber de gratia Christi et de peccato originali contra Pelagium et Coelestium*, his *De natura et gratia*, his various *Epistles* against the Pelagians, and similar writings. If it had not been for Augustine's zeal against

Pelagius and his penchant for setting up long quotations and then attacking them piecemeal, Pelagius would undoubtedly have disappeared even more completely. See note on 14/5–6.

22/10–13 **ita . . . sibi.** For examples of the sort of thing More has in mind, see 94/34–96/4, 100/29–102/2, and notes. There and elsewhere he singles out the dispute over the nature of the eucharist, which threatened to split the Reformation into warring factions, and the Peasants' Revolt, for which he found Luther directly responsible. Cf. also Cochlaeus, who sees Protestant discord and dissension—mental and spiritual ignorance, armies clashing, madwomen running naked through fields and groves raging like maenads—as God's direct expression of his anger and vengeance (*Responsio Cochlaei*, sig. D$_1$, quoted below, note on 100/19–30).

22/18–24/33 **Adeo . . . incendium.** The Peasants' Revolt—one of the bleakest, most disturbing events of the Reformation—was provoked in June 1524 by Countess Siegmund von Lupfen, who insisted that the peasants on her estate at Stühlingen, northwest of Schaffhausen, spend a holiday collecting snail shells for her to wind wool on. Instead the peasants rose up, took over the estate, and drew up a list of sixty-two grievances for which they demanded immediate relief. Most of the grievances were feudal and agricultural; not until later did religious motives become involved. Once the movement began, it immediately gathered momentum, and by August 1524 there were more than a thousand peasants in arms in Southern Germany under the command of Hans Müller of Bulgenbach. In October and November 1524 the peasants in the vicinity of Lake Constance rose up in revolt. The disturbance spread to the area northwest of Augsburg by February 1525, and in March the various bands met in a parliament of sorts at Memmingen to determine a unified plan of action. The result was the proposal of an Evangelical Brotherhood and the acceptance of the famous Twelve Articles, which call for a "new Gospel" whose essence was love, peace, patience, the unity of all men, and the removal or modification of unjust feudal burdens. In the meantime, the peasant armies pillaged and plundered some castles and even more churches and monasteries (which were more defenseless). By the end of April all Germany except the north and Bavaria in the south was in chaos. But the hope for economic justice and the beginning of a new era was short-lived, and the revolt was put down almost as quickly as it had arisen. In the north, for example, at Frankhausen, on May 15, 1525, Philip of Hesse slaughtered the forces of Thomas Münzer, who promised his troops immunity from enemy swords. They therefore offered no resistance and stood before the onslaught of the princes, singing hymns. In the south, in the same month, Truchsess massacred the Black Forest bands. A conservative estimate puts the total number of peasants killed at 100,000 (see notes on 149/15–25 and 149/18–23, below). The Diet of

Augsburg in 1525 attempted to moderate the vengeance of the princes, such as the episode at Kitzingen, near Würzburg, where the eyes of fifty-nine townspeople were put out and their friends and relatives forbidden to offer them assistance. But Augsburg produced few results, and the peasants in Germany remained for centuries the most miserable and wretched in Europe.

Like More, Cochlaeus holds Luther directly responsible for everything the peasants did in Germany and everything that was done to them. Cochlaeus speaks of recent events he himself witnessed, and the passage is one of the most highly charged and most moving in the entire work: "ubi obsecro praecipit uobis Deus tot contra totam Ecclesiam impietates docere, tot contra Principes et Praelatos in populo seditiones excitare, tot rusticorum utique supra centum milia corpora internitioni, animas inferno tradere. An ista negetis? At res iam gestae loquuntur, et tot miserrime seductorum agricolarum sanguis clamat contra uos de terra, neque cessabunt tot animarum querelae (cum Lutherus omnes occisarum [sic] animas Diabolo propria confessione tradiderit) contra uos in extremo iudicio quia propter nomen uestrum & uestrum propter Euangelium (hoc est, seditiosam impiamque doctrinam) occisi sunt, arbitrantes, se obsequium praestare deo si agerent secundum doctrinam uestram, quam iactitabat Lutherus non suam sed dei esse" (Responsio Cochlaei, sigs. C₂v-C₃).

22/34–24/1 **Et . . . iustitiam.** Matt. 5:10: "Beati qui persecutionem patiuntur propter justitiam: quoniam ipsorum est regnum caelorum." Bugenhagen had actually referred not to this verse, but to Matt. 5:11; see 16/9–10 and note, above.

24/9–10 **non . . . vendicant.** Gal. 3:27: "Quicumque enim in Christo baptizati estis, Christum induistis." Cf. Matt. 7:21.

24/11–18 **Quam . . . subuerti?** Cochlaeus makes the same point about the Peasants' Revolt: "satis constat nusquam perpetrata esse tam nefaria scelera, nisi ubi Luthericum praedicatum est Euangelium, utrinque uenditi ac lecti sunt libri. In caeteris uero prouincijs, quae uenena uestra non admiserunt, bene quieti, deuoti ac obedientes manserunt rustici" (Responsio Cochlaei, sig A₄). See note on 24/22–32.

24/22–32 **Integra . . . accendistis.** The military metaphor, the reference to rebellion, and the burning brand are all rooted in the Peasants' Revolt; see note on 22/18–24/33. See also 16/16–37, 98/18–30, 100/29–102/2, 102/3–19, and notes.

Cochlaeus also uses this section of the text to accuse Luther of responsibility for the Peasants' Revolt. Cf. "Qua obsecro fronte aut quibus verbis defendas, quae sub praetextu Euangelij Christianaeque libertatis hoc anno a Lutheranis Rusticis in plaerisque superioris Germaniae prouincijs perpetrata sunt? Neque tamen mox Deo Caesarique et Principibus excusati estis, si facta illorum iam non defenditis, quan-

doquidem ex doctrina uestra illi talia didicerunt. Quis enim simplicem
populum ad tam impia facinora induxit nisi Concionatores et libri
Lutherani sub falso uerbi dei libertatisque praetextu?" (*Responsio
Cochlaei*, sig. A₃v). The Peasants' Revolt is one of the minor themes in
More's *Letter*, recurring with some frequency, but in Cochlaeus it forms
the constant background against which the rest of the work is pro-
jected. One is never allowed to forget that no matter what the
Lutherans say or do, the civil chaos loosed in Germany is the real result
of their teachings. Cochlaeus, of course, is addressing a German audience in whose minds the events of the Peasants' Revolt were still
fresh, whereas More writes as an Englishman for whom they were not
quite as galvanizing or immediate. On More and Cochlaeus, see also
the Introduction, pp. xxxiv–xxxv.

26/1–4 **Hoc . . . Crucis.** See Appendix A, 398/16–19. Bugenhagen
has "uero miramur" rather than "certe miramur."

26/2–3 **ignorantes . . . mundo.**Cf. Luke 17:25, Mark 8:31.

26/3–4 **stultitiam . . . Crucis.**1 Cor. 1:18, 23.

26/13–15 **Is . . . prostrauerit.** Henry VIII's *Assertio semptem sacramentorum* (1521), a defense of the church's sacramental system, was written
in reply to Luther's *De captivitate Babylonica* (1520). The king's book
went through a number of editions in the early 1520s and earned him
the title of Fidei Defensor by papal bull delivered in full consistory. It is
doubtful that Henry wrote the book alone. He was probably aided by
various learned men at court, particularly Edward Lee. More always
spoke admiringly of the work, but his own role seems to have been a
minor one—perhaps that of editor or reader. In his letter to Cromwell
dated March 5 [1534], More understandably downplays his own involvement and praises the book as one who read it only after it was
finished and made a few suggestions for possible emendations. See
253/22–33 and note; see also Rogers, p. 498. In Roper, pp. 66–67,
More speaks of himself not as one of the makers of the book, but as one
who helped sort it out.

Luther replied to Henry's *Assertio* in 1522, in his *Contra Henricum
regem Angliae,* a particularly bold, outrageous attack on a head of state,
which ultimately drew More into the controversy. Luther was coun-
tered on an intellectual level by Bishop Fisher's *Defensio regiae assertionis
contra Babylonicam captivitatem* (1525), but it was More who was selected
or volunteered to answer Luther on his own level of invective. This was
the origin of More's *Responsio ad Lutherum* (1523), published not under
his own name, but under the pseudonym William Ross. See *CW* 5, 715–
31, 775–823.

26/17–20 **An . . . Wittenbergae.** Unless Bugenhagen's "episcopacy"
was merely part of More's irony about his apostolic pretensions (see

note on 14/8), More's information was incorrect. There were no Protestant bishops. Bugenhagen was pastor of the parish church in Wittenberg, a position to which he was recommended by Luther and elected
unanimously by the senate of the University and members of the city
council. He remained official pastor of the city from 1523 to 1557. The
imposition of hands was a regular part of episcopal ordination since at
least the third century (*DTC 11*, 1235–78).

26/21–22 **adiuncta . . . socia.** Bugenhagen was ordained to the priesthood in 1509. In October 1522 he married Eva Rörer, sister of George
Rörer. Luther had raised the question of marriage for the clergy in his
tract *An den christlichen Adel deutscher Nation von des christlichen Standes
Besserung* in 1520. This was followed by Lambert's sixty-six theses on
marriage and Luther's own *De votis monasticis,* both published in 1521.
A number of clergymen married almost immediately after these publications and at least one of them, Jacob Seidler, was imprisoned for
doing so and turned over to the local bishop. Karlstadt married in
January 1522, Bugenhagen in October 1522, followed by Lambert in
1523 and Luther in 1525. In 1525, the same year in which he wrote his
Epistola ad Anglos, Bugenhagen also wrote a treatise entitled *De coniugio
episcoporum et diaconorum,* defending such marriages. See Rogers, p.
326, n. on line 57, and "Sir Thomas More's Letter to Bugenhagen,"
Essential Articles, p. 450.

28/1–11 **Sed . . . exhalent.** In two German sermons on the holy cross
(September 14 and October 22, 1522), Luther makes some startling
remarks about relics of the true cross (*WA 10/3,* 332–34, 369–71).
Although a Latin translation of the first of these sermons was printed
in Strassburg in August 1526 (*WA 10/3,* xxi, clix), it is more likely that
More got his information about them from Cochlaeus' *Articuli .CCCCC.
Martini Lutheri, ex sermonibus eius sex et triginta . . .* (Cologne, 1525), a
Latin summary and refutation of thirty-six of Luther's German sermons. As Richard Marius has pointed out, More almost surely drew
upon the *Articuli* in *A Dialogue Concerning Heresies* (*CW 6,* 544–45; see
also the Commentary at 50/18–21 and 360/4–7). In his *Responsio* (sig.
A$_4$v) Cochlaeus repeats four of his *articuli* about the cross, giving (he
says) Luther's own words: "If I were given a piece of the holy cross (he
says), I would burn it to ashes. Item, I wish no crown of thorns, no holy
cross had ever come to light. If someone gave me a piece of the holy
cross, or if I held it in my hand, I would immediately hide it away in a
place never reached by the rays of the sun. Item. I want all crosses that
seem to sweat or bleed destroyed. Item. I would much prefer the cross
to be lost than found, humbled rather than exalted" (*Articuli .CCCCC.,*
nos. 231, 327, 328, and 338, sigs. H$_3$, L$_4$, M$_1$). See the note on 56/33–
58/3, below.
    In saying that Luther's sermon on the cross is "on sale almost every-
where" ("nusquam fere non prostent"), More is addressing a continen-

tal audience. It was well known that the sale of Protestant books was forbidden in England. Cf. Cochlaeus:"Luthericam doctrinam neque publice neque priuatim illic praedicare cuipiam licere, immo capitale sit Lutheri libros illuc importare aut uendere" (*Responsio Cochlaei,* sig. A₃; see also C₁v). The basis of the prohibition was the Papal bull *Exsurge Domine* (June 15, 1520), in which Leo X declared Luther's writings heretical and ordered them sought out and destroyed. The pope's order was supported in England by Henry VIII's anti-Lutheranism and two public bookburnings sponsored by Cardinal Wolsey, one on May 12, 1521, and the other on February 11, 1526, shortly after the publication of Bugenhagen's *Letter.* See the Introduction, p. xx–xxv.

28/14–17 **Quid ... peccator?** Bugenhagen reads "ne tu nolis" for "tu nolis." In his italicized quotations of Bugenhagen, More omits two sentences which occur in the printed texts of Bugenhagen between this quotation and the next one at 32/10–14: "cur non sequuntur Pauli regulam, Omnia probate, quod bonum est tenete? Si in hominum uel iustitiam uel iniustitiam respicere coepero, quando quaeso liberabor ab errore, quo fere perit mundus, & agnoscam tandem dei iustitiam?" (Appendix A, 398/23–27). But he explicitly refers to the first of these sentences at 30/30–32 as if he had quoted it.

28/18–28 **Quasi ... designare.**Cf. Cochlaeus: "Quae sunt illa de uobis mendacia propter Christum? an quod fidem Euangeliumque eius peruertitis? an quod sacramenta crucemque eius conculcatis? an quod genetricem eius amicosque eius apostolos debito fraudatis honore, immo inhonoratis iniuriosissime? an quod ecclesiam eius uniuersalem contemnitis? an quod oues eius ex ouili Petri, cui oues suas commisit, abducitis? . . . sanctitas autem uestra cernitur in sacrilegis ac promiscuis monachorum monialiumque et sacerdotum nuptiis. Miracula uestra apparent in ebrietate cereuisiaria, de qua gloriatur Lutherus, suum proficere Euangelium, dum Vuittenbergensem cum suo Philippo cereuisiam potat" (*Responsio Cochlaei,* sigs. A₄v–B₁). Cochlaeus often accuses Luther of drinking too much beer. More rarely does (*CW* 5, 56/29–33). He stresses instead his lust and "incestuous" marriage.

28/20–21 **Episcopus.** See note on 26/17–20.

28/22 **de ... erat.** For Lambert, see notes on 14/37–38 and 26/21–22.

28/24–26 **qui ... Monacham.**Luther married Katherine von Bora, a former Cistercian nun, on June 13, 1525. In canon law the marriage of a monk and a nun was regarded as incest (*CIC 1,* 100). More uses the marriage throughout his polemical works as a recurrent image of Luther's "beastly bitchery." See *Dialogue Concerning Heresies, CW 6,* 304/9–10, 346/13, 360/15–17; *Confutation, CW 8,* 925/10–926/37; *Dialogue of Comfort, CW 12,* 93/25–27. In the *Confutation* alone there

are more than sixty references to the idea; see *CW 8*, Commentary at
41/30–31.

According to Erasmus, Katherine von Bora was twenty-six when she
married Luther, having left the convent of Nimptschen near Grimma
with eight other nuns on April 4, 1523. They were assisted in their
escape by Leonhard Koppe of Torgau and supported afterward by
private funds donated by the elector of Saxony.

28/33–30/4 **quasi . . . salutis?** Cf. Cochlaeus: "Doctrinam suam
[Luther's] . . . non esse suam, sed Dei, suumque iudicium non suum,
sed dei esse. Tanquam ipse sit uerus Messias, qui sic loquitur in E-
uangelio Iohannis. Et quod impudentissimum est, ait sine doctrina sua
neminem saluari posse, tanquam nemo Christianorum ante hos
septem annos, quibus mundo male innotuit Lutherus, fuerit saluatus"
(*Responsio Cochlaei*, sig. A₃v).

30/7 **nec satis credamus idoneos.** Grammar would require an added
"vos."

30/12–13 **vt . . . mundum.** Cf. Rom. 7:5–6.

30/17–18 **Quare . . . tuum?** Ps. 49:16.

30/22–24 **Nam . . . haereses.** In a letter to Leo X prefaced to his
Resolutiones disputationum de indulgentiarum virtute (1518), Luther said
the rapid diffusion of his ninety-five theses seemed miraculous to him:
"Porro quodnam fatum urgeat has solas meas disputationes prae
caeteris non solum meis, sed omnium Magistrorum, ut in omnem terram pene exierint, mihi ipsi miraculum est" (*WA 1*, 528).

30/24–27 **facit . . . admittere.** *Monstrum* can mean either "a divine
omen of evil" or "monstrosity." Cf. More's first extant letter to
Cochlaeus (1528?), where he thanks him for keeping him informed of
current events in Germany, which is as bad as Africa in spawning
monsters: "Quae nunc neque minus assidua, et multo magis mon-
strosa, parit nobis Germania quam olim solebat Affrica" (Rogers, p.
395).

30/27–29 **Caeterum . . . cadere.** In the Oscott College copy of the text
Stapleton notes opposite this sentence "Sapienter." See note on 20/10–
12. "To fall like a stone" was proverbial (Whiting S781).

30/30–32 **Iam . . . tenete.** 1 Thess. 5:21. See note on 28/14–17.

32/6—7 **quae . . . seculi.** Matt. 28:20.

32/10–14 **Verum . . . venenum.** The printed text of Bugenhagen
reads "de cultu sanctorum defunctorum, etc." More's text specifies the
adoration of saints, not just the saintly dead, and changes "etc." to the
status of the dead and the existence of purgatory.

32/13–14 **sub . . . venenum.** See notes on 38/20–26 and 90/35.

32/24–32 **Quaeritur . . . gratia.** Such points were frequently discussed by scholastic theologians in commenting on Peter Lombard's *Sententiae*, I, dist. 36, 38–39; II, dist. 23–29.

34/19–25 **Quod . . . assequi.** For example, in *Contra Faustum Manichaeum* 11.5: "Ibi si quid velut absurdum moverit, non licet dicere, Auctor hujus libri non tenuit veritatem: sed, aut codex mendosus est, aut interpres erravit, aut tu non intelligis" (*PL 42,* 249). The idea is common in Augustine. See, for example, *PL 41,* 332–33; *34,* 38; *36,* 136; and *38,* 849. It is also common in More, particularly in the polemical works, where Augustine is consistently used as an authority for the church as the necessary interpreter of scripture. See *Dialogue Concerning Heresies, CW 6,* 127/27–33; *Confutation, CW 8,* 287/23–288/4, 331/5–15, 354/4–7. See also *Dialogue of Comfort, CW 12,* Commentary at 181/14–18.

34/28 **gnisiis.** A transliteration of γνήσιος, "legitimate" or "genuine." The word had been transliterated at least once before (*TLL 6,* 2124). Paul applies it to his "legitimate" sons in the faith (1 Tim. 1:2, Tit. 1:4). It is a favorite word of Chrysostom, who applies it to the sonship of Christ (Lampe, pp. 316–17). More applies the Greek word literally to a legitimate heir in one of his Latin poems (*CW 2/3,* 205/12).

36/2–6 **quae . . . patre**). John 16:13 and Matt. 28:20. The promise Christ obtained from his father through prayer is taken from John 14:16: "Et ego rogabo Patrem, et alium Paracletum dabit vobis, ut maneat vobiscum in aeternum." See also John 14:18, 25–26 and 15:25–27.

36/19–24 **Itaque . . . indubitatissimum.** Stapleton notes opposite 36/19–20 in the Oscott College copy "Simile." See note on 20/10–12.

36/31 ἀκίνητον. "Immovable, steadfast," applied by the Greek fathers to Christ, God the Father, the Trinity, and the angels (Lampe, p. 63).

36/33 αὐτὸς ἔφα. "He himself said it"—a proverbial expression derived from the authority of Pythagoras (Erasmus, *Adagia* 1487, *Opera omnia,* 2, 576EF; Diogenes Laertius 8.46). The disciples of Pythagoras gave this reply when asked the reasons for their beliefs (Quintilian 11.1.27; Cicero, *De natura deorum* 1.5.10).

38/4–5 **Quasi . . . scripturis.** Cf. 1 Cor. 2:4: "Et sermo meus, et praedicatio mea non in persuasibilibus humanae sapientiae verbis, sed in ostensione spiritus, et virtutis."

38/5–6 **quibus . . . potuerunt.** Cf. Matt. 16:18: "Et ego dico tibi, quia tu es Petrus, et super hanc petram aedificabo ecclesiam meam, et portae inferi non praevalebunt adversus eam."

38/7-8 **statuta ... Esaiae. 20.** The reference to Isaiah 20 is a typographical error. The printed text of Bugenhagen (Appendix A,
398/38) cites Isa. 29:14: "Et dixit Dominus: Eo quod appropinquat
populus iste ore suo, et labiis suis glorificat me, cor autem ejus longe est
a me, et timuerunt me mandato hominum et doctrinis; ideo ecce ego
addam ut admirationem faciam populo." The printed text of Bugenhagen has "deus" instead of More's "*Dominus.*"

38/8 **Christus, Matthaei. 15.** Matt. 15:8-9: "Populus hic labiis me ho-
norat, cor autem eorum longe est a me. Sine causa autem colunt me
docentes doctrinas et mandata hominum."

38/8-9 **Quid ergo veneni.** The printed text of Bugenhagen has
"Quod ergo uenenum" (Appendix A, 400/1).

38/11 **Dixti.** A colloquial shortening of *dixisti,* common in Plautus and
Terence.

38/13-16 **Quasique ... vllum.** This is not literally true, of course.
Luther and his adherents replied copiously to their opponents. More
means "not a word which validly refuted Henry and other anti-
Lutheran writers."

38/20-26 **Aut ... clarissimas.** Fowler's marginal note is essentially
correct. Cf. Hilary, *Ad Constantium Augustum* 1.3 (*PL 10,* 559): "Et nunc,
qui Ariana et pestifera contagione inquinati sunt, non cessant ore impio et sacrilego animo evangeliorum sinceritatem corrumpere, et rec-
tam apostolorum regulam depravare. Divinos prophetas non intel-
ligunt. Callidi et astuti artificio quodam utuntur, ut inclusam pernicio-
sam corruptelam inquisitorum verborum velamine contegant, et non
prius venenatum virus effundant, quam simplices et innocentes sub
praetextu nominis Christiani raptos atque irretitos, ne soli pereant,
participes horrendi criminis sui reos faciant" (see also 2.9 and *De trinitate* 4.7 and 9; *PL 10,* 569-70, 98-99, 100, 102). The poisoned cup
smeared with honey is proverbial: see Ambrose, *De Tobia* 9.35 (*CSEL
32/2,* 537) and *TLL 8,* 608, lines 74-79.

38/26-30 **Nam ... Pelagiani?** The Arian heresy was essentially a phe-
nomenon of the Eastern church, with major centers at Antioch and
Alexandria. It arose from various Gnostic speculations by authors such
as Valentinus, Tatian, and Paul of Samosata. Arius (d. 336) was born in
Libya and died in Constantinople after having been exonerated of all
unorthodoxy and received into full communion with the church. Although it took various forms and incorporated various shades of belief,
Arianism held in general that Christ was not of the same substance
(*homoiousion*) as the Father. God the Father alone was uncreated. The
Son, however, had been created by the Father out of nothing. He in
turn created all other things and thus stood in relation to them as
something like a first emanation or manifestation of the deity existing

before the world was created and not yet fully equal to God the Father. Fourteen general councils considered the question of Arianism from 341 to 360, and it was not until the Council of Constantinople (381) that it was finally defeated.

Pelagianism arose in the following century and was rooted not in Byzantine speculations concerning the abstract nature of the Trinity, but in Roman Stoicism. Minimizing the notions of grace and original sin, the Pelagians believed that the will of man was sufficient to follow God's precepts. Christ was regarded not as a mediator whose death redeemed mankind, but as a prime example of good as Adam was of evil. Pelagius, who first formulated the heresy, is believed to have been a native of Britain. Little is known of him outside the controversy itself. He appeared meteorically at Rome in 411 and disappeared just as rapidly in 418 after having been condemned by the Council of Carthage. His chief opponents were Orosius, Marius Mercator, and especially Augustine. Pelagius' theoretical principles were given precise theological definition by a eunuch named Coelestius, who had been a lawyer and a lay monk at Rome and was later ordained as a priest at Ephesus. Both Pelagius and Coelestius were regarded as coauthors of evil and were often lumped together in works such as Augustine's most important treatise on the subject, *De gratia Christi et de peccato originali contra Pelagium et Coelestium* (*PL 44*, 359–410).

38/30–32 **Pelagiani . . . Charybdim.** See Erasmus, *Adagia*, 404, *Opera omnia*, 2, 183E–184C. In his *Confutatio* (sig. V$_4$) John Fisher points out that by claiming that the just man sins in every good work Luther avoids one extreme only to fall into the other: "Sic enim dicens, quum pelagianorum haeresim vitare cupias, incidis in Manichaeos, quod est iuxta proverbium, vitare Scyllam et in Charibdem incidere."

40/25 **eris . . . Apollo.** More alludes to Virgil's *Eclogues* 3.104–5: "Dic, quibus in terris (et eris mihi magnus Apollo)/ tris pateat Caeli spatium non amplius ulnas." The implication is that the questions More asks are so unanswerable that it would take an oracle, like that of Apollo at Delphi, to answer them.

40/31–34 **Quod . . . fuerit.** A mocking allusion to Luther's doctrine of an "internal, spiritual, hidden church" ("ecclesia illa interna spiritalis, et occulta; quam solam definit ecclesiam"), as More describes it in the *Responsio* (*CW 5*, 174/15–16). Cf. *Dialogue Concerning Heresies:* "Peraduenture quod he there myght be sayd / that it nedeth not to assygne any place / where the very chyrche and true crysten congregacyon is. But syth euery place is indyfferent there vnto / it may be that all the good men and chosen people of god / that be predestynate to be saued / in what parte so ever they be / & how so euer they be scateryd / here one and there one / here two and there two / that these be the very chyrche of Cryste" (*CW 6*, 196/1–7). "Where there is the same gospel," Luther had written, "there is the same faith, hope, the same charity, the same spirit, and in fact everything is the same. This is the unity of the spirit, not of place, not of person, not of things, not of bodies." But where the gospel does not exist, "(as we see in the synagogue of the papists and Thomists), there you may know without a doubt that the church does not exist . . . ; but you may know that Babylon is there, full of sorceresses, satyrs, owls, ostriches, and other monsters" (quoted by More in the *Responsio, CW* 5, 175/28–37; the quotation is taken from Luther's attack on Ambrosius Catharinus, *WA* 7, 721/1–8). Sinners cannot be members of the true church, Luther argued. Thus the church was not an institution, but rather an invisible, scattered group that constituted the true body of the faithful (*WA* 7, 710–12). See note on 94/16–18.

42/3 **stipites.** Proverbial for stupidity (Otto, no. 1695). Whiting B353 cites More's "blont as a blocke" (*CW 8*, 719/27). Cf. Tilley B453.

42/4–7 **quum . . . imitandos.** The recognition that certain men are particularly beloved of God and therefore fit models for imitation seems rooted in Jewish tradition from the time of the patriarchs on through the Diaspora. See, for example, the famous passage in Ecclus. 44:1–50:23 praising the fathers of the Jewish people—Enoch, Noah, Abraham, Joshua, Caleb, David, Nathan, Elijah, Zorobabel, Seth, Shem, Adam, and others—as men of God whom the church will honor: "Corpora ipsorum in pace sepulta sunt, et nomen eorum vivit in generationem et generationem. Sapientiam ipsorum narrent populi, et laudem eorum nuntiet ecclesia" (44:14–15). *DTC* (*14*, 878) comments: "On imagine très bien que les panégyriques de ce docteur [the author of Ecclus.] . . . aient été utilisés dans les synagogues de la Dispersion, et l'on conçoit que l'Église chrétienne les ait adoptés pour ses offices. Ces panégyriques ne sont pas, sans doute, absolument des prières aux pères de la nation, mais une prière à Dieu, 'admirable dans ses saints.'" See also Exod. 32:13.

42/11–14 **eorum . . . declararit.** More mentions the church's major requirements for sainthood: martyrdom or heroic virtue and miracles performed after death (*DTC* 2, 1627–32, 1643–45).

42/32–44/4 **Et . . . humana.** More's text differs slightly from the printed text of Bugenhagen (Appendix A, 400/2–12).

44/1 **Christus . . . nostra.** Cf. Rom. 10:3–4: "Ignorantes enim iustitiam Dei, et suam quaerentes statuere, iustitiae Dei non sunt subjecti. Finis enim legis, Christus, ad iustitiam omni credenti."

44/1–2 **Nam . . . redemptio.** 1 Cor. 1:30.

44/5–27 **O compendium . . . eam?** Cf. Cochlaeus: "Mirabilis tu mihi sane dialecticus fueris, si ex uno isto articulo, quem proponis, iusta consequentia inferre atque probare possis omnem dogmatum uestrorum farraginem" (*Responsio Cochlaei*, sig. B₃). Instead of itemizing specific beliefs, Cochlaeus goes on to refer to the *Articuli .CCCCC.* he himself deduced from Luther's sermons and the various doctrines already refuted by Emser, Dietenberg, Eck, Faber, and others. The only specific items he mentions are the sacraments of the new law and baptism: "Quomodo enim sequitur si Christus est iustitia nostra, quod haereticum sit, dicere, sacramenta nouae legis dare gratiam, quod negare remanens post baptismum in pueris peccatum, sit Christum et Paulum conculcare."

44/6–8 **Hoc . . . complectitur?** See 94/22–98/27 and notes.

44/10 **in . . . panem?** In reading Pierre d'Ailly's commentary on Peter Lombard's *Sententiae*, Luther became convinced that the church was wrong in believing that the bread and wine in the eucharist were transubstantiated into the body and blood of Christ while retaining the outward form or accidents of bread and wine. In 1520 he thought that such a view was not an article of faith: "vidi Thomistarum opiniones, sive probentur a Papa sive a Concilio, manere opiniones nec fieri articulos fidei" (*WA 6,* 508). Luther argued instead that according to Occam's razor it was simpler and philosophically less contorted to believe that the body and blood of Christ are present in the bread and wine like fire in hot iron: "Cur autem non possit Christus corpus suum intra substantiam panis coninere sicut in accidentibus? Ecce ignis et ferrum duae substantiae sic miscentur in ferro ignito, ut quaelibet pars sit ferrum et ignis. Cur non multo magis corpus gloriosum Christi sic in omni parte substantiae panis esse possit?" (*WA 6,* 510). See the notes on 94/34, 94/34–96/2, 96/8–9, and 96/19–29. See also *Responsio, CW 5,* 452/3–462/11; *Dialogue Concerning Heresies, CW 6,* 353/34–354/13.

44/10–11 **nihil . . . Missam?** In *De captivitate Babylonica* Luther argued that the mass is not a good work from which priests could expect to receive money to relieve their necessities and pretend to relieve the necessities of others, living or dead. It is a promise of forgiveness of sins made to us by God and confirmed by the suffering and death of Christ. The true mass consists not of the ritual performed by the priest, but of the act of faith by which the individual accepts the promise of God in his heart and soul. The body and blood of Christ in the bread and wine are the external, sacramental sign of that internal act of faith. Hence no one can apply the benefit of the mass to someone else, living or dead, but only accept them for himself. But in arguing his case, Luther states his position so strongly as to deny that the mass can be applied even to the needs of the person attending mass: "Unde manifestus et impius error est, Missam pro peccatis, pro satisfactionibus, pro defunctis aut quibuscunque necessitatibus suis aut aliorum offere seu applicare" (*WA 6,* 521). More repeats the same charge in the *Dialogue Concerning*

Heresies, CW 6, 354/14–15, and discusses it at some length in the
Responsio, CW 5, 494–532. See note on 56/30–31, below.

44/11–12 **Ecclesiam ... Canone.** Luther objected to the canon or central part of the mass where the host is consecrated because it was
traditionally conceived of as a sacrifice representing Christ's passion
and death and not, as he thought it was, a series of signs signifying
God's promise of the remission of sins: "Canonem ego reieci," he wrote
in the *Contra Henricum,* "et reijcio, quod prorsus aperte contra euangelion, uocat sacrificia, quae sunt signa dei, promissionibus adiecta,
nobis oblata a nobis recipienda, non offerenda" (cited by More in the
Responsio, CW 5, 552/21–23). According to Luther, the gospels offer
the definitive proof. At the Last Supper, where the eucharist was first
instituted, Christ did not offer himself as a sacrifice to God the Father.
He sat among the disciples at table and offered them the sign and
promise of salvation. A promise is something we receive; a sacrifice is
something we offer (*WA 6,* 523–24). Priests must not be deceived,
therefore, by the words of the canon, which speak too much of sacrifice. The sacrifice refers not to the sacrament itself, which we receive as
a promise, but to the bread and the wine and the prayers we offer up to
God: "Quocirca observent sese sacerdotes ... ut verba Canonis maio-
ris et minoris cum collectis, quae aperte nimis sacrificium sonant, di-
rigant non ad sacramentum, sed vel ad ipsum panem et vinum con-
secrandum vel ad orationes suas. Panis enim et vinum antea offeruntur
ad benedicendum, ut per verbum et orationem sanctificentur. Postquam autem benedictus et consecratus est, iam non offertur sed ac-
cipitur dono a deo" (*WA 6,* 524–25). In *De captivitate Babylonica* Luther
cautioned against mistaking the accidental forms of the mass for its
true essence. They are no more important than the altar cloths or
monstrances in which the host is contained: "Nam quicquid ultra verbum et exemplum Christi accessit, accidens Missae est, quorum
quodlibet non alio loco ducere debemus, quam quo loco nunc ducimus
Monstrantias quas vocant et pallia altaris, quibus ipsa hostia con-
tinetur" (*WA 6,* 523). In the *De abroganda missa privata,* however, Luther
is more severe and comes closer to validating More's charge that he
considered the canon of the mass impious and sacrilegious: "Quis
etiam non videat eum esse compositum ab aliquo verboso et parum
spirituali? Quid enim attinet verbis ita superfluere? Haec dona, haec
munera, haec sacrificia. Item, hostiam puram, hostiam imma-
culatam. ... Negamus itaque et damnamus canonem in hac parte tanquam adversarium Euangelii" (*WA 8,* 449). See also *Dialogue Concerning
Heresies, CW 6,* 353/29–33 and Commentary.

44/12–13 **& ... figmentum?** Luther held that ordination to the
priesthood is not a sacrament because it was not instituted by God. It
was never mentioned in the New Testament, and despite Christ's saying that he would send the Holy Spirit to dwell within it, the church

does not have the authority to exceed the promises of God: "Ridiculum autem est asserere pro sacramento dei, quod a deo institutum nusquam potest monstrari. . . . Ecclesia enim . . . per promissiones dei constituitur, non promissio dei per ipsam" (*WA 6*, 560). The church itself cannot assure grace. Only God can do that. The church, therefore, cannot institute a sacrament: "Sit itaque certum, Ecclesiam non posse promittere gratiam, quod solius dei est, quare nec instituere sacramentum" (*WA 6*, 561). Luther himself thought of holy orders as a rite of the church ("ritum Ecclesiasticum") similar to the blessings bestowed on "vases, houses, clothing, water, salt, candles, herbs, wine, and things like that" (*WA 6*, 561). More's term *figmentum* (repeated at 71/4) is probably derived from Luther, who uses it a little further on in this same section of *De captivitate Babylonica:* "ut perspicuum sit, ordinem, qui, velut sacramentum, hoc hominum genus in clericos ordinat, esse vere, mere, omninoque figmentum ex hominibus natum" (*WA 6*, 565). See also *CW 6*, 353/20–21, 289/15–22; and *CW 5*, 654/19–662/5.

44/14–16 **mulier . . . Christi?** More exaggerates Luther's position, singling out women to make it seem more shocking. Luther actually believed in the priesthood of all Christians, men and women: "omnes sumus sacerdotes, quotquot Christiani sumus." Priests are simply representatives chosen to minister to the people in their name: "Sacerdotes vero quos vocamus ministri sunt ex nobis electi, qui nostro nomine omnia faciant, et sacerdotium aliud nihil est quam ministerium" (*WA 6*, 564). Ordination, therefore, is the ritual by which ministers are chosen. It is not a sacrament. Despite that, Luther never went so far as to suggest that women should actually serve as priests, although he thought that in an emergency they had the power to do so. As John Headley points out (*CW 5*, Commentary at 158/12–14), they were put in the same category as children. "With no priest available," Luther says in the *Assertio*, "even a child or a woman or any other Christian can give absolution" (*WA 7*, 121). Luther seems to be making a distinction here between women, children, and ordinary laymen and a priestly caste made up presumably of men. And yet he immediately follows that with an affirmation of the priesthood of all Christians and the indwelling spirit of God in all those who are baptized: "Qui enim baptisatus est, spiritum Christi habet: ubi autem spiritus Christi, ibi omnium potestas et libertas" (*WA 7*, 121). Cf. 94/24–25 and 96/12. See also *Dialogue Concerning Heresies, CW 6*, 289/20–22 and Commentary; 353/22–24, 26–27 and Commentary; *Responsio, CW 5*, 654/19–662/5.

44/17 **nullum . . . Purgatorium?** For purgatory and the doctrine of the sleep of the soul, see notes on 56/31–33 and 177/35.

44/17 **Et . . . arbitrium?** See notes on 48/6–9, 84/23–29, and 84/30–86/8.

44/18 **Et nulla . . . obligat?** Cf. *Responsio Cochlaei*, sig. C₃v: "Quasi sub nullo praecepto ecclesiae uiuere debeat homo Christianus, sed absque praecepto libere & sua sponte quilibet agere unicuique liceat, quicquid libeat. His et alijs hujusmodi uerbis incitatis uos indoctam plebem ad excutiendum iugum cuiuslibet obedientiae." See also sigs. A₃v and C₃. For Luther's concept of Christian liberty, see note on 98/10–14.

44/19–21 **sola . . . incredulitas?** See note on 62/4–6.

44/21–22 **ergo . . . vxorem?** See above, notes on 16/28–34 and 28/24–26.

44/24 **istam.** *Doctrinam* or *sententiam* must be understood. But after the series of neuters in "omnia dogmata . . . absurda," one would expect *illud*.

44/28–29 **esse . . . serpentes?** Matt. 10:16.

44/30–34 **sicut exhibuistis . . . sanctificationem?** Rom. 6:19.

44/34–35 **animam . . . suae?** Prov. 13:8: "Redemptio animae viri divitiae suae: qui autem pauper est, increpationem non sustinet." See also 74/12, where More quotes the verse again.

46/1–17 **Quisquis . . . abnegatio.** More's quotation differs from Bugenhagen's printed text in a few details, particularly the more correct "Pelagianae" for "Pelagiana" and "pietatis" for "sanctitatis." (See Appendix A, p. 395, n. 2, and 400/11–31).

46/2 **Pelagianae haeresis.** See note on 38/26–30.

46/5 **iustitiarij.** Here (and at 46/27, 80/33, and 84/20) More uses Bugenhagen's word (Appendix A, 400/16–17, 402/28). It signifies those who attempt to earn their salvation by good works as opposed to those who rely on Christ for their justification. Several modern dictionaries of medieval Latin give "justitiarius" as the title of various legal officers; only one gives the meaning "righteous," under the year 1461 (R. E. Latham, *Revised Medieval Latin Word-List from British and Irish Sources*, London, 1965). But in the glosses and scholia he prepared for his lectures on the epistle to the Romans in 1515 and 1516, Luther used the word several times (*WA 56*, 3/14–4/12, 68/5, 304/27, 334/28) and made its meaning quite clear: "superbi Iustitiarii, qui certi sunt de bonis operibus suis" (*WA 56*, 395/2–3). As Stephen Foley has pointed out to me, Luther used the same term in his *Tischreden* of 1533, where it is translated "Werkheiliger" (*WA TR 3*,52). In the anonymous English translation of Bugenhagen's letter (*A compendious letter which Ihon Pomerane sent to Englande*, 1536; *STC;* 4021), "iustitiarii" is translated "Pharises" (sig. A₄) and "Iustitiarios Phariseos" is rendered "Pharises supposynge them ryghteous by their works" (sig. A₆v). Cochlaeus also

notes that Bugenhagen calls Catholics *iustitiarii* because they pursue
righteousness by means of good works (*Responsio Cochlaei* sig. B₄v).

46/7–8 **Si . . . est.** Gal. 2:21: "Non abiicio gratiam Dei. Si enim per
legem iustitia, ergo gratis Christus mortuus est."

46/9–10 **Iustitia . . . Rom. 3.** Rom. 3:21.

46/10–11 **Qui autem . . . Rom. 9.** Rom. 9:31.

46/11–12 **Iustitiae . . . Rom. 10.** Rom. 10:3.

46/13–14 **Non . . . delictis.** Cf. 1 Cor. 15:3 and 1 Pet. 3:18.

46/33–34 **Inter . . . quisquam.** Cf. Cyprian, *Epistolae* 73.21 (*PL 3*,
1123): "salus extra ecclesiam non est."

46/35–48/2 **Ecclesia . . . gratiae.** According to Augustine, Pelagius
did not believe mankind required any particular grace whatsoever, but
only the knowledge of God's law and the free will to carry it out: "Isti
dicunt posse hominem in hac vita, praeceptis Dei cognitis, ad tantam
perfectionem justitiae sine adjutorio gratiae Salvatoris, per solum liberum voluntatis arbitrium pervenire, ut ei non sit jam necessarium
dicere, *Dimitte nobis debita nostra.* Illud vero quod sequitur, *Ne nos inferas
in tentationem* (Matth. VI, 12, 13), non ita intelligendum, tanquam di-
vinum adjutorium poscere debeamus ne in peccatum tentati deci-
damus; sed hoc in nostra esse positum potestate, et ad hoc implendum
solam sufficere voluntatem hominis" (*PL 33*, 763; see also 765, 772–73,
774, 816, 875). By "generali quodam influxu gratiae" More perhaps
means what Augustine calls "the grace by which we are created men":
"Etsi enim quadam non improbanda ratione dicitur gratia Dei qua
creati sumus, ut nonnihil essemus, nec ita essemus aliquid ut cadaver
quod non vivit, aut arbor quae non sentit, aut pecus quod non intelligit,
sed homines, qui et essemus, et viveremus. et sentiremus, et intel-
ligeremus, et de hoc tanto beneficio Creatori nostro gratias agere va-
leamus; unde merito et ista gratia dici potest, quia non praecedentium
aliquorum bonorum operum meritis, sed gratuita Dei bonitate donata
est: alia est tamen qua praedestinati vocamur, justificamur, glorifi-
camur" (*PL 33*, 767–68). Confronted with the traditional definition of
grace, Pelagius replied that grace does not extend beyond the gift of
man's created nature: "nihil aliud respondit, nisi naturam creati hominis referre gratiam Creatoris; atque ita se dicere, sine peccato impleri
posse justitiam per liberum arbitrium cum adjutorio divinae gratiae,
quod Deus hoc dederit homini ipsa possibilitate naturae" (*PL 33*, 768).

Instead of the grace of creation More is perhaps referring to the
grace of illumination, which Pelagius believed was available—despite
man's perfect nature—through prayer and the action of the Holy
Spirit. It was primarily a revelation of God's will for us—his law and

doctrine—which mankind would then oe able to bring to perfection through its own natural powers. See notes on 48/11–14 and 48/14–17.

48/2 **generali ... gratiae.** In his *Confutatio,* writing against Luther's view of free will, John Fisher contrasts God's help or grace in general with the special grace of God: "Patres enim asserunt, neminem posse quicquam boni velle sine speciali dei auxilio, nec sufficere generalem illum influxum. ... Nam iustus propter influxum, quem vocant gener-alem, habet auxilium dei speciale, simul et gratiam in eius anima prae-sentem, Communes vero peccatores gratia carent interna, sed praeter generalem influxum, non deest eis auxilium speciale, quo miris modis stimulantur ad reditum. Reprobi et indurati ita generalem dumtaxat habent influxum vt caeteris careant" (sig. ee₂v).

48/2–3 **sed ... peculiari.** In a synod of bishops in Asia held at Di-opolis, the ancient Lydia, in December 415, Pelagius is said to have recanted and condemned those who believe that God's special grace is not necessary for each and every good act: "ipse Pelagius cum episco-palibus gestis sine ulla recusatione damnaverit eos, qui dicunt gratiam Dei et adjutorium non ad singulos actus dari, sed in libero arbitrio esse, vel in lege atque doctrina" (Augustine, *De gratia Christi et de peccato originali contra Pelagium et Coelestium* 1.3, *PL 44,* 361; see also *PL 33,* 979). As a result of the hearings, Pelagius was exonerated of all charges of heresy and dismissed, the synod pronouncing him worthy of all future communion with the church. In 417 Augustine wrote an ac-count of the proceedings, *De gestis Pelagii* (*PL 44,* 317–60), based on the acts of the synod, pointing out that Pelagius had not abandoned the teachings he renounced at Diopolis. In the same year, when the newly elected Pope Zosimus was about to pronounce Pelagius once again free of all taint of heresy, a synod of African bishops hastily convened at Carthage begged the pope not to make a final pronouncement until Pelagius had confessed the need for interior grace for each and every good thought, word, and deed. This led in the next year to the con-demnation of Pelagius at the Council of Carthage (May 418), which officially labeled Pelagianism a heresy on nine points or canons (*DTC 12,* 691–700).

48/6–9 **eius ... artificis.** Fowler's sidenote refers to Luther's *Assertio omnium articulorum M. Lutheri per bullam Leonis X. novissimam dam-natorum* (1520). The quotation is taken from the title of article 36, which in turn was taken from the Heidelberg theses of 1518 (*WA 1,* 354): "Liberum arbitrium post peccatum res est de solo titulo, et dum facit, quod in se est, peccat mortaliter" (*WA 7,* 142). Luther goes on to quote Augustine: "Liberum arbitrium sine gratia non valet nisi ad peccandum" (*WA 7,* 142). He later corrects the phrasing of the title: "Male ... dixi, quod liberum arbitrium ante gratiam sit res de solo titulo, sed simpliciter debui dicere 'liberum arbitrium est figmentum in rebus seu titulus sine re'" (*WA* 7, 146; quoted by Erasmus, *De libero arbitrio*, p. 46). Luther also charges the church with Pelagianism for suggesting, among other things, that grace is given as a result of good works: "Verum Pelagium sub his studiis alunt. Quid enim refert, si neges gratiam ex operibus nostris et doceas tamen per opera nostra dari? . . . Neque enim Pelagiani alia opera docuerunt et fecerunt, propter quae gratiam dari voluerunt quam vos docetis et facitis . . . Desistite, quaeso, ab hac insania, misserrimi Pelagiani" (*WA* 7, 146–47). Bugenhagen refers to the Pelagians, but only in passing (46/2–3). In bringing up the issue of Pelagianism here, More seems to be replying not merely to Bugenhagen, but also to Luther, who stands behind him.

The simile of wax in the hand of an artist ("nec aliter a Deo formari, quam ceram a manu artificis") is attributed by Erasmus in *De libero arbitrio* (1524) to a position on free will that seems to be Karlstadt's rather than Luther's: "Sed durior est istorum opinio, qui contendunt liberum arbitrium ad nihil valere nisi ad peccandum, solam gratiam in nobis operari bonum opus non per liberum arbitrium aut cum libero arbitrio, sed in libero arbitrio, ut nostra voluntas hic nihilo plus agat, quam agit cera, dum manu plastae fingitur in quamcumque visum est artifici specimen" (*De libero arbitrio*, pp. 30–31). For Luther's belief in the passivity of the will, cf. *Assertio*, 36: "Rogo quae est ista libertas, quae non nisi in alteram partem potest eamque peiorem? Est hoc esse liberum, non posse nisi peccare?" (*WA* 7, 142). See also *De servo arbitrio, WA 18*, 783: "At nunc, cum Deus salutem meam, extra meum arbitrium tollens, in suum receperit, et non meo opere aut cursu, sed sua gratia et misericordia promiserit me servare, securus et certus sum, quod ille fidelis sit et mihi non mentietur." See note on 84/23–29.

48/10–11 **sed multo . . . Lutherani.** Cf. Fisher, *Confutatio:* "Tua nimirum haeresis deterior est, et magis ab Ecclesia dissidet, quam pelagianorum. Lege quotquot hacetenus contra pelagianos quicquam scripserunt, et hoc vbique testantur sibi cum pelagianis conuenire, quod praecepta dei possibilia sunt, et quod a libero possunt arbitrio seruari. Sed hoc dissidere quod pelagiani contendunt, id sine gratia fieri posse, orthodoxi contra, non sine gratia. Tu vero non solum praeceptorum possibilitatem negas, verumetiam arbitrij libertatem tollis funditus. Quare multo perniciosiorem hostem Ecclesiae te constituis, quam fuerant pelagiani" (sig. V$_4$).

48/11–14 **Nam . . . conditorem.** Pelagius attributed too much to nature in believing that all man needed to work out his own salvation was the knowledge of God's law, available through divine revelation, and his own natural attributes. Man's intelligence and free will—indeed, his very being—were regarded as free gifts of God earned by no prior merit, but apart from them the grace of God was not necessary to avoid sin. Pelagius also attributed too much to nature by failing to take into account the corruption of man's nature in the fall and the subsequent need for redemption through the passion and death of Christ. See Augustine's various letters against the Pelagians (*PL 33*, 764–78) and note on 46/35–48/2.

48/14–16 **Praeterea . . . gratia.** In his summary of Pelagian doctrines (*De haeresibus* 88.1–7, *CCSL 46*, 340–42), Augustine mentions that Pelagius was willing to admit that grace makes it easier for human nature to avoid sin: "Denique Pelagius a fratribus increpatus, quod nihil tribueret adiutorio gratiae Dei ad eius mandata facienda, correptioni eorum hactenus cessit, ut non eam libero arbitrio praeponeret, sed infideli calliditate supponeret dicens ad hoc eam dari hominibus ut quae facere per liberum iubentur arbitrum, facilius possint implere per gratiam. Dicendo utique: 'Vt facilius possint,' uoluit credi, etiamsi difficilius, tamen posse homines sine gratia diuina facere iussa diuina" (*CCSL 46*, 340).

48/14–17 **Praeterea . . . gratiae.** Pelagius believed that prayer for divine assistance was not necessary insofar as it affected will and action. Man should pray to God for the forgiveness of past sins and for the grace of illumination. Divine grace affects the intellect, the knowledge of law and doctrine revealed by the Holy Spirit, not the mysterious, interior motion of the will: "nullum auxilium gratiae credant, qua naturae possibilitas adjuvetur, nisi in lege atque doctrina: ita ut ipsas quoque orationes, ut in scripsis suis apertissime affirmat, ad nihil aliud adhibendas opinetur, nisi ut in nobis doctrina, etiam divina revelatione aperiatur, non ut adjuvetur mens hominis, ut id quod faciendum esse didicerit, etiam dilectione et actione perficiat. . . . Voluntatem autem et actionem nullo Dei adjutorio existimat indigere. Ipsum vero auxilium, quo possibilitatem naturalem perhibet adjuvari, in lege constituit atque doctrina, quam nobis fatetur etiam sancto Spiritu revelari, propter quod et orandum esse concedit." Similarly, Christ was regarded not as savior of mankind, but as a prime example of good, as Adam was of evil. With the example of Christ before us, it was easier to walk in the paths of righteousness. Thus grace was believed to assist nature: "ut videlicet tanquam via demonstrata, qua ambulare debeamus, jam viribus liberi arbitrii, adjutorio nullo alterius indigentes, sufficiamus nobis, ne deficiamus in via; quamvis et ipsam viam contendat etiam sola inveniri posse natura, sed facilius, si adjuvet gratia" (Augustine, *Liber de gratia Christi et de peccato originali contra Pelagium et Coelestium* 1.41, *PL 44*, 380–81; see also 1.7–8, *PL 44*, 364–65, and *De natura et gratia*, 18, *PL 44*, 256).

48/34—50/8 **Iam . . . Lutherus.** Cf. Cochlaeus, who makes the same point: Luther believes that God is responsible for both evil and good— the destruction of Judas and the conversion of Paul: "Vos autem ingratissimi estis Deo, dum donum eius, per quod ad imaginem et similitudinem eius creati estis, liberum arbitrium non agnoscitis. Estis et maxime blasphemi, dum negatis contra scripturas dei iustitiam, qua reddet unicuique mercedem secundum proprium laborem. Et quod adhuc blasphemius est, artibus humanis infertis necessitatem, ut omnia opera nostra tam mala quam bona referatis in uoluntatem praedestinationemque diuinam, ita ut non minus sit a deo principaliter ac effectiue perditio Iudae quam conuersio Pauli. Has et consimiles impietates uestras dum nos negamus, Pelagiani a uobis dicimur" (*Responsio Cochlaei,* sig. B₄). See also 96/34–98/7, and notes on 48/6–9 and 84/23–29.

50/10–16 **gratiam . . . aciem.** Erasmus used the same comparison to make the same point in *De libero arbitrio* (p. 30). Speaking of the grace of repentance, Erasmus agrees with those who believe God offers it to all: "Hoc autem putant esse in nostro arbitrio, ut voluntatem nostram applicemus ad gratiam aut avertamus ab ea, quemadmodum in nobis est ad illatum lumen aperire oculos ac rursum claudere." Later in *De libero arbitrio* Erasmus gives a more elaborate version of the same comparison (p. 83).

50/33–52/16 **Primum . . . concupiscentijs.** Cf. Cochlaeus, who also identifies Bugenhagen's "sects" ("omnis sectarum, quae hodie sunt," 46/4) with the religious orders in the church: "Primo itaque mendaciter sectas vocas, religiosorum sacros et approbatos ordines, qui non scinduntur in sectas, ut uos haeretici, sed unitatem Ecclesiae pulcra ordinum uarietate condecorant, ut Regina ac mater Ecclesia, iuxta Psalmistam sit circumamicta uarietatibus [Ps. 44:13]" (*Responsio Cochlaei,* sig. B₄).

52/12–14 **vendentes . . . Christum.** A combination of Mark 10:21 and Matt. 16:24.

52/15 **Agnum . . . sequentes.** Cf. Rev. 14:1–5.

52/15–16 **carnem . . . concupiscentijs.** Gal. 5:24: "Qui autem sunt Christi, carnem suam crucifixerunt cum vitiis et concupiscentiis."

52/17–20 **Quod . . . diffluat.** In the Oscott College copy of the text Stapleton wrote "Acuté" opposite this sentence.

52/22–25 **nisi . . . saeuiunt.** More is thinking not only of the Peasants' Revolt (see note on 22/18–24/33) but also of the suppression of religious houses in some Protestant territories.

52/30–33 **Neque . . . nobis.** Rom. 8:18.

52/35–37 **qui . . . fecimus.** Luke 17:7–10.

54/3–5 **si . . . vineam?** Matt. 20:1–16, used also by Erasmus, *De libero arbitrio,* p. 40.

54/8–10 **genimina . . . poenitentiae.** Luke 3:7–8. Cochlaeus cites the same text (see note on 60/34–36.).

54/11–13 **Sicut . . . peccatum.** Cf. Ecclus. 3:33: "Ignem ardentem exstinguit aqua, et eleemosyna restitit peccatis."

54/13–19 **Si . . . iustitiae.** 1 Cor. 11:31 and Rom. 6:19.

54/19–20 **Fac . . . viues.** Luke 10:28.

54/20–22 **Quorsum illud denique . . . exprobaturus?** Matt. 25:31–46, used also by Erasmus, *De libero arbitrio*, p. 40, and by Fisher, *Confutatio*, sig. hh$_1$.

54/24–56/2 **quin . . . tepidos.** Cf. Cochlaeus: "inique calumniaris nos de operum fiducia, tanquam sine Christo gratiaque Dei adiuuante confidamus in operibus nostris. Cum nemo nostrum non fateatur cum Paulo. Non esse nos sufficientes cogitare aliquid a nobis quasi ex nobis, sed sufficientiam nostram ex Deo esse. Non tamen sumus, ut uos, sic ingrati aut diffidentes atque infideles, ut non credamus datum esse nobis a Deo liberum arbitrium, per quod gratiae Dei ad bonum cooperari possimus" (*Responsio Cochlaei*, sig. B$_4$).

54/28–29 **si . . . est.** Jas. 2:24, 26: "Videtis quoniam ex operibus justificatur homo, et non ex fide tantum. . . Sicut enim corpus sine spiritu mortuum est, ita et fides sine operibus mortua est."

54/31–32 **neque . . . operibus.** Luke 18:9–14.

56/13–16 **At . . . vltimo.** More's quotation differs slightly from Bugenhagen's printed text (Appendix A, 402/1–6).

56/15–16 **quicquid . . . vltimo.** Matt. 28:20: "Docentes eos servare omnia quaecumque mandavi vobis."

56/25–26 **Dic . . . suo?** Stapleton (see note on 20/10–12) wrote "Acuté" in the margin opposite this sentence.

56/27–28 **Dic . . . voluntatem?** See notes on 48/6–9, 84/30–86/8.

56/28–29 **Vbi . . . castitatem?** See notes on 16/28–34 and 98/10–14.

56/29–30 **Vbi . . . Christi?** More is referring to a German sermon preached by Luther on the feast of Mary's nativity (September 8, 1522; *WA 10/3*, 315–16). Only German printed editions of it were available in 1526, but Cochlaeus gave excerpts from it in *Articuli .CCCCC*. The following consecutive sentences are an accurate translation of Luther's German: "Idcirco uelim, quod festum eius dimitteretur, Quia nihil de ea re habetur in scriptura. . . . Cum tamen a Christo dicamur Christiani, ut ab ipso solo pendeamus, ut simus dei filij atque haeredes & ita sumus aeque tanti, quanta est ipsa mater dei, ut, sumus Mariae sorores & fratres. Alioquin fit immutatio sacro sanguini Iesu Christi. . . . Quia per hunc sanguinem, omnes pariter expurgati sumus a peccatis, ac positi in coelestia bona, Si hoc ita est, sumus certe aeque sancti, sicut ipsa. . . Quod autem ipsa maiorem gratiam habet, hoc non est ex eius meritis factum, sed ex dei misericordia, quia non omnes possumus esse dei mater, Alias nobis similis est. Ita bene per sanguinem Christi oportuit ipsam ad gratiam uenire sicut nos" (sigs. E_4–F_1). See 16/27 and 96/33–34.

56/30–31 **Vbi . . . defunctis?** The mass is not a good work, Luther argued (see note on 44/10–11). It is a promise and testament received by faith in the minds and hearts of the faithful. Because it is essentially an interior motion of the soul which each individual must perform for himself, it is a mistaken notion to believe that one can offer up masses for the dead or any other special intention. See also *Dialogue Concerning Heresies, CW 6,* 354/14–15.

56/31–33 **Vbi . . . iudicij?** See 44/17 and 94/27–28. According to the detailed note in the *Dialogue Concerning Heresies, CW 6,* Commentary at 354/32–33, Luther did not categorically deny the existence of purgatory until 1530 (*WA 30/2,* 360–90), although the general drift of his thinking had been moving steadily in that direction since at least 1517, when he asked in one of his 95 theses why the pope does not release all souls from purgatory out of charity since he releases so many out of the lower motive of collecting money to build a church (*WA 1,* 237). By 1520 Luther had come to believe that no one actually knows what happens to the soul after death. In a German sermon (1522) reported by Cochlaeus (*Articuli .CCCCC.,* sigs. K_6–K_6v), Luther stated that the souls of the dead do not immediately ascend to heaven to be judged. They sleep in the bosom of Abraham until the Last Judgment, when they are united once again with the body and sentenced either to heaven or hell (*WA 10/3,* 192). This eventually became orthodox Protestant doctrine, effectively doing away with the idea of purgatory. See Helen Gardner, Appendix A in *John Donne: The Divine Poems,* 2nd ed. (Oxford, 1978), pp. 114–17. See also *Responsio, CW 5,* Commentary at 258/13; *Dialogue Concerning Heresies, CW 6,* 545, and note on 177/35, below.

56/33–58/3 **Vbi . . . scilicet?** More is referring to a passage in a German sermon of Luther's on the holy cross (*WA 10/3,* 334). Although a Latin translation of this sermon had appeared at Strassburg in August 1526 (*WA 10/3,* xxi, clix), More is probably drawing his information from Cochlaeus' *Articuli .CCCCC.* (sig. L_4), where articles 327–28 are as follows: "Ideo uelim quod nulla corona spinea, imo nulla crux sancta unquam in lucem ueniSset, Quia huc se conuertunt homines, & exornant auro & argento, & permittunt pauperes sedere uacuos. . . . Ideo si mihi frustum donaretur, imo si staret in manu mea statim illud eo abditurus essem, quo sol illud non multum circumfulgere deberet." See also *CW 6,* 50/17–51/19, where More takes up the same point once again, ridiculing Luther's "blered eyes" for not seeing how gold is not given to the poor, but frivolously squandered every day on much worse things than crosses—on cups, knives, swords, spurs, arras and painted cloths, posts of houses, and whole roofs. See note on 28/1–11.

58/5–8 **pauperes ... pauperibus.** John 12:1–8. This is the only version of the gospels that attributes the remark to Judas. The version More follows in John goes on to explain that Judas did not really care about the poor. He was concerned because he kept the purse for the disciples and used to steal cash donations: "Dixit [Judas] autem hoc, non quia de egenis pertinebat ad eum, sed quia fur erat et loculos habens ea quae mittebantur, portabat" (John 12:6).

Despite the egalitarianism of *Utopia,* More's personal opinion about social/economic reform seems to have been closely related to Christ's words, "The poor you have always with you." In the *Dialogue of Comfort,* More quotes the same words from Mark 14:7 and goes on to say that if the poor will be always with us, then rich men will also be needed to come to their relief. If there were a general redistribution of wealth, no one would have anything: "yf all the money that is in this countrey were to morow next brought to gether out of euery mans hand, & laid all vppon one hepe, and then dividid out vnto euery man a like: it wold be on the morow after worse than it was the day before. For I suppose whan yt were all egally thus devidid among all / the best shuld be left litle bettre than than almost a beggar is now" (*CW 12,* 180/3–8). Since the poor will always be with us, it is better to give the money directly to God than to squander it on the things of this world as most rich men do.

58/13–14 **Primum ... misit.** John 6:29; see also John 17:3. The printed text of Bugenhagen differs slightly from More's quotation (see Appendix A, 402/6–7).

58/19–25 **Lutherus ... fide.** See note on 62/4–6.

58/25–27 **ne ... tollit.** See notes on 66/31–68/5 and 94/22–24.

60/9–14 **Si ... prodest.** 1 Cor. 13:2–3.

60/16–18 **fides ... contremiscunt.** Jas. 2:26 (cited above at 54/28–29) and Jas. 2:18–19: "Sed dicet quis: Tu fidem habes, et ego opera habeo: ostende mihi fidem tuam sine operibus: et ego ostendam tibi ex operibus fidem meam. Tu credis quoniam unus est Deus: bene facis: et daemones credunt, et contremiscunt."

60/18–19 **frustra ... Apostolica.** In More's view the epistle of James was inconvenient to Luther ("incommoda") not only because of its stress on works but also because of its teaching on the sacrament of extreme unction (5:14–16) and what it had to say about Luther's own foul mouth and the raging fury inside his breast (3:16–18): "QVVM Lutherus urgeri se cerneret apertissimis uerbis ex epistola Iacobi, non solum in sacramento unctionis extremae, sed etiam in eo: quod eius maledicam linguam, et uirulentum pectus pulchre depinxit apostolus ... ; primum contempsit epistolam: deinde floccifecit apostolum" (*CW 5,* 70/4–10). The epistle of James was also regarded as a major piece of evidence for the Catholic position in the controversy over faith and good works; see Jas. 2:14–26. In his edition of the New

Testament Erasmus, relying on Jerome, suggsts that the author of the
epistle of James is perhaps not the same as James the apostle: "Et fieri
potest, ut nomen commune cum apostolo praebuerit occasionem, ut
haec epistola Jacobo Apostolo ascriberetur, cum fuerit alterius cu-
jusdam Jacobi." But Erasmus explicitly accepts it as inspired (*Opera
omnia*, 6, 1025–26). In *De captivitate Babylonica* Luther writes: "hanc
Epistolam non esse Apostoli Iacobi nec apostolico spiritu dignam multi
valde probabiliter asserant" (*WA 6*, 568). In the 1522 edition of the
German Bible, Luther states that James is clearly inconsistent with Paul
and the rest of scripture in arguing for works, not faith (*WA: Deutsche
Bibel 6*, 477–78). He also called it "an epistle of straw" (*6*, 444), a
statement that was omitted from later editions. More also accused
Luther, both here and in other works, of denying the canonical validity
of scripture wherever scripture witnessed against him; see *CW 6*,
149/6–7 and Marc'hadour, *The Bible, 3*,149–52.

More himself derived great consolation from the epistle of James
during his imprisonment in the Tower, particularly the verses referring to the righteous man who after a time of testing will receive the
crown of life (1:2–4, 12–14). Cf. *CW 12*, cli and Commentary at
101/10–13, 101/29–102/3, and 317/24–27.

60/20–21 **Adam non . . . seductus.** 1 Tim. 2:14: "Et Adam non est
seductus: mulier autem seducta in praevaricatione fuit."

60/25–34 **an . . . ferre.** Cf. Cochlaeus: "Si sufficiat, sola fide suscipere
Christum, Cur iis, qui in nomine Christi etiam prophetauerunt et
daemonia eiecerunt, multasque uirtutes fecerunt, quas profecto sine
fide non fecissent, dicet in illa die Christus dominus, iustus iudex.
Nunquam noui uos, discedite a me omnes qui operamini iniquitatem?"
(*Responsio Cochlaei*, sig. C₂).

60/27–31 **Domine . . . iniquitatem.** Matt. 7:22–23.

60/34–36 **nec . . . ignem?** More conflates Matt. 21:18–22, the parable
of the fig tree, with Matt. 3:10: "Omnis ergo arbor, quae non facit
fructum bonum, excidetur, et in ignem mittetur." Cf. Cochlaeus:"Negatis enim omne meritum, iustificatis uero sola fide. Quasi
non docuerint nos Christus et praecursor eius agere poenitentiam,
dignosque poenitentiae fructus facere. Omnis enim arbor quae non
facit fructum bonum, excidetur et in ignem mittetur. Fructus autem
bonus non est sola fides, sed charitas, gaudium, pax, patientia, benig-
nitas, continentia, castitas, etc." (*Responsio Cochlaei*, sig. C₂). In an earlier passage (sig. A₃v) Cochlaeus compares the fig tree to heretics in
general "Quos . . . maledixit Christus in ficu sterili, immo et succidi
iubet, ne frustra terram occupet."

62/4–6 **Nihil . . . fide.** The quotation is taken from the section on baptism in *De captivitate Babylonica*. Luther is exclaiming over the good

fortune of those who are baptized. No matter how much they sin, they cannot lose their salvation except through unbelief. Then follows the passage More refers to: "Nulla enim peccata eum possunt damnare, nisi sola incredulitas: caetera omnia, si redeat vel stet fides in promissionem divinam baptisato factam, in momento absorbentur per eandem fidem, immo veritatem dei, quia seipsum negare non potest, si tu eum confessus fueris et promittenti fideliter adhaeseris" (WA 6, 529). More's quotation is not exact, and he omits all references to baptism and the promise of God, which Luther regards as the essence of each of the sacraments. The promise in this case is the promise in Mark 16:16: "Those who believe and are baptized will be saved" (WA 6, 527). Cf. *Dialogue Concerning Heresies, CW 6,* 352/22–28, 33–34, where More uses the same reference and associates it directly with baptism.

62/29–30 **Si ... est.** See note on 46/7–8.

64/3–4 **id ... Mosaicae.** Rom. 3:20: "Quia ex operibus legis non justificabitur omnis caro coram illo."

64/5–7 **qui ... possunt.** See 46/10–12 and notes.

64/7–8 **Vbi ... admiscuisti.** Rom. 9:30–31: "Quid ergo dicemus? Quod gentes, quae non sectabantur iustitiam, apprehenderunt iustitiam, iustitiam autem quae ex fide est; Israel vero sectando legem iustitiae in legem iustitiae non pervenit." In context, Paul's sentence applies only to the Jews. Bugenhagen makes it seem as if Paul is speaking of Christians as well as Jews.

64/24 **Haec ... Christum.** See 46/12–13.

64/28–29 **Non ... tuis.** See 46/13–14.

66/1–5 **Igitur ... abnegatio.** See 46/14–17. The printed text of Bugenhagen reads "sanctitatis" for "pietatis" and "contra dei gratiam" for "contra Dei iustitiam." The substitution of "iustitiam" for "gratiam" is new; the other reading occurred before.

66/16–23 **Et ... coelorum.** This is More's first departure from the order of Bugenhagen's text. The section that should follow here is held off and a later passage quoted instead. See 80/7–28 and Appendix A, 402/19–29.

66/18–19 **Dimitte ... nostra.** Matt. 6:12.

66/19–20 **& ... reliquum.** Cf. Rom. 4:6 and 8: "Sicut et David dicit beatitudinem hominis, cui Deus accepto fert iustitiam sine operibus: ... Beatus vir, cui non imputavit Dominus peccatum."

66/20–23 **Non ... coelorum.** A conflation of Rom. 7:18, Matt. 9:13, and Matt. 21:31.

66/31–68/5 **In his ... demonstrant.** The reference is to the entire section on penance in *De captivitate Babylonica* (*WA 6*, 543–49), but More oversimplifies Luther's position, which was more complex than simply "sola fide cum oratione breuissima." Luther argued that faith must precede contrition: "fide autem obtenta contritio et consolatio inevitabili sequela sua sponte venient" (*WA 6*, 545). But it is not necessary to feel contrition for each and every sin. "Satis enim est, si ea doleamus peccata, quae praesente conscientia mordent et facili prospectu memoriae cognoscuntur". (*WA 6*, 545). Like contrition, confession is also necessary, and Luther rejoiced that it exists in the church to relieve the burden of guilt. But one need not confess to a priest, for Christ's words in Matthew 18:18, giving the power to absolve, were said of each and every Christian. Therefore Luther admonishes the Roman priesthood not to reserve confession to themselves: "de occultis audiendae confessionis facultatem permittant liberrimam omnibus fratribus et sororibus, ut peccator cui voluerit suum peccatum revelet, veniam et solatium, id est verbum Christi, ex ore proximi petiturus" (*WA 6*, 547). As for satisfaction, Luther argued that the only true satisfaction was a contrite heart, not the muttering of prayers or the purchase of indulgences or the performance of pilgrimages or other public signs of satisfaction, "ut arbitrentur sese posse deo per opera pro peccatis satisfacere, cui sola fide cordis contriti satisfit" (*WA 6*, 548). See note on 94/22–24.

66/35–68/1 **quippe ... sustulistis.** More refers to the three parts required in the traditional definition of penance: contrition ("deflendi"), confession ("confitendi"), and satisfaction ("satisfaciendi").

68/15–20 **Haec ... abnegatio.** See notes on 46/1–17 and 66/1–5.

70/23 **hypochrisin ... fidem.** More summarizes 46/14–17. See also 66/1–5 and 68/15–20.

72/16–17 **e fumo ... incidisti?** Cf. Erasmus, *Adagia* 405 (*Opera omnia*, 2, 184CD): "Fumum fugiens, in ignem incidi." Erasmus cites Lucian, Plato, Horace, and Plutarch. Cf. *Adagia* 3640 (*Opera omnia*, 2, 1106D); Whiting F696, Tilley S570. See *CW6*, Commentary at 192/8–9 and Charles Clay Doyle, "Looking behind Two Proverbs of More," *Moreana*, 33 (1986), 33–34.

74/7–9 **non vno ... mortua.** Cf. Jas. 2:17, 26: "Sic et fides, si non habeat opera, mortua est in semetipsa. ... Sicut enim corpus sine spiritu mortuum est, ita et fides sine operibus mortua est." See also 1 Cor. 13:2–3, Gal. 5:6.

74/12 **Redemptio ... suae?** Prov. 13:8 (see note on 44/34–35).

74/13–14 **Date ... vobis?** Luke 11:41.

74/15–18 **Non illud ... pauperes?** Matt. 25:31–46 (see note on 54/20–22).

74/26–29 **Quis ... agitat.** Cf. Juvenal 2.25–26: "Quis caelum terris non misceat et mare caelo, / Si fur displiceat Verri, homicida Miloni." The subject of the satire, as in More, is hypocrisy. See Erasmus, *Adagia* 281 (*Opera omnia*, 2, 142AC).

74/28–29 **qui ... incestu.** See note on 28/24–26.

74/29 **de virtute ... agitat.** Juvenal 2.19–21: "sed peiores, qui talia verbis / Herculis inuadunt et de virtute locuti / clunem agitant."

74/29–30 **subito ... demissus.** See Erasmus, *Adagia* 786 (*Opera omnia*, 2, 329BC) and Otto, nos. 287 and 516. Cf. *Richard III, CW* 2, 54/25–26, 132/4–5; *CW 15*, 424/9–10.

76/2–5 **Pudet ... vineam.** Matt. 20:1–16.

76/5–7 **Hic ... suspendio.** Stapleton (see note on 20/10–12) wrote in the margin opposite this sentence "Acuté." He later (p. 133) quotes this sentence in *Tres Thomae* as an example of More's clever sayings ("Acute et facete dicta vel responsa").

76/8–9 **e sublimi ... Prophetam.** Erasmus, *Adagia* 180 (*Opera omnia*, 2, 101A): "E sublime me derides."

76/9–11 **contempturusque ... retributionem?** Ps. 118:112: "Inclinavi cor meum ad faciendas justificationes tuas in aeternum, propter retributionem."

80/7–28 **Quisquis ... alienorum.** See Appendix A, 402/7–35. This is the continuation of Bugenhagen that follows 56/13–16 and 58/13–14. It incorporates at 80/16–23 the section quoted above, 66/16–23, which More inserted out of sequence. More's quotation differs from Bugenhagen's printed text in a number of details.

80/7–9 **Quisquis ... producit.** Matt. 7:16–20. See also Luke 6:43–45 and Ps. 1:3.

80/9–10 **Qui ... Dei.** Rom. 8:14.

80/10–11 **Sobrie ... mundi.** Tit. 2:11–12: "Apparuit enim gratia Dei Salvatoris nostri omnibus hominibus, erudiens nos, ut abnegantes impietatem, et saecularia desideria, sobrie, et iuste, et pie vivamus in hoc saeculo."

80/10–11 **adorabit ... veritate.** Cf. John 4:23.

80/18–19 **Dimitte ... nostra.** Matt. 6:12.

80/24–25 **Quisquis ... existam.** Deut. 18:19.

80/25–28 **Audiant . . . alienorum.** Matt. 17:5 and John 10:4–5.

82/28–32 **Haec . . . mulier?** Mark 14:6: "Jesus autem dixit: Sinite eam, quid illi molesti estis? Bonum opus operata est in me."

82/32–34 **An . . . facite?** John 8:39–40: "Responderunt [Iudaei], et dixerunt ei: Pater noster Abraham est. Dicit eis Iesus: Si filii Abrahae estis, opera Abrahae facite. Nunc autem quaeritis me interficere, hominem, qui veritatem vobis locutus sum, quam audivi a Deo: hoc Abraham non fecit."

84/4–6 **Esuriui . . . me.** Matt. 25:35.

84/15–18 **Quid . . . Deum?** Stapleton (see note on 20/10–12) notes in the margin opposite this sentence, "Mos haereticorum."

84/23–29 **Nisi . . . arbitrium.** Although he was at first impressed by a number of Luther's ideas for reform, especially those that matched his own, Erasmus became increasingly disturbed and alienated when he realized that Luther posed a threat to peace and the unity and universal harmony of the church. Finally, at the urging of Pope Adrian VI, he entered the controversy against Luther with his *De libero arbitrio* διατριβή *sive collatio,* written, Erasmus said, at one sitting and published on September 1, 1524, at Basel. This was a brief, ingenious, elegantly written attack on Luther's denial of the doctrine of free will in the Heidelberg theses of 1518 (*WA 1,* 354) and the *Assertio omnium articulorum M. Lutheri per bullam Leonis X. novissimam damnatorum* (1520), specifically article 36, asserting that free will is a mere fiction, and articles 31 and 32, that the performance of good works is sinful (*WA 7,* 142–49, 136–39; see also note on 48/6–9, above). A little more than a year later, in December 1525, Luther replied to Erasmus in the long, rambling, unsystematic *De servo arbitrio.* The volume was four times as long as Erasmus' *De libero arbitrio,* but it was so powerful and so fervent in its conviction that it seemed to overwhelm its opponent. Erasmus was stung and answered Luther once again at length in his *Hyperaspistes diatribae adversus servum arbitrium M. Lutheri,* the first volume of which was completed on February 20, 1526.

84/28–29 **furioso . . . arbitrium.** Perhaps More is thinking of the passage in *De servo arbitrio* in which Luther compares the human will to a horse which is ridden either by God or Satan and has no ability to choose or seek its rider (*WA 18,* 635).

84/30–86/8 **Quid . . . irrideat.** Erasmus argued in *De libero arbitrio* that scriptural passages such as Matt. 19:17 demonstrated the freedom of the will. Otherwise they would not have been put conditionally, with the clear implication that there was a choice: "Nonne frigent omnia praeclara praecepta Christi, si nihil tribuitur humanae voluntati? . . . *Si diligitis me, mandata mea servate.* Quanta apud Iohannem inculcatio mandatorum? Quam male coniunctio: si, congruit merae necessitati? *Si manseritis in me et verba mea in vobis manserint. Si vis perfectus esse*" (p. 39). Luther replied that such expressions are designed to show us things which we cannot do through our own free will, but which we may be enabled to do through the power of God dwelling within us. "Quo tropo intelligi datur utrunque, scilicet et nos nihil posse, et, siquid facimus, Deum in nobis operari." More's objection—that God orders man to keep his commandments while denying him the free will to enable him to do so—is never taken up directly by Luther, but he suggests an answer in what More would undoubtedly have seen as an absurd and circumlocutory paraphrase of Matt. 19:17: "Si volueris servare mandata, hoc est, si voluntatem aliquando habueris (habebis autem non ex te, sed ex Deo, qui tribuet eam cui voluerit) servandi mandata, servabunt et ipsa te." Not satisfied with that, Luther returns to it again a few lines later and tries a second version: "Si vis, si volueris, hoc est, si talis apud Deum fueris, ut voluntate hac te dignetur servandi praecepta, seruaberis" (*De servo arbitrio, WA 18,* 691).

84/31–32 **Si . . . mandata.** Matt. 19:17.

86/9–10 **Sardonio . . . risu.** A Greek term of obscure origin going back as far as Homer to describe any forced, scornful, bitter, or insane laughter. In his article in the *Adagia* Erasmus says that accounts of its origin and meaning are so confused and various that he is afraid whatever he might say about it will be greeted with the same sort of laughter he is trying to describe (*Adagia* 2401, *Opera omnia, 2,* 825–28: "Risus Sardonius"). In later Greek and Latin the term σαρδόνιος was substituted for σαρδάνιος in an attempt to explain its meaning by referring it "to the effects of eating a 'Sardinian plant' (*herba Sardonia*), which was said to produce facial convulsions resembling horrible laughter, usually followed by death" (*OED,* s.v. "Sardonian"). The *OED* designates "Sardonian" as obsolete. Its earliest recorded appearance in English was in 1586. *Sardonic,* on the other hand (in its more limited, contemporary meaning), was first used in English in 1638. Cf. *CW 5,* 490/27.

86/15–21 **Quin . . . spiritum.** Luther admitted in his letter to Erasmus at the beginning of *De servo arbitrio* that some people would never be convinced by what he said, no matter how logical, no matter how supported by scripture. One might as well plow the beach and sow seed in the sand or fill a leaky bucket with water. It required the inspiration of the Holy Spirit: "Illis enim, qui spiritum magistrum in nostris libellis hauserunt, satis abunde a nobis ministratum est, tuaque facile contemnunt, qui vero sine spiritu legunt, nihil mirum, si quovis vento, velut arundo, agitentur, quibus nec Deus satis dixerit, etiam si omnes creaturae in linguas verterentur." The Spirit is free, however, and blows where he wishes. "Quamvis enim res nostra talis est, quae externo doctore non est contenta, sed praeter eum qui plantat et rigat foris, etiam desyderet spiritum Dei, qui incrementum det et vivus viva doceat intus (quae cogitatio mihi imposuit) tamen cum liber sit ille spiritus, ac spiret non ubi nos volumus, sed ubi ipse vult, servanda fuerat regula illa Pauli, Insta oportune, importune, Non enim scimus, qua hora dominus venturus sit" (*WA 18*, 601–2).

86/31–88/4 **Quorum . . . fatemur.** Relying on Origen and Jerome, Erasmus explains in *De libero arbitrio* how such difficult texts as Exod. 9:12 (Induravitque Dominus cor Pharonis), Exod. 33:19, Isa, 63:17, and Rom. 9:14–18 are not inconsistent with free will (pp. 46–48).

88/5–8 **Sine . . . eum?** John 15:5 and 6:44.

88/14–16 **Quoties . . . noluisti?** Matt. 23:37. Fowler's marginal note is a mistake for Luke 13:[34–35], a slightly different version of the same saying.

88/20–22 **Quum . . . fecimus.** Luke 17:10.

88/25 **I nunc &c.** The expression is Juvenalian (6.306, 10.310, 12.57). For other uses of it by More see *CW 14*, Commentary 2 at 81/4. See also notes on 74/26–29, above.

88/30–90/2 **hypocrisin . . . fidem.** More paraphrases 66/1–5.

90/5–7 **Nam . . . sole.** Stapleton (see note on 20/10–12) notes opposite this sentence, "Simile." Cf. Tilley S996: "No sunshine but some shadow."

90/23 **dicto citius factum.** Otto, no. 529 ("dicto citius"). Erasmus, *Adagia* 1871 (*Opera omnia*, 2, 678DE): "Simul et dictum et factum."

90/26–29 **Quisquis. . . Dei.** See 80/7–10, where the passage is quoted more exactly.

90/35 **sub melle venenum lateat.** Ovid, *Amores* 1.8.104: "Impia sub dulci melle venena latent." Jerome was fond of this proverbial expression (Otto, no. 1085). Cf. 32/13–14 and note on 38/20–26, above.

92/9–12 **Sobrie . . . instituit.** See note on 80/7–28.

92/13 **At . . . lachrymae.** Cf. Terence, *Andria* 125–26: "attat hoc illud est, / hinc illae lacrumae, haec illast misericordia." Otto, no. 904.

92/15–16 **qui . . . adorare.** John 4:24: "Spiritus est Deus: et eos, qui adorant eum, in spiritu et veritate oportet adorare."

92/23–25 **At . . . extersit.** Luke 7:38. For the identification of the woman in this passage as Mary of Bethany, see John 12:3. The Latin church had traditionally identified Mary of Bethany with Mary Magdalene and the penitent woman in Luke 7:37–50. See Tertullian, *De pudicitia* 11 (*PL 2*, 1001); Gregory the Great (*PL 76*, 1189); and the

Glossa ordinaria (*PL 114*, 229). The Greek church, following Origen (*PG 13*, 1721–26), regarded them as three separate individuals. The unity of the three Marys was beginning to be questioned in More's time by Lefèvre d'Etaples and others. See Edward L. Surtz, *The Works and Days of John Fisher* (Cambridge, Mass., 1967), pp. 5–7, 274–89. More, however, held to the traditional view. Fowler's marginal note referring to Luke 6 is incorrect.

92/25–30 **Vobis . . . locustis,** Mark 1:6, Matt. 3:4.

92/30–31 **Sed . . . ieiunare.** The reference is vague, but More perhaps has in mind 1 Cor. 8:13: "Quapropter si esca scandalizat fratrem meum: non manducabo carnem in aeternum, ne fratrem meum scandalizem." See also Acts 27:33–34.

92/33–94/1 **At . . . illo.** David's dancing before the ark is described in 2 Kings 6:14–15. He was seen by Michol the daughter of Saul, who despised him in her heart and reproved him for dishonoring himself. She was punished by being unable to bear any children (2 Kings 6:16–23).

94/3–5 **Profecto . . . spiritu.** Cf. *De Tristitia Christi, CW 14*, 145/5–147/1 and Commentary 2.

94/6 **De . . . instituit.** More paraphrases 80/12.

94/11–13 **promissum . . . seculi.** Matt. 28:20.

94/16–18 **Ecclesia . . . nullam.** For Luther's view of the invisible church made up of a group of scattered individuals, "here one and there one / here two and there two," as More put it, see note on 40/31–34. For More's own view of the church, see Richard Marius' Introduction to the Confutation, *CW 8*, 1271–1363, and Brian Gogan, *The Common Corps of Christendom: Ecclesiological Themes in the Writings of Sir Thomas More*, Studies in the History of Christian Thought 26 (Leiden, 1982), pp. 148–70.

94/22 **Ordinem . . . figmento.** See note on 44/12–13.

94/22–24 **Quis . . . peccatis?** Contrition is the first of the three parts of the sacrament of penance, the other two being confession and satisfaction. Luther held that penance, like all sacraments, consisted essentially of God's promise of the forgiveness of sins, as in Matt. 16:19 or 18:18, and the faith of the penitent aroused by these words (*WA 6*, 543). The church taught that contrition, or sorrow for one's sins, could prepare a sinner to receive grace. In Luther's view this ignored the prior importance of faith: "Magna res est cor contritum, nec nisi ardentis in promissionem et comminationem divinam fidei, quae veritatem dei immobilem intuita, tremefacit, exterret et sic conterit conscientiam, rursus exaltat et solatur servatque contritam, ut veritas comminationis sit causa contritionis, veritas promissionis sit solacii, si credatur, et hac fide homo mereatur peccatorum remissionem." Faith alone merits remission of sins, and when faith is obtained, contrition inevitably follows: "Proinde fides ante omnia docenda et provocanda est, fide autem obtenta, contritio et consolatio inevitabili sequela sua sponte venient." Beware, then, Luther cautioned, lest you trust too much to sorrow and not enough to faith: "Cave ergo, in contritionem tuam confidas aut dolori tuo tribuas remissionem peccatorum. Non respicit te propter haec deus, sed propter fidem, qua minis et promissis eius credidisti, quae operata est dolorem eiusmodi" (WA 6, 545). See also Assertio, art. 6 (WA 7, 113–16); Dialogue Concerning Heresies, CW 6, 349/19–20; and note on 66/31–68/5, above.

94/24–25 **Quis . . . Confessionem?** An allusion to Luther's doctrine of the priesthood of all believers. See note on 44/14–16.

94/25 **Quis . . . contendit?** See 52/26–56/7, 58/33–64/17, and the second note on 44/17.

94/25–26 **Quis . . . ieiunia?** Luther objected to fasting because it restricted Christian liberty and led the common people to mistake shadows for substance, believing that it is "a greater sin to eat butter than to lie, to swear, or even to live unchastely" (WA 6, 447). See also Responsio, CW5, 686/26–30.

94/26 **Quis . . . Ecclesiae?** Luther objected to the canon of the mass (see note on 44/10–11) and the way in which the consecration was mumbled by the priest and not proclaimed aloud to the people. Luther also objected to the canonical hours, masses for the dead, prayer to the saints, and the whole notion of what he thought of as vain repetition, babbling prayers without knowing what they meant. The mass itself, moreover, was not a sacrifice or good work to be purchased and offered up for a special intention. Cf. De captivitate Babylonica (WA 6, 565): "abunde suo sacramento se satisfacere putat, si battologiam legendarum precum emurmuret et missas celebret, deinde eas ipsas horas nunquam oret aut, si oret, pro se oret. Atque missas suas (quae summa est perversitas) ceu sacrifitium offerat, cum missa sit usus sacramenti." See also Responsio, CW 5, 686/19–21 and Commentary.

94/26–27 **Quis . . . ornatum?** Since God is spirit, the reformers believed, he is to be worshiped in spirit by spiritual things, not by fasting or costly ornaments or any other material form of worship. Cf. More's paraphrase of John Ryckes' Ymage of Loue (1525), sigs. C_1v–E_1 in Dialogue Concerning Heresies, CW 6, 43/19–30: "the worshyppyng of god with golde and syluer & suche other corporall thynges ought not to be vsed amonge crysten people / but leuyng all that shadowe / we sholde drawe vs to the spyrytuall thynges / and serue our lorde onely in spyryte and spyrytuall thynges. For so he sayth hym self that god as

hym selfe is spyrytuall / so seketh he suche worshyppers as shall worshyppe hym in spyryte / & in trouthe / yᵗ is in fayth / hope / & charyte of
harte / not in yᵉ ypocrysy & ostentacyon of outward obseruaunce /
bodyly seruyce / gay and costely ornamentes / fayre ymages / goodly
songe / flesshly fastynge / & all yᵉ rable of suche vnsauoury ceremonyes." See also note on 56/33–58/3, above, and *CW 6*, 40/6–47/31.
The Ymage of Loue is discussed by E. Ruth Harvey in *CW 6*, Appendix A,
pp. 729–59.

94/27 **Quis . . . cultui?** See 96/32–33 and note on 16/27.

94/27–28 **Quis . . . Purgatorium?** See note on 56/31–33.

94/28–29 **Quis . . . Sacrificio?** Luther considered the mass to be a
promise received from God and not a ritual or sacrifice offered up to
God. See 96/10–11 and notes on 44/11–12 and 94/26.

94/32–34 **dogmata . . . Pontificis.** In *De captivitate Babylonica* Luther
notes that when he wrote his *Resolutiones disputationum de indulgentiarum
virtute* two years before, in 1518, he believed that indulgences should
not be rejected entirely because they were approved by the common
consent of all men. Now he is convinced that indulgences are simply
impostures and that all the books he had written on the subject should
be collected and burned: "postea . . . intellexi, eas aliud non esse quam
meras adulatorum Romanorum imposturas, quibus et fidem dei et
pecunias hominum perderent. Atque utinam a Bibliopolis queam im-
petrare et omnibus qui legerunt persuadere, ut universos libellos meos
de indulgentiis exurant et pro omnibus quae de eis scripsi hanc propo-
sitionem apprehendant: INDVLGENTIAE SVNT ADVLATORVM ROMANORVM
NEQVICIAE." Similarly, he had once argued that the pope at least had
human, if not divine, authority. Through the efforts of Eck, Emser,
and others, however, he is now convinced that the papacy is the kingdom of Babylon and the power of Nimrod, the mighty hunter. Everything he had written previously on the pope should be burned: "oro
librarios, oro lectores, ut iis quae super hac re edidi exustis hanc propo-
sitionem teneant: PAPATVS EST ROBVSTA VENATIO ROMANI EPISCOPI" (*WA*
6, 497–98).

94/34 **& ipsa item Eucharistia.** In *De captivitate Babylonica* (1520)
Luther says that when he published his sermon on the eucharist (1519)
he did not challenge the common belief of the church ("in usu communi haerebam"). But now that he has been forced into the arena (presumably by his excommunication a few months before, in June 1520),
he will speak his mind freely (*WA 6*, 502). He goes on to insist that it is
unscriptural and wrong to withhold the sacramental wine from the
laity, that transubstantiation cannot be proved from scripture, and that
the true bread and wine are present after consecration together with
the true body and blood of Christ (*WA 6*, 502–12). But he is still

unwilling to reject transubstantiation as heretical: "Permitto itaque qui
volet utranque opinionem tenere: hoc solum nunc ago, ut scrupulos
conscientiarum de medio tollam, ne quis se reum haereseos metuat, si
in altari verum panem verumque vinum esse crediderit, sed liberum
esse sibi sciat, citra periculum salutis, alterutrum imaginari, opinari et
credere, cum sit hic nulla necessitas fidei" (*WA 6*, 508). See note on
44/10.

94/34–96/2 **Carolostadius . . . panem.** In a series of German tracts
published at Basel in the fall of 1524, Karlstadt denied the physical
presence of Christ in the eucharist, denied even that the bread and
wine are sacramental signs (Ronald J. Sider, *Andreas Bodenstein von
Karlstadt: The Development of His Thought 1517–1525*, Studies in Medieval and Reformation Thought 11, Leiden, 1974, pp. 292–99). Ulrich
Zwingli also denied the real physical presence of Christ in the eucharist
in a letter to the Lutheran preacher Matthew Alber, first circulated in
manuscript and then published in March 1525; his conclusions resembled Karlstadt's, but his arguments were much more sophisticated.
His "De eucharistia," a section of *De vera et falsa religione commentarius*
(Zürich, 1525), was the source of George Joye's *The Souper of the Lorde*
(1533), to which More replied in *The Answer to the First Part of the
Poisoned Book* (1534). Oecolampadius also denied the corporeal presence of Christ in the eucharist in his *De genuina . . . expositione;* his
arguments were based mainly on the fathers, See *CW 11*, xxii–xxiv.

Zwingli was born at Wildhaus in the canton of St. Gall, Switzerland,
on January 1, 1484. Educated at the universities of Vienna and Basel,
where he studied theology, Zwingli was ordained and served as a parish priest at Glaris from 1506 to 1516. From 1513 to 1515 he served as
chaplain to the Swiss mercenaries employed in the Italian campaigns of
Pope Julius II. His work as a reformer began in 1518, when he joined
the Great Minster at Zürich and began to preach against fasting, the
worship of saints, and the need for celibacy among priests. Pope
Adrian VI requested the city of Zürich to remove Zwingli from its
midst, but Zwingli persuaded the city council to allow him to defend
himself in a public disputation, which he did so well that the city fathers
not only retained him but also separated the canton of Zürich from the
jurisdiction of the bishop of Constance. On April 2, 1524, Zwingli
publicly married Anna Reinhard. Believing that, since God is a spirit,
the worship of God should be essentially spiritual, Zwingli stripped the
churches of all sensory appeal—pictures, statues, organs, relics, altars.
Chalices and monstrances made of precious metals were melted down.
Indulgences, pilgrimages, the conception of the mass as a sacrifice, and
many of the sacraments were abolished. The break between Protestant
and Catholic eventually led to civil war. In February 1531, Zwingli
urged the Swiss Protestants to attack the five Forest Cantons, which
had remained Catholic. On October 10, 1531, the armies met at Kap-

pel, and Zwingli was killed waving a banner, urging his men forward in the name of God.

On Karlstadt and Oecolampadius see note on 14/37–38.

96/2–4 **Quod . . . Suinglius.** See note on 96/19–29.

96/5–8 **Nam . . . carnem.** The phrase "citra periculum" is apparently taken directly from a statement by Luther on the eucharist (quoted in the note on 94/34, above).

96/8–9 **Deinde . . . verti.** In *Contra Henricum regem Angliae* (1522) Luther condemned transubstantiation as wicked and blasphemous: "Antea posui nihil referre, sic sive sic sentias de transsubstantiatione, nunc autem visis rationibus et argumentis assertoris sacramentorum pulcherrimis decerno impium esse et blasphemum, siquis dicat panem transsubstantiari, Catholicum autem et pium, siquis cum Paulo dicat: Panis, quem frangimus, est corpus Christi" (*WA 10/2*, 208). More quotes this passage in *Responsio, CW 5*, 490/31–34, where the sidenote accuses Luther of inconsistency. See note on 94/34, above.

96/10–11 **Sacrificium . . . detraxit.** See note on 44/11–12.

96/12 **contrectandum . . . foeminis.** More exaggerates. Luther believed in the priesthood of all believers, but he also believed that not all men are given the vocation to exercise that power, but only those chosen to serve as representatives of the people. He never said that women should be permitted to consecrate the host. They were not even allowed to enter the priesthood although in an emergency women and children were allowed to hear confession and give absolution. See note on 44/14–16. See also *Responsio, CW 5*, Commentary at 158/12–14.

96/12–14 **in . . . tantum.** Luther disapproved of the veneration of the eucharist apart from reception (*WA 11*, 445). He considered it wrong to venerate the signs (bread and wine, the body and blood of Christ) apart from the words of the mass, which expressed the meaning of the signs (the promise of salvation through Christ). See *Dialogue Concerning Heresies, CW 6*, Commentary at 354/24–25.

96/14–18 **Imo . . . ingredienti.** More is misinterpreting a misleading passage in *De captivitate Babylonica*, where Luther says that, since the sacrament of the bread is a commemoration of the departure of Christ from this world, it is particularly appropriate for the dying, as baptism is for the newborn: "et sic distribuamus haec duo sacramenta, ut baptismus initio et totius vitae cursui, panis autem termino et morti deputetur, atque Christianus utroque exerceatur in hoc corpusculo, donec plene baptisatus et roboratus transeat ex hoc mundo" (*WA 6*, 572). More repeats the charge in *Dialogue Concerning Heresies, CW 6*, 354/19–21 and Commentary.

96/19–29 **An ... esse.** In a parallel passage in the *Dialogue Concerning Heresies,* More expresses the same invidious speculation: "Item Swynglius and Ecolampadius scolers of Luther ... teche that yᵉ sacrament of the auter ys not the very body or blood of oure lord at all. And Luther hym selfe all be yt he now wryteth agaynste theym there in / yet (as yt by many thyngys appereth) mynded and intended to putte forth by laysour the same heresye hym selfe / tyll he chaunged his mynd for enuye that he bare toward theym / whan he saw that they wold be hedys of a secte theym selfe (for that cowlde he suffer no man to be but hym selfe)" (*CW 6*, 354/3–11).

Cochlaeus also refers to Protestant confusion over the nature of the eucharist: "De abusu Eucharistiae quanta sit impietas uestra, horret profecto animus dicere. ... Num ignoras quam absurda et impia protulit male uxoratus uester Archidiaconus, quem Lutherus ipse reprobauit, Qualia uero sunt Lutheri? quando unquam constitit sibi ipsi?" (*Responsio Cochlaei*, sig. B₁v). Luther had publicly rejected Karlstadt's doctrine in late 1524, but he did not publicly attack the eucharistic teaching of Oecolampadius and Zwingli until the summer of 1526 (Mark U. Edwards, *Luther and the False Brethren*, Stanford, 1975, pp. 51–57, 89–93).

96/32–33 **& Sanctos ... blasphemat.** See 94/27 and note on 16/27.

96/33 **Crucem eius conspurcat.** See note on 28/1–11.

96/33–34 **& ... coaequat?** See note on 56/29–30; see also 16/27.

98/2–7 **clementissimum ... perniciosior.** See notes on 48/34–50/8 and 84/23–29.

98/10–14 **docet ... adulterum.** Luther's position on law is presented most clearly in his *Von der Freiheit eines Christenmenschen* (1520), where he argues the paradox that Christians are both totally free and totally subject—totally free from all laws of men that conflict with divine law and totally bound in obedience to the law of God. True Christians have no need of law because their faith leads them to obey the laws of God spontaneously and unerringly (*WA 11*, 250–51). In the section on matrimony in *De captivitate Babylonica,* Luther repeats his belief in Christian liberty, speaking of the laws governing marriage: "homo non habuit ius leges tales condendi et Christianis per Christum libertas donata est super omnes leges hominum, maxime ubi lex divina intercedit." He then goes on to discuss various impediments the church recognizes as bases for annulment—*impedimentum criminis, impedimentum ligaminis, impedimentum erroris,* and, among them, *impedimentum ordinis,* the impediment of ordination, which Luther regards as a human ordinance or tradition that crept into the church after the time of its first founding. "Est ergo inter sacerdotem et uxorem verum et inseparabile matrimonium, mandatis divinis probatum." In the case of an impotent husband, Luther suggests first a divorce, and if that is not possible because of "the tyranny of the laws" or the husband's refusal, the woman is no longer married in any real sense of the word and is therefore free to contract a secret marriage, which is a true marriage in the eyes of God and not an act of adultery. "An haec mulier salva sit et in statu salutis? Respondeo ego, quod sic, Quia error et ignorantia virilis impotentiae hic impedit matrimonium, et tyrannis legum non admittit divortium, et mulier libera est per legem divinam, nec cogi potest ad continentiam" (*WA 6*, 555–58). See also John Headley's explanation in *Responsio, CW 5*, Commentary at 688/9–12.

98/18–30 **Quum . . . adiungitur.** The soldiers, of course, were not members of a Lutheran army, but peasants who, More believed, were incited to riot and rebellion by Luther. For the Peasants' Revolt and the part Luther played in it, see note on 102/3–19. See also 16/16–25, 22/18–24/33 and note, 24/22–32. See notes on 149/18–23 and 149/28–30.

98/28–29 **obuijs . . . amplectimini.** Cf. Erasmus, *Adagia* 1854 (*Opera omnia*, 2, 675D): "Obviis ulnis."

100/2 **Ipsum audite.** See 80/26–27.

100/4–5 **Quisquis . . . Dominus.** More paraphrases. See 80/24–25.

100/13–15 **At . . . Christus.** Cf. Matt. 18:17: "Quod si non audierit eos: dic ecclesiae: si autem ecclesiam non audierit, sit tibi sicut ethnicus, et publicanus."

100/19–30 **Nam . . . seducti.** Cf. Cochlaeus: "diuina quoque uos ultio persequetur, quae percutit uos caecitate et amentia, non solum spiritali sed etiam corporali, ut non solum uiri, sed et mulieres quaedam furore correptae, uelut Menades Bacchi, nudae per agros et nemora sine mente, sine naturali pudore discurrant. Facit item concurrere Lutheranos contra Lutheranos, non modo contrarijs scriptis et opinionibus, uerum etiam aduersis signis, hostibus armis, instructis aciebus" (*Responsio Cochlaei*, sig. D$_1$).

100/19–24 **Nam . . . emendatorum.** The passage is prophetic of certain key concepts in *A Dialogue of Comfort*. More was convinced in the Tower that men were shadows or agents—*satellites,* as he calls them here—of a more ancient power of evil. "Our wrestlyng is not agaynst flesh and bloud," he says, quoting Paul; "it is the mydday devill hym selfe that maketh such incursion vppon vs, by the men that are his ministers to make vs fall for feare" (*CW 12*, 317/24–27). More also derived great consolation from Paul's statement, referred to here, that God is faithful and along with the temptation will provide a way out. It is one of the touchstones More keeps returning to throughout the *Dialogue of Comfort*. See, for example, *CW 12*, 162/4–9; 247/17–21;

278/27–279/2; and 22/26–30. The passage reads in full: "Tentatio vos non apprehendat nisi humana: fidelis autem Deus est, qui non patietur vos tentari supra id, quod potestis, sed faciet etiam cum tentatione proventum, ut possitis sustinere" (1 Cor. 10:13). The remainder of the sentence here is taken from Rev. 7:17: "Quoniam Agnus, qui in medio throni est, reget illos, et deducet eos ad vitae fontes aquarum, et absterget Deus omnem lachrymam ab oculis eorum" (cf. Rev. 21:4).

100/27–28 **spiritu . . . terrae.** A combination of 2 Thess. 2:8: "Et tunc relevabitur ille iniquus, quem Dominus Jesus interficiet spiritu oris sui, et destruet illustratione adventus sui eum," and Ps. 1:4: "Non sic impii, non sic: sed tanquam pulvis, quem projicit ventus a facie terrae." See also Isa. 11:4. The marginal note referring to 1 Thess. is incorrect.

100/29–102/2 **Cuius . . . redacti.** For the Peasants' Revolt, see 22/18–24/33 and note.

100/35–36 **ecce . . . interitus.** Cf. Ps. 28:3: "Vox Domini super aquas, Deus majestatis intonuit: Dominus super aquas multas," and 1 Thess. 5:3: "Cum enim dixerint, pax et securitas: tunc repentinus eis superveniet interitus, sicut dolor in utero habenti, et non effugient."

102/1 **plusquam septuaginta millia.** See note on 149/15–25, below.

102/3–19 **Qua . . . perdidit.** Cochlaeus makes the same point. Luther first stirred up the people by preaching a false gospel of Christian liberty and then turned against them in his "bloody little book": "Quis enim simplicem populum ad tam impia facinora induxit nisi Concionatores et libri Lutherani sub falso uerbi dei libertatisque praetextu? Id quod ego clarissime ostendi ex uarijs Lutheri libris et dictis, quando respondi sanguinario eius libello in rusticos" (*Responsio Cochlaei*, sigs. A₃v–A₄).

It was commonly believed that Luther was the prophet of revolution and that civil disorder and anarchy would inevitably follow unless he was suppressed. This was the charge in the Edict of Worms, it was repeated by the Papal Nuncio at Nürnberg, and by the time of the Peasants' Revolt it appeared as though it had all come true. Luther was immediately blamed for the turmoil by Catholic polemicists, and even the peasants themselves seemed to confirm the suspicion in March 1525, when at Memmingen they named Luther along with Melanchthon, Zwingli, and other reformers as arbitrators to determine whether the twelve articles they had drawn up were congruent with the teaching of scripture. Luther replied to this request in his *Ermahnung zum Frieden auf die zwölf Artikel der Bauerschaft in Schwaben* (*WA 18*, 279–334), in which he appealed for reason on both sides. The work was written in mid April 1525. By early May, when the tide was moving against the peasants, Luther reversed himself completely in a passionate, violent treatise entitled *Wider die räuberischen und mörderischen Rot-*

ten der Bauern (WA 18, 334–61). In this work Luther not only disassoci-
ated himself from the peasants but urged their utter destruction.
Condemning the violence perpetrated by roaming bands of peasants
ravaging the countryside "like mad dogs," and in particular Thomas
Münzer, "the archdevil of Mühlhausen," Luther wrote the book, he
says, to place the sins of the peasants before their eyes and to instruct
the civil authorities in their duty. The peasants merit destruction of
both body and soul because of three primary offenses against God and
man. First, they broke their vows of obedience to authority. Second,
they rose up in revolution and looted cloisters and castles. Third, they
committed these horrible sins under cover of the gospels. Since the
peasants have thus revealed themselves to be "faithless murderers,
perjurers," "armed robbers and blasphemers against God," the civil
authorities have a perfect right to strike them down and destroy them
"with a good conscience, as long as they have blood in their veins."
Luther's central attack against the peasants in his *Wider die . . . Rotten
der Bauern* was printed in May 1525, just as they were being butchered,
and it seemed as though he not only condoned the massacre, but had
perhaps arranged it or at least had sold them out. It immediately
earned Luther the same sort of criticism More and Cochlaeus level
against him: that he was a coward, a toady, a traitor, and betrayer of his
own people. Luther replied in *Ein Sendbrief von dem harten Büchlein
wider die Bauern (WA 18,* 362–401), defending his position. But it was
too late. The damage had already been done, and the book tended to
pass unnoticed, like an afterthought.

102/26–104/5 **Quod . . . gratulabimur.** More says nothing about the
final paragraph in Bugenhagen's printed *Letter* (Appendix A, 404/1–
8). See *CW 8,* 1154–55.

102/31–32 **Episcopatum.** See note on 26/17–20.

104/4–5 **& . . . gratulabimur.** Cf. Luke 15:6–7: "Et veniens domum
convocat amicos, et vicinos, dicens illis: Congratulamini mihi quia inveni ovem meam, quae perierat. Dico vobis quod ita gaudium erit in
coelo super uno peccatore poenitentiam agente, quam super nonagin-
ta novem justis, qui non indigent poenitentia."

104/9 **Cunerus . . . S. Petri.** Cuner Peeters (1531–1580) studied philosophy and theology at Louvain and taught theology at the Abbey of
Park near Louvain. In 1559 he became the pastor of St. Peter's in
Louvain. A year later he received his doctorate in theology, and in 1568
he was chosen rector of the University of Louvain. He was bishop of
Leeuwarden from 1570 to 1578, when he was expelled by the Protestants. He spent his last years writing and preaching at Münster and
Cologne. At Louvain he published Dutch books defending the traditional doctrine on purgatory (1566) and the eucharist (1567) and attacking the Anabaptists and other heretics (1568). He also published a

Latin book (Louvain, 1567) designating the church as the "colum-
na . . . et firmamentum Veritatis" and identifying it by fourteen properties. After 1568 he published several Latin books defending the
traditional doctrine on the mass, the celibacy of the clergy, grace and
free will, predestination, justification, indulgences, and the papacy.
The fullest account is in *Nieuw Nederlandsch Biografisch Woordenboek*, ed.
P. C. Mölhuysen, P. J. Blok, and L. Knappert, 10 vol.(Leiden, 1911–
37; reprint, Amsterdam, 1974), 5, 122–23; some additional information about his Dutch books can be found in *Biographisch Woordenboek der
Nederlanden*, ed. Abraham J. van der Aa, 7 vols. (Haarlem, 1852–78;
reprint, Amsterdam, 1969), 2, 283.

109/1 **soulys.** One would expect the definite article before "soulys", as
in *A Supplicacyon for the Beggers*, which More actually changed, perhaps
inadvertently, to *The Supplycacyon of beggars* (109/6). John Foxe refers
to Fish's pamphlet as *the booke of beggars* (twice), [*the booke*] *of the Beggars*,
or even *the Beggers booke* (Appendix D, 441/13–14, 442/1–17, 443/38–
39).

111/2–11 **In most pytuouse . . . hense.** This long sentence, with its
inversion, is a good specimen of the openings of official supplications
in Tudor England. A. W. Reed, *Early Tudor Drama* (London, 1926), p.
189, quotes More's brother-in-law's complaint to Henry VIII in 1529
against J. Ravyn: "Pitiously compleynyth unto yor gracious hyghness
yor pore subject John Rastell." Thomas Nash's *Pierce Peniles His Supplication to the Divell* (1592) is cast in the form of a supplication: Pierce
refers to More twice in his suit; see Germain Marc'hadour, "Thomas
Nashe and a Footnote to Thomas More," *Moreana, 26* (1970), pp. 40
and 72.

111/2–3 **pytuouse . . . pyte.** *Pity* and *piety*, different forms of one word
in More's English, were key words in his work generally and in *The
Supplication*. A wealth of meaning applies to the term, even when More
denounces Fish's "pretexte of pyte" (112/17), the "pyte" his bill "pretendeth" (112/19–20), "the cloke of pyte" (114/34) that conceals its
cruelty. It is well illustrated, for instance, in *CW 8,* 504/25 and in *CW 2*,
57/26. *Pituous* is More's spelling in his autograph prayer (*CW 13,*
226/17): "pytuously to call for his helpe." It designates a humble and
contrite heart, which arouses pity, deserving indulgence and compassion.

111/3 **cherite.** In *A Dialogue Concerning Heresies,* More had rebuked
Tyndale for using "the bare name of loue" where the New Testament
spoke of charity, the English name of "a good vertuous and well ordred
loue" (*CW 6,* 288/2–5).

111/4 **aquayntaunce** Perhaps a plural with the final *s* omitted. See
Delcourt, pp. 87–90, 138–41. But in More's time *acquaintance* was also

a collective noun with both singular and plural senses (*OED*, s.v. "acquaintance" 3). See note on 134/17.

111/6 **sely sowlys.** The stock phrase "silly souls," designating the souls in purgatory, owes its survival, at least partly, to alliteration. The suppliants call themselves thus again at 111/28, 112/8, 116/9, 136/31, 172/16, 219/4–5, and 225/17. Old English *saelig* ("holy, blessed") shifted toward "pitiful," "helpless," and on to "foolish." More's use of "silly souls," perhaps because the phrase was obsolescent, is echoed sarcastically in the works of his enemies Frith and Foxe. More uses 'sely' to mean 'foolish' in his *Letter against Frith* (241/25), *Debellation* (*CW 10*, 227/13), and *Dialogue Concerning Heresies* (*CW 6*, 287/35).

111/7 **abydyng.** Intransitive, though the verb could also be transitive (see 120/1).

111/8 **clensynge fyre.** The Council of Florence (1439), the most recent authority on purgatory in More's time, carefully avoided the word *fire*. But fire is the central element in 1 Cor. 3:12–15, a principal proof text for purgatory (see note on 187/10–17).

111/14 **yt may lyke you.** A formula of courtesy chiefly used in addressing a superior (also at 164/12). More begins his state letters with this phrase (Rogers, nos. 109, 110, 115–127, 136), and he often uses it at the beginning of a new paragraph (Rogers, p. 259, line 6; p. 276, lines 35 and 49; p. 277, line 70; p. 278, line 103; p. 314, line 74). He also uses its modern equivalent "yt may please you" (112/7), "yt myght please the kynge" (116/15).

111/17 **eased / holpen / and relieued.** More's redundancy suggests the official style of a supplication.

111/19 **masses.** The missal contained special masses for the dead, with variants according to the circumstances: mass for the day of burial, for one month after burial, for yearly anniversaries, for bishops and many special categories of departed souls, as well as for all souls on November 2 (*Sarum Missal*, cols. 956–60, 859*–85*). Moreover, at each mass there was a commemoration of the dead (*Sarum Missal*, col. 619).

111/19–20 **suffrages . . . relygyouse.** In monasteries and convents, whole communities, including nuns and monks or friars not in holy orders, were bound in duty to recite daily prayers for their deceased benefactors. These intercessory prayers for the souls, especially when they assumed a liturgical character, were called "suffrages."

111/21 **sprongen vp.** The old form of the participle was on its way out. More, in his *Dialogue*, had used it, one feels, to evoke older times, for instance the England of Duke Humphrey (*CW 6*, 86/16: "rongen . . . songen"). Here the departed souls, an average two or more generations ahead of their living bedesfolk, speak the English of yesteryear. They say "holpen (111/17, 111/23), as does More's father in an anecdote of the fifteenth century (*CW 6*, 86/8), and "comen" (114/2) as he does (*CW 6*, 86/14), and "founden" (114/21) and "holpe" (114/30). Such archaism also applies to syntactic elements such as "shall mow" (129/29 and 160/21), "when that" (130/16), "how often that" (131/7) and "after that" (168/4), all current in Chaucer. The souls continue also in the use and spelling of "mydle yerth" (134/3), "yerthly" (152/2), "inow" (134/7), "ynow" (149/4, 164/27), "ynowe" (157/32); the phrase "and we wold" for "if we would" (125/14, 135/3); "strenger" (141/11), "canneth" (140/10), "fader" (147/26), "send" for "sent" (148/1); and "thyng" as a plural (139/20).

111/21 **sedycyouse.** A key epithet for heresy (cf. "sedycyon" at 114/34). It recurs at 118/22, 149/16 and four times in the peroration at the end of the first book (166/19, 166/22, 168/23, 168/27).

112/29 **awne.** In the sixteenth century and later *awne* (instead of *own*) was a northern and Scottish form (*OED*, s.v. "own" a). That "awn(e)" is the usual spelling in *1529²* suggests that the compositor was from the north. See notes on 174/6, 186/10 and 223/16.

112/31 **almesse dede.** "Alms" comes from Greek *eleemosyne*, "compassion," and in More's day the word retained something of that broad meaning, close to "mercy"; see its ironic use in *CW 2*, 24/15 ("It wer almoise to hange them"); in *CW 6*, 392/35, 393/3 and *CW 8*, 404/12 More applies *alms* and *almsdeed* to all the works of mercy. See 142/20 where "theyre almoyse" practically means "their support," "the relief they afford."

112/31 **warkis.** The form "warkis" here and at 168/29 was a Scottish variant in the sixteenth century. See note on 112/29.

113/2–3 **wypyng . . . eyen.** Rev. 7:17 and 21:4, echoing Isa. 25:8. Many readers would recognize a sentence used in the mass for the very popular feast of the dedication of a church: "et absterget Deus omnem lacrymam ab oculis eorum" (*Sarum Missal*, col. 550).

113/8 **vngracyouse.** A strong epithet (repeated at 114/5, 137/17) directly opposed to "gracyouse" (112/30).

113/9 **repente & amend.** See *The Apology* (*CW 9*, 75/36–76/5), where More tells of Fish's conversion.

113/22–23 **goodys . . . sowle.** On the moral philosophers' well-known division of "goods" into those of the mind, body, and fortune (or external goods), see *CW 4*, Commentary at 160/16.

113/26 **hys boke ys nameles.** The anonymity of Fish allows More to nickname the author "the beggars' proctor," "the devil's proctor," or "the proctor of hell." He also used such nicknames in *The Answer to a Poisoned Book* (the Masker), *The Apology,* and *The Debellation* (the Pacifier).

114/7–8 **owre ... deuyll.** Cf. 1 Pet. 5:8: "aduersarius vester diabolus."

114/8–9 **he had set him ... boke.** The wording is ambiguous: (1) "he [the devil] had set him [Fish] to work on that book" (*OED,* s.v. "set" 112b); (2) "he [Fish] had set to work on the book" (*OED,* s.v. "set" 113b).

114/10–11 **enmyouse ... grynnynge.** Cf. Appendix D, 443/28–29.

114/11 **gnasshyng the teeth.** "Stridor dentium" is frequently associated with hell in the gospels (Matt. 8:12; 13:42, 50; 22:13, 24:51; 25:30; Luke 13:28). Cf. also Ps. 36:12.

114/14 **are.** For *ere* (= before); this reflects an obsolescent pronunciation. The souls say "parsons" for "persons" (121/22, 127/18, 149/24), "hard" for "heard" 134/5–6), "sarue" for "serue" (156/25); and more often than not the Latin prefix *per–* is spelled *par–*.

114/18 **yᵉ deuyll ... ly.** See John 8:44.

114/22 **labour loste.** Whiting, L11, Tilley L9.

114/25 **after ... forth.** A Latinate construction meaning "after the book was put forth." See Visser, *1,* 376–78.

115/15 **chanons.** The canons are correctly listed between the monks and the friars, since they pertain to both categories. They are cloistered and bound to the recitation of the divine office, as are the monks, but share some of the friars' freedom. (Erasmus' state as an Augustinian canon differed from that of Martin Luther and Robert Barnes, who were Augustinian friars and led an essentially active life as teachers and preachers.) *Canon* in Greek means "rule," so that the label "regular canon," as Erasmus loved to point out, is pleonastic, yet necessary because there are "secular canons," who constitute colleges such as cathedral chapters.

115/15 **pardoners.** These men had a license to collect the money given by the faithful in order to gain "pardons," or pontifical indulgences. With the banalization of indulgences after the holy year of 1300, and their gradual application to the souls in purgatory, the pardoner became a familiar figure in Christendom. A number of swindlers, armed with false bulls, thrived on popular credulity, but the very principle was coming under fire: all the odium of papal money-raising and disguised simony clung now to the pardoner. The word provided Sebastian Franck, when he translated Fish's pamphlet, with an opportunity to lash out at indulgences: he translated "pardoners" as "Verkuender der

indulgentz gnad vnd ablasz / das ist rechter warer poppen auszrieffer"
(Franck, *Klagbrieff*, sig. a₂v).

115/15 **sommoners.** The *sumpnour,* or *summoner,* was an ecclesiastical
officer in charge of summoning or citing people to appear before a
bishop's or archdeacon's court. He apparently was able to dispense
people from appearing by "releasing thapparaunce for money" (Appendix B, 413/10).

115/18–19 **tythys/ preuy tythys.** The open, that is public, official tithe
was one tenth of the annual harvest. The privy or petty tithe was levied
on such produce as eggs and fruit. In March 1517 More was appointed
an officer for the collecting of tithes; see Marc'hadour, *L'Univers,* p.
247.

115/19 **probatys of testamentes.** In England (and to some extent in all
of Christian Europe) wills were proved and their execution supervised
by the ecclesiastical—normally the diocesan—courts.

115/19 **offrynges.** Fish mentions "theire foure offering daies" (Appendix B, 412/31), presumably the ember days occurring four times a
year: in Lent, in the week before Pentecost, in September, and in
Advent. They were roughly contemporary with the other quartet of
annual terms: Lady Day, St. John's (midsummer), St. Michael
(Michaelmas), Christmas. For the offerings at pilgrimage shrines, see
CW 6, 54/7–17, 85/21–30, 98/20.

115/19–20 **masse pens.** For "mass-penny" the *OED* gives only the
meaning "an offering of money made at mass," but the meaning here,
at 224/25 and in some of the early examples given by *OED* is rather
"money given to a priest to say mass for someone." Cf. the proverb "No
penny, no paternoster" (Whiting P116, Tilley P199).

115/20 **mortuaryes.** A mortuary gift was the clergy's share in the goods
of a dead person, even a child; Hunne's refusal to pay this debt for his
dead baby was the beginning of his quarrel with the incumbent priest
(see *CW 6,* 318/5–8, and *CW 9,* 222).

115/20 **cytyng.** That is, summoning to appear before an ecclesiatical
tribunal. See the third note on 115/15.

115/20–21 **suspendyng & soylyng.** "Soylyng" or absolving (Appendix
B, 413/7) freed one either from a canonical censure or from the guilt of
sin (sacramental absolution). Suspension was generally a temporary
penalty, forbidding a priest to perform his sacred functions.

115/22–116/5 **they . . . labour not.** Appendix B, 413/11–23.

115/28 **hundred.** That is, "hundredth" (as also at 115/32–3 and
116/1). As late as the seventeenth century "hundred" could signify
both the cardinal and ordinal numbers.

115/33 **person.** More is echoing Fish, as he does again at 126/14, 16.

116/3–4 **hundreth . . . hundreth.** That is, "hundred." The spelling "hundreth" for the cardinal number was common in the sixteenth century.

116/5–7 **After . . . people.** Appendix B, 413/26–414/25.

116/18 **them.** That is, the clergy.

116/19 **spyrytuall law.** Ecclesiastical or canon law, as distinct from secular law.

116/25–27 **the byshop . . . wardmote questis.** Fish (Appendix B, 418/12) uses the form "warmoll," also retained by More when he returns to the subject at 132/4. In his edition of Fish's pamphlet (p. 9), Frederick Furnivall quotes "The Lamentacyon of a Christen against the Citye of London (1542): "There is a custome in the Cytye, ones a yeare to haue a quest called the *warnmall queste*, to redress vices." It was a commission of inquest, at district level, composed of London citizens and presided over by an alderman, to redress minor offenses, mostly misdemeanors relating to weights and measures. We have not been able to discover any record of the episode to which Fish refers.

116/27–30 **doctour Aleyn . . . benefyces.** See note on 131/22–34.

116/28 **by premunire.** Statutes of praemunire, limiting ecclesiastical jurisdiction, date back to 1353 (27 Edward III, c.1) and embody an antipapalist case. See W. T. Waugh, "The Great Statute of Praemunire," *English Historical Review, 37* (1922), 173–205; and Arthur G. Ogle, *The Tragedy of the Lollards' Tower* (Oxford, 1949), pp. 52–54. The defensive stand of the royal jurisdiction vis-à-vis the court of Rome ("out of the realm") is more perceptible in the Act of 1393 (16 Richard II, c. 5). How and why the writ was sought and issued is illustrated by the Hunne case; see *CW 6*, 318/35–324/17, and *CW 9*, Appendix B, 215–46.

116/31–117/10 **Richard Hunne . . . myche.** Appendix B, 418/12–14, 420/34–421/16. The bishop of London from 1506 to 1522 was Richard Fitzjames, a conservative scholastic who found traces of Lollardy even in John Colet's sermons (Erasmus to J. Jonas, June 13, 1521; Allen, *4*, 1211). Hunne was a merchant who, having lost a baby in 1514, refused to pay the mortuary fee, arguing that a child, owning nothing, owes nothing. The parish priest, Thomas Dryfield, sued his recalcitrant parishioner before the bishop's court, then headed by William Horsey. Hunne's retort was to accuse the church tribunal of trespassing on grounds that belonged to royal justice: he sued his pastor for a praemunire. The king's judges, however, acknowledged themselves incompetent in this case. Hunne was jailed in the Lollards' Tower under suspicion of heresy and was found dead there on De-

cember 5, 1514, strangled by his own sash. The coroner Thomas Barnewelt and a jury of Londoners concluded their inquest with a verdict not
of suicide, but of murder. Bishop Fitzjames claimed that the verdict
resulting from the London jury's "untrue quest" was dictated by the
king's council. Horsey was released; but Wolsey, perhaps in a spirit of
blackmail, made him pay a heavy fine, though the sum of £600 seems to
have been a guess, perhaps current before Fish gave it the authority of
print. Horsey was hardly "promoted," nor could he stay in London
after public opinion had labeled him a murderer. He received pre-
bends in the dioceses of Chichester and Wells, and a canon's stall in the
cathedral of Exeter, where he died in 1545.

On Hunne's posthumous trial as a heretic and on the debates this
cause célèbre provoked at court and in Parliament, More had spoken at
length in his *Dialogue Concerning Heresies* (*CW 6*, 318–30); and he would
return to it in his *Apology* four years later (*CW 9*, 126–27). He had a
good deal of information as a barrister, as undersheriff of London,
and as a member of Parliament, not to mention his brother-in-law's
close link with the affair as legal guardian of Hunne's children Mary
and Marget. See *CW 9*, Appendix B, 215–46.

117/3 **complyces.** Jerome Barlowe, like Tyndale and Frith, threw
Hunne's death into his indictment of the clergy. At least he claims that
he was "hanged / brent / and drownde"

> Because he had many a boke /
> In englysshe / of holy scripture
> Also he worshipped no ymages /
> And wolde not go on pilgremages. [*Rede me*, sig. h₃].

See note on 161/31–34. The chronology published in 1593 by one
John More, *A Table from the beginning of the world to this day* (London, J.
Legate; *STC² 18074*), under 1515 mentions neither More nor Erasmus
but reads "R. HVN murdered in the Lollardes Tower."

117/8–9 **promotyd hym forth wyth.** Fish has "promoted . . . with benefice vpon benefice" (Appendix B, 421/14–15); this would seem to
rule out the *1557* interpretation of "forth wyth" as the adverb
"furthwith."

117/24–26 **to get . . . Genesis.** Gen. 3:19. The error "furst" is repeated at 145/29 and 146/11. Fish (Appendix B, 422/15) has "Gene. iij."

118/8–9 **suttelte wythout substaunce.** This opposition occurs elsewhere in More (*Debellation*, *CW 10*, 178/9 and 204/25–26). The primary meaning of "suttelte" here is "cleverness" (*OED*, s.v. "subtlety" 2),
but there are overtones of the sense "tenuity" (*OED*, s.v. "subtlety" 8) in
contrast with solid substance.

118/15–16 **tyme . . . rekenynge.** Cf. Matt. 12:36 (see Marc'hadour,
The Bible, 2, pp. 40–41).

118/28–29 **As for . . . vntowched.** On the idiomatic omission of the expected pronoun "it" after "leue" in constructions beginning "as for" see Visser, *1, 33*–34.

118/35 **coueryng . . . suger.** Cf. Whiting P289, Tilley S958, and Ovid, *Amores* 1.8.104.

119/9–10. **as one . . . nother.** Cf. Whiting B187.

119/12 **proctours.** A proctor, from Latin *procurator,* was a proxy, a deputy; the term also designated people licensed to collect alms for hospitals or leper-houses.

120/6–21 **And furst . . . onys.** More's long sentence, incorporating almost verbatim the first sentence of Fish's pamphlet, is tortuous. Its syntactic looseness led *1557* astray. The main clause contains a less than happy anacoluthon: "vnto all those wordys . . . wold we . . . tell hym" (120/14–20). The nine clauses huddled between "were yt not" and "sayd trew" (120/15–19) are a long parenthesis, closed, as it were, by "els" (120/19), which connects "vnto all those wordys" with "let to tell." Even the *Dialogue Concerning Heresies* seldom gives such a vivid impression of oral speech, hastily couched on paper, in its unkempt form.

120/8–14 **the wretched . . . hunger.** See Appendix B, 412/4–10. The marginal colons indicating the excerpt from Fish begin two lines before the actual quotation.

120/14 **for very constraynte . . . hunger.** The souls will make a mocking refrain of this clause; see 121/17–18 and 121/38.

120/23 **he cannot yet.** *1557* was no doubt right in omitting the second "not" from "cannot not yet" of *1529.*

120/33 **they rayn not.** More almost certainly means "reign," not "rain." Fish (Appendix B, 416/7) has "reigne."

120/34–35 **the french pokkys .xxx. yere a go.** More echoes Fish's noun "pokkes" (Appendix B, 416/18), a plural that came to be spelled *pox,* denoting pustules on the skin. The name *syphilis* derives from Girolamo Fracastoro's poem *Hieronymi Fracastorii Syphilidis, sive de morbo gallico libri tres* (1530). In his *Dialogue Concerning Heresies,* apropos of St. Roch's being invoked for sores, More mentions the "great syknes" now added to the saint's patronage (*CW 6,* 227/5–6). The epithet "French" gained currency through Hutten's *De morbo gallico* (1519). Erasmus describes the horrors of the disease ("Diversoria," *Colloquia, ASD 1/3,* 335–36, *Lingua, ASD 4/1,* 235), remarking in 1524 that some people call it "poscas Gallicas," others call it "[poscas] Hispanicenses" (*Allen, 6,* 137/88–89). In 1509 John Fisher described people "vexed with the frensshe pockes, . . . lyenge by the hye wayes stynkynge and almoost roten aboue the grounde, hauynge intollerable ache in theyr

bones" (*English Works,* p. 240). Fisher, preaching more than two decades before the *Supplication,* bears out More's contention that the epidemic had not worsened but rather eased in recent years. More's "fyue
agaynst one" should not be interpreted too literally.

The *lues* (or *scabies*) *gallica,* or *morbus gallicus,* owed its commonest
name to its being brought north of the Alps by Charles VIII's soldiers
after their Italian campaign (1495). The French called it *morbus italicus,*
or *lues neapolitana,* because they caught it in Naples, which belonged to
the Crown of Aragon. Hence too the name *lues hispanica:* the Spaniards
are supposed to have brought it from the new world, though the disease may have existed in Europe in earlier times (Ralph H. Major, *A
History of Medicine,* 2 vols. Springfield, Ill., 1954, *1,* 364–68). A special
mass was composed *contra morbum gallicum,* which remained in the
Roman missal until Pius V's reform (*Milan Missal, 2,* 352). It was called
"St. Job's leprosy," in allusion to Job 2:7–8. Fish's beggars are a "foule
vnhappy sorte of lepres" (Appendix B, 412/5–6) who ask who can
"socoure vs pore lepres" (414/4–5); yet he distinguishes "the lepry"
from "the pokkes" (416/18–20). See William J. Brown et al., *Syphilis
and Other Venereal Diseases* (Cambridge, Mass., 1970), pp. 1–10.

121/20 **these dere yeres.** The years 1527–29 (see 122/1) were marked
by poor harvests and scarcity. See *CW 6,* 468 and *CW 8,* 3/7–8. At 145/3
below, More applies the phrase "dere yeres" (years of dearth) to the
famine in Egypt. A document from the Public Record Office, dated
about 1529 (in *Ballads from Manuscripts,* ed. Frederick J. Furnivall, 2
vols., London, 1868–73; reprint, New York, 1968, *1,* 18–19), speaks of
"theys vnseasonable yeres" due to "the kynges warres owtwarde," and
to three or four "mervelousse drye Sommers"; it reports that droughts
and frosts have combined to destroy fish and fowl and cause a great
murrain of cattle. A letter sent to Henry VIII about August 4, 1529,
from Cambrai evokes "the derthe and scasnes [*sic* = scarcity] . . . nowe
being in the worlde" (Rogers, p. 416, lines 19–20). Robert Fabyan
reported that in 1527 "corne beganne to faile" and in 1528 "corn was
verie dere" (*Chronicles,* pp. 698–99). In his *Chronick: Geschichte vnd
Zeitbuch* (n.p., 1585), it is under "Anno 1529" that Sebastian Franck
places the first peak of the gruesome "Theuwrung" (sig.Nn$_6$v).

122/6–7 **layd . . . byldyng.** The building metaphor is continued by the
frequent use of *laying* in the sense of alleging (122/13). The word
ground is repeated at 122/30, 122/34, 123/5, 123/25, 124/29, 125/12,
125/21: a sober continuity contrasting with Fish's jumping "from
fygure to fygure" (127/29).

122/24 **apostata.** The canonical term designates a professed religious
who has broken his vows and (according to the Greek etymology) "stays
away" from his community.

122/32 **make.** Perhaps a misprint for "maketh" or "makes," which both sense and syntax require.

122/35–123/1 **twoo . . . lye.** William Camden reports that, according to "the booke of Thomas Wolsey Cardinall, digested and written in the yeere 1520," there were 9,407 parish churches in England at that time (*Britain*, London, 1610; STC 4509, sig. O_1v). According to the *Valor Ecclesiasticus* of 1535, there were 8,838 rectories in England (Dom David Knowles, *The Religious Orders in England,* 3 vols., Cambridge, 1948–1959, 2, 291). As late as 1801 the total number of parishes was 10,141 (Wrigley and Schofield, p. 621). John Foxe's sidenote to his reprint of Fish's *Supplication* shows he was aware that Fish's figure of 52,000 parishes was grossly inaccurate (see Appendix B, p. 413, Foxe's sidenote to line 12.

123/4–5 **quarterage.** A quarterly payment. See 123/20, 123/32.

123/9 **euery of ye fyue ordres.** The phrase is from Fish (Appendix B, 413/17) and serves as a basis for all his statistics.

123/11–12 **.iiii. ordres . . . grey.** The mendicant orders, a new form of religious life born in the thirteenth century, departed from the traditional landowning and cloistered monasticism, leaving their convents to teach and preach and hear confessions. They were popularly distinguished by the colors of their habits: (1) the Whitefriars, or Carmelites, were contemplative monks established on Mount Carmel, who came to Europe with the retreating crusaders; the pope gave them the status of mendicants in 1245, when an Englishman, St. Simon Stock, was their general; (2) the Blackfriars, or Order of Preachers, founded by St. Dominic (1215), came to England as early as 1221; (3) the Austin or Augustinian friars owed their name to the fact that Pope Innocent IV (d. 1254) placed them under the rule of St. Augustine; (4) the Greyfriars were the Friars Minor of St. Francis of Assisi; they reached Kent in 1224.

More's appeal to "the comen people" about the number of mendicant orders is borne out by hundreds of testimonies. Chaucer's friar is peerless "in alle the ordres foure" (General Prologue to *The Canterbury Tales,* line 210). The first letters of the four orders (Carmelite, Austin, Jacobine [= Dominicans], and Minors [= Franciscans]) were satirically combined to form the name "Caim" (= Cain); a medieval poem against friars (*The Oxford Book of Medieval English Verse,* ed. C. and K. Sisam, Oxford, 1970, p. 368) has the lines:

> Thus grounded Caim these four ordours
> That fillen the world ful of errours
>   And of ypocrisy.

The number four was so proverbial that preachers likened the orders to the four rivers of paradise: "fons ille in Paradiso, vnde pro-

dierunt quatuor amnes, hoc est quatuor ordines Mendicantium"
(Erasmus to Wychman, Allen *4*, 571/8–10, alluding to Genesis 2:10–
14).

As an appendix to *Pierce the Ploughmans Crede* (Early English Text
Society, Original Series no. 30, London, 1867), W. W. Skeat edited an
anonymous poem (c. 1500), "God Spede the Plough," eight lines of
which decry the four orders with their "call for money . . . Whete or
barley . . . Corn or chese," while another stanza praises the Franciscans
Observant because they "been so holy." These were the reformed
branch of the Friars Minor, whose convent at Greenwich, founded by
Edward IV, served as chapel to the royal castle there. More thought
highly of them (*CW 15*, 294/20–23), and (according to Thomas Stapleton) considered joining their ranks (*Life*, p. 9).

123/16 **the crowched.** The Crutched or Crossed Friars, who owed
their name to the cross they bore on the top of their staves when they
first appeared in England, about 1230; later they wore a cross of blue
cloth on the breast of their habits. Julius II in March 1508 granted an
indulgence to their only priory in London, Holy Cross, to help them
raise money toward restoring their church, which had been destroyed
by fire. A *Letter of Confraternity* destined for benefactors was printed at
least five times in Latin or in English (*STC*² 14077c.51–55). The signer
is "Wilhelmus Bowri / Prior Monasterii ordinis fratrum sancte Crucis."
The last two (54 and 55) were published by the royal printer, Richard
Pynson, as late as 1528, in the very year of Fish's attack on "yᵉ fyue
ordres." Erasmus' colloquy *Funus* refers to five mendicant orders, including the Crutched Friars (*ASD 1/3*, 541; Thompson, *Colloquies*, p.
363). John Shaa in 1504 left money for 500 masses to be said by the five
orders (Wilbur K. Jordan, *The Charities of London, 1480–1660*, London,
1960, pp. 275–76). On July 12, 1529, Thomas Cromwell left bequests
to the five orders of friars in London to pray for his soul (*LP 4/3*, no.
5772). But many wills also refer to the four orders. William Bedell's
will, probated July 11, 1518, gives "to the iiij orders of ffreres in London . . . xxs to synge for me iiij trentalles" (H. L. R. Edwards, *Skelton:
The Life and Times of an Early Tudor Poet*, London, 1949, p. 300). In
August 1529 the estate of Sir Thomas Lucy gave sums to the four
orders for fetching him to church (*LP 4/3*, no. 5870). More's young
protégé Thomas Lupset, in *A Treatise of Charitie* (1530), analyzing the
relativity of "time," writes: "We saye . . . that the .iiii. orders of freres
beganne in christendome within a lyttell tyme paste" (John Archer
Gee, *The Life and Works of Thomas Lupset*, New Haven, 1928, p. 224).

124/11–12 **.vi. s. viii. d. . . . noble.** In 1526 the value of the angel noble
went from 6s. 8d. to 7s. 6d. See note on 125/14–20. See David Knowles
and R. Neville Hadcock, *Medieval Religious Houses: England and Wales*,
2nd ed. (New York, 1971), pp. 208–19, 212–13, 221, 230, 232, 239.

124/12 **the aungell noble.** The angel noble, a gold coin representing the archangel Michael and the dragon, was revalued at 7s. 6d. by royal proclamation issued at Westminster on November 5, 1526 (Hughes–Larkin, no. 112). The mark, worth 13s. 4d., was never a coin; it was money of account, much used for calculations. For details, see "Money and Weights and Measures, English and French," in *The Lisle Letters*, ed. Muriel St. Clare Byrne, 6 vols. (Chicago, 1981), 2, 669–70, and John H. Munro, "The Purchasing Power of Coins and of Wages in England and the Low Countries from 1500 to 1514," *CWE* 2, 308–45.

124/25 **playnesse.** This word probably means "clarity," though the context suggests that it might mean "fullness, completeness," as the adjective "playn" could mean "full" in the phrase "playn . . . rekenyng" (115/22). Nevertheless, the *OED* does not give this meaning for "plainness."

124/30 **.lii. thowsande paryshe churches.** See note on 122/35–123/1.

125/1–6 **euery asse . . . eares.** This flagrant sophism is built on a false major and a true minor.

125/14–20 **hys rekenynge . . . chaunged.** Revaluing old coinage and issuing new coins was the subject of two royal proclamations of August 22 and November 5, 1526 (Hughes–Larkin, nos. 111–12). In September 1526 Wolsey wrote to More that samples of the new coins were being sent to the king (Rogers, pp. 367–68, lines 62–71). On August 22, 1526, the value of the noble was raised to 7s. 4d., and on November 5 it was increased to 7s. 6d. so that one quarter of an angel became 22 1/2d., not 20d. as Fish had calculated. According to Foxe (Appendix D, 439/31–39), Fish left England in 1527 or 1528. Unless he deliberately used the old valuation for the sake of simplicity, he may well have left before August 1526, as More suggests. See also C. E. Challis, *The Tudor Coinage* (Manchester, 1978), p. 311.

125/18 **deserue.** *1529²* corrects the indicative preterite "deserued" of *1529¹* to a present subjunctive (Visser, *1, 260*).

125/22 **ragmannes roll.** A list or catalogue, usually of contemptible items. "Ragman" was not applied to a dealer in rags until later in the sixteenth century. In the expression "ragman's roll" it may be connected with a game of chance played with a written roll having strings attached to the various items in it, one of which each player drew at random (*OED,* s.v. "Ragman" 1, 2) and "ragman's roll"). More used the expression in his *Confutation* (*CW 8,* 181/30, 657/13).

125/27 **noble progenytours.** This is a readymade expression, transferred from the Latin, found in many proclamations and other royal documents both before and after 1529. See Hughes–Larkin, no. 121, pp. 177, 178; no. 122, p. 181.

125/27–29 **Brytons . . . Arthure.** Harking back to pre-Saxon Britain became the fashion with the advent of Henry VII, always conscious of his Welsh roots. Hence he gave the name Arthur to his eldest son, the Prince of Wales (d. 1502).

125/29–30 **Lucius the emperoure.** Lucius Tiberius, a legendary Roman emperor defeated by King Arthur at a great battle in Gaul (Geoffrey of Monmouth, *Historia regum Britanniae* 9.15–10.13).

126/12–14 **the clergye . . . persone.** Appendix B, 414/31–34. The colons in the margin of *1529* marking the excerpt from Fish begin two lines before the quotation (or close paraphrase) and extend one line too far.

126/16–21 **some folke . . . wyde.** More is probably referring to an unusual procedure adopted by Wolsey to collect unauthorized taxes. It was usual for Parliament to name commissioners for all the shires and towns to take a census of laymen in order to collect subsidies authorized by Parliament. But in 1522, while Parliament was not in session, Wolsey named commissioners to reckon up both laymen and clergymen in order to impose a subsidy (Edward Hall, *Chronicle*, London, 1809, pp. 645–46; *The Parliamentary or Constitutional History of England*, 2nd ed., 24 vols., London, 1762–63, *3*, 26–27). The attempt failed, and when a Parliament was called in 1523, More was chosen its speaker.

From modern population studies it is clear that Fish's proportion between clergy and total population is much too small. The total population of England in the 1520s was about 2,300,000 (Wrigley and Schofield, pp. 567–75). Fish's proportion of one clergyman in 400 persons would allow for only 5,750 clergymen. But there were over 9,000 monks, friars, and canons, not counting about 2,000 nuns and canonesses (Knowles and Hadcock, *Medieval Religious Houses*, p. 494). If the secular clergy were added to the regular clergy, the actual proportion would probably be close to one in 100.

127/10 **golophers.** Fish's spelling, "goulafres" (Appendix B, 419/3), is nearer to the French *goulafre/gouliafre*, from O.F. *gole* (animal's mouth), derived from Latin *gula*, the scholastic term for the deadly sin of gluttony. Another possible etymology is the sixteenty-century form *goulf(r)e* (today *gouffre*), "deep hole" or "whirlpool," the word used in connection with it (127/11). See *Dictionnaire de la langue française du seizième siècle*, 7 vols. to date (Paris, 1925–), *4*, 344.

127/15–21 **these . . . soner.** A paraphrase of Fish, Appendix B, 416/10–26.

127/26–27 **shypwrak of the comen welth.** Cf. *Utopia, CW 4*, 98/27–28.

128/24 **farne yeres.** The archaic "farne" is presumably meant to suggest a remote past by the use of an obsolete form (*OED*, s.v. "ferren").

128/25–129/8 **kyng Iohans days . . . neuer was.** By devoting more than one tenth of his pamphlet (Appendix B, 415/8–416/3) to John Lackland, Fish contributed to making that Angevin king a symbol of the "translation" of power from prince to pope. Tyndale, in *Obedience* (1528, sigs. V$_5$–V$_5$v), uses the same argument "Reade the cronycles of Englonde. . . . Considre the story of kyng Iohn / where I doute not but they [the clergy] have put the best and fayrest for them selves and the worst of kinge Iohn / For I suppose they make the cronycles them selves. . . . Did not the legate of Rome assoyle [absolve] all the lordes of the realme of their due obedience which they oughte to the kynge by the ordinaunce of God? . . . Sent not the Pope also vnto the kynge of France remission of his synnes to goo and conquere kynge Ihons realme[?] . . . Last of all was not kinge Iohn fayne to delyver his crowne vnto the legate & to yeld vp his realme vnto ye Pope / wherfore we paye Peter pence."

John was crowned king of England on May 27, 1199. In the elation of his early victories, he killed his nephew and rival, the adolescent Arthur of Brittany, at Rouen, on April 3, 1203. That crime, together with the loss of the French lands (1204–6) and the exactions by which he levied the money toward a reconquest, made him unpopular. After he was excommunicated by Pope Innocent III in 1209 he remained defiant but never broke off negotiations. The pope's legates Pandulph and Durand met him at Northampton (August 1211), and he himself sent an embassy to Rome in 1212. The papal threat to depose him (February 1213) and the French king Philip Augustus' plans to invade England (April 1213) brought John to bay. On May 15, 1213, in the House of Templars at Ewell near Dover, he resigned his double kingdom, receiving them back under the bond of fealty and homage and pledging a tribute of 1,000 marks, 700 for England, 300 for Ireland. The transaction was ratified in St. Paul's Cathedral on October 3, 1215, and is reproduced in Thomas Rymer, *Archiva Regia Reserata: sive, Foedera, Conventiones, et Cujusque Generis Acta Publica, inter Reges Angliae*, 20 vols. (London, 1703–35), *1*, 176–177. In his *Chronicle* (*1*, 240) Richard Grafton reported it as follows: "we offer and freely graunt to God, and to the Apostles S. Peter and Paule, and to our mother the Church of Rome, and to our holy father Pope Innocent the thirde, and to all the Popes that come after him, all the realmes, patronages of churches of England and of Ireland."

The two parties clearly saw the bond as one between feudal lord and vassal. Innocent himself was the vassal of several crowns for parts of his domain. When the barons and the clergy united in resisting John's tyranny, the king sought and obtained the patronage of his Roman overlord. Innocent IV treated John's heir and successor, Henry III, as a feudal vassal. Edward II also acknowledged himself as the pope's man. But Richard II declared that the king had never held England in fee from the pope. In 1365 Parliament, reminded by Rome that the tribute promised by John had long been in arrears, retorted that the king had no right to commit his subjects without their consent. "All the estates, including the prelates, . . . repudiated the papal claim to the feudal overlordship of England" (K. B. McFarlane, *John Wycliffe and the Beginnings of English Nonconformity,* New York, 1953, p. 55). By the end of the fifteenth century the claim had fallen into oblivion, as the Venetian ambassador Andrea Trevisan remarked; see *Relazioni di ambasciatori Veneti al senato,* ed. Luigi Firpo, Monumenta politica et philosophica rariora, Series 2, no. 8, vol. I (Turin, 1965), p. 72.

That John surrendered to Innocent and his successors the two islands of his kingdom is taken for granted by all early historians. Only later, when the mood of nationalism and antipapal feeling spread over medieval England, was the donation viewed as an unpardonable humiliation. Modern scholarship, in an attempt to rescue John from the caricature of his first chroniclers, has viewed the event with kinder eyes. Thus Warren Hollister sees him making a virtue of necessity and evincing "politic wisdom": "His surrender to Innocent III, for example, was accompanied by maneuvers which transformed the pope from a remorseless enemy into a valuable ally. . . . Far from being an act of humiliation, John's submission was a clever bit of diplomacy" (C. Warren Hollister, "King John and the Historians," *Journal of British Studies, 1* [1961], 7).

128/34–35 **kyng Iohans grete graundfather.** Henry I (1068–1135), but More wishes merely to suggest a long period of time.

128/36–129/7 **Now yf . . . wolde.** Though he admired More and had incorporated More's *Richard III* in his continuation of *The Chronicle of John Harding* (1543), Richard Grafton criticized this passage in his *Chronicle* 1569): "But Sir Thomas Moore knight wrytyng in a booke of his entituled, the supplication of soules, against the supplication of beggers, certeinly affirmeth that there was neuer any such tribute graunted, eyther for England or Ireland. And he sayth further, that neither Rome can shew any such graunt, nor neuer could, & if they could it were right nought worth: for neuer could any king of England geue away the Realme to the Pope, or make the lande tributary, though he would, and that no such money (sayth he) is there payd, nor neuer was. This saiyng I leaue to your iudgement. But I maruail much that maister Moore beyng a great learned man, would not for the auouchment of his credite, and the truth of so great a matter, in reprouing a thing so manifestly written by a great number of Aucthours, as namely Reynulph of Chester, Polydore, and a great number of other, which affirme the aforesayd History to be true, that he doth not allege so much as the testimonie and aucthoritie of some one aucthor, for the prouyng of his assertion: But as aforesaid I leaue this to the iudgement of the reader" (*1,* 240–41). Ranulf Higden of Chester (*Polychronicon, 8,* 190–92) does indeed say that John "totum regnum suum Angliae et Hiberniae, pro se et haeredibus, papae Innocentio ejusque catholicis successoribus in perpetuum obligavit, ita quidem quod ipse et haeredes sui deinceps forent feodarii ecclesiae Romanae, reddendo annuatim pro Anglia septingentas marcas, et pro Hibernia ducentas, ita quod si ipse vel aliquis heredum suorum ab hac conditione vel solutione deficiat, a jure regni cadat."

What More denies, however, is not that John made a grant of tribute to the pope for England and Ireland, but rather that he did in fact make them tributary. He did not because he did not have the power to do so, and there is no need for More to cite chronicles showing that John did not make the grant. Ranulph does not say that the money was ever paid, nor even that the grant was ever taken to Rome (though he implies that). More's careful statement is not mere hair-splitting, since neither the popes nor the kings of England ever considered the grant valid enough to take it seriously. Polydore Vergil (*Anglicae historiae libri XXVI*, Basel, 1534, sig. z_6) does not mention the tribute at all. He does say that John agreed to receive his crown from Pope Innocent III and made a law that his successors should receive their right to rule from the pope, but he immediately goes on to say that succeeding English kings did not recognize such a law and did not, according to the annals of England, receive their crown from the pope, so that it is clear the matter pertained to John alone.

128/36 **kynge.** The errata list in *1529*[1] changes "kynp" to "kyng" in this place, but the text itself has "kyng". See the Introduction, p. clxiv.

129/7–8 **no such money . . . neuer was.** Edward II and Edward III often promised to pay the pope several thousand marks for the arrears on the feudal rent, but in fact only 1,500 marks were paid (in 1333) from 1293 till the rent was abolished by Parliament in 1366 (O. Jensen, "The 'Denarius Sancti Petri' in England," *Transactions of the Royal Historical Society*, New Series, *15* [1901], 188–89).

129/8–12 **the peter pense . . . almes.** On the question of Peter's pence, More's view is endorsed by professional historians, though some details are still unclear. See Jensen, "The 'Denarius Sancti Petri' in England," pp. 171–247; and Paul Fabre, "Recherches sur le denier de Saint Pierre en Angleterre au moyen age," in *Mélanges G. B. de Rossi: Recueil de travaux publiés par l'Ecole française de Rome* (Paris and Rome, 1892), pp. 159–82. Polydore Vergil's term *vectigal*, "a tribute" (*Anglicae historiae libri XXVI*, Basel, 1534, sig. h_6), reflects the interpretation that came naturally to the Curia's canon lawyers in the period when one of the tiara's three crowns was seen to symbolize secular overlordship. The legates of Alexander II, after the Conquest, echoed that interpretation. But the Norman and Angevin kings found the practice to be traditional in England as in other realms, and to be clearly seen as a gratuitous gift, a penny per household, as Christendom's share in maintaining the papacy, especially the Schola Saxonum in Rome, which had been established in the eighth century. In 1115 Pascal II calls it *eleemosyna*, More's own word (*Regesta pontificum romanorum*, ed. Philipp Jaffé, 2nd ed., 2 vols., Leipzig, 1885–88, *1*, 757, no. 6450). Peter's pence was abolished on March 30, 1534, in the same session of Parliament that passed the Act of Succession, the preamble of which led More to refuse the oath. Mary Tudor did not succeed in restoring it.

129/12–33 **the archbysshop Stephen . . . theruppon.** Stephen Langton (c. 1155–1228) rose to eminence as professor in Paris and rector of the university. Innocent III, who had been his fellow student, called him to Rome and made him a cardinal. The account by A. L. Poole of his election as archbishop of Canterbury (*From Domesday Book to Magna Carta, 1087–1216,* 2nd ed., Oxford, 1955, pp. 442–47) bears out More's version of the election crisis (see also M. D. Knowles, "The Canterbury Election of 1205–6," *English Historical Review, 53* [1938], 211–20). When Hubert Walter, archbishop of Canterbury and chancellor of England, died (July 13, 1205), King John hurried to Canterbury. He tried to persuade the monks to postpone the election, but they secretly chose their subprior, Reginald, to succeed in the see and sent him to Rome for the pallium. On hearing of this, the king rushed back to Canterbury, and in his presence (December 11, 1205) the monks agreed to elect his nominee, Bishop John de Gray of Norwich. The pope quashed both elections as uncanonical and made it clear that the right to choose belonged only to the monks, who in December 1206, on the pope's recommendation, unanimously elected Cardinal Stephen Langton. The king in his rage seized the revenues of the see, thus driving the monks into exile (1207). In March 1208, Innocent III laid on England an interdict that was to last six years, and in November 1209 he excommunicated John.

Unable to enter England, Langton waited until 1213 at the Cistercian abbey of Pontigny, which forty years before had harbored the exiled Thomas Becket. Langton tried hard to be a fair arbitrator between King John and his unruly barons. His ambition was to have the coronation charter of Henry I honored, but the king's obstinacy forced him to side with the barons and to spearhead the movement that climaxed with the signing of Magna Charta in June 1215. Meanwhile Innocent III defended the authority of his royal protégé John by excommunicating the barons and suspending Langton.

129/25 **wold not of.** The errata list of *1529*[1] changes "wold of" to "wold not of" at this place, but the text already has "wold not of." See the Introduction, p. clxiv.

129/29 **ye shall mow.** The infinitive *mow* here and at 160/21, corresponding to the same root as *may* and *might* and meaning "be able," may be part of an attempt to give an old fashioned ring to the voices speaking from purgatory. See Visser, 2, 619, and 3, 834.

129/30 **dyuers cronycles.** In the chronicles, the fullest accounts of Stephen Langton's election to the see of Canterbury in 1206 are those of Matthew of Paris (*Chronica Major,* ed. Henry Richards Luard, 6 vols., London, 1872–82, 2, 492–96, 513–20) and Roger of Wendover (. . . *Flores historiarum ab anno domini MCLIV. annoque Henrici Anglorum regis secundi primo,* ed. Henry G. Hewlett, 3 vols., London, 1886–89, 2, 36–44). From these accounts it is clear that John objected to the election of Stephen primarily because his own candidate, John de Gray, bishop of Norwich, had been rejected by Innocent III. Under orders from Innocent, the monks of Christ's Church did elect Stephen canonically. John did not accuse Stephen of treason but complained that he had lived among his enemies (that is, in France) and was completely unknown to him. Substantially the same information is given in briefer form by Ranulf Higden (*Polychronicon, 8,* 186–88), Gervase of Canterbury (*The Historical Works of Gervase of Canterbury,* ed. William Stubbs, 2 vols., London, 1879–80, 2, 98–100), and Polydore Vergil (*Anglicae historiae libri XXVI,* Basel, 1534, sigs. z_2–z_3v). Polydore says that Stephen "a rege nullo suo in eum merito, odio habebatur" (sig. z_3v). The manuscript of Gervase was written at Canterbury and almost surely remained there until it came into the possession of Matthew Parker (1504–1575), archbishop of Canterbury, who gave it to Corpus Christi College, Cambridge (*Historical Works of Gervase, 2,* vii–viii).

129/30 **dyuers monumentis.** In doubtful cases, More recommends "suffycyent inquysycyon and serche" (*CW 6,* 88/22–23). He might have consulted original documents ("monumentis") preserved in Westminster, Lambeth Palace, and the metropolitan monastery of Christ Church, Canterbury. He was well placed to conduct these investigations. The state archives were in his keeping from 1521 to 1525 as part of his responsibility as undertreasurer. Lambeth was familiar ground to the former page of Archbishop Morton and to the man who had frequent dealings with Archbishop Warham over Erasmus' pensions and other matters. Canterbury he visited on his way to and from the Continent. His daughter Margaret married William Roper of Canterbury, and in April 1530 the prior and monks of Christ Church gave More and his wife letters of fraternity in gratitude for friendly patronage (Marc'hadour, *L'Univers,* p. 439).

In More's time many more documents concerning the election of Stephen were readily available than after the spoliation of the monasteries. Even today one letter from Innocent III to King John concerning the election of the subprior Reginald survives in the archives of Christ Church at Canterbury (C. R. Cheney, "A Neglected Record of the Canterbury Election of 1205–6." *Bulletin of the Institute of Historical Research, 21* [1946–48], 233–38). Forty-one letters concerning the election and its aftermath, dating from 1206 to 1211 and mostly written by Innocent III, King John, and Stephen Langton, are preserved in the British Library (Cotton Cleopatra E.1); see *Historical Works of Gervase,*

2, liv–cxv. In the late seventeenth century a volume of Canterbury annals and a "Chronicon Ecclesiae Christi Cantuariensis," both now lost, were available to Henry Wharton (*Historical Works of Gervase*, 2, xxviii–xxix). Modern scholars still disagree about some details of the dispute (Cheney, pp. 233–34) but it is clear that More's version is compatible with most of the surviving evidence and that Fish's crude misrepresentations are not.

130/3–5 **prynces . . . them.** The jurisdiction of the ecclesiastical courts was one of many sources of conflict among the king, the English clergy, and the papacy (Felix Makower, *The Constitutional History and Constitution of the Church of England*, 1895; reprint, New York [1960?], pp. 12–48). What More says here is certainly the truth, though hardly the whole truth. The principal royal documents establishing and refining the legal jurisdiction of the ecclesiastical courts were issued by William I (about 1070), Edward I (1285), Edward II (1316), and Edward IV (1462); see Makower, pp. 392–94. Magna Charta (1215), obtained by the nobles from King John, confirmed the legal rights of the church (Makower, p. 29). Under Edward III several laws defining the jurisdiction of spiritual courts were enacted by Parliament (Makower, p. 42), and the heresy statutes enacted by Parliament under Henry IV and Henry V clearly recognized ecclesiastical jurisdiction (*CW 9*, 251–60). The manifold competencies of the ecclesiastical courts are presented in detail by Makower (pp. 399–444).

130/16–20 **at the parlyament . . . assembled.** With a few exceptions, the language by which statutes were enacted in More's time was as he gives it here (see, for example, *Statutes of the Realm*, *3*, 6–7, 10, 14, 19, 32, 33).

130/26–27 **haue . . . compelle,** Because "pore men" is not set off by any punctuation in *1529*, the editor of *1557* did not understand that it is parenthetical and emended the text plausibly but incorrectly to "they haue no power to compell."

131/5–6 **to bere a fagotte.** A person who abjured heresy was required to bear a faggot publicly. It was a symbol of the fire to which relapsed heretics were condemned. Abjured heretics might also be enjoined to wear a faggot on their shoulder for a specified period of time (James Gairdner, *The English Church in the Sixteenth Century from the Accession of Henry VIII to the Death of Mary*, London, 1903, p. 53). On February 11, 1526, after John Fisher's anti-Lutheran sermon at St. Paul's Cross, Robert Barnes and the German heretics who were being abjured in the same public ceremony threw their faggots into the fire in which various Lutheran books and Tyndale's New Testament were being burned (*CW 8*, 1382–83).

131/7–14 **how often . . . playd.** A considerable number of priests were charged in ecclesiastical or civil courts, often for sexual offenses (Peter

Heath, *The English Parish Clergy on the Eve of the Reformation*, London and Toronto, 1969, pp. 104–34; and Ralph Houlbrooke, *Church Courts and the People during the English Reformation, 1520–1570*, Oxford, 1979, pp. 177–79).

131/10 **were . . . wyllynge.** A most willing victim is featured in one of More's Latin epigrams (*CW 3/2*, no. 167).

131/22–34 **doctour Aleyns . . . men.** According to *DNB*, John Allen (1476–1534) studied at Oxford and Cambridge and received his doctorate in law in Italy. About 1522 he became Wolsey's commissary and attracted unfavorable attention by acting as Wolsey's agent in the suppression of several small monasteries to provide income for Wolsey's colleges at Ipswich and Oxford. Under Wolsey's patronage he added several benefices to those he already held. In 1528 he became archbishop of Dublin, where he was murdered in 1534 during Lord Thomas Fitzgerald's rebellion. In 1531, like the rest of the English clergy, he paid a large fine for offending against the statutes of provisors and praemunire by recognizing Wolsey's legatine powers. This is the only charge of praemunire brought against him mentioned in *DNB*, but on October 12, 1517, John Allen and Christopher Plommer (chaplain of the queen) made a recognizance "in liquidation of a fine of 500 marks incurred under praemunire" (*LP 2/2*, no. 3741); nothing more is known about the circumstances of the case.

132/2 **the byshop.** The bishop of London in the year Fish refers to (1527) was Cuthbert Tunstal.

132/4 **the warmoll quest.** See note on 116/25–27.

132/21–22 **Rychard Hunne.** See note on 116/31–117/10.

133/10–11 **doctor Horsay.** See note on 116/31–117/10.

133/24–25 **thys croked . . . generacyon.** Cf. Phil. 2:15, Matt. 12:39, and 136/10, below.

134/7 **inow.** This relates to *enough* as *plow* to *plough*, and suggests that the phonetic shift to an *f* sound had not yet fully occurred, at least in the province of purgatory. The middle English spelling occurs again at 149/4, 157/32, and 164/27.

134/16 **exester.** More's family link with Exeter was his father's younger brother, Abel More, who died in 1486 (see *Moreana, 63/2* [1979], 14, 16). One of More's good friends in Wolsey's administration was John Veysey, bishop of Exeter (Rogers, no. 108).

134/17 **hepe of benefyce.** For the plural without final *s*, see note on 111/4.

134/31–32 **mortuary . . . law.** In the statute "Circumspecte Agatis" of 1285 (13 Edward I) the king's judges are ordered not to interfere with the bishop of Norwich if he hears cases in ecclesiastical courts concerning "such things as be meer spiritual," including "Mortuaries, in Places where a Mortuary hath been used to be given" (*Statutes of the Realm, 1,* 101). See also *CW 9,* Appendix B, pp. 240–41. The statute 21 Henry VIII, c. 6, passed by the Parliament that convened in November 1529, limited mortuaries to certain amounts and categories (for example, it rescinded mortuaries for children), but it continued to recognize their legality (*Statutes of the Realm, 3,* 288).

135/17 **chaunceller.** Horsey was the chancellor of the bishop of London.

135/19–26 **after . . . true.** See *CW 9,* Appendix B, pp. 215–46.

135/21–22 **as tyme . . . trouth.** See Whiting T326 and Tilley T338.

136/13 **innocentys.** The errata list of *1529*[1] changes "innocenty" to "innocentys" at this place, but the text already has "innocentys." See the Introduction, p. clxiv.

136/13 **ransaked vppe.** The *OED* says *ransack* is "rarely" used with *up;* but More has it in *The Four Last Things* (*EW,* sig. fg₆), here, and again in the *Confutation* (*CW 8,* 534/34).

136/24–25 **the greate . . . euyls.** Appendix B, 416/27–28.

136/25–26 **the wekenes . . . swerde.** Appendix B, 421/19.

136/26 **the translacyon . . . kyngdome.** Appendix B, 416/33–34, 418/22–23.

136/26–27 **the ruyne . . . crowne.** Appendix B, 415/26.

136/27–28 **Oh greuouse . . . exaccyons.** Appendix B, 413/23–24.

136/28 **oh case most horryble.** Appendix B, 415/30.

136/28–29. **oh greuouse . . . welth.** Appendix B, 417/17.

136/31 **pewlyng.** This addition to the stock phrase was singled out by Foxe as giving the tone of the souls' complaint; see Appendix D, 442/11 and 443/31.

137/1 **reformacyon.** In his convocation sermon of February 6, 1512, preaching on the text "Nolite conformari huic seculo, sed reformamini" (Rom. 12:2), John Colet shows how this word suggests putting a new "form" or soul into the church: "Via autem qua reformetur ecclesia & in meliorem formam restituatur: non est quidem condere nouas leges. . . . Non est opus ergo vt condantur noue leges & constitutiones: sed vt seruentur condite" (*Oratio habita . . . ad clerum in conuocatione,* 1511/12, *STC* 5545, sig. B₂).

137/12 **mad . . . hare.** The male hare is proverbial for its madness during the March mating season; Whiting H116, Tilley H148.

137/18 **an ape.** In Holbein's portrait of the More household, a long-tailed monkey is seen tugging at Dame Alice's gown; see also Erasmus' colloquy *Amicitia* about an ape in More's Bucklersbury garden (*ASD 1/3*, 706–7; Thompson, *Colloquies*, "Sympathy," p. 524). See also "The Ape as Metaphor," in Ernst Robert Curtius, *European Literature and the Latin Middle Ages*, trans. Willard R. Trask (Princeton, 1953), pp. 538–40.

138/13 **saynt Sauours.** An abbey in the borough of Southwark. See John Stow, *A Survey of London*, ed. Charles L. Kingsford, 2 vols. (Oxford, 1908), *2*, 66–67, 142. See *CW 9*, Commentary at 104/21, and *CW 11*, 159/10–12.

138/15–16 **alledgyth . . . appostles.** See Appendix B, 417/24–25 and Acts 4:34–35, 6: 5–6. Cf. *Utopia, CW 4, 218/5–6.*

138/26 **he layeth and lyeth.** *Lie* could be used transitively to mean "lay" (*OED*, s.v. "lie" *v.*[1]B, III, 15), though only in the sense "put," not "allege." In the sense "say falsely," *lie* was used only intransitively.

138/33 **relyef.** The primary sense is "alleviation" (*OED*, s.v. "relief[2]" 2) but there may be overtones of the sense "remains" (*OED*, relief[1]").

139/5 **meany.** The unusual spelling suggests that this word may stand for *meinie* (an obsolete word meaning "multitude") rather than for a substantive use of the adjective *many* (*OED*, s.v. "many" B 2).

139/6 **.iiii. shyres next adioynyng.** That is, Kent, Essex, Middlesex (where More lived at Chelsea), and Hertfordshire (where More's father lived at North Mimms).

139/6 **great . . . Hungary.** As a member of the royal council, More had direct news of the Turkish invasion, for instance through Johann Faber's mission to Henry VIII on behalf of King Ferdinand of Austria. See *CW 12*, cxx–cxxxv.

139/12–13 **thabbot of westmynster.** John Islip (d. May 1532). More important is the paradigmatic significance of the large monastery dedicated to St. Peter, a royal necropolis since the time of Edward the Confessor, surrounded by the organs of government and justice.

139/14 **a. .M.** This reading from *1529*[1] does not agree with Fish (Appendix B, 422/10), which, like *1529*[2], has ".M." But it is unlikely that anyone took the trouble to correct such a small detail.

139/20 **all thynge.** For *thing* as a plural see Visser, *1*, 45.

139/21 **his payntyd proces.** Cf. *Richard III, CW 2*, 38/9–10.

139/23 **It . . . se.** Whiting W658, Tilley W878. See also 185/6 and 198/3.

140/22–23 **the mocyon . . . parentys.** The gloss in *1557* refers to Caput 6 (beginning "Tanta est vis matrimonii") of Book 4, title 17 of Gregory IX's Decretals, entitled "Qui filii sint legitimi" (*CIC*, 2, 712). The first sentence may be translated: "So great is the force of matrimony that those begotten beforehand are considered legitimate after the marriage has been contracted."

140/26–28 **the constytucyon . . . cuntrees.** For ecclesiastical law, see note on 140/22–23. According to Roman law, children begotten before marriage became legitimate and capable of inheriting after the marriage of their parents (Codex Justinianus 5.27.5–11 in Theodor Mommsen and Paul Krueger, eds., *Corpus iuris civilis*, 3 vols., Berlin, 1912–28, 2, 217–19).

140/29 **that.** The sense seems to require a comma after this word.

141/7 **some . . . bene.** More was a member of Parliament in 1504 and Speaker in 1523 (Roper, pp. 7, 12–19).

141/9–12 **actes . . . stryue.** It is not difficult to think of acts passed by Parliament that were opposed by the clergy, notably the statutes of provisors and praemunire (1389/90 and 1392/93). But the only recent acts of Parliament to which the clergy might have taken exception were curtailments of the benefit of clergy (1488/89, 1496/97, and 1512). During the Reformation Parliament, which was convened on November 3, 1529, and prorogued the following December, stringent acts against the clergy concerning mortuaries, probate of testaments, pluralism, and nonresidence were passed by Parliament, but by that time More was no longer chancellor of the duchy of Lancaster (as he is identified on the title page of *The Supplication of Souls*).

141/16–18 **in theyr own conuocacyons . . . hym.** The provincial convocations of Canterbury, York, and Scotland granted Henry VIII generous subsidies in 1512, 1514, 1522, 1523, and 1529 (November); see Wilkins, *Concilia, 3,* 657–58, 698–99, 717.

141/25 **ryall.** "Royal," used of the king at 140/11 and 143/30, here used ironically (see also 142/12, 150/15).

141/32 **lordys & masters.** Titles addressing, respectively, the members of the upper and lower houses.

142/26 **vppon . . . harpeth.** Whiting S839, Tilley S936. See 158/21–22.

142/27 **Tyndals testament.** The translation of the New Testament into English, printed at Worms in 1526. See 161/25–26 and *CW 6*, 28/19–29/16, 284/28–293/11.

142/36 **the nunnys.** Another reason for their being left alone was their relative paucity.

143/4–5 **in the .xi. . . . heresy.** George M. Trevelyan (*England in the Age of Wycliffe,* London, 1925, p. 325) describes the dramatic trial and execution (1410) of the Lollard John Badby, who refused to recant his opinion that "Christ sitting at supper could not give his disciples his living body to eat," even though Prince Hal attempted to dissuade him at the place of execution in Smithfield. Trevelyan relies on the account given by Thomas Walsingham in *The St. Albans Chronicle 1406–1420,* ed. V. H. Galbraith (Oxford, 1937), pp. 51–52.

143/5–17 **And forthwyth . . . forward.** During the Parliament at Westminster in 1410, the commons submitted a Lollard-inspired bill to King Henry IV, advising him to expropriate church income and lands in order to support 15 earls, 1,500 knights, 6,200 squires, 100 almshouses, and 15 universities. The English text of the bill survives, in slightly different forms, in Robert Fabyan's *Chronicles,* pp. 575–76, and in *Chronicles of London,* ed. Charles L. Kingsford (Oxford, 1905), pp. 65–68. A Latin version is included in Thomas Walsingham's *St. Albans Chronicle,* pp. 53–56. The statistics and calculations in the bill, like Fish's, are detailed and elaborate, but they are inaccurate, as Walsingham noted (*Historia Anglicana,* ed. Henry T. Riley, 2 vols., London, 1863–64, 2, 282–83); they were apparently borrowed from John Purvey's *Fasciculi Zizaniorum.* The bill concludes with a paragraph of vituperation against the clergy. See Kingsford, pp. xxxvii–xxxviii, 295–96. In Walsingham's version, the last sentences of the bill assert that England has 46,822 parish churches; 52,000 towns; 17 bishopricks; and 32,215 knights' fees (feoda militum), of which 28,015 are in the possession of the religious orders. This bill was submitted again to the king in 1414 and 1431 (see notes on 143/31–35, 144/9–10). A "knight's fee" was the amount of land for which the services of an armed knight were due to the sovereign; but neither the amount of land nor its value was clearly fixed (*OED,* s.v. "knight's fee").

143/19–28 **So happed . . . burned.** *The Great Chronicle of London,* p. 91, gives the following account of this episode: "In this same yere [1413] the lord Cobham called sir John Oldecastel was dampned for a lollard and an heredyke by all holy chirche and commytted to the Toure of london where he brake a wey withynne fewe days. And anone after he and his complices conjecteden and conspireden not oonly the deeth of the kyng and of his bretheren But also the destruccion of all holy Chirche For they purposed hem to have assembeled to gedirs be nyght in Seynt Gyles felde a myle oute of the Cite for to have perfourmed here false ententes. But the kyng and his lordes havyng knowlege of here false purpose toke the felde rather than they awayting upon here comyng And so they toke mony of here preestes and Clerkes and other

lewde men that wern of the same secte of diverse coostes of Englond
wenyng to have founde there sir John Oldecastell. But they were foule
bygyled For anone after ther was drawen and hanged of hem xxxix up
on a day upon newe galowes made for hem upon the high way faste
beside the same felde where they thought to have assembled. Of the
which companye vij of the grettest lollardes wern brent bother they
and the galowes that they henge upon." See also *CW 6,* 409/24–410/6
and Commentary.

143/20 **yᵉ kynges . . . fyfte.** Henry VIII was not directly descended
from Henry V but from his widow Catherine, who married Henry
VIII's great-grandfather, Owen Tudor. Henry VIII's grandmother
Margaret Beaufort was descended from Henry V's grandfather, John
of Gaunt.

143/29–31 **at yᵉ parlyment . . . heretyques.** For the text of this statute
see *CW 9,* 257–60.

143/31–35 **so dyd . . . nought.** Edward Hall (*The Vnion of the Two Noble
and Illustre Famelies of Lancastre & Yorke,* London, 1548; reprint, London, 1809, p. 49) records that a bill originally submitted in Parliament
at Westminster in 1410 was resubmitted in Parliament at Leicester in
1414 but was deferred: "The effect of whiche supplicacion was, that
the temporall landes deuoutely geuen, and disordinatly spent by religious and other spirituall persones, might suffise to maintein to the
honor of the kyng and defence of the realme, xv. erles, xv.C. knightes,
vj.M. ii.C. esquires, and .C. almose houses for relief onely of the poore
impotente and nedy persones, and the kyng to haue clerely to his
cofers twentie thousande poundes." According to Hall, Henry
Chichely, archbishop of Canterbury, diverted Henry V's attention
from this bill by urging him to reclaim his lost lands in France. See
notes on 143/5–17 and 144/9–10.

144/1 **Rycharde howndon . . . heresye.** John A. F. Thomson (*The Later
Lollards 1414–1520,* Oxford, 1965, p. 146) gives all that is known about
him: "In 1430 there was another execution, of Richard Hunden, a
woolpacker of Mark Lane. All that is known of his heresies is that 'he
was of so large consciens that he wolde eten fleysh on Frydays.'" In his
continuation of Higden's *Polychronicon* (*8,* 561), Caxton mentions that
he was burnt at Tower Hill.

144/1–9 **And then . . . heddes.** More's account is close to the one given
in *Chronicles of London,* ed. Kingsford, pp. 96–97: "In the same yere
bytwene Ester and Whitsontyde, the duke off Gloucestre had wytyng
that ther was gadered a meyne of rysers at Abyngton, ayenst men of
holy chirche, ffor they seyde they wolde have thre prestes heedes ffor a
peny. And the name off her chyveteyn was Jakke Sharpe. And thanne
anone in alle haste the Duke of Gloucestre and his meyne redyn to

Abyngton; and ther was takyn Jakke Sharpe, and other men; and they were found defettyff, and therefore they were done to deth; and on the ffryday in Witson weke the hedde of Jakke Sharpe was brought to London, and hit was sette on London Brigge, and alle the remnant off his ffelisship that myht be takyn weren putte to deth at Abyngton." The incident is described in almost exactly the same words in *The Great Chronicle of London,* pp. 155–56. See Thomson, *Later Lollards,* pp. 58–61.

144/9–10 **And yet ... agayn.** In 1431 John Scharpe and others distributed bills in London, Coventry, Oxford, and other towns against the retention of property by religious orders (John Amundesham, *Annales Monasterii S. Albani ... Quibus Praefigitur Chronicon Rerum Gestarum in Monasterio S. Albani,* ed. Henry T. Riley, 2 vols. Oxford, 1870–71, reprint Wiesbaden, 1965, *1,* 63). The bill or "suplicatio" that Scharpe presented to the Protector, Humphrey duke of Gloucester (Amundesham, ed. Riley, *1,* 453–56), was a slightly altered version of the bill presented to Henry IV in 1410. In 1432, after Sharpe's death, during the Parliament of 1432, the commons petitioned King Henry VI "that all parsonages appropriated to some religious house, not endowing of vicars on the same, may be within 6 months unappropriated" (William Cobbett, *Parliamentary History of England from the Earliest Period to the Year 1803,* 36 vols., London, 1806–20, *1,* 368), but this was not nearly as sweeping as "the byll" More refers to. See notes on 143/5–17 and 143/31–35.

144/10–11 **And yet ... towre hyll.** Fabyan's *Chronicles,* which was printed by Richard Pynson in 1516 and by William Rastell in 1533, gives the fullest account of the execution of John Goose in 1474, an account that may have suggested More's gruesome jest about roast goose: "And in this yere was one Iohan Goos a Loller brent at the Tower Hylle for herysye; the whiche before dyner was delyueryd vnto Robert Byllydon, on the sheryffes, to put in execucion ye same afternoone; wherefore he, lyke a charytable man, had hym home to his house, and there exorted hym that he shuld dye a Cristen man, & renye his false errours. But that other, after longe exortacion harde, requyred ye sheryffe that he myght haue mete, for he sayd that he was sore hungryd. Thenne the sheryffe commaundyd hym mete, wherof he toke as he had eyled nothinge, & sayd to suche as stode about hym, 'I ete nowe a good and competent dyner, for I shall passe a lytell sharpe shower or I go to souper.' And whenne he had dyned, he requyred that he myght shortly be ladde to the execucyon" (*Chronicles,* pp. 663–64).

144/11–14 **And theruppon ... hym not.** More's phrase "that byll" seems to refer specifically to the bill on expropriating church lands first proposed in Parliament in 1410 and 1414. It was circulated and submitted to Duke Humphrey in 1431. See notes on 143/5–17, 143/31–35 and 144/9–10. But we have found no record of its being circulated ("to bere . . . a brode") in the years after 1474.

144/14–15 **some heretyques . . . abiured.** Cuthbert Tunstal, bishop of London, undertook the prosecution and abjuration of a considerable number of heretics in 1527 and 1528 (John Strype, *Ecclesiastical Memorials: Relating Chiefly to Religion, and the Reformation of it* . . . , 2 vols., Oxford, 1822, *1/1*, 113–34).

144/18–19 **byll . . . lyce.** Cf. More's *Letter to Brixius, CW 3/2,* 614/4–5.

144/28–145/2 **Holy . . . fote.** Possidius tells the story in his life of Augustine (*PL 32,* 52–53). See *CW 6,* Commentary at 216/9–11.

145/3–9 **When Pharao . . . wytnesse.** Gen. 47:20–23.

145/29 **fyrst . . . Genesys.** See note on 117/24–26.

145/36–146/1 **good . . . god.** The word "godly" between these two words seems to hover between "goodly" ("excellently") and "godly" ("in a godly fashion"). The spellings are the same in both 1529 editions and in *1557,* except that *1557* has "godlye." See note at 162/34–35.

146/10–11 **the precepte . . . Genesys.** See note on 117/24–26. In *A Dialogue Concerning Heresies* (*CW 6,* 139/6–9), More mentioned only three commands given by God to Adam and Eve before the fall: "Twayne commaundynge generacyon and etynge. The thyrde forbedynge the tre of knowlege." But in *CW 11,* 33/10–12, and *CW 13,* 12/28–30, he says that God "bad" or "bode" them to be occupied and work in tending the garden. The command to work was given after the Fall (Gen. 3:19).

146/14–18 **Moyses . . . handes?** See Num. 5:9–10, 18:20–21, 35:2–8; Deut. 18:1–4. Cf. *CW 6,* 41/35–43/15.

146/19–25 **saynt Powle . . . prechynge.** 2 Cor. 11:8–12, Acts 20:33–34.

146/25 **neyther . . . place.** Phil. 4:15–16.

146/26–30 **sayed . . . thynges?** 1 Cor. 9:6–18. Cf. *CW 5,* 500/1; *CW 8,* 629/33–630/4.

146/30 **chryst . . . mouth.** Such omission of expected prepositions is not uncommon in More (see, for example, *CW 6,* 123/31–33 and *CW 8,* 753/8–11). See also Delcourt, p. 216; Visser, *1,* 121.

146/30–31 **chryst . . . preests.** Matt. 8:4, Mark 1:44, Luke 5:14.

146/35–147/5 **chryst . . . beste.** Luke 10:38–42. Cf. *CW 12,* 185/6–15; *CW 13,* 201/30–202/1; *CW 15,* 300/23–24.

147/9–10 **goddes . . . face.** Gen. 3:19. See note on 117/24–26.

148/11–12 **they be commaunded . . . facys.** Gen. 3:19. See note on 146/10–11.

149/15–25 **vplandysh . . . .lx. M.** More describes the actions of the temporal lords during the Peasants' Revolt of 1525 in similar terms in his *Confutation* (*CW 8*, 483). He gives various estimates of the number of peasants killed: more than 60,000 here, at 166/20, below, and in *CW 8*, 483/34; "plusquam septuaginta millia" in *Letter to Bugenhagen* (102/1, above); more than 80,000 in *CW 8*, 56/30. For Cochlaeus' Latin pamphlet (1525) blaming the Lutherans for the uprising, see *CW 6*, 545–47. See also *CW 8*, Commentary at 56/25–31 and 59/28–60/4.

149/18–23 **set furste . . . them.** Actually the rebellion began with the sacking of the castle of the Count of Lupfen as well as some monasteries (E. Belfort Bax, *The Peasants' War in Germany 1525–1526*, London, 1899; reprint, New York, 1968, p. 45). But it is true that more churches and monasteries than castles were plundered, mainly because they were more defenseless. In the early stages of the rebellion in late 1524 and early 1525, the secular lords were prevented from moving vigorously against the peasants because most of their troops were with Charles V in Italy. After Charles's victory at Pavia on February 24, 1525, the returning troops enabled them to crush the peasants. But some of the German lords did try to use the anticlericalism of the peasants to gain control of church lands for themselves (Friedrich Engels, *The Peasant War in Germany*, originally published in 1850; trans. Moissaye J. Olgin, ed. Leonard Krieger, Chicago and London, 1967, pp. 97, 106, 115). See note on 22/18–24/33, above.

149/28–30 **nedy . . . rebellyons.** Several German nobles, the best known of whom is Götz von Berlichingen, became leaders of peasant armies. "It was a favorite scheme of Götz to divide up ecclesiastical property amongst the knightly order" (Bax, *The Peasants' War*, p. 145).

149/30–32 **Cobham . . . fyft.** See note on 143/19–28; *CW 6*, 409/24–410/6 and Commentary.

150/8 **appose.** The spelling "oppose" in *1529*[1] suggests that the typesetter was unfamiliar with the scholastic term.

150/9 **sawce malaperte.** The beggars' proctor is impudent because he demands answers from the king. Indeed Fish packs a large proportion of interrogative sentences into his pamphlet: there are at least fifty in its twenty small pages. Together with repetition it is the most striking feature of his rhetoric. At least twenty sentences begin with an interrogative "what," not to mention the exclamatory ones. He also likes "where" and "who." He has various other patterns, such as "Is it any merueille" (Appendix B, 414/4–5, 417/25), "haue they not" (418/20–22), and "did not" (418/15, 420/30–34).

150/12–13 **.iii. . . . placys.** See Appendix B, 416/10–13, 417/1–3, 422/26–27.

150/17–20 **These . . . realme.** Appendix B, 416/14–18, 416/22–23.

150/21 **these be these.** The second "these" probably represents what would now be spelled "they's." This phrase, here and at 150/27, should be taken as a unit that would now be set off within quotation marks.

150/28–31 **These . . . inhabytable.** Appendix B, 416/10–13.

151/19 **parell . . . to fall.** That is, "danger . . . of falling." See Visser, *1*, 318.

151/27–30 **But he . . . meane.** The *OED* gives the meaning "uninhabited" for *inhabitable,* citing this place in Fish as the first example, and giving only two later examples.

152/27–30 **How many seruauntys . . . contrary?** Hythloday included the large retinues in his indictment of European society (*CW 4*, 62/3–20 and Commentary). Wolsey's alone ran into the hundreds (George Cavendish, *The Life and Death of Cardinal Wolsey,* ed. Richard S. Sylvester, Early English Text Society no. 243, London, 1959, 18/26–21/18). To be fully available, these servants usually remained unmarried.

153/6 **yuell . . . byrdys.** Whiting C570. *Bird* in Middle English usually meant "little bird."

153/14 **in the wanyand.** *Waniand* was a northern present participle for *wanien,* our word *wane.* The waning of the moon was considered an unlucky time. Hence "in the waniand [moon]" was used as a vague imprecation or exclamation of anger or impatience (*OED,* s.v. "waniand").

153/18–25 **& yf . . . fyre.** The suffering souls have been jesting somewhat indelicately and now admit that their "wanton" mirth is not very appropriate for them ("do not very well with vs"). Though he enjoyed a good joke and told many of them, More believed that some jesting could be at least venially sinfull and so would need to be purged in purgatory (see 187/28–34, note on 187/29, and *CW 14*, 3/7–8). But even in their apology the souls are punning on words in the last sentence of their jest: "be nyce and play the wanton" ("be coy and dally"). The souls' words are "nyce and wanton" in the senses "loose-mannered" and "frivolous." Saved souls in purgatory are incapable even of venial sin, but More tries to make them human and their plea for pardon is poignantly ironic.

154/3–4 **be curatys of . . . soules.** That is, have care and charge of men's souls. More re-endows the term *curate* with its etymological sense, derived from *cura,* care.

154/8 **the sacrament.** That is, the eucharist. See *CW 13*, 152/18–27.

154/21 **marke . . . shoteth at.** On the shooting metaphor, cf. *CW 6*, 94/22–95/7 and 101/20–23.

154/32–33 **hys gracys excellent wrytynge.** See note on 162/32–33.

155/10–23 **then . . . endure.** Appendix B, 422/20–31. In *1529*[2] the colons marking the excerpt from Fish begin one line too late.

155/24 **Lo here here ye.** That is, "Lo, here hear ye."

156/8 **Dixit & facta sunt.** Ps. 32:9 and 148:5. Based on Gen. 1:3–31, the phrase is also echoed in Judith 16:17. Cf. *CW 14*, 197/9–10.

156/35 **as it were.** That is, "as it would be" (not "so to speak").

157/1 **incestuouse.** Cf. *CW 6*, Commentary at 165/16–19.

157/10–11 **seuen . . . vii. C. yere?** On seven and its multiples as mere superlatives, see 164/33–34 and cf. Gen. 4:24, Matt. 18:21–22, Luke 17:4.

157/12 **We knowe . . . dwelled.** Fish entered Gray's Inn about 1525. After he returned to England in 1529 he lived in London near the White Friars (*DNB*).

157/15 **the beste of theyre berdes.** Cf. Whiting B112. Friars did wear beards, as did the poorer classes throughout the Middle Ages.

158/21–22 **harpynge . . . strynge.** See note on 142/26.

159/4 **Ye . . . that.** That is, "Yes indeed, that, that is the point."

159/9–12 **saynt Hyerom . . . faders.** See *CW 6*, 526–35.

159/24–31 **tellyng you . . . lyberte.** This is one of More's many summaries of Luther's teaching; see others in his *Letter to Bugenhagen* (see note on 16/15–37, above) and *A Dialogue Concerning Heresies* (*CW 6*, 352–55, 374–77, 427–28). The key doctrine, justification by faith alone, is also discussed at greatest length in *A Dialogue Concerning Heresies*, especially *CW 6*, 378–402.

159/27 **there ys no purgatory.** See *CW 6*, Commentary at 354/32–33.

160/9–15 **Here . . . selfe.** Appendix B, 421/26–32.

160/14 **small enormytees.** An enormity was any transgression against a norm, so that a "small enormity" was not the oxymoron that it now is.

160/21 **mowe.** See note on 129/29.

160/31–32 **These be theys.** See note on 150/21.

161/8 **peccadulyans.** More appears to have coined this diminutive, which does not appear in *OED*. *Peccadillo* did not appear in English until the late sixteenth century.

352	COMMENTARY

161/10 **very hole . . . fayth.** The form "hole" could mean "holy" (see note on 175/7), but here it probably means "whole" and the phrase should be taken to mean "the true, complete body of the faith" or "the very entirety of the faith itself."

161/25–26 **Tyndals . . . testament.** See note on 142/27.

161/25–30 **Tyndals translacyon . . . selfe.** See *CW 6*, 284–93, 512–16.

161/31–34 **frere Roy . . . of the masse.** William Roy and Jerome Barlowe were Franciscans who left their Greenwich friary in 1525 and 1527 to go into exile at Strassburg. Roy was proficient in languages: in a letter of June 12, 1529, to Wolsey, Friars West and Lawrence speak of Roy as "sometime the familiar of our convent at Richmond" and "how he does speak all manner of languages." They mention "another with him, who had a red head . . . Jerome Barlow" (*LP 4/3*, 2503, no. 5667). At Strassburg he composed an English adaptation of a dialogue by Wolfgang Capito, himself a former Franciscan, *A Brefe dialoge bitwene a Christen father and his stobborne sonne* (*STC² 24223.3*, Hume, no. 4). It was published by J. Schott of Strassburg on August 31, 1527, and does not seem to have been known to More before he finished his *Dialogue Concerning Heresies.* On most points of the creed, the catechist "father" took the moderate line of Martin Bucer and Capito, but he did deny the real presence (Anthea Hume, "William Roye's 'Brefe Dialoge' (1527): An English Version of a Strassburg Catechism," *Harvard Theological Review, 60* [1967], 315–16). The *Dialogue* was reissued in London in 1550 by Walter Lynne.

The book which the souls call "the berying of the masse" is better known by its incipit as *Rede me and be nott wroth* (*STC² 21427*; Hume, no. 5). It features a priest singing a mock dirge for the mass. It was adapted by Jerome Barlowe from Niklaus Manuel's *Die Krankheit der Messe.* Purgatory is one of the targets, so inseparable is it from the mass. Says the priest: "The masse made us so stronge and stordy / that agaynst hell gates we did prevayle. Delyueringe soules out of purgatory / And sending theym to heuen with out fayle" (sig. b₂).

161/34–162/2 **Tyndals . . . obydyence.** Tyndale's *Obedience of a Christian Man* (*STC² 24446*; Hume, no. 7) discusses the real presence on sigs. M₁–M₂v. *The Parable of the Wicked Mammon* (*STC² 24454*; Hume, no. 6) does not deal with this matter. Cf.*CW 8*, 302/15–17 and *CW 11*, xxx–xxxi.

162/7 **beyng therby lernyd.** Here (and in quoting Fish at 160/13 and 163/9) More uses *learn* to mean "teach," a usage common in his time (*OED*, s.v. "learn" II 4). In the *Confutation* (*CW 8*, 846/10–22) More rebukes Barnes for translating "doceo" in 1 Cor. 4:17 as "I do lerne," but he does so because Barnes's intransitive use of *learn* is ambiguous and misleading. See Visser, *1*, 129, 219.

162/32–33 **thassercyon . . . Luther.** Henry VIII's *Assertio septem sacramentorum* (1521) was a defense of the seven sacraments against Luther's *De captivitate Babylonica* (1520). More's own *Responsio ad Lutherum* (1523) is a defense of the *Assertio* against Luther's *Responsio ad Henricum* (1522): see *CW* 5.

162/34–35 **godly . . . godly.** More seems to be punning on "godly" and "goodly." The primary senses seem to be "godly deed" and "goodly title." The spellings are the same in both 1529 editions and in *1557*. See note on 145/36–146/1.

162/35 **defensoure of the fayth.** Leo X gave Henry the title Defensor fidei on October 11, 1521, after being presented with a copy of Henry's *Assertio* (Wilkins, *Concilia, 3,* 693–95). The title was confirmed by Clement VII in a bull dated March 5, 1523 (Wilkins, *Concilia, 3,* 702–3). The book, however, was only the final motive for bestowing the title; since 1512 Henry had sought a special title (J. J. Scarisbrick, *Henry VIII,* Berkeley and Los Angeles, 1968, pp. 115–17).

164/13–21 **In one . . . apostles.** Appendix B, 417/17–25.

164/20 **rauenouse woluys.** A translation of "lupi rapaces" of Matt. 7:15 and Acts 20:29.

164/25–26 **in Hyerusalem.** The church of Jerusalem is the only one in Acts that is given as a model of total sharing (4:34–35). Only for "the poor brethren at Jerusalem" does Paul collect alms from other churches (Rom. 15:26–31, 1 Cor. 16:3).

164/32–33 **synnes . . . flode.** The phrase "as longe" seems to mean "as longe ago," but we cannot find any precedent for this usage. See Whiting N117.

165/11–12 **many places . . . genesys.** Gen. 47 has already been invoked at 145/3. Melchisidek was a non-Jewish king and priest (Gen. 14:18, Hebr. 7:1); Baal's prophets were also sacrificing priests (3 Kings 18:19–22).

165/14 **thousandes . . . alledgeth.** The book is the Acts of the Apostles. More's "thousandes" is hyperbolic, since Moses, who organized the Jewish priesthood, lived less than two thousand years before Acts was written.

165/15 **lyuynge . . . prouyded for.** See note on 146/14–18.

165/18 **hys boke.** That is, "the book he alleges, the Acts of the Apostles."

165/21–22 **dyd dystrybute . . . nede.** Acts 4:34–35. Cf. *CW 8,* 634/36–635/8.

166/4–7 **tother place . . . more.** See Appendix B, 422/23–24.

166/5–6 **after . . . cast out.** See note on 114/25.

166/19–21 **that slew . . . Almayn.** See note on 149/15–25.

166/28 **then . . . more.** See Appendix B, 422/29.

167/1 **great pokkys.** See note on 120/34–35.

167/9–10 **blaspheme . . . fathers.** See Luther's *Contra Henricum* (*WA 10/2*, 215, quoted in *CW 8*, Commentary at 623/30–624/5).

167/34 **after . . . caste owte.** See note on 114/25.

169/2 **be able.** That is, "are able."

169/5 **enseygned.** Derived from Latin *insignare*, the word meant "to mark with a sign." Three of the sacraments, baptism, confirmation, and holy orders, leave a mark or indelible character on the soul. See Thomas Aquinas, *Summa theologica*, III, q. 63, aa. 1–6; *Commentum in quatuor libros sententiarum*, IV, dist. 4, q. 1, aa. 1–4; and *CW 4*, Commentary at 218/16.

170/16 **thys .xv. C. yere.** Cf. 167/14, 198/9, 212/16–17. John Frith, after quoting this sentence, at once alleges that in the time of Augustine, who "was iiii hundred yeare after Chryste," purgatory was not yet "fullye & fastly beleued" (*A Disputation*, sigs. F₇v–F₈). In support of his argument, he translates a sentence from Augustine's *Enchiridion* 64 (*CCSL 46*, 87/74–75).

170/26–29 **the dyuels badge . . . people.** More views Christ and the devil as captains of two armies, their soldiers or knights wearing respectively the badges of hatred and of charity. For the same metaphor, suggested by John 13:35, see *CW 8*, 12/12 and 250/2.

170/30–171/1 **to loue . . . enmy.** Matt. 5:44.

171/2 **Saracene.** Not altogether synonymous with "Turk," since More and others frequently couple the two terms. The Turks were the Ottomans, non-Arabic Muslims whose irresistible advance haunted Christendom and provided a frame for More's *Dialogue of Comfort*. The Saracens were the Muslims of North Africa, familiar to Europe through their conquest of Spain and inroads deep into France.

171/19 **Thys ways.** That is, "These ways." *This* could be used as a plural (Delcourt, p. 147).

171/22 **colour.** *Color* was a technical term in common law for "an apparent *prima facie* right, as in *Color of title.*" It also designated "a probable but really false plea, the design of which was to draw the decision of the case from the jury to the judge" (*OED*, s.v. "colour" 12 c).

172/29 **fallen . . . man.** The pagans of Utopia also consider as sub-human, and treat accordingly, disbelievers in immortality (*Utopia*, *CW 4*, 160/30–162/4). Scriptural support for their natural theology is provided mainly by Rom. 1:20 and especially Hebr. 11:6. In canon 20 of his *Enchiridion*, Erasmus refuses not only the name of Christian, but the name of man, to any person who doubts the immortality of the human soul (Holborn, p. 119).

172/32 **after . . . deceased.** See note on 114/25.

173/2 **punyshed and pourged.** In his retort Frith, no doubt unwittingly, altered the order to "purged & punyshed" (*A Disputation*, sig. F₈v). He sees this universal consensus as one more reason not to believe in purgatory and urges believers in Jesus Christ to part company with these miscreants.

173/7 **fyrst . . . reuelacyon.** The notion of an essential creed given to Adam in Eden and to Noah after the Flood and to pagans such as Job, and disseminated in the world outside Judaism, was postulated by many Christian humanists, especially Cabbalists like Pico and Reuchlin, who sought to supplement biblical revelation through the Pythagorean and Hermetic traditions. See More's cautious words on the primeval revelation in *CW 8*, 155/29–156/7.

173/11 **nature and reason.** From More's "leffe and an halfe" under this heading "Rastell toke all his boke," says Frith (*A Disputation*, sig. G₁v).

173/11–12 **perceyue . . . bylefe.** See the Introduction, p. clxii.

173/18 **dystrusted.** Although all editions agree on a past form, the present "dystrusteth" would be more natural.

173/19 **ryghtuousenes . . . goodnes.** These two attributes of God together, his mercy tempering his justice, require purgatory besides heaven and hell, as the souls are going to explain, varying the terms to include "bounte" (174/11), or coupling them differently, as in "mercy and goodnes" (175/25), or in the redundant "ryghtuouse iustyce" (175/24), "goddys iustyce & ryghtuousenes . . . goodnesse & mercy" (176/1–2).

173/26 **by due penaunce.** A grace More seeks for himself in his autograph prayer, "gladly to bere my purgatory here" (*CW 13*, 226/26).

174/6 **marcy.** The *OED* ("mercy" *sb.*) gives this as a Scottish form of *mercy* in the sixteenth century. See notes on 112/29, 112/31, (second note) 186/10, and 223/16.

174/27 **theyr onely . . . baptysm.** This Lutheran assertion rests on Mark 16:16, "Qui crediderit et baptizatus fuerit salvus erit," which the Messenger in the *Dialogue Concerning Heresies* (*CW 6*, 390/33–391/2) quotes to prove the sufficiency of faith alone; More had already quoted it in *Responsio* (*CW 5*, 294/15–16).

174/34–35 **.iii. or .iiii. wordys.** Cf. *CW 12,* 92/9–16 and Commentary.

175/7 **hole.** The spelling "hole" was a recognized variant of *holy,* which may well have been the meaning here (in spite of the reading "whole" in *1557*). See note on 182/3–6, variants at 162/16, note on 236/28, and Appendix F, p. 476.

175/19–20 **brydle . . . synne.** Cf. Ps. 31:9.

176/22 **Ezechias.** Isa. 38:1–3, 4 Kings 20:1–3. See the Introduction, pp. lxxv–lxxvi. Frith (*A Disputation,* sig. K₃) claims that More "toke his worke out of my lord of Rochesters," that is, John Fisher's. Refuting this first scriptural argument, Frith says Ezechias "wept for feare of deeth and not for purgatorye" (sig. G₂).

176/24–26 **dyuers doctours . . . dye.** Rabanus Maurus (*PL 109,* 260) and the *Glossa ordinaria* in the *Biblia latina* on 4 Kings 20:3 and Isa. 38:3 rely on Jerome's commentary on Isaiah (*CSEL 73,* 443). Jerome says Ezechias "fleuit autem fletu magno, propter promissionem Domini ad Dauid, quam uidebat in sua morte perituram. . . . Ergo iste omnis est fletus quod desperabat Christum de suo semine nasciturum. Alii asserunt, quamuis sanctos uiros morte terreri, propter incertum iudicii et ignorationem sententiae Dei, quam sedem habituri sint."

176/26–177/5 **auncyent doctours . . . purgatory.** In commenting on Ezechias' canticle (Isa. 38:18), Jerome suggests that Ezechias uses *infernus* to designate what would come to be called *limbus patrum,* to which Christ would descend to release the souls of the patriarchs: "Qui enim in inferno est, non exspectat iudicii ueritatem, sed misericordiam Dei; maxime cum Saluator ad inferna descenderit, ut uinctos de inferis liberaret" (*In Esaiam* 10.38, *CSEL 73,* 449). In *Biblia latina* Nicholas de Lyra on Isa. 38:10 says that Ezechias' words "vadam ad portas inferi" refer to the *limbus patrum:* "Et ideo non dicit hic ad infernum sed ad portas inferi: quia limbus ille a sanctis dicitur esse in superiori parte inferni." See note on 179/21.

176/27–28 **lothe . . . deth.** It is this dread that saddens the death of some Utopians and reveals their lack of virtue (*CW 4,* 220/21–29).

177/13 **lyfe.** The sense requires a question mark after this word.

177/26–27 **such . . . thus.** Cf. 176/24–26.

177/35 **soulys . . . slepe.** Soul-sleep was debated not just between Catholics and Lutherans, but also among the reformers; cf. *CW 6,* 544–45; *CW 9,* Commentary at 88/9–10; and Norman T. Burns, *Christian Mortalism from Tyndale to Milton* (Cambridge, Mass., 1972), pp. 7–41.

178/19–20 **wordys . . . reducit.** 1 Kings 2:6. To refute More's interpretation of this text, Frith devotes over three pages to exposing More's lack of acquaintance with "the phrase and manner of speache of the Scripture" (*A Disputation,* sigs. G₂v–G₃v).

178/26–28 **wordys . . . aqua.** Zach. 9:11. Frith gives a cogent refutation of the argument for purgatory from this verse (*A Disputation*, sigs. G₄v–G₆).

179/1 **gaolers of god.** Thomas Aquinas argued that the devils are not the actual ministers of pain in purgatory, but he thought it possible that they accompany souls to purgatory and stand nearby to observe and enjoy their suffering (*Commentum in quatuor libros sententiarum*, IV, dist. 21, a. 1).

179/5–9 **our sauyour . . . tonge.** Luke 16:19–31.

179/16–17 **by his precyouse . . . church.** Cf. Heb. 9:14–15.

179/20–21 **in yᵗ hell . . . redempcyon.** See *CW 6*, Commentary at 136/18–22.

179/21 **in limbo patrum.** Literally "in the border-district of the fathers." These "fathers" are the generations from Adam to Christ, abiding in *limbus*, "a place of derknes nye to hell," to quote the *Pilgrimage of Perfection* (London, Pynson, 1526, *STC* 3277, sig. O₅). In the *Confutation* (*CW 8*, 366/9, 407/19, 881/21), More describes *limbus patrum* and likens souls there to children who die unbaptized: they are "out of pain" yet somewhat frustrated by not enjoying the sight of God. This *limbus patrum* is the hell that the risen Christ "harrowed," that is plundered, claiming his booty from the city where the souls of the righteous were held captive and taking them with him to heaven at the time of his own ascension. "The harrowing of hell" was part of the Easter cycle of mystery plays, notably in Chester; and Christian art represents the new Adam taking mankind's first couple out of the age-old confinement. See 186/18.

179/27–33 **the places . . . batayle.** 2 Macc. 12:39–46. This is the first argument of St. Thomas Aquinas (*Commentum in quatuor libros sententiarum*, IV, dist. 21, q. 1, a. 1) and of the Council of Florence in 1438 (d'Alès, pp. 11–12).

180/5–6 **shote anker.** Cf. *CW 6*, 196/11, 229/6–7.

180/15–16 **Luther . . . Iamys.** See note on 60/18–19, above. Cf. *CW 5*, 70–72, 294–96, 302–4; and Marc'hadour, *The Bible, 3*, 149–52.

180/18–19 **they deny yt for scrypture.** See *CW 8*, 156/27–28 and Commentary. See the Introduction, pp. lxxix–lxxxi, above. Frith, after granting scriptural authority to the books of the Maccabees, offers no fewer than nine ways out of More's net, ending with the contention that the text here alleged makes no sense if purgatory exists (*A Disputation*, sigs. G₆–H₂).

180/19 **scrypture.** The sense requires a question mark after this word.

180/20–25 **They neyther do . . . before.** The acceptance of the deu-

terocanonical books of the Old Testament, including the two books of
the Maccabees, as inspired is not nearly as unanimous among the
Greek and Latin fathers as More asserts here, though the use of them
in the liturgy was almost universal and many of the fathers who deny
their canonicity nevertheless cite them as scripture. See *DTC* 2, 1574–
82.

180/24 **saynt Hyerome . . . Austayn.** Jerome is quite as emphatic in
denying the canonicity of the books of the Maccabees (*PL 28*, 1242–43)
as Augustine is in affirming it (*PL 34*, 41; *De civitate Dei* 18.36, *CCSL 48*,
632). The second of the two prologues to Maccabees, which are no
longer accepted as Jerome's, places the two books among the inspired
canon: "Machabeorum libri licet non habeantur in canone hebreorum
tamen ab ecclesia inter divinorum voluminum annotantur historias"
(*Prologi sancti Hieronymi in Bibliam,* Paris, Guy Marchant, March 12,
1495 or 1496, sig. d₄v). In his edition of Jerome's works (Basel, 1516),
Erasmus listed these prologues among the doubtful works, saying
"mihi non videtur hoc opus esse Hieronymi" (vol. 1, sig. γ₃v); they are
not included in the edition. In the Leipzig disputation of July 1518,
Luther admitted purgatory exists and is mentioned in scripture but
insisted it is never mentioned in such a way as to convince unbelievers;
Maccabees can offer no persuasive proof because it is not included in
the canon. Eck replied that Augustine in book 18 of *De civitate Dei* and
Ivo in his *Decreta* had included it in the canon. Luther replied that he
knew the church receives Maccabees but that the church cannot give
them more authority than they have by their own nature, no more than
it can to the books of the fathers. Eck then quoted the sentence given
above from Jerome's second prologue to Maccabees. Luther replied
that Jerome and Eusebius disagree with Augustine about the canonicity of Maccabees; he said he didn't remember that Jerome's prologue includes Maccabees among the "divine volumes." Luther later
refers to the *prologus galeatus* in which Jerome clearly places the books
of the Maccabees among the Apocrypha (*WA* 2, 339). See *Disputatio,*
sigs. K₃v–L₁v (*WA* 2, 324–29).

181/2 **put . . . gospell.** For similar reasoning, see *CW 8*, 744–745. The
gospel of John was treated in medieval Christendom with more honor
than any other portion of the Bible; its opening verses (1:1–14) were
read at the end of each mass (*Sarum Missal,* cols. 61–62) and its opening
words were used to drive away demons (Chaucer, General Prologue to
The Canterbury Tales, line 254; see Morton Bloomfield, "The Magic of
In Principio," *Modern Language Notes, 70* [1955], 5, 59–65). A copy of it
was carried hanging around the neck to ward off diseases or other
misfortunes, a superstition Erasmus denounced (Allen, 5, 169/253–
55; cf. canon 5 of *Enchiridion, Opera omnia,* 5, 30F; Holborn, p. 73).
Erasmus was brutally attacked because he changed "In principio erat
verbum" to "In principio erat sermo" (Allen, 4, 310–11; 7, 15/43–44).

181/14 **valyaunt capytayne.** Judas Maccabaeus was well known as one of the "nine worthies" (see J. Huizinga, *The Waning of the Middle Ages*, London, 1924, p. 61).

181/16 **festum enceniorum.** See 1 Macc. 4:52–59. Cf. *CW 8*, 350/30.

181/19–21 **our sauyour . . . Iohan.** John 10:22.

181/31 **Sapyence . . . insypyentys.** The book of Wisdom was written in Greek for Jews of the diaspora and was never part of the Hebrew canon.

182/3–6 **the hole psalter . . . church.** The spelling "hole" may mean "holy" (in spite of the reading "whole" in *1557; 1529*[1] has "holy"; see note on 175/7 and Appendix F, p. 476). On the importance of the psalms in More's life and writings see Marc'hadour, *The Bible, 1*, 101–4. To More, as to Luther and to the whole Christian tradition, each psalm, in addition to its literal meaning, which alone interests the Jews, carries a prophetic sense, made "lyghtsome" (that is, illumined) by its fulfillment in the life and especially the Passion of Christ. The psalms are also the most important scriptural part of the divine office.

182/14–23 **Luther . . . church.** In 1520 Luther took it for granted that the church alone was competent to decide what writings were authentic documents of Christian revelation. In chapter 12 of his *Assertio* (1521) Henry VIII quoted from Luther's *De captivitate Babylonica* (1520) the following passage: "Hoc sane habet Ecclesia, quod potest discernere verbum dei a verbis hominum, sicut Augustinus confitetur, se Euangelio credidisse motum autoritate Ecclesiae, quae hoc esse Euangelium praedicabat" (*WA 6*, 561). More quoted the same passage in his *Responsio* (*CW 5*, 110/24–28). Augustine's sentence, "Ego vero Euangelio non crederem, nisi me catholicae Ecclesiae commoveret auctoritas" (*Contra epistolam Manichaei* 1.5, *PL 42*, 176), is frequently cited by More in his polemical works (see *CW 5*, 735–36, 741–43; and Marc'hadour, *The Bible, 4*, 201–6).

182/25–27 **the church . . . shall.** Cf. John 14:16–17, 15:26, and 16:13.

183/15–16 **saynt Hyerome . . . doctours.** See note on 180/24.

183/22 **to y^e hard wall.** Whiting W21, Tilley W15.

183/28 **to the worldys ende.** Cf. Matt. 28:20.

184/4–7 **Est . . . that.** 1 John 5:16; see the Introduction, p. lxxxiii. Frith devotes three pages to quoting and refuting this argument (*A Disputation*, sigs. H$_3$v–H$_4$v).

184/7–8 **Thys synne . . . impenytens.** De Lyra in *Biblia latina* defines "peccatum ad mortem" in 1 John 5:16 as "finalis impenitentia qua quis in peccato mortali moritur" and comments on "et est peccatum ad mortem" in the following verse: "si quis in peccato perseueret vsque ad finem vite inclusiue." Gregory (*In Librum I Regum* 6.38, *CCSL 144*, 572) and Jerome (*In Hieremiam* 3.33, *CCSL 74*, 140–41) take "peccatum ad mortem" to mean impenitence. Arguing against the rigorist Novatians, Ambrose insists 1 John 5:16–17 does not mean that certain sinners are incapable of penitence (*De poenitentia* 1.10–13, *PL 16*, cols. 480–86). In *De correptione et gratia* 12.35 (*PL 44*, 938), Augustine defines it as abandoning throughout life the faith that works through charity. He expresses a similar opinion (qualified in his *Retractationes* 1.19.10) in *De sermone Domini* 1.22 (*CCSL 35*, 82–83; quoted in the *Glossa ordinaria* in *Biblia latina*). He goes on to associate "peccatum ad mortem" with the despair of Judas (*CCSL 35*, 83–84).

184/20–25 **I haue harde . . . lamb.** Rev. 5:13. More here follows Erasmus' Latin translation or the Greek rather than the Vulgate. The Clementine Vulgate of this passage is as follows: "Et omnem creaturam, quae in caelo est et super terram et sub terra, et quae sunt in mari, et quae in eo, omnes audivi dicentes: Sedenti in throno et Agno benedictio et honor et gloria et potestas in saecula saeculorum." The same version is given in the copy of the Vulgate included in the Hatfield manuscript of Erasmus' translation (*Un inédit d'Erasme: la première version du Nouveau Testament copiée par Pierre Meghen 1506–1509*, ed. Henri Gibaud, Angers, 1982, p. 540). Other Latin texts, like Froben's *Biblia latina* of 1498, the copy of the Vulgate included in the Oxford manuscript of Erasmus' translation, and the Vulgate given in the 1527 edition of Erasmus' *Novum Testamentum*, have: "subtus terram et mare et quae in eo sunt, omnes." Some Latin manuscripts have "in ea" for "in eo," but only one has the "in eis" required by More's translation (*Novum Testamentum Latine . . . Editio Minor*, ed. John Wordsworth and Henry White, London, 1911, p. 588); and none has the required "omnia" instead of "omnes." Erasmus' *Novum Instrumentum* of 1516 has the following translation: "Et omnem creaturam quae in coelo est, et quae super terram, et sub terra et in mari, et quae in eis sunt, omnia audiui, dicentes, sedenti in throno et agno, benedictio et honor et gloria et potestas in saecula saeculorum." This agrees with Erasmus' Greek (which remains constant in the first four editions) except that the Greek places the comma after "omnia (πάντα)" rather than before it, and this correction is in fact made in the next three editions of Erasmus' translation (1519, 1522, and 1527). More seems to take "omnia" both with the preceding clause and as an object of "audiui." Erasmus' *Annotationes in Novum Testamentum* of 1516, 1519, 1522, and 1527 do not comment on the passage. The Greek καὶ ἐπὶ τῆς θαλάσσης ἅ ἐστι lends some credence to More's interpretation that it refers to those sailing on the sea (184/36).

184/30 **as the deuyll doth.** On the psychology of the fallen angels, see *CW 13*, 14–20.

184/35–185/18 **the creaturys . . . creaturis.** Nicholas de Lyra in *Biblia latina,* commenting on the literal sense of Apoc. 5:13, remarks that irrational and inanimate creatures are said to praise Christ insofar as they are the matter and occasion of praising Christ, because through them intellectual creatures ascend to the knowledge of God and hence to praising and glorifying him. Ambrose (*In Apocalypsin expositio, PL 17,* col. 811) interprets the sea and the fish in it literally but he goes on to make the point that "all creatures on land" does not literally mean "all men," since sinners do not praise God; the elect, not the reprobate, are meant. He also says that the sea can mean the church, the waters of the sea the multitude of the faithful, and the fish the doctors of the church. Alcuin (*Commentarius in Apocolypsin 3.5, PL 100,* 1123), like others after him, says that "Mare, et quae in eo sunt, praesens saeculum designat." Primasius (*Commentarius super Apocalypsim 2, PL 68,* 834) remarks that in this text "creatura" refers only to men: "creaturam homines significare frequenter novimus, sicut Apostolus: Nam et ipsa, inquit, creatura liberabitur a servitute corruptionis in libertatem gloriae filiorum Dei (*Rom.* viii). Et Dominus (*Marc.* xvi): Praedicate Evangelium omni creaturae. Omnia enim quae universis competunt creaturis, inveniuntur in homine: esse, vivere, moveri, sentire, intelligere. Ergo et hic omnem creaturam dicit omne humanum genus. . . ." But no one, so far as we know, interprets the creatures on the sea as sailors.

184/36 **or saylynge in the se.** See note on 184/20–25.

185/6 **yt . . . se.** See note on 139/22.

185/8–12 **They sey . . . lamb.** Frith understands the text so: "By this texte I vnderstonde . . . euen all beestes, fishes, wormes, and other creatures do prayse the lorde" (*A Disputation,* sigs. H₅–H₅v). But we have not been able to discover an example of this interpretation before 1529.

185/14 **our Ladyes . . . Iudas too.** Even though the Assumption of the Virgin was not then a proclaimed dogma, all of Christendom agreed that at least her soul shared Christ's bliss in heaven and needed no praying for. As for Judas, More shared the general conviction that he was damned in hell, because of Jesus' words: "It would have been better for this man not to have been born" (Matt. 26:24, Mark 14:21), and because of Peter's sinister obituary of the traitor (Acts 1:25).

185/15–16 **he sent . . . creature.** Matt. 28:19–20.

185/24 **therin.** That is, in "mannys redempcyon" (185/22–23).

185/26–27 **theyr iust . . . ryghtuousnes.** In the letter to Alice Alington (at least coauthored by More), Margaret reports what More said to her: "And if he suffre me for my faultes to perish, yet shall I than serue for a praise of his iustice" (Rogers, p. 531, lines 656–57).

185/30–33 **Peter . . . losed.** Acts. 2:24. See the Introduction, pp. lxxxiii–lxxxiv, and Frith, *A Disputation*, sigs. H$_6$–H$_7$.

185/30 **chapiter.** The reading "boke" in *1529*[1] is corrected by hand in all surviving copies, possibly by William Rastell himself; see R. Keen, "A Correction by Hand in More's *Supplication*, 1529," *Moreana*, 77 (1983), 100.

186/1 **oure sauyour . . . euerlastyng.** Mark 9:43–48. See note on 179/20–21.

186/2–3 **limbo patrum.** See note on 179/21.

186/4–5 **in quiete . . . reste.** In the *Dialogue of Comfort* (*CW 12*, 319/1–4) "poor Lazare" has "eternall blysse" in Abraham's bosom (Luke 16:20–22).

186/10 **ony.** According to the *OED, ony* was a northern and Scottish form of *any*. See notes on 112/29, 112/31, 174/6, and 223/16.

186/12–16 **And therfore . . . hell.** More refers to the Apostles' Creed, which Erasmus expounded in his *Inquisitio de fide* (first printed in the *Colloquia* of 1524) and in his *Explanatio Symboli* (Basel, 1533). The more common wording is "descendit ad inferos" (*Inquisitio, ASD 1/3*, 368/174; *Explanatio, ASD 5/1*, 215/266), but Erasmus also has "descendit ad inferna" (*ASD 5/1*, 257/544), and scriptural texts associated with this article of the creed often use various forms of *infernus* (*ASD 5/1*, 258/571–76). Erasmus thought the scriptural support for this article to be weaker than for the others, but he accepted it on the authority of the church (*ASD 1/3*, 369/175–84; *5/1*, 260/601–3).

186/15–16 **englyshe . . . hell.** The phrase in the Apostles' Creed is translated "descended to hel" in the earliest English primer of 1534 (*STC*[2] 15986, sigs. C$_6$–C$_6$v). A revision of this primer issued in the same year changed the translation to "descended to the helles" (*STC*[2] 15988, sig. F$_1$). A 1543 translation of the same phrase in the Athanasian Creed is "descended to hell" (William Maskell, *Monumenta ritualia ecclesiae Anglicanae*, 3 vols., Oxford, 1882, *3*, 259).

186/22–25 **Whych word hell . . . ground.** More refers to the first meaning given in *OED* ("the lower world regarded as a place of existence after death"), which cites this place among many others.

186/27–29 **thys word hell . . . punyshed.** More refers to the second meaning given in *OED:* "The abode of devils and condemned spirits."

187/1 **And in lymbus . . . paynes.** See note on 179/21.

187/4–6 **saynt Poule . . . exposycyon.** Cf. *CW 6*, 343/29–35 and *CW 8*, 363/33–34.

187/8–9 **Cryste . . . saluacyon.** 1 Cor. 3:11. In his *Responsio* (*CW 5*, 234/6–236/3, 238/26), More discusses Luther's appeal to this verse.

187/10–17 **If any . . . fyre.** 1 Cor. 3:12–15. See the Introduction, pp. lxxxiv–lxxxvi. In his *Disputation* (sigs. H_7–H_8) Frith contends that the reckoning Paul evokes applies only to preachers, "And therfore maye the temporaltye be of good comforte" (sig. I_1v). But this was the key text in St. Gregory's *Dialogorum libri quatuor* (*PL 77*, col. 396; see 190/34–191/2, below) and the third proof produced at the Council of Florence (see d'Alès, pp. 17–19); and Eck used it in his Leipzig disputation of July 9, 1519 (*Disputatio*, sig. k_4v).

187/18 **hys very lyuely fayth.** That is, "his true, vital faith," "lyuely" ("alive") opposing it to that "faith without works" which is dead, in James's words (Jas. 2:20), often quoted by More (see 54/29, 74/8–9, and note on 60/18–19, above; see also *CW 6*, 386–88).

187/25 **criste the fundacyon.** 1 Cor. 3:11.

187/29 **ydle wordys.** Cf. Matt. 12:36.

187/29 **wanton myrth.** In his autograph prayer, More begs for grace "To estew lyght folysh myrth & gladnesse" (*CW 13*, 227/12).

187/32 **he.** The masculine form, repeated in the next lines until 188/35, confirms the impression that the speakers are mostly men, especially lawyers and merchants speaking to their peers on earth. That women are included may account for the grammatically incongruous "them" of 188/2.

188/4–5 **lak . . . prayoure.** See *CW 14*, 139–43, 313–27.

188/15–21 **For here . . . gone.** For some intriguing but inconclusive speculation about the influence of this passage on Shakespeare's *Hamlet* I, v, 10–13 see Vittorio Gabrieli, "'Hamlet' and 'The Supplication of Souls'" and Robert F. Fleissner "*Hamlet* and *The Supplication of Souls* Reconvened," *Notes and Queries* (Oxford), New Series, 25 (1978), 120–21, and 32 (1985), 49–51.

188/24 **Poule.** A very rare instance of More's using a saint's name bared of its title.

189/7–12 **If there . . . folke.** More himself had by now crossed the Channel at least seven times both ways: c. 1508, 1515, 1517, 1520, 1521, 1527, 1529.

189/11 **walowyng.** Cf. *CW 6*, 80/6.

189/13 **humours.** In the *Dialogue of Comfort*, More shows the devil basing his strategy on each person's humors (*CW 12*, 150/8–28).

189/28–29 **as a small . . . great.** A probable echo of Virgil's "si parva licet componere magnis," *Georgics* 4.176.

189/36 **frete owt.** *Fret* in its active transitive use, after its appearing twice in a passive sense (189/25, 34).

190/4 **Corynthyes.** The more usual form in More, though he also used "Corinthians" (see Marc'hadour, *The Bible, 3,* 51).

190/5–7 **some doctours . . . other sensys.** Both Augustine and Gregory give alternative interpretations (see notes on 190/32–34 and 190/34–191/2.

190/7–9 **dyuerse sensys . . . otherwyse.** More alludes to the traditional four senses, including the technical categories under the vague "otherwyse." Like Erasmus, he avoided making systematic use of the method, which had been used and abused, but the main division into literal and moral was essential to Christian exegesis. See Marc'hadour, *La Bible, 3,* 459–61.

190/11–12 **fyre . . . dome.** Cf. Rev. 16:8–9.

190/15–21 **yet letteth . . . punyshement.** The literal sense, which applies "properly" speaking (190/16–17) because it was meant by the divine author (even if unsuspected by the human writer), is the prophetic sense; see note on 182/3–6. For other instances of More's (and his masters') reading Christ and his church into the psalter, see Marc'hadour, *The Bible, 1,* under Ps. 2:2, 18:5, 21:2b and 7a, 33:1, 39:7, 44:8b, 54:13–14, 67:7, 81:6, 84:9a, 103:15, 109:1. His boldest allegory is applied to Ps. 136:9.

190/17–18 **properly . . . sum.** Ps. 37:18, which can be translated "I am prepared for scourging." More includes this hemistich, indeed all of Ps. 37, which was the third penitential psalm, in his *Imploratio, CW 13,* 220/1–221/4. In his sermon on Ps. 37, Fisher applies the saying to the penitent soul (*English Works*, p. 84), while in *The Myrrour or Glasse of Christes Passion* (London, R. Redman, 1534; *STC²* 14553) the Brigittine monk John Fewterer places the words on the lips of Christ and translates them "I am prepared and redy to receyue beatynges" (sig. Q₅).

190/19–21 **many . . . punyshement.** More himself chose that key for the praying of the entire Psalm 37: "psalmus efficax ad consequendam veniam" he wrote in the margin of his Latin Psalter (dₛv). See *Thomas More's Prayer Book: A Facsimile Reproduction of the Annotated Pages*, ed. L. L. Martz and R. S. Sylvester (New Haven and London, 1969), p. 74.

190/28–31 **Orygene . . . purgatory.** In at least three places Origen interprets the fire of 1 Cor. 3:11–15 as referring to purification in the afterlife of souls who have not sinned gravely but who are tainted by contact with fleshly desires: *Homilia 6 in Exodum* (*PG 12,* 334–35),

Homilia 3 in Psalmum 36 (PG 12, 1337), and *Homilia 25 in Numeros (PG 12,* 769–70). Origen's reliance on this Pauline text was important for the later development of the doctrine of purgatory; see Gustav Anrich, "Clemens und Origenes als Begründer der Lehre vom Fegfeuer," *Theologische Abhandlungen: eine Festgabe zum 17. Mai 1902 für Heinrich Julius Holtzmann,* ed. W. Nowack et al. (Tübingen, 1902), p. 109. The collected works of Origen in Latin translations, edited by Jacques Merlin, were published at Paris in 1512 (with later editions in 1519 and 1522). Erasmus' edition of Origen's works (Basel, Froben, 1536) appeared after Erasmus' death.

190/32–34 **saynt Austayne . . . purgatory.** When Augustine considers 1 Cor. 3:11–15, which he finds to be a difficult text, he is usually concerned mainly with refuting those who hold that "ligna, fenum, et stipulam" refers to grave, persistent, and unrepented sins and that such sinners, as long as they remain on the foundation of Christ (that is, continue to believe), will finally be saved by fire after their deaths because of their faith alone. According to Augustine, "ligna, fenum, et stipulam" refers to persons who are too attached to worldly things but not so much as to prefer them to the love of Christ, the foundation. The "quasi per ignem" of the text refers to the pain such persons experience when forced to give up their worldly attachments. Or it may refer to other tribulations in this life or to the pain of death itself. But Augustine also regularly presents the interpretation that "quasi per ignem" applies to pain suffered after death to purge such faults; and he finds such an interpretation acceptable, though he does not insist it is necessary. See *De fide et operibus* 15.26–16.29 (*PL 40,* 214–17), *De civitate Dei* 21.26 (*CCSL 48,* 796–99), and *Enchiridion* 18.68–69 (*CCSL 46,* 86–87). Outside the context of the necessity of both faith and works, Augustine at least once interprets "quasi per ignem" as meaning primarily pain suffered by a saved soul after death in order to purge himself (*Enarratio in Psalmos 37, 3, CCSL 38,* 384). In his *Novum Testamentum (Opera omnia, 6,* 671–72), Erasmus draws upon Origen, Ambrose, Augustine, Gregory, Theophylactus, and Chrysostom, as well as certain syntactical and lexical features of the Greek, in interpreting the text. He stresses tribulation in this life as the meaning of "quasi per ignem" and is technically correct in saying that Augustine makes no mention of the place "purgatorium" in discussing the text. But Augustine does use such expressions as "per ignem quendam purgatorium" (*Enchiridion* 18.69, *CCSL 46,* 87) and "emendatorio igne" (*Enarratio in Psalmos 37, 3, CCSL 38,* 384) and he clearly believes that the text can rightly be applied to purgative pain suffered after death by saved souls. Actually Erasmus is in agreement with Nicolas de Lyra (*Biblia latina,* 1 Cor. 3:12–16) in stressing that "ligna, fenum, et stipulam" applies, in the immediate literal sense and according to the context, not to wrong acts but to imperfect doctrine. But de Lyra also applies "quasi per ignem" in the literal sense to the pain such imperfect teachers will suffer after death in purgatory.

190/34–191/2 **saynt Gregory . . . purgatory.** In establishing that lighter sins are punished after death in purgatory, Gregory relies mainly on Matt. 12:31. He says that "quasi per ignem" of 1 Cor. 3:15 can be taken to mean tribulation in this life or the fire "futurae purgationis" (*Dialogorum libri quatuor* 4.39, *PL 77*, col. 396).

191/11–14 **there ys . . . cum?** Matt. 12:32. Frith retorts (*A Disputation*, sig. I₁v), "Althoughe this argument be a verye Sophysme / yet is there neyther one rule in Sophystrye that can proue this argument / nor yet one Sophyster so folyshe as to graunte it."

191/11–192/14 **a certayne synne . . . wretchys.** Thomas Aquinas summed up the three main opinions about the sin against the Holy Spirit: (1) blasphemy against the Trinity as distinct from blasphemy against the manhood of Christ (Athanasius, Hilary, Ambrose, Jerome, Chrysostom); (2) impenitence (Augustine); (3) malice that rejects the means of avoiding or repenting for sins (Peter Lombard and other scholastics). See *Summa theologica* IIᵃ–IIᵃᵉ, q. 14, a. 1. More follows Augustine, who found the problem perhaps more difficult than any other in scripture and approached it with great hesitation (*Sermones* 71.5.8, *PL 38*, 449). He thought the best answer was lifelong hardness of heart that rejects God's calls to penitence. But like More he pointed out that before death penitence is always possible (*Sermones* 71.12.20–13.21, *PL 38*, 455–56).

191/14 **Now as for to dyspute.** That is, "as for disputing"; but we have found no precedent for this use of the infinitive.

192/1–3 **Ex te . . . grace.** Hosea 13:9. The modicum of paraphrase completing the translation shows that More is not here engaged in proving but in edifying, a pious digression as the souls admit (192/21–32). Cf. *CW 15*, 302/11–22.

192/8 **such . . . unkyndenes.** That is, "in such a sort of kind of unnatural hatred." The pleonasm of "maner [of] kynde of" was perhaps caused by straining after the pun.

192/10 **knokkyng.** An allusion to Rev. 3:20: "the knocking of our lord, which alway standeth at the dore of mans hert and knocketh," as More had written in the *Four Last Things* (*EW*, sig. fg₂). He often quoted this verse, which so vividly illustrates the freedom of man's response to God's advances and the powerlessness of grace when human will does not cooperate (see Marc'hadour, *The Bible, 3*, 185).

193/4–8 **For when . . . come.** Gregory made the same point about this text in his *Dialogorum libri quatuor* 4.39 (*PL 77*, col. 396): "Sed tamen de quibusdam levibus culpis esse ante judicium purgatorius ignis creden-

dus est, pro eo quod Veritas dicit, quia si quis in sancto Spiritu blas-
phemiam dixerit, neque in hoc saeculo remittetur ei, neque in futuro
(*Matth.* XII, 31). In qua sententia datur intelligi quasdam culpas in hoc
saeculo, quasdam vero in futuro posse laxari. Quod enim de uno nega-
tur, consequens intellectus patet, quia de quibusdam conceditur." Fisher quoted this passage from Gregory in his *Confutatio* (sig. ii₂v).

193/9 ar . . . euery synne. Delcourt (p. 89) suggests the resistance of
neuter and feminine nouns (such as *mother, sin,* and *thing*) to pluraliza-
tion in *s* as a possible reason for the frequent appearance of apparently
singular nouns with plural verbs in More's English.

193/31–32 men . . . word. Matt. 12:36: "Dico autem vobis quoniam
omne verbum otiosum quod locuti fuerint homines, reddent rationem
de eo in die iudicii." Frith protests vehemently against both Fisher and
More for applying to purgatory a text that postpones the reckoning till
"the day of judgment" (*A Disputation,* sig. I₂v): the quarrel arises from
his assumption that there is no private judgment following each individual death.

194/7 saynt Peter. More forgot to list his proof from Paul (187/3–30,
210/26–27); "the sentence of saynt Poule" is duly mentioned in the
second recapitulation (210/26–27). A corrector of the copy of *1529*²
used to set *1557* (probably William Rastell) changed "Peter" to "Paule"
(See Appendix F, p. 475).

194/14–16 dicentes . . . folys. Rom. 1:22. Applying this verse to More
on the title page of his *Subversion of More's False Foundation* (1534, *STC*²
14829), George Joye also renders "stultus" as "starke foole," and adds
for good measure that the Greek is *Moros.*

194/23 many . . . texte. Apart from the texts More cites, the following
texts from the Old Testament (not all of them, certainly, "playne")
were cited as evidence of purgatory: Gen. 3:16–19, 21:23, 23:2–4,
37:35; Lev. 24:18; Num. 14:16 and 26, 20:11–12, 31:23, 35:25; 2
Kings 1:22, 12:13–23; Tob. 1:9, 4:18, 12:8–9; Job 19:21, 23:2, 24:19;
Ps. 6:2 and 6, 15:8–10 (quoted in Acts 2:22 and 13:35), 34:13, 35:7,
37:2, 39:13, 65:12, 129:2, 141:7–10; Prov. 10:12, 24:12 and 16; Cant.
8:6; Sap. 11:17; Ecclus. 3:33; Isa. 4:4; Mic. 7:7–9; Hab. 3:2; Mal. 3:2–
3. From the New Testament: Matt. 3:11, 5:22 and 25–26, 6:14, 6:20,
7:12, 10:28 and 42, 16:9 and 27, 25:40–41, 27:3; Mark 3:29, 7:47;
Luke 7:47, 8:55, 11:41, 12:48, 15:9, 16:9 and 26, 23:40–42; John
15:12; Acts 2:27–31; Rom. 2:6; 1 Cor. 15:12–22, 34–35, and 51–57;
Phil. 2:10; 1 Thess. 1:8, 4:13–18; 2 Tim. 1:16–18; Heb. 9:27; Jas. 2:13;
1 Pet. 3:18–20; 1 John 3:17; Rev. 2:27, 5:3, 14:13.

194/32–33 deny . . . blakke. The two birds and their colors were
proverbial: Otto, no. 495; Whiting C566, S930, S935; Tilley C844,
S1027; Erasmus, *Adagia* 3635, *Opera omnia,* 2, 1105. Cf. especially

Tilley C853: "He will say the crow is white." See also *CW 6*, 255/30–32, and *CW 15*, 10/22–23.

195/1–4 **saynt Austayn . . . theym.** More does not seem to claim all of these canonized church fathers as witnesses to belief in purgatory, but as supporting scriptural interpretations denied by modern heretics. On More's use of such lists of the fathers, see *CW 6*, 526–35.

195/13 **our blessyd lady . . . cryst.** By not daring to deny Mary's perpetual virginity, which Christendom had taken for granted time out of mind, the early reformers endorsed a "dogma" that had no explicit grounding in scriptures, and thus treated oral tradition and consensus as a source of the Christian faith on that point. Erasmus had used the argument in his debate with Luther (see *CW 6*, 463), as had Henry VIII in two chapters (10 and 12) of his *Assertio septem sacramentorum* (*CW 5*, 88/16–21, 102/27–104/3), and More returns to it several times (*CW 8*, 287–88, 473–74, 481–82, 1005–6; *CW 9*, 18, 315–16; *CW 11*, 58/21–61/23).

195/22 **Eluidius.** Helvidius' learned challenge of the already popular belief in Mary's perpetual virginity was refuted by Jerome. Henry VIII had alleged the precedent in chapter 10 of his *Assertio:* "De qua [virginitate perpetua], adeo nihil invenit [Lutherus] in scripturis: ut Heluidius non aliunde quam ex scripturarum uerbis, arripuerit ansam decernendi contrarium" (*CW 5*, 88/19–21). See note on 195/13, above.

195/34–196/1 **aske why . . . theym.** There is a fine irony in the fact that the *Supplication* itself is the souls' answer to the question.

196/9–10 **as Abraam . . . hell.** Luke 16:29.

196/10–13 **the myscreaunte . . . destroye hym.** John 12:9–11.

196/15–17 **apparycyons . . . purgatory.** Apparitions of souls in purgatory are a common theme in folklore (Stith Thompson, *Motif-Index of Folk-Literature*, Bloomington, Ind., and London, 1955–58; reprint, 1966, E341.3, E755.3, E755.3.1, T251.1.2). See note on 203/6, below. More in his dedication of his translation of Lucian's *Philopseudes* (*CW 3/1*, 4/28–6/20) and Erasmus in his colloquy *Exorcismus* (*ASD 1/3*, 417–23) had made fun of the credulity and superstition associated with apparitions and ghosts. In More's translation of Gianfrancesco Pico's life of his uncle Giovanni Pico, Savonarola revealed in a sermon that "Picus had after his death appered vnto him, all compassed in fire: and shewed vnto him, that he was such wise in purgatorie punished for his negligence, and his vnkindenesse" (*EW*, sig. a$_5$v). Jacques Le Goff gives many examples from the twelfth and thirteenth centuries (*Purgatory*, pp. 177–201, 295–332).

196/24–26 **in the bokis . . . them.** See preceding note.

196/27–29 **the apostles . . . Iewys.** Luke 24:37.

196/30–32 **y^e better . . . actys.** Acts 25:9.

197/4–5 **those Iewes . . . Belzabub.** Matt. 12:24.

197/6–11 **saynte Thomas . . . wyth.** John 20:24–29.

197/6–7 **Thomas of Inde.** The apostle Thomas was, and still is, considered the founder of the church in Malabar (present Kerala); hence the label "of India" used to distinguish him from Becket and Aquinas (see "Thomas More's Biblical Namesake," in Marc'hadour, *The Bible, 4,* 13–18). Thomas's missionary work is recorded by Jacques de Voragine, *Legenda aurea,* ed. Th. Graesse (Dresden and Leiden, 1846), pp. 33–39.

197/8–9 **some hardnes . . . resurreccyon.** John 20:24–25.

197/12–19 **as dyd . . . dede.** Matt. 12:38–40, more explicit than Luke 11:29–30.

197/22–24 **Beati . . . saw yt.** John 20:29.

197/24 **in thys world.** This should mean the world beyond death, where the souls now are; but the context shows it means the world of men living on earth.

198/3 **it . . . see.** See note on 139/23.

198/5–7 **they now . . . slepe.** On this perplexed question of the state of souls between death and the general resurrection, see note on 177/35. The first major expression of Luther's belief in soul-sleep is in his 1523 sermon on Dives and Lazarus (*WA 18,* 261). More returns to the problem in the *Confutation* (*CW 8,* 626/1–8) and *The Apology* (*CW 9,* 88/7–13).

198/8–9 **Iudas . . . in hell.** See note on 185/14.

198/10–14 **Then say . . . onys.** See Appendix B, 419/18–24. The argument appears in Frith, as he answers More (*A Disputation,* sigs. I_5–I_6), and again at the end of his reply to Fisher, using Fish's words "cruel tyraunt" (sig. L_7).

198/29–30 **he myght yf he lyst.** Frith retorts: "God can delyuer no man . . . vntyl hys iustice be countrepaysed" (*A Disputation,* sig. I_5v), which the souls more than imply too. More, here and at 199/12–13 ("he may do hys pleasure"), leans to the Scotist view in ascribing to God a *potentia absoluta;* for More's reliance on Scotus see *CW 14,* Commentary at 533/9–535/2, and Edward Surtz, *The Praise of Pleasure* (Cambridge, Mass., 1957), pp. 185–87.

199/10 **of god . . . set.** See the Introduction, pp. clxii–clxiii.

199/14 **as.** That is, "such as."

199/22–23 **as we . . . byfore.** See 174/24–36.

200/2 **runne on the brydle.** Whiting B539. We cannot find this expression in the *OED* but the examples of the proverb confirm that it means "run unbridled, have free rein."

200/6–7 **For he . . . chyld.** Prov. 13:24.

200/7–10 **god . . . hym.** Heb. 12:6–7.

201/1 **in person.** That is, in the single second person of the Trinity.

201/4–6 **Wherfore . . . saued?** Rom. 1:10 and 15:30.

201/8–9 **at the deliuery . . . hym?** Acts 12:5.

201/27–29 **For yf thy . . . iourney.** The unusual second person singular pronouns give the statement a universal or proverbial ring.

201/30–202/3 **saynt Austayne . . . grace.** More paraphrases a passage from *De cura pro mortuis*, 1.18.22 (*PL 40*, 609). Augustine expresses the same doctrine in his *Enchiridion* 109–110 (*CCSL 46*, 108–9), and in *De civitate Dei* 21.24 (*CCSL 48*, 789–93).

202/17–18 **more very . . . church.** The phrase "mystical body" applied to the church derived from Eph. 5:23. See *CW 5*, 202/12. The adjective reflects the μυστήριον of Eph. 5:32, rendered by "sacramentum" in the Vulgate. For "mystical members" of Christ's body, see 257/34, below. *CW 5*, 202/12; *CW 13*, 142–43, 175; and *CW 14*, Commentary at 347/1–2.

202/31–32 **specyall . . . masse.** Gregory the Great places special emphasis on the efficacy of offering masses for the souls in purgatory (*Dialogorum libri quatuor* 4.54–56, *PL 77*, cols. 416–24).

203/2–3 **he confesseth . . . trew.** In refuting translated excerpts from Luther's vernacular sermon on the rich man and Lazarus, Cochlaeus pointed out that Luther's insistence that no dead soul has ever appeared to anyone from the beginning of the world contradicts what he had written elsewhere: "Et Lutherus alibi ait. Multa leguntur exempla, in quibus habetur, nonnullas animas sui status incertitudinem confessas fuisse. Apparuerunt enim tanquam euntes uocati ad iudicium, ut de sancto Vincentio &c. Rursum leguntur multa, in quibus certitudinem suam sunt confessae" (*Articuli .CCCCC.*, sigs. L₁v–L₂).

203/3–4 **could . . . him.** Double negatives are not uncommon in More (Visser, *1*, 251) but not in such phraseology as "could not nor," as *1557* recognized by omitting "nor." Possibly *1529*[1] omitted a word such as "believe" or "accept" after "not."

203/6 **wrytten . . . sayntys.** In his *Dialogorum libri quatuor*, Gregory tells the story of deacon Paschasius of Rome, who became ensnared in a disputed papal election and died with the church against him. Condemned to labor as an attendant in the baths of Angulus as punishment for his disobedience, Paschasius' soul was freed by the prayers of Germanus, bishop of Capua (*PL 77*, cols. 396–97). Gregory also recounts two other appearances of souls released from the pains of purgatory through masses offered for them by the living (*PL 77*, 416–21). Bede tells of a man who came back from the dead and recounted his vision of purgatory, noting that the souls there are helped by the prayers, alms, and fasting of the living, and especially by masses (*Historia ecclesiastica* 5.12, *PL 95*, 248–50). Gregory's accounts are repeated in the *Legenda aurea* (Venice, 1512, sigs. Z_6–Z_7), which also explains that the feast of All Souls was established because of a vision of needy souls in purgatory and gives three other visions of purgatory (sigs. A_4v–A_6). In a chapter refuting the assertion that prayers for the dead are useless, St. Bernard repeats Gregory's account of Paschasius (*Liber contra Waldenses, PL 204*, 829–30). The *Revelations* of St. Bridget of Sweden (see note on 209/24) include the visionary account of an Ethiopian soldier who is told that the length of his punishment in purgatory is dependent upon the intercessory good works of the living (Nürnberg, 1500, sig. L_5). She also relates a visionary experience in which her dead husband tells her what the souls in purgatory suffer and begs prayers for them (sig. F_4).

203/10–17 **Iudas Machabeus . . . synnys.** 2 Macc. 12:39–46.

203/21–23 **stopped . . . out.** According to Thomas Tusser's *Five Hundred Pointes of Good Husbandrie* (1580, ed. W. Payne and Sidney J. Hentage, London, 1878, p. 42), repairing gaps in hedges is one of the usual rural tasks assigned to September.

203/26 **saynt Austayn.** Augustine is quite clear and unambiguous on this point. In *De cura pro mortuis gerenda,* for example, after citing 2 Macc. 12:43 to support offering sacrifice for the dead, he goes on to assert: "Sed et si nusquam in Scripturis veteribus omnino legeretur, non parva est universae Ecclesiae, quae in hac consuetudine claret auctoritas, ubi in precibus sacerdotis quae Domino Deo ad ejus altare funduntur, locum suum habet etiam commendatio mortuorum" (*PL 40*, 593). See also his *Sermones* 172 (*PL 38*, 936–37).

203/27 **saynte Damascene.** *De iis qui in fide dormierunt: quomodo missis et eleemosynis et beneficientiis quae pro illis fiunt, adjuventur,* a work wrongly accepted as John Damascene's in More's time, argues that the efficacy of prayers for the dead has been held "firmly and without any controversy at all" by "the apostolic and catholic church of Christ and of God which is spread to the ends of the earth, from that time [of the apostles] up to this day and will continue to be held while the world still lasts" (*PG 95*, 249–50). Thomas Aquinas quotes several passages from a Latin translation of this work, which he accepts as Damascene's (*Commentum in quatuor libros sententiarum*, IV, dist. 45, q. 2, aa. 1–3). Oecolampadius, who also accepted the attribution to Damascene, published his Latin translation of it at Augsburg in 1520 (Ernst Staehelin, "Oekolampad-Bibliographie: Verzeichnis der im 16. Jahrhundert erschienenen Oekolampaddrucke," *Basler Zeitschrift für Geschichte und Altertumskunde, 17* [1918], 1–119; reprint, Nieuwkoop, 1963, no. 28).

204/9–13 **There remayneth . . . soules.** Prayers for the dead occur several times in both the liturgies attributed to Basil (*PG 31*, 1641, 1656, 1662, 1672, 1675). The same is true of the liturgy attributed to Chrysostom (*PG 63*, 905, 917). In *De veritate* John Fisher makes frequent use of the liturgies of Basil and Chrysostom (for example, 2.14 and 2.19, sigs. H₁v and H₅v). He mentions that Tunstal had provided him with a book containing Basil's liturgy in Greek and Chrysostom's in Latin (1.20, proem 3, and proem 4, sigs. D₆, M₂, and Q₁). He also mentions that sixteen years earlier Erasmus had presented him with "Chrysostomi missam graece scriptam, et in latinum sermonem traductam" (proem 3, sig. M₂). This was probably the "Officium Chrysostomi" which Erasmus sent to Colet in September 1511 but which was apparently first printed by Wechel at Paris in 1537 (Allen, *1*, 467).

204/9–10 **There remayneth . . . masse.** The phrase "and bokys ynow therof" is parenthetical.

204/14–17 **Chrisostheme . . . dirige.** The dirge, which takes its name from the first word of matins for the dead ("dirige"), usually consisted of vespers and matins of the office of the dead, which preceded the funeral mass. The first psalm of vespers for the dead was Ps. 114 (*Brevarium ad usum insignis ecclesiae Sarum,* fasc. 2, Cambridge, 1879, col. 270). In *De sanctis martyribus* . . . , Chrysostom notes that Christians should look on death joyfully: "idcirco psalmos super mortuos psallimus, qui nos cohortantur, ut mortem non timeamus. *Convertere* enim, inquit, *anima mea, in requiem tuam, quia Dominus benefecit tibi* (*Psal.* 114.7)"; *PG 50*, 634. Cf. *CW 4*, 222/19–224/2.

204/20–22 **he sayth . . . selfe.** In *In Epistolam ad Philippenses commentarius,* cap. 1, homilia 3, 4, Chrysostom says that prayers at mass to help the souls of the dead were legally established by the apostles (*PG 62*, 204).

204/26–28 **they say . . . waged.** Here, as at 198/10, More responds to Fish, who plays the reporter of what "men of greate litterature and iudgement" say, repeating "they sey also" for the pope and "lyke wyse saie they" for the clergy (Appendix B, 419/10–25).

205/2–3 **other suffragys . . . vs.** For liturgical commemoration of the dead, see *Sarum Missal,* cols. 619, 639, and *Milan Missal, 1*, pp. 200, 208.

205/8 **desyre theym thereto.** That is, "ask them to [do] it," taking "thereto" in the sense of "to or for it" (*OED*, s.v. "thereto" 1). But "thereto" in the sense "also" (*OED*, s.v. "thereto" 3) would also make good sense. The parallelism with "therefore" (205/9) tends to support the meaning "for it" for "thereto." Cf. "hyred therto" (204/32), meaning "hired to [do] it."

205/25 **vertuose.** The sense seems to require a plural noun (virtues) rather than an adjective, but the spelling is unusual for the noun. The spelling "vertuose" for the plural noun also occurs in *CW 12*, 127/16 and in *The Answer to a Poisoned Book* (*CW 11*, 38/30).

207/17–24 **yt fareth . . . fole.** This is the only "merye tale" noted in the *Supplication* by the marginal glossator of *1557*. The friar must have belonged to the Franciscan Observants, the only friars who went barefoot in More's England. The temper of social relations is evoked by the gallant's use of the familiar "thou" and the friar's very polite form of address, surely ironic in a sentence calling him "a mych more fole."

208/3–7 **sayd . . . purgatory.** See Appendix B, 419/10–18.

209/14–18 **saynt Austayne . . . proctour.** Cf. *CW 6*, 530. The pairing may not be a random one. Luther was an Augustinian friar; "Husken" (Oecolampadius) by 1529 had become virtually the ruler of Basel, as Ambrose had been of Milan; "Pomeranus" (Bugenhagen) was Stiftpfarrer (or principal pastor) of the kind of new Rome Wittenberg was becoming. See note on 14/37–38.

209/15 **frere Lambert.** François Lambert, a Franciscan of Avignon (c. 1487–1531), was the first French friar to marry. His wife was Christina of Ertzeberg, who was in the service of August Schurf, a physician at Wittenberg. He justified his conduct in *De sacro conjugio* (Strassburg, 1524) and led a rather obscure life of teaching. See note on 14/37–38, *CW 9*, 29/10 and Commentary.

209/15–16 **frere Husken.** See note on 14/37–38. Johann Hausgen or Hausschein (1482–1531), who translated his surname into the Greek Oecolampadius, a name More avoided, as he also objected to the Greek coinage Melanchthon for Schwarzerdt; see *Apology*, *CW 9*, 326–27.

209/16 **preeste Pomeran.** John Bugenhagen (1485–1558), pastor of Wittenberg, is called merely "preeste" because he was a member of the secular clergy, not of a religious order. See the Introduction, p. xviii, notes on 26/17–20 and 26/21–22, and *CW 6*, Commentary at 434/15–18.

209/23 **saynt Anastace . . . Luthers wyfe.** St. Anastasia's name was familiar, as having been mentioned in the Roman canon since the days of Pope Damasus, Jerome's patron. At least three Roman virgins went by that name, the most famous having been martyred under Diocletian:

her basilica in Rome was the seat of a cardinal's title, and she was
commemorated on December 25 at the dawn mass. Having succeeded
in remaining a virgin though married, she contrasted sharply with
Katherine von Bora, who had vowed perpetual chastity as a Cistercian
nun before becoming Luther's wife. See note on 28/24–26. See also
Germain Marc'hadour, "Thomas More and His Foursome of 'Blessed
Holy Women,'" *Thomas-Morus-Gesellschaft Jahrbuch 1983–84*, ed. Hermann Boventer (Düsseldorf, 1984), pp. 115–16.

209/24 **saynt Hildegardes.** St. Hildegard (1098?–1179 or 1180; feast
on September 17) entered the Benedictine convent of Rupersberg,
near Bingen in the Rhine valley, where she became abbess. She was a
traveling reformer, not unlike her correspondent St. Bernard. She also
exchanged letters with Pope Eugenius III, a former Cistercian. Her
Scivias, a book of twenty-six visions, was approved by episcopal, then by
papal experts. She wrote saints' lives, a morality play, and hymns that
she also put to music. See Marc'hadour, "Thomas More and His Foursome of 'Blessed Holy Women,'" pp. 117–19.

209/24 **saynt Brygyte.** More refers to St. Bridget of Sweden (1302 or
1303–73) rather than to St. Brigid of Ireland (c. 450–523), since his list
seems to be chronological and since the souls in purgatory were a major
devotion of the Brigittines. This was an order founded by the Swedish
noblewoman during her widowhood. Her daughter Karin (Catherine),
who died in 1381 and though never canonized was venerated as a saint,
was abbess of the mother monastery at Vadstena, Sweden. Bridget's
Ordo sanctissimi salvatoris, with a rule derived from Augustine and approved by Pope Urban V in 1370, spread throughout Europe and was
followed by some eighty houses in the early sixteenth century. Its only
English foundation, endowed by Henry V in 1415, was at Syon, near
Isleworth (now Hownslow), within walking distance from Chelsea. As
usual, it was a twin monastery under an abbess. More had two good
friends there, both university men: Richard Whitford, who had tu-
tored Mountjoy during his early years in Paris, and St. Richard Reynolds, "England's most learned monk," as Reginald Pole called him
when he wrote of his martyrdom (May 4, 1535) for refusal of Henry
VIII's supremacy over the church. More often visited Syon, which had
an excellent library; there he had his first interview with Elizabeth
Barton. The popular impact of the Brigittines came through devotional works in English, and especially through the *Revelations* of their
foundress. They stressed "the Savior" in his passion and in the blessed
sacrament, and Our Lady's compassion, and compassion for the souls
in purgatory. "The Fifteen O's" were Bridget's contribution to the lay
Catholic's book of hours. James K. McConica, "The Patrimony of
Thomas More," in *History and Imagination,* ed. Hugh Lloyd-Jones et al.
(London, 1981), stresses Syon's emphasis on study and points out that

"the monastery was the chief centre for the production of English works of devotion, especially from the pens of Richard Whitford, William Bonde, Thomas Betson and John Fewterer. . . . The library, rich in theology, sermons and devotional literature, was notably strong in biblical and patristic texts. . . . There were literary works by Aeneas Sylvius and Valla and the letters of Ficino, while Gianfrancesco Pico was one of the thirteen authors represented by ten or more works, along with Cicero, Cyprian, and Hugh of St. Victor" (p. 61). See Marc'hadour, "Thomas More and His Foursome of 'Blessed Holy Women,' " pp. 119–24.

209/25 **saynt Katheryn of senys.** The dictated revelations of Catherine of Siena (1347–80) were contained (in a Middle English translation) in the *Orchard of Syon.* Phyllis Hodgson sees in it "a forerunner in England of such later devotional writers as Sir Thomas More who explicitly integrated their devotion to the Person of our Lord with the Mass, and were constantly aware of the mystical Body of the Church" (McConica, p. 62). Syon's "spiritual programme . . . was marked by an intimate relation between clerical professionals and a coterie of educated and influential laymen" (p. 62). Catherine persuaded Pope Gregory XI to move back to Rome from Avignon. She refused marriage but did not enter the cloister, only joining the third order of St. Dominic. She learned Latin against opposition, for the purpose of reading the Bible, and especially for praying the psalms intelligently. Though she chided the pope in God's name, she sought from him a plenary indulgence, and on her deathbed she asked to have it read out to her. Her *Dialogue,* dictated in ecstasy, is really a kind of catechism which exposes mystically the elements of Christianity. See Marc'hadour, "Thomas More and His Foursome of 'Blessed Holy Women,' " pp. 125–28.

209/25 **senys.** "Senis" is one of the Latin names of Siena; "Sena" is the more usual Latin name. See *Orbis Latinus: Lexikon lateinischer geographischer Namen des Mittelalters und der Neuzeit,* ed. J. G. Theodor Graesse, Friedrich Benedict, and Helmut Plechtl, 3 vols. (Braunschweig, 1972), *3*, 362.

210/6 **saynt Austayne.** See note on 203/26.

210/6–7 **saynt Hierome.** Jerome does not say anything very explicit about purgatory, but he did teach that some Christians who died in sin would be purged by fire and be finally saved (*In Isaiam* 56:24, *PL 24,* cols. 677–78; *Epistolae* 119.7, *PL 22,* col 973). Jerome praised Pammachius for giving alms for the sake of his dead wife (*Epistolae* 66.5, *PL 22,* cols. 641–42).

210/7 **saynt Ambrose.** Ambrose, whose eschatology was strongly influenced by Origen, provides for a category of Christians who die in sin but who are finally saved after a period of purgatorial suffering (*DTC 13*, 1215–18). He clearly recommends prayer as helpful for the souls of dead Christians (*PL 16*, cols. 1099, 1381, 1397).

210/7 **saynt Gregory.** See notes on 202/31–32 and 203/6.

210/8 **saynt Chrisostem.** Cf. the liturgy of ps.-Chrysostom, *PG 63*, 905, 917; and notes on 204/9–13 and 204/20–22.

210/8 **saynt Basyle.** For Basil's prayers for the dead, see *PG 31*, 1641, 1655, 1662, 1672, and 1675; and note on 204/9–13.

210/8–9 **those holy women.** For St. Bridget, see note on 209/24. More has perhaps extended her example to the others, whom he does not cite as authorities, on this matter.

210/10 **doctour Oregene.** See note on 190/28–31. Origen indicates the attitude we should bear toward the dead in *Commentum in Epistolam ad Romanos* 9 (*PG 14*, 1220).

210/11 **Gregorius Nasianzenus.** Gregory does not seem to have had a consistent view concerning purgatory: he claims that the punishments after death are eternal with no purgation, but also that there will be a judgment (*Oratio 16 In Patrem Tacentem, PG, 35*, 943–46). He claims also that Christ brought with him a purifying fire to purge the vile matter and vicious feelings from the soul, and also that there is a fire which punishes instead of purifying, and which burns sinners eternally (*Oratio 40 In Sanctum Baptisma, PG 36*, 409–14).

210/12 **Gregorius Nissenus.** Gregory of Nyssa argues for the existence of purgatory chiefly in *De mortuis* (*PG 46*, 523–26, 535–38).

210/12 **Gregorius Emissenus.** The grouping of the three Gregories, all Greek saints and doctors, make it all but certain that the third is Gregory of Neocaesarea (213–70), called the Miracle-worker, though we know no reason why he should be called "Emissenus." Nor does he seem to be a proponent of purgatory or prayer for the dead.

210/12 **saynt Cyryllus.** Cyril of Alexandria presents a doctrine of purgatory in *In Johannis Evangelium* 10, *PG 74*, 352. The importance of praying for the dead is stressed by Cyril of Jerusalem in *Catechesis 23 Mystagogica* 5, 9–10 (*PG 33*, 1115–18). More probably had in mind only the better known Alexandrian.

210/13 **saynt Damascene.** See note on 203/27.

210/13–14 **saynt Cipryane.** Cyprian does not present a doctrine of purgatory per se, but one is implied in his distinction between martyrs, who join God immediately upon death, and everyone else, who must wait below for such a union (*Ad Fortunatum*, praef. 4, *CCSL 3*, 185). During this waiting period the soul is either rewarded or punished according to one's conduct in life (*Epistola 10 ad Antonianum* 20; *PL 3,* 785–86). Cyprian mentions the practice of praying for the dead in *Epistola* 66 (*PL 4,* 410–11).

210/14 **saynt Hylary.** Hilary differs from Cyprian in claiming that all souls descend to purgatory upon death, with the just reposing in the lap of Abraham, the others being punished by the fire of judgment, which he claims is a form of baptism in that it purifies sinners (*Tractatus in Psalmum 2 48, PL 9,* 290; *Tr. in Ps. 51 22, PL 9,* 322; *Tr. in Ps. 57 5–7, PL 9,* 371–73; *Tr. in Ps. 121 1, PL 9,* 660–61; *Commentarius in Matthaeum 5, PL 9,* 948–49). He does not seem to have been concerned, at least in his extant writings, with prayers for the dead.

210/14 **saynt Bede.** See note on 203/6.

210/14 **saynt Thomas.** Aquinas is quite clear in affirming the existence of purgatory and the efficacy of prayers for the dead (*Commentum in quatuor libros sententiarum,* IV, dist. 45, q. 1, a. 3; q. 2). See note on 203/27.

210/24 **ye fere of Ezechyas.** See 176/22–24.

210/24 **the boke of the kyngys.** See 178/19–25.

210/24–25 **the wordes . . . zachary.** See 178/26–30.

210/25 **the fayth of Machabeus.** See 179/26–33.

210/25–26 **ye authoryte . . . Iohan.** See 184/3–25.

210/26 **the wordys . . . Peter.** See 185/28–33.

210/26–27 **the sentence . . . Poule.** See 187/3–17.

210/27 **ye testimony . . . Mathew.** See 193/30–194/3.

210/27–28 **the playne . . . cryste.** See 191/11–14 and 193/1–8.

211/6–7 **from Alexander . . . sober.** The phrase was originally applied to Alexander's father, Philip (Valerius Maximus 6.2, ext. 1; Tilley P252). But it had been transferred to Alexander in the Middle Ages (George Cary, *The Medieval Alexander,* ed. D. J. A. Ross, Cambridge, 1956, p. 100). Whiting A85 gives only this passage from More.

211/26–212/3 **But when . . . scrypture.** In *Resolutiones disputationum de indulgentiarum virtute* of 1518 (a defense of his ninety-five theses addressed to Leo X), Luther wrote: "Mihi certissimum est, purgatorium esse, nec multum me movet quid blatterent haeretici, quando iam mille et plus centum anni sunt, quod B. Augustinus in suarum confessionum li: ix, pro matre et patre suo orat et orandum petit, Et eadem sancta mater eius moriens (ut ibi scribit) memoriam sui optaverit ad altare domini, sed et a B. Ambrosio id factum narrat. Quod si etiam tempore

Apostolorum non fuisset purgatorium (ut superbit fastidiosus Pighardus), nunquid ideo credendum est haeretico vix quinquaginta annos nuper nato et fidem tot saeculorum falsam fuisse contendendum?" (*WA 1*, 555–56). But in this work Luther does not deny that purgatory can be proved from scripture; and in fact, he cites scripture to prove that the punishment in purgatory consists in feelings of fear, horror, and desperation that spring from a lack of faith (*WA 1*, 54, 56). And he prefaced his defense with the profession that he does not wish to hold any doctrine that is not founded in scripture, the fathers, or the canons and papal decretals (*WA 1*, 529–30). Later in 1518 he still professed that all beliefs ought to conform to the faith professed by the Roman church, though he also asserted that the Roman church is ruled by the faith and does not rule it (*WA 1*, 662). In July 1519 at Leipzig, during his dispute with Eck, Luther said he firmly believed in purgatory, indeed he knew it existed and could easily be persuaded that it is mentioned in scripture (*WA 2*, 324). But he also said that the existence of purgatory could not be proved from scripture and that scripture said nothing about it (*WA 2*, 323–24, 330). At Leipzig Luther did not say that no doctrine could be taken as true unless it could be proved by clear and evident scripture, and he spent much time arguing about the pronouncements of councils and of the fathers. But in his later defense of his arguments at Leipzig (*Resolutiones Lutherianae super propositionibus suis Lipsiae disputatis*, 1519), he explicitly falls back on *sola scriptura:* "certum est, in manu Ecclesiae aut Papae prorsus non esse articulos fidei statuere, immo nec leges morum seu bonorum operum, quod haec omnia in sacris literis sint tradita." But he immediately goes on to say: "Ideo reliquum est, ut articulorum declarandorum tantummodo potestatem habeat [ecclesia] . . ." (*WA 2*, 427).

212/9 **as we . . . before.** See 194/4–195/16, above.

212/12 **sow dronk.** Whiting S534. See 212/25.

212/15–16 **& beyng . . . old.** Luther was born on November 10, 1483.

212/17–18 **besydys . . . before.** The second edition of 1529 reduced the number of years between Christ and Adam from 7,500 to 4,500. Estimates were extremely various, from Jerome's 3,941 to Lactantius' 5,801 (G. De Mortillet, *Dictionnaire des sciences anthropologiques*, vol. 1, Paris, 1889, p. 298). In his *Heptaplus* Giovanni Pico della Mirandola says that the Jews calculate 3,508 years between Adam and Christ; see his *Opera omnia* (2 vols., Basel, 1572; reprint, Turin, 1971), *1*, 52. But 4,500 was clearly a better approximation than 7,500.

212/19–25 **sermon . . . dome.** In *Articuli .CCCCC.* (1525) Cochlaeus translated and refuted excerpts from thirty-six vernacular sermons preached by Luther in 1523. In the sermon on the rich man and Lazarus, Luther says: "Sciendum est, quod hominis anima aut spiritus nullum locum aut requiem habet, ubi manere queat, quam uerbum dei, donec ipse in nouissimo die ad claram contemplationem dei peruenerit. . . . Ideo nos existimamus sinum Abrahae nihil aliud quam verbum dei, quo, Gene. 22. Christus promittebatur, nempe, in semine tuo benedicentur omnes gentes. . . . Ita omnes presentes ante Christi natiuitatem in sinum Abrahae decesserunt, hoc est, in morte cum firma fide manserunt in isto dicto dei, & in verbum illud obdormierunt, recepti & custoditi, sicut in que[n]dam sinum. Et dormiunt adhuc in eo usque ad nouissimum diem. . . . Quemadmodum & nos quando morimur, nos committere & dedere debemus cum firma fide in verbum Christi, ubi dicit, Qui credit in me non morietur in aeternum, Aut consimile, Et ita super hoc mori, obdormire, & in sinum Christi recipi atque custodiri usque ad nouissimum diem" (sigs. $K_3v–K_4$; K_3 missigned K_5). In his refutations Cochlaeus points out that Luther here contradicts some of his earlier statements about purgatory and prayers for the dead (sigs. $L_1–L_1v$). To Luther's flat statement that all clergymen are corrupt and greedy, Cochlaeus replies: "Scriptum est, nolite iudicare, & non iudicabimini &c. Matt. 7 Non omnes ecclesiastici mali sunt, nec omnes laici boni. Vtrique homines sunt, & humana patiuntur. Et scripsit alibi Lutherus, se non in uicia, sed in falsas doctrinas ecclesiasticorum inuehi. Si multi sunt auari, sunt certe etiam plerique eleemosynarij, & plura in pauperes & pias causas distribuunt, quam aequalium opum laici" (sigs. $K_3–K_3v$; K_3 missigned K_5).

212/25 **sow dronken.** See note on 212/12.

212/31 **lyeth . . . myre.** Whiting M573, Tilley M989.

213/10–15 **Tyndall . . . bygan.** Tyndale's main attacks on purgatory come on sigs. K_3, $L_2–L_2v$, N_5v, P_6v, R_1 of his *Obedience* (1528).

213/31 **statute . . . mortmayn.** Literally, in French, "dead hand," designating corporations that never died (or married). *Mortmain* is defined in John Rastell's *Expositiones Terminorum* (London, 1527, sigs. $K_1v–K_2$) as follows: "Mortmayn est lou terres sount dones a vn meason de religion ou a vn auter company que sont corporat par le grannt le roy donqzs cest terre est deuenuz in mortmayn & donques le roy ou le seigniour de qui le terre est tenuz puit entre com apert in le statute de relygiousis id vide statutum. Auxi si vn fait feffement sur confidens a certeyn persons all ops de vn meason de religion ou all ops de ascun gild ou fraternite corporate donqzs il serra dit mortmain & il incourage meme le payne vt patet per statutum anno xv. R. II." In sum, mortmain applies to all lands or feoffments given to a religious house or some other legally incorporated moral person such as a guild or fraternity. These goods became "dead," as it were, by never changing hands and being inalienable, so very seldom did the guild or monastery go out of existence. That is why as early as 1215 legacies in favor of the church were limited by Magna Charta, and a mortmain statute was passed in

1279. To compensate the rights that accompanied all changes of ownership, the crown levied a special tax on mortmain goods. The statute *De viris religiosis* of 1279 completed the 1252 Provisions of Westminster and was in turn completed by further legislation, which extended the legal strictures to valuables vested in secular corporations.

214/7 **eschete.** *Escheat* comes from the Latin *ex-cadere* via the French *escheoir:* "to escheat" is literally "to fall to" (by inheritance). In John Rastell's *Expositiones Terminorum* (London, 1527), *eschete* is defined as "vne brefe & gyst lou vn tenaunt tyent dune seignour sauns mesne et face felony pur quel il est pendu ou abiure le realme ou vtlage [*sic*] de felony murder ou pety treson ou si le tenaunt murrust sauns heyr general ou special donqzs le seigniour puit enter par voy de eschet." In sum, escheat takes place when a tenant holding his property from a lord is hanged for felony, abjures the realme (forfeits his nationality), or dies without heirs. In these cases the lord, who may be a moral person, has the right to enter, that is to reclaim the fief, by way of escheat. The property thus reverting to the lord was also called escheat. As the crown possessed more lordships than any other seignieur, more fiefs reverted to it, especially through attainder, since an attainted subject had no legal heirs. On escheat and mortmain and other legal terms, see David M. Walker, *The Oxford Companion to Law* (Oxford, 1980).

This strict sense of escheat could not apply to lands held in mortmain, because the corporations or religious houses could not commit the crimes causing escheat. But "escheat" was sometimes used in the broader sense of "forfeiture," and the mortmain statutes did provide for the forfeiture of lands held in mortmain if the proper licenses had not been obtained (see note on 215/34–216/18). The escheator-general and his assistants, who were under the jurisdiction of the undertreasurer (an office held by More himself from 1521 to 1525) was responsible not only for reporting all escheated properties to the crown but also for confiscating for the crown lands held illegally in mortmain. See Raban, pp. 73–77, 83–95.

214/8–9 **what lawes . . . landys.** Apart from the regulations of the religious orders themselves, English laws of the thirteenth century forbade the alienation of ecclesiastical land, but exceptions were also allowed for (Raban, pp. 35–38).

214/21–24 **in the cytee . . . testamentes.** The city of London had obtained an exemption from the mortmain statutes which gave them the freedom to devise in mortmain (Raban, pp. 102–4).

214/27–30 **now a days . . . whyle.** Edward IV's foundation of the Observants (Greenwich, 1485) was the last erection of a large religious house. By 1500 the passage of land into mortmain because it had been given to religious houses had almost entirely ceased (Raban, pp. 155, 168–70).

214/30–31 **excepte . . . vnyuersytees.** More is not defending the universities, although Luther had denounced them as the gates of hell: "To subvert and put downe the gospell Sathan cowld never have found a more sotle and craftie invention," his attack reads in the English of "Brightwell," that is, John Frith (*A Pistle to the Christen reader*, 1529; *STC* 11394; Hume, no. 11, sig D₇v).

The three colleges founded at Oxford over the last two decades were endowed chiefly with money or land already in ecclesiastical hands. (1) Brasenose was founded by Bishop William Smyth of Lincoln and commonlawyer Richard Sutton, steward to the Brigittine abbey of Syon. It received a royal charter in 1512. Lands were given by Mrs. Morley, John Cocks, and other lay benefactors. (2) Corpus Christi, founded by Bishop Richard Fox of Winchester, helped by his friend Bishop Oldham of Exeter, received its charter in 1517. Fox's steward, William Frost, was a generous contributor. Erasmus congratulated John Claymond, first president of Corpus Christi, for the full support given to Fox's foundation by Wolsey, Campeggio, and Henry VIII (Allen, *3*, 620/10–14; *CWE 6*, 405/12–15). (3) Cardinal College, planned by Cardinal Wolsey as early as 1523, was endowed through the suppression of various monasteries. On September 1, 1527, Guillaume Budé, answering a nonextant letter from More, praises its generous and secure resources: "gymnasium nobile . . . opimisque redditibus certissimisque fundatum" (Rogers, p. 383, lines 68–69). The hall was ready for use in 1529. Cardinal Campeggio, bishop of Salisbury and in 1529 Wolsey's joint legate in the tribunal court appointed by Clement VII to hear of "the King's great matter," donated timber for the construction. As chancellor, More used his influence with the Privy Council to save Wolsey's foundation. Wolsey's "wise provision" of public readerships at Oxford was praised by Erasmus in letters to Mountjoy as early as 1519 (Allen, *3*, 584/10–14; *CWE 6*, 362/14–16) and to Wolsey himself (Allen, *3*, 588/33–34; *CWE 6*, 367/40–41). Among the beneficiaries were John Clement, Thomas Lupset, and Juan Vives. At Cambridge Christ's College and St. John's had been founded by the will (1509) of Lady Margaret Beaufort and the efforts of John Fisher.

215/4–5 **benefycys . . . theym.** If the income of a benefice was assigned to a religious house, the benefice was said to be "impropered" or "impropriated" to it.

215/16–18 **yet myght . . . all.** On the Continent there were laws and regulations broadly similar to the mortmain legislation in England (Raban, pp. 21–23).

215/34–216/20 **Whyche . . . temporall.** According to *The Dictionary of English Law*, ed. William Allen Jowitt and Clifford Walsh (London, 1959), the "statutes prohibiting alienation in mortmain, in the strict sense of the word, that is, alienation of land to corporations, are Magna Charta, 1215, the statute *De viris religiosis*, 1279, the Statute of Westminster II, 1285, and the statute 1391, 15 Ric. 2, c. 5. These statutes prohibited not only direct grants of land to corporations, whether sole or aggregate, but also several contrivances by which the religious houses (against which the statutes were especially directed) attempted to elude their provisions. Their effect was that if land was granted to a corporation without a licence from the Crown, and from the feudal lord of whom it was mediately or immediately held, then within a certain time the immediate lord might enter on or take possession of the land, which thus became forfeited to him; or, if he failed to do so, each lord paramount had the right to enter in his turn, and in default of all of them the Crown" (pp. 1194–95).

216/2–8 **he shall fynd . . . church.** Modern scholarship confirms the intent of the mortmain statute of 1279 as More summarizes it here (Raban, pp. 18–28).

217/29–30 **not onely . . . and.** One would expect "but also" instead of "and." Perhaps a phrase such as "but also the belief" was omitted before "and."

218/24 **owte of syght . . . mynde.** Whiting S307, Tilley S438.

219/1 **neglygence.** See the Introduction, p. clxiii, n. 1.

219/14–15 **let . . . wysdome.** Cf. Whiting F404.

219/17–18 **he that . . . hym self.** Whiting C24, Tilley C45.

219/26–29 **For mich . . . handys.** Though he is speaking of sharing in the eucharist rather than of almsgiving, Gregory the Great makes much the same point: "Inter haec autem pensandum est quod tutior sit via ut bonum quod quisque post mortem suam sperat agi per alios, agat ipse dum vivit per se" (*Dialogorum libri quatuor* 4.48, *PL* 77, col. 425).

219/30–32 **gold ryngys . . . funerallys.** Erasmus' Folly also complains of worldlings who take an inordinate interest in the pomp and ceremony of their own funerals (*ASD 4/3*, 126/23–28 and commentary). In his *Four Last Things* (*EW,* sig. e₅v) More reminds the reader of the devil's wiles in tempting the dying man not to look to his sins and ready himself for heaven but rather to "provision for somme honorable burying, so many torches, so many tapers, so many black gownes, so many mery mourners laughyng vnder black hodes, and a gay hers with delite of goodly and honorable funeralles."

220/11 **hersys.** A hearse was "an elaborate framework originally intended to carry a large number of lighted tapers and other decorations over the bier or coffin while placed in the church at the funerals of distinguished persons" (*OED,* s.v. "hearse" 2 a).

220/15 **monthys mynde.** A special memorial mass said for a departed soul one month after burial. See note on 111/19.

220/16–19 **fond fantesy . . . brydeale.** G. R. Owst (*Preaching in Medieval England*, Cambridge, 1926, p. 329, n. 1) reports punning on the name of the deceased in the funeral oration for Edward the Black Prince: "Edwardus, dum vixit, nos wardavit." On the tendency toward extravagant rhetoric and lavish pageantry at funerals, see Owst, pp. 265–68.

220/18–19 **made . . . brydeale.** The present form "take" is not parallel with "deuysed" (220/14) and "made" but rather depends on "made": "we made men merry and made them take. . . ."

220/35–221/1 **Gabryell . . . lady.** Luke 1:28.

222/1 **grynned.** The *1529*[1] reading "gyrned" is a variant form of "grynned." Both forms were common in More's time and both meant the same. The compositor of *1529*[2] may have made the change quite thoughtlessly.

222/24 **rap and rend.** That is, "seize and grab away." The alliterative doublet was common in the sixteenth century.

222/24 **catche . . . can.** Whiting C112, Tilley C189.

222/25 **holde . . . catcheth.** Cf. Whiting H412, Tilley H513.

223/1 **late . . . neuer.** Whiting L89, Tilley L85.

223/16 **awne slewth.** Both words are northern forms. See notes on 112/29, second note on 112/31, 174/6, and 186/10.

223/22–23 **warnynge . . . selfe.** Cf. Jas. 1:22.

224/8 **pastis.** See note on 224/15.

224/15 **pastys.** We can find no precedent for this word (also used in the same sense at 224/8) as applied to some article of feminine apparel. But the context here makes it likely that it refers to ornamental headdresses, regularly worn by women of station in More's time, such as are to be seen in the Holbein sketches of the women in More's family. Perhaps it refers only to the sidepieces of such headdresses.

225/18–19 **dark fyre.** The classic text for the dark fire of hell is by Basil (*Homilia in psalmum 28, PG 29*, 298), who suggests that in the afterlife the brightness of fire will be separated from its heat to contribute to the glory of heaven, leaving the dark burning for the damned. In answering affirmatively the question whether the damned are in physical darkness, Thomas Aquinas quotes Basil's explanation (*Summa theologica,* supplementum, q. 97, a. 5). In his *Life of Picus* More mentions "the darke fire of purgatorie" (*EW*, sig. a₅v); there is no equivalent in the Latin he is translating.

226/12–13 **blynd man . . . colours.** See *CW 6*, 86/13–87/7.

226/30–32 **ryche gloton . . . tonge to.** Luke 16:24.

233/1 **you.** The person addressed here is unknown. More may have sent him at the same time a six-line Latin poem (see *CW 3/2*, Commentary at 280/1–6. More uses the formal "you," not "thou."

233/7–12 **the kynges . . . see.** Henry issued these orders in a proclamation of June 22, 1530, 22 Henry VIII (Hughes–Larkin, *1*, 193–97, no. 129; see also no. 122 of March 6, 1530 [wrongly dated 1529 by Hughes–Larkin], pp. 181–86). See *CW 11*, Commentary at 6/12.

233/22–23 **dyuerse . . . abrode.** After his return to England in 1532 but before his arrest later that year, Frith wrote *The Testament of master Wylliam Tracie esquier (STC² 24167)* and *An other boke against Rastel (STC 11385);* see Hume, no. 40, p. 1091). In the Tower (apart from his two sacramentarian tracts) Frith wrote *A letter vnto the faythfull followers of Christes gospel (STC 11386), A myrroure or lokynge glasse wherin you may beholde the Sacramente of baptisme described (STC 11391),* and *A mirrour or glasse to knowe thy selfe (STC 11390).* None of these five works was printed until after Frith's death in 1533 (Hume, pp. 1089–91); they presumably circulated in manuscript copies. Like *A christen sentence,* they tend to be shorter than the works of Frith that were printed in 1532 or earlier *(STC 12732;* Hume, nos. 11, 24).

233/30–31 **as the scrypture . . . & more.** Cf. Rev. 22:11: "Qui nocet noceat auduc, et qui in sordibus est sordescat adhuc."

233/33–34 **saynte Poule . . . canker.** 2 Tim. 2:17. More applies the same text to heresy in *The Debellation of Salem and Bizance (CW 10, 71/14–15)* and *The Answer to a Poisoned Book (CW 11, 4/34–37).*

234/15–16 **as it hath . . . tother.** More is thinking of such outbursts as the Peasants' Revolt in Germany and the religious war in Switzerland; see notes on 22/18–24/32, 94/34–96/2, and 102/3–19.

234/19–20 **a wors . . . make.** See *CW 3/2*, Commentary at 280/1–6.

234/22 **wyclyffe.** The eucharistic doctrine of John Wyclif the Oxford theologian (c. 1320–84) is intricately enmeshed in subtle metaphysical distinctions. He did deny transubstantiation and taught (like Luther) that the substance of the bread and wine remains after consecration. But he did not deny the real corporeal presence of Christ in the eucharist. Nevertheless, some of his followers did and some of Wyclif's unguarded language left him open to the accusation that he denied the real presence, which was in fact leveled against him at the Council of Constance. See *DCT 15*, 3601–4. His long works on the eucharist were written in his later years: *Tractatus de apostasia* and *De eucharistia tractatus maior.* See *CW 11*, Commentary at 136/18.

234/22 **Huyskyn.** For John Hussgen's (Oecolampadius') denial of the real presence, see note on 14/37–38. See also *CW 11*, xlviii–liv.

234/22–23 **Tyndale.** As More admitted elsewhere (*CW 8*, 116/2–11), it is not possible to prove from the somewhat ambiguous statements in Tyndale's writings that he explicitly denied the real presence. But More thought it likely that he did (see *CW 11*, xxx–xxxi).

234/23 **zuinglius.** For Zwingli's denial of the real presence see notes on 94/34–96/2 and 96/19–29, and CW 11, xxiii–xxiv, xlvii–xlviii.

234/24–25 **affermyng . . . Luther doth.** For Luther's eucharistic doctrine see notes on 44/10, 94/34, 96/8–9, and 96/19–29.

234/29–31 **he sayth . . . vnconsecrated.** *A Christian Sentence*, Appendix C, 433/17–23.

234/34–235/2 **thynge . . . strength.** Christ, the founder of the sacraments and the source of the grace conferred by them, is himself present in the eucharist.

235/11–12 **My flesh . . . drynke.** John 6:56.

235/13–21 **Chryste . . . me.** Matt. 26:26–28, Mark 14:22–24, Luke 22:19–20, 1 Cor. 11:23–25.

235/30–236/20 **But now sayth . . . promyse.** Appendix C, 430/8–34, 431/16–432/13.

235/30–33 **our sauyoure . . . braunchys.** John 15:1–6.

235/33–34 **he calleth . . . dore.** John 10:7.

235/39 **Iacob . . . Israel.** The marginal gloss is intended to refer to Gen. 35:7, but the passage actually meant is Gen. 33:20

236/1–3 **Iacob . . . god.** Gen. 32:30.

236/3–4 **pascall lambe . . . lorde.** Exod. 12:11, 21. The marginal gloss is inaccurate.

236/5 **saith.** The sense requires a comma after this word.

236/17–20 **brydegrome . . . promyse.** The comparison with the bridegroom's ring (as well as the analogies with Christ as the vine and the door) is presented in Cornelis Hoen's brief treatise against the real presence, which exerted a decisive influence on Karlstadt and Zwingli and was first published by Zwingli in Zürich in 1525; it has been edited in *CRZ, 4*, 505–11. See also *CW 11*, xx–xxii.

236/22–23 **cyrcumuented . . . deuyll.** Cf. 2 Cor. 2:11.

236/28 **hole.** The meaning is probably "holy" rather than "whole" (236/29). See note on 175/7.

236/33–34 **god . . . declared.** In the *Confutation* (*CW 8*, 608/23–27), More noted Zwingli's death in battle as an example of how the crimes of the heretics have fallen back on their own heads. See note on 94/34–96/2.

237/13 **whole substaunce.** There are strong overtones here of the doctrine of transubstantiation, though More does not use that word here or in *The Answer to a Poisoned Book.* The entire substance of the bread and wine is changed into the substance of Christ's body, but the accidents (such as color and weight) which inhere in the substances do not change.

238/12–239/21 **For suche . . . ensample.** More employs a similar analogy between the Arians' handling of scripture and that of the reformers in *A Dialogue Concerning Heresies* (*CW 6*, 159–61) and *The Answer to a Poisoned Book* (*CW 11*, 41/11–22).

238/27–28 **as thys . . . phrase.** Appendix C, 431/15. More is glancing at Frith's pretentiousness in using an exotic new word. The *OED* gives 1530 as the earliest use of *phrase.*

238/30–31 **god . . . Pharao.** Exod. 7:1.

238/32–33 **thou . . . goddes.** Exod. 22:28.

238/33–35 **I saye . . . all.** Ps. 81:6.

239/27–36 **Hierom . . . cotes.** *Dialogus adversus Luciferianos* 28 (*PL 23*, cols. 181–82): "brevem tibi apertamque animi mei sententiam proferam, in illa esse Ecclesia permanendum, quae ab Apostolis fundata, usque ad diem hanc durat. . . . Nec sibi blandiantur [haeretici], si de Scripturarum capitulis videntur sibi affirmare quod dicunt, cum et diabolus de Scripturis aliqua sit locutus, et Scripturae non in legendo consistant, sed in intelligendo. Alioqui si litteram sequimur, possumus et nos quoque novum nobis dogma componere: ut asseramus in Ecclesiam non recipiendos, qui calceati sint, et duas tunicas habeant." The marginal gloss refers to Luke 3:11, but Jerome was probably thinking of Matt. 10:10.

240/17–18 **the thing . . . were.** Though the subject is singular, "were" is not modal but factual; More may use this form because he is reporting the statements of the fathers (Visser, *1*, 297).

240/24–241/2 **the very circumstances . . . in dede.** The author of *The Souper of the Lorde* (1533) attempted to confute this argument from the differing contexts of the texts. More responded at length in *The Answer to a Poisoned Book* (1533), *CW 11*, 149–77.

240/34–37 **he sayed . . . blood.** John 6:54–56.

241/15–17 **Many . . . scrypture.** More devoted the whole first book of

The Answer to a Poisoned Book (1533) to a long and detailed exposition of John 6:26–72 (*CW 11*, 21–95).

242/10–33 **For he confesseth . . . possyble.** Appendix C, 429/5–430/2.

243/22–23 **no thynge . . . god.** Luke 1:37.

243/25–246/4 **How be it . . . speke of them.** More discussed this sentence from Augustine once again in *The Answer to a Poisoned Book,* (*CW 11*, 194/1–195/5 and Commentary). The sentence is from Augustine's *Tractatus in Iohannem* 30.1 (*CCSL 36*, 289, where the reading "potest" is accepted rather than "oportet") and refers not to Christ's presence in the eucharist but to his visible presence on earth as a teacher (as Melanchthon had pointed out in his *Sententiae veterum aliquot scriptorum de coena Domini,* Wittenberg, 1530, Corpus Reformatorum 23, 747). In his reply to More's *Letter against Frith* (*A Boke . . . answeringe vnto M mores lettur,* sigs. F₁v–F₂), Frith admitted he had taken the sentence from Gratian's *Decretum* (*De consecratione* 2.44, *CIC 1*, 1330). The passage in Gratian is a conflation from three different works of Augustine.

243/28 **loke . . . medew.** Whiting N71, Tilley N97.

244/18–20 **Nonne . . . suam?** Luke 24:26.

244/21–23 **he myghte . . . or no.** John 10:18.

244/26–27 **He was . . . hym selfe.** Isa. 53:7.

245/25–27 **good storyes . . . ascensyon.** There is scriptural warrant for at least two appearances of Christ after his ascension (Acts 7:54–56 and 9:3–15; 1 Cor. 15:8). See *CW 13*, 83/20–21; *CW 14*, 185/11–12.

246/5 **Now as for . . . reasonynge.** For the ellipsis of the subject see Delcourt, pp. 214–15, and Visser, *1*, 33–35.

246/6–9 **For fyrste . . . his is.** Appendix C, 429/8–11.

246/16–21 **our sauyour . . . god.** Mark 10:25, Mat. 19:24, Luke 18:25. Cyril of Alexandria and a few late Greek manuscripts have the variant reading κάμιλος, for κάμηλος, but modern scholars agree that the correct meaning is "camel," not "cable" (*The Interpreter's Bible,* ed. George A. Buttrich et al., 12 vols., New York, 1952–57, 7, 806). More could have known of it from Theophylactus' remark in Aquinas' *Catena aurea* (*Opera omnia,* 25 vols., Parma, 1852–78; reprint, New York, 1948–49, *11*, 398): "Camelum siquidem oportet intelligere aut ipsum animal, aut funem illum crassum, quo naves magnae utuntur." The camel/cable crux is not mentioned by Nicolas de Lyra and the other commentators in the *Biblia latina* (Basel, Froben, 1598), but Erasmus discusses it at length in his *Annotationes in Novum Testamentum,* beginning in the 1516 edition (sig. aa₂, on Matt. 19:24) and adding a few embellishments in the later editions. He agrees with Jerome that "camel" is the correct interpretation (see *Opera omnia,* 6, 102). In *A Dialogue of Comfort* More gives both alternatives without deciding between them (*CW 12,* 170/29–171/3 and Commentary). So too in *The Four Last Things:* "our saviour Crist said it were as harde for the riche manne to come into heauen, as a great cable or a Camel to go through a nedles eye" (EW, sig. fg₅v).

247/7–9 **as he dyd ... pylgryme.** Mark 16:[12], cited in the gloss, mentions the episode briefly but More must have had in mind Luke 24:13–35, which mentions the detail that the two thought Jesus was a pilgrim (Luke 24:18).

248/1–8 **ascrybynge ... repugnant.** More had discussed the problem of God's foreknowledge and man's free will in the *Confutation* (*CW 8,* 938/30–939/16 and Commentary) and would do so again at greater length in *The Answer to a Poisoned Book* (*CW 11,* 84/25–86/30 and Commentary).

248/5 **pore blynde.** That is, "purblind," meaning "totally blind."

248/17–18 **myracles ... scrypture.** In a passage translated from Cyril, More gave some examples of miraculous transformation in scripture in *The Answer to a Poisoned Book* (*CW 11,* 65/1–14).

248/20–26 **one face ... onys.** More defended this passage at length in *The Answer to a Poisoned Book,* particularly the analogy of one face appearing in many mirrors (*CW 11,* 206/2–210/9). The similes of the voice and of the broken mirror appear in Innocent III's *De sacro altaris mysterio* 4.8 and 27 (*PL 217,* 861, 875). The analogy of the broken mirror is repeated by Bonaventure, Albertus Magnus, and Aquinas (see *CW 11,* Commentary at 207/14–28). In *A Dialogue Concerning Heresies* (*CW 6,* 66/6–68/3), More gives other feats of craftsmen which might seem impossible, including the manufacture of glass from fern roots.

248/36–37 **two bodyes ... not.** As, for example, when Jesus passed through locked doors (John 20:19–26).

249/17–21 **Now hys laste ... onys.** Appendix C, 429/27–30. More discussed this argument at greater length in *The Answer to a Poisoned Book* (*CW 11,* 188/18–193/31).

249/34 **varyeth his extremytes.** That is, there is no term common to the first and last (or "extreme") propositions.

249/36 **rather haue.** The compositor of *1532* falsely anticipated (and then repeated) "haue." More's syntax does not allow for a construction with two *haues* after "must" (Visser, 2, 632; 3, 864–65).

250/4 **bothe ... antecedent.** That is, the major and minor propositions of the syllogism.

250/16–19 **but yf . . . creaturs.** That is, such a conditional proposition may be valid if the antecedent depends on possibility, not on fact (if one man can be a stone, all men can), or if the consequent is in itself necessary, apart from the antecedent (all men are living creatures).

251/16–19 **rauysshed . . . god.** 2 Cor. 12:2 and Rom. 11:33. The marginal gloss is inaccurate.

251/20–27 **But yet . . . styll.** Appendix C, 429/30–430/2.

251/22–23 **angell . . . here.** Mark 16:6.

251/24–26 **Cristes . . . erth.** Acts 1:9.

251/31 **roten . . . rype.** Whiting R142, Tilley R133.

251/34–36 **sophyster . . . peruise.** That is, when he was a second- or third-year student of logic at a public disputation.

252/14–15 **Beware . . . phylosophy.** Col. 2:8.

252/17–22 **he sayth . . . lyst.** Appendix C. 428/1–22.

252/27–29 **many . . . receyue hym.** 1 Cor. 11:29–30.

253/22–33 **kynges hyghnes . . . we do.** In the *Responsio ad Lutherum* (*CW* 5, 492/14–20), More quotes Henry's words from *Assertio septem sacramentorum:* "At Lutherus ipse fatetur nihil esse periculi: si quis hac in re sentiat, quod tota iam sentiat ecclesia. Sed contra, tota ecclesia censet haereticum esse eum: qui sentiat cum Luthero. Non debet ergo Lutherus animare quenquam, cui bene cupit: ut secum sentiat, cuius sententiam tota condemnat ecclesia: sed debet his suadere, quos amat: ut accedant illis, quos ipse quoque iudicat in nullo uersari periculo." See note on 26/13–15.

253/33 **whom . . . well.** That is, "who you wish would do well" (see Visser, *1*, 290–91).

254/4–11 **thys yonge man . . . vnsayd.** Appendix C, 432/24–37.

254/16–18 **And therfore . . . selfe.** Discussing Judas's reception of the eucharist at the Last Supper, Chrysostom remarks: "Quam ob rem constat, in nostro esse arbitrio, an saluemur, an perdamur" (*PG 59*, 268; *Opera omnia*, Basel, 1530, *3*, sig. G*G$_2$). More later translated the whole passage in *The Answer to a Poisoned Book* (*CW 11*, 93/16–33).

254/31–33 **putteth . . . diner.** 1 Cor. 11:29.

255/3–4 **stoppe . . . incantacyons.** An allusion to Homer's Odysseus, who sealed his men's ears with wax against the magical and destructive song of the Sirens (*Odyssey* 12, 165–200).

255/5–6 **peple . . . doctryne.** Eph. 4:14.

255/5–7 **with yᵉ wynde . . . wethercok.** Whiting W158–60, Tilley W223.

255/8–10 **that euyll . . . Galathyes.** In chapter 3 of his letter to the Galatians, Paul is writing against some Judaizers who insisted that Christians fulfill all the requirements of the Mosaic law.

255/14 **open myracles.** For examples see *CW 11*, Commentary at 203/9–11.

255/20–21 **Berengarius . . . errour.** Berengarius of Tours (c. 1000–88), *scholasticus* at St. Martin's School at Tours (1031) and archdeadon of Tours (1041), initiated the first major controversy about the physical presence of Christ in the eucharist. Until the nineteenth century his doctrine was known mainly from such opponents as Lanfranc and Guitmund; he clearly denied transubstantiation (which was only beginning to be formulated in his time) and also seemed to assert that Christ was sacramentally present in the consecrated bread and wine only through his effect on the mind of the recipient. His teaching on the eucharist was condemned at several councils (Vercelli, 1050; Paris, 1051; Rome, 1059 and 1079). He recanted several times but repudiated his recantations more than once. After the Council of Bordeaux (1080), he made a final retraction, retired into solitude, and died in union with the church. See *CW 11*, xviii and Commentary at 179/15–16; *The Catholic Encyclopedia,* 15 vols. (New York, 1907–14), 2, 487–89; *The New Catholic Encyclopedia,* 16 vols (New York, 1967–74), 2, 320–21.

255/25 **Cronica cronicarum yᵉ .cxc. lefe.** Richard Schoeck ("The 'Cronica Cronicarum' of Sir Thomas More and Tudor Historians," *Bulletin of the Institute of Historical Research, 35* [1962], 85) points out that More here is not referring to the abridged *Cronica cronicarum* (Paris, 1521 and 1532) but rather to Hartmann Schedel's *Liber Cronicarum* (Nürnberg, 1493). Folio 190 presents Berengarius as follows: "Berengarius doctor natione turonensis andegauensis archidiaconus per hec tempora cum diu sanctitate et doctrina insignis et clarus fuisset, ob doctrine sue amplitudinem primo confusus in eucharistie sacramento turpiter errauit. et multorum animos ipso suo errore infecit. Sed diuina postea illustratus gratia errorem suum publico concilio vercellis habito emendauit. vt in decretis habetur de cons. di. 2 c. ego berengarius [*CIC 1,* 1328] Emendacioneque facta. statim sophistice discipline studio omisso. primo omnia pauperibus erogauit. factusque pduperrimus [i.e., pauperrimus] labore manuum suarum quoad vixit viuere voluit. et vniuersum vite sue tempus sanctissime contriuit." In the edition of *Liber cronicarum* printed at Augsburg on February 1, 1497, the passage occurs not on fol. 190 but on fol. 212.

255/25–256/7 **frere Barns . . . contented wyth.** In the first part of the *Confutation* (1532), More had accused Barnes, in passing, of holding the sacramentarian position of Zwingli on the eucharist (*CW 8*, 302/10–12). This passage in the *Letter against Frith* is all we know of Barnes's letter. Barnes apparently never carried out his promise to write a book against More on the eucharist (*CW 8*, 1395).

256/15–18 **the herers . . . from hym.** John 6:66–68.

256/20 **folosophy.** A coinage suggested by μωρόσοφος, used by Lucian (*Alexander* 40), Erasmus (*Moriae encomium*, *ASD 4/3*, 74/76 and Commentary), and More (*Utopia, CW 4*, 64/2). Cf. "folosophers" in *The Answer to a Poisoned Book, CW 11*, 179/31.

257/5–6 **the scisme . . . wrytyng.** In *A Christian Sentence* (Appendix C, 432/14–20), Frith mentions the doctrine of utraquism, the insistence on reception of the eucharist under both species, but he does not insist on it. Utraquism arose among the Hussites of Bohemia in the early fifteenth century and flourished mostly there until the time of Luther. In his *Supplication* of 1531 Barnes held that the eucharist must be received "in both kindes vnder the payne of deedlye synne," but in his revision of the *Supplication* in 1534 he omitted that doctrine (*CW 8*, 1389, 1397–98). More never wrote a book against Barnes's utraquism.

257/13 **yᵉ paryng of a pere.** Whiting P29.

257/15 **therefore.** That is, "for that purpose, in order to make it." The reading "therfro" in *1557* is a plausible but unnecessary emendation. But Frith, quoting this passage in *A Boke . . . answeringe vnto M mores lettur* (Hume, no. 30), gives "therefro" (sig. I₂v).

257/21 **presentely.** The temporal sense—"at that very time"—seems to be predominant; (*OED*, s.v. "presently" 2 c); but the overtones of Christ's real presence are also evoked (*OED*, s.v. "presently" 1).

257/23 **vnworthy of her self.** That is, "not worthy in and of herself" but because of God's grace.

258/14–16 **the mouthes . . . prayse.** Ps. 8:3.

258/18 **Cryste . . . noster.** Matt. 6:9–13.

258/28 **more than all your owne.** Cf. "Plus quam totus tuus," the closing formula of two of More's letters to Francis Cranevelt (Rogers, pp. 311, 317).

APPENDIX A

John Bugenhagen's *Epistola ad Anglos*

Johann Bugenhagen, by Lucas Cranach the elder (reduced)

APPENDIX A

John Bugenhagen's *Epistola ad Anglos*

This reprint of Bugenhagen's *Epistola ad Anglos* is based on the edition printed by Simpertus Ruff at Augsburg in 1525.[1] Minor misprints have been silently corrected,[2] and in a few places the punctuation has been silently changed to make the sense clearer. The italic typeface of our copy-text appears here as roman, except for the sidenotes, which have also been indented into our text. Periods at the ends of sidenotes have been uniformly omitted.

---

[1]Geisenhof, no. 181. The Wittenberg edition of 1525 (Geisenhof, no. 182) and the other edition of 1525 (n.p., Geisenhof, no. 183) have also been completely collated and reveal no substantive variants, except that they have no sidenotes; and Geisenhof, no. 183, has "hi filij dei sunt" at 402/11. We have used microfilms of Geisenhof, nos. 181–82, from the Deutsche Staatsbibliothek in Berlin (German Democratic Republic) and of Geisenhof, no. 183, from Germanisches Nationalmuseum, Nürnberg. Three editions in German also appeared in 1525 (Geisenhof, nos. 185–87). A copy of the fourth Latin edition (Geisenhof, no. 184, 1530?) in the Beinecke Library at Yale has also been examined and reveals no substantive variants. An English translation was printed in 1536 (Geisenhof, no. 188; *STC* 4021).

[2]At 398/4 "Anglis" has been corrected to "Anglia," the reading in More's quotation (12/12), in the Wittenberg edition of 1525, in the other edition of 1525, and in the fourth edition (Geisenhof, no. 184). Also, at 400/13, "Pelagiana," which has been changed to the more correct "Pelagianae," might possibly have been intended by Bugenhagen.

EPISTOLA
IOANNIS BVGENHAGIJ POMERANI
ad Anglos.

M. D. XXV.

A LETTER OF JOHN BUGENHAGEN OF POMERANIA
to the English

1525

IOANNES BVGENHAGIVS POMERANVS,
pastor Ecclesiae Wittenbergensis
Sanctis in Christo qui sunt
in Anglia.

5 GRATIA uobis & pax a deo patre nostro et domino nostro Iesu
Christo. Non potuimus non gaudere quando audiuimus et in Anglia
Euangelium gloriae dei apud quosdam bene audire. Caeterum & illud
nobis nunciatum est, multos infirmiores adhuc auerti, propter rumores nescio quos, qui isthic feruntur ab illis qui Euangelio dei aduer-
10 santur de nobis. Haec est gloria nostra, tantum abest ut mendatia in
Euangelij professores iactata refellenda duxerim, alioqui in quo
uideretur illa beatitudo, Beati estis cum maledixerint uobis?

Neque tamen defendimus si qui alibi pretextu Christianae libertatis
quid designent non Christianum, quandoquidem non omnes Chris-
15 tum induerunt qui Christi nomen sibi uendicant.

Hoc uero miramur cur sacrum Christi Euangelium quidam isthic
uerentur suscipere, propterea quod de nobis mala dicuntur, ignorantes quod oportet filium hominis reprobari a mundo & stultitiam
haberi predicationem crucis. Quid si uerum esset quod de nobis [A₂]
20 mentiuntur propter Christum? ipsi scilicet ideo non susciperent oblatum a deo Euangelium salutis? Quid stultius, quam ut magis curiosus
sis ad meam iniquitatem quam ad tuam salutem? Ideo ne tu nolis esse
Christianus quia ego sum peccator? cur non sequuntur Pauli regulam,
Omnia probate, quod bonum est tenete? Si
1 thes. 5
25 in hominum uel iustitiam uel iniustitiam
respicere coepero, quando quaeso liberabor ab errore, quo fere perijt
mundus, & agnoscam tandem dei iustitiam?

Verum aiunt rudiores, quis ista tam uaria capere poterit? disputatur enim de libero arbitrio, de uotis & sec-
Objectio
30 tis monasticis, de satisfactionibus, de abusu
uenerandae eucharistiae, de cultu sanctorum defunctorum, &c. Alij
aiunt, Veremur ne sub ista uarietate lateat uenenum. Quasi uero nos
agamus persuasibilibus humanae sapientiae uerbis, & non manifestissimis scripturis, quibus ne portae quidem in-
1. cor. 2
35 ferorum hactenus preualere potuerunt?
aut quasi aduersarij nostri aliud contra nos producant quam statuta &
traditiones humanas, quas damnat deus Esai. 29. & Christus Math. 15.

JOHN BUGENHAGEN OF POMERANIA,
Pastor of the Church of Wittenberg,
To the Saints in Christ who are
in England.

Grace be to you and peace from God our Father and our Lord Jesus Christ. We could not but rejoice when we heard that in England too the gospel of the glory of God has been well received by certain persons. But we have also been told that many weaklings still reject us because of vague rumors reported of us there by those who oppose the gospel of God. This is our glory. I consider it unnecessary to refute the lies told about those who proclaim the gospel. How else could we experience in our own lives the beatitude, Blessed are you when they revile you?

But we make no defense if men elsewhere perform unchristian acts under the pretext of Christian liberty, since not everyone who claims for himself the name of Christ has put on Christ.

What surprises us is this: why it is that some people there are afraid to receive the holy gospel of Christ because evil is spoken of us, not remembering that it behooves the son of man to be reproved by the world and the preaching of the cross to be esteemed foolishness. What if the lies that men tell about us for Christ's sake were true? Would they therefore not accept the gospel of salvation offered to them by God? What could be more foolish than to be more concerned with my wickedness than with your own salvation? Will you therefore be no Christian because I am a sinner? Why do they not follow the

1 Thessalonians 5

rule of Paul: "Test all things, and hold fast to what is good"? If I begin to regard man's righteousness or unrighteousness, when (I ask you) will I be freed from error, which the whole world almost perished in, and acknowledge at last the righteousness of God?

But, the less educated will say, Who is able to understand all these

Objection

different arguments? Men dispute about free will, about vows and monastic orders, about works of satisfaction, abuse of the holy eucharist, the worship of the saintly dead, etc. Others say, We are afraid that poison is hidden

1 Corinthians 2

under all this disagreement. As if we deal in the enticing words of human wisdom and not the palpable evidence of scripture, against which even the gates of hell have not yet been able to prevail. Or as if our adversaries brought forth anything against us except human statutes and traditions, which the Lord condemns in Isaiah 29 and Christ in Matthew 15.

Quod ergo uenenum hic timebis, dum in occulto agimus nihil, &
omnia nostra toti mundo iudicanda proponimus? Et ne uarietatem
doctrinae excuses breuiter dico, unum tantum articulum a nobis doceri, [A₂v] utcunque quotidie multa praedicemus, multa scribamus,
5 multa agamus contra aduersarios ut & ipsi salui fiant.

Est autem articulus ille,
CHRISTVS EST
IVSTITIA NOSTRA.

Nam is factus est nobis a deo sapientia, iustitia, satisfactio, redemp-
10   *1 Cor. 1*   tio. Quisquis hoc non dederit nobis, non
                                 est Christianus, quisquis autem fatebitur
nobiscum, apud eum statim cadet alia quaecunque iustitia humana.
            Pelagii   Nihil hic erit Pelagianae haeresis, qua licet
                                 mutatis uerbis infecti sunt qui uel solos se
15 Christianos gloriantur, nihil ualebit omnis sectarum quae hodie sunt
& operum fiducia, quam abnegato crucis Christi scandalo nostri iustitiarij nobis inuexerunt, dum opera pro Christo nobis uenditarunt.
Contra quos & contra totum Satanae regnum hoc argumentum fortissimum cum Paulo producimus. Si ex operibus & nostro arbitrio
20   *Gala. 2*   iustificamur, ergo gratis Christus mortuus
                                 est.
Iustitia haec quae Christus est, testimonium habet in lege & prophetis, Rom. 3. Qui autem suam iustitiam sequuntur ad ueram
iustitiam, ut Iudei, non peruemiunt, Rom. 9. Iustitiae enim dei subijci
25 non possunt, [A₃] Rom. 10. Haec iustitia dei tua est, dum per fidem
suscipis Christum: non enim pro se mortuus est, aut pro suis delictis,
sed pro te & tuis delictis.
Igitur quicquid aliud tentaueris ad iustitiam, id est, unde iustificeris
& liber sis a dei iudicio, peccatis, morte & inferis, hypocrisis erit, men-
30 dacium & impietas, quacunque sanctitatis specie fulgeat, pugnabit
enim contra dei gratiam, & Christi erit abnegatio.

What poison then are you afraid of, since we do nothing in secret and set all our works before the whole world to be judged? And lest you plead as an excuse the variety of our teaching, let me briefly say that we teach but one article of faith no matter how often we preach every day, no matter how much we write and how much we do against our opponents so that they too may be saved.

And this is that one article,
CHRIST IS
OUR RIGHTEOUSNESS.

For God made him our wisdom, justice, satisfaction, redemption.

1 Corinthians 1 Whoever does not grant us this is no Christian; whoever agrees with us in this will soon give over all righteousness of man. There will be no trace

Pelagius' [heresy] left here of the Pelagian heresy, by which (although the words are changed) they have been infected who boast that they are the only ones who are Christians. Each of the sects that exists today will count for nothing, nor will the trust in good works, which our self-justifiers have thrust upon us, rejecting the stumbling block of Christ's cross, peddling works instead of Christ. Against them and against the entire kingdom of Satan we bring forth with Paul this most powerful argument: If we

Galatians 2 are made righteous by works and by our own free will, then Christ died in vain.

This righteousness which is Christ is testified to by the law and the prophets (Romans 3). A man who follows his own righteousness will, like the Jews, not arrive at true righteousness (Romans 9). They are not able to submit to God's righteousness (Romans 10). This righteousness of God is yours when you receive Christ through faith. For he did not die for his own sake or for his own sins, but for your sake and for your sins.

Whatever else, therefore, you have tried in order to arrive at righteousness—that is, to become righteous and free from the judgment of God, from sin, death, and hell—will be hypocrisy, lies, and wickedness, no matter how it shines with a semblance of piety. For it will strive against the grace of God and deny Christ.

At forte interrogabis quid de moribus, cultu dei, sacramentis & huiusmodi sentiamus & doceamus? Respondeo,

De externis

Christus qui factus est iustitia nostra factus
est & doctor noster. Quicquid is suo ore nobis prodidit, hoc docemus

5 *Ioan. 6*

seruandum, quemadmodum & praecepit
Matthei ultimo. Primum autem docuit hoc
esse opus dei, ut credamus in eum, quem pater nobis misit. Quisquis
autem in eum crediderit, arbor bona est, & non poterit suo tempore
non ferre fructum bonum, non quem fructum hypocrisis fingit, sed

10 quem spiritus Christi illic sua sponte producit. Qui enim spiritu
Christi aguntur hi sunt filij dei. Sobrie ita-

Rom 8
Ioan. 4
Gal. 4
Colos. 2

que pie & iuste uiuet, adorabit deum in
spiritu et ueritate, non in elementis mundi,
cibis & uestitu, aut alia hypocrisi, sentiet de

15 sacramentis quod Christus docuit & in-
stituit, seruiet proximo doctrina, consilio, oratione, rebus, etiam cum
dispendio uite, nec solum ami[A₃v]co, sed etiam inimico. Haec docuit
Christus, ad haec trahit natura spiritus corda credentium, & nos haec
omnia docemus facienda, & quia in carne

Rom. 8

20 adhuc sumus quicquid ex his non fit aut
non satis fit, & quicquid adhuc peccatur, docemus cum Christo, ut
iugiter oretur delicti uenia, quemadmodum orare praecepit. Dimitte
nobis debita &c. & propter istam fidutiam in deum non imputari peccatum quod est in carne reliquum. Non

Rom. 7
25 *Matthe. 9*
Luc. 5

enim inuenio in me, id est, in carne mea
bonum. Sed gratia deo quod Christus
uenit non propter iustos, sed propter pec-
catores, & publicani & meretrices praecedunt iustitiarios Phariseos in
regnum coelorum. Quid hic ogganniet os iniquum, quod non alia

30 docemus? Deus per Mosen dicit, Quisquis

Deut. 18
Ioan. 4

prophetam illum, id est, Christum non audierit, ego ultor existam. Audiant hoc con-
tra se dei iudicium Euangelij hostes. Et pater clamat super Christum,
Hunc audite. Et Christus, Oues, inquit, meae uocem meam non alien-

35 orum audient.

But perhaps you will ask what we think and teach about morals, the

On externals worship of God, the sacraments, and things of that sort. I answer that Christ who became our righteousness also became our teacher. Whatever he has revealed to us with his own mouth, this we teach must be observed, even as he commanded in the last chapter of Matthew. First of all

John 6 Christ taught that this is the work of God, that we believe in him whom the Father sent us. Now whoever believes in him is a good tree, and cannot fail to bear good fruit in its season. Not the fruit imagined by hypocrisy, but the fruit which the spirit of Christ produces there of its own accord.

Romans 8
John 4
Galatians 4
Colossians 2

For those who are moved by the spirit of Christ are the sons of God. Such a one will live soberly, piously, and justly, adoring God in spirit and truth, not in the elements of this world, in food, clothing, and other hypocrisy. About the sacraments he will believe what Christ taught and established. He will serve his neighbor with instruction, advice, prayer, material possessions, even at the cost of his life. And this not only for friends, but also for enemies. Such are the things Christ taught us; the nature of the spirit draws the hearts of believers to

Romans 8 these things; and these are the things that we teach must be performed. And because we are still in the flesh, whatever of these we do not do or do not do well enough, and whatever sins we still commit, we teach with Christ that one should pray constantly that his sins will be forgiven, just as he taught us to pray: forgive us our trespasses, etc. And because of this trust in God, we teach that whatever sin still remains in the flesh will

Romans 7
Matthew 9
Luke 5

not be imputed to us. For I discover in me—that is, in my flesh—no good thing. But I give thanks to God that Christ came not for the righteous, but for sinners. And publicans and prostitutes will enter into the kingdom of heaven before self-righteous Pharisees. Why do wicked backbiters grumble

Deuteronomy 18
John 4

because we do not teach otherwise? God says through Moses, Whoever will not hear that prophet (meaning Christ), I will take vengeance on him. Let the enemies of the gospel hear this judgment of God against them. And the Father cries aloud over Christ, Hear him. And Christ says, My sheep will hear my voice and not the voice of strangers.

Haec ad uos breuibus scripsi fratres, ut gaudium meum de uobis testarer uobis, et simul rationem redderem de ea quae in nobis est spe, contra illos qui omnia nostra impudentibus mendacijs apud ignorantes peruertunt. Vos autem orate deum pro nobis & pro omnibus

5   sanctis & pro aduersarijs nostris, ut uerbum [A$_4$] dei crescat & inuulgetur mundo, in gloriam ipsius & hominum salutem, per Ihesum Christum dominum nostrum, cui gloria & imperium in omnia secula seculorum, Amen.

I have written this to you, brothers, in few words to witness to you the joy I have of you and also to give you reason for the hope that is in us against those who destroy all that we do by impudently lying to the ignorant. But pray to God for us and for all the saints and for our enemies that the word of God may increase and be made evident throughout the world for his glory and the salvation of man, through Jesus Christ our Lord, to whom be the glory and the power forever and ever, Amen.

APPENDIX B

Simon Fish's *A Supplicacyon for the Beggers*
with John Foxe's Sidenotes

APPENDIX B

Simon Fish's *A Supplicacyon for the Beggers* with John Foxe's Sidenotes

We reprint here the first edition of *A Supplication for the Beggers* (Hume, no. 8; *STC* 10883), which was probably printed by Johannes Grapheus of Antwerp early in 1529.[1] Our copy-text is a microfilm of the only known copy, in the British Library. The abbreviation indicating "m" or "n" after a vowel has been silently expanded. At the beginnings of sentences lowercase "s," "h," "y," and "w," which may have been lacking or in short supply in the printer's italic font, have been silently capitalized. The pilcrow, which indicates paragraphs in the copy-text, has been replaced by indentation. Obvious misprints, such as turned letters, have been silently corrected,[2] and in a few places the punctuation has been emended to make the sense clearer. John Foxe's sidenotes in *Acts and Monuments* (1583)[3] glossing his reprint of Fish's text are reprinted here as footnotes.

The entire book, and especially a specific paragraph denying the existence of purgatory,[4] were condemned and prohibited in a proclamation produced at an assembly called by Henry VIII at Westminster on May 24, 1530.[5] The assembly was presided over by William War-

---

[1] For the printer see Wouter Nijhoff and M. E. Kronenberg, *Nederlandsche Bibliographie van 1500 tot 1540*, 3 vols. ('s-Gravenhage, 1923–71), no. 3032. Hume (*CW 8*, 1072) points out that in a *Supplication of Souls* (161/34–162/22), which was in press by October 24, 1529, More clearly implies that *A Supplication for the Beggers* was published after Tyndale's *Obedience* (October 2, 1528; Hume, no. 7).

[2] At 415/34 "maner" may be a misprint for "mater."

[3] See Appendix D, p. 437 and 442/3–4.

[4] "But there be . . . al holy scripture" (419/10–18).

[5] Wilkins, *Concilia, 3*, 733, 736. On November 3, 1526, William Warham, archbishop of Canterbury, ordered all copies of Tyndale's New Testament to be confiscated and burned. His order concludes with a list of other forbidden books, including "The supplication of beggars" (Wilkins, *Concilia, 3*, 706–7). But the list was a later addition to the order, since it includes books such as Tyndale's *Wicked Mammon* (1528), not published till after 1526. The name "Simone Fishe" appears in a list of heretical authors in the statutes issued by the convocation of Canterbury which was held in London between November 5, 1529, and April 29, 1530 (Wilkins, *Concilia, 3*, 720); but the statutes also mention John Frith's *Disputation of Purgatory* (1531), which must have been added later.

ham (archbishop of Canterbury) and Cuthbert Tunstal (bishop of Durham) and included More himself together with many counsellors and learned men. The book was also prohibited in a royal proclamation against heretical books dated June 22, 1530.[1]

It was reprinted together with *A supplication of the poore Commons* in 1546 (*STC* 10884) and as part of "The Story of Simon Fish" (see Appendix D) in John Foxe's *Acts and Monuments* in 1563, 1570, 1576, 1583, and 1596 (*STC* 11222–26). It was also reprinted at least five times in the nineteenth century (not including the many editions of Foxe between 1596 and our day) and twice in the twentieth century.[2]

[1]Hughes–Larkin, *1*, 194; Wilkins, *Concilia, 3*, 740.

[2]London, 1845: London, 1871, ed. Frederick J. Furnivall; London, 1878, ed. Edward Arber; Westminster, 1895, ed. Edward Arber; New York, 1898. See *National Union Catalogue [of the Library of Congress]: Pre-1956 Imprints*, 754 vols. (London and Wisbech, England, 1968–81), *173*, 550; *Tudor Poetry and Prose*, ed. J. W. Hebel et al. (New York, 1953), pp. 565–73; and *English Historical Documents*, ed. David C. Douglas et al., 12 vols. (London, 1955–77), *5*, 669–76.

A Supplicacyon for the Beggers.
[₁v]

TO THE KING OVRE
souereygne lorde.

Most lamentably compleyneth theyre wofull mysery vnto youre high-
nes youre poore daily bedemen the wretched hidous monstres (on
5 whome scarcely for horror any yie dare loke) the foule vnhappy sorte
of lepres, and other sore people, nedy, impotent, blinde, lame, and
sike, that live onely by almesse, howe that theyre nombre is daily so sore
encreased that all the almesse of all the weldisposed people of this
youre realme is not half ynough for to susteine theim, but that for
10 verey constreint they die for hunger. And this most pestilent mischief
is comen vppon youre saide poore beedmen by the reason that there is
yn the tymes of youre noble predecessours passed craftily crept ynto
this your realme an other sort (not of impotent but) of strong puissaunt
and counterfeit holy, and ydell beggers and vacabundes whiche syns
15 the tyme of theyre first entre by all the craft and wilinesse of Satan are
nowe encreased vnder your sight not onely into a great nombre, but
also ynto a kingdome. These are (not the herdes, but the rauinous
wolues going in herdes clothing deuouring the flocke) the Bisshoppes,
Abbottes, Priours, Deacons, Archedeacons, Suffraganes, Prestes,
20 Monkes, Chanons, Freres, Pardoners and Somners. And who is abill to
nombre this idell rauinous sort whiche (setting all laboure a side) haue
begged so importunatly that they haue gotten ynto theyre hondes
more then the therd part of all youre Realme. The goodliest lord-
shippes, maners, londes, and territories are [₂] theyrs. Besides this they
25 haue the tenth part of all the corne, medowe, pasture, grasse, wolle,
coltes, calues, lambes, pigges, gese, and chikens. Ouer and bisides the
tenth part of euery seruauntes wages, the tenth part of the wolle, milke,
hony, waxe, chese, and butter. Ye and they loke so narowly vppon
theyre proufittes that the poore wyues must be countable to theym of
30 euery tenth eg or elles she gettith not her ryghtes at ester, shalbe taken
as an heretike. Hereto haue they theire foure offering daies. Whate
money pull they yn by probates of testamentes, priuy tithes, and by

---

4 *Foxe sidenote:* A libell called the supplication of beggars   18 *Foxe sidenote:* Strong,
valiant, sturdy & idle beggars   27 *Foxe sidenote:* More then the third part of the realme
in the spiritual mens hands

mennes offeringes to theyre pilgremages, and at theyre first masses? Euery man and childe that is buried must pay sumwhat for masses and diriges to be song for him or elles they will accuse the dedes frendes and executours of heresie. Whate money get they by mortuaries, by hearing of confessions (and yet they wil kepe therof no counceyle) by halowing of churches, altares, superaltares, chapelles and belles, by cursing of men and absoluing theim agein for money? What a multitude of money gather the pardoners in a yere? Howe moche money get the Somners by extorcion yn a yere, by assityng the people to the commissaries court and afterward releasing thapparaunce for money? Finally, the infinite nombre of begging freres whate get they yn a yere? Here if it please your grace to marke ye shall se a thing farre out of ioynt. There are withyn youre realme of Englond .lij. thousand parisshe churches. And this stonding that there be but tenne houshouldes yn euery parisshe yet are there fiue hundreth thousand and twenty thousand houshouldes. And of euery of these houshouldes hath euery of the fiue ordres of freres a peny a quarter for euery ordre, that is for all the fiue ordres fiue pens a quarter for euery house. That is for all [2v] the fiue ordres .xx. d. a yere of euery house. Summa fiue hundreth thousand and twenty thousand quarters of angels. That is .cclx. thousand half angels. Summa .cxxx. thousand angels. Summa totalis .xliij. thousand poundes and .cccxxxiij. li. vi. s. viij. d. sterling: whereof not foure hundreth yeres passed they had not one peny. Oh greuous and peynfull exactions thus yerely to be paied. From the whiche the people of your nobill predecessours the kinges of the auncient Britons euer stode fre. And this wil they haue or els they wil procure him that will

---

12 *Foxe sidenote:* Peraduenture the common count of the parishes of England, among men, and in Mappes of the olde time so went. And albeit the sayd Parishes do not amount now to the same rate of 52000 yet neuertheless the number (no doubt) is great, and therefore the quarterage of the Friers canne not be litle, but riseth to a great pennye through the Realme. Whereupon the scope of this mans reason soundeth to good purpose. For althoughe he hit not perfectly on the iust summes, yet it cannot be denyed, but the Fryers had very much, and much more, then they deserued. Agayne, neyther can it be denyed, but the more they had, the lesse redounded to the impotent needy beggars in deede. And what reason is it, that such valiaunt beggars, whiche may worke, & yet will nedes be idle, should reape any peece of the crop, whiche beare no burden of the haruest, but wilfully do sit idle, & serue no vse necessary in the common wealth 19 *Foxe sidenote:* Admitte the summa totalis came not to so much, yet it came to more then the Friers deserued, which coulde well worke & would not, & would needes begge, & needed not, wherof read herein the storye of Armathanus 23 *Foxe sidenote:* Oh greuous, &c. these wordes, sayth M. More, the soules themselues did heare euen into Purgatory. Belyke M. More himselfe stoode behinde Purgatorye doore the same time, or els how could he tell, that the soules did heare hym?

not giue it theim to be taken as an heretike. Whate tiraunt euer oppressed the people like this cruell and vengeable generacion? Whate
subiectes shall be abill to helpe theire prince that be after this facion
yerely polled? Whate good christen people can be abill to socoure vs
5   pore lepres, blinde, sore, and lame, that be thus yerely oppressed? Is it
any merueille that youre people so compleine of pouertie? Is it any
merueile that the taxes, fiftenes and subsidies that your grace most
tenderly of great compassion hath taken emong your people to defend
theim from the thretened ruine of theire comon welth haue bin so
10 sloughtfully, ye painfully leuied? Seing that almost the vtmost peny
that mought haue bin leuied hath ben gathered bifore yerely by this
rauinous cruell and insatiabill generacion. The danes nether the saxons yn the time of the auncient Britons shulde neuer haue ben abill to
haue brought theire armies from so farre hither ynto your lond to haue
15 conquered it if they had had at that time suche a sort of idell glotons to
finde at home. The nobill king Arthur had neuer ben abill to haue
caried his armie to the fote of the mountaines to resist the coming
downe of lucius the Emperoure if suche yerely exactions had ben taken
of his people. The grekes had neuer ben [3] abill to haue so long
20 continued at the siege of Troie if they had had at home suche an idell
sort of cormorauntes to finde. The auncient Romains had neuer ben
abil to haue put all the hole worlde vnder theyre obeisaunce if theyre
people had byn thus yerely oppressed. The Turke nowe yn youre tyme
shulde neuer be abill to get so moche grounde of cristendome if he had
25 yn his empire suche a sort of locustes to deuoure his substaunce. Ley
then these sommes to the forseid therd part of the possessions of the
realme that ye may se whether it drawe nighe vnto the half of the hole
substaunce of the realme or not, so shall ye finde that it draweth ferre
aboue. Nowe let vs then compare the nombre of this vnkind idell sort
30 vnto the nombre of the laye people and we shall se whether it be
indifferently shifted or not that they shuld haue half. Compare theim
to the nombre of men, so are they not the .C. person. Compare theim
to men wimen and children, than are they not the .CCCC. parson yn
nombre. One part therfore yn foure hundreth partes deuided were to
35 moche for theim except they did laboure. Whate an vnequal burthen is
it that they haue half with the multitude and are not the .CCCC. parson

---

16 *Foxe sidenote:* He meaneth all this onely of idle Fryers   29 *Foxe sidenote:* An vnequal
diuision that the Fryers should haue halfe with the multitude, they being not the 4.
hundreth person of the number

of theire nombre? Whate tongue is abill to tell that euer there was eny comon welth so sore oppressed sins the worlde first began?

And whate do al these gredy sort of sturdy idell holy theues with these yerely exactions that they take of the people? Truely nothing but exempt theim silues from thobedience of your grace. Nothing but translate all rule power lordishippe auctorite obedience and dignite from your grace vnto theim. Nothing but that all your subiectes shulde fall ynto disobedience and rebellion ageinst your grace and be vnder [3v] theym. As they did vnto your nobill predecessour king Iohn: whiche forbicause that he wolde haue punisshed certeyn traytours that had conspired with the frenche king to haue deposed him from his crowne and dignite (emong the whiche a clerke called Stephen whome afterward ageinst the kinges will the Pope made Bisshoppe of Caunterbury was one) enterdited his Lond. For the whiche mater your most nobill realme wrongfully (alas for shame) hath stond tributary (not vnto any kind temporall prince, but vnto a cruell deuelisshe bloudsupper dronken in the bloude of the sayntes and marters of christ) euersins. Here were an holy sort of prelates that thus cruelly coude punisshe suche a rightuous kinge, all his realme, and succession for doing right.

Here were a charitable sort of holy men that coude thus enterdite an hole realme, and plucke awey thobedience of the people from theyre naturall liege lorde and kinge, for none other cause but for his rightuousnesse. Here were a blissed sort not of meke herdes but of bloudsuppers that coude set the frenche king vppon suche a rightuous prince to cause hym to lose his crowne and dignite, to make effusion of the bloude of his people, oneles this good and blissed king of greate compassion, more fearing and lamenting the sheding of the bloude of his people then the losse of his crowne and dignite agaynst all right and conscience, had submitted him silf vnto theym. O case most horrible that euer so nobill a king, Realme, and succession shulde thus be made to stoupe to suche a sort of bloudsuppers. Where was his swerde, power, crowne, and dignite become wherby he mought haue done iustice yn this maner? where was their obedience become that shuld haue byn subiect vnder his highe power yn this mater? Ye where [4] was the obedience of all his subiectes become that for mainteinaunce of the

5

10

15

20

25

30

35

---

10 *Foxe sidenote:* The rule of kinges empayred by the Popes Clergye   27 *Foxe sidenote:*
K. Iohn submitted himselfe vnto the Pope, read before

comon welth shulde haue holpen him manfully to haue resisted these
bloudsuppers to the shedinge of theyre bloude? Was not all to gither by
theyre polycy translated from this good king vnto theim? Ye and what
do they more? Truely nothing but applie theym silues by all the
5   sleyghtes they may to haue to do with euery mannes wife, euery
mannes doughter and euery mannes mayde, that cukkoldrie and
baudrie shulde reigne ouer all emong your subiectes, that noman
shulde knowe his owne childe, that theyre bastardes might enherite the
possessions of euery man to put the right begotten children clere be-
10 side theire inheritaunce yn subuersion of all estates and godly ordre.
These be they that by theire absteyning from mariage do let the generation of the people wherby all the realme at length if it shulde be
continued shall be made desert and inhabitable.
     These be they that haue made an hundreth thousand ydell hores yn
15 your realme whiche wolde haue gotten theyre lyuing honestly, yn the
swete of theyre faces, had not theyre superfluous rychesse illected
theym to vnclene lust and ydelnesse. These be they that corrupt the
hole generation of mankind yn your realme, that catche the pokkes of
one woman and bere theym to an other, that be brent wyth one woman,
20 and bere it to an other, that catche the lepry of one woman, and bere it
to an other, ye some one of theym shall bost emong his felawes that he
hath medled with an hundreth wymen. These be they that when they
haue ones drawen mennes wiues to suche incontinency spende awey
theire husbondes goodes, make the wimen to runne awey from theire
25 husbondes, ye, rynne awey them silues both with wif and goodes, bring
[4v] both man wife and children to ydelnesse theft and beggeri. Ye who
is abill to nombre the greate and brode botomles occean see full of
euilles that this mischeuous and sinful generacion may laufully bring
vppon vs vnponisshed? Where is youre swerde, power, crowne, and
30 dignite, become that shuld punisshe (by punisshement of deth euen as
other men are punisshed) the felonies, rapes, murdres, and treasons
committed by this sinfull generacion? Where is theire obedience become that shulde be vnder your hyghe power yn this mater? Ys not all
to gither translated and exempt from your grace vnto theim? Yes
truely. Whate an infinite nombre of people might haue ben encreased

3 *Foxe sidenote:* If this be not true in the whole, I would the greatest parte were not suche
14 *Foxe sidenote:* 100000, idle whores made in England by the Popes Clergye   35 *Foxe
sidenote:* The realme of England is diminished & decaied by the number of 200000
persons at least, or els replenished with so many whores & whoremaisters, by restraining
of marriage from priestes, Monkes, Friers, Nunnes, Colleges, Hospitalles, Beadmen, &
such like orders within the realme of England. The increase of which number might be
recouered, and the realme more peopled, and also Gods Commaundements better
kepte, if these vowes of bondage were broken, & matrimony permitted free to all men

to haue peopled the realme if these sort of folke had ben maried like other men. Whate breche of matrimonie is there brought yn by theim? suche truely as was neuer sins the worlde began emong the hole multitude of the hethen.

Who is she that wil set her hondes to worke to get .iij. d. a day and may haue at lest .xx. d. a day to slepe an houre with a frere, a monke, or a prest? What is he that wolde laboure for a grote a day and may haue at lest .xij. d. a day to be baude to a prest, a monke, or a frere? Whate a sort are there of theime that mari prestes souereigne ladies but to cloke the prestes yncontinency and that they may haue a liuing of the prest theime silues for theire laboure? Howe many thousandes doth suche lubricite bring to beggery theft and idelnesse whiche shuld haue kept theire good name and haue set theim silues to worke had not ben this excesse treasure of the spiritualtie? Whate honest man dare take any man or woman in his seruice that hath ben at suche a scole with a spiritual man? Oh the greuous shipwrak of the comon welth, whiche yn auncient time bifore the coming yn of these rauinous wolues [5] was so prosperous: that then there were but fewe theues: ye theft was at that tyme so rare that Cesar was not compellid to make penalite of deth vppon felony as your grace may well perceyue yn his institutes. There was also at that tyme but fewe pore people and yet they did not begge but there was giuen theim ynough vnaxed, for there was at that time none of these rauinous wolues to axe it from theim as it apperith yn the actes of thappostles. Is it any merueill though there be nowe so many beggers, theues, and ydell people? Nay truely.

Whate remedy: make lawes ageynst theim. I am yn doubt whether ye be able: Are they not stronger in your owne parliament house then your silfe? Whate a nombre of Bisshopes, abbotes, and priours are lordes of your parliament? are not all the lerned men in your realme in fee with theim to speake yn your parliament house for theim ageinst your crowne, dignite, and comon welth of your realme, a fewe of youre owne lerned counsell onely excepted? Whate lawe can be made ageinst theim that may be aduaylable? Who is he (though he be greued never so sore) for the murdre of his auncestre, rauisshement of his wyfe, of his doughter, robbery, trespas, maiheme, dette, or eny other offence

---

11 *Foxe sidenote:* Priestes and Doues make foule houses   16 *Foxe sidenote:* The Popes clergy a shipwracke to all common wealthes   22 *Foxe sidenote:* The cause of so many beggars, theeues and idle people in England   27 *Foxe sidenote:* The popes clergy stronger in Parliamente, then Princes, as hath appeared by their cruell lawes against the poore Gospellers   34 *Foxe sidenote:* No lawe nor remedye against the clergie

dare ley it to theyre charge by any wey of accion, and if he do then is he by and by by theyre wilynesse accused of heresie. Ye they will so handle him or he passe that except he will bere a fagot for theyre pleasure he shal be excommunicate and then be all his accions dasshed. So captyue

5 are your lawes vnto theym that no man that they lyst to excommunicat may be admitted to sue any accion in any of your courtes. If eny man yn your sessions dare be so hardy to endyte a prest of eny suche cryme, he hath or the yere go out suche a yoke of heresye leyd in his necke that it maketh him wisshe [₅v] that he had not done it. Your grace may se

10 whate a worke there is in London, howe the bisshoppe rageth for endyting of certayn curates of extorcion and incontinency the last yere in the warmoll quest. Had not Richard hunne commenced accyon of premunire ageinst a prest he had bin yet a lyue and none eretik at all but an honest man.

15 Dyd not dyuers of your noble progenitours seynge theyre crowne and dignite runne ynto ruyne and to be thus craftely translated ynto the hondes of this myscheuous generacyon make dyuers statutes for the reformacyon therof, emong whiche the statute of mortmayne was one? to theintent that after that tyme they shulde haue no more gyuen

20 vnto theim. But whate avayled it? Haue they not gotten ynto theyre hondes more londes sins then eny duke yn ynglond hath, the statute notwithstonding? Ye haue they not for all that translated ynto theyre hondes from your grace half your kyngdome thoroughly? The hole name as reason is for the auncientie of your kyngdome whiche was

25 bifore theyrs and out of the whiche theyrs is growen onely abiding with your grace? and of one kyngdome made tweyne: the spirituall kyngdome (as they call it) for they wyll be named first, and your temporall kingdome. And whiche of these .ij. kingdomes suppose ye is like to ouergrowe the other, ye to put the other clere out of memory? Truely

30 the kingdome of the bloudsuppers for to theym is giuen daily out of your kingdome. And that that is ones gyuen theim comith neuer from theim agein. Suche lawes haue they that none of theim may neither gyue nor sell nothing. Whate lawe can be made so strong ageinst theim that they other with money or elles with other policy will not

35 breake and set at nought? Whate kingdome can endure that euer gy[₆]uith thus from him and receyueth nothing agein? O howe all the

---

4 *Foxe sidenote:* All lawes and actione captiue to the clergy men 9 *Foxe sidenote:* Of Richard Hunne read before pag. 806 15 *Foxe sidenote:* The statute of Mortmayne
22 *Foxe sidenote:* Halfe the profite of the realme in the clergies handes

substaunce of your Realme forthwith, your swerde, power, crowne, dignite, and obedience of your people, rynneth hedlong ynto the insaciabill whyrlepole of these gredi goulafres to be swalowed and devoured.

Nether haue they eny other coloure to gather these yerely exaccions 5 ynto theyre hondes but that they sey they pray for vs to God to delyuer our soules out of the paynes of purgatori without whose prayer they sey or at lest without the popes pardon we coude neuer be deliuered thens, whiche if it be true then is it good reason that we gyue theim all these thinges all were it C times as moche. But there be many men of 10 greate litterature and iudgement that for the love they haue vnto the trouth and vnto the comen welth haue not feared to put theim silf ynto the greatest infamie that may be, in abiection of all the world, ye yn perill of deth to declare theyre oppinion in this matter, whiche is that there is no purgatory but that it is a thing inuented by the couitousnesse 15 of the spiritualtie onely to translate all kingdomes from other princes vnto theim and that there is not one word spoken of hit in al holy scripture. They sey also that if there were a purgatory, and also if that the pope with his pardons for money may deliuer one soule thens: he may deliuer him aswel without money: if he may deliuer one, he may 20 deliuer a thousand: yf he may deliuer a thousand he may deliuer theim all, and so destroy purgatory. And then is he a cruell tyraunt without all charite if he kepe theim there in pryson and in paine till men will giue him money.

Lyke wyse saie they of all the hole sort of the spiritueltie that if they 25 will not pray for no man but for theim that gyue theim money they are tyrauntes and lakke charite, [₆v] and suffer those soules to be punisshed and payned vncheritably for lacke of theyre prayers. These sort of folkes they call heretikes, these they burne, these they rage ageinst, put to open shame and make theim bere fagottes. But whether 30 they be heretikes or no, well I wote that this purgatory and the Popes pardons is all the cause of translacion of your kingdome so fast into

5 *Foxe sidenote:* The most good that the Popes clergye doth in England is to pray mens soules out of Purgatorye   14 *Foxe sidenote:* Purgatory denyed   25 *Foxe sidenote:* If the Pope may deliuer soules out of Purgatory for money, hee may then as well deliuer them without money, as it pleased him.

Agayne, if he deliuer one, he can deliuer a thousand, if he can deliuer a thousand, he can deliuer all, and so make a gaile deliuerie, and a cleane dispatch of all Purgatorie, if hee woulde: and if he will not when he may, then is there no charitye in him.

their hondes wherfore it is manifest it can not be of christ, for he gaue
more to the temporall kingdome, he hym silfe paid tribute to Cesar, he
toke nothing from hym but taught that the highe powers shuld be
alweys obeid, ye he him silf (although he were most fre lorde of all and
innocent) was obedient vnto the highe powers vnto deth. This is the
great scabbe why they will not let the newe testament go a brode yn
your moder tong lest men shulde espie that they by theyre cloked
ypochrisi do translate thus fast your kingdome into theyre hondes, that
they are not obedient vnto your highe power, that they are cruell,
vnclene, vnmerciful, and ypochrites, that thei seke not the honour of
Christ but their owne, that remission of sinnes are not giuen by the
popes pardon, but by Christ, for the sure feith and trust that we haue in
him. Here may your grace well perceyue that except ye suffer theyre
ypochrisie to be disclosed all is like to runne ynto theire hondes and as
long as it is couered so long shall it seme to euery man to be a greate
ympiete not to gyue theim. For this I am sure your grace thinketh (as
the truth is) I am as good a man as my father, whye may I not aswell
gyue theim as moche as my father did. And of this mynd I am sure are
all the loordes knightes squirs gentilmen and yemen in englond, ye and
vntill it be disclosed all your people will thinke that your statute of
mortmayne was never made with no good conscience, seing that it
taketh a [7] wey the liberte of your people in that they may not as
laufully by theire soules out of purgatory by gyuing to the spiritualte as
their predecessours did in tymes passed.

Wherfore if ye will eschewe the ruyne of your crowne and dignite let
theire ypocrisye be vttered and that shalbe more spedfull in this mater
then all the lawes that may be made be they never so stronge. For to
make a lawe for to punisshe eny offender except it were more for to
giue other men an ensample to beware to committe suche like offence,
whate shuld yt avayle? Did not doctour Alyn most presumptuously
nowe yn your tyme agaynst all his allegiaunce all that ever he coude to
pull from you the knowlege of suche plees as long vnto your hyghe
courtes vnto an other court in derogacion of your crowne and dignite?
Did not also doctor Horsey and his complices most heynously as all the

---

1 *Foxe sidenote:* Christ submitted himselfe vnder temporall gouuermente. The cause
touched, why the Popes clergy will not let the new Testament goe abroad in the mother
tongue   15 *Foxe sidenote:* M. More here playeth the cauiller, noting the authour of this
supplication to desire leaue to raile of the whole clergye, as though the hipocrisie of ihe
[*sic*] Friers coulde not otherwise be disclosed without railing of the Whole clergye   30
Foxe sidenote: Of Doctour Alen the Cardinalls Chauncellour read before, pag. 986. Of this
Doct. Horsey, the Bish. of Londons Chauncellour, read before pag. 807

world knoweth murdre in pryson that honest marchaunt Richard
hunne? For that he sued your writ of premunire against a prest that
wrongfully held him in ple in a spiritual court for a mater wherof the
knowlege belonged vnto your hyghe courtes. And whate punisshement was there done that eny man may take example of to beware of   5
lyke offence? truely none but that the one payd fiue hundreth poundes
(as it is said to the bildinge of your sterre chamber) and when that
payment was ones passed the capteyns of his kingdome (bicause he
faught so manfully ageynst your crowne and dignite) haue heped to
him benefice vpon benefice so that he is rewarded tenne tymes as   10
moche. The other as it is seid payde six hundreth poundes for him
and his complices whiche forbicause that he had lyke wise faught so
manfully ageynst your crowne and dignite was ymmediately (as he had
opteyned your most gracyous pardon) promoted by the [7v] capiteynes
of his kingdome with benefice vpon benefice to the value of .iiij. tymes   15
as moche. Who can take example of this punisshement to be ware of
suche like offence? Who is he of theyre kingdome that will not rather
take courage to committe lyke offence seying the promocions that fill to
this men for theyre so offending? So weke and blunt is your swerde to
strike at one of the offenders of this croked and peruers generacyon.   20
    And this is by the reason that the chief instrument of your lawe ye the
chief of your counsell and he whiche hath youre swerde in his honde to
whome also all the other instrumentes are obedient is alweys a spirituell
man whiche hath euer suche an inordinate loue vnto his owne kingdome that he will mainteyn that, though all the temporall kingdoms   25
and comon welth of the worlde shulde therfore vtterly be vndone.
Here leue we out the gretest mater of all lest that we declaring suche an
horrible carayn of euyll ageinst the ministres of iniquite shulde seme to
declare the one onely faute or rather the ignoraunce of oure best
beloued ministre of rightousnesse whiche is to be hid till he may be   30
lerned by these small enormitees that we haue spoken of to knowe it
pleynly him silf. But whate remedy to releue vs your poore sike lame

---

10 *Foxe sidenote:* IO. tymes, that is, 10. times as much as he had in benefices before, & not
as he payde to the king. And althoughe these murtherers of Hunne were not recompensed with 10. times, or withe 4. tymes as muche (which More denieth) yet can he neuer
be able to denie the substaunce of the story, that is, that Hunne by these was broughte
hys death, & that they being put to their fines, wer afterward sufficiently recompensed
with benefices vpon benefices   21 *Foxe sidenote:* Unconuenient for a spirituall man to
be Lord Chauncellour   27 *Foxe sidenote:* More expoundeth this to meane the abuse of
the sacrament of the altar

and sore bedemen? To make many hospitals for the relief of the poore
people? Nay truely. The moo the worse, for euer the fatte of the hole
foundacion hangeth on the prestes berdes. Dyuers of your noble predecessours, kinges of this realme, haue gyuen londes to monasteries to
5 giue a certein somme of money yerely to the poore people wherof for
the aunciente of the tyme they giue neuer one peny. They haue lyke
wise giuen to them to haue a certeyn masses said daily for theim wherof
they [8] sey neuer one. If the Abbot of westminster shulde sing euery
day as many masses for his founders as he is bounde to do by his
10 foundacion, .M. monkes were to fewe. Wherfore if your grace will
bilde a sure hospitall that neuer shall faile to releue vs all your poore
bedemen, so take from theim all these thynges. Set these sturdy lobies a
brode in the world to get theim wiues of theire owne, to get theire
liuing with their laboure in the swete of theire faces according to the
15 commaundement of god .Gene. iij. to gyue other idell people by theire
example occasion to go to laboure. Tye these holy idell theues to the
cartes to be whipped naked about euery market towne til they will fall
to laboure that they by theyre importunate begging take not awey the
almesse that the good christen people wolde giue vnto vs sore impotent
20 miserable people your bedemen. Then shal aswell the nombre of oure
forsaid monstruous sort as of the baudes, hores, theues, and idell
people decreace. Then shall these great yerely exaccions cease. Then
shall not youre swerde, power, crowne, dignite, and obedience of your
people, be translated from you. Then shall you haue full obedience of
25 your people. Then shall the idell people be set to worke. Then shall
matrimony be moche better kept. Then shall the generation of your
people be encreased. Then shall your comons encrease in richesse.
Then shall the gospel be preached. Then shall none begge oure almesse from vs. Then shal we haue ynough and more then shall suffice
30· vs, whiche shall be the best hospitall that euer was founded for vs. Then
shall we daily pray to god for your most noble estate long to endure.

Domine saluum fac regem.

---

2 *Foxe sidenote:* Priestes turne the Hospitals to their owne profite   16 *Foxe sidenote:* What
wealth and goodness commeth to the realme, by putting out Monkes, Fryers, and
Chauntries

APPENDIX C

A Christen Sentence

BY JOHN FRITH

APPENDIX C

A Christen Sentence

The text of Frith's first treatise on the eucharist, to which More replied in his *Letter against Frith,* is here reprinted from a microfilm of the Bodleian copy of an edition printed by Richard Wyer in London about 1548 (*STC*² 5190).[1] Germain Marc' hadour first pointed out that Wyer's two editions printed about 1548 represent Frith's treatise,[2] of which no extant manuscript is known. Though More does not quote the treatise *in extenso,* the correspondence between the printed editions and More's reply is very full and close; there can be little doubt that they present Frith's text with substantial accuracy. Moreover, in *A Boke . . . answeringe vnto M mores lettur* (1533; *STC* 11381; Hume, no. 30), sigs. A₃v–A₄, Frith quotes a passage from his first treatise that agrees exactly with the opening of *A Christian Sentence* (428/11–42).

In this reprint abbreviations have been expanded (except for "&," "yᵉ," and "yᵗ"). The punctuation and capitalization have been silently corrected in a few places to make the sense clearer. A cross between two pointing hands has been omitted after "Amen" (433/26). The pilcrow on the title page and the two pilcrows in the colophon have also been omitted. The puzzling phrase "Contra Parisienses, de contemptu mundi" above the colophon (433/27–28) may derive from a manuscript in which Frith's treatise was followed by a work with some such title or catchword.

---

[1]Richard Wyer printed another edition about the same time (*STC*² 5190.3). Nati Krivatsy of the Folger Library, which has copies of both editions, has informed us that not only the title pages but also the sheets of *STC*² 5190.3 differ from those of *STC*² 5190, but which edition is prior is still unknown.

[2]Marc'hadour, *La Bible,* pp. 298, 302.

A christen sen-
tence and true iudgement
of the moste honora-
ble Sacrament
of Christes bo-
dy & bloude
declared
both
by the auctorite of the
holy Scriptures
and the aun-
cient Doc-
tores.

Very necessary to be redde in this
tyme of all the faythfull. [A₁v]

Concernynge the dyscorde and varyaunce that is spronge and daylye
increaseth of the sacrament of vnitie and vnderstandynge of yᵉ wordes
of our sauyour christ iesu, that no man shulde be disquieted or troubled in conscience, me thought it necessarye to wryte a shorte instruc-
5   tion wherin by gods grace I shall so pacyfye both the parties that
without contencion they shall admytte eche other into brotherly loue
according to christes exhortacion, whiche wolde haue vs to loue eche
other as he hath loued vs and wolde haue loue to be the token of his
very disciples and faythfull folowers. [A₂]

10   The fyrste Chapter proueth that it is none article of our fayth necessarye to saluacion. Fyrst we must all acknowleg that it is none article of
our fayth whiche can saue vs neyther which we are bound to beleue
vnder the payne of eternall dampnacion, for yf I shulde beleue yᵗ his
verye naturall body both fleshe & bloude were materyally in the breade
15 & wyne, that shulde not saue me seynge many beleue that, & receyue it
to theyre dampnacion. For it is not his presence in the bread that can
saue me, but his presence in my harte thorowe fayth in his bloud, which
hath washed out my synnes and pacefied the Fathers wrathe [A₂v]
towardes me. And agayne yf I do not beleue yᵗ his bodely presence is in
20 the breade and wyne that shall not dampne me. For it is not his absence
out of the breade that can dampne me, but the absence out of my hart
thorowe vnbelefe. now yf they wolde here obiecte yᵗ thoughe it be truth
that yᵉ absence out of the bread of it selfe could not dampne vs, yet are
we bounde to beleue it because of godes worde, which who beleueth
25 not as moche as in hym is, he maketh god a lyar. And therfor of an
obstinate mynde not to beleue his wordes may be an occasion of dampnacion. To this we may answere yᵗ we beleue goddes worde and knowledge that it is true, but in this we dissente whether it be true in the sence
that we take it in, or in yᵉ sence that ye take [A₃] it in, And we say agayne
30 yᵗ though ye haue as it appeareth vnto you the euident wordes of
Christ, and therfore consyst in the barke of the letter, yet are we compelled by conferryng of the scriptures togither to enter within the letter
and to searche out the mynde of our sauiour whiche spake the wordes,
and we saye thyrdly that we do it not of an obstinat mynde for he that
35 defendeth a thynge obstinately whether it be true or false, is euer to be
reprehended but we do it to satisfie oure consciences whiche are compelled by other places of Scripture reasons and doctors so to iudge of it
And euen so ought you to iudge of your parte and to defende your
sentences (not of an obstinacy for then ye offende) but for to satysfie
40 your consciences as touching [A₃v] the Scriptures whiche cause you so
to take it. And so ought nether parte to dispise the other, for eche
seketh the glory of God, & the true vnderstandynge of the scripture.

The seconde Chapter sheweth the reason and scriptures whiche
cause vs otherwyse to take it then ye common multitud at this tyme do.
Regarde we therfore the precepte of our mayster christ euer norishyng
brotherly loue in peace and vnitie, & yf ye can not otherwyse beare vs,
yet admytte vs as weake brethern. And as touchynge the causes which   5
compell vs so to iudge, we knowe y^t Christ before his passion had a
naturall body, which he receyued of the vyr[A$_4$]gyn Mary thorow the
power of y^e holy ghost. This body we say was natural and not phantasticall, but had the qualyties of an other body in all thynges saue
synne, nether was it more possible for that naturall body so beyng   10
mortal and not gloryfied to be in dyuers places at once, then for myne.
So that when we heare these wordes spoken, this is my body, and se that
they were spoken before his body was gloryfied, knowyng also that a
natural body vngloryfied can not be in many places at once, and that yf
these wordes were vnderstanden as they sounde he shuld haue ben at   15
y^e least in .xii. or .xiii. places at once in his Disciples mouthes, and
syttynge at the table with them, It causeth vs to loke better vpon it, and
so to search out the pure vnderstandying[A$_4$v]. Nowe yf ye obiect that
he myght be in diuers places at once, Then may we answere by the
auctorytie of saynt Austen whiche sayth, Corpus in quo resurrexit in   20
vno loco esse oporteth. His body wherin he rose must be in one place,
and after determyneth that it contynueth in heauen, and shall so do
vntyll the tyme that he shall come to iudge both quycke & deade. Nowe
seyng saynt Austen sayth that his body (wherin he rose must be in one
place which was his glorified body) then may we wel say that his body   25
not gloryfied can not be in many places at once. And so must it nedes
folowe that he can not be there in fleshe & bloude. Besydes that ye can
shewe no reason why he shulde be in many places at once, and not in
all, but in all places at once he can [A$_5$] not be, wherfore we must
conclude that he can not be in many places at once. If ye say that he   30
maye be in all places at once because he is also God, we answere that the
angel at the sepulchre sayd. Surrexit non est hic .i. He is rysen, and is
not here. Wherfore yf ye say that he is in all places, then make ye the
Angell a lyar. Furthermore what tyme he ascended the scripture testi-
fieth that a cloude toke hym out of theyr syght, & that two men stode by   35
the Disciples and sayd ye men of Galiley why stande ye gasynge vp into
heauen? This same Iesus whiche is taken vp from you into heauen shall
so come euen as you haue sene hym go into heauen. Here we thynke
verily that Christ ment good earnest. And y^t in dede he was taken vp
from them into heauen [A$_5$v] as the Angell testyfieth, & y^t from thense   40
he shall come to iudge the quicke and dead, as our Crede teacheth.
Nowe yf ye can perswade your owne consciences and vnderstande the
Scriptures y^t he playde boo pype with his Disciples, and dyd but make

hym selfe inuisible onely, than may ye take your pleasures, for Christe
teacheth vs not to be contentious.

The thyrde Chaptre declareth why Christe vseth suche maner of
speache, and the pure vnderstandynge of Christes wordes. If ye wolde
5   then axe vs why christ shulde so saye: & vse these playne wordes yf he
wolde that it shulde be spiritually vnder[A₆]stande, to this we answere
that it is the maner both of christ and his scriptures so to speake for
dyuers consyderacions: Christe calleth hymselfe a very vyne & his
disciples vyne braunches wherwith he hath so perfectly set out his
10 power, that a thousande wordes coulde not expresse hym so lyuely. For
where he sayeth I am a very vyne there declareth he sensyble that as
verely as the braunches of a naturall vyne can brynge forth no frute
except they contynewe in the vyne, euen so can his disciples do nothyng
except they abyde in hym. Now where he sayth that he is a very vyne, he
15 wolde not haue you bounde to beleue for an artycle of the fayth, that he
were a naturall vyne. But had leuer that ye vnderstande it mistically
that there is a [A₆v] certein propertie in this vine which doth so lyuely
expresse hym that he can put no difference (for yᵗ poynte) betwene a
vine & hym selfe but calleth hym selfe euen a very vyne. We vse it also in
20 common speache. If a man se his neyghboures horse hauynge a certen
properte which his horse hath, then wyll he say this is my horse vp and
downe, not meanynge that the substaunce of his neyghbours is his own
horse, but that there is a certaine propertie in his neyghbours, whiche is
so lyke his that they coulde not decerne the one from the other.
25 Lykewyse Christe calleth hym selfe a doore, not that he hym self is a
material doore, but bycause the dore hath a certen propertie which
doth well describe hym. For as no man can come within a strong holde
but [A₇] by the doore, Euen so can no man come vnto the father but
thorow Christ, and for this propertie doth he call hym selfe a doore.
30 And this doth he to expresse euen to our outwarde senses what powre
he hath and what profyte commeth to vs thorowe hym And euen so in
this Sacrament he calleth the breade his body and the wyne his bloude
not that the breade and wyne are his naturall fleshe and bloude, but for
certayne properties whiche are in them.
35   For he toke the bread and brake it and commaunded them to eate it,
sayng this is my body which shall be gyuen for you. This do in remembraunce of me. As thoughe he shuld haue sayd these wordes.
Nowe is the tyme come yᵗ I muste departe from you. Neuerthelesse I
shall [A₇v] gyue you suche a perfyct token before I go, that ye shall not
40 doubte but that I am yours. Loo I shall be put to death and my body
broken euen as ye se this bread broken. Neuertheles be ye not dis-
mayde. Take this bread, and eate it, and swalow it downe into your

belyes for this breade shall be vnto you euen my very body which shall
be gyuen for you. For as verely as ye ar partakers of this bread which by
youre senses ye knowe ye haue within you, euen as surely shall ye be
partakers of my bodye whiche shall be crucyfied for you, thoughe it
were done a thousande myle from you, wherfor ye nede not to doubt 5
nor feare in myne absence, seynge that the frute of my death shall be as
verelye youres, as this breade whiche ye haue within you, but yf [A₈] ye
shuld fal into any mystrust, then breke ye amonge youre selues this
bread, & eate it in the remembraunce of me, that it maye certyfie euen
your senses yᵗ you are partakers of my body thorowe fayth, as verely as 10
ye are partakers of this bread thorowe eatynge of it.

The fourth Chapter noteth an other maner of speache & proueth
our exposytion by a proper simylytude of the brydgrome & bryde. This
is the pure vnderstandyng of Christes wordes, whiche manye auc-
toryties cause vs to receyue, and also that it is the common phrase of yᵉ 15
scripture no man can deny, whiche is but meanelye exercysed in it. We
rede yᵗ Iacob [A₈v] buylded an alter, & called it God, the god of Israell,
we rede also yᵗ Iacob wrastled with an angell & called the place
Pemell .i. The face of God, we reade yᵗ the pasch lambe was called the
passynge by of the Lorde with infynite other of such Phrases. Howe be 20
it I thynke no man so innocent that he wolde contende and affyrme yᵗ
the very alter was the god of Israell, or yᵉ place where he wrastled to be
the verye face of God, or the naturall lambe to be the passynge by of the
Lorde, but such names are gyuen that as soone as we heare them we
myghte knowe what was ment by them. As by example he called alter 25
the god of Israell, that euen the very name it selfe shulde testyfie that it
was made to put vs in remembraunce of the very God of Israell.
Lyke[B₁]wyse the place where he wrastled was called the face of God,
that yᵉ very name it selfe myghte put vs in remembraunce that there
Iacob had wrastled with God, & had sene hym face to face. Also the 30
lambe was called pasouer or the passyng by of the lorde, that the very
name it selfe myght put vs in remembraunce that the lorde passynge by
had slayne all the fyrste begotten in Egept. And euen so to oure purpose the bread is called the bodye, that the very name it selfe, myght
put vs in remembraunce that his very body was broken for vs And is as 35
verely ours thorowe fayth as the bread is ours by eatyng of it. And
therfore added he also these wordes This do in remembraunce of me,
whiche thynge expoundeth all togyther yf we had wytte. [B₁v] If a
brydegrome whiche had promysed fayth & trouth to his bryde shulde
depart into a farre countree for necessary busynes that he hath then to 40
comfort his brydes harte he wolde saye on this maner. I must departe

into a farre countree for vrgent maters. Neuerthelesse I shal leaue you
such a token that ye shall be as sure of me, as though I were here
present with you. Take this rynge & put it on youre fynger for it is my
fayth & my trouth whiche I haue promised to kepe with you And
5   therfore kepe it in remembraunce of me. And as surely as you haue this
rynge on youre fynger, so sure may you be of me that I shall not
dyceyue you. So that yf ye shulde any thyng mystrust me, then beholde
the ryng which is my fayth and trouth, & it shall certyfye euen [B₂] your
outwarde senses that I am youres. And moche more is this trew in the
10   Sacrament, for a man may repent hym of his promes, & dyceyue his
bryde, but Christe can not repent hym of his gracious fauour, wher
with he loueth vs, he can be no lyar, nether can deceyue vs. And
therfore we nede not to doubt of his promes.

The fyfth Chapter sheweth the maner how it ought to be receued.
15   Here also muste we touche some what as concernyng the receyuyng of
it for therin are many vexed. Some be so fearfull to breake Christes
institution, whiche gaue it in both the kyndes that they wholly abstayne
& dare [B₂v] not come at it, excepte the priest wold gyue it consecrat in
both kyndes, and some there are that neuer stycke at it, but receyue
20   they wote not what hauyng no respecte vnto Christes institution. And
both are deceyued, albeit the fyrst are more to be alowed, bycause they
most sorow to breake Goddes ordinaunce. But I wyll shewe you a
meanes how ye shall euer receyue it accordyng to Gods institution,
although the priest wold withdraw it from you. Fyrste ye nede to haue
25   no respect vnto yᵉ priestes wordes which mynistreth it. For yf ye remembre for what entent Christ dyd institute the sacrament and knowe
that it was to put vs in remembraunce of his body breakynge and
bloude shedyng, & that it was done for oure wealthe, & we as sure of it
thorow [B₃] beleuynge it (accordyng to his promesse) as we are sure of
30   the breade by eatynge of it. If as I say ye remembre this thing (for which
entent onely the priest speaketh these wordes) then yf yᵉ Priest leaue
out these wordes or parte therof he can not hurte you, for ye haue
already the effecte and fynall purpose for which he shulde speake
them. And agayne yf he shuld wholy alter them yet can he not deceyue
35   you, For then are ye sure that he is a lyar. And therfore when he
bryngeth the Sacrament vnto me, I wyll consyder christes mynde &
institution & not yᵉ priestes wordes. And wyll thanke my heuenly father, saying on this maner. Blyssed be thou most dere and mercyfull
father, which of thy tender fauour and benignitie (not withstandyng
40   our greuous enor-B₃v]myties commytted against yᵉ) vouchsauedest to
send thyne owne dere and onely sone to suffre most vyle death for my

redemption. Blessed be thou Christe Iesu my lorde and sauyour, which of thyne abundaunt pytie consyderynge oure myserable estate wyllyngly toke it vpon the to haue thy moste innocent body broken and bloud shede to purge and washe me whiche am laden with iniquite. And to certyfie vs therof haste lefte vs not onely thy worde, whiche may instructe oure hartes but also a visible token to certyfie euen our outwarde senses of this great beneficte that we shuld not doubt but that thy body and frute of thy passion are oures as surely as the bread whiche by our senses we know that we haue within vs. Blessed be also that spirit of veri-[B$_4$ misnumbered B$_5$]tie, whiche is sent from God oure father thorowe our sauyour christ Iesu to lyghten our darke ignoraunces and led vs thorowe fayth into the knowledg of hym which is all veritie, strenght we besech the our fraile nature & encrease oure fayth that we may prayse God our most mercyfull Father, and Christe his sone our sauyoure and redemer, & the (with them) which arte our comforter to whom be all honour and prayse Amen.

Thus shalte thou receyue it accordynge to Christes institution & though thou se that the priest bringeth wyne vnconsecrate, yet neuer stycke at that, for as surely shall it certyfie thy consyence & outward senses though he consecrate it not (so that thou knowe what is ment therby) as though he made a thou[B$_4$v]sande blessynges ouer it, and loke what we haue spoken of the bread and euen the same mayst thou verify on the wyne. So that we nede to be no longer.

But commytte you to God desyrynge hym to open his lyght more abundauntly vnto vs all that we may walke therin praysynge hym eternally. Amen.

Contra Parisienses, de
contemptu mundi.

God saue the Kynge.

Imprynted by me
Rycharde Wyer.

Cum priuilegio
Ad imprimendum
solum.

APPENDIX D

The Story of Simon Fish
from
John Foxe's *Acts and Monuments*

APPENDIX D

The Story of Simon Fish

Almost all we know about Simon Fish derives from the account of him given in John Foxe's *Acts and Monuments* together with his reprint of Fish's *A Supplication for the Beggars*. The first edition of *Acts and Monuments* (1563) contains only the first version of how Fish's book came to the attention of Henry VIII (439/19–441/12). The 1570 edition added another version, obtained from one of Henry's footmen named Moddys. Fish may have studied at Oxford as well as Gray's Inn (A. B. Emden, *A Biographical Register of the University of Oxford A.D. 1501 to 1540,* Oxford, 1974, p. 205). He was probably the "Mr. Fyshe" who sold copies of Tyndale's English New Testament to Robert Necton and others (*LP 4/2,* 1791, no. 4030; John Strype, *Ecclesiastical Memorials,* 6 vols., Oxford, 1822, *1/2,* 63–65). In his *Apology* More reports that Fish renounced his heresies and was reconciled to the church (*CW 9,* 75/36–76/5). He died of the plague in 1531.

The copy-text of this reprint is the copy of the 1583 edition of *Acts and Monuments* (*STC* 11225) in the Beinecke Library at Yale University. All abbreviations except "&," "yᵉ," and "yᵗ" have been silently expanded. At 443/32–33 commas have been added after "grinning" and "scoffing." Foxe's marginal glosses have been italicized and inset in the text.

At 443/25–26 Fox refers to the proverbial use of *nasturtium* to mean "stimulant" (Pliny, *Natural History* 19.44.154). See also Otto, no. 1197 and Erasmus, *Adagia* 754, "Ede nasturtium" (*Opera omnia,* 2, 319). Erasmus uses *nasturtiari* to translate καρδαμίζειν.

The Story of M. Symon Fish

Before the time of M. Bilney, and the fall of the Cardinall, I should haue placed the Story of Simon Fish with the booke called the Sup-

plication of Beggars, declaring how and by what meanes it came to the kynges hand, and what effect therof folowed after, in the reformation of many thinges, especial-ly of the Clergy. But the missing of a few yeares in this matter, break-eth no great square in our story, though it be now entred here which shold haue come in six yeares before. The maner and circumstaunce of the matter is this:

After that the light of the gospell working mightely in Germany, began to spread his beames here also in England, great styrre & al-teration folowed in the harts of many: so that colored hipocrisy, and false doctrine, & paynted holynes began to be espyed more and more by the reading of Gods word. The authority of the Bishop of Rome, and ye glory of his Cardinals was not so high, but such as had [TTt₁v] fresh wits sparcled with Gods grace, began to espy Christ from Anti-christ, that is, true sincerity, from counterfait religion. In the number of whom, was the sayd M. Simon Fish, a gentleman of Grayes Inne. It happened the first yeare that this Gentleman came to London to dwel, which was about the yeare of our Lord 1525. that there was a certayne play or interlude made by one M. Roo of the same Inne gentleman, in which play partly was matter agaynst the Cardinall Wolsey. And where none durst take vpon them to play that part, which touched the sayd Cardinall, thys foresayd M. Fish tooke vpon him to do it, wherupon great displeasure ensued agaynst him, vpon the Cardinals part: In so much as he being pursued by the sayd Car-

dinall, the same night that this Tragedy was playd, was compelled of force to voyd his owne house, & so fled ouer the sea vnto Tindall: vpon occasion wherof the next yeare folowing this booke was made (being about the yeare .1527.) and so not long after in the yeare (as I suppose) 1528. was sent ouer to the Lady Anne Bulleyne, who then lay at a place not farre from the Court. Which book her brother seing in her hand, tooke it and read it, & gaue it her agayne, willing her earnestly to geue it to the king, which thing she so dyd.

This was (as I gather) about the yeare of our Lord .1528. The king

The booke of the supplication of beggars geuen to the king

after he had receiued the booke, demaunded of her who made it. Whereunto she aunswered and said, a certayne subiect of his, one Fish, who was fled out of the

5 Realme for feare of the Cardinall. After the king had kept the booke in his bosome 3. or 4. dayes, as is credibly reported, such knowledge was geuen by the kinges seruaunts, to the wife of the sayd Simon Fish, that she might boldely send for her husband, without all perill or daunger. Wherupon she therby being incouraged, came first & made

10 sute to the king for the safe returne of her husband. Who vnderstanding whose wife she was, shewed a maruellous gentle & chearefull countenance towardes her, asking where her husband was. She answered, if it like your grace, not farre of. Then sayth he, fetch him, and he shall come and goe safe without perill, & no man shall do him

15 harme, saying moreouer that he had much wrong that he was from her so long: who had bene absent nowe the space of two yeares and a halfe. In the which meane time, the Cardinall was deposed, as is aforeshewed, and M. More set in his place of the Chauncellorship.

Thus Fishes wife being emboldened by the kinges words, went im-

20 *M. Fishe brought, and gently entertayned of the king*

mediatly to her husband being lately come ouer, and lying priuily within a myle of the Courte, and brought him to the king: which appeareth to be about the yeare of our

Lord 1530. When the king saw him, and vnderstood he was the au-
25 thor of the booke, he came and embraced him with louing countenance: who after long talke: for the space of 3. or 4. houres, as they were riding together on hunting, at length dimitted him and bad him take home his wife, for she had taken great paynes for him. Who aunswered the king agayne and said, he durst not so do, for feare of
30 Syr Thomas More then Chauncellour, & Stoksley then Bishop of London. This seemeth to be about the yeare of our Lord .1530.

The king taking his signet of his finger, wylled hym to haue him

M. Fishe rescued by the king

recommended to the Lord Chauncellor, charging him not to be so hardy to worke
35 him any harme, M. Fish receiuing the

kinges signet, went and declared hys message to the Lord Chauncellour, who tooke it as sufficient for his owne discharge, but he asked him if he had any thing for the discharge of his wife: for she a litle before had by chaunce displeased the Friers, for not suffering them
40 to say theyr Gospels in Latine in her house, as they did in others vnlesse they would say it in English. Whereupon the Lord Chaun-

Syr Thomas More persecuteth M. Fishes. wife

cellor, though he had discharged the man, yet leauing not his grudge towardes the wife, the next morning sent his man for her to appeare before him: who, had it not bene for her young daughter, which then lay sicke of the plague, had bene like to come to much trouble. Of the which plague her husband,

M. Fishe dyeth of the Plague

the sayd M. Fish deceasing within halfe a yeare, she afterward maryed to one M. Iames Baynham, Syr Alexander Baynhams sonne, a worshypfull knight of glostershyre. The which foresaid M. Iames Baynham, not long after was burned, as incontinently after in the processe of this story, shall appeare.

And thus much concerning Symon Fishe the author of the booke of

The summe of the Scripture translated by M. Fyshe

beggars, who also translated a booke called the Summe of the Scripture, out of the Dutch.

Now commeth an other note of one Edmund Moddys the kinges footman, touching the same matter.

This M. Moddys being with the king in talke of religion, and of the new bookes that were come from beyond the seas, sayd if it might

M. Moddys the kinges footman

please his grace to pardon hym, & such as he would bring to his grace, he shoulde see such a booke, as was maruell to heare of. The king demaunded what they were. He sayd, two of your Marchauntes, George Elyot, & George Robinson. The king poynted a

The booke of Beggars brought to the king by George Elyot and George Robinson

time to speake with them. When they came afore his presence in a priuy closet, he demaunded what they had to say, or to shew him. One of them said y^t there was a book come to their hands, which they had there to shew his grace. When he saw it, he demaunded if any of them could read it. Yea sayd George Elyot, if it please your grace to heare it. I thought so, sayd the king, for if need were thou canst say it without booke.

The whole booke being read out, the king made a long pause, &

The kinges answere vppon the booke of beggars

then sayd, if a man should pull downe an old stone wall and begin at the lower part, the vpper part thereof might chaunce to fall vpon his head: and then he tooke the book and put it into his deske, and commaunded them vpon theyr allegiance, that they should not tell to any man, that he had seene the booke .&c. The Copy of the foresayde booke, intituled of the Beggars, here ensueth.

[*A Supplication for the Beggers* is reprinted at this point. Foxe's sidenotes to this reprint are given in Appendix B.]

5 [TTt₃] Against this booke of the Beggers aboue prefixed, being written in the time of the Cardinall, another contrary booke of supplication, was deuised and written shortly vpon

The supplication of
Purgatorye, made by
Syr Tho. More,
10 *agaynste the*
booke of beggars

the same, by one Sir Thomas More knight,
Chauncellour of the Duchy of Lancaster,
vnder the name and title of the poore sely
soules pewling out of Purgatory. In the
which booke, after that the sayd M. More
writer therof, had fyrst deuided yᵉ whole world into foure partes, that
is into heauen, hell, middle earth, and purgatory: then he makes the
15 dead mens soules by a Rhetorical *Prosopopoea* to speake out of Purgatory pynfolde, sometimes lamentably complayning, sometimes pleasauntly dalying & scoffing at the authour of the Beggers booke, sometimes scoldyng and rayling at him, calling him foole, witlesse, frantike,
an asse, a goose, a mad dog, an hereticke, & all that nought is. And no
20 maruell if these sely soules of purgatory seeme so fumish & testy. For
heat (ye know) is testy, & sone inflameth choler, but yet these Purgatory soules, must take good heed how they call a man a foole, and
hereticke so often. For if the sentence of the Gospell doth pronounce

Math. 5
25

them guilty of hell fyre, which say *fatue*,
foole: it may be doubted lest those poore
sely melancholy soules of Purgatory, calling this man a foole so oft as
they haue done, doe bring themselues therby out of purgatory fire, to
the fire of hel, by yᵗ just sentence of the ghospell: so that neither the
.5. woundes of St. Fraunces, nor all the merites of S. Dominicke, nor
30 yet of all the Friers can release them poore wretches. But yet for so
much as I doe not, nor cannot thinke, that those departed soules,
eyther would so farre ouershoote themselues if they were in purgatory, or els that ther is any such fourth place of Purgatory at all

Vtopia
35 *that is to say,*
Nusquam, no place

(vnlesse it be in M Mores Vtopia) as Mayster Mores Poeticall vayne doth imagine, I
cease therefore to burden the soules departed, and lay all the witte in maister
More the authour and contriuer of this Poeticall booke, for not keeping *Decorum personae*, as a perfect Poet

40 *A Poete*
sayeth Horace,
Reddere personae sit
conuenientia cuique

should haue done, They that geue pre-
ceptes of Arte, do note this in all Poeticall
fictions, as a special obseruation to foresee

and expresse what is conuenient for euery person, according to his
degree and condition to speake and vtter. Wherefore if it be true that
M. More sayth in the sequele of his booke, that grace & charity increaseth in them that lye in the paynes of Purgatory, then is it not
agreable, that such soules lying so long in Purgatory, should so soon   5
forget their charity, and fall a rayling in their supplication so fumishly
both against this man, with opprobrious & vnsitting termes, & also
agaynst John Badby, Richard Howndon, John Goose, Lord Cobham
and other Martirs of yᵉ Lord burned for his word: also agaynst
Luther, William Tindall, Richard Hunne and other moe, falsly bely-   10
ing the doctrine by them taught & defended: which is not like that
such charitable soules of Purgatory would euer doe, neither were it
couenient for them in that case, which in dede though theyr doctrine
were false, shoulde redound to the more encrease of theyr payne.
Agayne, where the Bishop of Rochester defineth the Aungels to be   15
ministers to Purgatory soules some will thinke peraduenture M. More
to haue missed some part of his *Decorum* in making the euill spirite of
the author & the deuill to be messenger betwene middle earth, &
Purgatory, in bringing tidings to the prisoned soules, both of the
booke, and of the name of the maker.   20

Now, as touching the maner how this deuil came into Purgatory,

M. Mores Antickes　　laughing, grinning, and gnashing his teeth,
　　　　　　　　　　　in sothe it maketh me to laugh, to see the
merye Antiques of M. More. Belike then this was some mery deuil,

Satan nasturciatur　　or else had eaten with his teeth some *Nas-*   25
　　　　　　　　　　　turcium before: which commyng into Pur-
gatory, to shewe the name of this man, could not tell his tale without
laughing. But this was (sayth he) an enmious and an enuious laughing
ioyned with grinning and gnashing of teeth. And immediatly vpon
the same, was contriued this scoffing & rayling supplication of the   30
pewling soules of Purgatory, as he himselfe doth terme them. So then
here was enmying, enuying, laughing, grinning, gnashing of teeth,
pewling, scoffing, rayling, and begging and altogether to make a very

A Blacke Sanctus　　black *Sanctus* in Purgatory. In deed we
in Purgatorye　　read in Scripture, that there shall be weep-   35
　　　　　　　　　　　ing and gnashing of teeth in hell, where
the soules and bodyes of men shalbe tormented. But who would euer
haue thought before, that the euill aungel of thys man, yᵗ made the
booke of Beggers, being a spirituall and no corporall substaunce, had
teeth to gnashe, and a mouth to grinne? But where then stood M.   40
More I meruaile all this meane while, to see the deuill laugh with hys
mouth so wide, that the soules of purgatory might see all his teeth?
Belike this was in Vtopia, where M. Mores Purgatory is founded, but

because M. More is hence departed, I leave him wyth hys mery An-
The answere of tiques. And as touching his book of Purga-
Iohn Fryth agaynst tory, which he hath left behynde, because
M. Mores purgatorye Iohn Frith hath learnedly and effectually
5   ouerthrowne the same, I will therefore referre the reader to hym, while I repayre again (the Lord willing) to
the history.

APPENDIX E

Popular Devotions Concerning Purgatory

BY GERMAIN MARC'HADOUR

APPENDIX E

Popular Devotions Concerning Purgatory

The pained surprise which More's souls express that one "shulde nede nowe to proue purgatory to crysten men" (170/13–14) stems from a long-established sense that purgatory was "an vndowted artycle" (170/16). An excellent witness to this unshaken belief, which needed only exhortation to make it grow and fructify, is a small anonymous devotional treatise, *A lytell boke . . . of Purgatorye*, printed in London by Robert Wyer a year or more before More's death.[1] Its use of verse to describe and exhort is consonant with its catechetical intent. Purgatory is defined in the terms one expects as

> a clensynge place / soules in to dwell
> That haue done synne / and haue contrycyon
> And ben in the waye / of saluacyon. [sig. A₁v]

The least pain there is greater than the greatest pain on earth, the author says, citing the Latin of a "great clerke,"[2] and then adding:

> Betwene the payne of hell / certaynly
> And betwene the payne / of Purgatorye
> Is no dyfference / but certes that one
> Shall haue an ende / and that other none. [sigs. A₁v–A₂]

The netherworld is imagined as having four levels: "hell pyt," *limbus* of

---

[1]*Here begynneth a lytell boke, that speketh of Purgatorye: & what Purgatorye is & in what place / and of the paynes that be therin / and whiche soules do abyde therin tyll they be pourged of synne / and whiche abyde not there. And for what synnes a soule goth to hell / & of the helpe that soules in purgatorye may haue of theyr frendes that be on lyue: & what pardon aueyleth to mannes soule* (London, [1534?]; *STC* 3360). The date of publication, here derived from the revised *STC*, may be somewhat earlier; see P. B. Tracy, "Robert Wyer: A Brief Analysis of His Types and a Suggested Chronology for the Output of His Press," *The Library*, 6,2 (September 1980), 293–303.

[2]The Latin reads: "Minima pena Purgatorii maior est maxima pena mundi" (sig. A₁v). The "clerke" is Augustine, who in discussing the intensity of purgatorial pains wrote: "Ita plane quamuis salui per ignem, grauior tamen erit ille ignis, quam quidquid potest homo pati in hac uita" (*Enarrationes in psalmos* 37, *CCSL* 38, 384).

unchristened children, purgatory, and *limbus patrum* (sig. A$_2$v). There is also a form of purgatory on earth in which sins are purged by a sufferer's willing acceptance of tribulation (sig A$_3$v). The author goes on to describe the seven pains of purgatory (sigs A$_3$v–B$_4$v) in terms of bodily suffering, justifying this figurative approach with the story (Luke 16:19–31) which More calls "the ryche gloton & pore nedy Lazarus" (226/30). Whether it is simply figurative to speak of Lazar and Dives as possessing finger and tongue (Luke 16:24), or whether souls have bodies of air to suffer pain, as the treatise's author suggests (sig. B$_2$), such references are, as More says, an accepted "maner of spekynge" (226/27).

Predictably we find in the treatise an echo of 1 Cor. 3:12–15: "they must brenne . . . as woode and haye . . . and stoble" (sig. B$_3$), as well as the image of the jail, with jailers provided from the lowest province of the underworld (yet less permanently present, it seems, than in More's picture): the souls are in "prysone"

> bounde / both handes & fete
> In hote brennynge fyre . . .
> Amonge foule fendes / that there haue leue
> Some tyme the soules / to tourment and greue. [sigs. B$_3$v–B$_4$]

The torments, as in Bede's *History*,[1] include storms of hail and rain (sig. B$_4$). The souls' greatest pain, however, is not of the senses, but "The moche coueytyse / that they haue to se / The swete face of God" (sig. B$_4$–B$_4$v).

No doubt for mnemonic purposes, and as a bow to the number of God's commandments, the treatise recommends ten ways of purging away, while on earth, the spots of venial sin which would otherwise burden the soul and after death lengthen its stay in purgatory. The methods offered are the use of holy water, almsgiving, fasting, housel (receiving Holy Communion), reciting the Pater Noster, general shrift, bishop's blessing, smiting upon the breast, kissing of the ground, and the last anointing (sig. C$_2$). These serve to counter the accumulation of sins into which the good man daily falls, described in the words of Prov. 24:16: "Septies in die cadit justus" (sig. C$_3$).[2] There are also four gener-

---

[1] Bede, *Historia ecclesiastica* 5.12 (*PL* 95, 248–50).

[2] The words "in die," which are not in the Vulgate but were commonly inserted into the text (perhaps from Ps. 119:164), are added also by More in the *Responsio ad Lutherum* (*CW* 5, 152/7) and in the 1529 *Dialogue Concerning Heresies* (*CW* 6, 395/24). In the more vigilant *Confutation of Tyndale's Answer* this addition is avoided (*CW* 8, 844/36–37).

al ways in which the living may help the souls already in purgatory (sigs. D_1–D_4v), summarized as "almes dede and prayers / penaunce and masse" (sig. D_4v). Coming thus to the aid of these souls is an expression of Christian solidarity:

> For they ben all / as lymmes of one bodye
> That ben in erth here / and tho in purgatorye. [sig. D_2]

The author then touches on worthily purchased indulgences or pardons granted for sin. These lie chiefly in the pope's gift, for he "bereth the Kaye" (sig. E_1). Finally, the last half-page of the "lytell boke" is devoted to listing authorities: Innocent, Augustine, "mayster Raymonde" (de Pennafort, presumably), and "Thomas Alquin . . . In a boke . . . called / Ueritas theologye" (sig. E_3).

At one point (sig. D_3v) the author of the treatise links the evocation of purgatory with that of heaven and hell, as does More in the prayer he wrote in the margin of his psalter during his imprisonment in the Tower.[1] The optimistic linkage of purgatory with heaven—reflected in devotional exhortation, as in the pious tag "whose soul God assoil" added to every mention of the deceased—and other practices current throughout Christendom indicate a consensus of the faithful which would free More from reliance on the official pronouncements of the church, since he viewed church unanimity as the supreme criterion of doctrinal infallibility.[2]

Far more widespread and important than *A lytell boke . . . of Purgatorye* was a book that probably had no rival on the bookshelves of pre-Reformation households: its very name, the *Golden Legend*, proclaims the appreciation of medieval Christendom.[3] Saints' lives are only part of the book. It has many pages of sacred, that is, biblical, history: it contains, for example, almost all of Genesis. For important feasts, the author of the *Golden Legend*, Jacobus de Voragine (c. 1230–98), a "friar preacher," provides model sermons. His section "De commemoratione

---

[1]The appeal and guide to action in favor of needy friends beyond the grave is also in a way a preparation for death. In More's "A godly meditacion," the request "gladly to bere my purgatory here" adjoins that "To have ever a fore myn yie my deth that ys ever at hand" (*CW 13*, 226/26 and 227/2).

[2]See *Dialogue Concerning Heresies, CW 6*, 498–501.

[3]References to the *Legenda sanctorum* (written c. 1260 and commonly known as the *Legenda aurea*) are to the 1503 Strassburg edition; those to the *Golden Legend* are to the edition printed by Wynkyn de Worde, August 27, 1527 (*STC*² 24880). For further information about purgatory in Jacques de Voragine's work, see Le Goff, *Purgatory*, pp. 321–24.

omnium fidelium defunctorum," a compendium of traditional information and legends about purgatory, yields more than eighteen columns in Caxton's translation.[1] The sermon recalls the origins of the
feast in the Cluny of Abbot Odilo (c. 962–1049).[2] The important text
of 1 Cor. 3:10–15 is referred to not as proof—none is needed—but to
explain how the hay and stubble represent the perishable attachments
of the flesh, and why purgation can be a slow process: wood is long in
"brennynge" (sig. $2m_1$). Augustine is the authority on the exquisite,
unparalleled cruelty of the pain.[3] Not the good angels, but "the euyl
aungels turmenten the euyll chrysten soules."[4] The location is a matter
of dispute: most of the experts say "by hell," some "in y^e ayre," "in
torrida zona,"[5] or in yet other locations, including an icy one, or at the
scene of the soul's sinning.[6] This last opinion is supported by Gregory
the Great,[7] whose *Dialogues* are cited frequently. The four traditional
suffrages are examined: prayer, for instance the *De profundis;*
almsgiving, an element already present in the collection organized by
Judas Maccabaeus (2 Macc. 12:43–46); the eucharistic sacrifice ("sa-
lutaris hostie immolatio," sig. D_8v); and fasting (sigs. $2m_1v$–$2m_3$). The
principle of commutation, which justifies the granting of indulgences,
is illustrated by the story of a knight who goes on crusade: "And in lyke
wyse auayleth the indulgences of the chirche" (sig. $2m_3$). Purgatory's
denizens are the "mediocriter boni" (sig. E_2), neither good nor bad,
"myddle & bytwene bothe," as Caxton puts it (sig. $2m_3$).

Hardly second to the *Golden Legend* in popular circulation, and probably more personal in the use made of them, were the mass books
compiled for the faithful. They are all alike in substance, as is shown by
a comparison of the fifteenth-century texts of various provenance
gathered in *The Lay Folks Mass Book.*[8] Before the canon, already, there
is a brief prayer "for the soules, that hennes be past" (p. 27). The

---

[1]Sigs. D_7v–E_2v of the 1503 Latin edition; sigs. $2l_8$–$2m_4v$ of the 1527 English edition.
[2]Sig. $2l_8$–$2l_8v$. See Le Goff, *Purgatory*, pp. 125–27.
[3]Sig. $2m_1$, see Augustine, *Enarrationes in Psalmos*, 37:3 (*CCSL 38*, 384).
[4]Sig $2m_1$. See Le Goff, *Purgatory*, pp. 205, 322.
[5]Sig. D_8. This refers to the "gloomy and dismal region" on both sides of the equator,
for which Raphael Hythlodaeus also uses the epithet *torridas, CW 4*, 52/4, 53/5. Caxton
was put out by *zona*, and renders the phrase awkwardly: "in a place brennynge & rounde"
(sig. $2m_1$).
[6]Sig. $2m_1$–$2m_1v$. On the location of purgatory, see Le Goff, *Purgatory*, passim.
[7]Gregory the Great, *Dialogues* 4.40, 55 (*PL 77*, 396–97, 417).
[8]*The Lay Folks Mass Book, or The Manner of Hearing Mass*, ed. Thomas Frederick Simmons, Early English Text Society, Original Series no. 71 (1879; reprint, Oxford, 1968).
In my quotations, the "thorn" character is transcribed as *th*.

"memento of the dead" proper comes after the Elevation, where the missal devotes some ten lines to listing the souls who must have "part of this messe" (pp. 42–45): fathers, mothers, and so on, enumerated again in the "Bidding Prayers" (pp. 66–67, 72, 74, 80). The worshipers are urged to pray

> for all the sowles that ye or I be bownde to praye for, and specyally for all the sowles whose bones are buryed in this chirche or in this chirche yerde: or in any other holy place, and in especyall for all the sowles that bydes the great mercy of almighty god in the bytter peynes of Purgatory: that god for his great mercy releas them of theyr peyne if it be his blessyd wyll. And that our prayers may sumwhat stande them in stede: Every man and woman of your charite / helpe them with a Pater noster and an Ave maria.[1]

The *De profundis* is also recommended, and the bidding prayers end, as do the hours of the breviary, with the words "Fidelium anime per misericordiam dei in pace requiescant."[2]

The *Ordo Missae* in a York Minster manuscript, dated c. 1425, is identical with the Roman Missal. Its *Memento* for the dead is the text still used in the first eucharistic prayer of the Catholic liturgy. It represents the exact wording already spoken by Alcuin in Charlemagne's court, by Erasmus wherever he celebrated, and by every priest who might belong to More's mighty chorus of "Souls." The original Latin is as follows:

> Memento etiam, Domine, famulorum famularumque tuarum N. qui nos praecesserunt cum signo fidei, et dormiunt in somno pacis; ipsis, Domine, et omnibus in Christo quiescentibus locum refrigerii, lucis, et pacis ut indulgeas deprecamur. Per eundem Christum, Dominum nostrum. Amen.[3]

The education of the faithful in true charity, not limited to kin or acquaintance, is achieved through regularly praying for them "that

---

[1] *The Lay Folks Mass Book*, p. 80; quoted by Simmons from *Manuale quoddam secundum usum matris ecclesie Eboracensis*, printed by Wynkyn de Worde in 1509 (STC² 16160).

[2] *The Lay Folks Mass Book*, p. 80. The word order varied a little. Thus, the last three words are more usually "requiescant in pace."

[3] *The Lay Folks Mass Book*, p. 110. Simmons provides this translation: "Remember also, O Lord, thy servants and handmaidens N, who have gone before us with the sign of faith, and sleep the sleep of peace; unto them, O Lord, and to all that rest in Christ, we entreat that thou wouldest grant a place of refreshing, light, and peace; through the same Christ, our Lord. Amen" (p. 111).

haue most nede and leste helpe" since they have "none to praye for
them."[1] Their sense of justice is formed by the special mention of the
souls from whom "ye have your lyvynge and your sustenance" through
inheritance, or else some lesser good by bequest (p. 346).

The book of hours in the margins of which More jotted his own
"Godly Meditation" contains special prayers "For thy fader and moder
deed," "For thy frende that is deed," "For the lyuynge and deed," and
"For our benefactours qwyk and deed."[2] These departed souls reap-
per in the *suffragia*, which conclude both morning and evening
prayers. Compline ends with the *De profundis* (Ps. 129): "Out of the
depths I cry to thee, O Lord. . . ." These depths suggest the dark
dungeon of purgatory, whose entire population is explicitly remembered at the close of the psalm: "God haue mercy on all cristen soules.
Amen" (sig. e_7). More's household was not unusual in reciting the *De
profundis* each evening at bedtime: the night rest symbolized death, and
dying well is "falling asleep in the Lord," the biblical phrase[3] which had
become a cliché of the martyrology and of the *Golden Legend*.

Books of hours normally included "Vigils of the Dead." These texts
were themselves a continuing education, prayer shaping belief. Indulgences, which their denouncers have associated primarily with money,
were available day after day to the faithful who recited these prayers.
What was stipulated in every pardon-granting bull is made explicit also
in the book of hours: an indulgence for one of the prayers requires that
it be prayed "deuoutly" by people who are "penitente and trewly confessed of all theyr synnes" (sig. e_5). The indulgence is sometimes defined as a shortening and a mitigation of purgatorial pains. Indulgences were also used as incentives to reading: Henry VIII's *Assertio*
prints a "sum of the indulgences granted to those who read the king's
book."[4]

The drafting of last wills, the proving of their validity by the bishop's
court, and their execution were occurrences when masses and obits for
the dead came inevitably to the fore. Sir John More's will is typical.[5]
More's father bestows more money on masses to be said for his soul

---

[1] *The Lay Folks Mass Book*, p. 343; cf. p. 74.

[2] Sigs. C7–C7v. Published in 1530 in Paris by Francis Regnault (*STC* 15963); see *Thomas
More's Prayer Book*, ed. Louis L. Martz and Richard S. Sylvester (New Haven, 1969).

[3] Cf. "obdormivit in Domino" (Acts 7:59).

[4] The 1521 edition prints a "Summa indulgentiarum, libellum ipsum regium legen-
tibus, concessarum" (sigs. A1, C3v; *STC* 13078).

[5] The "Will of Sir John More, knight," signed February 26, 1527, and proved on
December 5, 1530, is printed in Appendix B of Margaret Hastings, "The Ancestry of Sir
Thomas More," in *Essential Articles*, pp. 101–3.

than on any other purpose: £5 (or more) per year for seven years for two priests studying divinity, one at Oxford, the other at Cambridge; an annual obit at St. Lawrence Jewry for ten years; and a trental of masses (in addition to a dirge and requiem) to be said by each of the four orders of friars. Along with his own soul, the old judge lists those of his wives and their former husbands, his parents, and Edward IV; he includes seven more names and adds "all other that I haue hadd / any goodes of or am charged in conscience to doo eny thinge for / and for all cristen soules" (p. 101). The last phrase, repeated later in the testament, was a stock formula. More's purgatorial inhabitants hear their children say, amid their carefree piping, "god haue mercy on all crysten sowlys" (222/13), a routine tag that "lyeth but in the lyppys" (222/14–15). The mention of any dead person in everyday life was automatically followed by a formula such as "on whose soul God have mercy," "whose soul God pardon," or "God assoyle his/her soul." The liturgical "May they rest in peace" (*Requiescant in pace*) led to the prayer "God rest all christian souls," which must have still sounded familiar to Elizabethan Londoners when uttered, for instance, by the nurse in *Romeo and Juliet*.[1] More himself never omits this ritual memento, and he uses the whole gamut of formulae: "whose both soules our lord pardon," "our Lord . . . haue mercy on the soule of mine other good sonne," "God [or our Lord] assoyle his soule."[2]

Late medieval and early Tudor poems and ballads yield hundreds of references or allusions to purgatory as a reality hardly less present in popular imagination than heaven and hell. To take but one contemporary of More, William Dunbar, addressing Scotland's king, defines purgatory as "living in pain with hope of glory,"[3] a rhyme that recurs when he evokes the mediation of the angel Gabriel leaving "heaven's glory" to visit "them that are in purgatory."[4]

---

[1] I, iii, 18. Weever, in *Funeral Monuments*, records that epitaphs which "began with an *Orate pro anima N*, or concluded *cujus animae propitietur Deus*" suffered especially during the Reformation (quoted by Chambers, p. 386). The *Lisle Letters*, of More's day (ed. Muriel St. Clare Byrne, 6 vols., Chicago, 1981), reflect a tendency to say "Jesus" instead of "God." An example is "whose soul I pray Jhesu pardon" (*1*, 664).

[2] *Richard III*, *CW 2*, 49/24; Rogers, p. 481, line 15; p. 517, lines 116–18, 161 (letter of Margaret Roper); *Dialogue of Comfort*, *CW 12*, 109/30. This "soyling" in the *Supplication* (for example, 115/21) looks archaic in comparison with Fish's "absolving" (413/7). *Soyl* and *assoyl* are More's preferred forms; they occur dozens of times in his writings.

[3] *The Poems of William Dunbar*, ed. James Kinsley, Oxford English Texts (Oxford, 1979), p. 126, no. 42, ll. 81–82: "As saule in to purgatorie / Leifand in pane with hoip of glorie."

[4] *Poems of Dunbar*, p. 75, no. 22, ll. 75–76: "Dois go betwene fra hevinis glory / To thame that ar in purgatory."

More's first English book, the *Life of John Picus,* contains all the elements of an All Souls sermon. True to the Latin *vita* he is translating, More quotes two revelations made by Savonarola after the death of Pico. One relates that the young earl, for shrinking from the labor of a monastic vocation, was "adiudged for a while to ye fyre of purgatorie, there to suffre paine for a season" and the Florentines "shoulde now w^t their praiers, almes, and other suffrages helpe hym" (*EW,* sig a₅v). The other is "that Picus had after his death appered vnto him, all compassed in fire" (sig. a₅v). The biographer in his turn begs the readers' prayers for his uncle: "Let euery christen body shew their charitie vpon him to helpe to spede him thether, where. . . after the darke fire of purgatorie (in which, veniall offences be clensed) he maie shortly (if he be not alreadie) entre the inaccessible and infinite light of heauen."[1] The essential points are brought to the unlearned reader's mind: in purgatory, venial sins are punished and cleansed away; and souls can appear to the living, who should speed them on their way to heaven through prayers, alms, and other means.

---

[1] *EW,* sig. a₅v. "Fra Hieronymo" himself asked a fellow friar attending his execution: "Say a few masses for me after my death," while his companion Fra Silvestro said: "Pray that God give me life everlasting without any purgatory [*senza el purgatorio*]." Quoted by Olga Zorzi Pugliese, "A Last Testimony by Savonarola and His Companions," *Renaissance Quarterly, 34* (1981), 10.

APPENDIX F

The Printer's Copy for the Supplication of Souls
in the 1557 English Works

BY RALPH KEEN

APPENDIX F

The Printer's Copy for the Supplication of Souls *in the 1557* English Works

The Beinecke Library at Yale University possesses the copy of More's *Supplycacyon of soulys* that was used in the printing house of either John Cawood or (more likely) Richard Tottel to set the type for the reprint of the *Supplication* in the 1557 edition of More's *Workes . . . in the Englysh tonge* (sigs. t_4v-y_6).[1] This printer's copy provides a rare glimpse into the workings of a major printing shop and illuminates some aspects of the printing, or rather reprinting, process in sixteenth-century England.

Of the two early editions of the *Supplication of Souls,* both probably printed in 1529 (but neither bearing a date), the rarer edition (Gibson, no. 72; *STC* 18093 = *STC²* 18092) was long considered to be the second, and the more common edition to be the first (Gibson, no. 71; *STC* 18092 = *STC²* 18093). The signatures and the arrangement of the text and errata make it clear that in fact *STC²* 18092 must be considered the first of the two.[2] There is no reason to believe that both were not printed in the same year, and the year 1529 may be established on the authority of the words "made, Anno. 1529." inserted after the title in the heading of the 1557 reprint.[3] In this appendix the two editions

---

[1]*English Works* was published jointly by John Cawood, Richard Tottel, and John Whalley, and although Cawood's monogram appears on the title page (he was the queen's printer), he seems to have been typographically responsible for only the front matter (Frank Isaac, *English & Scottish Printing Types 1535–58 * 1552–58,* Oxford, 1932, s.v. "John Cawood"). My examination of the paper and types throughout the volume has not indicated any means of identifying a division of labor between Whalley and Tottel. Sheets with the very common watermark of hand and star (which was Tottell's sign and the address given in the colophon) are randomly mixed with those marked with a water-jug, which was not then a printer's sign (so far as I can tell).

[2]See the Introduction, p. clxii.

[3]Both editions must have appeared by October 25, 1529, since More is still "chauncellour of hys [the King's] Duchy of Lancaster" on both title pages (the same title appears in the *1557* heading, but it is retained merely in order to locate the book at a period in More's life when he was not yet chancellor of England). The *Dialogue Concerning Heresies*

457

are distinguished as *1529*[1] and *1529*[2], and the reprint of the *Supplication* in *English Works* as *1557*.[1] *1529*[2] was used as the copy-text for *1557;* and one of the two Yale copies of this edition (Beinecke If/M81/+S529) was the printer's copy.

PHYSICAL MAKEUP

The pages are 18 cm wide by 27 cm high and the signatures are A–L[4], followed by an additional page with "the fawtes escaped in the pryntynge." This errata sheet is not for the *Supplication* but rather for the second edition of the *Dialogue Concerning Heresies* (1531), also printed by William Rastell; and in fact it follows that text in the other Yale copy of *1529*[2], which is bound with the *Dialogue*. The errata for the *Supplication* are printed after the text on sig. L[4]. The book is correctly foliated in roman numerals; the title page is unnumbered, A[2] is numbered i, and the final leaf is xliii. The text begins on the verso of the title page.

The book is now in a modern binding it received before acquisition by Yale,[2] but it seems to have been in loose sheets for a long time before that, since all the leaves are separated from each other and the inner margins of the earlier leaves are considerably frayed. Some of the inner margins have been trimmed and all the leaves have been fastened to strips of new paper for the present binding. The book must have been unbound in 1557; whether it had been bound before and

---

was published probably in June of 1529 by John Rastell, and the *Supplication* probably came shortly thereafter as the first product of William Rastell's press. Germain Marc'hadour suggests September 1 for the publication date, but that seems a bit late for a second edition to have been called for within two months (*L'Univers*, p. 427). There is no reason why William could not have been engaged with the first edition of the *Supplication* while his father was working on *Heresies*. The *Supplication of Beggers* had already been out for more than a year, according to Foxe (Appendix D, 439/32–34).

The phrase "made, Anno. 1529." could refer to the year the book was written rather than the year it was printed, but for More's other polemical works there was no long delay between the writing and the printing. It is true that later editions sometimes merely reprinted the information given in the first, but there is no other instance of this in Rastell's editions of More's polemical works, and when he reprinted *A Dialogue Concerning Heresies* in 1530 or 1531 he duly noted that More had since become lord chancellor of England.

[1]The following abbreviations are also used in this appendix: t, v, x, y = the gatherings in *English Works* signed with those letters; T, V, X, Y = the compositors of those gatherings.

[2]It was bound by the Lakeside Press, Chicago, and bears the bookplate of Henry Cunliffe. It was purchased for the More Project at Yale on June 26, 1960, but no records of the transaction can be found either in the files of the Beinecke Library or in published records of book sales for that period.

then unbound is impossible to say. The extra sheet, containing the errata for the *Dialogue Concerning Heresies,* had been folded horizontally, perhaps to prevent its being printed with the *Supplication;* likewise the final leaf (sig. L₄) had been folded back so that the errata of the *Supplication* also would not be reprinted in *1557.*

Casting Off and Composition

When a compositor received copy to set up in type, he did not automatically, or even normally, begin at the beginning and proceed to the end in one uninterrupted sequence. Usually the compositor simply did not have enough type at his disposal to have many gatherings standing at once. Moreover, when more than one compositor worked simultaneously on a book, they would have to estimate accurately the amount of copy that would fill successive gatherings: the end of the first compositor's gathering was a fixed starting point for the second compositor. Each had to estimate how much of his copy would fit into a single new page of type and mark off in his copy enough pages to fill a gathering. Thus for a folio in eights like *English Works,* each compositor marked or cast off sixteen segments in his copy, one for each page of the new gathering he was to set. In reprinting the *Supplication* of 1529 in the large collection that is *English Works,* the task was complicated by the fact that *1529²* was set in a 43-line page, which had to be transformed into a double-columned page of 60 lines per column. The compositor could have followed either of the two methods given by Joseph Moxon in *Mechanick Exercises on the Whole Art of Printing* (1683):[1] (1) set up a line of copy in the composing stick and calculate from how much longer or shorter the resulting type is than the line of copy, or (2) calculate from an average line the total number of letter-spaces in the copy and use the number of letter-spaces in the new line length to calculate the number of lines and pages in the reprint. It turned out that the compositors of the *Supplication* had to mark off about 36-1/2 lines of *1529²* for every column of *1557.* In fact they already had the necessary proportion because the preceding work in *English Works, A Dialogue Concerning Heresies,* had just been set from a format identical to that of the printer's copy of the *Supplication.*[2]

Many scholars in recent decades have noticed and studied the marks and symbols used in the process of preparing printer's copy for the

---

[1] Edited by Herbert Davis and Harry Carter (London, 1958), pp. 239–42.
[2] *A Dialogue* was set from William Rastell's 1531 edition (see *CW 6,* 575–77).

press.[1] In all cases a single text was being prepared for printing, but the markings are not uniform throughout the printer's copy; there is evidence of more than one typesetter's work in most of the texts. Usually the division of labor was made according to the gatherings, each man being assigned to set a separate one.[2] The table of contents of *English Works* lists twenty-four works, and the allocation of work was made by gatherings rather than by individual works. When the *Supplication* came up in the sequence of texts to be included, it was cast off and set not by one man, but by three: one each for gatherings t, v, and x; and y was prepared by the same typesetter as t. Where the *Supplication* begins in *English Works* it is preceded by 287 pages of prose, and possibly also by an unpaginated gathering of early poetry.

We must assume that the compositor of gathering t had his starting point set for him by the compositor of s, who finished his gathering at the beginning of the thirtieth line of sig. C_3v of the 1531 *Dialogue Concerning Heresies*. Compositor T would have recognized immediately that there was not enough copy left in the *Dialogue* to fill his gathering, and so began his casting off to the end of that text and into the *Supplication*. He counted off groups of 36 lines, making short strokes with his pen in the right margin marking first 20, then another 10, and

---

[1]A chronological sample of the more important recent studies: W. W. Greg, "An Elizabethan Printer and His Copy," *The Library*, 4th Series, *4* (1924), 102–18 = *Collected Papers*, ed. J. G. Maxwell (Oxford, 1966), pp. 95–109; Gavin Bone, "Extant Manuscripts Printed from by W. de Worde with Notes on the Owner, Roger Thorney," *The Library*, 4th Series, *12* (1931–32), 284–306; H. C. Schulz, "Manuscript Printer's Copy for a Lost Early English Book," *The Library*, 4th Series, 22 (1941–42), 138–44, which is followed up by his "A Middle English Manuscript Used as Printer's Copy," *Huntington Library Quarterly*, *29* (1966), 325–36; Robert W. Mitchner, "Wynkyn de Worde's Use of the Plimpton Manuscript of *De proprietatibus rerum*," *The Library*, 5th Series, *6* (1951), 7–18; Margery M. Morgan, "Pynson's Manuscript of *Dives and Pauper*," *The Library*, 5th Series, *8* (1953), 217–28; James E. Blodgett, "Some Printer's Copy for William Thynne's 1532 Edition of Chaucer," *The Library*, 6th Series, *1* (1979), 97–113; W. Speed Hill, "Casting Off Copy and the Composition of Hooker's Book V," *Studies in Bibliography*, *33* (1980), 144–61, cited hereafter as "Hill"; and C. M. Meale, "Wynkyn de Worde's Setting-Copy for *Ipomydon*," *Studies in Bibliography*, *34* (1981), 156–171. The reason why most extant printer's copy is manuscript is that manuscript texts were lent by their owners to the printer and then returned still in good condition. Printed copy could be used for reprints and second editions, just as *1529*[2] was printed from *1529*[1]; but the copy would be the printer's own and would not be as valuable as a manuscript. There would be no special reason to preserve it once it had been used as copy.

[2]For a description of this practice see R. B. McKerrow, *An Introduction to Bibliography for Literary Students* (Oxford, 1927), pp. 128–29.

finally another 6. Reflecting this practice, the number "20" is written in ink on sigs. A_2, A_3v, A_4, and A_4v. In the outside margins he wrote "T" followed by the appropriate number and simply "col" for the second column of each page. Since the *Supplication* begins in the middle of t_4v, the only numbers that appear in *1529²* are "T9" through "T16." When the compositor reached t_8v he wrote "T16" after the usual 36 lines but canceled it and moved it back three lines, perhaps so as to keep the text from being crowded in the gathering. At T16 he also placed a square bracket for the first time at the beginning of the line. This bracket does in fact correspond to the beginning of t_8v in *1557*. On the other hand, he marked the end of t_8v with another bracket before a word that occurred fortuitously in the middle of a line in *1529²*, the word "poynte" in line 7 of B_4v. In other words, the actual beginning of t_8v was determined by the compositor's deliberate choice to begin setting t_8v at the beginning of a line in *1529²*, but the end of t_8v was determined only by the actual setting of the page. This conclusion follows from W. Speed Hill's first "axiom" of casting off: "If a break falls *within the line* of the manuscript, and *not* at a punctuation break, it marks the point *to which* actual composition had come and stopped. . . . Conversely, breaks marked at the *beginning of a line* in the left-hand margin, or at *punctuation breaks* within a line, are normally casting-off marks and indicate the point *from which* composition of a given page would have begun."[1] We may assume, therefore, that the setting of t_8v was the last step in casting off. Moreover, t_1 was probably set at the beginning of casting off or after t_8v to make up the first forme ready to be printed.

Because it was not the intention of the compositor to have his casting-off marks match the breaks exactly—a practice that would be possible but unnecessarily difficult—he made another set of marks to indicate the end of the pages as they were actually set, and these he made in pencil to distinguish them from the casting-off marks. The procedure that was followed in composition makes clear how necessary such signals were. Whether a gathering was being set from the outside in, from the outermost sheet or forme to the middle, or from the inside out (a more common order), the compositor could not proceed in the normal sequence of the text, and so needed to indicate the point to which his composition had already come and from which he had to start when he returned to it for the next sheet or forme. For this reason penciled bracket marks appear in *1529²* at the exact break points for each new

---

[1]Hill, pp. 150–51.

page in t; because both columns were always set together, no such pencil marks appear at the breaks of the second columns.[1]

Although the position of the break mark for the end of t_8v indicates clearly that that page was composed early, the relation of the penciled break marks to the casting-off marks indicates that the rest of this gathering was not composed from the outside in. Instead what seems to have happened is that the compositor returned from t_8v to the center of his gathering, t_4v, which contains the end of the *Dialogue Concerning Heresies* and the beginning of the *Supplication*. He would have known from his cast-off copy of the 1531 *Dialogue* where to begin the final page of that text, and so he composed that and the beginning of *Supplication* then and there. Since that page (t_4v) is the first page of the inner forme of the innermost sheet, it was natural enough for him to compose the conjugate page (t_5) next. If he had gone directly on and set t_5v next, there would have been no need for him to pencil in the break mark for the end of t_5. But since the beginning of the next page is so marked, he seems next to have set t_4, the penultimate page of the *Dialogue,* and t_5v after that, so as to complete the outer forme of the inner sheet. The fact that penciled breaks are indicated in the series t_5– t_8 shows that he proceeded from the inside out, even though the outermost forme was already composed. Had he composed from the outside in, the pages in the second half of the gathering would have begun with ink casting-off marks at the beginning of lines instead of penciled break marks within the lines. The printer's copy of the *Dialogue* presumably had casting-off marks in ink corresponding to the actual page divisions, because that part of the text was composed from the inside out and the only point at which to begin a page in such a process is the estimated place one finds by casting off.

If the ordinary procedure could always be executed without problems, there might be no need to describe printer's copy in detail. But it is the hitches that help us to sympathize with the printer's task and to understand the procedure more clearly. Examples of difficulties in *1529*[2] occur from the very beginning. At A_1v, for example, the mark "15" appears at the right of line 7 (not counting the heading, "⁋To all good christen people," as a line of text) and "11" at the right of line 20.

---

[1]This circumstance is analogous to Hill's second axiom: "If a page break is marked twice within the manuscript and if one of these is cancelled and the other corresponds to the break as it appears in the printed text, the first will usually (but not invariably) be the casting-off mark made prior to setting type, the second, the one made in the course of actual composition to fit copy in when the page ahead is already in type" (Hill, p. 151).

In line 30 "your[self" is bracketed strongly in ink as a break, and the symbol "T 9" is in the left (outer) margin slightly below it. The "15" corresponds to line 14 of the first column of the *1557 Supplication* text on t_4v (again, not counting the heading or title) and the "11" to line 11 of the second column. The "your[self" is within line 3 of the next page, t_5. Because it is also within a line of the text in 1529^2, we would expect it to correspond (like the penciled brackets) to the exact beginning of a page.

The latter discrepancy may be accounted for in this way. It is possible that the compositor had failed to take into account the size of the initial letter in the first column. A block letter of that size is able to displace 20–25 words of type, which would be the equivalent of $2\frac{1}{2}$ or 3 lines. Hence it may well be that 3 lines from t_4v were shifted to t_5. When t_4v was first set up, it had more text, possibly without the block initial or beginning higher in the chase. The new beginning crowded two and a half lines at the end of the original setting onto the following, conjugate page, t_5.[1] As I have said, compositor T sometimes wrote numbers in ink as he counted off segments of 36 lines each. He also probably wrote "41" at the fourteenth line of A_2, which matches line 44 of the first column of t_5 and thus may have preceded the shift of $2\frac{1}{2}$ lines onto t_5.[2]

The numbering on the title page of 1529^2 seems to be for determining the starting point of the *Supplication* in the middle of t_4v. The first mark is a "30" next to the line "¶Against the supplycacyon of beggars." This number is crossed out and a "33" is written below the line. The line in *1557* is 32 lines down in the page, and 30 lines up from the bottom. In thinking that he had 33 lines left, if that is what this number is supposed to indicate, the compositor must have assumed that the title would have been set higher in the page. At the top of A_1v is the number "27," above the line "¶ To all good Chrysten people." Includ-

---

[1] The two half-columns of the *Supplication* on t_4v must have been at least partially reset, for if the compositor had merely shifted two or three whole lines onto t_5, the inked bracket in "your[self" would have remained at the beginning of line 3 or 4 on t_5, whereas it actually occurs a little after the middle of line 3.

[2] In a different, larger hand and in pencil is a "20" at line 21 of B_2 (which is the twentieth line from the page break on t_7v in *1557* and not in 1529^2) and a "60" at line 6 of that page (which is sixtieth from nothing in particular in 1529^2 but does match line 60 of the second column of t_7). Of these two numbers, marked probably after the gathering was already printed, the "20" is hard to explain. The "60" at least could be from another compositor's calculation of how much text of 1529^2 would fit into a sixty-line column in *1557*; but it is also entirely possible that both marks were made by a later reader comparing 1529^2 with *1557*.

ing the blank line between this heading and the beginning of the main text, there are 27 lines in the remainder of t_4v.

The next gathering, v, is indicated in the margin of 1529^2 by the letter "V" and the symbol for "prima pagina."[1] This compositor has also made two sets of marks, the first in ink and the later one in pencil. At twelve points are bracket-style casting-off marks in ink at the beginnings of lines; at three points the mark is at midline, but at a punctuation mark in the line; these lines begin with continuations of hyphenated words. The last of these marks is also coincident with the true beginning of v_8v, and thus shows that v_8v was composed first. The fact that the beginning of the page is indicated by an actual break mark in ink instead of in pencil, as the others have, strongly suggests that the outer forme v_1-v_8v was composed immediately after the gathering was cast off. Because of the large amount of text that fits on a page of 1557 and the fact that pages in *English Works* have two columns, this compositor also found it useful to make casting-off marks for the second column of each page as well as for the page itself, and accordingly there are ink brackets at the beginning of lines to indicate his estimate for the column breaks. For v_1 the actual breaks for the ends of both the first column and the page (which occur at midline in 1529^2) are marked in ink; thus the first page was marked as it was set or after it was set and not before. On the other hand, the point corresponding to the second column of v_8v, which one might expect to match its forme-mate in the way it is marked, has a break indicated in the middle of the line, albeit at a punctuation mark, but it does not match the actual column break and is thus a casting-off mark rather than a break mark made during the course of setting. Hence v_1 was set in type and then marked, but the column break for v_8v, which is the next page in the order of typesetting, was still estimated before it was set. After he had set v_1 the compositor indicated each new page in the margin with a "v" and the number of the page in the signature, from 2 to 16; and the new column within each page is designated "Col"; this is a standard procedure, although this compositor differs in making these marks in the lefthand margins of both recto and verso, so that the labeling on recto pages is in the gutter of the book and somewhat obliterated both by wear before binding and by the binding itself.

After setting forme v_1-v_8v, compositor V went on to set the rest of the gathering; but the ink and pencil marks do not enable us to say with

---

[1]Percy Simpson, *Proof-reading in the Sixteenth, Seventeenth and Eighteenth Centuries* (Oxford, 1935), p. 49.

certainty in what order he set up the text. We would expect the true breaks to match the ink brackets in one-half of the gathering and the penciled brackets in the other if the gathering was set by formes from the inside out or from the outside in. If a gathering or part of it had been set seriatim there would have been no need for the ink brackets to coincide and no need at all for penciled brackets marking true breaks. But in this gathering there is no consistent coincidence of ink brackets and true breaks (or even page beginnings, if we allow for shifted lines) in either half of the gathering; and penciled brackets coinciding with true breaks run through both halves of the gathering. The ink brackets coincide with the true beginning of a page (or line) only for v_1, v_1v, v_3 (line 4), v_7v (third line up on v_7), and v_8v. The penciled breaks coincide with page (or line) breaks for v_2, v_2v, v_3v, v_4, v_4v, v_5v (second line up on v_5), v_6 (line 2), v_7 (second line up on v_6v), v_7v, and v_8.[1] It is barely possible that compositor V first set v_1-v_8v and then set v_1v-v_8 seriatim, marking true breaks in pencil out of convenience, not necessity. That hypothesis would at least account for the evidence, though it is hard to guess why he should have done so.[2]

On v_5-v_7 the penciled brackets do not coincide with the true beginnings of pages. Instead, they mark the beginnings of lines either before or past the page break. Specifically, the beginning of v_5v is two lines past the penciled bracket, that of v_6 is two lines before it; that of v_6v is two lines before the bracket, and that of v_7 is two lines past the bracket. There seems to have been a shift of lines such as might have occurred if four lines on v_7 had been overlooked in setting the type and were inserted after it and v_6v had been composed and thus marked off. Similarly, four lines that later had to be inserted in v_5v would have displaced its original lines by pushing two lines back to v_5 and two forward to v_6. This may account for the fact that the first column of v_5 has one extra line, 61 instead of the normal 60. Sig. v_5v originally began with the line "hereafter by gods grace" and ended with "that lieth in the fire:"; what may have been omitted and later inserted, shoving these lines off the page, is now impossible to tell.

---

[1] For the beginning of v_3v the word "hospytall" is bracketed twice in pencil: "[hos[pytall." The catchword at the bottom of v_3 is "hos-" and the compositor made the minor slip of thinking that he needed to start the next page with just the second half of the broken word.

[2] If he set seriatim he could begin distributing type after the inmost forme v_4v-v_5 was printed. But the same broken letter, a dented "l", appears on v_3 (in 'temporall' at D11) and v_4v (in "labour" at D7), so that it is hard to see how they could have been standing in type at the same time.

The innermost sheet of the gathering, v_4-v_5v, survives in two distinct settings. Since the penciled bracket for v_4v in the printer's copy coincides with the beginning of the page in the Yale copies of *1557* but not in the other setting, it is all but certain that the Yale copies of *1557* contain the earlier setting.[1] The second setting, which is found in at least six copies,[2] differs from the first only in accidentals, except for a few careless misprints.[3] Neither the columns nor the lines match exactly in the two settings: naturally, the opening and closing words of the sheet match, but no other page beginning does so except that on v_5v. The easiest explanation for this duplicate setting is that for some reason not enough sheets were made when the sheet was first set and printed. By the time the deficiency was discovered, the type had already been distributed and had to be reset from one of the sheets already printed.[4] The match in page beginnings on v_5v shows that the pages were reset in the order v_5v, v_4, v_4v, v_5: once the last page was set, the first page finished the outside forme, which was printed first; moreover, the first three pages could be set seriatim with no concern for matching any page breaks except the final one to meet the fourth page.

In gathering x, in the second column of the first page, the first book of the *Supplication* ends and the large-type heading for the second is given. This page was set at the very beginning of casting off: it ends with an ink bracket in the phrase "vppon [the tother" within the line in *1529*[2], and the ink bracket for the second column is within the line and corresponds with the actual break in *1557*.[5] The compositor then cast

---

[1]It is also found in copies at Trinity College (Cambridge), Princeton University, Ushaw College, Harvard University, Trinity College (Dublin), the University of Illinois, the Berg Collection at the New York Public Library, the Cambridge University Library copy reprinted by Scolar Press (London, 1978), and one of Germain Marc'hadour's copies in Angers. Father Marc'hadour first pointed out the double setting in "More's *English Works:* Toward a Census and an Anatomy," *Moreana, 13* (1967), 76–78.

[2]The copies at the Folger Shakespeare Library, Princeton University, the National Library of Scotland, All Souls College (Oxford), the Boston Public Library, and the other Marc'hadour copy.

[3]They are as follows: "of of hys" for "of hys" (146/20), "haue then" for "haue thē [= them]" (146/32), "gestinst" for "gestyinge" (147/6), "thinketh yet" for "thinketh yt" (146/15), "al these" for "al hys these" (150/26–27), "earthly" for "yerthly" (152/2). On the other hand, the second setting might be thought to have improved the spelling (and perhaps the sense) by changing "beast" to "beste" at 147/5 and "precure" to "procure" at 149/11.

[4]Not from *1529*[2]: the misprint at 146/32 ("then" for "them") derives from "thē" in *1557*[a]; *1529*[2] has the unambiguous "theym."

[5]This correspondence occurs nowhere else in this gathering. None of the compositors had any need to hit any of the column brackets exactly.

off the rest of the gathering, marking page and column breaks with ink brackets at the beginnings of lines in his copy.[1] He wrote "x" followed by his version of the abbreviation for "prima pagina" in the margin at the beginning of the first page and continued through the gathering, marking "x" followed by 2 through 16 and "col"—always in the outer margins.[2] Ink brackets coincide with the true beginnings of pages (or nearby lines) on x_1, x_1v, x_3, x_4, x_5v, x_6v (line 4), x_7 (line 2), x_7v, x_8, and x_8v.[3] Penciled brackets[4] mark the true page breaks on x_2v, x_3v, x_4, x_6 (line 2), x_6v, and x_7. Though the pattern is not perfectly regular, the compositor pretty clearly set by forme from the outside in the following sequence: 1, 8v, 8, 1v, 2, 7v, 2v, 7, 3, 6v, 3v, 5v, 6, 4, 4v, 5. We would have expected a penciled bracket to mark the beginning of x_3, but the compositor seems to have just happened to end x_2v at an ink bracket.[5] After he set x_3v we would have expected him to set its forme-mate x_6, but the lack of correspondence between the ink bracket and the true beginning of x_6 shows that he must have set x_5v (which does have the correspondence) and gone right on to x_6. The difficulty may have sprung from hitting the correct number of lines on x_5v, x_6, and x_6v, for according to the break marks, the first three lines of what is now x_6v were transferred from x_6, and the first line of what is now x_6 was marked (and presumably set) as the last line of x_5v.

Unlike V and X but like T, the compositor of gathering y did not cast off pages and columns by placing a bracket at the beginning of the lines he had counted off, but simply made short strokes in the right margin, marking off twenty, then ten, and finally six or seven lines to fill each column. At the beginning of his first page he wrote "y" followed by the symbol for "prima pagina"[6] and continued writing "y 1," "col," "y 2," and so on through "y 11," where the *Supplication* ends at the top of y_6. Penciled brackets mark the actual beginnings of pages (or nearby lines)

---

[1]He placed seven of these brackets slightly before or after the beginning of a line so as to avoid placing it within a hyphenated word or in order to place it after a strong mark of punctuation.

[2]He wrote "3," "10," and "11" before the "x" rather than after it.

[3]The bracket for the beginning of x_5 occurs in "re-[sembled." In actual setting the compositor set the whole word.

[4]The first word for x_4 is bracketed twice: "[ac[counted." The first is in ink; the second, in pencil. The significant bracket is the one in pencil, for the preceding page (before the catchword) ends "ac-." The penciled bracket marking the end of a page already set happened to fall in a word bracketed in ink during casting off. When the typesetter returned to pick up setting at the pencil mark, he inadvertently set the whole word.

[5]We can see that he came within one syllable of doing this at the beginning of x_4.

[6]His symbol is quite different from that of compositor X.

¶ Sette nowe to thys place the tother place of hys in the ende and conclusyon of hys boke / where he sayth that after the clergy spoylyd onys and cast out / then shall the gospell be preched / and then shall we Beggars haue ynough and more. lo lyke as in the tone place he sheweth that all beggary cam in wyth the clergy that brought in þ fayth / so she weth he in the tother that there shuld wyth the clergy all beggary go forth agayn / yf they were so clene cast out that Crystys gospell beyng cast out wyth them / and the fayth whych cam in wyth them / they myghte haue that gospell preched as they say they shulde and as in dede they shuld whych they call the gospell / that is to wit Luthers gospell and ¶ Tyndallys testament / prechynge the dystruccyon of Crystys very fayth and hys holy sacramentys / auauncyng and settyng forth all boldenes of synne and wrechydnes / and vnder the false name of cryste fredome / spurryng forward the dpuylysh vnbrydeled appetyte of sewd sedycyouse and rebellyouse lyberte / that sew in one somer as we shewed you before aboue. lx. M. of þ pore vplandysh Luteranes in Almayn. And thys ys all that these heretykys loke for as the frute of theyr se dpcyouse bolys and beggars byllys / trustyng by some such wayes to be eased of theyr beggary / whych they now sustayn beyng ronne oute of the realm for heresy. for yf they might (as they fayn wold) haue þ clergy cast out / and Crystys gospell cast of / and theyr owne gospell preched: the hope they to fynde that word trew where he sayth: then shall we haue ynough and more.

¶ For of all that euer he hath sayd / he hath not almost sayd one trew word saue thys. And surely this word wold after theyr gospell onys prechyd and recepuyd be fonden ouer trew. for then shuld the beggers / nat such beggars as he semeth to speke for that be syk sore and lame / but such bold presumptuouse beggars as he ys in dede / hole and strong in body but weke and syk in soule / þ haue theyr bodys clene fro skabbys and theyr soulys foule infect wyth vgly great pokkys and lepry: these Beggars wold hope to haue and except good men take good hede wolde not fayle to haue ynough and a great deale more. for after that they myght (the clergy furst dystroyd) bryng in onys after þ the prechyng of Luthers gospell and Tyndales testament / and myght wyth theyr herysyes and fals fayth infect and corrupt the people / causyng them to set the blyssed sacramentys asyde / to set holy days and fastyng days at nought / to contemne all good workys / to gest and rayle agaynst holy vowed castyte / to blaspheme the olde holy fathers and doctours of Crystys church / to mok and scorne the blyssed sayntys and martyrs þ dyed for Crystys fayth / to reiect and refuse þ fayth that those holy martyrs lyued and dyed for / and in the stede of þ true fayth of cryst contynued thys. xv. C. yeres / to take nowe the false fayth of a fond frere / of olde condemnyd and of new reforgyd wythyn so few dayes
wyth

fore/neuer so many/neuer so myscheuouse/neuer long so cótynued/
yet they shall neuer bere payn therfore: but by theyr onely fayth and
theyr baptysm wyth a short retuine agayn to god/shall haue all theyr
synne ¶ payn also clene forgeuen and forgotté/nothyng els but onely
to cry hym mercy as one womã wold ¶ tredyth on a nothers trayne:
thys way wolde as we sayd gyue the worlde great occasyõ ¶ corage
not onely to fall boldly to synne and wrechednes/but also carelesse to
contyne w therin/presumyng vppon that thyng that suche heretykes
haue parsuaded vnto some mē all redy/that.iii.or.iiii. woldys ere they
dye shall suffycyently serue them to brynge them strayghte to heuen.
Where as besydys the fere that they shulde haue lest they shall lak at
last the grace to turne at all/and so for faut of those.iii.or.iiii. woldys
fall to the fyre of hell:yf they beleue ther wyth the thyng ¶ trewth is
bysyde/that ys to wyt that though they happe to haue the grace to re
pent ¶ be forgeuen the synne ¶ so to be delyueryd of the endlesse payn
of hell/yet they shall not so frely be deliuered of purgatory/but that
besyde the generall relyefe of Crystys hole passyon extended vnto
euery man not after the valure therof but after the stynt and rate ap
poyntyd by goddis wysdom/great and long payn abydyth them here
amonge vs/Wherof theyre wyllyngly taken penaunce in the world/
¶ afflycyon there put vnto them by god/¶ there pacyently borne and
suffred wyth other good dedys there in theyr lyfe done by theym/¶
fynally the merytys and prayours of other good folkys for thē/may
mynyshe and abbrydge the payne/Whyche wyll ellys hold them here
wyth vs in fyre and turmentys intollerable onely god knowyth how
long:thys thyng we say as yt ys trew in dede/so yf the world well ¶
frmely for a sure trewth beleue yt/can not fayle to be to many folke
a good brydle and a sharpe bytte to refrayne theym from synne. And
on ¶ tother syde ¶ cótrary belyefe wolde sende many folke forward
to synne/¶ therby in stede of purgatory in to euerlastynge payne.

¶ And therfore ys thys place of our temporall payne of purgatory
not onely cósonaunt vnto hys ryghtuouse iustyce/but also the thyng
that bryghtly declareth hys greate mercy and goodnes/not onely for
that the payn therof though and sore yet/ys yet lesse then owr synne
deserueth:but also moste especyally in that by the fere of payn to be
suffred and susteyned here/hys goodnes refrayneth men from the
boldenes of synne and neclygence of penaunce/¶ therby kepeth and
preserueth theym from payne euerlastynge: Where as the lyght for
geuenes of all to gether/wold geue occasyon by boldenes of synne
and presumpsyon of easy remyssyon/myche people to runne downe
hedlynge thyther,And therfore were as we sayed that way very far
cótrary not onely to goddys iustyce ¶ ryghtuousenes/but also to hys
goodnesse ¶ mercy. Wheruppõ as we sayd byfore it must nedys folow
that

for y_1v (line 2), y_2, y_2v, y_3, y_3v, and y_4.[1] Though we lack printer's copy for the last five pages of the gathering (the beginning of the *Confutation*), the penciled brackets once more suggest setting by formes from the outside in. But after he had set y_3v, he did not go on to its formemate y_6, which has no bracket to mark its beginning.[2] The reason was probably that y_6 was not easy to estimate because it has a four-line title in three type sizes extending across the whole page and a column-wide subtitle in two type sizes. Instead he seems to have set y_4 through y_6 seriatim: no page breaks are marked for y_4 through y_6, and setting by formes would have required them at least for y_4v, y_5v, and y_6.

In his version of casting off toward the end of the *Supplication*, he counted lines in three's on the last page of *1529*[2], drew the stroke, and marked "20" (one of only two marginal numbers in this gathering) at the right of the last line. This is the twenty-second line of L_4 in *1529*[2], the twenty-fifth past the "y 11" mark, and the twenty-first of the second column on y_6 in *1557*. Evidently he was figuring the space that the two partial columns on the last page would require, and came commendably close in his estimate. The only other number is a faded "46" at the right of line 6 of L_3. This is the twenty-ninth after the "col" mark, but it is line 45 in y_5, column 2. Like the "60" in gathering t, this seems to have been part of someone's calculation of text, but more than that we cannot say.

The method of this compositor is entirely similar to that of T, and the hand is the same, so far as can be determined from the meager marginal markings. Thus it seems that the *Supplication* was prepared by three men, one assigned to the outer two gatherings and two to the center of the book. At this point *English Works* was being set by a team of three men, and it may well be that all or most of the volume was set in the same way.

THE THREE COMPOSITORS

That gatherings t and y were set by the same man and that each of the three had distinctive habits of composing type can be seen from a comparison of certain features of spelling and punctuation in different

---

[1] All of these except the one for y_3 fall within lines, wherever the page being set happened to end. On y_3 the penciled bracket just happened to fall at the beginning of a line. The penciled bracket for line 2 of y_1v suggests that y_1 originally had sixty-one lines in one of its columns so that the last line was shifted to y_1v.

[2] In fact the marginal "y" occurs a few lines before the actual page break.

gatherings. Since the sixteenth-century compositor was virtually autonomous in these matters, they serve as a good measure by which to detect differences among compositors.

One of the most obvious changes in the reprint is the proportion of commas to virgules. In 1529^2 the virgule or slash indicates a pause or half-stop roughly equivalent to our comma; by 1557 the comma had replaced it.[1] The amount of articulation by means of either mark was usually not the prerogative of the author but of the compositor. The following table lists the number of virgules in each compositor's section of the 1529^2 text, the number of commas in the corresponding gatherings of 1557, and the percentage of commas over virgules.

Passage equal to 1557 sig.	1529^2 virgules	1557 commas	% increase
t	431	586	35.96
v	679	718	5.74
x	675	781	15.70
y	493	681	38.13

These figures certainly seem to indicate that there were different typesetters at work; and since t and y are alike both in their 1529^2 markings and in their punctuation, it is fair to assume that in the preparation of 1529^2 for reprinting and in the actual setting of 1557, the same individual marked and set gatherings t and y.

Another indication of different compositors at work may be found in the use of typographical abbreviations. In order to condense and justify lines more easily, compositors were accustomed to use superscript abbreviations instead of adscript letters: the most common abbreviation was a line over a vowel to indicate a following "m" or "n." Likewise a subscript ligature of "p" was used to abbreviate *per–*, *pro–*, and *pre–*. A superscript "t" over a "w" could stand for "with" and save the space of three letters. The Old English letter thorn had disappeared by the sixteenth century, but a vestige of it remained in the

---

[1] R. B. McKerrow, *An Introduction to Bibliography for Literary Students* (Oxford, 1927), 315.

abbreviation "y^e" for "the" and "y^t" for "that." Following are the figures for all such abbreviations except "y^t".[1]

Passage equal to 1557 sig.	1529^2	1557	% change
t	289	174	−39.79
v	479	626	30.69
x	506	507	0.20
y	378	185	−51.06

Of the four gatherings, it is clear from this table that the compositor of t and y, if we may now assume it was the same man, was the most sparing in his use of such abbreviations, whereas V was the most liberal with them. And X was the most consistent with 1529^2. It is interesting that the use of abbreviations is in almost inverse proportion to the

---

[1]An anomaly does arise, however, in their respective uses of "y^t" for "that." The frequency of the alternate form does indeed differ with the gatherings, but not in the pattern established by the other tabulations.

Passage equal to 1557 sig.	1529^2	1557	% change
t	31	56	80.65
v	91	102	12.09
x	81	121	49.38
y	53	37	−30.19

It may be that the compositor of t and y had become aware of the confusing similarity of y^e and y^t in this typeface or had run short of y^t characters; but such explanations are purely speculative.

A further indication of different hands at work in the composition of *EW* is the fractional differences in column width among the gatherings. Such differences can be expected, as Fredson Bowers describes in "Bibliographical Evidence from the Printer's Measure," *Studies in Bibliography*, 2 (1949), 153–67. The most striking variation in *EW* is the sheet XX$_4$–XX$_5$v, with columns over 6.5 cm wide, in contrast with the average 6 cm elsewhere in the book (see Ralph Keen, "More Bibliographical Notes," *Moreana, 97,* 1988, 141–42). In our text the columns of t are all between 6 and 6.2 cm wide; those of v are fractionally thinner—6 cm or under. The columns in x are on average 6.25 cm, and those of y are, like t, between 6 and 6.2 cm wide. These widths are constant in four copies measured (three at Yale and the one at the New York Public Library) and so are not due to differences in paper shrinkage.

increased use of commas by each compositor. Of the three compositors, V set six misprints; X, three; and TY, none at all.[1]

Another method for distinguishing compositors is a simplification of one that Charlton Hinman formulated in 1941[2] which relies on preferences in spelling by the different compositors. While it is true that each was autonomous in the spelling of his text, different spellings of the same word could be used, like contractions, for reasons of space. Nevertheless, of all the spellings of particular words in a given compositor's passage, several were used with a frequency that would indicate a personal preference for such spellings. Among the most common forms of alternate spellings are word endings. The compositors differ in their use of the variant forms of "–ing" and "–ly," as the percentages in the following table show.[3]

Word ending	t	v	x	y
–ly	63.33	73.77	74.14	66.10
–lye	34.44	18.18	21.98	32.20
–li	2.22	0.76	3.02	0.85
–lie	—	5.30	0.86	—
–ing	72.58	66.66	50.24	76.00
–yng	11.29	6.23	41.38	11.20
–inge	8.60	19.41	2.96	7.20
–ynge	7.53	6.59	5.42	5.60
–enge	—	0.73	—	—
–eng	—	0.73	—	—

Both endings show that gatherings t and y were set by the same compositor; his preferences are consistent and markedly different from those of the other two compositors. The "–ing" endings also reveal that

---

[1] See the variants at 131/1, 131/24, 134/7, 140/21, 150/29–30, 154/9, 170/21, 177/6, 179/10.

[2] "Principles Governing the Use of Variant Spellings as Evidence of Alternate Setting by Two Compositors," *The Library*, 4th Series, *21* (1941), 78–94. My application in this test is much simpler than Hinman's because there are other sources of evidence.

[3] A similar calculation for the ending "-ike" and seven of its variant forms reveals no significant differences among the compositors except that V shows a marked preference for "–ique" and "–yque."

compositor V had a distinct preference for "–inge," while compositor X strongly favored "–yng."

OTHER MARKS

The final leaf of *1529²* contains a printed list of eleven errata that were written into the text of this copy by someone other than the compositor at some time between 1529 and 1557. These corrections are rendered in *1557* as follows:

1529² sig.	Line	Error	Correction	1557 sig.	Col.	Line	Reading
A_2v	14	enuoyuse	enuyouse	t_5	2	56	enuious
A_3	31	pryoure	prayoure	t_5v	1	34	prayer
A_4	29	to	so	t_6	2	51	so
B_4v	43	in hys	in thys	v_1	1	60	in hys
C_1v	38	he	the	v_1v	2	17	y^e
F_1v	37	at yought	at nought	v_8v	2	57	at ynought
F_2	26	withdrade	wythdraw	x_1	1	50	withdraw
F_2v	31	euerlystyng	euerlastyng	x_1v	1	10	euerlastingly[1]
F_4v	1	long to	so long	x_2	2	42–43	so long
G_2v	7	hole	holy	x_3v	1	32–33	holy
I_4	10	hys	thys	y_1	1	50	this

The errors in making the corrections may be explained by the fashion in which the corrections were made. On B_4v the "t" was inserted before the "hys" in a clumsy manner (this corrector did not use carets to indicate insertions). The printer, thinking it was merely an inkblot (for which it could easily be mistaken), ignored the mark and set only the printed word. The correction at F_1v was made by scratching out the descender of the "y" and drawing a second downstroke on the right of the letter in the attempt to make it an "n." Here the compositor assumed that the original "y" was defective and that the correction was to insert an "n" between "y" and "o." The correction of "hys" to "thys" on I_4 has the "t" written before the word as at B_4v; the whole word was then crossed out and "this" written in a different hand between the lines, with a caret.[2] The other corrections were printed as marked,

---

[1]The "–ly" is in the following line in *1529²*.

[2]The form and hand of this correction are very similar to those of William Rastell and the corrector of *1529¹*; see Ralph Keen, "A Correction by Hand in More's *Supplication*, 1529," *Moreana*, 77 (1983), 100.

allowing as usual for the compositor's personal preference in spelling.

Apart from the errata list, other corrections have been made either by writing over the incorrect letter or word or by crossing out the incorrect word and writing the correction above it. In all cases but one the revised form was the reading printed. These alterations are set forth in Table 1. The reading of the first edition, 1529^1, is indicated by an asterisk. At several points letters have been darkened in ink for greater clarity, but the spelling has not been changed, and neither has the reading in *1557:* "swarmeth" at D_1v line 10, "tree" at D_2 line 2, "this" at D_2 line 23, "contrary" at F_4v line 42, "that" at I_4 line 22, and "payne" at I_4 line 42.

Most of these corrections are quite basic and need little explanation. It is nevertheless clear that the corrector was working without a copy of the first edition, since the majority of corrections are not common to 1529^1. Furthermore, those corrected forms that 1529^1 also has are not in any way unusual enough to suggest that any comparison of the two versions was made. Two of the corrections, that of "sessyons" on B_4v and of "prayours" on F_4v, seem to have been made in a different, brown ink, possibly by a different person or by the same person at two different times. Certainly it is not possible to identify the source of a mere couple of strokes.

The corrector's youth is suggested by the changing of "mowe" to "nowe" on B_4 and E_3. Although it was obsolete by 1557, the use of this form for "be able to" was still current in More's time; and the usage "ye shall mowe perceiue" in the sense "you will be able to perceive" was not uncommon.[1] But a younger printer, or one otherwise unfamiliar with the usage, would have seen in it only a misprint for "now," and thus made the blunder of printing "now soon" at v_7. A similar change was made at K_3 in the correction of "token" to "taken." The participle "token" was current enough usage in 1529 but may have begun to sound archaic by 1557, especially to a younger man. The retention of the reading "here" on G_1 is likewise interesting. First, the "t" inserted is so indistinct that the compositor could not be sure that it was not merely an inkblot. Second, it indicates that while the corrector noticed the error and rectified it, the compositor himself was not aware of the point that the speakers are in purgatory and referring to the world as beyond their reach. At E_1v the corrector himself wrongly changed "ye" to "he" and the compositor accepted his error.

A third set of corrections consists of large crosses written in the

---

[1]See note on 129/29.

TABLE 1

1529[2] sig.	Line	Printed text	Correction	1557 sig.	Col.	Line	Reading
A₁	2	Made*	Made Aº. 1529[1]	t₄ᵛ	1	21	made, Anno. 1529.
A₂	12	pryour	prᵉour[1]	t₅	2	42–43	prayoure*
A₄ᵛ	34	vnto*	Vnto	t₆ᵛ	2	8	Vnto
B₄	25	mow*	now	t₈ᵛ	2	20	nowe
B₄ᵛ	10	haue pore men no way to compelle*	haue no pore to compelle	v₁	1	5–6	haue no power to compell
B₄ᵛ	14	wyll	well*	v₁	1	11	well
B₄ᵛ	25	sessynos	sessyons*	v₁	1	29	sessions
C₂ᵛ	41	as marche*	as a marche	v₂	2	46	as a march
D₁ᵛ	9	cowhed	cowched*	v₄	1	2–3	couched
D₃ᵛ	34	thays (these*)	they	v₅	2	30	thei
E₁ᵛ	12	ye*	he	v₆	2	40	he
E₃	28	men /*	ment	v₇	2	34	meint,

E₃	41	mowe*	v₇	2	nowe	57	now
E₃v	41	obydyence	v₇v	2	obedience*	10–11	obedience
F₃	20	effeccyon	x₁v	1	affeccyon*	46	affeccion
F₄v	23	preyoure*	x₂v	1	prayours	20	prayers
F₄v	34	hough and sore ys yt*²	x₂v	1	though great and sore it is	38	though great & sore it is
G₁	35	here	x₂v	2	there*	52	here
G₂	8	gaolers*	x₃	2	gaylers	25	haylers
G₂v	25–26	take take*	x₃v	2	take (1st deleted)	4	take
G₃v	25	hamelesse*	x₄	2	shamelesse	21	shameles
H₃v	7–8	Peter*	x₆v	1	Paule	18	Paule
H₄v	36	godnes*	x₇	2	goodnes	22	goodnes
I₂	38	men	x₈	1	man*	54	man
K₁	8	no	y₁v	2	not*	14	not
K₃	10	nother	y₃	1	other*	13	other
K₃	18	token*	y₃	1	taken	25	taken
K₃	35	be be	y₃	1	be*	54	be
L₂v	12	that	y₅	1	the*³	40	the

[1]This may be either an inkblot or an attempt to make an "a" out of the "y". In either case the "y" is obliterated.

[2]"ys" is omitted after "yt" in 1529¹, whereas 1529² reads "hough and sore ys yt / ys"

[3]1529¹ has a "ye" that could easily have been mistaken for a "ye" by the compositor of 1529².

margin beside the errors, which have been underlined but not changed in the text.

1529^2 sig.	Line	Underlined word(s)	1557 sig.	Col.	Line	Reading
C_4v	12	to	v_3	2	44	so*
D_1v	25–26	entre in to one fote*	v_4	1	29–30	entre into one foote
F_4v	17	hole (holy*)	x_2v	1	10	whole

Of these three corrections, the first was necessary and obvious: "be they never so strong" is the only possible reading, as the compositor of 1529^1 also realized. The second phrase is puzzling at first: it might seem to mean "that his heart would serve him to enter into on foot" or "enter in on foot." The compositor simply changed "in to" to "into," which does not change the sense: what is meant is that he would enter into the possession of one foot of land, and the reading in both 1529^1 and 1529^2 was correct as it stood. The third correction, concerning the phrase "Christ's whole passion," is a mistake. "Hole" can be a variant spelling of either "holy" or "whole";[1] clearly the corrector, who was perhaps the compositor himself, felt that the correct word of the two possible should be less ambiguously spelled. Thinking that the word was meant in the sense of "whole," the compositor printed that. But "holy" was the correct word: the Passion is more likely to be thought of as sacred rather than as complete; and in fact 1529^1 has "holy." The printer of 1529^2 saw "holy" but simply spelled it differently, as he was entitled to do; but the compositor of 1557 saw "hole," did not realize which word was meant, and spelled the word according to what he thought it meant, without consulting the other edition or thinking there was anything odd about the Passion's being more complete than sacred.

Another set of markings is more mysterious, since they have little in common with each other and there is nothing unusual at these points either in 1529^2 or in 1557. These are groups of words, of varying length, enclosed by a box and indicated by the drawing of a hand pointing with a grotesquely long finger to the box. The passages thus highlighted are:

[1]See note on 175/7.

E_1, 9–10   on the tone day: and then knele to hym / and confesse to
hym
E_1, 33   be borne by the kynges hyghnes
F_1, 37   to consyder what he wold haue you
F_1v, 25   saue thys. And surely this word
F_4, 9   hys goodnes whyche scant the deuyll hym selfe denyeth /
purgatory
I_4, 14   and all / and after that heuen
   One possible explanation for these lines' being singled out is that the
printer at one time wished them to be noted with the pointing-hand
sign; but there is nothing particularly interesting about any of these
passages, and the hand is not used as a marginal mark in *English Works*
anyway.[1] Since they are neither sense units nor typographical units,
they may have been made by the compositor to mark the point where
he stopped for some reason, even though they occur in the middle of
columns and are sometimes quite close to one another. Alternatively,
they may not have originated in the printing shop but may have been
drawn in by an earlier or later owner for some reason, however in-
scrutable today.

MARGINAL NOTES

The hand that made at least two of the textual corrections is also
responsible for the sidenotes written in the margins of *1529*[2] (which
has no printed sidenotes): the interlinear correction "this" on F_4 and
the change from "hough and sore ys yt" to "though great and sore it is"
on F_4v are almost certainly by the same hand that wrote the sidenotes.
The notes are generally drawn directly from the text and follow the
spelling of *1529*[2] fairly consistently: as much, that is, as *1557* itself does.
The notes are pertinent to the passages but reflect no independent
insight. The glossator provides numerous scriptural references, in
both Latin and English, and one reference to canon law at p. 301 (sig.
v_3)C. The character and orientation of the glossator are not reflected in
the notes, but there are enough words to provide a good sample of his
hand. While it cannot be matched with another manuscript that would
identify its author beyond all doubt, it does very clearly resemble markings made in the manuscript of the *Dialogue of Comfort against Tribulation* at Corpus Christi College in Oxford. That MS was not printer's
copy, but it was augmented and corrected as if for printing; and the

---

[1]It is used as a quotation mark to indicate passages from More's adversaries in *The
Answer to a Poisoned Book, The Apology,* and *The Debellation of Salem and Bizance.*

author of those annotations was almost surely William Rastell himself.[1] Only the appearance of the Tottel edition of the *Dialogue of Comfort* in 1553, which became the copy-text for *English Works,* prevented the Corpus Christi manuscript from having also been used as printer's copy for *English Works.*

If the textual corrections, such as "though great and sore," are all by Rastell, it is interesting that he should have made such changes as that from "mowe" to "nowe" on B_4; we would have expected a finer sense of his uncle's language. The error is even more glaring at E_3, where he sets "now" and "soon" side by side. We may make allowances for Rastell's being thirty years younger than More, or we may see the hand of more than one corrector here. Another textual addition which is possibly also in Rastell's hand is the "A? 1529" inserted in the title. Rastell would have remembered or had a record of its printing date (it was the first book he published) and would have had to know the date More wrote the book in order to determine its place in the collected volume. We do not know whether Rastell wrote "Made A? 1529" on *1529*[2] in 1529 or later; but if it was dated early the book would have done a good bit of traveling by 1557 and Rastell would not have had to shop for a copy on his return to England. Whenever he supplied the date, his authority for it and the Lancaster title are the best evidence we have for the year in which the book was written.

INDEXING

While the sidenotes could have been written at any time (Rastell had been planning an edition of More's works before the accession of Mary Tudor, when the possibility of such a publication in England was little more than a dream),[2] another step was necessary before *English Works* could be bound and published. Thomas Paynell (fl. 1528–65), an Augustinian friar of Merton College, Oxford, took up the task of preparing a "table of many matters contained in this book" on sigs. $\P_4$–$\P_9$v. This is in effect a listing of selected marginal notes from the various texts and does not prove that Paynell himself actually read through all of *English Works* in the preparation of his index. During Queen Mary's brief reign he published six books of his own;[3] and since the composi-

---

[1]See the Introduction to *CW 12*, xix–lvii.

[2]The story of Rastell's career is told by A. W. Reed in "The Editor of Sir Thomas More's English Works: William Rastell," *The Library,* 4th Series, *4* (1924), 25–49, and with minor changes as chapter 3 of his *Early Tudor Drama,* pp. 72–93.

[3]This number includes works that have been only conjecturally attributed to him. There is a brief but accurate survey of his life in *The Complaint of Peace by Erasmus* (Paynell's translation), with introduction by W. J. Hirten (New York, 1946), pp. xiii–xxi.

tion of Rastell's collection could not have been started before 1555, Paynell must have worked at a rapid pace indeed.

There are more than a hundred sidenotes to the *Supplication* itself, but only about half of them are actually explanatory glosses. The rest are either scriptural citations or highlights such as "Note" or "A merry tale." The "Table of matters" incorporates about fifty of the sidenotes. It is interesting to examine the variations between Paynell's table and the sidenotes as they are printed in *1557*. The following list excludes variants merely of spelling, the initial use of "the," and the occasional interchange of singular and plural. In this list the first line is the entry in the "table," the second one the actual printed sidenote. And since Paynell keyed his entries to the numbers and letter divisions of the pages, it is convenient to do so here as well.

288D	Soules in purgatory cale vnto vs for helpe
	The sely soules in purgatorie call vnto vs for help
288G	Soules in Purgatory be releued and howe
	Howe the soules in purgatorie be releued
296B&D	Of Peter pense, and when they were payde
	B: Peter pense D: Peter pense were payd before the conquest
302F	Properties of heretiques
	The veri propertie of heretiques
306G	Preistes that do mary are of yᵉ worste sort (table reads 906G)
	The worste sort of prists do mary
310E	Tindals translation of the new testament
	Tindals translation of the new testament purposely corrupted
315A	The painims belieued that there was a purgatorye
	Paynims beleue that there is a purgatorye
318B	Heretikes, and theyr shameles boldnes
	The shameles boldnes of heretikes
323B	Grace and what it is
	Grace
324E	The churche beleueth yᵗ there is a purgatorye
	The churche hath alway beleued purgatorye
325F	Reuelacions and why they are not commen
	Why reuelacions be not comen
326E	Pope the generall vycarre of Christ in his church
	The Pope Christs vicar
331G	All good Christen beleue that there is a purgatory
	Al good Christians haue beleued purgatorie
333E	Charitie waxeth cold
	Whereby charitie waxeth colde

Anyone who has ever indexed a book, or even used indexes regularly (and this may be the first index in an English book), will recognize familiar practices of the indexer. The key word of the gloss will if possible be the first word of the index entry. Similarly certain key words, such as "purgatory" for the *Supplication,* will be picked up regularly by the table. Paynell lists certain glosses more than once when they contain more than one key word. The following list contains those sidenotes which are indexed more than once, with the italicized words indicating the points at which they are listed in the index.

314E   The *Badge* of the *Sedicious*
316B   Good folkes prayers abbredge yᶜ *payn* of *purgatorye*
319A   The *Churche* can not fayle in the *choyce* of *scripture*
321B   Euery mans *worke* shalbe *proued* by fyre
324E   The *churche* hath alway beleued *purgatorye*
328E   The *apostles* dyd institute to *pray* for the dead
328F   *Luthers priestes* are no very priestes
331G   *Luther* sayth ther is a *purgatorie*
332B   *Luther* sayth there is no *purgatory* [wrongly cited as 331B]

Finally, though Paynell relied almost entirely on the sidenotes, there are entries in the table which do not appear as marginal notes to the text of *Supplication.* These are:

294B   *Beleue* the *churche*
295A   *Due* obediens of the *peple*
297H   Richard Hun conuicted of heresy
336G   *Good* dedes done by our *executors* God doth accept [second entry cited as 339G]

Only the last two of these four are accurate. The entry "Beleue the churche" is a simple misprint: the sidenote "Belieue Christes churche" is on 394B, but that form and number do not appear in the table. The error of the second entry is less clear, but it may represent the sidenote "Christen obedience" at 364F, which is not in the table; but how it was given the number 295A is hard to say. There are no other sidenotes for either "belief" or "obedience" in *English Works.*

This examination reveals certain facets of the printing process in the middle of the sixteenth century. The reprinting of a text like the *Supplication,* within a large collection of texts, took place in roughly the following sequence. First, the sidenotes in the margins could have been entered at any time after Rastell decided to collect and publish his uncle's works. The Corpus Christi MS of the *Dialogue of Comfort* illustrates that the final text was not necessarily determined before Rastell went to work on it.[1] Second, the corrections both from the errata sheet and from context were entered, possibly at different times and probably by different people, one of whom certainly seems to have been Rastell. The corrections from the errata sheet, of course, could have been made by anyone; since they are in a different ink it may be that they were made by a previous owner or by a member of the staff. Third, the copy was unbound and distributed to the compositors, who proceeded to cast off their copy. Then they set their copy, each being completely independent in the use of punctuation or abbreviations. While the type was being set, certain other corrections could be made, such as inserting the block letter at the beginning, which displaced about two and a half lines. Finally, once the text was set up and printed, a copy was given to Thomas Paynell, who scanned the sidenotes and added the more important ones to his index, very rarely adding passages which had not been sidenoted but which he or Rastell thought important enough to include. When the whole book had been printed, his index (which like the youthful poems is unpaginated and signed only "¶," and which like the poems was often left out)[2] was included in the gatherings before they were ready to sell.[3]

---

[1]See *CW 12*, xxxvii.

[2]Although Gibson and Constance Smith (*An Updating of R. W. Gibson's St. Thomas More: A Preliminary Bibliography*, Sixteenth Century Bibliography, no. 21, St. Louis, 1981) do not list variations among copies, numerous booksellers' catalogue clippings preserved in the More Project at Yale and by me indicate inclusion or lack of these sections, usually described as "often wanting."

[3]I wish to thank Georges Edelen, Speed Hill, and especially Clarence Miller for helping me figure out exactly what went on in the process described and then helping me explain it in what I hope is a comprehensible form.

APPENDIX G

Table of Corresponding Pages:
The Sixteenth-Century Editions
and The Yale Edition

APPENDIX G

Table of Corresponding Pages:

SUPPLICATION OF SOULS

Signatures in second 1529 Edition	Page numbers in 1557 Edition	Page numbers in Yale Edition
A$_1$	288	109
A$_1$v	288–289	111
A$_2$	289	112–113
A$_2$v	289–290	113–115
A$_3$	290	115–116
A$_3$v	290–291	116–118
A$_4$	291–292	118–119
A$_4$v	292	119–120
B$_1$	292–293	120–121
B$_1$v	293	121–123
B$_2$	293–294	123–124
B$_2$v	294–295	124–126
B$_3$	295	126–127
B$_3$v	295–296	127–129
B$_4$	296	129–130
B$_4$v	296–297	130–131
C$_1$	297–298	131–133
C$_1$v	298	133–134
C$_2$	298–299	134–136
C$_2$v	299	136–137
C$_3$	299–300	137–138
C$_3$v	300–301	138–140
C$_4$	301	140–141
C$_4$v	301–302	141–142
D$_1$	302	142–144
D$_1$v	302–303	144–145
D$_2$	303–304	144–146
D$_2$v	304	146–148

Signatures in second 1529 Edition	*Page numbers in 1557 Edition*	*Page numbers in Yale Edition*
D_3	304–305	148–149
D_3v	305	149–151
D_4	305–306	151–152
D_4v	306–307	152–153
E_1	307	153–155
E_1v	307–308	155–156
E_2	308	156–157
E_2v	308–309	157–159
E_3	309–310	159–160
E_3v	310	160–162
E_4	310–311	162–163
E_4v	311	163–164
F_1	311–312	164–166
F_1v	312–313	166–167
F_2	313	167–168
F_2v	313–314	168–170
F_3	314	170–171
F_3v	314–315	171–173
F_4	315	173–174
F_4v	315–316	174–176
G_1	316–317	176–177
G_1v	317	177–178
G_2	317–318	178–180
G_2v	318	180–181
G_3	318–319	181–183
G_3v	319	183–184
G_4	319–320	184–185
G_4v	320–321	185–187
H_1	321	187–188
H_1v	321–322	188–189
H_2	322	189–191
H_2v	322–323	191–192
H_3	323–324	192–193
H_3v	324	193–195
H_4	324–325	195–196
H_4v	325	196–198
I_1	325–326	198–199
I_1v	326	199–200
I_2	326–327	200–202
I_2v	327–328	202–203

Signatures in second 1529 Edition	Page numbers in 1557 Edition	Page numbers in Yale Edition
I$_3$	328	203–205
I$_3$v	328–329	204–206
I$_4$	329	206–207
I$_4$v	329–330	207–208
K$_1$	330–331	208–210
K$_1$v	331	210–211
K$_2$	331–332	211–213
K$_2$v	332	213–214
K$_3$	332–333	214–215
K$_3$v	333–334	215–217
K$_4$	334	217–218
K$_4$v	334–335	218–219
L$_1$	335	219–221
L$_1$v	335–336	221–222
L$_2$	336–337	222–223
L$_2$v	337	223–225
L$_3$	337–338	225–226
L$_3$v	338–339	226–228
L$_4$	339	228

Signatures in 1532 Edition	*Page numbers in 1557 Edition*	*Page numbers in Yale Edition*
a_1	833	231
a_1v	833	232
a_2	833	233
a_2v	833	233
a_3	833	233
a_3v	833	233–234
a_4	833	234
a_4v	833	234
b_1	833–834	234–235
b_1v	834	235
b_2	834	235
b_2v	834	235–236
b_3	834	236
b_3v	834	236
b_4	834	236
b_4v	834–835	236–237
c_1	835	237
c_1v	835	237
c_2	835	237–238
c_2v	835	238
c_3	835	238
c_3v	835	238–239
c_4	835	239
c_4v	835–836	239
d_1	836	239–240
d_1v	836	240
d_2	836	240
d_2v	836	240
d_3	836	240–241
d_3v	836	241
d_4	836–837	241
d_4v	837	241–242
e_1	837	242
e_1v	837	242

Signatures in 1532 Edition	Page numbers in 1557 Edition	Page numbers in Yale Edition
e_2	837	242
e_2v	837	242–243
e_3	837	243
e_3v	837–838	243
e_4	838	243–244
e_4v	838	244
f_1	838	244
f_1v	838	244–245
f_2	838	245
f_2v	838	245
f_3	838	245–246
f_3v	838–839	246
f_4	839	246
f_4v	839	246
g_1	839	246–247
g_1v	839	247
g_2	839	247
g_2v	839	247–248
g_3	839–840	248
g_3v	840	248
g_4	840	248–249
g_4v	840	249
h_1	840	249
h_1v	840	249
h_2	840	249–250
h_2v	840–841	250
h_3	841	250
h_3v	841	250–251
h_4	841	251
h_4v	841	251
i_1	841	251
i_1v	841	252
i_2	841	252
i_2v	841–842	252
i_3	842	252–253
i_3v	842	253
i_4	842	253
i_4v	842	253–254
k_1	842	254
k_1v	842	254

Signatures in 1532 Edition	Page numbers in 1557 Edition	Page numbers in Yale Edition
k_2	842–843	254–255
k_2v	843	255
k_3	843	255
k_3v	843	255
k_4	843	255–256
k_4v	843	256
l_1	843	256
l_1v	843	256–257
l_2	843–844	257
l_2v	844	257
l_3	844	257–258
l_3v	844	258
l_4	844	258
l_4v	844	258

GLOSSARY

GLOSSARY

This glossary serves for both the *Supplication of Souls* and *A Letter against Frith*. It is intended to contain only words whose meanings or forms (not merely spellings) are obsolete or archaic according to *The Oxford English Dictionary*. It also includes a few words which might be puzzling because of their spelling or some other ambiguity. In general, if a word recurs more than twice, only the first instance, followed by "*etc.*," is given. Unusual spellings of proper names have also been included.

a *prep.* to 148/1 *etc.*
abhorre *v.* shrink back from 200/16
able *adj.* suited, adapted 151/27
about, abowte *prep.* on account of 128/25, 144/20; with 147/5, 168/33
abowt(e) *adv.* about, around 123/14 *etc.*
abuse *v.* deceive 113/21
abyde *v.* wait through, endure 120/1; *ppl. a.* **abydyng** dwelling 111/7
acceptacyon *n.* acceptance 162/34
accompte *n.* computation 125/7
accompte *v.* regard, account 154/14 *etc.*; *pr. 3 s.* **accounteth** 182/12 *etc.*; *pp.* **accompted, accounted, accountyd** regarded 180/19 *etc.*
aduenture *n. at aduenture* at random 198/36 *etc.*
aduyse *v. refl.* take thought, reflect 206/28; *pr. 3 s.* **aduyseth** considers 160/19
aferde *ppl. a.* afraid 238/4
affeccyon *n.* disposition, attitude 171/5 *etc.*
affeccyonate *adj.* partial to 172/22
a fore, afore *adv.* earlier 121/11 *etc.*
afore *prep.* before 133/5, 223/26
afrayed *pp.* alarmed 125/25
after *adv.* afterward 118/7
after *prep.* according to 120/33 *etc.*
after as *conj.* according to whether 189/21
after that *conj.* since 178/11; after 135/19 *etc.*

agayn(e), ageyn *adv.* back, in return 117/13 *etc.*
agaynst *prep.* in contrast to 121/1
aggreueth *v. pr. 3 s.* aggravates 127/6
agre *v. pp.* **agreed** agreed to 155/4
agreable *adj.* fitting, appropriate 199/26
alakke the whyle *interj.* alas the day 114/23
albe, albe it, albe yt, albeyt (y^t), all be yt *conj.* although 112/26 *etc.*
alledge *v. pr. 3 s.* **alledgyth, alledgeth** cites as evidence or authority 138/15 *etc.*
all onely *adv.* solely, only 213/28
allowed *pp.* approved of 220/2
all to gether *n. phr.* everything taken together 196/20
all way, allway(e), allwey, alway *adv.* always 111/16 *etc*; without exception 172/31 *etc.*; after all, still 209/1
Almaygne, Almayn *n.* Germany 149/15 *etc.*
almes dede, almoyse dede *n.* the practice of almsgiving, charity 198/18 *etc.*
almesse, al(l)mes, almoyse, almys *n. pl.* alms 111/26 *etc.*
alyen *v.* make over, transfer 216/21; *pp.* **alienyd, alyened** 214/16 *etc.*
amend *v.* rectify 113/9; *pp.* **amended** recovered 189/18
amendys *n. pl.* compensation 216/16
among *adv.* from time to time, occasionally 214/24, 221/24

493

an *prep. an horsbake* on horseback 221/18
and, & *conj.* (even) if 125/13 *etc.*
angelles *n. pl. See* **aungell**
angell noble *n. See* **aungell**
anker *n. at an anker* at anchor 189/11
antecedent *n.* premises of a syllogism 249/24
any thyng(e) *adv. See* **eny thyng**
apostata *n.* apostate 122/24, 28. *See note*
apparaunt *adj.* self-evident 256/21
appere *v.* be evident 119/30 *etc.: vbl. n.* **apperyng** appearance 196/28
appose *v.* interrogate 150/8. *See note*
aquayntaunce *n. pl.* acquaintances 111/4
are *conj.* ere, before 114/14
arte *v. pr. 2 s.* are 207/22
as *conj.* so that (result clause) 118/32 *etc.*
as *rel. particle* such as 199/14 *etc.*
assay *v.* try 162/9 *etc.; pt.* **assayd** 161/24–25
assercyon *n.* vindication 162/32, 253/23
assygne *v.* specify, point out 242/39
assystent *adj.* aiding 163/34; present 181/7
at *prep.* in 112/4 *etc.;* on occasion of 201/12,14
ate *prep.* at 168/7
attempred *pp.* balanced 189/13
auauncyng *ppl. a.* promoting 166/16
aught *pron. See* **ought**
augrym *n.* arithmetic 139/8
aungell, angell noble *n.* gold coin 124/6 *etc.; pl.* **angelles, aungellys, aungels** 124/4 *etc. See note on* 124/12
auoyde *v.* refute 185/29, 195/8; *vbl. n.* **avoydynge** putting an end to 233/8
austayne *adj.* Augustinian 123/12
Austeyne(e), Aust(a)yn, Austayn(e) *n.* St. Augustine 144/28 *etc.*
awne *adj.* own 112/29 *etc. See note*
awter, aulter, aultare *n.* altar 146/28 *etc.*
axaccyon *n.* excessive impost 130/24; *pl.* **exaccyons** 125/26 *etc.*

bare *v. pt.* bore 172/19, 220/14
be *pp.* been 215/8
because that *conj.* since 187/4
bederoll *n.* catalogue of persons to be specially prayed for 115/13; list 120/24
beggar *n. sturdy beggars* able-bodied per-

sons begging without cause and often with violence 115/16
behauour *n.* conduct 192/4
behofe *n.* benefit, advantage 245/1
beholden *pp.* seen, beheld 248/20
bendyd them selfe *v. refl. pt.* formed a party 140/18
bene *v. pr. 3 pl.* are 189/33
bene *pp. been in hand* been occupied with 143/3
bere bench *n.* drinking bench 211/4
bere *v.* support 123/24; *bere . . . in hand* assert 125/2 *etc.; bere hym bolde of other* behave abusively toward others 168/16
beryeng *vbl. n.* burying 161/34 *etc.*
bestely *adj.* bestial 172/30
bestow *v.* expend, put to use 215/29 *etc.*
beynge *vbl. n. at hys laste beynge here* the last time he was here 255/28
blesse *n.* bliss 113/4
blood suppers *n. pl.* bloodsuckers 127/8, 142/28
blynde *adj.* deceitful 247/35
blyssyd, blyssed *adj.* holy 113/5 *etc.*
boch *n.* sore 121/10
body *n.* person, individual 144/23
Bohemys *n. pl.* Bohemians 257/5
boldnes *n. take boldnes* venture 206/22
boone *n.* entreaty 177/9
bo pepe *n.* peek-a-boo 251/26
boste *n.* pomp, show 220/3
boste *v. trans.* brag about 114/10 *etc.; pp.* **bosted** 114/7
boteth *v. impers.* helps, profits 184/15
bought *pp.* redeemed 113/5
bounde(n) *pp.* required, obliged 139/14 *etc.;* tied 145/15 *etc.*
boystuouse *adj.* violent 144/35
brake *v. pt.* broke 112/1
brastyng *vbl. n.* bursting 172/15
bratte *n.* makeshift cloak, rag 225/6
brek(e) *v.* break up 222/30, *to breke . . . maryage* to break the marriage vow 157/22,24
brethern, brothern *n. pl.* brothers 119/18, 170/2
bringeth vp vppon *v. pr. 3 s.* produces against 150/25
brothern *n. pl. See* **brethern**
brotle *adj.* transitory 219/32

brydeale *n.* wedding feaste 220/19

brynger *n.* messenger 233/2

brynge vp *v.* introduce, start 239/33

burgeyses *n. pl.* members of Parliament for a borough 141/3–4

busye *adj.* solicitous 147/5

busynes *n.* ado, trouble 144/20 *etc.;* mischievous activity 147/18

but *conj.* but that 113/15; *but only* except 201/33

but if, but yf *conj.* unless 122/25 *etc.*

but . . . that *conj.* except (that), unless 205/29–30, 222/31–32

by *prep.* about, with respect to 121/6 *etc.;* in (the writings of) 180/24 *etc.;* through 202/24 *etc.; by longe tyme* for a long time 135/20; *by all to gether* entirely 217/4

by(e) *v.* purchase 179/31, 203/11

by & by *adv.* immediately 138/32 *etc.*

bycause yᵗ, because that *conj.* because 135/29 *etc.*

bycum *v.* betake oneself, go 220/34; *where ys . . . bycome* what has become 127/31–32; *pr. 3 s.* **bycummeth** suits, befits 218/7

byelded *v. pt.* built 235/39; *pp.* **by(e)lded** built 187/15 *etc.*

byleued *v. pt.* held as true the existence of 195/5

bymyred *ppl. a.* befouled 233/30

byrdys *n. pl.* nestlings 153/6. *See note*

byreue *v.* deprive of 172/21, 200/22

bysely *adv.* fervently 192/32

by that *conj.* because, by the fact that 118/33 *etc.*

bytyme *adv.* in good time 147/22

canker *n.* gangrene 233/28 *etc.*

canneth *v. pr. 3 s. canneth . . . skyll* have knowledge 140/10

careyn *adj.* rotting 220/23

carnall *adj.* material, secular 146/29

car(r)ayn(e), carryn *n.* corrupt mass, something vile 160/10 *etc.*

case *n.* event 136/28; *in the case* in the position (to) 118/18–19

caste *pp. caste in oure teeth* reproached us with 221/31–32

cauillacion *n.* verbal trickery, sophistry 238/14 *etc.; pl.* **cauyllacions, cauyllacyons** 239/2 *etc.*

cause *n.* case 118/17

certayn *n. a certayn* a restricted number, some 209/12

chanons *n. pl.* canons 115/15. *See note*

chapiter, chapyter *n.* chapter 146/11 *etc.*

charge *n.* expense 220/3; *lay . . . (vn)to his charge* blame him for 120/16–17 *etc.*

chatte *n.* idle talk 239/19

Chelchith *n.* Chelsea 258/26

chepe *adv.* See **good** *adv.*

chese *v.* choose 221/15

chydynge *vbl. n.* quarreling 222/16

chyldhed *n.* childhood 120/26

clene *adj.* free 166/35, *etc.*

clene *adv.* completely 112/34 *etc.*

clensynge *ppl. a. clensynge tyme* time of purgation 221/6

clere *adv.* clearly 170/20 *etc.*

clerk(e) *n.* cleric 148/27; scholar 190/28

close *adj.* hidden 234/19

close *adv.* secretly 233/23

cloth *n.* clothing 119/28

clowte *v.* mend 154/10

colorable *adj.* specious, plausible 257/3

colour(e) *n.* semblance, pretext 115/1 *etc.;* allegeable reason 180/3 *etc.*

combred *v. pt.* troubled 133/25–26; encumbered 254/29

comen, comon, commune *adj. of comen course* as a rule 201/25; *comon sense* usual meaning 242/8

comen *pp.* come 114/2

comen crede *n.* Apostles' Creed 186/12

comen howse, comen house *n.* House of Commons 130/21 *etc.*

comens *n. pl.* common people 128/28 *etc.*

com(m)en welth(e), comen weale *n.* common good 127/27 *etc.*

commodytees, commoditees *n. pl.* benefits, comforts 117/29 *etc.; sing.* **commodyte** well-being 140/25; advantage 145/22; benefit 245/1

companyons *n. pl.* partners, accomplices 152/33

compassyng *vbl. n.* planning 233/25

complayne vppon *v.* grumble against 218/26

complyces *n. pl.* accomplices 117/3 *etc.*

compt *n.* tally, calculation 125/9, 10; *cast a*

compt add up an account 123/27; *vbl. n.* **comptyng** 124/8

concluded *ppl. a.* overcome in argument 195/32, 210/30

concludeth *v. pr. 3 s.* confutes 253/34

condycion *n.* moral character 150/26

condygne *adj.* merited, fitting 176/33

condyscended v. pt. acceded 177/10

conferre *v.* bring together, compare 164/12

connyng(e) *vbl. n.* learning 146/11 *etc.*

connynge, cunnyng *ppl. a.* learned 177/29, 239/25

consecrate *ppl. a.* consecrated 254/5 *etc.*

consequent *n.* logical conclusion 173/28, 249/23

conster *v.* interpret 190/6, 7

conteyn *v.* withhold oneself 172/15

conuay(e) *v.* guide, lead 221/9 *etc.; ppl. a.* **conuayd** brought about 130/33

conuenyent *adj.* proper, appropriate 113/4 *etc.*

conueyaunce *n.* cunning manner of expression 154/30

copyouse *adj.* numerous 197/32

corage *n.* boldness 174/22; *take corage* be bold, dare 133/22, 136/7

corne *n.* grain 121/20

corps *n.* body, bulk 161/10; body of people 198/20; corpse 204/16, 220/23

corrupted *ppl. a.* diseased 189/23

Corynthyes *n. pl.* Corinthians 187/7, 190/4. *See note on* 190/4

cosyn *n.* kinsman 156/7

cote armours *n.* coats of arms 220/12

coueenaunt *n.* bargain 222/8

couent *n.* monastery 129/19

councell, counsell *n.* council 140/2 *etc.*

counseyl *n. of hys . . . counseyll* in his confidence 114/1

countenaunce *n. make a countenaunce* make a show of action 199/6; *in countenaunce* seemingly 200/20

counterpaysyth *v. pr. 3 s.* equals in power 140/12

couored *ppl. a.* hidden from view 149/26

course *n. of comen course* ordinarily 201/25

cowched *ppl. a.* phrased 114/29 *etc.*

crowched *ppl. a.* crossed 123/16. *See note*

crymes *n. pl.* accusations, charges 127/7

crysten *adj.* Christian 114/20 *etc.*

crystendom *n.* state of being Christian 228/11

cum *v.* come 191/14; *pr. 3 s.* **cummeth** 115/21 *etc.; cummeth owt* is uttered 222/13

cumber *v.* burden 119/35

cumfort(e) *n.* support, relief 177/12 *etc.*

cumpanyes *n. pl.* guilds 214/25

curatys, curates *n. pl.* parish pastors entrusted with the care of souls 116/26 *etc. See note on* 154/3

cure *n.* care 201/31

cursyng *vbl. n.* anathematizing 115/20

curtesye *n. of your owne curtesye* by your favor (as distinct from legal duty) 159/30

curyouse *adj.* cautious 196/34

customably *adv.* customarily 203/34

cyrcumstaunce *n.* context 177/25; *pl.* **cyrcumstances** contextual clues 241/1

cytyng *vbl. n.* summoning to appear in an ecclesiastical court 115/20

dase *v.* become stupefied 211/26

daunger, daungeour *n.* liability (to punishment) 113/19; power 146/21

declaracyon *n.* elucidation 213/22

declare *v.* reveal 187/12, 188/15

declyne *v.* deviate 198/5, 242/2

decypher *v.* reveal 208/31

dede *adj. were dede* died 179/32

dede *n. in dede, yn dede* in fact 122/18–19 *etc.; in very dede* undoubtedly, without question 199/7 *etc.*

dedely *adv.* fatally 114/31 *etc.;* to the death, implacably 171/8

defaced *ppl. a.* discredited 158/6

defaut, defawt *n.* failure 126/29 *etc.;* want, lack 115/12, 130/28

def(f)enso(u)r(e) *n.* defender 162/35, 164/1

dele *v. dele surely* act prudently 253/31

deliuery *n.* release 201/8

delycates *n. pl.* delicacies 179/9–10

delyuernesse *n.* agility 226/21–22

demeryte *n.* desert 191/28

departe *v. departe with* part from 244/24

dere *adj. dere yeres* years of dearth 121/20, 145/3

desert, desart *adj.* deserted 150/31, 151/7

desperacyon *n.* despair 184/8

desperate *adj.* in despair 192/13

despyght *n.* malice 220/21

detectyd *pp.* accused 132/25, 29

determined them selfe *v. refl. pt.* resolved 162/9

determineth *v. pr. 3 s.* fixes 245/16

deuised *pp.* imagined 252/20 *etc.*

deuyce *n.* devising 117/16; scheme 155/4; intention 223/1

deuyse *v. See* **dyuyse.**

dirige *n.* office of the dead 204/17; *pl.* **dyryges** 205/2. *See note on* 204/14–17

discouer *v.* make known 113/34

dispyghtfull *adj. See* **dyspytefull.**

diuers *adj. See* **dyuers(e)**

doctour *n.* learned priest 220/14

dole *n.* distribution 158/27

dome *n.* Last Judgment 190/12

dowsy *adj.* stupid 212/11

dowt(e) *n.* uncertain matter 167/20; uncertainty 170/17 *etc.; in euery dowt* if in doubt 206/33

draw *v. draw to* incline toward 199/29; *draw . . . to* pervert, misinterpret 239/12

drawen *pp.* drafted in due form 130/20

drawghte *n.* drink 211/21

dreue *v.* drive 243/1 *etc.*

dreuen *pp.* driven 146/4 *etc.;* forced 242/31; *dreuen of* put off, postponed 223/15

dronken *ppl. a.* drenched 142/28

dryft *n.* ruse, stratagem 118/35

dryuynge *ppl. a.* putting off 223/20

dutyes *n. pl.* payments owed to the church 146/31

dyd *v. subj.* would do 223/12

dyed vp *pp.* died off entirely 122/2

dyryges *n. pl. See* **dirige**

dyscernyng *vbl. n.* distinguishing 252/27–28

dyscorage you to dyspose discourage you from disposing 223/30

dyscoueryng *vbl. n.* disclosing 172/17

dysease *n.* discomfort, pain 189/31

dyspeplyng *vbl. n.* depopulation 163/30

dyspleasure *n.* trouble, discomfort 189/20, 219/34

dyspose *v.* bestow 148/35 *etc.*

dyspycyons *n. pl.* debates 121/2; disputations 213/21

dyspyte *n.* hatred 135/2 *etc.*

dyspytefull, dyspyghtfull, dispyghtfull *adj.* cruel 112/16 *etc.;* contemptuous 221/31

dyspytuouse *adj.* pitiless 112/16 *etc.*

dystrusted *v. pt.* doubted 173/18

dyuers(e), diuers *adj.* several 129/30 *etc.*

dyuyse, deuyse *v.* scheme 114/30 *etc.;* conceive 165/6; bequeath 214/23; arrange for 220/14; *vbl. n.* **deuysyng** inventing 147/17

dyuysers *n. pl.* inventors 233/17

eate *pp.* eaten 258/5

effectual *adj.* effective 116/14, 141/30

effectually *adv.* effectively 181/6

efte sonys *adv.* soon afterward 143/32, 33

eleccyon *n.* choice 180/28, 183/9

els, elles, ellys *adv.* otherwise 120/19 *etc.*

Eluidius *n.* Helvidius 195/22. *See note*

empropred *pp.* assigned as a possession 215/5. *See note*

enduce *v.* infer, deduce 249/35

endyghted *v. pp.* composed 210/5–6

enmy *n.* adversary, foe 171/1 *etc.; pl.* **enmy(e)s, enymyes** 171/10 *etc.*

enmyouse *adj.* hostile 114/10, 172/14

enmyte *n.* hostility 172/19

enormytees, enormyties, enormytyes *n. pl.* transgressions 160/14 *etc.*

enprent *v.* print 233/13

ensample *n.* example 172/10 *etc.; pl.* **ensaumples** 117/10 *etc.*

enseygned *v. pt.* marked 169/5. *See note*

entent *n. to thentent yᵗ* in order that 216/12

entre in to *v.* take possession of 145/1, 216/12

enuyouse *adj.* envious 225/27

eny thyng, any thyng(e) *adv.* in any way, to any extent 116/8 *etc.*

ere *conj.* before 117/31 *etc.; or ere* before 138/13

ere *n.* ear 212/29, 226/20

ergo *adv. (Lat.)* therefore 250/11 *etc.*

erronyouse *adj.* deviant, straying from truth and virtue 142/25, 195/26

Esay, Esaie *n.* Isaiah 244/25 *etc.*

eschete *n.* lapsing of land to lord or king 214/7. *See note*

eschew *v.* avoid 141/29

especyall *adj.* particular 213/22; *in especyall* particularly 161/12

estate *n.* rank, position 155/22; condition 170/4, 176/28

este(e)me *v.* value 116/8 *etc.;* consider, deem 243/23; *pp.* **estemed** 143/18; *pt.* **estemyd** 176/32

ete *v. pt.* ate 257/29

eth(e) *adj.* easy 142/23, 178/33

ether *adj.* *of ether syde* of both sides 209/27

euen *adj.* *euen crysten* fellow Christians 112/23

euery *pron.* each 123/9, 124/31

euerychone *pron.* everyone 122/2

euydent(e)ly *adv.* clearly 173/15 *etc.*

euyn *adv.* precisely, just 180/16

exaccyons *n. pl. See* **axaccyon.**

except(e) *conj.* unless 125/15 *etc.; except that* unless 183/12

excusyng *vbl. n.* defending 196/31

expoune, expowne *v.* interpret, explain 190/23; *pp.* **expowned** 190/25; *pr. 3 s.* **expowneth** 190/33; *vbl. n.* **expounynge** 238/16–17

exquysyte *adv.* excruciating 113/18

extremytes *n. pl.* 249/34. *See note*

eyen *n. pl.* eyes 113/3 *etc.; at eye* with one's own eyes 197/33

face *n.* pretense 118/33, 164/6

faculte *n.* profession 119/2

fader *n.* father 147/26; *pl.* **faders** 159/12

fagot(te) *n. bere a fagotte* renounce heresy 131/6, 157/8. *See note on* 131/5–6

faint, faynt *adj.* weak 170/13; unconvincing 250/13

fall *v. fall to* lapse into 167/25 *etc.; fall from* turn away from 242/31

fall *pp.* become 209/36

fallen in to *pp.* become involved with 209/1

fall to, fall a *v.* take to, start in with 117/28 *etc.;* turn into 151/19, 152/21; befall 170/10

fall vppon *v.* come across 119/21

fallyng from *vbl. n.* departing from 183/12

fals(e)hed *n.* deceitfulness 114/24, 114/33; falsity, error 131/6, 165/8

familier *adj.* pertaining to a family or household 228/8

famyshyng(e) *vbl. n.* starving 121/32, 36

fantastyke *adj.* imaginary 227/4

fantesy, fantasy *n.* ingenious fiction 191/4 *etc.;* illusory appearance 197/3; imagination 212/21, 226/11; *pl.* **fantesyes, fantasyes** ingenious fictions 198/4; inclinations, fancies 224/18

fare *v.* deal 121/6; *impers.* happen 121/6 *etc.; pr. 3 s.* **fareth** behaves 137/20, 237/16

farforth(e), ferre forth, ferforth *adv. so farforth* to such a degree 119/5 *etc.*

farne *adj.* bygone, remote in time 128/24. *See note*

farr(e) *adv.* extremely, to a great degree 114/19 *etc.;* by far 189/15; *farre an other thing* completely different matter 122/19

farre *adj.* distant 208/25

farsed *ppl. a.* crammed full 172/11

fassyon, fasshyon *n.* way of acting 154/6, 252/32; form 163/19 *etc.*

fast(e) *adj.* steadfast 210/19, 211/24

faste *adv.* zealously 180/2

fastly *adv.* firmly 170/15

faughten *pp.* fought 117/7

faut(e), fawlte, fawt(e) *n.* fault 115/12 *etc.;* lack 152/2 *etc.;* offense 177/3 *etc.*

fawtelesse *adj.* innocent 136/18

fawty *adj.* guilty 126/31

fayle *v. fayle of* be deficient in 128/1, 145/11; *pr. 3 s.* **fayleth** is lacking 148/26

fayn(e) *adj.* well pleased, well disposed 120/25 *etc.;* obliged 172/15 *etc.*

fayn(e) *adv.* gladly 137/26 *etc.*

fayned *v. pt.* made out falsely 115/7; *pr. 3 s.* **fayneth** 141/19

faynt *See* **faint**

faynyd, feynyd *ppl. a.* fictitious 164/2; imaginary 225/14

fee *n.* estate, property 143/9 *etc. See note on* 143/5–17

feed *pp.* hired for a fee 140/2, 141/1

felow(e)s *n. pl.* companions 202/19, 20; worthless persons 208/27, 228/17

felyshyp(e), felishyp *n.* company 119/2 *etc.; pl.* **felyshyppys** guilds 214/26

ferforth *adv.* See **farforth(e)**

fest(e) *n.* feast 142/12 *etc.*

festing *ppl. a.* feasting 228/21

festum enceniorum *n.* Hanukkah 181/16. See *note*

festyng *vbl. n.* feasting 220/17

fet *ppl. a.* drawn from 150/22

feynyd *ppl. a.* See **faynyd**

flesshely *adj.* worldly 223/16

florysheth *v. pr. 3 s.* embellishes 118/1; *vbl. n.* **floryshyng** blossoming 118/8

flowre *v.* flourish 168/31

flowres *n. pl.* rhetorical figures 128/2

flyt(te) v. get away 160/6; deviate 183/10 *etc.*

foded forth *ppl. a.* nourished and led on 218/14

folosophy *n.* foolish wisdom 256/20. See *note*

fond(e) *adj.* foolish 113/9 *etc.*; doting 164/6

for (that) *conj.* in order that 113/29 *etc.*; because 205/22 *etc.*

for(e) *prep.* on account of 113/20 *etc.*; in the character of, as 122/28 *etc.*; as for, as regards 182/7, 210/21; in favor of 252/9; for the sake of 253/39

forbare *v. pt.* did without 221/1; *ppl. a.* **forberyng** 151/23

forbede *v. subj.* forbid 192/29; *pt.* **forbade** 199/1–2; *pp.* **forbeden, forboden** 203/13, 233/10

forborne *pp.* done without, spared 222/29

for bycause *conj.* because 240/32

force *n.* concern 228/19; *make lyttel force of* attach little importance to 176/12; *of . . . force* of necessity 238/3

force *v.* be concerned, mind, care 171/15 *etc.*; hesitate, scruple 249/8; *pr. 3 s.* **forceth** is concerned, cares 134/21, 258/23

forgate *v. pt.* forgot 218/27

forsayd *ppl. a.* aforesaid 155/11

forslouth *v.* neglect out of laziness 173/27; *ppl. a.* **forslouthed** 218/14

forth *adv.* forward 209/19

for to *prep.* in order to 116/22 *etc.*

for why *conj.* because 243/27

fostred *v. fostred vs vp* brought us up 224/27

fote *n.* foot (of land) 145/2, 214/12

fou(w)le *adv.* grievously 167/1, 219/6; shamefully 251/34

foundacyon *n.* charter of establishment 139/14

founden, fow(n)den *pp.* found 114/21 *etc.*; invented 191/4; founded 214/33–34

frame *n. out of all frame* completely out of order 204/4–5

frantyke *adj.* delirious 159/32, 213/20

frely *adv.* without labor or cost, gratis 146/20 *etc.*

frere *n.* friar 122/28 *etc.*; *pl.* **frerys** 115/15

frete *v.* give way to anger 142/32; *pr. 3 s.* **freteth, fretyth** eats out 111/8 *etc.*; is consumed with vexation 142/24 *etc.* See *note on* 189/36

fro *prep.* from 121/31 *etc.*

frote *v.* foam at the mouth 142/32

frowarde *adj.* perverse 256/23

frowardly *adv.* perversely 238/24

frowardnes(se) *n.* perversity 194/31–32; wrongheadedness 256/31

full *adv.* exceedingly, very 128/23 *etc.*; completely 195/9, 209/2

furste *adj. the furste* in the first place 116/24

fyft(e) *adj.* fifth 123/13 *etc.*

fylth *n.* impurities 187/21

fylthy *adj.* disgraceful 223/9

fynd(e) *v.* provide (food) for 115/9 *etc.*; *fynd out* invent 239/22 *etc.*

fyndyng *vbl. n.* providing for one's living 115/12

fyne *adj. of fyne force* by absolute necessity 246/26

gageleth *v. pr. 3 s.* cackles 144/16

gagling *vbl. n.* cackling 144/13

galand, galant *n.* fine gentleman 207/18 *etc.*

Galathyes *n.* Galatians 255/10

gapyng(e) *vbl. n.* eager longing 159/5, 6

gat *v. pt.* obtained 161/20

gatheryng *vbl. n. made that gatheryng* took up that collection 203/15–16

gay *adj.* specious 118/2 *etc.*; showy 220/10 *etc.*

generacyon *n.* procreation 127/5 *etc.*

generaltye *n. for the generaltye* for the most part 221/6–7

gere *n.* stuff and nonsense 141/24, 253/8; material goods 144/24; doings, matter 197/24; apparel 224/14

geste *n.* laughingstock 153/32

gested *ppl. a.* entertained as a guest 147/7

gestynge *vbl. n.* entertain as a guest 147/6

get(e) *v.* beget 151/14 *etc.*

geue, gyue *v.* give, grant 129/6 *etc. gyue ouer* give up 183/31; *geue sentence* pronounce an opinion 211/18

geuer *n.* giver 148/29 *etc.*

glasse *n.* mirror 248/21 *etc.; pl.* **glassys** 248/20

glose *n.* a note in a commentary 180/3 *etc.*

godly *adj.* godly, goodly 162/34–35 *etc. See note*

godly *adv.* excellently, in a goodly fashion 145/36. *See note on* 145/36–146/1

goeth about *v. pr. 3 s.* attempts 251/20

goeth very farr wide *v. pr. 3 s.* is extremely inaccurate 126/21

go forth *v.* go away 166/10

golophers *n. pl.* gluttons 127/10. *See note*

good *adv. as good chepe as* just as cheaply as 144/6

good *n.* property, goods, wealth 222/30 *etc.*

goodly *adj.* handsome, striking 136/14 *etc.;* splendid 237/17

good will *n.* hearty consent 216/14

go(o)stely *adj.* spiritual 111/19 *etc.*

go to *v. imper.* come on 156/22; *v. phr.* consider 122/20, 123/30

gracyouse *adj.* endowed with divine grace, godly 162/30

gratytude *n.* free gift 129/12

grefe *n.* pain 121/10

gre(a)t(e) *adj.* great 116/25 *etc.; comp.* **greter** 207/36; *superl.* **grettyst** 182/13

greued *v. pt.* afflicted with pain 121/11

grote *n.* coin, originally four pence 138/3, 142/7

ground(e), grownd *n.* reason, basis 115/29 *etc.;* foundation (of a building) 122/6

grudge *n.* uneasiness, scruple 178/4, 219/12

grynde *v.* sharpen 136/17

grynnes *n. pl.* snares 168/26

grynnynge *ppl. a.* displaying his teeth 114/11

gyft *n.* transference (of property) 148/28

gyse *n.* custom 204/20

gyue ouer *v. See* **geue**

haft *n.* handle 171/18

handell *n.* excuse 208/32–33

handelynge *vbl. n.* treatment 239/10 *etc.*

hand *n. pl. at hys own hand* at his own disposal 216/16; *set hand* undertake 228/27

hangeth *v. pr. 3 s.* depends 250/21

happe *v. impers.* happen 151/7 *etc.*

happely *adv.* perhaps 146/21–22 *etc.*

hard *v. pt.* heard 132/11; *hard speke* heard tell 134/5

hardnes *n.* difficulty 197/8

harm(e) *n.* pain 187/35; *take harme* sustain injury 254/17

harneyse *n.* armor 220/13

hedlynge *adv.* headlong 175/33

help(e) *n.* remedy 141/24 *etc.*

helpe vs hense *v.* help us get out of here 221/13

helth(e) *n. in helth(e)* sound of body 220/8, 223/28

hepe *n.* pile of material wealth 222/31

herawdys *n. pl.* heralds 220/11

here saye *v.* hear from others 233/21

hersys *n. pl.* hearses 220/11. *See note*

heuely *adv.* grievously 115/10 *etc.*

heuy *adj.* grievous 114/17 *etc.;* weighty 136/6

heuynes, heuenysse *n.* sadness, grief 112/15 *etc.; heuynes of hart* heartfelt sadness 191/20

heuynward *n. to heuynward* for gaining heaven 258/2

Hierom, Hyerom(e) *n.* St. Jerome 239/27 *etc.*

Hierusalem, Hyerusalem *n.* Jerusalem 164/26 *etc.*

hinder *v.* impair 174/7

hit *pron.* it 235/15 *etc.*

hold(e) *v.* refrain 172/15; *holde for* consider to be 253/36; *pp.* **holden** held 124/17 *etc.;* considered 234/32; espoused 255/22

holde *n.* support 180/11, 240/2; *in holde* in confinement 113/16

hole *adj.* entire 112/13 *etc.;* healthy 166/34 *etc.;* holy 175/7 *etc. See note on* 175/7

hole *adv.* fully, completely 195/9, 209/3

holpe *v. pt.* helped 114/30

holpen *ppl. a.* helped 111/17 *etc.*

homly *adj.* rudely familiar 134/8

hopyd *v. subj. hopyd of* hoped for 205/31

hospytall *n.* charitable institution for the needy 142/9, 155/21; *pl.* **hospytals** 117/17 *etc.*

hotely *adv.* eagerly 132/32

how(e) be it *adv.* however 212/11 *etc.*

howsell *n.* the reception of the eucharist 257/18

huker moker *n. in huker moker* in secret 233/22

humours *n. pl.* elementary bodily fluids 189/13

hundred *adj.* hundreth 115/28 *etc. See note*

hundreth *adj.* hundred 116/3–4, 245/24. *See note on* 115/28

husbandes *n. pl.* managers, stewards 214/13–14

hyduouse *adj.* hideous 120/8

Hyerom(e) *n. See* **Hierom**

Hyerusalem *n. See* **Hierusalem**

hygh harted *ppl. a.* arrogant 195/30, 197/11–12; *comp.* **hygher harted** 224/12 *etc.*

hyghnous *adj.* heinous 127/22

hym selfe *pron.* he himself 129/26 *etc.*

hyndryng *vbl. n.* impairment 161/1

hyt *pron.* it 132/12

hys *poss. pron.* its 186/23 *etc.*

illumynyd *pp.* enlightened intellectually 163/36

imagynacyon, ymagynacyon *n.* mental image 188/36–189/1, 249/11

immedyate *adj.* dealing directly, without intermediary 216/11

imperfyte *adj.* flawed 188/19

importeth *v. pr. 3 s.* signifies 198/23

importunatly *adv.* inopportunely 112/3; exceedingly 115/17

importune *adj.* vexatious 205/27

impugnacyon *n.* refutation 169/12

impugnynge *ppl. a.* attacking 231/3

in *prep.* on 245/24 *etc.*

incontynency(e) *n.* unchastity 116/26 *etc.*

incredulyte *n.* lack of Christian faith 196/5

indifferent, indyfferent *adj.* impartial 145/29–30 *etc.*

induceth *v. pr. 3 s.* leads 247/35

indyfferently *adv.* impartially 216/18

infect *pp.* afflicted 167/1; contaminated 172/23

inhabytable, inhabitable *adj.* uninhabitable 150/31 *etc.*

inough, ynoughe, ynow *adv.* enough 239/19 *etc.*

inough *pron. See* **yno(u)gh(e)**

inow(ghe), inough, ynough, ynow *adj.* enough 120/13 *etc.; ynoughe to* sufficient for 193/25

instytute *pp.* instituted 204/21

instytucion, institucyon, instytucyon *n.* words used in the consecration of the eucharist 254/19; establishment of the eucharist 254/10 *etc.*

insypyentys *n. pl.* fools 181/31. *See note*

interdyccyon *n.* laying (a place) under interdict 128/34

interprysynge *vbl. n.* attempt 137/18

Iohan *n.* John 128/29 *etc.; poss.* **Iohans** 128/25

iust *adj.* exact 123/30

keene *n. pl.* cows 185/17

kepe *v.* provide for 121/31; *kepe away* hold back 237/19; *pr. 3 s.* **kepeth** protects 175/30

kepers, kepars *n. pl.* guardians 222/5 *etc.*

kinred, kynred *n.* blood relationship 228/13, 19

knowledge *v.* acknowledge 258/21

knytteth *v. pr. 3 s.* concludes 136/5–6, 150/21; *pp. knyt* joined 258/7

kokered *pp.* pampered 224/18

kyll *v.* do away with 154/18; *kyll up* kill off completely 144/6

kynred *n. See* **kinred**

kyrtels *n. pl.* gowns 224/6

laborers *n. pl.* ones performing or executing something 116/19

laboureth . . . to *v. pr. 3 s.* endeavors to persuade, entreats 116/12–13

lak(ke) *v.* be lacking 149/28 *etc.*

lapped *ppl. a.* wrapped up 221/18

largely *adv.* generously 165/15, 170/30

larger *adj. comp.* more abundant 146/16
laste *n. at the laste* finally 242/24–25
late *adv.* recently 121/8 *etc.*
laud(e) *n.* praise 185/12, 258/16
lay *n.* layman 148/27
lay *v.* allege, bring forward as evidence
 157/9 *etc.; lay . . . (vn)to his charge* attribute to him, blame him (for) 120/16–17
 etc.; pr. 3 s. **lay(e)th** attributes (to),
 blames (on) 115/10 *etc.; charges,* alleges
 116/23 *etc.; layeth he from* does not attribute to 135/10; *pt.* **lay(e)d** *layed out*
 distributed 135/8; *layed . . . for theyr parte*
 alleged on their side 140/26; *layd vp* put
 away, saved 221/30
laysour, leys(o)ure *n.* opportunity 118/15,
 177/3; deliberation 257/16; *at your
 leysure* at your pleasure 112/7
Lazare *n.* Lazarus 196/12
ledde *ppl. a. sone ledde* easily led 215/12
lefte of *v. pt.* abandoned 138/4
lene . . . to *v.* rely on 178/11
lenger *adv. comp.* longer 176/31 *etc.; superl.*
 lengest 188/27
lengthyng *vbl. n.* extension 177/11
leprye *n.* leprosy 167/1
lerned, lernyd *v. pt.* taught 160/13 *etc.*
le(e)se *v.* lose 142/21 *etc.*
lesse *adj. comp.* fewer 136/24
lessed *pp.* diminished 188/35
lest(e) *adj. superl. at the leste wyse* to even a
 minimal degree 119/21 *etc.*
let(te) *v.* omit or forbear to do something
 120/19 *etc.;* hesitate 147/14, 208/6;
 hinder 150/29; cease 180/13; *pr. 3 s.*
 letteth stops 190/15 *etc.; pp.* **letted**
 hesitated 224/31
letterd, lettred *ppl. a.* learned 208/5,
 208/13
leue *n.* permission 221/16, 251/10
leue *v.* leave off, stop 206/20; abandon
 242/6 *etc.; pr. 3 s.* **leueth** leaves off, stops
 134/12; *pt. subj. left of* forsook 138/4
leuer *adv.* rather 142/18
lewd(e) *adj.* wicked, base 126/27 *etc.*
lewd(e)nes *n.* wickedness 141/26, 199/29–
 30
ley *adj.* secular, nonclerical 159/17
leys(o)ure See **laysour**
limbo patrum, lymbus patrum *n.* region

of hell for the just who died before
 Christ's coming 179/21 *etc. See note*
lo(o) *interj.* behold 136/10 *etc.*
loke *n.* appearance 219/8
loke *v.* expect 118/29 *etc.;* look for 243/28
longe *adv.* long ago 164/33. *See note on*
 164/32–33
lose *v.* loosen, remove 186/33; *pp.* **losyd**
 203/17
loth(e) *adj.* unwilling 125/17 *etc.*
lothenes *n.* unwillingness 176/25
lowd *adv.* blatantly 134/21
lowd(e) *adj.* blatant 131/2, 134/29
lust *n.* desire, inclination 118/15
lustely *adv.* gladly, willingly 199/29
lusty *adj.* cheerful 189/14; self-confident
 203/7
lybert(y)e *n.* permission 116/16; *putteth . . .
 at lybertye* allows 253/10–11
lycence, lycense *n.* permission 116/13 *etc.*
lyen *pp.* lain 111/28
lyght *adj.* easy 175/31 *etc.;* unthinking,
 frivolous 178/7; quick 188/25
lyght *adv.* frivolously, lightly 235/4
lyght *n. comme vnto lyght* come into the
 open 234/7
lyghtnes(se) *n.* readiness 174/22; frivolity
 241/24 *etc.*
lyghtsome *adj.* clear 182/4
lyke, like *adj.* likely 135/7, 153/7; *such other
 thyngys lyke* other similar things 187/29–
 30; *lyke (vn)to* similar to 189/2 *etc.*
lyke *adv.* equally 256/27; *lyke as* even as
 187/35 *etc.*
lyke *v.* please 111/14 *etc.; pr. 3 s.* **lyketh**
 approves of 256/12
lyke wyse as, lykewyse as *conj.* in the same
 manner as, just as 143/29 *etc.*
lyklyhod, lykelyhed *n. of lyklyhod* in all
 probability 122/2 *etc.*
lykyng *vbl. n. lyking of* delight in 176/29 *etc.*
lymbus patrum *n. See* **limbo patrum**
lymmes *n. pl. lymmes of the deuyll* agents of
 the devil 236/22–23
lymyteth *v. pr. 3 s.* specifies 216/26
lymytour *n.* regulator 122/25
lyppe *n. make a lyppe* express vexation or
 merriment at 125/7
lyst(e) *v.* wish, desire 121/1 *etc.; what him
 lyste* as he pleases 248/34

lyue by *v. lefte you to lyue by* left you something to live on 222/9

lyuelod *n.* means of living 134/27

lyuely *adj.* living 187/18. *See note*

magnyfyeng(e) *vbl. n.* extolling 173/32, 174/6

maior *n.* major premise of a syllogism 249/33

make *v. make the mater strange* make difficulties 153/19; *make lyttel force of* attach little importance to 176/12; *make as pretend that* 176/17; *make vs very sure* assure ourselves 191/17; *make as though* act as if 251/24; *pr. 3 s.* **maketh** counts, avails (of evidence) 165/18 *etc.;* *maketh nothynge for* lends no support to 243/31

make bate *n.* breeder of strife 130/7

makynge *vbl. n. in makynge* in the course of being composed 114/28

malaperte *adj.* presumptuous, insolent 150/9. *See note*

maner *n.* fashion 123/26 *etc.;* custom 140/7; *maner (of)* kind of 160/27 *etc.; in a maner* in some way or degree 234/30; *in maner* as it were 235/2; *by some maner meanes* somehow 247/13; *pl.* **maner** 189/16

manhed *n.* state of being human 201/2

ma(e)yntenaunce *n.* supporting, abetting 194/35, 236/27

many *adj.* many of 210/4

marcy *n.* mercy 174/6 *etc. See note*

marcyfull *adj.* merciful 199/5, 222/34

margentes *n. pl.* margins 133/7

marked *v. pt.* noted 137/29; *pp.* heeded 234/14

markys *n. pl.* coins equal to 160 pence each 129/2

marrars *n. pl.* spoilers 127/4

marred *v. pp.* hampered 125/31

maruelo(u)se, meruaylouse, meruelous *adv.* wonderfully 174/16 *etc.*

mary *interj.* to be sure 159/4. *See note*

masse pens, masse pennys *n. pl.* money given to a priest to say mass for someone 115/19–20, 224/25. *See note on* 115/19–20

mat(t)er *n. maketh hym lytell mater* is of little consequence to him 254/26–27

maundy(e) *n.* Last Supper 242/15 *etc.*

maynteyne *v.* support 250/16

mayre *n.* mayor 132/11

mayster *n.* teacher 258/19

maystershyp(pe) *n.* the personality of a master or gentleman 133/30, 207/24

maystred *pp.* controlled 234/11

mean(e) *n.* method, means 195/7 *etc.; pl.* **meanes, meanys** intercession 111/10, 218/21; method, way 157/17 *etc.*

meane *adj.* middle 215/21

meane season *n.* meantime 158/30

meany *adj.* many 139/5. *See note*

medew *n.* meadow 243/28

medyate *adj.* acting through an intermediate person 216/11

member *n.* part 198/20–21

memoryall, memoreall *n.* something by which a person is remembered 237/12 *etc.*

mend(e) *v. intrans.* improve, correct oneself 201/24 *etc.*

ment of *v. pt.* intended to refer to 185/19, 190/11

meruayle *n.* wonder 248/21 *etc.*

meruayle, meruayll, merueyll *v. I meruayle me* I marvel 238/3 *etc.*

meruaylouse, mervelous *adv. See* **maruelo(u)se**

mete *adj.* proper, appropriate 136/33 *etc.*

mete *n.* solid food, meal 115/9 *etc.*

meteles *adj.* without food 142/13

metely *adv.* fairly, tolerably 236/33

mich *adv. See* **mych(e)**

mich *pron. See* **mych**

minor *n.* minor premise of a syllogism 249/33

misshappe *v.* have the misfortune (to do something) 188/29; *pt.* **myshappenyd** 192/29

mo *pron.* more 134/5 *etc.*

mo(o) *adj. comp.* more 124/17 *etc.*

mo(o) *adv.* more, besides 123/15 *etc.*

moch(e) *adj. and adv. See* **mych(e)**

mok *n. maketh a mok at* derides 226/33

mok *v.* deride 167/11; trifle 176/15

mokkage *n.* mockery 221/31

mokkys *n. pl. makyng mokkys . . . at* deriding 178/2

moneth *n.* month 121/11

monument *n.* record 181/23; *pl.* **monu-mentis** records 129/30

more *adj. comp.* greater 119/7, 207/24

mortall *adj.* deadly 172/23 *etc.*

mort(e)mayn, morte mayne *n.* condition of lands held unalienably by an ecclesiastical or other corporation 213/31 *etc. See note*

mortuary *n.* a customary gift claimed by a parish priest from the estate of a deceased parishoner 115/20 *etc. See note*

most(e) *adj. superl.* greatest 113/11 *etc.*

mote *v.* may 228/24

moued *pp.* proposed 140/20; *v. pt.* 140/24

mouth *n.* *hys awne mouth* from his own mouth 146/30; *of mouth* in spoken words 190/20–21; *pl.* **mouthis** *vppon other mennys mouthis* on the basis of what others have said 117/4. *See note on* 146/30

mow(e) *v.* be able to 129/29, 160/21. *See note on* 129/29

mowes *n. pl.* derisive grimaces 178/2

multytude *n.* number 148/4

murtheryd *pp.* murdered 117/2; *v. pt.* **murdred** 134/34

mych, mich *pron.* much 116/4 *etc.*

mych(e), moch(e) *adj.* much 112/21 *etc.;* many 175/33, 205/2

mych(e), mich, moch(e) *adv.* greatly 111/15 *etc.*

myddys *n.* *a myddys of* into the middle of 188/3

mydle yerth *n.* the world as supposed to occupy the center of the universe 134/3

myght *v. subj.* would be able 125/4 *etc.*

mynd(e) *n.* idea, thought 116/10 *etc.;* opinion 208/7 *etc.; hygh mynde* arrogance 241/27; *was . . . in mynde* intended 257/4–5 *etc.; pl.* **myndis** intentions 178/6; *monthys mynde* a mass celebrated for someone a month after his death 220/15. *See note on* 220/15

myndeth *v. pr. 3 s.* intends 118/21 *etc.; ppl. a.* **myndyng** caring about 112/20; *ppl. a.* **mynded** inclined 113/35

mynysh(e), mynysshe *v.* diminish 172/21 *etc.; pp.* **mynysshed** 158/7

myny(s)sh(e)ment *n.* lessening, diminution 112/12 *etc.*

mynyster *v.* administer 154/4; *pp.* **mynystred** 154/15; *vbl. n.* **mynystryng** 161/11

myred on *pp.* bespattered with filth 233/31

myscheu(e)ouse *adj.* injurious 150/24 *etc.*

myschyefe, myschef(e) *n.* evildoing 112/21 *etc.*

myscreaunt(e) *adj.* unbelieving 172/27, 196/11

myscreauntes *n. pl* infidels 173/5

myshap *n.* bad luck 119/20

myshappenyd *v. pt. See* **misshappe**

myslyke *v.* dislike 160/7; *pp.* **myslyked** 220/5

mysse *n.* loss 152/12

mysseconster *v.* misinterpret 132/30

mysse vnderstanders *n. pl.* those who misunderstand 195/20

mystaketh *v. pr. 3 s.* misconstrues 164/24

naked *adj.* *naked to the shew* for all to see 119/26–27

nat(te) *adv.* not 141/8 *etc.*

naturall *adj.* without Christian faith 171/1; inborn 171/5; having natural feelings or intelligence 205/25 *etc.;* based on the order of nature 246/5; *naturall folys* born fools 252/10

naught *pron. See* **no(u)ght**

naughty, noughty, nawghty *adj.* bad, wicked 153/9, 156/27; worthless 208/30 *etc.*

nay *adv.* no 142/4 *etc.; say nay* express dissent 133/30

necessyte *n.* need 202/22, 213/20; time of need 208/34

neclygence *n.* neglect 175/29

nede *adj.* necessary 153/5 *etc.*

nede *n.* distress, emergency 145/6 *etc.; pl.* **nedys** wants 165/23

nede *v. impers.* be necessary 183/26; *pr. 3 s.* **nedeth** is necessary 184/15; *what shall me nede* why will it be necessary for me 246/24–25

nedys, nedes, nedis *adv.* of necessity 111/25 *etc.*

nere *adv.* closely 112/27; close 181/1

nere *adv.* never 135/15; not at all 154/13 *etc.*

neuer the more *adv.* not at all the more 188/35

new *adj.* *of new* recently 167/15

new(e) *adv.* recently 142/33, 191/4

noble *n.* old English gold coin 124/29; *pl.* **nobles** 124/26

Noes *n. poss.* Noah's 164/33

no(u)ght *adj.* bad, worthless 126/33 *etc.*

no(u)ght, naught *pron.* nothing 129/5 *etc.*

nomber *v.* ascertain the amount of 150/23

none *adj.* no 129/17 *etc.*

none *pron. none other* nothing else 161/9 *etc.*

not and *conj.* not even if 221/4

nother *adj.* other 152/4, 214/26; *neyther nother* neither the one nor the other 226/32

nother *adv.* neither 123/19

nothyng(e), nothing, no thing, no thyng *adv.* not at all, in no way 113/31 *etc.*

noughty *adj. See* **naughty**

noyaunce *n.* trouble, harm 115/3

noyous *adj.* vexing, troublesome 254/28

nyce *adj.* coy 153/18; loose-mannered 153/21. *See note on* 153/18–25

nygh *adj.* close 112/23

oblyuion, oblyuyon *n.* forgetfulness 218/17, 227/34

obtayne *v. intrans.* prevail 140/28; *pt.* **obtaynyd** 161/20

occasyon *n.* cause (for) 174/22 *etc.; by occasyon of* through the incidental agency of 186/7; *pl. vppon greate occasyons* for important reasons 126/17

of *adv.* off 119/26 *etc.*

of *prep.* on account of 111/15 *etc.;* from 119/9 *etc.;* by 120/11 *etc.;* off of 120/11; concerning, about 124/27 *etc.;* out of 174/11; in consequence of 187/5, 198/32; on (our side) 211/24; *belefe of* belief in 113/12 *etc.*

offyce *n.* duty, task 199/25

ofrynge vp *ppl. a.* presenting 220/11

oft(e) *adv.* often 247/5; *as oft as* whenever 198/25

olde *adj. of old* formerly 167/15

one *adj. all one* the same thing 234/29–30

onely *adj.* sole 115/12 *etc.; onely fayth* faith alone 159/29, 174/27; mere 176/32 *etc.*

ones, onys *adv.* once, at one time 113/8 *etc.*

ony *adv.* any 186/10

onys *adv. See* **ones**

open *adj.* clear, evident 183/21 *etc.*

opened *ppl. a.* made manifest 176/19

order *n.* customary procedure, rationale 140/8 *etc.*

orderlesse *adv.* without order 198/36

or ere *conj.* before 138/13

orient *adj.* precious, excellent 224/21

other *conj.* either 199/18

other *pron. pl.* others 170/30 *etc.*

otherwese *adv. none otherwese* in no other way 238/19

ouchys *n. pl. See* **owchis**

ouer *adv.* too, excessively 166/31, 199/11

ouer, over *prep.* beyond 113/11 *etc.*

ouer go *v.* surpass 203/7

ouer match *v.* defeat 140/31

ouermych *adj.* excessive 176/29

ouer se *v. refl.* blunder 137/15; *pp.* **ouersene** 251/35

ouersene *adj.* rash, mistaken 255/13

ouerture *n.* disclosure 160/4

ought *adv.* anything at all 216/31

ought, aught *pron.* anything 149/12 *etc.*

our self(e) *pron.* ourselves 169/11 *etc.; we ourselves* 227/14

ow *v.* have or cherish 206/1

owchis, ouchys *n. pl.* clasps, brooches 224/7 *etc.*

owt(e) *adv. owt of questyon* in no doubt 133/3; *owt of* free from 146/18

pacyence *n. take pacyence . . . of* accept patiently 120/2

pagea(u)nt *n.* scene on a stage 131/14 *etc.*

paraduenture, peraduenture *adv.* perhaps 120/19 *etc.*

parceiue, parceyue, perceyue, percyue *v.* comprehend fully 117/33 *etc.; pp.* **perceyued** recognized 213/14

parcell meale *adv.* bit by bit 112/7

parceyuable *adj.* perceptible 152/12

parceyue *v. See* **parceiue**

parde *adv.* assuredly 158/34

pardoners *n. pl.* preachers of indulgences 115/15. *See note*

parformyd *pp.* carried into effect 117/29; completed 177/5

parsuaded vnto some men caused some men to believe 174/34

parsuasyon *n.* conviction 174/8

part(e) *n.* party, faction 149/9 *etc.;* share 138/29, 184/29; side of an argument 180/12 *etc.; vppon the tother parte* on the other side 170/4; *take a parte* take sides 178/8; *for our parte* on our side 190/24 *etc.; the great parte* most 197/33 *etc.; on the contrary part* on the other hand 228/5–6

parted *ppl. a.* departed, deceased 201/31

partelettes, partelettys *n. pl.* ruffs, collars 224/7 *etc.*

parteners *n. pl.* See **partyners**

particuler *adj.* individual 188/13

partye *n. partye defendaunte* defendant 135/29; *pl.* **partyes** individuals 174/20

partyners, parteners *n. pl.* partakers, sharers in 184/35 *etc.*

paruerse, peruerse *adj.* wicked 133/25, 136/10

paryng *n.* peeling 257/13

passe *n.* completion 217/16

passe *v.* surpass 160/26, 203/7

passed *ppl. a.* in the past, former 130/3; past 224/22

pastis, pastys *n. pl.* ornamental head-dresses 224/8 *etc. See note on* 224/15

pater noster *n.* (*Lat.*) the Lord's Prayer 258/18

payn(e) *n.* punishment 157/8 *etc.; vppon payn of heresye* or else be punished by being charged with heresy 157/8

payned *pp.* punished 185/35

paynted *pp.* rhetorically adorned 257/16

payntyd *ppl. a.* specious, feigned 139/21

paynym *adj.* pagan 194/14

Paynym *n.* pagan 171/2 *etc.; pl.* **Paynyms** 165/6 *etc.*

peason *n. pl.* peas 224/21

peccadulyans *n. pl.* minor sins 161/8. *See note*

pece *n.* sample 133/26; portion 228/13

pens(e), pennys *n. pl.* pence 115/20 *etc.*

peraduenture *adv. See* **paraduenture**

percase *adv.* perhaps, maybe 221/10

perceyue, percyue *v. See* **parceiue.**

perceyuynge *vbl. n.* being perceived 247/7

perle *n.* the substance of pearls 224/8

perled *ppl. a.* decorated with pearls 224/14–15

person *n. See notes on* 115/33 *and* 201/1

pertayne *v.* belong as a legal right 134/32

peruerse *adj. See* **paruerse**

peruise *n.* public, academic disputation 251/36

peruse *v.* consider one by one 118/5

pestylent(e) *adj.* pernicious, noxious 233/9 *etc.*

peter pense *n. pl.* tax paid to the papal see 128/30 *etc.*

pewlyng *ppl. a.* whining 136/31

phisyk *n.* medical treatment 225/24

phrase *n.* phraseology 238/28

place *n.* a short passage of a book 160/21 *etc.; haue (good) place* be (very) valid 154/23–24 *etc.; gyue place* yield 183/34

play(e)d *pp.* acted out 131/14, 148/2

playing *ppl. a.* enjoying onself 228/23

playn(e) *adj.* full 115/22, 139/16; clear, obvious 123/1 *etc.;* fully assembled 130/5; open 168/20

playne, plaine *adv.* clearly, absolutely 165/4 *etc.;* openly, plainly 237/23 *etc.*

playnesse *n. See note on* 124/25

ple *n.* legal suit 133/3 *etc.*

pleasure *n.* favor 253/10

plentuouse *adj.* abundant 215/16

plentuously *adv.* abundantly 165/10

plumpes *n. pl.* bands, bunches 167/24

plyght *n.* state, condition 218/16, 220/9

pokkys *n. pl.* pustules 167/1; *french pokkys* syphilis 120/35. *See note on* 120/34–35

polytyke, polytyque *adj.* judicious 139/23; scheming 155/3

pore blynde *adj.* totally blind 248/5

poynt *n.* jot, whit 228/12, 15; article 238/2; *in some poynt* in some way 198/19; *in that poynt* in that feature 199/35–200/1; *hygh poynt* crucial matter 216/4, 216/33–34

pray *v. trans.* beseech 153/22

preace *n.* crowd, throng 220/23. *See note on* 153/26

preacyth *v. pr. 3 s.* urges 153/26.

premunire, premunyre *n. See note on* 116/28

presentely *adv.* just then 257/21

presthed, presthod *n.* priesthood 204/36 etc.

presupposed *pp.* presupposing 198/23

pretended *v. pt. refl.* claimed to be 131/19

preue *v. See* **proue**

preuy tythys *n. pl. See note on* 115/18–19

probable *adj.* worthy of belief 178/16; demonstrable 240/2

probatys *n. pl. See note on* 115/19

proces *n.* legal action 129/32; line of argument 139/32, 152/3

proctour(e) *n.* official agent, proxy 119/27 *etc.; pl.* **proctours** 119/12. *See note on* 119/12

procure *v.* cause, bring about 113/31 *etc.;* take measures (to do something) 149/11

profe *n.* proving 121/16 *etc.*

profyte *n.* benefit 254/10 *etc.; pl.* **profettes** revenues 122/14

proll *v.* prowl 139/19

proper *adj.* fine looking 144/17; personal 227/18

proper *adv.* handsomely 164/5

property, propertie *n.* distinguishing attribute *sidenote* 234/5 *etc.*

proue, preue *v.* show, demonstrate 135/13 *etc.;* turn out 162/14 *etc.;* show by testing 187/13, 188/15

prouoke *v.* urge, spur on 204/24–25

prouydeth *v. pr. 3 s.* makes provision 137/29

prouys, proues *n. pl.* proofs, arguments 118/5 *etc.*

prowd *adv.* proudly 224/14

prykketh *v. pr. 3 s.* grieves 216/4

prysoned *ppl. a.* imprisoned 208/29

purpose *n.* proposition 164/28 *etc.; to purpose* to the point 214/20–21; *to thys purpose* concerning this issue 246/2

purpose *v.* intend, plan 119/34 *etc.; pr. 3 s.* **purposeth** presents 160/8

put *v. put lyttel dowte* raise little doubt 181/12; *put in* submitted 143/6, 143/32; *pp. put forth* distributed, published 114/25, 130/20; *pr. 3 s.* **putteth** asserts 123/2, 245/8; *putteth . . . owt of questyon* establishes unquestionably 179/26–27; *ppl. a. put vp(p)* presented 115/7 *etc.*

pykynge vp *vbl. n.* acquiring 224/8

pyll *v.* despoil, pillage 217/18

pyth *n.* logical force, pertinence 241/20

pyththy *adj.* full of significance, substantial 136/5

pytuo(u)se *adj.* pious 111/2, 115/6; compassionate 199/34, 200/13; pitiful 205/26. *See note on* 111/2–3

pytuously *adv.* pitiably, lamentably 241/24

quaftyng *vbl. n.* drinking heavily 211/12

quarell *n.* complaint 218/9

quarterage *n.* quarterly payment 123/4–5 *etc.*

quenchyd *ppl. a.* extinguished 149/26

quest(is) *n. See* **wardmote questis**

questyon *n. owt of questyon* in no doubt, undoubtedly 133/3 *etc.; in questyon* unresolved 135/14, 156/22–23

questyonlesse *adj.* unquestionable 217/36

quikened *pp.* roused, stirred up 218/16

quoth *v. pt.* said 207/21, 23

quycke, quyk *adj.* alive 115/4 *etc.*

quyet, quiete *n. in quyet* in a peaceful state 128/11, 186/4

quykly *adv.* vigorously 201/32

rable *n.* mob 144/2

race *v.* erase, wipe out 228/1, 18

ragmannes roll *n.* list 125/22. *See note*

ransaked vppe *v. pt.* searched through 136/13. *See note*

rap *v.* snatch 222/24

rate *n. after such rate* on such a scale 120/33–34; *after that rate* according to that valuation 124/11 *etc.; vpon the same rate* at the same valuation 125/16–17

rather *adv. ye rather* sooner, more quickly 111/10 *etc.; the rather* all the more 168/34

rauenouse *adj.* rapacious 149/28, 164/20. *See note on* 164/20

rauyne *n.* pillage 144/26

rauysshed *pp.* carried away 251/16

raylers *n. pl.* calumniators 141/25

rayn, reygne *v.* hold sway 120/33; *reygne vppon* hold sway over 127/34

reame, realm(e) *n.* kingdom 121/25 *etc.*

reason *n. as reason ys* as is reasonable 135/30; *of reason* rightly 199/16

rebownd *v.* return 227/33
receyued *pp.* accepted, permitted 239/11
receyuyng *vbl. n.* acceptance 182/27
reche *n.* comprehension 251/17
reche vnto *v.* comprehend 242/36
recommended, recommendyd *v. pt.* committed 111/17, 203/34
reconyng *vbl. n.* financial accounts 122/25, 31
recouer *v.* rescue 197/11
rede *v.* interpret, decipher 160/16
redemyng *vbl. n.* compensation 177/16
reele *v.* stagger 211/35 *etc.*
referr *v. refl.* appeal 122/3
refrayne *v. trans.* keep (from) 175/19 *etc.; pp.* **refrayned** restrained 156/31
refused *v. pt.* rejected 256/16–17
regarde *v.* esteem, value 198/1; *pt.* **regardyd** 227/21
rehersall *n.* recounting 119/35
reherse *v.* cite, quote 178/17 *etc.;* recount, recite 117/34–35 *etc.*
rek(en) *v.* consider, judge 122/28 *etc.;* count 126/7; *pr. 3 s.* **rekeneth, rekenyth** counts, estimates 125/15, 139/33
reke (oute) *v.* fume out 234/8
rekenyng(e), rekening(e) *vbl. n.* accounting, calculation 115/22 *etc.*
releue *v.* assist 142/9; pp. **relyued** 169/1
relyef(e) *n.* assistance 138/33, 210/21. *See note on* 138/33
relyeue *v.* set free 208/26
relygyous(e) *adj.* belonging to a religious order 111/19–20 *etc.*
relyued *pp. See* **releue**
remeaneth *v. pr. 3 s.* remains 181/22
remembraunce *n.* memory 235/21; reminder 236/16 *etc.;* commemorative discourse 181/23; *put you in remembraunce of* recall to your mind 189/4
remembryd, remembred *pp.* recounted, mentioned 161/7, 190/29–30
remnaunt(e), remenaunt, reman(n)aunte *n.* remainder, rest 118/22 *etc.*
remyt *v.* send back 120/25
rend *v.* grab 222/24. *See note*
repenteth *v. refl.* repents 222/32
repete *v.* recount 117/32
report *v. refl.* appeal 122/3

reproche *n. in my reproche* in order to reproach me 255/33
reprofe *n.* refutation 119/35; censure 194/13
reproue *v.* refute 170/25; *pp.* **reproued** 178/15; *vbl. n.* **reprouyng** rejecting 217/26
repugnant *adj.* contradicting 247/32 *etc.*
repugnaunce *n.* contradiction, inconsistency 247/30 *etc.*
repute *v.* consider 255/32
require, requyre *v.* request 119/10 *etc.; pt* **requyred** 196/9–10
resembled *pp.* compared 189/6, 30; *pr. p.* **resemblyng** comparing, likening 239/3
reserued *ppl. a.* preserved 181/24
resoned *ppl. a.* argued for 177/23
respecte *n.* consideration 145/21, 199/13–14; *for the respecte of* for the sake of 112/29
rest *v. pr. 3 pl.* are left over 193/11
reste *n.* peace 186/5; *in reste* at peace 179/21–22
restrayned *pp.* restricted 186/27
resydew *n.* remainder 139/1
resydew *adj.* remaining 152/22
ret(h)oryk(e), retoryque *n.* rhetoric 118/9 *etc.;* eloquence 125/23 *etc.*
reuoke *v.* retract 183/24
reygne *v. See* **rayn**
roll *v.* luxuriate 151/29; *ppl. a.* **rollynge** 127/29
rolles *n. pl.* rolls of written parchment 136/14
romys *n. pl.* positions 249/6
ronne *v. ronne to* fall upon 216/31; *pp.* driven 151/22, 163/21; *pt. ouer ronne hym selfe* exceeded his capacities 241/26; *pr. 3 s.* **ronneth** *ronneth vp to* goes back to 128/25
rosted *ppl. a.* roasted 144/11
rowghteth *v. pr. 3 s.* snores 212/27
rowtes *n. pl.* crowds of people 167/24
rude *adj.* inexpert 125/22
runne *v. runne on the brydle* run unbridled 200/2. *See note*
rustye *adj.* morally foul 111/9
ryall *adj.* royal 140/11 *etc.*
ryche *adj.* valuable 237/18

rychesse *n.* wealth 158/24 *etc.*
ryddyth *v. pr. 3 s.* sets free 198/13
ryflyng *vbl. n.* plundering 168/19
ryght, right *adv.* quite 121/8 *etc.*
ryseth *v. pr. 3 s.* arises 205/10; *ryseth vppon* is based on 242/30
rysshe *n.* rush 237/20

sad(de) *adj.* serious, sober 125/10 *etc.*; mature 243/16
sadly *adv.* earnestly 211/12
sa(y)eth *v. pr. 3 sg. See* **say**
safe *adj.* saved 187/16
saith *v. p. 3 s. See* **say**
sample *n.* example, instance 139/12 *etc.*
Sapience *n. boke of Sapience* Book of Wisdom 181/31
Saracene *n.* Saracen, Muslim 171/2. *See note*
sarue *v. See* **serue**
satysfaccyon *n.* performance of good deeds to make up for the temporal punishment due to sin 177/6 *etc.*
saue *prep.* except 134/19 *etc.*
saue *v.* prevent 139/27
sauourly *adv.* wisely 140/9
Sauours *n. poss.* Savior's 138/13. *See note*
sauynge *conj.* except 192/22 *etc.*
saw *n. olde sayd saw* maxim, proverb 218/24
sawce malaperte *n.* presumptuous sauciness 150/9. *See note*
say *v.* speak (for or against) 190/24 *etc.; say so well by* speak so well of 222/20; **sa(y)eth, saith, sayth** *v. pr. 3 s.* states, says 126/15 *etc.; pp.* **sayed** 146/26 *etc.; ppl. a.* **saynge, seynge** 130/2 *etc.*
scant(e) *adv.* hardly 156/20 *etc.*
scantly *adv.* scarcely 193/3
scarce *adj.* stingy 199/11
scryuener *n.* notary 119/22
season *n.* time 221/8; *for the season* for the time being 172/13; *at seasons* at times 227/13
secret(e) *adj.* beyond ordinary apprehension 151/5; disguised 160/4
see apostolyque *n.* papal see 163/1
sekynge *vbl. n.* trying to find 147/17
self(e) *pron.* itself 118/4 *etc.*
selfe *adj.* selfsame 234/33

sely *adj.* pitiable, helpless 111/6 *etc.*
semblaunce *n.* appearance 249/2
semyng of . . . reason what seems right to reason 248/9
send *pp.* sent 148/1
sensuall *adj.* perceptible by the senses 192/17
sentence *n.* meaning, sense 114/32; opinion, testimony 210/26 *etc.*
senys *n.* Siena 209/25. *See note*
serue, sarue *v.* treat 156/25; suffice 174/35; avail 200/28 *etc.*
seruyse *n.* liturgy 203/33
sessyons *n.* periodic sitting of the justices of the peace 131/8, 131/14
set(te) *v. set hym a wurke wyth:* see note on 114/8–9; *set out* deck out 142/9; *sette at nought* have total disregard for 163/13–14 *etc.; set so lyt(t)le by* have so little esteem for 163/24, 171/29; *sette . . . to* add . . . to 166/4; *set nought by* have no esteem for 168/17; *set hand* undertake 228/27; *ppl. a.* **settyng forth** promoting 166/16
seynge *ppl. a. See* **say**
shamfastnes *n.* ashamedness 227/20–21
sharpe *adj.* severe 199/35
shew *n.* display 133/27, 177/12; *at a sodayne shew* at first glance 118/2–3; *naked to the shew* for all to see 119/26–27
shew(e) *v.* declare 118/21 *etc.; pp.* **shewed** shown 116/24 *etc.*
shift *n. See* **shyft(e)**
shold(e) *v. mod. See* **shuld(e).**
shone *n. pl.* shoes 154/11, 222/12
short *adj.* hasty 174/27; immediate 199/29; *in short* concisely 118/4
shortly *adv.* in a short time 233/18
shote anker *n.* emergency anchor 180/5– 5. *See note*
shrew(e) *n.* rascal, villain 237/19 *etc.*
shrewd *adj.* wicked 214/13
shuld(e), shold(e), shud *v. mod.* should 113/10 *etc.; pl.* **shulden** 170/24
shyft(e), shift *n.* evasive device 180/4 *etc.; made ryght hard shyft* found it hard 121/20; *for a sodayn shyft* in a hasty makeshift way 149/8–9
shyfted *pp.* distributed 126/11, 138/27

shyfte ouer *v.* change positions 176/15

shypwrak(e), shyp wracke *n.* shipwreck 127/26–27

similitudes *n. pl.* similarities 236/6

simple. See **symple.**

skabbys *n. pl.* skin diseases 166/35

sklaunder of *n.* persons who are a disgrace to 153/4

skouchyn *n.* shield with armorial bearings 220/12

skyll *n. See* **canneth**

slewth *n.* sloth 223/16

sleyght *adj.* insignificant 163/31

sleyghte *adv.* slightly, poorly 235/3

smale *adj.* minor 163/7

smote *v. pt.* struck 170/12

smowdreth *v. pr. 3 s.* smoulders 188/26

sodayn *adj. at a sodayn shew* at first glance 118/2–3

sodaynly *adv.* extemporaneously 257/19

solempne *adj.* of great dignity 210/10; sumptuous 219/31–32

solempnely *adv.* ostentatiously 220/9–10

solycyte *v.* push forward 149/11

som(m)e, summe *n.* highest attainable point 182/4

som(e)tyme, sumtyme *adv.* once, formerly 149/30; sometimes 187/5 *etc.*

som(e)what *pron. See* **sumwhat**

sondry *adj.* distinct for each respectively 113/3, 189/16; various 141/10, 173/13

sone *adv.* immediately 134/15, 189/10; quickly, easily 215/12

songen *pp.* sung 204/16

sophisticacion *n.* use of sophistry 238/13

sophyster *n.* university student of logic 251/34

sore *adj.* distressed 115/7 *etc.;* in pain 138/14; grievous 149/32 *etc.*

sore *adv.* greatly, extremely 115/8 *etc.;* grievously 116/19 *etc.*

sorow *v.* lament 119/20

sorte *n.* manner 126/25

so that *conj.* so long as 142/21

soukyng *ppl. a.* nursing 258/15

sow *n. sow dronk(en)* extremely drunk 212/12, 212/25. *See note on* 212/12

soylyng *vbl. n.* absolving 115/21. *See note*

spake *v. pt.* spoke 179/3 *etc.*

sparyng *vbl. n.* forbearing 113/20

spech *n.* power of speech 226/22

specyall *adv.* especially, in particular 202/31, 224/10

spede *n.* success 117/34

spede *v. intrans.* succeed 144/17; *pp.* **sped(de)** brought to a successful conclusion 118/31 *etc.*

spedefull *adj.* efficacious 141/30

sportyng *vbl. n.* taking one's pleasure 228/24

spoyle *n.* spoliation, pillage 112/13, 142/20

spoyled, spoylyd *pp.* pillaged 153/27, 166/6

sprongen *pp. are sprongen* have sprung 111/21

spyrytualte, spyrytual(l)tye *n.* clergy 117/7 *etc.*

staggar *v.* waver, doubt 170/17; *pt.* **staggared**

stand(e) *v.* depend (on) 243/3; *stand . . . in stede* be of use or advantage 184/10–11 *etc.; stande in suche case* are in such a position 218/6–7; *stande (ther)wyth* be consistent with 211/34, 243/4; *stande to gyther* be logically consistent 247/33 *etc.; pt.* **stoode all by** was entirely established by 215/3; *subj.* **stode** would stand 183/4; **standen** *pp.* stood 220/22

stede *n. in (the) stede of* in place of 167/13 *etc.*

stode *v. subj. See* **stand(e)**

stomake *n.* feelings 218/22

store *n.* abundant supply 135/13

storyes *n. pl.* historical accounts 165/11, 245/25

strange *adj. make the mater strange* is reluctant, makes difficulties 153/19

strayght *adj.* strict 199/12

strechyd *v. pt.* pressed forward 149/19

strenger *adj. comp.* stronger 141/11

strenght(e) *n.* force (of authority) 195/14, 239/30

stryue *v.* compete 141/12

study *n.* deliberate effort 233/25

studyeng *vbl. n.* meditating 147/21

studyouse in *adj.* attentive to 243/15

stycke, styk(ke) *v.* haggle, delay 241/17; *styk therat* hesitate at it 153/3; *stykke styf* persist obstinately 194/18; *styk in theyr teeth* resist utterance 203/9

styf *adv.* obstinately 194/18

styffe *adj.* stubborn 210/29

styk(ke) *v. See* **stycke**

styll *adv.* without change, always 145/8 *etc.;* continually 189/28 *etc.*

stynt *n.* allotment 175/9

styrre *v.* move, induce 118/20

substancyall *adj.* solid 243/16

substancyally *adv.* in a sound maner, on a solid basis 203/5–6

substaunce *n.* wealth 134/27 *etc.; whole substaunce: see note on* 237/13

sue *v.* sue *to* make a petition to 216/13; *pt. sued a praemunire* asked a court to issue a writ of praemunire 116/31–32

suertye *n.* safety 128/11

suffer *v. suffer hym abuse* allow him to deceive 113/21; *pp.* **suffered** tolerated 238/1

sufferaunce, sufferauns *n.* patient endurance 190/20; permission 221/11

suffragans *n. pl.* auxiliary bishops 115/14

suffrages, suffragis, suffragys *n. pl.* prayers for the souls of the dead 111/19 *etc. See note*

summa *n.* total 123/32 *etc.*

summary *adj.* general, overall 160/20

summa totalis *n.* sum total 124/23, 125/6

summe *n. See* **som(m)e**

summeth *v. pr. 3 s.* totals 126/4

sumtyme *adv. See* **som(e)tyme**

sumwhat, som(e)what *pron.* something 192/27 *etc.*

sure *adj.* affording safety 142/9

surety *n.* certainty (of attaining some end) 202/19, 208/16

surmysynge *ppl. a.* charging 130/24–25; *pp.* **surmysed** legally submitted as a charge 131/10; falsely devised 204/3

surrepcyon *n.* unperceived stealing in upon one's mind, a sudden temptation 188/6

suspendyng *vbl. n.* temporary deprivation of one's office 115/20. *See note*

sustayn, susteyn *v.* keep 121/31, 35

suster *n.* sister 218/19

sute, suyt *n.* litigation 129/32 *etc.;* legal prosecution 132/33; kind, sort 210/3, 15

sutely *adj.* suitable, matching 155/29

suttelte *n.* cleverness 118/8. *See note on* 118/8–9

suyt *n. See* **sute**

swarmeth *v. pr. 3 s. swarmeth full of* swarms entirely with 144/19

swerd(e), sworde *n.* sword 133/24 *etc.*

symple, simple *adj.* unsophisticated, uneducated 113/12 *etc.;* slight 187/27

synysterly *adv.* unfavorably 132/30

systern *n. pl.* sisters 170/2

syth *conj.* since 113/23 *etc.; syth that* since 111/20 *etc.*

syth *prep.* from the time of 151/9

take *v.* undergo, receive 207/2, 20; *take theym* betake themselves 180/5; *take theyr faut to them self* assume the blame themselves 184/29–30; *pr. p.* **takyng** considering to be 235/2–3; *pr. 3 s. taketh . . . for* considers to be 254/26

takelynge *n.* gear 180/5

taken *pp.* arrested 131/17; accepted 239/23

takyng *vbl. n.* acceptance (of a word) 186/30

tale *n.* account, story 128/9 *etc.;* message 194/29; *by tale* counting one by one 155/31; *pl.* **talys** falsehoods 178/1

taryed *v. pt.* remained 251/27

tay *v.* tie 117/26

teeth *See* **caste**

temperyth *v. pr. 3 s.* regulates 197/25

temporall, temporyll *adj.* secular, civil 116/18 *etc.;* temporary 173/23–24 *etc.*

temporaltye *n.* the whole body of laymen 126/30 *etc.*

tere *v.* lacerate 225/31

testament *n.* will 223/13

testifyed, testyfyed *pt.* proved, confirmed 255/14–15 *etc.*

than *adv.* then 234/18 *etc.*

thank(e) *n.* gratitude or expression thereof 134/19; *ye brydegromys thank* gratitude owed to the bridegroom 237/24–25

that *conj.* because 198/14; *as well for that* both because 205/22

that, thet *rel. pron.* that which 197/33 *etc.*

thays *pron.* "they's" 150/27. *See note on* 150/21

the *pron.* you 201/28

the(y)m self(e) *pron.* themselves 170/26
etc.; they themselves 194/34 *etc.*

then *conj.* than 111/13 *etc.*

then *prep.* than 112/19 *etc.*

thense *adv.* from there 178/21 *etc.*

therefore *adv.* to that end 165/28; for it
192/32 *etc. See note on* 257/15

therfro *adv.* from that or it 160/6 *etc.*

therin. *adv. See* **theryn**

therof *adv.* of that 114/26 *etc.;* from it or
that 219/16

theron *adv.* on that or it 187/15

ther(e)to *adv.* to that or it 118/4 *etc. See note
on* 205/8

therup(p)on, there vpon *adv.* from that
117/30, 238/11; about that 121/3

therwyth, therwith *adv.* besides 204/30–
31 *etc.;* with that 211/34

theryn, therin *adv.* about it 192/27, 257/8

these *pron. these be these* "these be they's"
150/21. *See note*

thet *rel. pron. See* **that**

thorow(e) *prep.* throughout 115/23 *etc.;*
through 171/18 *etc.;* by means of 177/1

thorowly *adv.* completely 188/32

thou *pron.* you 207/22

thoughte *v. pt.; me thoughte* it seemed to me
256/35

though yᵗ, though that though 138/28,
214/21

thyder *adv.* thither 140/16, 198/15

thyngys, thyngis *n. pl.* matters 117/31 *etc.;*
considerations 118/1; *all thyng(e)* all
things, everything 139/20 *etc.*

thys *pron.* these 171/19. *See note*

thy self *pron.* yourself 192/2; you yourself
201/27

to *adv.* too, in excess 116/4 *etc.*

to *adv.* too, in addition 140/13 *etc.*

to *prep.* so as to produce 220/16; *geuyng
counseyll . . . to the makyng* advising to
compose 114/4; *to godwarde, to god ward*
toward God 215/11, 223/17; *to the world
ward* toward the world 223/17

to gyder, togyder, togyther, to gether *adv.*
together 167/23 *etc.*

token *pp.* taken 214/34

told *ppl. a. thre tymys told* counted three
times, times three 212/18

tolter *v.* flounder, toss 189/24, 225/20

tonne *n. pl.* casks 179/11

too *prep.* to 246/11

too *n. from top to too* from head to toe
225/30

torned *pp. See* **tourned**

touche *v. See* **towch(e)**

tourne *v. refl. See* **turne**

tourned *v. pt.* converted 165/2; *pp.* **torned**
torned into converted to 163/35

toward *prep.* in store for 177/8; with regard to 200/29; *toward vs ward* as it concerns us 223/25

towch(e), touche *v.* affect 112/27; rebuke
198/28; *ppl. a.* **towchynge** injuring
192/24; *vbl. n.* **towchyng** *towchyng of*
treatment of 137/26, 162/12; *as towchyng*
concerning 238/2 *etc.*

translacyon *n.* removal 136/26

translated *pp.* removed 155/14, 158/14;
transferred 215/1, 237/30

translatyng(e) *vbl. n.* removal 127/27 *etc.*

trauayle *v.* work hard 111/22

traynes *n. pl.* snares 168/26

treasure *n.* store, stock 199/17

trew(e) *adv. sayd trew* spoke the truth
120/19

trewe *adj.* truthful 114/25

trewthe *n. of trewthe* in fact 132/24 *etc.*

troble *v.* molest 116/19; *pp.* **trobled** 117/13

trone *n.* throne 184/24

trow *v.* think, believe 163/9, 234/20

tryacle *n.* antidote 112/9

tryfle out *v.* put off idly 239/15

tryflynge *ppl. a.* feigning 176/16

turne, tourne *v.* repent 175/1; *refl. tourne
vs* turn 169/9, 218/3

twayn(e) *pron.* two 121/27 *etc.*

tyme *n. by longe tyme* for a long time
135/20; *one tyme or other* at one time or
other 204/7; *old tyme* ancient times 204/7

tythys *n. pl. preuy tythys* 115/19. *See note*

valure *n.* worth 175/8

vauntage *n. for the vauntage* in addition
210/23

venemed *pp.* poisoned 114/31; *ppl. a.*
venomed 172/23

very *adj.* true 156/24 *etc.; comp.* **more very**
more genuine 202/17

veryfyed *pp.* asserted as true 190/14, 19

vnacquaynted *ppl. a.* not personally known 111/5

vnclennes *n.* impurity 171/25–26

vncogitable *adj.* incomprehensible 226/22

uncontrolled *ppl. a.* unchecked 132/19

vnderstande(n) *pp.* understood 159/13 *etc.*

vnderstandyng *vbl. n.* meaning, sense 237/30 *etc.*

vndoutable *adj.* indubitable 217/17

vnfallyble *adj.* infallible 217/30

vnfaythfull *adj.* lacking religious faith 206/1

vngracyouse *adj.* wicked 113/8 *etc.*

vnhappy *adj.* causing trouble 112/26, 113/28; unfortunate 120/9

vnkynd(e) *adj.* unnaturally wicked 192/4; uncharitable 219/9, 13

vnkynd(e)nes(se) *n.* unnatural enmity 114/3 *etc.*

vnlykelyhed *n.* unlikelihood 216/6

vnmete *adj.* unfitting 169/9, 258/18

vnmynyshed *ppl. a.* undiminished 187/22–23

vnperfayte *adj.* deficient, imperfect 137/20

vnpourgeable *adj.* unable to be cleansed 189/33–34

vnsatysfyed *ppl. a.* uncompensated for 206/13

vnseasonable *adj.* untimely 112/4

vnsurety *n.* uncertainty 183/5

vnthryfty *adj.* idle, good for nothing 156/26

vnthryftynesse *n.* dissoluteness 168/13–14

vnthryftys *n. pl.* good-for-nothings 168/15

vntowched *ppl. a.* not treated, written of 118/29

vntreuth, vntrewth, vntrouth *n.* dishonesty 118/28 *etc.*

vntrew *adv.* falsely 120/16 *etc.*

vntrouth *n. See* **vntreuth**

voyd from *v.* get away from 185/7

vpholden *pp.* maintained 151/11

vplandysh *adj.* rustic 149/15, 166/20–21

vp(p)on *prep.* according to 125/16; on the basis of 132/4 *etc.;* after 189/10; in pursuit of 228/2

vppe *adv.* thoroughly 251/14; *vppe and downe* in every respect 235/37–38

vre *n. in vre with* in the habit of using 226/17; *brought in vre* put into practice 239/11

vse *v.* observe 199/16; *ppl. a* **vsed, vsyd** practiced 171/24 *etc.*

vs ward *adv. toward vs ward* directed toward us 223/25

vttermoste *n.* fullest extent 251/14–15

vyage *n.* journey 189/14

vylanous *adj.* demeaning 162/5

vylany(e) *n.* insulting degradation 153/16, 154/19

vysage *n.* appearance, semblance 150/2, 213/27

wach *n.* watch, vigil 228/22

wade *v.* go 192/21

waged *pp.* paid, hired 204/28

wake *v.* stay awake 152/20

walowyng *ppl. a.* being tossed about helplessly 189/11. *See note*

walter *v.* stumble 189/23, 225/20

wamble *v.* feel nauseous 189/26

want *v.* lack 142/14

wanton *adj.* frivolous 153/22 *etc.;* spoiled 224/19. *See note on* 187/29

wanton *n. play the wanton* dally 153/18–19. *See note on* 153/18–25

wantonely *adv.* through self-indulgence and lack of discipline 173/27

wantonnes *n.* overindulgence 218/27

wanyand *ppl. a. in the wanyand* on top of all that 153/14. *See note*

warantyse *n.* guarantee 139/4

wardmote questis, warmoll quest *n.* judicial inquiry made during the meeting of the citizens of a ward 116/27, 132/4. *See note on* 116/25–27

wardys *n. pl.* minors entrusted to guardians 216/6

ware *adj.* cognizant 125/18

ware *n.* goods 157/20

ware *v. imper.* guard against; *Nay ware of y*ᵗ No, let's have none of that! 142/4

ware *v. subj.* wore 171/31

warkis *n. pl.* deeds 112/31, 168/29. *See note on* 112/31

washed *ppl. a.* soaked, drunk 211/25

wasteth *v. pr. 3 s.* devastates 234/10

wax(e) *v.* become 151/25 *etc.; pp.* **waxen** 131/2

way *n. at the wurst way* at worst 211/1; *whyche waye* whatever 252/22

way *v.* consider, judge 114/32, 178/14; amount 166/2; *subj.* **wayd** counted for 216/31

wayted on *pp.* attended to 234/13

weale *n.* welfare 112/20 *etc.*

well *adv. as well grekys as latyns* both Greeks and Latins 190/27–28

welth *n.* happiness 173/3. *See also* **com-(m)en welth(e)**

wene *v.* think, imagine 112/11 *etc.; ppl. a.* **wenyng** 118/26; *pp.* **went** 143/9

were out *v.* eliminate gradually 177/7–8

what *adv.* how 222/26

what so euer *adj.* whatever 188/28

when *conj. when that* when 130/16

where *conj.* whereas 207/10; *where that* inasmuch as 215/22

wherin, wheryn, whyrin *conj.* in which 117/17 *etc.*

wherof *adv.* of which 117/13, 220/20; *interr.* to what end 201/3

wherof, wher of *conj.* from which 217/10; concerning which 203/10, 204/32

wherto *adv. interr.* to what end 177/13 *etc.*

wherwyth *conj.* with which 116/6 *etc.*

wheryn *conj. See* **wherin**

whether *adj.* which of the two 207/2

which(e), whyche *rel. pron.* who 233/21 *etc.*

who *rel. pron.* who *y^t* one who 117/12

whom *pron.* whomever 139/11

whyle, while *n. the whyle* in the meantime 114/23; *for the while* for the meantime, temporarily 118/3 *etc.; of good whyle* for some time 214/30; *thys great whyle* since long ago 214/32, 215/6–7; *to lytell whyle* for too short a time 251/13

whyrin *conj. See* **wherin**

whyther *conj.* whether 147/10 *etc.; whyther y^t* whether 209/34

whyther *pron.* which of the two 154/13

whyther so euer *adv.* wherever 221/16

wit *n. See* **wyt(t)(e)**

wit *v. See* **wyt(te)**

without *conj.* unless 204/32

wo *adj.* wretched, miserable 198/7, 224/17

woars *n. pl.* wooers, suitors 222/5

wold(e) *v. pt.* would, wished 112/4 *etc.*

wonder *n.* matter for amazement 170/23; *in . . . a wonder* amazed 240/38

wonderouse *adv.* wonderfully 153/33

wonne *pp.* gained 249/28

wont(e) *ppl. a.* accustomed (to) 111/13 *etc.*

work(e), wur(c)k *n.* disturbance, fuss 132/2, 13; labor 156/13 *etc.;* job, occupation 156/14 *etc.; set hym a wurke wyth: see* note on 114/8–9; *a work(e)* to labor(ing) 155/16 *etc.*

world(e) *n. at ye wyld world* toward open ground 156/32; *in ye worlde* at all 165/5–6; *yt ys a world(e)* it is a remarkable thing 185/6, 198/3

worldly *adj.* living in the world below 113/5

worshypfull *adj.* distinguished 118/7

worth(e), worthy *adj.* legally valid 133/2; valid 139/21; of value 159/28; *nothynge worthe* invalid, worthless 133/1–2 *etc.;* deserving of 199/1

wot(e) *v.* know 123/4 *etc.; pr. 3 s.* **wot(t)eth** 130/26 *etc.*

wrechydnes, wrechednes *n.* vice 166/17, 174/32

wrekk *n. goth all to wrekk* is being wrecked 180/7

wrought *pp.* worked 147/11; done 187/33 *etc.*

wur(c)k *n. See* **work(e)**

wurkynge *vbl. n.* operation 114/29

wurshyp *n.* honor 224/32

wyll *n. by his wyll* willingly 217/24; *pl.* **wyllys** *by theyr wyllys* intentionally 206/3

wyll *v.* desire, want, wish 123/27 *etc.; pr. 3 s.* **wylleth** 171/8

wynne *v.* accomplish 162/18

wysdome *n.* a wise thing 132/18; *pl. your wys(e)dom(e)s* you wise men 117/32, 213/6

wyse *n.* manner, way 111/2 *etc.; at the leste wyse* to the least degree 119/21 *etc.;* at least 219/3; *none other wyse* in no other way 129/17; *in no wyse* in no way 135/33, 142/5; *in eny wyse* by all means 150/6; *in lykewyse* in the same manner 218/27 *etc.*

wyse *n.* wise man 142/14

wysely *adv.* cunningly 152/1

wyt(t)(e), wit *n.* understanding, reason, sense 118/10 *etc.; pl.* **wyttys** understanding 178/13

wyt(te), wit *v.* know 111/14 *etc.; to wyt(te)* namely 121/17 *etc.; imper.* 114/17, 170/5; *pt.* **wyst(e)** 120/15 *etc.; ppl. a.* **wyttyng** 135/6

wyth *prep.* by 140/2

wythall, wyth all *adv.* therewith 132/26

wythdrawen vs *pp.* taken away from us 218/13

wythstanden *pp.* withstood 168/22

wyttys *n. pl. See* **wyt(t)(e)**

ye *adv.* yea 159/4; yes 207/23. *See note on* 159/4

yelde *v.* render 193/31

yere *n. pl. thys four hundreth yere* for the past four hundred years 131/19

yerth(e) *n.* earth 134/3 *etc.*

yerthly *adj.* earthly 152/2

yet *adv.* still 132/23 *etc.;* as yet 142/36; even 164/33; *nor yet* and also not 189/35; *not yet . . . byreue* still do not deprive 112/3

yf that *conj.* if 200/12

ymagynacyon *n. See* **imagynacyon**

ynions *n. pl.* onions 224/20

yno(u)gh(e), inough, ynow(e) *pron.* sufficient number, quantity, or amount 145/13 *etc.*

ynough, ynow *adj. See* **inow(ghe)**

ynoughe, ynow *adv. See* **inough**

yongely *adv.* immaturely 252/7

your self(e) *pron.* yourselves 151/15, 169/7; you yourselves 183/14 *etc.*

ys *v. pr. 2 s.* are 226/17

ywysse *adv.* indeed 222/8; certainly 222/18

zelator *n.* zealous supporter 136/11

ze(a)le *n.* fervent affection 137/21, 171/22

INDEX

INDEX

Aa, Abraham J. van der, 322

Abbeys and other religious houses: benefices, 381; lands, 214–15, 379–80, 381–82; suppression of, lxvii, 302. *See also* Anticlericalism; Clergy; Friars

Abington, 144, 346–47

Abraham, souls in his bosom, cx, 179, 196, 226, 362, 377, 379

Act of Succession, 338

Adam, clxvi, 146–47, 292, 301, 348, 355, 357, 378

Adams, R. P., 273

Adrian VI, Pope, 310, 316

Aeneas Sylvius, 375

Ailly, Pierre d', 294

Alber, Matthew, 316

Alberigo, Giuseppe, xcvi n., cxxxviii n., 263

Albertus Magnus, 388

Albigensianism. *See* Cathars

Alcuin, 361, 451

Alexander II, Pope, 337

Alexander the Great, 211, 377

Alington, Alice, xxxi, 361

Alington, Giles, xxx–xxxi

All Souls, feast of, xcii, xcvii, c, ciii, cviii, cxii, 323, 371, 449–50, 454

Allegories and figurative language, in Scripture, cxxxv–cxxxvi, cxliv, cxlv, cxlvii, 235–43, 245, 247, 249, 430–31. *See also* Scripture

Allen, John, 116, 131, 341, 420

Allen, P. S., lxxiv, lxxxii n., 264, 331–32, 358, 372, 381

Allison, A. F., 270

Almsgiving: to benefit souls in purgatory, xcviii, ci, 119, 168–69, 205, 218, 219, 224, 382, 449, 450; by clergy, 422; Fish's attitude toward, 117, 142, 158–59, 422; leads to salvation, 74, 222–23; scale of, 121–22, 304, 305; in Scripture, 74, 164, 353. *See also* Beggars; Works

Ambrose, Saint, cvi, 159, 195, 209, 291, 360, 361, 365, 366, 373, 375–76, 377

Amundesham, John, 347

Anabaptists, cxxxix, 278, 279

Anastasia, Saint, 209, 373–74

Angel noble (coin), 124, 125, 332–33

Angels: fallen, *see* Devils; good or guardian, xcviii, xcix, c, cx, 202, 227

Anrich, Gustav, 365

Anselm of Laon, 263

Anticlericalism: economic motives for, lxxii–lxxiii, 117, 143; in England generally, lxvii, 336; Henry VIII's attraction for, lxvii–lxviii, lxix; and heresy, lxviii, lxix, 142–45; in law, 216, 327, 344, 382, 420–21; Luther's, lxx, 379; during the Peasants' Revolt, 98, 284, 302, 349; purgatory doctrines motivated by, lxxii, cv, cxxix, 116, 206. *See also* Church; Clergy; Hunne, Richard; Protestantism

Antony, Marc, 272

Antwerp, lxvi, cxxiii, cxxxii, 274

Apelles, 4, 271

Apostles' Creed, 186, 362

Apparitions of the dead, lxxv, lxxx, lxxxix, ci, cii, cxv, cxlvi, 195–98, 202–03, 221, 368, 370–71, 454. *See also* Purgatory

Aquinas. *See* Thomas Aquinas

Arber, Edward, 410 n.

Arianism and Arius, cv, cxliv–cxlv, 38, 238–39, 291–92, 386

Arthur, Duke of Brittany, 335

Arthur, King of Britain, 125, 334, 414

Arthur, Prince of Wales, 334

Athanasian Creed, 362

Athanasius, Saint, cix, 366

Augsburg, Diet of, 284–85

Augustine of Hippo, Saint: on anticlericalism, 144–45, 348; on Church and scripture, lxxix n., lxxx, 34, 182, 290, 359; on the eucharist, cxlv–cxlvii, cliv, 242–46, 387, 429; on grace and free will, 299; on heretics, xlix–l; Luther's preference for, lxxx; on Maccabees, lxxvii, lxxix n., lxxx, cviii, 180; More mentions, 34, 144–45, 159, 180, 182, 190, 195, 201–

Augustine of Hippo, Saint (*continued*)
202, 203, 209, 210, 242–46; on Pelagianism, 283–84, 292, 298, 299, 301; on purgatory, lxxxv, lxxxviii, xcv, ci, cii, cvi, cvii–cviii, cxi, cxvii, 190, 195, 201–202, 203, 354, 360, 364, 365, 370, 371, 377, 447 n., 449, 450; on the scriptural canon, 358; on the sin against the Holy Spirit, 366; mentioned, cl, 159, 209, 210, 278
Augustinian friars, xxii, 331, 373, 374

Babington, Churchill, 266
Badby, John, 143, 345, 443
Bainham, James, 441
Baptism, 48, 96, 294, 306–07, 317, 354, 355, 377
Baravellus, Ferdinandus (More pseudonym), xxi n.
Barker, Nicholas, 271
Barlow, William, xliv n., 12, 275–76, 282–83
Barlowe, Jerome, 161, 263, 275, 328, 352
Barnes, Robert, xxii, xxv, cxx, cxxxi, cxxxiii–cxxxix, cl–cli, 255–56, 257, 325, 340, 352, 390–91
Barnewelt, Thomas, 328
Barton, Elizabeth, 374
Basel, 279–80, 373
Basil, Saint, xcv, 159, 195, 204, 209, 210, 372, 376, 383
Bax, E. Belfort, 349
Beaufort, Margaret, 346, 381
Beda, Nicholas, xci n.
Bede ('The Venerable'), Saint, lxxxix, cix, cxv–cxvi, 210, 371, 448
Bedell, William, 332
Bedouelle, Guy, lxxxi n.
Beggars: clerical activities and, 137–38, 155–56, 164–65, 413, 414, 422; and economic conditions generally, lxxiii, 121–22, 305; numbers of, 115, 120–22, 138, 148, 412; origin of, 164–66, 417; souls in purgatory worse off than, 119, 225. *See also* Almsgiving; Fish, Simon
Beinecke Library. *See* Yale University Library
Bellay, Jean du, lxxii–lxxiii
Bellendorpe, Helbert, xxxii
Benedict, Friedrich, 375

Berengarius, cxxxvii, cl, 255, 390
Bergenroth, G. A., cxxx n., 264
Bernard of Clairvaux, Saint, lxxix n., lxxxix–xc, 159, 371, 374
Bessarion, metropolitan of Nicaea, xciv
Betson, Thomas, 375
Beza, Theodore, 274
Bible, editions of: *Biblia latina* 263, 356, 359–60, 361, 365–66, 387; Douay, lxxvii n., lxxix n., lxxxi n.; Erasmus' *Novum Testamentum*, xxiii n., lxxxiv, xci, cxx, cxxi, 279, 305–06, 358, 360, 365, 387–88; Jerusalem, 266; Luther's, xviii, xxiii n.; Reims, lxxxi n., lxxxiii; Septuagint, lxxx; Tyndale's *New Testament*, xxiii, xxv, xxvi, xxvii–xxviii, lxxx, lxxxvi, cxx, cxxiii, cxxxviii, 142, 161, 167, 168, 322, 340, 344, 409 n., 420, 437; Vulgate, lxxv, lxxix n., lxxxi, lxxxiii, lxxxiv n., 360, 370, 448 n.. *See also* Scripture
Biblical quotations, major: Gen. 3:19, 117, 145, 146, 147, 148, 328, 348, 349; Gen 33:20, 235–26, 385; Gen. 47:20–23, 145, 165, 348, 353; Deut. 18:19, 100, 309, 402; 1 Kings 2:6, lxxvi, 178, 356; 2 Kings 6:14–15, 92–94, 313; 4 Kings 20:1–7, lxxv, 176–78, 356; Ps. 37:18, lxxii, 190, 364; Ps. 129, xcix, cxi, 450, 451, 452; Prov. 13:8, 44, 74, 297, 308; Isa. 29:14, 38, 398; Isa. 38:9–20, lxxv, lxxvi, 176–78, 356; Isa. 53:7, cxlvii, 244, 387; Zech. 9:11, lxxvi–lxxvii, cxv, 178–79, 357; 2 Macc. 12:39–46, lxxv, lxxvii–lxxix, lxxxii, lxxxiv, lxxxvii–lxxxviii, xciv, cviii, 179–80, 357, 371, 450; Matt. 12:32, lxxxvi, xciv, cvi, cvii, 191–93, 366–67; Matt. 12:36, lxxxvi, cvii, 193–94, 328, 363, 367; Matt. 20:1–16, 54, 76, 302, 309; Matt. 25:31–46, 54, 74, 84, 303, 309, 310; Matt. 28:20, 32, 36, 56, 94, 289, 290, 303, 313, 359, 361, 402; Mark 10:25, 246–47, 387–88; Luke 16:19–31, lxxvi–lxxvii, lxxi, ci, cvii, cx, 179, 196, 226–27, 357, 362, 368, 369, 370, 378–79, 384, 448; Luke 17:7–10, 54, 88, 302, 312; Luke 24:26, cxlvi–cxlvii, 244, 387; John 4:24, 92, 312, 402; John 6:56, cxliv, 235, 240, 385; John

10:18, cxlvii, 244, 387; John 10:22, lxxxi, 181, 359; John 12:1–8, 58, 92, 305,
312; John 16:13, 36, 290, 359; Acts
2:24–28, lxxxiii–lxxxiv, 185–87, 362;
Rom. 3:21, 46, 298, 400; Rom. 6:19, 44,
54, 297, 303; Rom. 8:18, 54, 302, 402;
Rom. 9:31, 46, 298, 307, 400; Rom.
10:3, 46, 293, 298, 400; 1 Cor. 1:30,
xcviii n., 293, 400; 1 Cor. 3:12–15, lxvi
n., lxxvi, lxxxiv–lxxxvi, lxxxvii–lxxxviii,
lxxxix, xciv–xcv, cvi, cvii–cviii, 187–88,
190–91, 323, 363, 364–66, 448, 450; 1
Cor. 10:13, clii, 100, 319–20; 1 Cor.
11:29–30, 252, 254, 389; 1 Thess. 5:3,
100–102, 320; 2 Tim. 2:17, 233–34,
384; Jas. 2:18–19, 60, 305; Jas. 2:26, 60,
303, 305, 308; 1 John 5:16, lxxxiii, cvii,
184, 359–60; Rev. 5:13, lxxxiii, cvii,
184–85, 360–61; Rev. 7:17, 100, 320,
324. See also James; Maccabees; Psalms;
Scripture
Bilney, Thomas, xxii n., cxx, 439
Blackfriars. See Dominicans
Blanchard, André, 272
Blodgett, James E., 460 n.
Blok, P. J., 322
Bloomfield, Morton, 358
Blount, William Lord Mountjoy, 381
Bodleian Library. See Oxford University
Bohemia, utraquism in, 257
Boleyn, Anne, lxvii, lxxiii, clv, clvi, 275,
439–40
Boleyn, Thomas, cxxx
Bolt, Robert, xlviii
Bonaventure, Saint, 388
Bonde, William, 375
Bone, Gavin, 460 n.
Books, heretical: banned, 409–10;
burned, xx, xxi, xxii, xxiv, xxv, xxxii,
xlix n., 288, 409 n.; import forbidden,
xx, xxiii–xxv, xxvi, xxxii, lxv, cxviii,
cxxiii, cxxx, cxliii, 233, 288; More men-
tions, 28, 233. See also Heresy; Tyndale,
New Testament
Books of hours, lxxvi, 451–52
Bora, Katherine von, xviii, 288–89, 374
Boston Public Library, 466 n.
Bourrilly, V.-L., lxxiii n.
Boventer, Hermann, 374
Bowers, Fredson, 470 n.

Bowry, William, 332
Bradner, L., 267
Brandon, Charles, Duke of, lxvii
Brewer, J. S., xxiv n., 266
Bridget of Sweden, Saint, xcvi, cii, 209,
371, 374–75, 376
Bridgett, T. E., cxvi n.
Brightwell, Richard. See Frith, John
Brigid of Ireland, Saint, 374
British Library, 409
Brodie, R. H., xxiv n.
Bromehill, 275
Brown, William J., 330
Bucer, Martin, 352
Budé, Guillaume, 381
Bugenhagen, John (Pomeranus): bio-
graphical details, xviii, 270, 287; De con-
iugio episcoporum et diaconorum, 287; and
Luther, xvii–xix; pseudonym, 270; sta-
ture, xvii–xix; in Wittenberg, xvii–xviii,
xix, 286–87, 373; mentioned, 209
— Epistola ad Anglos, 395–405; argument
of, xxxvi–xlii; intended audience, xix,
xxv–xxvi, xxvii–xxviii, xxx, xxxvii, xlii,
li, 276, 398; and Luther's letter to Henry
VIII, xxv–xxx, xxxvi, xlii; More's impression of, xxvi, xxx, xxxiv n., xlii, li;
More obtains copy, xxxi, xxxii, xliv; as
Pauline epistle, xix, xxv, xxviii, xxxvii,
xxxix, xlii; popularity, xvii, xix–xx, xxx;
publishing history, xvii, xxx, 263, 270,
281, 395; rhetorical strategy of, xxxvi–
xlii, li; structural divisions within,
xxxv n., xxxvi; version used by More,
xliv n., clxi, 12, 275, 276, 280, 283, 289,
395 n.
Burns, Norman T., 356
Butterworth, Charles C., lxxxv n.
Buttrich, George A., 387
Byrne, Muriel St. Clare, 333, 453 n.

Cabbalism, 355
Calvin, John, 274
Cambrai, Treaty of, lxvi
Cambridge University: endowed colleges,
381; Greek at, cxxii; libraries, 466 n.;
Lutheranism at, xxii–xxiii, xxiv, xxv,
xxvi, cxx–cxxi, cxxii. See also Universi-
ties
Camden, William, 331

Campeggio, Cardinal, lxvii–lxviii, cxxix, 381

Canon law. *See* Spiritual law

Canons, 325

Canterbury, 339

Capito, Wolfgang, 352

Carey, George, 377

Carmelites, 123, 331

Carter, Harry, 459 n.

Catharine of Aragon, cxxviii, cxlii, cxliii, 8, 273. *See also* Henry VIII, divorce

Catharine of Valois, 346

Catharinus, Ambrosius, lxxi, lxxii

Cathars, lxxi, xc, cxxxviii, cxxxix

Catherine of Genoa, Saint, xc

Catherine of Siena, Saint, 209, 375

Cavendish, George, 350

Cawood, John, 457

Caxton, William, lxxxi, 346, 450

Celibacy, vows of, liii, 26, 56, 98, 127, 153, 281. *See also* Marriage

Cesarini, Cardinal Guiliano, xciii

Challis, C. E., 333

Chambers, R. W., xxi n., xxxi n., 263, 266, 282, 453 n.

Chantries, lxix, cxvi, 214. *See also* Prayer for the dead

Chapuys, Eustace, cxxx–cxxxi, cxxxii, clv

Charles, Cardinal of Lorraine, 271

Charles V, Emperor, xx, cxxx, clv, 273, 275, 349

Charles VIII, King of France, 330

Charles the Fat, lxxxix

Chastity. *See* Celibacy; Marriage

Chaucer, Geoffrey, lxxvii, 324, 331, 358

Chelsea (Chelcith), xxx, cxl, clxviii, 258, 275, 343, 374

Cheney, C. R., 339, 340

Chester, Allan G., lxxxv n.

Chichely, Henry, 346

Chomarat, Jacques, 272

Christ: after the ascension, 245, 387; his commandments, 56–58, 92, 94, 402; figurative language used by, cxxxv–cxxxvi, cxliv, cxlv, cxlvii, 235–41, 247, 430–31; heretical views of, cxliv, 238–39, 291–92, 301; More's personal devotion to, cxxvii; his natural body, and transubstantiation, cxxxv, cxlv–cxlix,

cliv, 242, 243–47, 249, 429. *See also* Eucharist; God; Trinity

Christ, only source of righteousness: in Bugenhagen, xxviii–xxix, xxxvi, xxxix–xl, 42–46, 56, 400–402; and justification by faith, lvii, xl–xli, 64; More's response, xliii n., liv, lvii, 44, 56–58, 60. *See also* Faith alone, justification by

Christ Church, Canterbury, 339

Christ Church College, Oxford, cxxi

Christ's College, Cambridge, cxvi

Christian II, King of Denmark, xix, xxvi–xxvii

Christian III, King of Denmark, xviii

Christina of Ertzeberg, 373

Church: authority in, xliii n.; composed of living and dead, lxix, lxxviii, xc, xcvii, xcix, 202, 449; consensus of, cxxv, cxliii–cxliv, cxlix, 18, 32, 38–40, 56–58, 94, 100, 195, 203–04, 208–10, 212–13, 217, 239–42, 243, 253, 255, 368, 371–72, 447, 449; faith rules, 378; Holy Ghost guides, xlviii, 34–36, 58, 94, 100, 182, 210, 295; mystical body, 370; no holiness outside of, 46; property held by, lxvii–lxix, 115, 122, 143, 144–45, 148–49, 213–17, 345, 346, 347, 379–80, 412, 418; Protestant definition of, xxi n., 40–42, 94, 292–93, 313; Scripture authorized by, lxxiv, lxxix n., lxxx, cv, cvi, cxlv, cxlix, 18, 34–40, 180, 182–83, 239–40, 290, 358, 359; sin causes schism within, cii; unity of, cxxv. *See also* Anticlericalism; Clergy; Papacy

Churches, numbers of, 122–23, 124, 331, 345, 413

Cicero, 272, 290, 375

Cistercians, lxxxix–xc

Claymond, John, 381

Clebsch, William A., xvii n., xx n., xxii n., xxiii n., xxiv n., xxv n., cxxi n., cxxiv, cxxx n., 263

Clement VII, Pope, lxxii, 275, 353, 381

Clement, John, 381

Clergy: faults of, 126, 153, 171; labor by, 145–48, 156, 157; lands held by, lxvii–lxix, 115, 122, 143, 144–45, 148–49, 213–17, 345, 346, 347, 379–80, 412, 418; moneys collected by, 115–16, 126, 138, 412–14; not divided from laity in

purgatory, xc; number of, 115–16, 121, 126, 138–39, 334, 414–15; obedience to the crown of, lxvii, 127–28, 139–42, 158, 415–16, 418–19, 420–21, 422; origin of, 164–65; in parliament, 130, 139–40, 417; Protestant, 286–87, 296, 314, 317; responsibility for beggary, 137–38, 155–56, 164–65, 413, 414, 422; and the sacraments, cxxxvi, cxlix–cl, 154, 161, 234, 254, 432, 433; sexual misconduct by, 126, 131, 341, 416; temporal law against, 216, 327, 344, 382, 420–21. *See also* Anticlericalism; Church; Friars; Ordination; Papacy; Spiritual law
Clericus, J., lxxxiv n., 264
Cluny, 450
Cobbett, William, 347
Cochlaeus, John: *Articuli .CCCCC. Martini Lutheri*, 263, 287, 294, 304, 370, 378–79; correspondence with More, 289; on the Fathers, 282; on free will, 301–02, 303; on good works, 297–98, 303; on Luther's vices, 288; pamphlet on the Peasants' Revolt, 349; on the Peasant's Revolt, 285–86, 320, 349; on Protestant dissension, 284, 318, 319; on purgatory, xci, 378–79; on relics, 287; rhetoric, xxxiv–xxxv n., 277, 280–81; on solafideism, 306; on suppression of Lutheranism, xxiii, 288; translation of Fisher, civ; on Tyndale's testament, xxiii
— *Epistola Iohannis Bugenhagij . . . Responsio Cochlaei*, 263 date, xvii n., xxxiv; on Bugenhagen's audience, xix, xxx, 276; on Bugenhagen's language, 278; compared to More's *Letter to Bugenhagen*, xvii, xix, xxx, xxxiv–xxxv n., xlvii, 276, 277, 278, 280–81, 282, 285–86, 288, 289, 293–94, 297, 301–302, 303, 306, 318, 319, 320; incorporates text of Bugenhagen, xvii, xxxiv, xxxv n., xliv, 277; More's knowledge of, xxxiv, xxxv n.; style, xxxiv–xxxv n., xlvii, 280–81
Cocks, John, 381
Cockx-Indestege, Elly, 270
Coelestius, 292
Coinage, English, xxxi–xxxii, 332–33
Colet, John, cii, 327, 342, 372

Colley, Dorothy, 270
Comestor, Peter, lxxxix, xc–xci
Commons, House of, 130, 139–41. *See also* Parliament
Confession. *See* Penance
Confirmation, 354. *See also* Sacraments
Consubstantiation, cxxvi, cxxviii, cxxxiv, cxxxvi–cxxxvii, cxlix, 96, 234, 294, 384. *See also* Eucharist
Cope, Alan, 6, 272
Councils, church: Basel (1431–37), cix; Bordeaux (1080), 390; Carthage (418), lxxx, 292, 299; Constance (1414–18), 384; Constantinople I (381), 292; Florence (1439), lxxxvii, xcii–xcvi, cix, 323, 357, 363; Lateran IV (1215), cxxxvii, cxxxviii n.; Lateran V (1512), civ; Lyons II (1274), lxxxvii, xcii; Trent (1563), lxxxvii, xcvi, civ, 271; Vatican II (1962), xc
Coverdale, Miles, xxii n.
Cramner, Thomas, Archbishop of Canterbury, xx, xxii n., xxiii, cxlii, clv, clvi, clvii
Cranevelt, Francis, 391
Crawford, Charles W., clx n., 283
Cross, Jesus', 26–28, 56–58, 281, 287, 304
Crossed Friars. *See* Crutched Friars
Cromwell, Thomas, cxxix, cxxxii, cxxxiii, cxlii, clv, clvi, 275, 286, 332
Crutched Friars, 123, 332
Cunliffe, Henry, 458 n.
Currein, Dr., clv
Curtius, Ernst Robert, 343
Cyril of Alexandria, Saint, 210, 376, 387, 388

d'Alès, Adhémar, xciii n., xciv n., xcv n., 264, 357, 363
Dante Alighieri, lxxxix, xc
Darcy memorandum, lxvii
Davis, Herbert, 459 n.
Death, contemplation of, ci–cii. *See also* Purgatory
Delcourt, Joseph, 264, 322, 348, 354, 367, 387
Deutsch Staatsbibliothek, Berlin, 395 n.
Devils and demons, lxxxiii, 363; Catholic clergy, 412; jailers of purgatory, lxxvi, 114, 179, 221–22, 225–26, 357, 443, 448, 450; Luther possessed by, lix–lxii, 84, 86, 282; More's belief in, lxi–lxii,

Devils and demons (*continued*)
319, 360; source of heresy, xlviii, li, lvi,
lvii, lix, lx–lxii, lxiii, cxxv, 24, 68, 100,
114–15, 118, 170, 233, 319, 354; tor-
tured by fire, xci. *See also* Hell
Dickinson, F. H., 267
Dietenberg, Johnannes, 294
Diogenes Laertius, 290
Dionysius the Areopagite, cix
Diopolis, synod of, 299
*Disputatio . . . D. Iohannis Eccij & D. Martini
Lutheri Augustani quae cepit.IIII.Iulij*, 264,
358, 363
Dobneck, John. *See* Cochlaeus
Doernberg, Erwin, xxvii n., xxxv n., 264
Dominic, Saint, 331, 442
Dominicans, 123, 331
Donatists, cl
Döring, Matthias, 263
Dormer, Jane, 273
Dorp, Martin van, lxxxvi
Douay, 270, 283
Douglas, David C., 410 n.
Doyle, Charles Clay, 308
Dryfield, Thomas, 327
Dualism, cxxxvii–cxxxix, cxlviii
Dunbar, William, 453

Eck, John, xxxi, lxxi, 264, 278, 294, 315,
358, 363, 378. *See also Disputatio*
Economic conditions, lxx, lxxii–lxxiii,
121–22, 305, 330. *See also* Beggars
Edelen, Georges, 481 n.
Edward I, King of England, 340
Edward II, King of England, 335, 337, 340
Edward III, King of England, 337, 340
Edward IV, King of England, 332, 340,
380
Edwards, H. L. R., 332
Edwards, Mark U., 318
Egli, Emil, lxxii n., 269
Ehses, Stephen, lxvii n.
Election, 48–50. *See also* Faith alone, justi-
fication by; Saints
Elizabeth I, Queen of England, 270, 275,
282
Ellies Du Pin, M. L., xcvi n.
Ellis, Henry, cxxii n., 264
Elyot, George, 441
Ember days, 326

Emden, A. B., 437
Emser, Hieronymus, 294, 315
Engels, Friedrich, 349
England: anticlericalism in, lxvii, 336;
Catholic state, xix, xx, cxix, clv, clvi, 26–
28; first Protestants in, xix, xxii–xxvi,
cxx, cxxix–cxxx, cxxxii, 398; general
conditions, lxx, lxxii–lxxiii; Luther's
perception of, xxvi–xxx, xxxvi, 16, 26,
40, 280. *See also* Henry VIII
Erasmus: correspondence with Jonas,
327; correspondence with More, lxxiv;
correspondence with Wychman, 331–
32; on Fisher, civ n.; on grace, 302; influence, cxx, cxxi, cxxii; introduces Holbein to More, xxxi n.; last will, cxvi; on
Luther, 289, 310; on Mary's virginity,
368; More mentions, lix, 84–86; on natural theology, 355; pensions, 339; and
popular piety, cxxvii, 358; on purgatory,
xci, 365, 451; referred to in *Letter to
Bugenhagen*, lx; and *Responsio ad Lutherum*, xxi n.; scriptural interpretation,
364; on the universities, 381; mentioned, 273, 277, 325
— works: *Adagia*, 290, 292, 308, 309, 311,
312, 319, 367, 437; *Amicitia*, 343; *Colloquia Familiaria*, cxxvii, 264, 329, 332,
343, 362, 368; *The Complaint of Peace*,
478 n.; edition of Chrystostom, 372; edition of Jerome, 279, 358; edition of Origen, 365; *Enarrationes*, lxxxi–lxxxii; *Enchiridion*, xci n., 355, 358; *Exorcismus*,
368; *Explanatio Symboli*, 362; *Funus*, 332;
Hyperaspistes, xxx n., 310; *De immensa dei
misericordia*, 271; *Inquisitio de fide*, 362;
De libero arbitrio, 84–86, 264, 279, 299,
302, 303, 310–11, 312; *Novum Testamentum*, xxiii n., lxxxiv, xci, cxx, cxxi, 279,
305–06, 358, 360, 365, 387–88; *The
Praise of Folly*, 382, 391
Escheat, 214, 216, 380
Etaples. *See* Lefèvre d'Etaples
Eucharist: Church tradition and, cxliii–
cxliv, cxlix, 94 (*see also* Transubstantiation); faith the primary element, 428,
431; Frith's views, cxviii–cxix, cxxvi–
cxxviii, cxxxiii–cxxxix, cxlii–cxlix, 428–
33; Henry VIII's views, cxlii, cxliii, cxlix;
Luther's views, lviii, cxix, cxxiii, cxxvi–

cxxvii, cxxviii, cxxxiv, cxxxv, cxxxvi–
cxxxvii, cxlix, 94–96, 234, 294, 315–16,
317, 385; More's personal attitude,
cxxxvi, cxli, cli–clii, clviii; in popular
piety, cli–clii; priest's role, lxix, cxxxvi,
cxlix–cl, 254, 432, 433; the primary sacrament, 234–35; Protestant dissension
concerning, cxviii–cxix, cxxiii, cxxvi–
cxxvii, cxxxiii–cxxxv, cl–cli, clii, 94–96,
278, 280, 284, 318, 385, 428; Protestant
plots against, 161–62; token of Christ,
cxxxvi, 234, 236, 237, 385, 431–33. See
also Consubstantiation; Masses; Sacramentarianism; Transubstantiation
Eugenius III, Pope, 374
Eugenius IV, Pope, xcv n.
Eusebius Gallicanus, 358
Exeter, 134, 341
Exsurge Domine (bull), xx, ciii–civ, cix, 278,
288
Extreme unction, 305. See also Sacraments

Faber, Johannes, 294, 343, 355
Fabre, Paul, 337
Fabyan, Robert, 264, 330, 345, 347
Faith: apart from good works, 58–62;
merit of, 197; necessary for salvation,
76–78, 90, 313–14, 428; superior to
reason, 36, 242–43, 248
Faith alone, justification by: Augustine on,
365; good works forbidden, xlv–xlvi,
54–56, 64, 68–70, 78, 310, 400; good
works inevitable, xl–xli, lvii, cxxvi, 58–
62, 80, 90, 402; importance for More,
xxxiv n., xliii n., liii n., 351; license for
sin, lvi, lvii–lviii, 58–60, 62, 64–70, 72,
78, 90, 173–75; penance unnecessary,
58, 66–68, 308; in Protestant doctrine
generally, xix, xxix, xl–xli, 278; purgatory doctrine and, lxx, 159; scriptural
arguments, 60, 62, 64, 66, 355. See also
Christ, only source of righteousness;
Free will; Works
Fasting, xxxii, xcviii, ci, 94, 314, 450
Fathers of the Church: endure, lv, 20–22,
42; on the eucharist, cxliv, cxlvi, cxlix,
cliv, 239–40, 243, 252–53, 386; and
Henry VIII's divorce, cxli; heretics opposed by, l–li, lv, 18, 36, 208–10, 282;
Lutheranism opposed to, 18–20, 30–

32, 38, 40–42, 86, 94, 159, 368; on pur-
gatory, lxxvi, lxxvii n., 190–91, 195, 204,
208–10, 356, 368, 370–72, 375–76; and
the scriptural canon, lxxx, 180, 183,
357–58. See also Augustine, Jerome
Fen, John, cxi n., cxii n.
Ferdinand, Emperor, 272, 273, 343
Ferguson, Charles W., lxxiii n.
Ferguson, F. S., xvii n., clxix n., 268
Fewterer, John, 375
Ficino, 375
Field of the Cloth of Gold, cxii, cxiii
Figurative language. See Allegories and
figurative language
Fire, in purgatory: doctrine, lxxxviii, xc,
xci, xciv, xcv, cix, cxv, 375, 376, 377, 383;
nature of, lxxxviii, lxxxix, xc, xci, cvii–
cviii, cxiii, cxvii, 225; More's belief, 111;
in Scripture, lxxvi–lxxvii, lxxxiv–
lxxxvi, lxxxviii, lxxxix, xciv, cvii–cviii,
cxv, 179, 187–88, 323, 442
Firpo, Luigi, 336
Fish, Simon: biographical, 333, 351, 409 n.,
437, 439; and Henry VIII, cxxix, 409 n.,
437, 439–40, 441–42; The Summe of the
Scripture, 441; mentioned, xxxiv n.
— More on: his anonymity, 113–14, 324–
25; his conversion, 324; his intentions,
112, 114–15, 118, 128, 137, 142, 154–
55, 160–64, 166–68, 170–72, 206, 213,
217; his statistics, 115–16, 120–26,
138–39, 151–52
— Supplication for the Beggars: condemned,
409–10; date, lxv, clxi, 333, 409, 458 n.;
Foxe's sidenotes, 331, 409; influence,
lxvii–lxviii; motives for, lxix–lxx; publication, 327, 409–10, 437; rhetoric,
349; translation, 325–26
Fisher, John, bishop of Rochester and
Saint: anti-heretical spokesman, xx,
xxi–xxii, xxiii, xxiv, xxv, xlix, lx, 340;
and Cambridge, 381; on the eucharist,
280; influence on More, ciii, cvi, 356;
polemical style, xlvii, xlix; on purgatory,
lxxvi, xci, xcix n., ciii–cxvii, 367, 443; on
syphilis, 329–30; use of Psalms, lxxxii;
mentioned, ci n.
— works: Assertionis Lutheranae confutatio,
xxii, ciii–cx, cxvi n., cxvii, 265, 292, 299,
300, 303, 367; Defensio regiae assertionis

Fisher, John (*continued*)
  contra Babylonicam captivitatem, xxii,
    xxxiv n., 286; funeral sermon for the
    countess of Richmond, cxi; funeral ser-
    mon for Henry VII, cxi; *The Myrrour or
    Glasse of Christes Passion*, 364; *Sacri sacer-
    dotii defension contra Lutherum*, xxii; ser-
    mons against Luther, xx, xxi–xxii, xlix,
    cxiv; sermon on Ps. 37, 364; *Spiritual
    Consolation*, cxiv–cxv; *Treatise concerynge
    the fruytfull saynges of Dauyd*, cix n., cx–
    cxi; *Two fruytfull sermons*, cxi–cxiv; *De
    unica Magdalena*, ciii n.; *De veritate cor-
    poris et sanguinis Christi in eucharista*, 265,
    372
Fitzgerald, Thomas, 341
Fitzjames, Richard, 116, 132–33, 327–28
Floeissner, Robert F., 363
Foley, Stephen M., 267, 297
Folger Shakespeare Library, clxix n.,
    425 n., 466 n.
Fowler, John, xvii n., xix, xxxiii, clx, 2, 4,
    8–10, 270, 271, 274, 275–76, 283; mar-
    ginal notes to *Letter to Bugenhagen*, 291,
    299, 312, 313
Fox, Alistair, liii n., lxv n., 265
Fox, Edward, cxx
Fox, Richard, 381
Foxe, John: *Acts and Monuments*, xxii n.,
    265; on Barnes, cxxxiii n., cxxxiv; cites
    More, 323, 413 n.; Fish biography, lxvii,
    cxxix, clxi, 322, 410, 437–44; on Frith,
    cxix, cxx–cxxi, cxxii–cxxiii, cxxiv, cxxix,
    cxxx, cxxxi–cxxxii, cxxxiii n., cxxxiv,
    clii, clv, clvi–clvii, clviii n.; mentions
    More, cxxx, cxxxiv, clii, 442–44; side-
    notes to Fish, 331, 333; mentioned,
    458 n.
Francastoro, Girolamo, 329
Francis I, King of France, lxxii
Francis of Assisi, Saint, 331, 442
Franciscans, 123, 331, 332, 351, 373
Franck, Sebastian, 265, 325–26, 330
Frarinus, Petrus, 274
Frederick, Duke of Saxony, xxvi, xxvii,
    289
Freedom, Christian: and law, 318; and the
    Peasants' Revolt, 22–24, 100, 166, 320;
    and Protestant license, xxxvii–xxxviii,
    22–24, 30, 48, 50, 159, 166, 297

Free will: dissension concerning, 32–34,
    98, 310–11; and God's responsibility for
    evil, 48–50, 96, 98, 301–02, 311; good
    works and, 82–86, 90–92, 292; grace
    and, 46, 48–50, 56, 86–88, 298–300,
    366; repugnant to reason, 248; Scrip-
    ture on, 82–84, 88, 310–11, 312
Friars, 325, 351; Luther on, cx; money col-
    lected by, 115, 122–26, 130–31, 157,
    413–14; More on, 50–52, 121; numbers
    of, 121; orders of, 123, 331–32, 413;
    and popular piety, cx, cxxvii; Protestant
    attacks on, 98, 302; purgatory and, cx.
    See also Clergy; individual orders
Friedberg, Emil A., 263
Frith, John (Richard Brightwell): charac-
    ter, cxix–cxx, cxxi, cxxiv–cxxv, cxxxi;
    death, cxix, cxxiv, clvi–clviii; on double
    justification, cxxv–cxxvi; education,
    cxx, cxxi–cxxii; on the eucharist, cxviii–
    cxix, cxxvi–cxxviii, cxxxiii–cxxxix,
    cxlii–cxlix; on Fisher, ciii, civ, cv, cvii,
    cxvii; and Henry VIII, cxxix–cxxxiii,
    cxxxix, cxli–cxliii, clv–clvii, clviii; heret-
    ical declarations, cxxviii, cxxx–cxxxi,
    cxxxiv–cxxxv, cxli, cl–cli, clvi–clvii; im-
    prisonment, cxviii, cxix, cxxiii, cxxiv,
    cxxx, cxxxii–cxxxiii, cxli, clii–cliii, clv,
    clvi, 384; joins heretics, xxii n., cxx–
    cxxi; marriage, cxxiii–cxxiv; on More,
    ciii, cxv; publication of his works, 384;
    on purgatory, lxxii, cxxviii, cxxix, 354,
    356, 357, 367; on sin, cxxxviii; travels,
    cxxiii, cxxv, cxxix–cxxx, cxxxii; and
    Tyndale, cxx–cxxi, cxxiii–cxxv, cxxviii,
    cxxx, cxxxii, cxxxiii; mentioned, 323,
    328
— works: *Antithesis wherin are compared to
    geder Christes actes aqnd oure holye father the
    Popes*, cxxviii; *A boke . . . answeringe vnto
    M mores lettur*, cliii–clv, clviii, 265, 387,
    391, 425, 444; *A Christian Sentence*,
    cxviii–cxix, cxxxiii–cxl, cliii, clxviii, 265,
    384, 385, 391, 425–33; *Disputation of
    Purgatory*, ciii, cv n., cvii n., cxv, cxxviii,
    265, 354, 355, 356, 357, 361, 362, 363,
    366, 367, 369, 409 n.; *A letter vnto the
    faythfull followers of Christes gospel*, 384; *A
    mirrour or glasse to knowe thy selfe*, 384; *A
    myrroure or lokynge glasse wherin you may*

beholde the Sacramente of baptisme described,
384; *An other boke against Rastel,* 384; *A
Pistle to the Christen reader,* 381; reply to
Fisher, 369; *The Revelation of Antichrist,*
lxxii, cxxviii; *The Testament of master Wyl-
liam Tracie esquier,* 384
Froben, John, 263, 279, 360
Frost, William, 381
Fulop, Robert E., cxxi n., cxxii n., cxxiii,
cxxx, cxxxii n., cxxxiii n., clvii, 265
Funerals, 219–20, 382–83
Furnivall, Frederick, 327, 330, 410 n.

Gabriel, archangel, 220–21
Gabrieli, Vittorio, 363
Gairdner, James, xxiv n., 340
Galbraith, V. H., 345
Galen, 271
Gardiner, Stephen, cxx, cxli–cxlii, clii–
cliii, cliv, clv–clvi, clvii
Gardner, Helen, 304
Gee, John Archer, 332
Geisenhof, Georg, xvii n., clxi n., 265,
395 n.
Geoffrey of Monmouth, 334
Germanisches Nationalmuseum, Nürn-
berg, 395 n.
Gerson, Jean, xcvi–ciii, 265
Gervase of Canterbury, 339–40
Gibaud, Henri, 360
Gibson, R. W., xxi n., clxi, clxii n., clxviii,
265, 457, 481 n.
Gill, Joseph, xcii–xciii n., xcv n., xcvi n.,
265
Glorieux, Geneviève, 270
Gnosticism, cxxxviii, 20. *See also* Dualism
God: all things possible to, cxlv, cxlvii,
246–47, 249, 252 (*see also* Miracles); re-
leases souls from purgatory, 112–13,
198–200, 369; responsibility for evil,
48–50, 96, 98, 301–02, 311. *See also*
Christ; Holy Ghost; Trinity
Gogan, Brian, 313
Golden Legend. See Legenda aurea
Goldhammer, Arthur, lxxxvii n., 266
Goose, John, 144, 347, 443
Gospel, in Protestant sense, 14–16, 26,
28–30, 42, 52, 159, 162, 163, 166, 398.
See also New Testament; Scripture
Götz von Berlichingen, 349

Goudge, H. L., lxxxv, lxxxvi
Grace: church cannot assure, 296; and
free will, 46, 48–50, 56, 86–88, 298–
300, 366; and good works, 46–48, 50,
54–56, 64, 72, 78, 202, 299–300, 400;
heretics' lack of, 86–88; necessary to
overcome sin, 191–92, 292, 301; of re-
pentance, 301, 302; of souls in purgatory, cx, 227. *See also* Christ; Faith
Graesse, J. G. Theodor, 369, 375
Grafton, Richard, 265, 335, 336
Grapheus, Johannes, 409
Gratian, cxlvi n., 387
Gray, John de, 338, 339
Greek Church: on Mary Magdalen, 313;
prayer for the dead in, xci–xcii, xciv;
purgatory in, lxxi, xc, xci–xcvi, cv, cix,
190–91, 210; scriptural canon, lxxx n.
Greek language, study of, cxx, cxxii
Greg, W. W., 460 n.
Gregory I (Gregory the Great), Saint and
Pope: on bequests, 382; and conversion
of England, cxv; More mentions, 159,
190–91, 195, 209, 210; on purgatory,
xciv, xcv, cvi, 190–91, 360, 363, 364,
365, 366–67, 370–71, 450; mentioned,
312
Gregory IX, Pope, 344
Gregory XI, Pope, 375
Gregory of Nazianzus, Saint, 210, 376
Gregory of Neocaesarea, Saint, 210, 376
Gregory of Nyssa, Saint, xciv, 210, 376
Grente, Georges, 272
Greyfriars. *See* Franciscans
Groote, Gerhard de, cii
Grüninger, Johann, xcvi n.
Guitmund, 390
Guy, John A., xxx n., xxxi n., xxxii n.,
lxvi n., lxvii n., 266, 267

Hadcock, R. Neville, 332, 334
Hägglund, Bengt, 282
Hall, Edward, 334, 346
Hallett, Philip E., xliv n.
Hanseatic League, xxxi. *See also* Steelyard
Harpsfield, Nicholas, xxi, 266, 272
Harris, Alice, 270
Harris, John, clx, 270
Harvard University Library, 466 n.
Harvey, E. Ruth, 315

Hastings, Margaret, 452 n.
Haupt, G. E., 267
Hazlitt, William, lxiii n.
Headley, John M., lv, 267, 296, 319
Heath, Dr., clvii
Heath, Peter, 341
Heaven: not a physical location, cxlvi, 220–21, 244, 245; no punishment in, 193, 194; proof of, 196; Protestants seek to deny, 206; purgatory and, 449. *See also* Purgatory
Hebel, J. W., 410 n.
Hell: entrance into, c, 192, 198, 442; God's power over, 198; harrowing of, lxxxiv, 179, 185–86, 357; location of, 220–21, 447; nature of, lxxxiii, lxxxviii, xcv, cix, cxvi, cxvii, 179, 442; no relief in, lxxxvi, lxxxviii, cvii, cxi, 193, 194, 202; proof of, 196; Protestants seek to deny, 206; synonym for purgatory, lxxxiv, ci n., cxvi, cxvii, 178, 184–86, 362. *See also* Devils; Purgatory
Helvidius (Elvidius), cv, 195, 368
Henry I, King of England, 128, 336, 338
Henry III, King of England, 335
Henry IV, King of England, 143, 340, 345, 347
Henry IV, King of France, 273
Henry V, King of England, 143, 149, 340, 346, 347, 374
Henry VII, King of England, cxi, 334
Henry VIII, King of England: ancestry, 346; and Anne Boleyn, lxvii; and church property, lxvii–lxviii; Defender of the Faith, lxix, cxliii, 26, 154, 162–64, 286, 353; divorce, xxii, lxvii, cxxviii–cxxix, cxxxi, cxxxiii, cxli–cxlii, clv, 273, 275; and English Lutheranism, xxiv, xxv–xxvi; on the eucharist, cxlii, cxliii, cxlix, 253, 389, 421; and Fish, 439–40; Fish invokes, 127–28, 132, 133, 134, 136–37, 139–40, 150, 154–55, 158, 162–64, 349, 412–22 *passim*; and Frith, cxxix–cxxxiii, cxxxix, cxli–cxliii, clv–clvii, clviii; heresy and, xxii, xxvi, lxviii, cxviii, cxxix, cxxxi, cxli–cxliii, clv–clvi; and the Hunne case, 134–36; on indulgences, cvi n.; and Luther, xx–xxi, xxvi–xxx, xxxv–xxxvi, 277; More's letters to, lxvi; and Oxford, 381; public opinion and, cxix, cxliii, clv, clvi; and spiritual law, 116–17; struggles with Catholicism, cxxiii, cxxix, cxxxi, cxli, clv; subsidies granted to, 344; mentioned, 343. *See also* England; Royal authority
— works: *Assertio septem sacramentorum adversus M. Lutherum*, xx, xxi, lxxi, lxxiv, cvi n., cxlii, cxlix, 26, 38, 162, 164, 253, 276, 286, 353, 359, 368, 389, 452; letter to Luther, xxxv–xxxvi
Hentage, Sidney J., 371
Heresy: charges, trumped-up, 116–17, 130–32, 412–14, 418; danger to society, l, cxxvi, cxliii, 16, 22–24, 137, 143–44, 148–49, 166–68, 324; diabolical origin, xlviii, li, lvi, lvii, lix, lx–lxii, lxiii, cxxv, 24, 68, 100, 114–15, 118, 170, 233, 319, 354; disunity of, cxxv, 22, 44 (*see also* Protestantism, dissension); does not endure, 20–22, 283–84; Fathers of Church oppose, l–li, lv, 18, 36, 208–10, 282; God's purpose in permitting, 100; Henry VIII's flirtation with, xxii, xxvi, lxviii, cxviii, cxxix, cxxxi, cxlii–cxliii, clv–clvi; laws, lxviii, clvi, 130–31, 142, 158, 340; madness, xxvi n., xxx, xxxiv n., xxxvi, xlvi, lii, lv, lvi, lix–lxi, lxiii, cxlix, 36, 84–86, 137, 153, 206; minority compared to Catholics, 208–09; More's general attitude toward, xxxi, xxxiv n., xliii, xlviii–li, liv–lv, lxiii–lxiv, lxvi, cxviii, cxl, clviii–clix; offical English response to, xx–xxv, xxxi, cxxii–cxxiii, clv–clvii, 233, 288, 348, 384, 409–10; Philip II and, 273; Protestants' "revival" of old, xx, cxliv, 18, 3, 40; punishment for, xxiv, xxv, xlviii–li, cxxiii, 340, 418; traditional Catholic attitude toward, xlviii–li, 20. *See also* Arianism; Books, heretical; Pelagius and Pelagianism; Protestantism
Hering, Hermann, xviii n.
Hervet, Gentian, 6, 271
Hewlett, Henry G., 339
Hexter, J. H., 267
Hezekiah, lxxv–lxxvi, lxxviii, 176–78, 356
Higden, Ranulf, 266, 336–37, 339, 346
Hilary, Saint, 38, 210, 291, 366, 377
Hildebert of Lavardin, lxxxix n.
Hildegard, Saint, 209, 374

Hill, W. Speed, 460 n., 461, 462 n., 481 n.
Hinman, Charlton, 471
Hirten, W. J., 478 n.
Hitchcock, Elsie Vaughan, xxi n., xlviii n., 266, 268, 272
Hodgson, Phyllis, 375
Hoen, Cornelius, cxxxvi, 385
Hofmann, Georg, xciii n.
Holbein, Hans, xxxi, cxxvii, 4, 343, 383
Holborn, Annemarie and Hajo, 264, 355, 358
Hollister, C. Warren, 336
Holt, William, cxxxiv
Holy Ghost: comforts souls in purgatory, cx; grace and, 298; informs the Church, lxviii, 34–36, 58, 94, 100, 182, 210, 295; Luther on, 311–12; sin against, lxxv, lxxxvi, 191–93, 366; torments heretics, xlix
Homer, 389
Hope, lxii. See also Faith
Hopman, F., lxxvii n.
Horace, 308
Horsey, William, 116–17, 132–36, 327–28, 342, 420–21
Hospitals, 117, 142, 422
Houlbrooke, Ralph, 341
Howard, Thomas. See Norfolk
Huett, Andrew, clvii–clviii
Hugh of St. Victor, xc, 375
Hughes, Paul L., 266, 333
Hughes, Philip, xxii n., xxiii n., 266, 410 n.
Huizinga, J., lxxvii n., 359
Hume, Anthea, lxxxiii n., cxxviii n., 263, 266, 269, 275, 352, 381, 391, 409, 425
Humphrey, Duke of Gloucester, 346–47
Hunden, Richard, 144, 346, 443
Hunne, Richard, 116–17, 132–36, 326, 327–28, 418, 420–21, 443
Huntington Library, California, clx
Huskyn, John. See Oecolampadius, John
Hussites, 391
Hutten, Ulrich von, 329
Hythlodaeus, Raphael, 350, 450 n.

Iconoclasm, 274, 278
Imitation of Christ, xcvi
Immortality, 172–73, 354–55. See also Purgatory
Incarnation, and transubstantiation,

cxxxvii–cxxxix, cxlvi, cxlviii, cli, 257–58. See also Christ
Indulgences: Catholic defense of, ci, cviii–cix, cxvi, 198; history of, lxx–lxxi, xcvi, cvi, 325–26, 375; in popular piety, cxxviii, 315, 325, 449, 450, 452; Protestant opposition to, lxxi, lxxii, cv, cviii–cix, 198, 315, 325–26, 419–20, 452. See also Purgatory
Innocent III, Pope, xc, cxxxvii, 128–29, 335–37, 338–39, 388, 415, 449
Innocent IV, Pope, lxxxix n., 331, 335
Irenaeus of Lyons, cxxv
Isaac, Frank, clxiii n., clxix n., 457 n.
Islip, John, 343
Ivo of Chartres, Saint, 358

Jackson, W. A., xvii n., 268
Jacob, 235–36, 431
Jaffé, Philippe, 338
James, Epistle of, lxxix–lxxx, 60, 180, 305–06, 363. See also Biblical quotations
James V, King of Scotland, 275
Jamnia, Jewish Synod of, lxxx
Jensen, O., 337
Jerome, Saint: Dialogus Aduersus Luciferianos, clxix, 239, 386; on free will, 312; on Mary's virginity, 368; More mentions, lxxxvi, 159, 180, 183, 195, 209, 210, 239; on purgatory, lxxxvi, cvi, 195, 356, 360, 375; and the scriptural canon, lxxx, lxxxi, lxxxii, cvii, 180, 183, 306, 358; on scriptural interpretation, 239, 386, 387–88; on the sin against the Holy Spirit, 366; mentioned, 312, 378
Jesus. See Christ
Jews: belief in afterlife, 172, 196; clergy among, 165; More mentions, 26, 42, 64, 82, 154, 171, 197; pray for the dead, lxxix n., lxxxviii; "saints" of, 293; scriptural canon and, lxxix–lxxxi, 180–82, 359
Job, cii
John, Gospel of, authority of, lxxx–lxxxi, lxxxiii, 181, 183, 358. See also Biblical quotations; New Testament; Scripture
John I, King of England, 128–29, 334–37, 338–39, 340, 415
John the Baptist, Saint, lxxxviii, 54, 92
John Chrysostom, Saint, xciv, xcv, cvi, cix,

John Chrysostom, Saint (*continued*)
    159, 195, 204, 209, 210, 254, 290, 365,
    366, 372, 376, 389
John Damascene, Saint, lxxi, 203, 210,
    371–72
John of Gaunt, 346
Jonas, J., 327
Jordan, Wilbur K., 332
Jowitt, William Allen, 381–82
Joye, George, xxii n., lxxxv, cxxiv, cliii, 367.
    See also The Souper of the Lorde
Judaism. *See* Jews
Judas, 305, 360, 361, 389
Judas Maccabaeus, lxxvii–lxxix, lxxxvii,
    179, 203, 359, 450. *See also* Maccabees,
    books of
Judgement: of individuals, xcv, cix, 188,
    367, 376; last, xcv, cxvi n., 54, 56, 188,
    245, 304, 367. *See also* Purgatory
Julius II, Pope, 316, 332
Justice, purgatory required by, c, 173–76,
    198–200, 355
Justification: double, cxxv–cxxvi; More
    on, lvi, lvii–lviii. *See also* Christ, only
    source of righteousness; Faith alone
Juvenal, 309, 312

Karlstadt, Andreas Bodenstein von, xix,
    lviii, 14, 94–96, 278, 287, 300, 316, 317,
    318, 385
Kawerau, Gustav, xviii n.
Keen, Ralph, clxvii n., 267, 362, 472 n.
Kelly, J. N. D., cxliv n.
Kesler, Nicolaus, xcvi n.
Kingsford, Charles L., 343, 345, 346
Kinney, D., 267
Kinsley, James, 453 n.
Knappert, L., 322
Knight, William, xxix n.
Knowles, M. David, 331, 332, 334, 338
Koelhoff, Johann, xcvi n.
Koppe, Leonhard, 289
Krieger, Leonard, 349
Krivatsky, Nati, 425
Kronenberg, M. E., xxxii n., 409 n.
Krueger, Paul, 344

Lactantius, 378
Lambert, François, xix, liii, 14, 28, 209,
    278–79, 287, 288, 373
Lambert, John, cxx, cxxxiv, cxlii, cl

Lambeth, 339
Lampe, G. W. H., 266, 290
Lanfranc, 390
Langland, John, Bishop of Lincoln, xxiv n.
Langton, Stephen, clxiv, 129, 338–39, 415
Larkin, James F., 266, 333, 410 n.
Last Supper, cxxxv, 235, 246–47, 429. *See
    also* Eucharist; Masses
Latham, R. E., 297
Latimer, Hugh, xxii n., xxiii, lxxxv, cxx
L'Aubespine, Claude de, 271
Law. *See* Mortmain; Parliament; Praemu-
    nire; Spiritual law; Temporal law
Lawler, Thomas M. C., xlix n., lx–lxi, 267
Lay Folks Mass Book, The, 450–52
Le Goff, Jacques, lxxxvii–xci, 266, 368,
    449 n., 450 n.
Lee, Edward, xxxv, 286
Lefèvre d'Etaples, lxxxi, cii, 313
Legenda aurea, 371, 449–50, 452
Leo X, Pope, xx, 278, 289, 353, 377. *See
    also Exsurge Domine*
Lepanto, battle of, 273
Leprosy, 330, 412. *See also* Beggars
Liberty. *See* Freedom
Limbo, lxxvii n., c, cxii, 179, 186–87, 196,
    356, 357, 447–48. *See also* Purgatory
Linacre, Thomas, 271
Lippe, Robert, 267
Lisle Letters, 453 n.
Liturgies, 323, 324, 358, 372, 450–52. *See
    also* Masses
Lloyd-Jones, Hugh, 374
Logic: Frith's use of, cxxxv, cxlv, 249–52,
    429; More's use of, lv–lvi, cxlv–cxlix,
    249–52, 333, 388–89. *See also* Miracles;
    Reason; Scholasticism
Lollards, 345–46, 384. *See also* Protestant-
    ism
Lombard, Peter, xc, 290, 294, 366
London, City of, 214, 380
Longland, John, clvii
Lord Chancellor: office of, 421; More as,
    lxv, lxvi, cxviii, cxxx, cxxxii, cxxxiv, clxi,
    277, 381, 440, 458 n.
Lords, House of, 139–40. *See also* Parlia-
    ment
Luard, Henry Richards, 339
Lucian, 308, 391
Lucius Tiberius, 125, 334, 414
Lucy, Thomas, 332

Lumby, Joseph, 266
Lupset, Thomas, 271, 332, 381
Lusardi, James P., xxii n., xxv n., cxxxiv n., 267
Luther, Martin:
—biographical: Augustinian friar, 325, 373; and Barnes, cxxxiv; and Bugenhagen, xvii–xix; excommunication, xx, xxiv, 315 (*see also Exsurge Domine*); and Henry VIII, xx–xxi, xxvi–xxx, xxxv–xxxvi, 277; and Karlstadt, 278; and Lambert, 279; marriage, xviii, xxvi, xxvii, liii, 281–82, 287, 288–89, 374; opinion of More, lxiii–lxiv; polemicist, xx–xxi, xlvii, 291; and Tyndale, xxiii n., xxvi
— theological: on the appearence of dead souls, 370; on baptism, 306–07; on the church visible and invisible, 292–93, 313; on the eucharist, lviii, cxix, cxxiii, cxxvi–cxxvii, cxxviii, cxxxiv, cxxxv, cxxxvi–cxxxvii, cxlix, 94–96, 234, 294–95, 315–16, 317–18, 385; on fasting, 314; Fisher on, ciii–cx, cxiv; on free will, 84–86, 299–300, 310–12, 318; on indulgences, 315; justification by faith, 297; on law, 318–19; on marriage, 318–19; on Mary, 303–04; on the mass, 294–95, 304, 314, 315, 317; on ordination and the priesthood, 295–96, 314, 317, 318, 379; on penance, 308, 313–14; on the pope, 315, 378; on purgatory, lxx–lxxi, cv, cvi–cx, cxiv, cxvi, cxvii, 198, 211–13, 304, 358, 369, 377–79; on relics, 281, 287; on sacraments and the church, 295–96, 313; on saints, 281; *scriptura sola*, 378; and the scriptural canon, lxxix–lxxx, 180, 203, 305–06, 358, 359
— More on: aims, lxiii–lxiv, lvii–lviii, 24, 30, 58, 62, 66–68, 96–98, 351; the Christ of Lutherans, 16, 28, 36, 62, 96; demonic, lix–lxii, 84, 86, 282; inconsistency, lviii, civ, 94–96, 317, 102; insane, lix–lxi, 84–86, 203; marriage, 28, 56, 96, 151, 209, 281, 288–89; and the Peasants' Revolt, lviii–lix, 102, 285, 286, 319, 321; quotes, 20; mentioned, 159, 163, 164, 166, 167, 168, 177, 208, 209
— works: *De abroganda missa privata*, 295; *Adversus execrabilem Antichristi bvllam*, civ n.; *Assertio omnium articulorum M. Lutheri per bullam Leonis X*, civ n., cvi–cx nn., cxvi n., 48, 266, 296, 299–300, 310, 314; Bible translation, xviii, xxiii n.; *De captivitate Babylonica*, xviii, xx, cxxxvi, cxlix, 68, 96, 162, 253, 281–82, 286, 294, 295–96, 306–07, 308, 314, 315, 317, 318–19, 353, 359; *An den christlichen Adel deutscher Nation von des christichen Standes Besserung*, 287; commentary on Psalms, lxxxii; *Contra Henricum regem Angliae*, xxi, xxvii, xxxv, 276, 282, 286, 295, 317, 354; *Disputatio . . . D. Iohannis Eccij & D. Martini Lutheri Augustani quae cepit.IIII. Iulij*, 264, 358, 363; *Ermahnung zum Frieden auf die zwölf Artikel der Bauerschaft in Schwaben*, 320; *Von der Freiheit eines Christeumenschen*, 318; *De libertate Christiana*, xviii; letter to Henry VIII, xxxv–xxxvi; *Ad librum . . . Ambrosii Catharini . . . responsio Martini Lutheri*, lxxii; ninety-five theses, 289, 304, 377; *Offenbarung des Endchrists*, cxxviii; *Repeal of Purgatory (Der Widerruf vom Fegefeür)*, lxx; *Resolutiones disputationum de indulgentiarum virtute*, 289, 315, 377–78; *Resolutiones Lutherianae super propositionibus suis Lipsiae disputatis*, 378; *Ein Sendbrief von dem harten Büchlein wider die Bauern*, 321; sermon on the cross, 28, 287–88, 304; sermon on Dives and Lazarus, lxxi, 370, 378–79; sermon on the eucharist, 315; sermon on the feast of Mary's nativity, 303; *De servo arbitrio*, xxx n., lxi, 84–86, 300, 310–12; *Table-Talk*, 266, 297; *De votis monasticis*, 282, 287; *Wider die räuberischen und mörderischen Rotten der Bauern*, 320–21
Lutheranism. *See* Heresy; Luther, Martin; Protestantism
Lynch, C. A., 267
Lynne, Walter, 352
Lyra, Nicholas de, 263, 356, 359–60, 361, 365–66, 387. *See also* Bible: *Biblia latina*
Lytell boke . . . of Purgatorye, a, 447–49

Maccabees, books of: canonicity of, lxxiv, lxxix–lxxxi, cviii, 180–83, 203, 357–58; More's use of, lxxiv, lxxv, lxxvii, lxxxiv; on purgatory, 179–80, 203. *See also* Bib-

Maccabees, books of (*continued*)
lical quotations; Judas Maccabaeus;
Scripture
McConica, James K., 374–75
McCue, James F., cxxxvii
McFarlane, K. B., 336
McGugan, Ruth, 267
McKerrow, R. B., clxix n., 460 n., 469 n.
McLean, Andrew M., 276
Magna Charta, 338, 340, 379, 381
Major, J. E. B., xx n.
Major, Ralph H., 330
Makower, Felix, 340
Mandeville, Sister Scholastica (Helen I.),
267
Manichaeanism, cxxxvii, cxlviii
Manley, Frank, 267
Manuel, Niklaus, 352
Marburg Colloquy, cxxiii, cxxviii, 279, 280
Marcellus II, Pope, 271
Marc'hadour, Germain P., xxxiv, xxxv n.,
liii, lxxix n., lxxxii n., cxii n., cxxxv n.,
clxi n., 266–67, 268, 270–71, 280, 282,
306, 322, 326, 328, 339, 357, 359, 364,
366, 369, 374, 375, 425, 458 n., 466 n.
Margaret, Countess of Richmond, cxi, cxvi
Marius, Richard, xxxv n., cxxxii n.,
cxxix n., 267, 287
Marius Mercator, 292
Markos Eugenikos, metropolitan of
Ephesus, xciv, xcv
Marlowe, Christopher, lix
Marriage: of clergy, urged by Fish, 150–
54, 156–57, 416–17, 422; Henry VIII's,
xxii, lxvii, cxxviii–cxxix, cxxxi, cxxxiii,
cxli–cxlii, clv, 273, 275; laws, 140, 281,
318–19, 344; Luther's, xviii, xxvi, xxvii,
liii, 281–82, 287, 288–89, 374; of Prot-
estants, xviii, liii, 16, 26, 28, 74, 209, 278,
279, 280, 281–82, 287, 373; of servants,
152, 350. *See also* Celibacy
Martin, John, clvii
Martyrs, 376–77. *See also* Saints
Martz, Louis L., xliii, 267, 364, 452 n.
Mary, the Blessed Virgin, ci, cii, 56, 195,
227, 281, 303–04 361, 368, 429
Mary I, Queen of England, clvi, 275, 338,
478
Mary Magdalen, Saint, 147, 312–13
Maskell, William, 362

Mass books. *See* Missals
Masses: fees for, lxxix, 204–06, 224, 294,
326, 413, 422; and forgiveness of sin,
294–95; good works, 294, 304, 314;
necessary with transubstantiation, lxix;
prayers for the dead in, 205, 323, 372,
450–53; Protestant alterations, 96, 278,
294–95, 304, 314, 317; as sacrifice, 295,
314, 315, 450; for souls in purgatory,
xcviii, ci, 56, 111, 202, 204–06, 224, 227,
323, 352, 370, 371, 382, 422, 449, 450;
symbolic, cxxxiv; wills provide for, 139,
332, 452–53. *See also* Eucharist
Matthew of Paris, 339
Maxwell, J. G., 460 n.
Mayor, John E. B., cxv n., 265
Meale, C. M., 460 n.
Melanchthon, Philipp (Schwarzerdt), xviii,
cxlvi n., 320, 373, 387
Melchisidek, 353
Merchants: economic conditions and,
lxxiii; raid on Steelyard, xxiv, xxv, xxxi–
xxxii
Mercy, God's, and purgatory, 173–74,
175–76, 198–200, 355
Merlin, Jacques, 365
Meyer, Carl S., xx n., xxxii n.
Michael Palaeologus, Emperor, xcii
Michel, A., lxxxvii, lxxxix n.
Migne, J.-P., xlix n., 268
Milan Missal, 372
Miller, Clarence H., 267, 481 n.
Miracles: apparitions and, 197–98; of
Catholic saints, 42; in popular religion,
cxxvii, cxxviii; the Protestant "revela-
tion" and, 30; repugnance toward, 247–
49, 388; transubstantiation, cxxviii,
cxlvii, 247–49
Missals, 323, 324, 358, 372, 450–52. *See
also* Masses
Mitchner, Robert W., 460 n.
Moddys, Edmund, 441
Mölhuysen, P. C., 322
Mommsen, Theodor, 344
Monica, Saint, lxv–lxvi, lxxxviii, cii
More, Abel, 341
More, Dame Alice, xxx, 343
More, Cecily, xxx
More, Elizabeth, xxx
More, John, 328, 452–53

More, Margaret. *See* Roper, Margaret

More, Thomas:

— biographical: chancellor of Lancaster, xxxi, lxv, clxi, 277, 344, 457 n.; execution, 272; high steward of Cambridge, xxxi; and the Hunne case, 328; imprisonment, lxii, 306; keepership of foreign exchanges, xxxii; lord chancellor of England, lxv, lxvi, cxviii, cxxx, cxxxii, cxxxiv, clxi, 277, 381, 440, 458 n.; portraits, xxxi, 4, 271, 343, 383; and Luther's letter to Henry VIII, xxix–xxx; reputation, 277; residence at Chelsea, xxx, 275; secretary to Henry VIII, xxix–xxx; self-chastisement, xlvii; speaker of Parliament, 334, 344; Steelyard raid, xxiv, xxv, xxxi–xxxii; tithecollector, 326; travels, lxvi, 275, 363; undertreasurer of the Exchequer, xxxi, 277, 339, 380

— literary and theological: anti-heretical activities in general, xxxi, xxxiv n., xliii, xlviii–li, liii n., lxiii, lxv, lxvi, cxviii, cxxx, cxxxiv–cxxxv, cliii, clviii–clix, 276; on Greek studies, cxxii; and Henry's *Assertio*, xxxv–xxxvi, 276, 286; as historian, 337, 339–40; humor, 277, 350, 353, 366; metaphors, xlv–xlvi, xcix n., 330; monastic urges, 332; nationalist, xxxiv n., xlv; pacifism, 273; personal piety, xlvii–xlviii, cxxvii, cxxxvi, cli–clii; polemicist, xxi, xliii, xlv–xlviii, l–lii, lxii–lxiv, cxli, cxlii, 277; prayer book, lxxvi n., 322, 355, 364, 449, 452; pseudonyms and hoaxes, xxi, xxxii–xxxiii, xlvi, 276–77, 286; puns on his name, 270–71, 272; scripture use, xxi, lxxiv–lxxxvii, 364 (*see also* Biblical quotations); violence and anger, xxi, xlv–xlviii, l–lii, lxii–lxiv, cxli

— *Letter to Bugenhagen* (*see also* Bugenhagen, John): date of composition, xvii, xxii, xxx–xxxi, xlviii, clx, 277, 281; compared to Cochlaeus, xvii, xix, xxx, xxxiv, xxxiv–xxxv n., xlvii, 276, 277, 278, 280–81, 282, 285–86, 288, 289, 293–94, 297, 301–302, 303, 306, 318, 319, 320; errata and mistakes, 280, 291, 312, 313, 320; humor, xlv–xlvii, lix, 277; intended audience, xxxiii, 281;

manuscript, 270; More's identification as author, xxxii–xxxiii, 12, 277; persona, xxxi n., xxxii–xxxiii, xliv–xlv, xlvi, 12–14, 275, 276–77; publication history, xvii, xxxiii–xxxvi, clx, 274; quotation from Bugenhagen, xxxiv, xxxv n., xlii–xliv, xlv, lii, clxi, 14, 16, 24, 26, 28, 32, 38, 42–46, 56, 58, 64–66, 68, 80–82, 88–90, 92, 94, 100, 280, 285, 288, 289, 291, 293, 297, 303, 305, 307, 309; rhetoric, xxvi n., xxxiv–xxxv n., xliii–lxiii; sidenotes, clx; structure, xxxiv, xxxv n., xlii–xliv, liii, 280; style, xxxiii, xxxiv n., xliii, xlv, liv; texts, clx–clxi, 270, 289; translation, xvii; version of Bugenhagen used, xlii n., clxi, 12, 275, 276, 280, 283, 289, 395 n.; violence, xlv–xlviii, l–lii, lxii–lxiii

— *Letter against Frith*: addressee, 384; date of composition, cxii, cxviii, cxl, clxviii; distribution, cxl–cxli, cxlii–cxliii, clii, cliv; errrata and mistakes, clxix, 385, 388, 389, 391; quotation from Frith, 425; publication, clxviii–clxix; purpose, cxviii–cxix, cxxxv, cxl, cxlii–cxliii, clix; treatment of Frith personally, cxviii, cxix, cxxxi, cxxxix–cxl, cxli, cxlii, clviii

— *Supplication of Souls*: archaisms in, 323–24, 325, 334, 338, 341, 343; date of composition, lxv–lxvi, clxi, 457–58 n.; errata and mistakes, lxvi, clxi n., clxi–clxvii, 327, 329, 330, 337, 338, 340, 342, 343, 349, 351, 362, 367, 383, 459, 466 n., 472–76, 481; Fisher's influence, ciii, cvi, 356; index, 478–81; intended audience, lxvi, lxviii, lxxiii–lxxiv; and persecution of Fish, 440–41; printer's copy for *English Works*, 457–81; publication history, lxv–lxvi, clxi–clxiii, 324, 457–58, 481; quotations from Fish, clxviii, 322, 328, 329, 334, 343; scripture in, lxxiv–lxxxvii; sidenotes, 478–81; souls in purgatory, literary device of, lxviii–lxix, 111, 442–44; structure, lxxiv–lxxv

— correspondence: with Barnes, cl–cli; with Cochleaus, 289; with Cranevelt, 391; with Cromwell, 286; with Erasmus, lxxiv; with Henry VIII, lxvi; with Wolsey, 333

More, Thomas (*continued*)
— other works: *The Answer to a Poisoned Book*, xci, cxl, cliii, clviii, clxviii, clxix, 275, 316, 325, 373, 384, 386–87, 388, 389, 391, 477 n.; *The Apology*, lxiii n., cxxxix–cxl, cxli, cxlii, clii–cliv, clviii, clxix, 324, 325, 328, 369, 373, 437, 477 n.; prayers in *A Brief Fourme of Confession*, 270; *The Confutation of Tyndale's Answer*, lxxxiii, lxxxiv n., lxxxv, xci n., ciii n., cxvi n., cxliii, clxi n., 277, 282, 288–89, 290, 313, 333, 342, 349, 352, 357, 369, 386, 388, 390–91, 448 n.; *The Debellation of Salem and Bizance*, lxv n., xci, 323, 325, 328, 384, 477 n.; *A Dialogue of Comfort*, xliv n., xlvi, xlvii n., lxii, lxxv n., lxxvi, lxxxvi, xcvi, c, ci, 270, 271, 273, 277, 288, 290, 305, 319–20, 354, 362, 363, 388, 453 n., 477–78, 480–81; *A Dialogue Concerning Heresies*, xlvii n., lx, lxv, lxvi, lxviii, lxxiv, ciii, civ, cxxiv, cxxv, cxxvii, cxlvii n., clxi n., clxiii n., clxiv, 280, 281, 282, 287, 288, 290, 292, 294–95, 296, 304, 307, 314, 317, 318, 322, 323, 328, 329, 348, 351, 352, 355, 386, 388, 448 n., 449 n., 457–58 n., 458, 459, 460, 462; *The Four Last Things*, ci, 342, 366, 382, 388; "A godly meditacion," lxxvi n., 322, 355, 364, 449, 452; *The History of Richard III*, lxv n., lxxxiii n., 309, 336, 343, 453 n.; *Imploratio diuini auxilij*, lxxxii n., 364; Latin poems, 290, 341; *Letter to Brixius*, 348; *Life of Picus*, lxxx n., lxxxiv, xcix n., 368, 383, 454; Lucian translations, 368; *Responsio ad Lutherum*, xxi, xxxi, xliv n., xlv, lxv n., lxxi, lxxiv, lxxxiv, ciii n., cvi n., cxiv n., 276–77, 278, 280, 281, 282, 286, 292–93, 294–95, 296, 304, 314, 317, 319, 353, 355, 359, 363, 389, 448 n.; *A Treatise on the Blessed Body*, 270; *A Treatise on the Passion*, lxxxiii; *De Tristitia Christi*, lxxv n., clviii, clxiii n., clviii n., 313; *Utopia*, xxi, xxxiii, xliv n., xlvi, lxv n., cxliii, cxlvi, cxlvii n., 277, 305, 334, 343, 354–55, 356, 391, 442, 443; Valencia autograph, clxiii n., clxviii n.; *Workes . . . in the Englysh tonge*, 457–81
Morgan, Margery M., 460 n.
Morison, Stanley, xxxi n., 271

Morley, Mrs., 381
Morris, Eileen, clxi n.
Mortillet, G. de, 378
Mortmain, 213–17, 379–80, 381–82, 418, 420
Morton, John, Cardinal, archbishop of Canterbury, 339
Mortuaries, 133, 134, 326, 327, 342, 344, 413
Moses, 353
Mountjoy, Lord William Blount, 381
Moxon, Joseph, 459
Mozley, J. F., cxxi n., cxxiv n., 267
Müller, Hans, 284
Munro, John H., 333
Münzer, Thomas, 284, 321
Murray, J. A. H., 267
Mynors, R. A. B., 264

Nash, Thomas, 322
National Library of Scotland, 466 n.
Necton, Robert, 437
New Testament: Erasmus' translation, xxiii n., lxxxiv, xci, cxx, cxxi, 279, 305–06, 358, 360, 365, 387–88; More's use of, lxxiv, lxxvi; and Old, lxxx–lxxxi, lxxxii–lxxxiii; Tyndale's translation, xxiii, xxv, xxvi, xxvii–xxviii, lxxx, lxxxvi, cxx, cxxiii, cxxxviii, 142, 161, 167, 168, 322, 340, 344, 409 n., 420, 437. *See also* Bible; Biblical quotations; Scripture
New York Public Library, 466 n., 470 n.
Nicholas de Lyra. *See* Lyra, Nicholas de
Nijhoff, Wouter, 409 n.
Norfolk, Thomas Howard, Duke of, lxvii, cxxx, cxxxi
Notre Dame, school of, xc
Novatians, 360
Nowack, W., 365
Ntedika, Joseph, lxxxviii n.
Nuns, 142–43, 334, 345. *See also* Clergy; Friars

Obedience. *See* Royal authority
Odilo, Abbot of Cluny, 450
Oecolampadius, John (Huskyn), 267; biography, 279–80, 317, 373; on the eucharist, lviii, cxxvi, cxxxv, 94–96, 316, 318, 385; More mentions, xix, lviii, cxix,

14, 94–96, 209, 234, 236, 240, 241; on
    St. John Damascene, lxxi, 372
Ogle, Arthur G., 327
Old Testament: More's use of, lxxiv, lxxv–
    lxxvii; and New, lxxx–lxxxi, lxxxii–
    lxxxiii. *See also* Bible; Biblical quota-
    tions; Scripture
Oldcastle, John Lord Cobham, 149, 345–
    36, 443
Oldham, bishop of Exeter, 381
Olgin, Moissaye J., 349
Oliver, R. P., 267
Ombres, Robert, lxxxviii–lxxxix, xc,
    xcii n., 268
Ordination, 281–82, 295–96, 318, 354.
    See also Clergy; Sacraments
Ordo Missae, 451–52
Origen, lxxxviii, lxxxix, xciv, cvii, cix, 190,
    210, 312, 313, 364–65, 375, 376
Orosius, 292
Oscott College, clx, clxix n., 282, 283, 289,
    290, 302
Otto, August, 268, 293, 309, 312, 367, 437
Ottomans. *See* Turks
Ovid, 312, 329
Owst, G. R., 383
Oxford University: endowment, 381;
    Greek at, cxxii; libraries, clxi n., clxix n.,
    425, 466 n., 477–78, 480–81; Lutheran-
    ism at, xxiii, xxvi, cxxii. *See also*
    Universities

Pace, Richard, xx n., xxx n.
Pammachius, 375
Pantzer, Katherine F., xvii n., 268
Papacy: infallibility, xxxii; Luther on, 315;
    Peter's pence, 128–29, 337–38; power
    over purgatory, lxx–lxxi, lxxii, c, cv, cix,
    198–99, 200, 213, 419, 449 (*see also* In-
    dulgences); property of, lxviii; and royal
    authority, cxxxi, 128–29, 327, 335–37,
    338. *See also* Church; Clergy; individual
    popes
Pardoners, 325–36, 412, 413
Parker, Matthew, 339
Parliament: anti-clericism in, 140, 141,
    143–44, 344, 345, 346, 347–48; au-
    dience for *Supplication of Souls*, lxvi,
    lxxiii; clerics in, 130, 139–40, 417; and
    ecclesiastical jurisdiction, 130, 140, 340,

344; and fealty to Rome, 335–36; House
    of Commons, 130, 139–41; House of
    Lords, 139–40; taxation by, 334. *See also*
    Temporal law
Pascal II, Pope, 337
Pascal lamb, 236, 431
Paschasius, 370–71
Patrick, J. Max, xxi n., 265
Paul, Saint and Apostle, Protestant prefer-
    ence for, lxxxiv, 14, 277–78. *See also* Bib-
    lical quotations
Paul IV, Pope, 274
Paul of Samostata, 291
Paulus de Santa Maria, bishop of Burgos,
    263
Payne, W., 371
Paynell, Thomas, 478–81
Peacock, Stephen, clvii
Peasants' Revolt: Bugenhagen on, xxxvii–
    xxxviii; Christian freedom and, 22–24,
    100, 166, 320; Cochlaeus on, 285–86,
    319, 321; history, xlviii, 279, 281, 284–
    85, 320, 349; Luther and, xxvi, lviii–lix,
    319, 320–21; More mentions, lii–liii, liv,
    lvi, lviii–lix, lxii–lxiii, 16, 22–24, 100–
    102, 149, 166, 234, 282, 302, 320, 349,
    384
Peeters, Cuner, 104, 321–22
Pelagius and Pelagianism, xli, 38, 46–48,
    50, 283–84, 292, 298–302, 395 n., 400
Pelikan, Jaroslav, cl n.
Penance: by the living on behalf of the
    dead, xcviii, 200, 449; Luther on, 308,
    313–14; owed by the dead, xciii, xcv, cx–
    cxi, 173–74, 193; to avoid purgatory, ci,
    cvi, 175–76, 177; unnecessary under
    doctrine of justification by faith, 58, 66–
    68, 173–75. *See also* Purgatory; Sacra-
    ments
Pennafort, Raymond de, 449
Persecution: of heretics, xlviii–li; of More,
    lxii n.; of Protestants, predicted in Scrip-
    ture, xxix n., xxxviii–xxxix, cvii, 16, 22–
    24
Peter, John, 263
Peter's pence, 128–29, 337–38
Petri, Cunerus. *See* Peeters, Cuner
Pharaoh, 145
Philip II, King of Spain, 8–10, 273–74,
    283

Philip Augustus, King of France, 335
Philip of Hesse, Landgrave, 279, 284
Pico, Gianfrancesco, 375. *See also* More,
    Life of Picus
Pico, Giovanni, 355, 378. *See also* More,
    Life of Picus
Piers the Plowman's Creed, 332
Piety, popular. *See* Public opinion
Pilgrimage of Perfection, 357
Pilgrimages, 326, 413
Pius V, Saint and Pope, 330
Plato, 308
Plautus, 291
Plechtl, Helmut, 375
Pliny, 437
Plommer, Christopher, 341
Plutarch, 272, 308
Pole, Arthur, 271
Pole, Reginald, Cardinal, 271, 374
Polemics, xx–xxi, xxviii, xxxvii–xxxix, xli,
    xliii, xlv–xlviii, l–lii, lxii–lxiv, cxli, cxlii,
    277, 291
Pollard, A. W., xvii n., 268
Polydore Vergil, civ n., 336, 337, 339
Pomeranus. *See* Bugenhagen, John
Poole, A. L., 338
Poor. *See* Beggars; Poverty
Pope. *See* Papacy
Population: of beggars, 115, 120–22, 138,
    148, 412; of clergy, 115–16, 121, 126,
    138–39, 334, 414–15; of England, 334,
    413; general, reduced by clerical celiba-
    cy, 127, 150–53, 157, 416. *See also* Statis-
    tics, Fish's use of
Possidius, 348
Poverty, 58, 305. *See also* Almsgiving; Beg-
    gars; Economic conditions
Powell, Edward, xxxv
Praemunire, lxvi, 116–17, 131, 132–33,
    327, 341, 344, 418, 421. *See also* Spiritual
    law; Temporal law
Prat, Fernand, lxxxv n.
Prayer, necessity of, 48, 66, 80, 301
Prayer for the dead: charity, 119, 205–06,
    225, 451–52; customary in the church,
    203–04, 210, 376–77, 450; fees for,
    lxxix, 204–06, 419; in the Greek
    church, xci–xcii, xciv; institutional, 323;
    in Maccabees, lxxviii–lxxix, lxxxii; in
    masses, 205, 323, 372, 450–53; in the

New Testament, lxxxii–lxxxiii, 184;
    purgatory doctrine and, lxix, lxxi–lxxii,
    lxxxvii–lxxxviii, xc, xcvii–ci, cxi, 111,
    184, 199, 200–202, 218, 219, 224, 227,
    371, 376, 449; wills provide for, xcvii, c–
    ci, cxvi, 332, 452–53. *See also* In-
    dulgences; Purgatory
Priests. *See* Clergy
Primasius, 361
Princeton University Library, clx, 466 n.
Proctors, 119, 329
Protestantism: dissension concerning the
    eucharist, cxviii–cxix, cxxiii, cxxvi–
    cxxviii, cxxxiii–cxxxv, cl–cli, clii, 94–96,
    278, 280, 284, 318, 385, 428; dissension
    in general, cxxv, 44, 221; in England,
    Luther's perceptions of, xxvi–xxx,
    xxvi, 16, 26, 40, 280; in England, rise of,
    xix, xxii–xxvi, cxx, cxxix–cxxx, cxxxii,
    398; Henry VIII's divorce and, xxii,
    cxxviii–cxxix, cxxxiii; persecution of,
    predicted in Scripture, xxix n., xxxviii–
    xxxix, cvii, 16, 22–24; propaganda
    against, xxxvii–xxxix, xli, xliii n., lii,
    cxix, 16–18, 22, 28–30, 398–400, 404;
    and royal authority, lxvii, cxxvi, cxxxviii,
    cxxxix; spiritual emphasis of, cxxvii,
    cxxxviii–cxxxix, 314–15, 316. *See also*
    Anticlericalism; Heresy; Luther, Martin
Psalms, Book of: xxxviii, lxxxi–lxxxii, cx–
    cxi, cxxxviii, 182, 359, 364; *De Profundis*
    (Psalm 129), xcix, cxi, 450, 451, 452
Public opinion: Henry VIII and, cxix,
    cxliii, clv, clvi; popular piety, cxxvii–
    cxxviii, cli–clii
Pugliese, Olga Zorzi, 454 n.
Purgatory: belief in necessary for salva-
    tion, 113, 118, 170, 175; consensus of
    the church on, 195, 203–04, 208–10,
    212–13, 371–72, 447, 449; and the con-
    templation of death, ci–cii; dogmatic
    definition, xcii–xciii, cxiv, cxvii, 323,
    447; on earth, xcvi, 355, 448; fear of,
    discourages sin, 174–76, 199–200, 206;
    in Fish, 159, 419; harrowing of, lxxxiv,
    179, 185–86, 357; history of doctrine,
    lxx–lxxii, lxxxvii–xci, cv–cvi, cix, 56,
    354; importance in Catholic doctrine,
    lxviii–lxix, lxxxvii, cxvii, 194–95; im-
    portance for More, lxviii–lxix, xc, cxvii;

justice requires, c, 173–76, 198–200, 355; Luther on, lxx–lxxi, cv, cvi–cx, cxiv, cxvi, cxvii, 198, 211–13, 304, 358, 369, 377–79; masses for, xcviii, ci, 56, 111, 202, 204–06, 224, 227, 323, 352, 370, 371, 382, 422, 449, 450; natural men believe in, 172–73, 355; neglect of, 111, 218–19, 227–28; no anger in, 219; opposition to, based on indulgences, cv; pains of, lxxxvii, c, cix, cx, cxiii, cxvii, 111, 188–90, 221–22, 225–27, 447, 448, 450; physical nature of, lxxvi–lxxvii, lxxxiv–lxxxvi, lxxxvii–xci, xcix, c, cvii–cviii, cix, cxv, 220–21, 226, 383, 450; Pope's power over, lxx–lxxi, lxxii, c, cv, cix, 198–99, 200, 213, 419, 449; in popular piety, cxxviii, 447–54; prayer for the dead and, lxix, lxxi–lxxii, lxxxvii–lxxxviii, xc, xcvii–ci, cxi, 111, 184, 199, 200–202, 218, 219, 224, 227, 371, 376, 449; as prison, lxxvi, cxii–cxiii, cxvii, 178–79, 448; prudent to believe in, 206–08; as purification, lxxxv–lxxxvi, lxxxviii, xc–xci, c, cvi, cx, cxii–cxiii, 111, 187–88, 365–66, 375–76, 377, 447, 448, 450, 454; in Scripture, lxx, lxxv–xci, xciii–xcv, ciii, cv, cvi–cviii, cx–cxi, 176–80, 184–88, 190–94, 203, 210, 212, 356–57, 359–67, 377–78, 448. *See also* Apparitions of the dead; Fire; Hell; Indulgences; Limbo

Purvey, John, 345
Pynson, Richard, xxi n., xxvii n., 332, 347, 357
Pythagoras, 290

Queen's College, Oxford, clxvii
Quentel, Peter, xxiii n.
Quintilian, 290

Raban, Sandra, 268, 380, 381, 382
Rabanus Maurus, 356
Rabelais, François, 272–73;
Rastell, John, clxi n., clxiii, 322, 379, 380, 458 n.
Rastell, William, cxii, clxi, clxiii, clxvi–clxvii, clxviii, clxix, 275, 283, 347, 355, 362, 367, 458, 459 n., 472 n., 477–79, 481
Ravyn, J., 322

Raymond de Pennafort, 449
Reason: faith superior to, 36, 242–43; miracles and, 248–49; supports theology, 32–36. *See also* Logic; Scholasticism
Redemption: faith and, 313–14; the mass as a promise of, 294–95; original sin and, 300–01. *See also* Christ, only source of righteousness; Sin
Redgrave, G. R., xvii n., 268
Reed, Arthur W., clxiii n., 268, 322, 478 n.
Regnault, Francis, 452 n.
Reinhard, Anna, 316
Relics, 26–28, 56–58, 281, 287, 304
Resurrection of the dead, lxxvii, lxxviii, lxxx, xcv. *See also* Purgatory
Reuchlin, Johannes, 294, 343, 355
Reusell, Hans, xxxii
Reynolds, E. E., cxii n.
Reynolds, Saint Richard, 374
Richard II, King of England, 335
Richter, Emil L., 263
Ridley, Nicholas, cxx
Riley, Henry T., 345, 347
Rinck, Hermann, xvii n.
Robinson, F. N., lxxvii n.
Robinson, George, 441
Roger of Wendover, 339
Rogers, D. M., 270
Rogers, Elizabeth, xxxiv, xxxvi n., lxvi n., lxxxi n., ciii n., clx n., clxviii, 267, 268, 286, 287, 323, 330, 332, 333, 348, 361, 381, 391, 453 n.
Rolle, Richard, cii
Roo, Mr., 439
Roper, Margaret (More), xlvii, ciii n., 270, 339, 361, 453 n.
Roper, William, xlviii, 268, 286, 339
Rörer, Eva, xviii, 287
Rörer, George, xviii, 287
Rosenblatt, Wilibrantis, 280
Ross, D. J. A., 377
Ross, William (More pseudonym), xxi, xxxiii, 276–77, 286
Rouschausse, Jean, cxii n.
Roy, William, 161, 352
Royal authority: clergy's obedience to, lxvii, 127–28, 139–42, 158, 415–16, 418–19, 420–21, 422; heresy subverts, l, cxxvi, cxliii, 16, 22–24, 137, 143–44, 148–49, 166–68, 324; More on, lxxv, lx-

Royal authority (*continued*)
    xviii; and papal jurisdiction, cxxxi, 128–
    29, 327, 335–37, 338; Protestantism
    and, lxvii, cxxvi, cxxxviii, cxxxix; spir-
    itual law and, 129–30, 133, 136–37,
    139, 158, 418. *See also* Henry VIII
Royal council, 140–41, 277, 328, 343
Ruff, Simpertus, xvii, 395
Rupp, E. G., 275, 276
Russell, Joycelyne G., cxii n.
Russell, Thomas, 269
Ruysbroeck, Jan van, cii
Ryckes, John, 314–15
Rymer, Thomas, 335

Sacramentarianism: arguments   for,
    cxxxv–cxxxvi, 428–31; eucharist is a
    token, cxxxvi, 234, 236, 237, 385, 431–
    33; Frith's career and, cxxvi–cxxvii,
    cxxxiii–cxxxiv, cxlii; Henry VIII and,
    cxlii; history, cxxxvii, cxli, cl, 280, 316–
    17, 345, 352, 391; More on, 234, 258;
    and purgatory, xci. *See also* Eucharist;
    Transubstantiation; Zwingli
Sacraments: Bugenhagen on, xl, 92–94,
    402; and the church, 295–96, 313; eu-
    charist the primary, 234–35; faith's role,
    313–14; Fish on, 159, 161, 163; and
    God's presence in creation, cxxxvii–
    cxxxix, 385; indelible, 354; priest's role,
    cxxxvi, cxlix–cl, 154, 161, 234, 254, 432,
    433; promises of God, 307, 313–14;
    Protestant reduction of, cxxvii, 204–05,
    281, 294, 295–96, 316, 402. *See also* Bap-
    tism; Eucharist; Marriage; Penance
St. Austin, order of, 123, 275, 331
St. John's College, Cambridge, cxvi
St. Saviours abbey, 138, 343
Saints: adoration of, 281, 289, 293; their
    holiness is recognized, 42; prayers of,
    202, 227; Protestant use of, 12, 142, 293,
    398. *See also* Fathers of the Church
Salvation. *See* Christ; Faith; Heaven;
    Redemption
Salviati, Giovanni, lxvii
Saracens, 354. *See also* Turks
Sarum Missal, 323, 324, 358, 372
Satan. *See* Devils
Saulnier, Verdum L., 272
Savonarola, Girolamo, lxxx n., 368, 454

Scarisbrick, J. J., lxxiii n., 353
Scharpe, John, 347
Schedel, Hartmann, 390
Schoeck, Richard J., 267, 390
Schofield, R. S., 269, 331, 334
Scholasticism, cxlv, 20, 32–36, 290. *See also*
    Logic; Reason; Thomas Aquinas
Schoneugiensis, Eckbertos, cxxxviii n.
Schott, J., 352
Schultz, H. C., 460 n.
Schurf, August, 373
Schuster, Louis A., xxxiv, lxv n., cxxiv n.,
    267
Schwarzerdt. *See* Melanchthon
Scotus, John Duns, 369
Scripture: allegories and figurative lan-
    guage in, cxxxv–cxxxvi, cxliv, cxlv,
    cxlvii, 235–43, 245, 247, 249, 430–31;
    canon of, lxxiv, lxxix–lxxxiii, cvii, cviii,
    180–83, 203, 306, 357–59; the church
    authorizes, lxxiv, lxxix n., lxxx, cv, cvi,
    cxlv, cxlix, 18, 34–40, 180, 182–83,
    239–40, 290, 358, 359; literal interpre-
    tation, 185, 237–43, 245, 249, 359, 361,
    364; manipulated by Protestants, lvi–
    lvii, lxxv, lxxxiv, cv, cxliv–cxlv, 18, 38–
    40, 84, 94, 190, 194; More's use of, xxi,
    lxxiv–lxxxviii, clxix, 364; proper inter-
    pretation of, 34–38, 190, 239–40, 364;
    sole reliance of Lutherans, xxxix, lxx,
    lxxxiv, cxxii, cxlv, 38, 176, 378, 402. *See
    also* Bible; Biblical quotations; New Tes-
    tament; Old Testament
Seidler, Jacob, 287
Seneca, cii
Septuagint, lxxx
Shaa, John, 332
Shakespeare, William, lxxvii n., cxv n.,
    363, 453
Sharp, Jack, 346–47
Sherley-Price, Leo, cxv n.
Sider, Ronald J., 316
Siegmund von Lupfen, Countess, 284
Simmons, Thomas Frederick, 450 n.
Simon, W. G. H., lxxxv n.
Simpson, Percy, 464 n.
Sin: forgiveness of, promised by the mass,
    294–95; grace necessary to overcome,
    191–92, 292, 301; justification by faith
    encourages, lvi, lvii–lviii, 58–60, 62, 64–

70, 72, 78, 90, 173–75; original, 292, 300–301; purgatory discourages, 174–76, 199–200, 206; venial, lxxxv, lxxxvi–lxxxvii, lxxxviii, cvi, cxii, cxiii, 187–88, 193–94, 350, 448, 454. *See also* Hell; Redemption

Sisam, C. and K., 331

Sixtus IV, Pope, lxx

Skeat, W. W., 332

Smith, Constance, clxvii n., 481 n.

Smyth, William, 381

Solafideism. *See* Faith alone

Soul-sleep, lxxi, xcv, 56, 177, 198, 212–13, 304, 356, 369. *See also* Luther; Purgatory

Souper of the Lorde, The, clviii, 275, 316, 386. *See also* Joye, George

Southern, A. C., 270

Spalatin, George, xxvi–xxvii

Spirit, Holy. *See* Holy Spirit

Spiritual law: on heresy, lxviii, clvi, 130–31, 142, 158, 340; jurisdiction, 132–33, 134, 326, 340–41; on marriage, 288; parliament and, 130, 140, 340, 344; royal authority and, 129–30, 133, 136–37, 139, 158, 418; trumped-up charges, 116–17, 130–32, 412–14, 418. *See also* Mortmain; Praemunire; Temporal law

Staehelin, Ernst, 372

Stapleton, Thomas, xliv n., xlvii n., cxv n., clx n., 268, 270, 271, 272, 277, 282–83, 332; marginal notes to *Letter to Bugenhagen*, 283, 289, 290, 302, 309, 310

Star Chamber, 421

Starvation, 121–22, 138, 412. *See also* Beggars

Statistics, Fish's use of, lxviii, 115–16, 120–26, 138–39, 151–52, 331, 334, 345, 412–14

Steelyard, More's raid on, xxiv, xxv, xxxi–xxxii

Stock, Saint Simon, 331

Stoddard, John L., lxxxv n.

Stoicism, 292

Stokesley, John, bishop of London, clvi, clvii, 440

Stow, John, 343

Strabo, Walafrid, 263

Strype, John, 348, 437

Stubbs, William, 339

Stuchs, Georg, xcvi n.

Sturm, Johann, 279

Suffolk, Charles Brandon, Duke of, lxvii

Suffrages, 111, 323

Sullivan, Marie Denis, cxii n.

Summoners, 326, 412, 413

Supplications, official, 322, 323

Surtz, Edward, civ n., cvi n., cxvi n., 267, 313, 369

Sutton, Richard, 381

Sweating sickness, lxxii, lxxiii, 279

Sylvester, Richard S., xxxiv n., 267, 268, 350, 364, 452 n.

Syon monastery, 374–75, 381

Syphilis, lxxiii, 120–21, 329–30, 416

Tanner, Thomas, 272

Tatian, 291

Tauler, Johann, lxxi

Taxes, 414. *See also* Tithes

Temporal law: against the clergy, 216, 327, 344, 382, 420–21; property, 379–80, 381–82; and trumped-up heresy charges, 116–17, 130–32, 412–14, 418. *See also* Mortmain; Parliament; Praemunire; Spiritual law

Terence, 291, 312

Tertullian, xlviii–xlix, 312

Thecla, Sr. Mary, clxi n.

Theophylactus, 365, 387

Thomas, Saint and Apostle ('of India'), 195, 369

Thomas, A. H., 265

Thomas Aquinas, Saint, xc, cxxxvii, 159, 210, 354, 357, 366, 371–72, 377, 383, 387, 388, 449

Thomas à Becket, Saint, 338

Thompson, Craig R., 264, 267, 343

Thompson, Stith, 368

Thomson, John A. F., 268, 346, 347

Thornley, I. D., 265

Thuasne, Louis, 272–73

Tilley, Morris P., 268, 293, 308, 312, 325, 326, 329, 342, 343, 344, 359, 367–68, 377, 379, 382, 383, 387, 389, 390

Tithes, 122, 326, 412

Torquemada, Tomás de, xciv–xcv

Tottel, Richard, 457, 478

Townsend, George, 265

Tracy, P. B., 447 n.

Transubstantiation: clergy necessary for,

Transubstantiation (*continued*)
  lxix, cxxxvi, cxlix–cl, 254; consensus of
  the church, cxliii–cxliv, cxlix, 94, 239–
  42, 243, 253, 255; Henry VIII's view,
  cxlii, cxliii, cxlix, 253, 389, 421; heresies
  concering, 255–57; history of doctrine,
  cxxxvii–cxxxviii, cxlvii, 386, 390; and
  the incarnation, cxxxvii–cxxxix, cxlvi,
  cxlviii, cli, 257–58; Luther's views, 315–
  16, 317; miracle, cxxviii, cxlvii, 248–49;
  not impossible, 242–51; not necessary
  for salvation, 428; prudent to believe in,
  253–54, 389; scriptural support, 235,
  240–41. *See also* Eucharist; Consubstantiation
Trapp, J. B., cxxviii n., clvi n., 267
Trask, Willard R., 343
Trevelyan, George M., 345
Trevisan, Andrea, 336
Trinity, 256, 291–92. *See also* Christ; God;
  Holy Ghost;
Trinity College, Dublin, 466 n.
Tudor, Owen, 346
Tunstal, Cuthbert, bishop of London,
  xxiii, xxxiv n., lx, lxv, lxvi, cxxi, 341, 348,
  372, 410
Turks, xci, 125, 171, 172, 273, 343, 354,
  414
Tusser, Thomas, 371
Tyndale, William: and Bugenhagen's *Letter to the English*, xvii, xxvi; on the eucharist, cxviii, cxix, cxxviii, cxxxii,
  cxxxiii–cxxxiv, cxxxvii, cxlii, 234, 235,
  236, 240, 241, 352, 385; and Fish, 439;
  on Fisher, ciii n.; and Frith, cxx–cxxi,
  cxxiii–cxxv, cxxviii, cxxx, cxxxii, cxxxiii;
  and Henry VIII, cxxix, cxxxi–cxxxii;
  on John I, 335; and Luther, xxiii n.,
  xxvi; on miracles, cxxviii; on purgatory,
  379; on sin, cxxxviii; mentioned, xxii n.,
  lxxx n., 328, 443
— More on: marriage, 151; on purgatory,
  213; word use in his New Testament,
  322; mentioned, 159, 163, 164, 177,
  208, 209
— works: *An Answer to Sir Thomas More's
  Dialogue*, lxvi, cxxiv; *The exposition of the
  fyrste Epistle of seynt Ihon*, lxxxiii; *New Testament*, xxiii, xxv, xxvi, xxvii–xxviii,
  lxxx, lxxxvi, cxx, cxxiii, cxxxviii, 142,

161, 167, 168, 322, 340, 344, 409 n.,
  420, 437; *The Obedience of a Christian
  Man*, lxvii, lxviii, lxix–lxx, clxi, 162, 269,
  335, 352, 379, 409 n.; *The Parable of the
  Wicked Mammon*, 161–62, 352, 409 n.

Union Theological Seminary, New York,
  NY, clxvii
Universities: bequests to, cxvi, 381; Protes-
  tantism at, xxii–xxiii, xxiv, xxv; mort-
  main and, 214, 381. *See also* Cambridge;
  Oxford
University of Illinois Library, 466 n.
Urban V, Pope, 374
Ushaw College Library, 466 n.
Utraquism, 257, 391, 432. *See also*
  Eucharist

Vaissière, P. de, lxxiii n.
Valencia autograph, clxiii n., clxviii n.
Valentinus, 291
Valerius Maximus, 377
Valla, 375
Vaughan, Stephen, lxvi, cxxxii
Venial sins, lxxxv, lxxxvi–lxxxvii, lxxxviii,
  cvi, cxii, cxiii, 187–88, 193–94, 350,
  448, 454. *See also* Purgatory
Veysey, John, 341
Virgil, 292, 364
Visaigier, Jean, 6, 272–73
Visser, F. T., 269, 325, 329, 338, 343, 348,
  350, 352, 370, 386, 387
Vives, Juan, 273, 381
Vogt, Karl, xviii n.
Voragine, Jacques, 369, 449–50. *See also
  Legenda aurea*

Waldensians, lxxi, xc
Walker, David M., 380
Walsh, Clifford, 381–82
Walsingham, Thomas, 345
Walsyngham, Edmund, cxxxii–cxxxiii
Walter, Hubert, 338
Walther, Johannes von, 264
Warham, William, archbishop of Canter-
  bury, cxxii, cxxiii, cxxx, cxlii, 339, 409–
  10
Warnmall quest, 116, 132, 327, 418
Waszink, J. H., 264
Waugh, W. T., 327

Wechel, Chrétien, 372
Weever, John, 453 n.
Westminster, Provisions of, 380, 381–82
Westminster Abbey, lxxxiii n.
Whalley, John, 457 n.
Wharton, Henry, 340
White, Henry, 360
White Horse Tavern, xxii, cxx, cxxi
Whitefriars. *See* Carmelites
Whitford, Richard, 374, 375
Whiting, Bartlett J., 269, 289, 293, 308, 325, 326, 329, 342, 343, 344, 350, 351, 359, 367, 370, 377, 379, 382, 383, 387, 389, 390, 391
Wilkins, David, 269, 344, 353, 409 n., 410 n.
William I, King of England, 340
Wills, bequests in: for education, cxvi, 381; for masses, 139, 332, 452–53; for prayers, xcvii, c–ci, cxvi, 332, 452–53; purgatorial suffering and, 219, 222–23
Wimpheling, Jacob, xcvi n.
Wingfield, Richard, 277
Wisdom, Book of, lxxx, 181, 359
Wittenberg, xvii–xviii, xix, xxv, xxvi, xxvii, xxviii, cxxxi, cxxxiii, 24, 26, 278, 286–87, 373
Wollin, 270
Wolsey, Thomas Cardinal: anti-heretical activities, xx, xxiii, xxiv, xxv, xxxii, 288; and church property, lxviidi; correspondence with More, 333; fall, lxvi–lxvii, lxxiii; Foxe mentions, 439, 440; and Henry VIII's divorce, cxxix; and Henry VIII's letter to Luther, xxxvi; and the Hunne case, 328; Ipswich college, 275, 341; and Oxford, cxxi–cxxiii, 341, 381; retinue, 350; tax-collection, 334; travels with More, 275; unpopularity, 341; mentioned, xvii n., xxix n., 331, 352
Worde, Wynkyn de, 449 n., 451 n.
Wordsworth, John, 360

Works, good: Catholic reliance on, xli, 50, 52, 297–98; and Christ's righteousness, 44–46; faith makes them inevitable, xl–xli, lvii, cxxvi, 58–62, 80, 90, 402; in Fish, 159; free will and, 82–86, 90–92, 292; grace and, 46–48, 50, 54–56, 64, 72, 78, 202, 299–300, 400; hypocricy and, cxxvi, 68–70, 88, 92–94; justification doctrine and, 58–60, 297–98; mass as, 294, 304, 314; meaningless without faith, 62–64, 70–72; necessary for salvation, 72–78; Protestant attacks on, xlv–xlvi, 54–56, 64, 68–70, 78, 310, 400; purgatory and, lxxxvi, cxxviii, 111, 112, 200–202, 221, 227, 371, 448–49; scriptural arguments, 54, 60, 62, 64, 66, 74, 76, 82–84, 305–06. *See also* Almsgiving
Worms, Edict of, xx, 320
Wright, Thomas, 276
Wrigley, E. A., 269, 331, 334
Wyclif(f), John, lxx, cxix, 234, 236, 240, 241, 384
Wyer, Richard, 425, 433
Wyer, Robert, 447

Xenophon, 271

Yale University Libary, clxvi, clxvii, clxix, 395 n., 437, 457, 458, 470 n.

Zosimus, Pope, 299
Zwingli, Huldreich: biography, 316–17, 386; dualism in, cxxxviii–cxxxix; on the eucharist, lviii, cxxiii, cxxvi–cxxvii, cxxviii, cxxxiv, cxxxv, cxxxvi–cxxxvii, cxxxviii–cxxxix, cxliv, cl, 94–96, 234, 280, 316, 318, 385, 390; More mentions, lviii, cxix, 94–96, 234, 236, 240, 241; and the Peasants' Revolt, 320; on purgatory, lxxi–lxxii; mentioned, 279